THE KILLING FACTORY

THE KILLING FACTORY

The top secret world of germ and chemical warfare

JOHN PARKER

SMITH GRYPHON
PUBLISHERS

First published in Great Britain in 1996 by
SMITH GRYPHON LIMITED
12 Bridge Wharf, 156 Caledonian Road
London N1 9UU

A CIP catalogue record for this book is available from the British Library

ISBN 0 85685 121 4

Typeset by Computerset, Harmondsworth
Printed in Great Britain by Butler & Tanner Ltd, Frome

CONTENTS

ACKNOWLEDGEMENTS

IT WILL BE be evident from the text that many people have given time and effort to the author with interviews and the provision of archive material, along with many others whose request for anonymity has been respected. A special note of appreciation is due to Mr Michael Roche, founder of the Porton Down Volunteers Association (PDVA), and his various members who agreed to be interviewed for this book, and recount their experiences. Thanks are also due to Mr Alan Care of the London firm of solicitors Leigh, Day & Co., representing the PDVA, and Ms Hilary Meredith of Donn & Co., Manchester, a leading member of the group of lawyers representing Gulf War Veterans. Thanks are also due to the staff and information desk at the Public Record Office at Kew in guiding the author towards relevant material and retrieving it rapidly from the archives during searches over many days, and to the Crown Copyright Department at the PRO for permission to reprint extracts from selected documents. Also great appreciation is due to Senator Donald Riegle, who headed the Senate Committee on Bank, Housing and Urban Affairs, and particularly for the efforts and assistance of his chief investigator, Mr James Tuite; the reports of both men were invaluable to this work. Many other sources in Britain and the US were readily forthcoming and are listed in the chapter notes and bibliography.

Photographs: cover, Associated Press; inside section provided by Associated Press, Yardley Collection, Foto Germany, Public Record Office, London, *Daily Mirror* and the photograph of Jayce Hanson, Derek Hudson, Paris.

PROLOGUE

'GAS. It's gas . . . Level Four. Level Four. Not a Drill, repeat NOT a drill.' The words were shouted often as thousands of chemical detectors and alarm systems positioned across the Saudi Arabian desert among the tented cities of the Coalition forces screamed the alert and sent troops diving for cover. Sweating buckets in their protective suits, drugged to the eyeballs with a cocktail of 13 separate vaccines and tablets, breathing air heavily polluted by sand, dust, diesel fumes, jet fuel, pesticides, bug sprays and depleted uranium tips of armour-piercing shells, the massed armies of Desert Storm were on the very edge of their nerves.

Saddam Hussein's expected chemical blitz would surely come. The fear of it, as one Gulf War military commander recalled, was worse than the sound of the howling big guns or the barrage of Saddam's Scud missiles. Mustard gas, phosgene, nerve gas, anthrax, cholera, bubonic plague . . . any one of a dozen lethal man-made horrors whose basic ingredients were shipped to Iraq from the West before the war, could have been loaded into the Scud warheads. There had been so much talk of it, so much preparation, the tension could be sliced with a blunt bayonet. Saddam's Scud attacks were launched on 19 January 1991 in response to the start of the Coalition heavy bombardment of Baghdad. Every Scud attack was met with a 20-minute wait while the air was tested. Sirens were sounding. The cry would go up: 'Level Four, Level Four.' And the troops pulled on their gas masks, buttoned down their protective suits and found cover where they could, sometimes for up to eight hours at a time.

The insidious nature of Chemical and Biological (CB) weapons and the vivid memories of Saddam Hussein's trial run with chemical attacks, which killed up to 7,000 of his own Kurdish people in 1988, ensured a built-in scare factor that some who experienced it would say was far greater than that for conventional hardware.

They need not have worried.

There was no gas.

Nor were there any of those deadly germs loaded into Saddam's warheads. There was none blowing down on the wind from the bombed Iraqi CB plants, either.

Or, at least, not according to the official history of the Gulf War written by the British and American defence administrations. They repeatedly insisted that 'no chemical or biological agents were found within the theatre of operations.' There are many who beg to differ.

Dale Glover was a Staff Sergeant with the US 1165th Military Police Company who made a report which was logged by a senior officer in charge of recording all such incidents: 'I was awakened at 3:30 on the morning of January 20 by the noise of a sonic boom. The Battalion NCO was announcing that we were under chemical attack. I went out to check the M43 detector for signs of chemicals and found the visual display was blinking. I knew there were several possible causes that could have set off the alarm, like a sonic boom, pesticides or even strong vehicle exhaust fumes. The Battalion NCO and myself conducted tests with a standard Army issue 256 A1 detector kit. Both received a positive pale red colour on the nerve agent test spot. The NCO ordered a Level Four – and we took cover for four hours.'

Richard Turnbull, RAF corporal, based at Dharan, Saudi Arabia: 'I was in a nuclear and biological cell, building shelters and training others in the use of protective gear and instruments, such as the Nerve Agency Infantry Advanced Detectors (NAIAD) and Chemical Agent Monitors (CAM). On 20 January, there was a Scud attack around 8pm. It landed on the airfield and within seconds every NAIAD and CAM blasted off chemical warnings. We were placed on the highest alert. We all had to put on our masks and protective clothing, literally thousands of us. Afterwards, we were told not to worry. The alarms had gone off, they said, because of unburnt fuel from aircraft taking off. But, as we all knew, aircraft were taking off all the time. There were two other Scud attacks that night. One at Al-Jubayl and one at Tabuk. The alarms went off at three units. The nerve gases tabun and sarin were among the chemicals detected by French and Czech units that night. I'm pretty sure they've affected me.'

Harold Jerome Edwards was the US chemical NCO in charge of the NBC team (Nuclear, Biological and Chemical unit) for the Naval Mobile Construction Battalion 24 Air Detachment at the King Abdul Aziz Naval Air Station: 'I conducted three M256 tests for chemical agents on the evening of January 20 after an Iraqi Scud raid. Two of the three tests conducted were positive for chemical blister agents. The negative test was taken in an area in between a number of rows of tents. I reported this information to my unit commander. One member of the unit, Tom Muse, blistered in the area under his watch. Eventually, the all-clear was given from a higher command.'

Fred Willoughby of Columbus, Georgia, who was with the Naval Mobile Construction Battalion: 'At about three in the morning, I was hanging out outside my tent when I heard a long, loud explosion. Shortly afterwards, the siren sounded and I went to get my gas mask. By the time I came out, people were yelling, "Level 4, not a drill." Immediately, my mouth, lips, and face became numb all over, a sensation like Novocain at the dentist's. I stayed in the bunker for about an hour or an hour and a half. When I came out I and others in my unit were told by the officers that what they had heard was just a sonic boom. The next day, the unit was told not to talk about it; at the same time the unit's protective gear was collected and replaced.'

Roy Morrow of Phoenix City, Alabama, assigned to the Air Detachment, King Abdul Aziz Stadium: 'I heard two explosions between 3:00 and 3:30am. We went to the bunker for 25 to 30 minutes until the all-clear was given. When I came out, there were Marines running and screaming, "Level 4." The siren sounded again. As I started to run for cover, I began to feel a burning sensation on my arms, legs, the back of my neck, ears and face. My lips felt numb. Next day, the head of the decontamination team came round. He told us that the two explosions were sonic booms, nothing more, and we were ordered not to talk about it. All of our chemical protection gear was collected and replaced with new equipment.'

William Brady, Battalion Logistics NCO with the US 217th Maintenance Battalion: 'There was a deafening sound, a flash of light, everything shook. I checked the chemical litmus paper in my contamination kit; it had turned red and I got a positive reading from an M256 kit. My nose began to run. I smelled and tasted sulphur and I began coughing up blood a couple of days after the attack.'

The area from which most of these reports emanated was outside the range of all Iraqi delivery systems except for Scuds. On 20 January four Scuds landed near Al-Jubayl, two of them about 35 miles away and two about 58 miles away. Another 'live' find was confirmed in the official records of the US Marines, detailing its involvement in the Gulf War, published in 1993 by its History and Museums Division. One item related to a discovery in February 1991: 'At approximately 0656, the FOX chemical reconnaissance vehicle at Red 1 detected a trace of mustard gas, originally thought to be from a chemical mine. The alarm was quickly spread throughout the division. Since everyone had been told to don his protective outer garments and boots the previous evening it was only necessary to hurriedly pull on a gas-mask and protective gloves to attain Level 4 protection. A second FOX vehicle was sent to the area, and confirmed the presence of an agent . . . it was still sufficiently strong to cause blistering on the exposed arms of two AAV crewmen. Work continued on the clearance of the lanes, and the protection alert was reduced to Level 2 after about a half-hour.' The chemicals were found in an area not occupied by the Iraqis until after August 1990.

Then there is the mystery of the contents of a large storage tank that a British Army unit tested positive for mustard gas. The reports of its commanding officer remain classified in the UK but copies were obtained in the US. The tank had been sited by Iraqi troops in the grounds of a girls' school in south-eastern Kuwait, well inside the Kuwaiti theatre of operations and eventually occupied by US and British forces. By then the tank was riddled with bullet holes and was leaking a brown oily substance. Lieutenant Colonel Saleh Al Ostath of the Kuwaiti Army reported it to an officer of the Royal Ordnance Corps.

British Army Major John Watkinson was ordered to take his unit, the 21st Explosive Ordnance Disposal Squadron, 33 Royal Engineers, to the site of the Sabahiyah High School for Girls to examine the tank, which had a capacity of approximately 2,000 litres. Watkinson immediately ordered all personnel to move up wind, and after putting on his three-layered rubber chemical protective clothing, approached the container and tested the liquid with a chemical agent monitor. It gave a reading of eight bars on H, for mustard agent – a maximum reading indicating a highly concentrated agent – and no bars on G, indicating no nerve agent was present. Watkinson made two further tests and both readings gave positive for mustard gas. On a second visit, he inserted a wire into one of the bullet holes, and according to his report, wiped the oily substance on the wire on two types of detector paper and again achieved a positive reading.

He sealed the holes with masking tape and left to fetch an M18A2 chemical detector kit. He tested again, and achieved a total of ten positive readings for mustard. The bullet holes were resealed using industrial silicone filler and plaster of Paris bandages and guards placed around the area.

Now the Americans became involved. The Commander of the 11th Armoured Cavalry Regiment was ordered to send two FOX chemical reconnaissance vehicles to the site. Since this was a joint and combined live-agent chemical-detection mission, involving both US and British forces, detailed rehearsals were carried out to ensure that no accidents occurred. One FOX team moved to the area near the container and began to insert a detection probe fitted to the FOX vehicle into the ground to a depth of about 4cm. The mass spectrometer showed chemical mustard agent in the ground. A second collection team in full heavy-duty protective clothing, covering them from head to toe, walked to the container, estimated to contain between 800 and 1000 litres, or about 250 gallons, of liquid carrying assorted detection equipment. They removed the storage container's seals and there was a discharge of pressurized vapour into the air.

Captain Michael Johnson, one of the US team, said in his report of the incident that he saw amber-coloured vapour escaping from the hole. The chemical agent monitor again registered eight bars, confirming highly concentrated mustard agent. Captain Johnson's unit pushed a medical syringe with a catheter tube into the tank to extract liquid for testing. Johnson reported that each of the mass spectrometer analyses confirmed mustard gas and further analysis by the system also showed traces of phosgene. In all, 21 tests conducted by Watkinson and Johnson showed the presence of mustard gas.

When the unit began to prepare for the removal of the tank and its contents, a member of the British team was injured when some of the liquid dropped on his left wrist. Johnson reported: 'The soldier suffered immediate pain and was believed to be going into shock.' He was quickly taken to a decontamination site and cut out of his chemical protective clothing. The medical team doused the soldier with a decontamination solution. Within one minute, a small blister was observed forming on his left arm, the size of a pinhead. About five minutes later, the blister had already reached 2in across and he was sent to the field hospital for further treatment. The soldier was one of Watkinson's men, Lance Corporal Robert Jones. An eye witness to the whole incident was another British soldier, James Alan McQuoid from

Birmingham, who was a sergeant in the 21st Squadron until he left the Army in 1992, with a letter from the Queen and a British Empire Medal citing him as a resolute leader in dangerous situations.

Given the opportunity, McQuoid would testify on oath in a court of law that the liquid that burned its way through Jones's three-layered rubber protective suit was mustard gas. 'Everything pointed to it – the machines identified it, the litmus test confirmed it, the oily consistency of it told us.'

It was also McQuoid who cut Jones from the protective suit. He is adamant that the suit was thrown to the ground and later burned for safety reasons, along with everything else that had been contaminated. 'I would have known if the suit had been retained or asked for,' he said. Yet when the British Ministry of Defence was approached about the incident – still classified in their eyes – they claimed that the protective suit had been collected up and taken to the Chemical and Biological Defence Establishment (CBDE) at Porton Down for tests. No gas agents were found, and the suit was subsequently burned there. Almost five years later, a British Commons Select Committee accepted a letter from Porton Down stating that the suit was contaminated by nitric acid – not mustard gas.

This view became the official line, repeated by the British MoD and the US Department of Defense: it was nitric acid, not mustard gas. The men were mistaken. The equipment must have been faulty. By then, other evidence had vanished. After completing their testing, the US FOX team leaders were ordered to remove the tapes from the mass spectrometer of the FOX vehicles by Lieutenant Colonel Killgore, the chemical officer for Task Force Victory. The tapes were the paper records of the chemical breakdown of the liquid or vapours, produced by the mobile mass spectrometer in the FOX vehicle. They were handed to personnel who 'suddenly appeared from nowhere' wearing desert camouflage uniforms with no rank or distinguishing patches.

Captain Johnson does not know what happened to the tapes or samples. He was ordered from the scene after his unit's mission was completed. From that moment, both the British and the US defence departments appeared to want to keep this discovery under wraps. A team of United Nations observers assigned to the area were informed that it was in the hands of scientists under the supervision of Porton Down. The UN could produce no written records of their findings at the site.

While the US Department of Defense and the British were denying the presence of chemical agents in Kuwait, the Kuwaiti, US and British governments all received classified reports on this recovery of bulk chemical agents. Yet the MoD and the DoD consistently maintained that no chemical agents were located in areas occupied by Coalition forces.

A contrasting view would eventually be available from an unusual source – in a recommendation for an Army Commendation Medal presented to Sergeant James Warren Tucker for 'participating in the mission that located stores of chemical agents'. Tucker was in a unit commanded by Captain Johnson who was awarded a Meritorious Service Medal for his actions. Two soldiers and as many as six others from the 54th Chemical Troop of the United States Army's 11th Armoured Cavalry Regiment were given Army medals for 'the positive identification of suspected chemical agents' – which was the citation presented to Captain Johnson.

Reports retrieved from two separate NATO countries that were Coalition members during the Gulf War contained a detailed analysis of the discovery of the chemical agents, along with the testimony of nuclear, biological and chemical officers who were there. Still further evidence would eventually come from the records of a Czech military chemical decontamination unit, which had been flown in specifically to assist the under-staffed Saudi Arabian Army. The 180-strong unit was placed under the direct command of His Royal Highness General Khaled, a nephew of King Fahd, Commander of the Joint Forces and Theatre of Operation.

Long after the end of the war, and as hundreds of Gulf War veterans began to fall ill, the Czech Minister of Defence announced that its chemical decontamination unit had detected the nerve gas sarin in areas of northern Saudi Arabia during the early phases of the Gulf War. They had attributed the detection to fall-out from Coalition bombing of Iraqi chemical-warfare factories. The US Department of Defense publicly poured scorn on the findings, supported by the British MoD, and insisted that there was no evidence that troops were exposed to chemical-warfare agents.

However, after a visit to the Czech capital by an American investigations team, led by a US senator, a senior DoD medical officer admitted that chemical and biological exposure had not been explored 'because it was the position of military intelligence that such exposures never occurred'. Finally, on 10 November 1993, the Pentagon acknowledged that the Czech government did detect chemical agents. But after analysing the results of the Czech report, the Department of Defense concluded that the detection was unrelated to the 'mysterious health problems suffered by some of our veterans'.

For that conclusion, the Pentagon clearly placed great score by views of British scientists attached to Porton Down. A Pentagon memo, viewed for this work, used the words of Dr Graham Pearson, director of Porton Down CBDE, to support its own rejection of a chemical presence. The memo read:

'Dr Pearson, head of the British Nuclear, Biological and Chemical [NBC] labs and the foremost expert on chemical agents . . . has said there was no evidence to validate positive chemical detection incidents . . . monitors gave some alarms which resulted in the use of more capable detectors . . . all of the monitor alarms were ruled to be false alarms as the detectors never produced a positive reading.' Yet one further mystery came up. During the hearings of a US Senate Committee of inquiry, its chairman Senator Donald Riegle discovered that chemical agent detectors used by US forces during the Gulf War were not sufficiently sensitive to detect sustained low levels of chemical agent and to monitor personnel for contamination.

It was admitted that the levels for the alarms were set at a rate 1,000 times greater than the minimum at which exposure was considered in US safety regulations to be hazardous to people if exposed over a long period of time. Riegle also uncovered one other glaring miscalculation: that the US did not possess effective biological agent detectors. The military commanders had ruled out any exposure to biological weapons (BW). Yet when Riegle collected up samples of equipment from veterans themselves and had them independently analysed by a leading US research institute, traces of BW agents were found in gas-masks.

Riegle, whose staff interviewed hundreds of veterans and war commanders, was angrily explicit in his assessment. He said:

'The information provided by the veterans indicated that exposure to chemical and possibly biological agents was widespread – widespread! Detections were confirmed by chemical specialists deployed in Saudi Arabia, in Kuwait and in Iraq.' The chemical alarms went off so frequently, it was reported, that some were even turned off. They were activated by small amounts of nerve agents released by the bombings of Iraqi chemical facilities, storage depots and bunkers, but troops were often told that there was no danger.

One more piece of evidence was turned up by the Senate Committee's chief investigator, James Tuite. He discovered that the US Department of Veteran Affairs had conducted a confidential survey of CB specialists with the 1st Marine Division. They were asked specifically if they had encountered any CB munitions during the Gulf War. Out of the experts questioned, 71 said no, 32 said yes and 9 declined to answer.

Meanwhile, the British and the Americans continued to assert that no troops were exposed to any CB agents in the war theatre – a claim that, as will be seen in ensuing chapters, is vehemently challenged. Not least by the 45,000 Gulf War veterans who registered some form of post-war illness in themselves or their families. As those numbers began to mount, and devastating effects appeared among troops and in the deformities of many of their children, the Pentagon memo once again deferred to Porton for blunt rejection of such claims:

'Dr Pearson says British studies determined that there are no long-term effects from small doses of chemical agents. American studies agree. Therefore it is not useful to worry if Allied forces ever encountered chemical agents . . . the British reject the idea of a new disease. The military actually suffered fewer health problems during the war . . . much of this is attributable to the reduced consumption of alcohol . . . thus the British conclude that it would not be useful to investigate more deeply reports of a new Gulf War disease.'

The British word on such matters is the one that few are prepared to challenge. 'When you are talking CB technology,' said a source for this work, 'all roads lead to Porton Down. It is a miniscule operation compared with what the Americans and the Russians have, but Porton has consistently led the field. They wrote the gospel in terms of CB technology and the Americans treat them with great respect.'

It goes much deeper than that. As will be seen in the ensuing pages, Britain and America have maintained an active partnership in their CB research, dating from the first use of gas by the Germans in 1915. The links were formalized at the end of World War II when joint Anglo/US teams swept through Germany and the Far East gathering up the spoils of war. They brought home mountains of research documents, photographs, laboratory samples of animal and human organs, along with tons of equipment plundered from the Nazi and Japanese CB installations, concentration camps and PoW compounds. And many senior Axis scientists were granted immunity in exchange for their knowledge.

From the late 1940s, the partnership developed, with a constant interchange of information and staff, predominantly to develop Hitler's secret nerve gas and Japanese biological weapons, which Allied intelligence feared had also fallen into Russian hands. The association has continued throughout the second half of the century to match the Russians. They have co-operated on many joint missions: while the US biological chemists were spraying bacteria over San Francisco to test its spread, Britain equipped two special ships to float hundreds of animals tethered on rafts in the waters off the Bahamas to test more virulent agents. When US scientists spread bacteria through the New York City subway, Britain did the same in the London Underground. Controversial 'mind-control' experiments with LSD, which so occupied the CIA in 1960s, were pursued in Britain on a mass basis, using detachments of soldiers. Results of horrific experiments on animals routinely carried out at Porton produced vital research data used by their US counterparts.

When the British government halted the stockpiling of nerve gas, America carried on, using Porton-developed gas of the highest potency. The American military was conducting aerial tests with that very strain when in 1968 they released a cloud of it across the Great Salt Lake Desert in western Utah and killed 6,000 sheep.

When the use of human volunteers to test nerve gas was banned in the US in the 1970s, British researchers continued to herd up to 200 men a year into Porton laboratories, for which it re-equipped itself with a new £3.5 million gas chamber complex, opened in 1996. It does so in spite of a mounting toll of ill health among many earlier volunteers who have provided personal testimony for this work.

They tested suits and medication that would be used in the Gulf War – for which the combined expertise of the US and British CB experts was marshalled once again, both in Allied efforts to protect Coalition forces from Saddam Hussein's much-feared CB attack, and in playing down the consequences.

1

THE HAUNTED GARDEN

IT IS PERHAPS the absolute paradox that the place that for eight decades has experimented with some of the most deadly poisons known to man is to be found within one of Britain's most coveted and protected nature reserves. 'It is,' said Richard Harvey, a local activist and former peace campaigner who has lived beside it for most of his adult life, 'a Jekyll and Hyde of a place – sinister, compellingly so, and yet engulfed in a natural beauty that is rarely surpassed anywhere in Britain.'

That is why the Ministry of Defence calls it 'The Jewel in our Crown', which is a reference both to its 80-year record in contributing to the defence capabilities of the British armed forces against chemical and biological attack, and to the environs and habitat in which it is situated.

Porton Down has been the home of the Chemical and Biological Defence Establishment (CBDE) since it was hurriedly founded to combat a German gas attack in World War I. It is set within 7,000 acres of the glorious, rolling countryside of Wiltshire. It is also one of the most secretive and sensitive installations anywhere in the United Kingdom and although its presence becomes immediately obvious to visitors who flock to this region to enjoy the tranquil beauty of its villages and the unspoiled charm of its towns, few have any real idea of what goes on inside. High fences topped with barbed wire protect much of its perimeter. The landscape is dotted with the tall, white painted flagpoles carrying pennants of Red for Danger. 'Keep Out' notices are displayed in profusion.

The area is kept under constant surveillance, electronically and manually, by patrols of police and security guards and plain-clothed officers. Helicopters and low-flying aircraft are often in the air above it. Anyone stopping on the country lanes that criss-cross the open areas of the Porton landscape can expect an inquisitive guard to swoop in from nowhere. 'It has always been that way,' said Richard Harvey, 'to the point of being a nuisance, a fear and at times a threat to local residents. There has always been an air of paranoia about Porton – less so now than when the militant animal-rights campaigners were at the peak of their extremism, blowing up members of staff and sending threatening letters to others. It's understandable, I suppose, that the Porton staff should be protected almost as prodigiously as the secret projects they are working on. But for those of us who regard the use of animals for experimental purposes as abominable – though do not resort to extremist methods to make the point – Porton Down is a place haunted by the ghosts of the millions of creatures who have been, to use the term of the scientists themselves, sacrificed there.'

It is precisely because of the activities within the complex that the estate became the so-called 'jewel'. The security cordon protected it from the trampling of the masses, and it was left untouched by the vagaries of modern land management and, ironically, completely free of the pesticides that have been the subject of great scrutiny by the scientists who work there. Large areas of the site have been left the way nature had perfected them, with archaeological monuments that date from the early Neolithic period.

In 1977, Porton Down was scheduled by the Nature Conservancy Council as a Site of Special Scientific Interest and, in 1992, English Nature signed a management plan with CBDE to ensure the future preservation of about half the Porton site. It is a massive garden of unspoiled natural beauty, with tree-lined lanes and lush pastures containing relics and sites of prehistoric man which until recent times have received few visitors from the outside world. Recently, however, the establishment has been listed as a Special Protection Area under the European Commission Directive on conservation and is playing host to visits by natural history groups from all over Britain, with limited access, of course, to the Porton estate – but well away from the test sites and laboratories.

It *is* a fascinating place. More than 200 sites of archaeological relics dating from early prehistory have been recorded. Some have been excavated but most remain undisturbed. They include cemeteries, flint mines and 100 mineshafts, which provide an unrivalled example of Neolithic life and industry, dating to around 3300 BC. There are 115 round barrows of the Bronze Age, 2300 BC, including the largest bell barrow known in Wiltshire, over 15km of late Bronze Age linear earthworks, Celtic field systems from the early Iron Age, around 1200 BC, and sites of pit cremations from 1740 BC.

Many of the areas of downland have never been tilled and the lack of any chemicals has resulted in a rich and diverse growth of chalk grasslands where flora and fauna of a kind that has long become extinct elsewhere in the British Isles are found in profusion. It has become, for example, the most important site for juniper, with more than 18,000 bushes, 20 per cent of the juniper population of southern England. Fifteen different species of wild orchid have been recorded there, along with rare continental species of candytuft originating from the Iberian peninsula. Many varieties of fungi and lichens, which have disappeared elsewhere, are thriving.

The plant life has provided a haven for five significant communities of invertebrates, four of which have been listed as being of national importance. It supports a population of yellow ants estimated at around three million in mounds that are up to 100 years old. It has the largest spider community of any similar site in Britain, containing 194 different species, including some of the rarest ever found in the British Isles.

Over the years, 87 per cent of all British butterfly species have been recorded at Porton. It has the largest colonies of both the Silver Spotted Skipper and the Dark Green Fritillary, of which there were about a million. There are nationally important colonies of the Marsh Fritillary, the Duke of Burgundy and the Adonis Blue.

The wildlife population provides an equally exciting list of inhabitants: 96 different species of birds including the endangered stone curlew, which here enjoys one of its last remaining breeding habitats, along with deer, badgers, rabbits and squirrels.

It is here, too, that experiments have been conducted on hundreds of thousands of animals of many species – and humans. The figures are beyond estimation but approaching three million since Porton was first opened, as its scientists sought to create, test and perfect some of the deadliest weapons known to man; where enough supplies of a biological agent capable of wiping out the entire nation can be stored in an exceedingly small jar.

Since its inception, Porton has been surrounded by the most

secure measures of confidentiality, especially over its use of animals and humans in experiments. They have become an integral part of its history, creating a moral dilemma that, in a way, has been fundamentally overwhelmed by the place itself. It is steadfastly proud, almost arrogantly so, that it was charged with first creating, and then spearheading a defence against, CB weapons capable of far greater devastation even than was ever imagined at the height of the nuclear age.

It all began at a place that was the Kuwait of the World War I, the little town of Ypres, in Belgium – the town that died twice as Germans and the Allies fought ferocious battles in the early months of the Great War. It lay in a small pocket on the Flanders plain three miles inside German lines and became a citadel of courageous resistance, known to all as 'Wipers'. Its strategic location as the gateway to the Channel ports meant that Ypres was under constant attack.

The first Battle of Ypres raged through the autumn of 1914. British, French, and Belgian troops, heavily outnumbered, resisted a German offensive aimed at the French ports of Calais and Dunkirk on the English Channel. After 34 days of fighting, thousands lay dead in the Flanders mud. Ypres was mercilessly bombarded, yet as the troops went to ground during the dreadful winter of 1914/15, its people drifted back as the battlefield around them fell temporarily silent, with the Germans preoccupied at Neuve-Chappelle and Champagne.

The Allies held the front but Flanders was devastated, a sea of mud as the shelling broke down the natural drainage of the land. The dead of the previous autumn lay still unburied between the lines on the thin strip of No Man's Land, just a few hundred yards wide. 'An acrid smell of death infected the air, which even the chloride of lime failed to make endurable,' records an official British history. Even so, life began again among the wreckage of the town, in the cellars and the bombed-out buildings. The soldiers drank vin rouge as the bistros reopened and lorries were soon rumbling through the cobbled streets once again. The respite was briefly taken, and on 17 April 1915 the second Battle of Ypres began when the British Royal West Kents captured what was known as Hill 60 and occupied the German trenches.

Their success was short lived. The German High Command furiously ordered an immediate counter-attack and within three days Hill 60 had become a mound of shell craters strewn with bodies. Next, the offensive was turned once again to Ypres, upon which the Germans rained a heavy attack of Jack Johnsons – the 17in howitzer shells fired in pairs every 20 minutes.

Ypres was crushed for the second time and the surviving civilians fled once more, leaving the soldiers to battle it out. What followed was, in the words of Sir John French, commander of the British Expeditionary Force, 'practically indescribable'. Thursday, 22 April was a glorious spring day and the hedgerows of Northern France were beginning to glisten with the white of blossoms, and in the fields wild flowers bloomed around the crater scars. The day had passed relatively quietly, but just before 5pm the Germans began their bombardment again. Heavy mortar fire pummelled Ypres and the villages in front of it.

Then, the French territorial and coloured colonial troops on the northern shoulder of the salient heard what they would describe as a 'loud hissing sound' coming from the German lines. A cloud of whitish vapour appeared along the German front. It was, as Beatrix Potter wrote in *The Battle Book of Ypres*, an uncanny vision. The hissing continued for about ten minutes and the whitish vapours seemed to change colour. To some, it was a bluish-white mist; others saw it as a greenish-yellow cloud, which gathered to the height of three men and rolled along the ground towards them, propelled on a gentle breeze.

The cloud increased in intensity until it was estimated to be at least five miles wide and half a mile in depth, a massive man-made fog of poisonous fumes, heading inexorably towards the unsuspecting troops. In the first ever use of poisonous gas in war, the Germans had placed 5,730 cylinders containing 160 tons of chlorine along a four-mile stretch of the front. It was a devastating chemical that attacked the lungs of its victims, producing an instant accumulation of liquid in the windpipe, frothing into the mouth and blocking the lungs so that the casualties actually drowned in their own fluids.

On the northern flank of the Allies' Ypres salient, the 45th Algerian Division and the 87th French Territorials were the first to be enveloped by the poisonous shroud, with catastrophic results. Their eyes began streaming uncontrollably and then the soldiers were choking and coughing, spitting blood and retching in agony. Dozens died where they fell. Others who dared to stand on the parapets escaped the worst effects, for the greatest concentration of the gas was at ground level and in the trenches.

As the cloud began to knock down the enemy, German infantry, faces masked with moist gauze tied across mouths and noses, advanced firing at will, but even they were shocked by the scenes of sheer horror that confronted them. Bodies littered the battlefield. Men with faces of tortured agony had collapsed gasping for air. Those who were still alive were heaving up the terrible yellow fluid from their lungs. Their weapons, the metal buttons on their uniforms and even their watches had turned green.

The attack led to an immediate rout of the French. In his account of the resultant battlefield mayhem, Colonel E.D. Swinton wrote: 'Behind the wall of poisonous vapour which had swept across fields, through woods, came the German firing line . . . allowing sufficient time for the fumes to take full effect, the Germans charged forward over a practically unresisting enemy and, penetrating the gap thus created, pressed on silently and swiftly south and west . . . and then when their infantry had reached well behind the enemy lines, the Germans opened hot artillery fire with a bombardment of high explosive shell and shrapnel of various calibres and also with projectiles containing more asphyxiating gas.'

The French colonial soldiers who had taken the brunt of the gas attack were, Swinton wrote, confused and mortified. Those still able to move, many of them already blue with cyanosis fled, crying, 'Gaz!' Some did not stop running until they reached a town six miles away, and all around was 'wild confusion' as panicking soldiers and civilian refugees swarmed along the roads.

Medical teams with their wagons began collecting up the survivors and bringing them to the field hospitals. 'Soldiers lying on the floors with faces of a blue or ghastly green colour, gasping for air in their struggles with death . . . with the faintly metallic smell of chlorine everywhere,' wrote one American surgeon, Harvey Cushing, serving with the American Ambulance Service. He recorded that of 1,000 men of the Bataillion d'Afrique only 60 had escaped. One of his colleagues, William Boyd, wrote in his diary: 'I saw a sight which for sheer ghastliness equals anything . . . in a courtyard were 200 men on stretchers. Some were in a state of stupor, flies buzzing around their faces; some were sitting up gasping for breath with hands and faces of a deep dusky hue. A few had fallen back and with gurglings in the back of the throat were passing away into the undiscovered country. They were the first gas cases from Ypres.'

It was many hours before the Allied commanders were able to assess the scale of the disaster that had overwhelmed them. Even the German commanders who had ordered its use as an experiment had no real idea of the outcome. It was a battlefield try-out and they had no reserve supplies immediately available to exploit the attack. Even so, the gas had scorched a four-mile hole in the Allied lines.

Sir John French, the British commander, wrote: 'It was impossible to realize what had actually happened. Fumes and smoke obscured everything and within an hour of it being launched the whole position had to be abandoned along with 50 guns.' Casualties were officially put at 15,000 of whom 5,000 were dead, though in reality the figure was far higher. French immediately telegraphed the War Department in London, urging 'immediate steps be taken to supply similar means of most effective kind for use by our troops . . .. Also essential that our troops should be supplied with adequate protection.'

French also called for the immediate despatch of scientific advisers to suggest temporary solutions to the gas. The contingent arrived at the front on 27 April, and among them was Professor John Scott Haldane, the Scottish physiologist who was to play a major part in the inauguration of the Allied response to the German gas. The scientists, like the military, could offer no immediate solution. All the men could do was to hold moistened cloth over their faces during a gas attack. In the trenches, soldiers had to urinate on socks, handkerchiefs or any other pieces of material they could rip from their battledress to tie around their faces.

The Germans, buoyant with their success, began planning a new onslaught. Within 36 hours, they were ready to attack the Allied lines held by the Canadian divisions. As the official Canadian Record Officer noted in his account of the battles: 'On Saturday morning just before dawn a German airship appeared in the sky to the east of our line and at this point dropped four red star flares which floated downwards for some distance before they died out. When our men, whose eyes had not unnaturally been fixed on this display of pyrotechnics, again turned to their front it was to find the German trenches rendered invisible by a wall of greenish-yellow vapour which was bearing down upon them on the breeze, travelling at perhaps seven or eight miles an hour. Through this, the German started shooting. The stupefying gas was launched on several occasions on that day, but the attack was not pursued very quickly. The reason given by a German prisoner is that many of the enemy's own infantry were also so affected by the fumes that they could not advance.'

With officers shouting 'Stand Firm' the men held moistened cloth over their faces and watched the coloured mist rolling towards them. 'We waited until the vapour reached our trenches,' the Canadian account goes on, 'and then we charged through it and met the advancing Germans with the bayonet as they swarmed over the parapets.'

Canada, the record officer wrote, had a 'large graveyard in Flanders, very large'. The combined gas, artillery and infantry attacks killed 5,000 men. Among them was the first casualty on whom a post mortem examination was conducted, one Sergeant Grindley of the Canadian 15th Battalion, whose body was to provide the doctors with their first insight into how to treat gassed soldiers. The report, by Lieutenant McNee of the Royal Army Medical Corps, lodged in the Public Record Office at Kew, read: 'On opening the chest, the two lungs bulged forward. On removing the lungs there exuded a considerable amount of frothy light yellow fluid, evidently highly albuminous, as slight beating was sufficient to solidify it like the white of an egg. The veins on the surface of the brain were greatly congested.'

The first British troops to face the gas on 1 May were from the 1st Dorset Regiment. By then, military commanders were desperately pleading with their war offices and scientists for protection. The gas attacks continued on May 6, 10 and 24. Yet five more weeks of fighting around Ypres secured no breakthrough. A stalemate had been reached and the Germans brought the battle to an end. German losses totalled 35,000 officers and men; Allied casualties were about 60,000. In those five weeks around Ypres, the Germans had released 500 tons of chlorine from 20,000 canisters. As the Second Battle of Ypres was being left for historians to record and assess, the first chapter in the history of chemical warfare had been written.

It had started two years earlier, when the 'fathers' of modern chemical warfare, Professor Fritz Haber of the Kaiser Wilhelm Institute and Professor Walther Nernst of the University of Berlin, were conducting experiments for the use of gas on the battlefield. The German High Command was half-hearted about using gas. Haber, a 40-year-old chemist and, incredibly, a future Nobel Prize Winner, persisted even after losing his assistant, Professor Sachur, who was blown up in an early laboratory experiment. And it was Haber who brought to fruition the threat that had lingered for centuries – that some time, some where chemicals would be used in war.

There was nothing new in the concept. Incendiary weapons were originally invented by the Greeks, Hannibal used to hurl bottles of poisonous snakes on to the ships of his enemies, the Spartans burnt sulphur and pitch to produce sulphur dioxide, a gas that hit the throat and lungs. Even Napoleon envisaged the use of a crude form of germ warfare when he flooded the ground around Mantua to try to spread malaria. Toxic gases were more seriously proposed during the American War of Independence and the Crimean War.

In fact the French were the first to use chemicals in World War I, when they fired tear gas at the Germans in August 1914, though without great effect, and the Allied generals ridiculed the idea. Now, it was a reality. Germany had done what no one believed any nation would do and there was uproar, panic and a massive outcry of moral indignation among the Allied nations. Even Professor Haber's wife pleaded with him to give up his work. He refused and was already experimenting with a new gas, phosgene, to be unleashed on the Eastern front in the summer of 1915. On the night he left to oversee the new attack, she committed suicide.

The Allies, meantime, were desperately attempting to form a response and a defence to the Germans' new weapons. It would be almost a year before the British were able to manufacture crude protective helmets and respirators and many of those were ineffective, as the Germans had already discovered to their cost. Dozens of German corpses, soldiers who had died from the effects of gas, still in their respirator hoods littered the battlefields. In this mêlée of anger and confusion, the first moves were made towards the birth of Porton Down chemical experimental station, as the British led the Allied nations into efforts to match the Germans gas capability.

The War Office gathered all available experts from the military and the chemicals industry. A scientific advisory committee was set up to supervise the production of a suitable gas, hampered though it was by the lack of industrial capability and a suitable testing site, not to mention ignorance. It became a matter of supreme urgency, according to War Office documents of the day, to set up a 'ground for experimental purposes'. Several sights were visited, in Dorset, Hampshire and Wiltshire before they settled on Porton, then a tiny village close to Salisbury Plain.

Scientists were co-opted by the War Office and were placed under the charge of the Royal Engineers to create, amid great secrecy, Britain's first chemical warfare unit. RE Major Charles Foulkes was promoted to the rank of Lieutenant Colonel and given the title of Gas Advisor to the Commander in Chief of the British Expeditionary Force. Foulkes was already a legendary figure in the British Army, in which he had served for 23 of his 40 years, with battle-zone experience in various parts of the world. His appearance bore the marks of a fighter; his mud-stained uniform torn and dishevelled and his cap split by shrapnel.

He was sent immediately to London to liaise with the scientific committee and returned to France with orders to form Special Companies – so called to conceal their purpose – each with two officers and 80 men. By early July 1915 four companies of soldiers with scientific experience or qualifications had been gathered. The mystery surrounding them was further enhanced when they were eventually posted to the front, identifiable only by their brassards of pink, white and green – colours that were to be incorporated in the Porton Down mess tie.

They began work at an experimental site at Helfaut in France; while in Britain chemical and engineering factories were working around the clock to produce chlorine gas and cylinders to carry it. By August, the first of the stockpile of gas-filled cylinders was on its way to France and by mid-September Britain's retaliatory effort was being demonstrated to the British commanders, five months to the day after the first German attack.

Needless to say, there were problems, not to mention great indifference – and fear – among many of the military commanders, and their men of all ranks. The first British gas attack was directed from the battle headquarters. By then, Foulkes had amassed a force of 1,400 in his Special Companies and by mid-September they had placed 5,500 gas canisters containing 130 tons of chlorine along the Western Front.

After several delays and anxious reports about wind changes, the attack was finally given the go-ahead for 5am on 25 September 1915, but even then all did not go according to plan. On one section of the front, the gas company discovered they had the wrong-sized spanners and could not release the nuts on their canisters. On another section, one of the officers refused to give the order to open the cylinders because of wind change. He was ordered to obey the command immediately, and the gas blew straight back into the faces of the British troops.

The Germans, realizing that Allies were launching gas, opened fire on the emplacements and several canisters were hit and the gas spread through the British trenches. Several men of the Special Companies died from their own chemicals. Those mishaps apart, the bulk of Britain's gas stock was released, the hissing cloud sent forwards, the men watching it roll steadily towards the German lines. There was more than a touch of fiasco, resentment and fear in the British act – as vividly recalled by Robert Graves in *Goodbye to All That*.

The British Trench Warfare Department was pushing ahead with plans for its new experimental station at Porton Down and by the winter had acquired an initial 2,886 acres there, to which a further 4,000 acres would be added. A distinguished chemist and academic, Arthur Crossley, a professor of organic chemistry at King's College, London, was appointed to the role of commandant and superintendent of operations, for which he was given the rank of Lieutenant Colonel.

After spending some time at the front in France, he arrived at Porton to discover that his new base consisted of two Army huts, which had no running water, no electricity and no roads. In a copse nearby – later to be nicknamed by the locals as Gas Wood – lay the first consignment of 116 industrial cylinders containing hydrogen chloride, which had been prepared at Oldbury, Birmingham. Each one was 5ft 8in long and weighed 30lb, and had been sent by rail and moved from Porton station by local labour. A civilian watchman had been hired to stand guard until Crossley and his military back-up team arrived.

Sergeant Major Dobbs of the Royal Engineers reported for duty on 11 April. He was given the task of recruiting 13 civilian workmen and training them for gas experiments in the Porton countryside. Another six civilians from a mine rescue team, trained in the use of breathing sets, arrived at Porton to act as 'samplers' who would go into the gas clouds as they were released for testing. This contingent represented the first of many thousands of servicemen who would become human guinea-pigs in the decades of experiments using humans that followed at Porton. Within a month of his arrival, Crossley had set up his laboratory, and his first experiments began with gas cylinders set up in a mock war front. A system of trenches had been dug, into which were placed dozens of rats in cages.

The field trial viewed by the new Chemical Advisory Committee of scientists and military experts was judged to be 'highly successful'. Unfortunately for the British, the Germans were already one step ahead. Professor Haber had perfected the new and deadlier phosgene gas and was experimenting with shells instead of canisters, so that the gas could be fired directly into enemy lines.

Phosgene introduced a new level of fear for the Allied troops. It was, first of all, almost 20 times as powerful as chlorine and far less easy to detect. Troops were not immediately struck down by it; the effects might not become apparent for 24 hours or more. A victim of severe gassing would just collapse and die without warning; for others it was a slow and painful death, with men evacuating up to half a gallon of foul, yellow liquid uncontrollably from their mouths every hour. On the first day it was used, more than 1,000 men were gassed, of whom 116 died within 48 hours. The survivors would suffer the consequences for years to come.

The British, once again in haste, switched to phosgene and launched their first massive attack with the new gas at the Battle of the Somme. The huge cloud, released among the Allied front of almost 20 miles, rose 60 feet in the air and travelled on the breeze, reaching the German lines a dozen miles beyond, killing all wildlife that came in its path. 'Birds were falling from the trees,' contemporary news reports stated, 'and hundreds of dead rats are found in the trenches after each attack.'

Germany was extending its trials on shell-delivered gas, for greater accuracy. Porton experiments, on the other hand, still concentrated on gas from cylinders, an aspect that detained its scientists for far too long, although one of the Special Company commanders, Captain Livens, had invented a projectile, which was first tested on the Porton ranges in the early months of 1917.

In his report on the effectiveness of his canister-firing projectile, Livens clinically estimated that the device was so simple it could be manufactured by mass production so that 'the cost of killing Germans would be reduced to sixteen shillings each'. The Livens projectile and the small gas canisters it would fire went into immediate production and they were first used in the Battle of Arran in April 1917.

In his book *Gas: The Story of the Special Brigade*, published in 1936, Charles Foulkes recalled: 'there was a muffled roar as 2,340 of these sinister projectiles hurtled through the air . . . twenty seconds later they landed in masses in the German positions and after a brief pause the steel cases were burst open by the explosive charges and nearly fifty tons of liquid phosgene were liberated which vaporized instantly and formed a cloud so dense that Livens who watched the discharge from an aeroplane noticed it still so thick as to be visible as it floated over Vimy and Bailleul villages.'

Quite apart from the fear that the exploding canisters brought to the German lines, one of the other unexpected side effects was that the gas cloud killed or disabled hundreds of the horses and mules that were dragging the German supply carts to the front. Their soldiers soon began to run out of ammunition and while the gassing of troops on both sides of the infamous No Man's Land produced the most terrifying experiences, it must be said that conventional heavy metal continued to incur by far the most devastation.

At least, that was certainly the case until the Germans unleashed one final escalation in the chemical battle. Like Britain, they had been experimenting with many new agents such as phosgene and arsenal smoke and harassing chemicals. By the summer of 1917 they had perfected another calamitous new gas – what became known among the troops as HS – Hun Stuff or Yellow Cross, from the marking on its shells – otherwise known as mustard gas.

It was judged by German scientists to be a 'highly efficient' weapon not because of its mortality rate – only 2 per cent of those affected died immediately – but because it could injure men even if they were wearing respirators. It was also noticed that because mustard gas had little immediate effect and was so insidious in its approach, inexperienced troops paid little heed to it, and died as a result.

Within an hour or two, eyes were streaming and were subsequently blinded with painful conjunctivitis, the throat became sore as severe laryngitis set in, followed by vomiting and then breathing difficulties. After the first attack using mustard gas, once again at Ypres, it became common to see files of men, being led through the battlefields to the medical station, each with one hand on the shoulders of the man in front.

The casualties would be covered by severe blistering and skin burns, fluid from which soaked their clothes. In the worst cases, the effects on the soldier's breathing would subside into a fatal attack of bronchopneumonia. As the Germans had said, it was a most effective weapon and the Allies hurriedly sought to match it.

In February 1917, the nucleus of what was to become the Porton Battery of the Royal Artillery arrived with the two-fold task of firing experimental trials and proving Britain's own gas shells. Laboratories were operating around the clock to perfect the most effective form of chemical weapons and, secondly, to design efficient protective suits and respirators for both military and civilian use.

The British government, fearing an aerial attack over London, had ordered the mass manufacture of gas-masks developed through Porton trials. The entire output of a dozen factories had been turned over to their production. They were produced in vast quantities, and by the beginning of 1918 respirators and hexane helmets were made under special contract by factories in London and Nottingham.

Porton Down had, in the meantime, taken on the appearance of a small village with more than 1,000 servicemen and women and 500 civilians working inside its perimeters. Lines of barrack huts had been built, along with a new research block. The station's work was already forming a pattern that would continue for the remainder of this century. In his reports on Porton's activities, camp commandant Arthur Crossley recorded that civilian 'workmen were used extensively for experimental work' – in other words, they were the human guinea-pigs. Tests were also performed on a variety of animals, but particularly on goats, whose respiratory volume was similar to that of humans. Demand for experimental animals – at a time when food was in short supply – meant that Porton had to acquire its own farm, with the dual role of making the unit self-sufficient and breeding enough animals for research purposes.

For that, the nearby 314-acre Arundel Farm was commandeered. While all the usual farm animals were raised for food, goats were required on a daily basis; 600 were bred and housed at the farm as experiments in medical and toxicological research became increasingly important to the war effort. The first strains of Porton white mice, rats, guinea-pigs and rabbits were also introduced. Early Porton Down research documents, classified until the late 1950s, set out the theories that would become the blueprint for the future – that experiments using animals and humans were vital in assessing the 'lethality of gas in both concentration and period of exposure and [were] critical to a proper understanding of gas poisoning and its treatment'.

The story of gas and chemical warfare of that era – on all sides – was set against a background of uncertainty, crudely assembled laboratories and research teams with inadequate knowledge, certainly in Britain. Those days and nights of tired, weary scientists with the ever-anxious military machine breathing down their necks for answers produced the basis of the future of chemical warfare the world over. In the remaining two years of the war, Porton scientists tested 147 separate toxic substances for possible use.

By then, running in tandem with the chemical labs, the first physiological laboratory was set up in 1917 to monitor experimental animals and to report on the clinical effects and pathology of gas. Much use, according to the declassified documents, was also made of 'the human observer who was unmasked but with his respirator at the ready to act as the ultimate sensor and recorder of the effects on man'.

A true estimate of how many of those 'observers' died in later life as a result of that exposure is beyond calculation. At the time, the health of volunteers who might be permanently damaged was hardly one that could be allowed to stand in the way of science, considering the thousands of lives that were at stake. There is little or no evidence in the available reports of that period of even a shadow of doubt in the minds of those working on the various chemical projects that the discomfort and injury to personnel and animals caused in the testing was a matter for serious contemplation.

The Porton documents merely record 'the nation's great appreciation to these men whose courage enabled the country to meet the German gas threat'. In this reaction to chemical warfare, the British had been joined by the Americans, who entered World War I in June 1917. The American military set up its own chemical warfare establishment at Edgewood Arsenal, Maryland, towards the end of 1917 and were producing vast quantities of gas and researching new forms of weaponry.

As the Americans began their own research, in close co-operation with the British, the Germans had already perfected the delivery of the liquid mustard gas by shells, achieving incredible accuracy and producing a long-lasting poison that lay in pools on the ground and contaminated huge areas. The Germans had saved their major attack with mustard gas for 1917 until they had amassed a stockpile of more than a million shells. There were so many casualties that the field hospitals were simply unable to cope.

In the last months of the war, a quarter of all shells were being loaded with the Hun Stuff. Porton did not perfect its own brand of mustard gas until the late summer of 1918, by which time the hostilities were almost over. The Allies did not go short of their own poison bombs, however. In the final battles, with their troops under increasing bombardment after the Germans had made peace with the Russians, the Americans' production of chemical weapons was fully operational at Edgewood, which produced 100,000 bombs a day.

Those final months of the Great War saw a tally of horrifying statistics. Mustard gas, phosgene, chlorine and many other substances had taken their place in the arms race, and many nations would seek to include them in their chemical armoury. In all, 54 separate substances had been tested on the battlefield by both sides by the end of the war. Around 130,000 tons of gas and other chemicals had been dispersed by the two sides, using about 20,000 specially trained troops.

The final toll of casualties would show that 1,250,000 men were victims of gas attacks; a tenth of them were killed and an unknown but large percentage of the remainder would spend their lives fighting debilitating illness. Mustard gas, deemed to be five times as effective as either high explosives or shrapnel, accounted for 400,000 casualties alone and was placed at the top of the shopping list of the major nations, now alerted to the effects of chemical warfare.

In the longer term, beyond this war, which had wiped out a generation of young men in Europe, lay the result of Germany's decision to disregard the international Hague Convention of 1889: a dash to chemical armament. If there was a moment of particular poignancy at Porton, it came on the day of the Armistice, when, according to the unpublished memoirs of one of Porton's leading scientists, the men in charge of the experimental animals released 'a considerable number of monkeys' into the Wiltshire countryside. They mistakenly believed the animals would never be needed again.

There was one other vision totally contrary to those optimistic ideals that peace had come at last and never again would there be such a war. Among the battle-weary and humiliated enemy troops heading back towards their homeland was a 29-year-old corporal in the Bavarian reserve infantry, who, temporarily blinded by chemical gas, was vowing revenge for the stinging wounds: Adolf Hitler.

2

THE HUMANE KILLER

PUBLIC REACTION TO the sheer scale and horror of gas casualties was, for a time, judged to be sufficient to bring warring nations to their senses – and pledge that never again would such weapons be used. It was, ran the famous phrase, the war to end all wars. Porton, singled out for a particular recognition of its wartime work with a visit from King George V, was left with a 'sense of anti-climax'. For a while it seemed that the place might be shut, or at least scaled down. The Germans had been defeated and there were international moves to ensure that the signatories of the Hague Convention on chemical warfare reverted to their pre-war position.

The reality was exactly the reverse. While Allied nations on the one hand joined as one to decry Germany for starting the chemical conflagration, ambitions ran high among the military men to go on producing chemical weapons. They were supported by a growing body of scientists promoting the remarkable theory that chemical weapons were actually more humane than conventional arms. Figures produced by an international study group claimed that, apart from deaths during the early gas attacks and those among unprotected troops, the mortality rate was far lower than could be expected from conventional hardware.

It became a particularly emotive issue, especially among those who had experienced gas in the trenches, hundreds of whom would be scarred and incapacitated for life. The scientists answer to that was: 'Well, at least you are still alive.' That, in a nutshell, was the theme of a report to the British Cabinet in May 1919, which charted the possibilities resulting from the continued chemical threat in the future – a prospect that was comparable in its significance then as was the nuclear threat left hanging over from World War II.

The post-war exodus of personnel from Porton was immediately halted. In 1920, pending a decision by the League of Nations on disarmament, the British Cabinet approved plans to proceed with an expansion of the Porton establishment, and the Americans did the same at Edgewood. In that year, the future of chemical warfare research was set in stone. The Edgewood plant, built in two years at a cost of the then astronomical sum of $47 million, made the British equivalent look like a Boy Scout operation.

Scientific and military journals and even newspapers carried recruitment advertisements, extolling the virtues of the US Chemical Warfare Service 'located at Edgewood on the beautiful Chesapeake Bay in Maryland'.

Some of the best scientific brains in the US were enlisted to join a research and technical team of 1,200 and almost 1,000 support staff, assembled by the early 1920s. Edgewood mushroomed, with more than 200 buildings, in which hundreds of new chemical substances were being researched. Inside its perimeters were 30 miles of railway and 15 miles of roads, the largest capital investment on any military project in the US until the arrival of the rocket and nuclear technology towards the end of World War II.

Today it remains a monument to the first chemical war in history and, almost 80 years on, its self-promoting literature still portrays it, like Porton in Britain, as one of the jewels of the American defence network. The French also built their own chemical facility, centred mainly at the Atelier de Pyrotechnie de Bouchet, near Paris. The Italians had their Servizio Chemico Militare, north of Milan. The Japanese put their research into chemical weapons in the hands of the military scientific group under the control of the Japanese Navy and the Russians, latecomers to the race because of their own turmoil following the 1917 Revolution, founded the Military Chemical Division of the Red Army at the beginning of 1924.

Archive documents, so secret that they came into public view only in recent years, provide an insight into the early research work of these establishments. What stands out is the scientists' pride in their work, a significant and familiar aspect of those engaged in the development of Chemical and Biological Warfare (CB.W) down the years. The cost in terms of the massive use of animals and the hefty reliance on human 'observers' for testing was invariably swept aside, was barely a consideration. Unlike the hardware, where the effectiveness of explosives and gun carriers could be tested and monitored from a safe distance, virtually every aspect of chemical development needed to be tried out on some form of living being. The scientists would say there were no alternatives.

Almost bankrupted by the war, Britain had little money to spare. Even so, a gradual programme of new building at Porton was begun almost immediately. Those who doubted the efficacy of this development were merely pointed towards the same arguments as applied during the nuclear age of the 1950s and 1960s – that possession was also a form of deterrent. Among those early supporters was Winston Churchill, who had visited the front at the height of the gassing in France and had expressed himself to be 'exceedingly impressed' by the British effort. He would be joined by many eminent people in both political and scientific circles, as was evident from the membership list of Britain's Chemical Warfare Committee and the later Chemical Defence Committee that would oversee the development of Porton.

The list of those associated with the early development of Porton reads like a Who's Who of the world of science and medicine; many were household names of the day. Among them was the German-born physicist Professor Frederick Lindemann (later to become Lord Cherwell), who was the wartime director of the Royal Flying Corps Experimental Physics Station at Farnborough. An early pioneer of experiments on atomic heat at the Sorbonne, his work had attracted international acclaim. He was in no doubt of the importance of the chemical defence strategy, a view shared by his close friend Winston Churchill, who made him his personal scientific adviser in World War II.

Another was Professor John Scott Haldane, the Scottish physiologist, one of the early advisers on the British chemical response. His two children were also to make a name for themselves, in other ways. His daughter was the author Naomi Mitchison and his Oxford-educated son, John Burdon Sanderson Haldane, was among eminent scholars who were prepared to argue publicly the case for chemical weapons as against conventional warfare.

J.B.S. Haldane had become an atheist during the war and later was a committed Marxist and a director of the Communist newspaper, the *Daily Worker*. He would write many books in his distinguished career, among them (with J.A.S. Huxley) *Animal Biology*. In 1924, Haldane, then a reader in biochemistry at Cambridge conducting research into enzymes, published a work entitled *Callinicus: A Defence of Chemical Warfare*. He argued that: 'future wars being accepted as inevitable, I am in favour of anything which will impose the will upon the enemy speedily without taking his life or injuring him permanently.'

Apparently primed by several military scientists, Haldane argued that if wars were conducted with the use of chemical weapons, properly protected troops would suffer far less in terms of fatal casualties. The same applied to civilian populations under attack. The wholesale issue of gas-masks and other protection in towns and cities would save many thousands of lives. He wrote: 'In London, for example, high explosives and incendiary bombs dropped from aeroplanes would do far more harm than gas bombs. Houses are far more vulnerable to explosives and do far more damage to their occupants in collapsing, besides being inflammable. On the other hand they contain far more refuges that could be made gas proof.'

He noted that on the nights of 11 to 14 March 1918, the Germans fired 150,000 mustard gas shells into villages and valleys in the Cambrian salient, causing 4,500 casualties, of whom only 50 died, all because they took off their respirators.

Though controversial, Haldane's views were widely supported among leading military and political figures of the day, although the long-term effects of gas poisoning were then unknown, as was the fact that in thousands of cases it would cause long and lingering deaths to dozens of victims through cancer and other chemical-induced illnesses. His battle rules for the future called for the banning of the conventional hardware and its replacement with shells containing only chemicals and a small bursting charge. He concluded:

'Until 1915, the soldier's business was to push and throw pieces of metal at the enemy. Various devices were employed for throwing them fast and far, thanks in the main to the genius of the unforgotten Major General Shrapnel. The future is in the hands of the chemists.'

Perhaps the most incredible of his recommendations came from his case studies, which he maintained had shown that certain men were immune to the effects of blistering agents in mustard gas attacks. His assessment was accepted with rather less of an outcry than would be the case later in this century. It was discovered, he said, that 20 per cent of white men and a remarkable 80 per cent of black men were shown to be resistant to mustard gas burns – just as they might be to sunburn. 'It looks, therefore, as if after a slight preliminary test it should be possible to obtain enough coloured troops who would be resistant to gas blistering in concentrations harmful to most white men. Enough whites ought to be available to officer them.'

Gas was the 'humane killer' said Haldane, a weapon that would win battles in which many will be incapacitated but few slain. Such was the ignorance abroad at the time. Even so, Haldane's thesis was never dismissed, and certainly not by the scientists at Porton Down and Edgewood as they assembled in the 1920s to satisfy the military's continuing fascination with chemical weaponry, not to mention their own.

Against that thesis was an equally strong body of international anti-CW campaigners who were seemingly rewarded in 1925 when 38 major nations signed the Geneva Protocol, acknowledging that the use of poisonous gases in war had justly been condemned by public opinion in the Western world. Nations who signed the treaty would accept the prohibition of the use of such chemicals. In reality it wasn't worth the paper it was written on. Fifty years would pass before Japan and America even ratified the protocol and, in any event, most of the major nations around the world – Britain, America, France, Italy, Japan – were as deeply committed to chemical research as ever.

In Britain, the anti-gas lobby generally led public opinion and the government's intentions for Porton were largely unknown to the outside world. A self-contained scientific village was emerging within a closed-off region of Wiltshire countryside. New laboratories were built, including three huge gas chambers, and an extended farm breeding unit was added to provide an ever increasing need for animals.

Civilian staff numbers were doubled in five years, and doubled again by the end of the 1920s as the station grew in importance. Work on mustard gas, temporarily lapsed at the end of the war, was resumed and volunteers had to be found to expose their skin 'fearlessly in the gas chamber tests'. The reports of Porton scientists of that era clearly recognized that the task was unpleasant and dangerous.

Experiments with mustard gas and protective measures against it had been stepped up, more or less in line with J.B.S. Haldane's theories. It was widely considered in that secret world that sufficient stocks of both the gas itself and respirators to supply to large civilian populations should be available to meet the threat of a new chemical war. The post-war upsurge in the aircraft industry had added a new dimension to these possibilities.

One of the first tasks of the new Porton Down Chemical Defence Establishment was to test the nation's complete stock of gas-masks and respirators, which had lain largely unused since they were turned out in their millions at the height of the World War I. A large number of human 'volunteers' recruited from the services to test a sample selection of approximately 100,000 respirators was sent to Porton. The only way of proving their effectiveness, according to Porton's official history, was to use 'the human experience' as had been the case from the beginning and, on occasions, Porton's scientists led from the front in that respect.

One famous incident is recorded in previously classified documents at the Public Record Office. The Quarterly Reports to the War Office from the Commandant of Porton (September, 1928) carries an account of an experiment conducted personally by Sir Joseph Barcroft, head of the physiology department at Porton, to resolve a dispute between his own team and their counterparts in France over the effectiveness of hydrogen cyanide (HCN), a particularly awful poison. The French had tested the gas on dogs, all of which had died. Porton tried it on goats, which survived.

Late one evening after everyone else had left, Barcroft decided to test it on himself. With an army corporal as a witness, he took a dog into a gas chamber and, without masking himself, released a 1 in 2,000 concentration of hydrogen cyanide. This is his account of what happened:

'I remained standing and took a few steps from time to time while I was in the chamber. In about thirty seconds the dog began to get unsteady, and in 55 seconds it dropped on the floor and commenced characteristic distressing respiration which heralds death from cyanide poisoning. One minute thirty seconds after the commencement the animal's body was carried out, respiration having ceased and the dog being apparently dead. I then left the chamber. As regards the result upon myself, the only real effect was a momentary giddiness when I turned my head quickly. This lasted about a year and then vanished. For some time it was difficult to concentrate on anything for any length of time.'

What became known as the Barcroft Dog Incident was brought to the attention of Prime Minister, Lloyd George, who, upon hearing it, immediately dictated a memo congratulating him on his 'gallantry and devotion . . . which obtained information of quite exceptional value'. Brave, perhaps, but also foolhardy and an action with little perception of what possible reaction he might sustain in the future; research into the long-term effects of gassing was then virtually non-existent and a fascination with cyanide, like Barcroft's, would remain one of the features of Porton experiments for years to come.

Safety boundaries were pushed to the very edge of acceptable risk and occasionally beyond as Britain sought to match the German capability. Two Porton-linked colonels died conducting experiments on themselves and, as the Porton history records, 'sufferings were endured in a manner which was only possible by men of high morale under the urge of war'. Hundreds of men submitted themselves for testing purposes in an atmosphere of trial and error in the early days. One set of experiments was to test the limits of tolerance to an arsenic gas: 'twenty men were placed in the chamber for ten minutes . . . they [experienced] dull aching at the roots of the teeth . . . gnawing pain at the back of the face, numbness, cold of fingers, dryness of throat, retching and nausea . . . the men feel definitely ill . . . they lie down, sigh and roll about . . . keep moving in attempt to find relief.'

In the post-war era, testing of the nation's stock of respirators was no riskless task, either. The volunteers wearing the masks were sent into gas chambers filled with irritant arsenical smoke. The shock came when many of the respirators were found to be at the very least, 'penetrable'. The result was, says the Porton history with some resignation, that many of those involved in the tests were subjected to 'some physical and physiological strain'.

The tests proved that much of the national stock of gas-masks was useless. There were calls by the services for replacements, with specialist designs to cover all eventualities. Porton developed a general-purpose respirator for the services, which went into production in 1926, and between then and the end of World War II, more than 25 million were made. The government-sponsored Chemical Defence Committee also pressed for new designs for civilians, on which Porton began working at the same time, as the possibilities of aerial bombing of cities grew with each passing year.

Within a few years, a design was perfected at Porton which would be used to produce military and civilian gas masks. The continued strength of the chemical-war lobby was sufficient for the British and Americans to redouble their efforts, literally, and this was done on the single-sentence pretext – the same one that is widely used today – which, in a nutshell, states that all possible chemical permutations have to be trialed and tested in order to develop an efficient defence.

It was only towards the end of the 1920s that the hidden implications of chemical experiments began to come home to roost. Ten years after the end of the war, the first assessments were made of the many thousands of veterans who were by then drawing disability pensions directly as a result of wartime gassing. Porton was called upon to investigate and concluded that the prognosis for the gas victims was poor: virtually without exception they suffered from lung diseases, pneumonia, impaired vision – all of which would 'gradually get worse . . . it is only a matter of time before a cardiac condition develops.'

The Porton report, now in War Office documents at the Public Record Office, added: 'the evidence suggesting mustard gas is the cause appears to be conclusive'. One year later, a further 70 men were examined by Porton physiologists and were found to be suffering from a list of half a dozen illnesses – all apparently resulting from mustard gas poisoning. These conclusions and statistics were not for public consumption, nor would they be for a further 50 years.

Contemporary newspaper reports claiming the permanent disability of gas attack victims were widely dismissed by government health ministry officials as scaremongering. However, a World Health Organization study years later would discover what the British knew but refused to admit – that as of 1 January 1930, 80 per cent of the surviving veterans who had been exposed to mustard gas poisoning in the war were suffering from chronic respiratory problems, and many subsequently died from lung cancer.

The truth about the long-term effects of gas was finally dawning. Just as 'top secret' then, as now, were the statistics concerning the use of animals. In 1982, the first details of some of those early experiments were finally revealed among 9,000 documents released for historical assessment into the Public Record Office, covering the period to 1929. They showed that virtually every kind of animal available to British scientists was used in experiments whose descriptions make upsetting reading for those concerned with animal welfare. As ever, they carried the preamble that it was done in the name of science, in order to make life less hazardous for troops and civilians alike who might one day face these chemicals in reality.

Even then, in the early days, although Porton's animals were considered vital to their work, J.B.S. Haldane noted that many of the soldiers who worked at the station had an exceedingly strained relationship with the physiologists because they 'objected so strongly' to the experiments on animals. Monkeys and baboons, especially, were used for studying the effects of gas on the skin.

They had chemicals squirted into their eyes, noses and ears, rubbed into shaven areas of skin, smeared over their genitalia. Goats, sheep, cats and dogs, along with countless thousands of rats, mice and guinea-pigs, were tethered or caged in the Porton ranges to test gas in the trenches, or inside in the gas chambers. Others were subjected to research designed to aid the treatment of soldiers wounded by conventional weapons. Larger animals were regularly subjected to the 'firing squad' to receive varying degrees of bodily damage, ranging from mere gashes in their flesh to traumatic and eventually fatal wounds.

The blanket of security surrounding this activity, which had attracted the attention of anti-vivisectionists and animal-welfare groups, naturally had an effect on those involved in the work. To some degree, they were to become excluded from the rest of society, and inside the Porton compound itself a quite remarkable lifestyle developed as the inmates settled down to their various tasks, increasing in numbers through the decade of the 1920s and on into the 1930s.

The Porton station became an area prohibited to the public. All who had access to it were diligently vetted and sworn to uphold the Official Secrets Act. Everyone who worked there in whatever capacity was left in no doubt that the Act would be rigorously applied and pursued through the courts. 'Secrecy in all that we do' became the official motto of the establishment and every written contact with the outside world was subject to security checks.

Virtually all government reports that included mention of chemical defence were immediately given a 'classified' rating and very little of Porton's own documentation escaped into the public domain until well into the second half of the century. Much of it is still regarded as being too sensitive to release and will not be available until well into the next century – if ever.

The obsessional regard for secrecy was taken to extreme lengths. Even a rather parochial history of Porton, written by Lieutenant Colonel A.E. Kent, who had served in the Special Brigade Royal Engineers in the 1914–18 war, and had worked there as a civilian until 1956, did not see the light of day for nearly 30 years. Kent had kept a diary of his work with the unit for many years and wanted to write his memoirs, or a book on Porton. Permission was refused.

In 1961, however, he was paid a modest £250 to write an authorized version and 'a brief history' was published for limited circulation within the defence community. It remained a 'classified document' until 1987, long after Kent's death. The larger history that he had intended for the general public was barred from publication and the original typescript he presented for approval remains to this day filed away at the establishment.

From Kent's accounts of Porton, relatively innocuous after

screening by the security staff, and from other unpublished records, it is possible to glimpse the fascinating, if worrying, style of life that gradually built up within its fenced perimeters. It was from the beginning a closed society, in almost every respect. Barrack-style accommodation was available for single technicians while the staff in married quarters had more space. They were allotted a small garden and allowed to keep poultry. All food, bread, meat, disinfectants and general groceries could be drawn from the Barrack Services and Supplies store.

The Portonians, as they called themselves (and thus, those who left were Old Portonians), had their own church and camp padre, staged their own entertainment through the Porton Musical and Drama Society and, of course, had their own cricket team, which was kept with a busy fixture list by the chairman of the, by now, many sub-committees of the controlling Chemical Warfare Committee that had developed by the early 1930s.

Later they would get their own cinema, which was also used by the scientists to run film of their experiments. There were occasional incidents of black humour such as the time the married quarters were accidentally sprayed with a dye during an aerial bombing simulation, resulting in the discovery of pink-spotted babies left outside in their prams and pink-spotted washing.

The main thrust of their work remained as serious as ever and in that the British government, like most others, was quite cynically prepared to disguise the fact that, on the one hand, it had approved the Geneva Protocol of 1925 but, on the other, it was working away to improve its own chemical defence strategy. As the Porton documents from the era acknowledged, development of weapons had to be 'done under the rose'. The language and description of its work was altered to provide some form of recognition of the Convention. The term chemical warfare was, as a matter of policy, deleted from the public pronouncements and substituted with 'chemical defence'.

In reality, it was business as usual. The only difference was that the whole operation was now paraded under the heading of defensive rather than offensive necessity. Field trials became renowned among visiting top brass from the military. Its official history boasts that during the inter-war years, 'the anti-gas defence of the United Kingdom and its forces had been brought to a level which was superior to that of any other nation'. Experiments simulating virtually every scenario of gas attack had been acted out around the Porton ranges.

They had Vickers tanks for testing – with volunteers – the vulnerability of tank crews. Light aircraft were used to spray coloured simulants on marching troops to discover the strength of chemicals as droplets reached the ground. Porton tested attacks of mustard gas at high altitudes, when wearing respirators would not be practicable. It researched dozens of items of clothing and protective shields for both soldiers and horses – ranging from an anti-gas oilskin cape, protective dubbin for boots, a sleeve detector for the presence of chemicals, gas identification sets and, for the animals, anti-gas covers for horses, mules and war dogs. Even a prototype gas-mask for horses was produced. All these inventions were proved and tested in the Porton chambers and on the ranges to make British troops, says the Porton history, better equipped in anti-gas protection than any force in the world.

In the chemical labs, research work concentrated on discovering new CW agents and perfecting defences against them. Scientists there were also experimenting with riot-control gases for use by British police and military forces in various parts of the British Empire where unrest occasionally flared.

No large stockpiles of any gas were maintained in Britain. Elsewhere, the build-up was blatant. America, Russia, Japan and Italy were already heavily committed to CW production, building large stocks of mustard gas and lewisite. As one military analyst described it, chemical warfare had become a huge slumbering giant, growing fat and expansive, protected by politicians and fed by scientists. One day, it might explode.

3

HITLER'S SECRET AGENT

THE GIANT BEGAN to stir in the early 1930s and with it came a new threat: biological warfare. The Russians led the way, and Japan was close behind. Britain would soon join the race. Crude experiments with germ-carrying containers were already being tested by Soviet scientists in the Siberian waste. What horrors were perpetrated on human guinea-pigs under the Stalin regime will never be known but many hundreds are thought to have died in experiments. Put in it simplest form, germ warfare was a way of overcoming enemy troops and civilian resistance by spreading killer diseases such as anthrax, cholera, typhoid, tetanus and a host of others, even syphilis. The idea, like gas, had been around for centuries, dating from the earliest recorded history of war when soldiers used to poison the water of their enemies by throwing human bodies and dead animals into their wells.

In this century, the first attempts at primitive forms of biological attack were made by Germany during World War I, when it attempted to halt the Allies by killing their horses with a highly infectious disease called glanders, which would also transfer to man. At the same time, Germany had accused the Russians of attempting to spread plague bacteria across the German lines in 1916. After that, little was heard of biological attack; the scientists were too busy discovering new forms of chemical weapons.

However, the use of bacteria to spread fatal and quick-acting disease came back to the international warfare agenda in the late 1920s. Poland, aware of experiments being conducted across the border in the USSR, had successfully proposed that 'bacterial warfare' should be included in the 1925 Geneva Protocol although at the time there was very little research – and even less knowledge – in the West of how biological agents might be used.

Japan's interest, as documents retrieved after World War II would show, became almost an obsession after its own troops had fallen victim to what was in effect the world's first major attack using BW agents. Captured Japanese General Shiro Ishii claimed that five Russian spies were arrested by the Japanese military in southern China in the early 1930s. They were part of a well-trained sabotage unit, armed with ampoules containing cholera and anthrax. Under interrogation they had admitted they had already carried out attacks near Shanghai, which – according to the Japanese general – resulted in the deaths of 5,000 Japanese troops from cholera and 2,000 horses from anthrax.

Ishii himself, then a 40-year-old military scientist with the rank of major, was dispatched on a secret mission to Europe, touring the capitals of the West in an attempt to discover the extent of BW research. He returned in 1934, convinced that biological weapons held 'the greatest promise' in future wars.

Ishii became, according to a post-war intelligence assessment produced by the Americans, the most dominant force in the development of the Japanese BW capability. He promoted his theories in government circles and finally won approval to establish a germ warfare research centre at a military hospital at Pingfan, 50 miles from Harbin, in south Manchuria. It was initially conducted under the guise of a water-purification plant. Though some regarded his work as unimportant, his military masters became intrigued by his theories for the production of an anthrax-filled bomb that could wipe out an entire city without structural damage. He also drew up models for sabotage techniques, using specially trained units to go behind enemy lines spreading disease and poisoning water supplies.

The Japanese began pouring money into his research programme, and by 1939 when the research centre was completed, they had installed a detachment of 3,000 troops, scientists and laboratory workers – capable of producing several tons of bacteria a month. It was there, as will be seen in future chapters, that Ishii tested his research on British, Australian and American prisoners of war.

Early intelligence reports of Japanese activity in this field began to surface in the West in the mid-1930s and prompted a response in Britain. The potential threat of BW was first discussed among Chiefs of Staff in the autumn of 1933. At another CoS meeting on 12 February 1934, Sir Maurice Hankey, one of the nation's most powerful mandarins, was ordered to begin 'very secret' inquiries among the scientific community about the possibilities of this kind of warfare.

Hankey, a dour, intense man of 57, was secretary to both the Cabinet and the Committee for Imperial Defence. He had an extensive knowledge across the whole spectrum of Britain's military and defence policy and his advice was highly regarded. The Cabinet was informed of his informal soundings and gave its approval. Outside Whitehall, however, he found less than an enthusiastic response, especially from the Medical Research Council, whose secretary, Edward Mellanby, issued a point-blank refusal to co-operate with any such project.

One ally did emerge, however, in the shape of Dr Paul Fildes, the dictatorial head of the council's Bacterial Metabolic Unit, who agreed to assist Hankey in compiling a report on the practicalities of BW and why Britain should work on counter-measures. The upshot was that Hankey went back to the Chiefs of Staff fully convinced that BW research was 'a priority for Britain'. The Committee for Imperial Defence gave the go-ahead for the creation of a Microbiological Warfare Committee with Hankey as its chairman. In its first report, the committee concluded that immediate steps should be taken to create a defence against possible attacks using bacteria such as plague, anthrax and foot-and-mouth disease.

After a long series of consultations with leading scientists, the Medical Research Council and directors and deans of leading medical faculties, the British government formally and secretly authorized work on biological research in Britain by a small group of experts, to be based at Porton Down.

Results of that work, and its implications, lay in the future. Like the Japanese and the Russians, Porton had to build its experimental research base, and that would take several years. For the time being, the bulk of its effort continued to be focused on chemical weaponry, which had once again become an area of intense activity. Japan was moving rapidly on that front. In 1932, it had opened the Army Chemical Warfare School at Narashimo, near Tokyo, specifically to train its young scientists and army specialists. By the end of the decade, the centre had produced 3,200 experts who were given jobs in the burgeoning Japanese chemical plants with more than a dozen factories sited around the country, primed to produce mustard gas and phosgene while continuing experiments with other forms of chemical attack weapons. The stockpiles being mounted were to be trialed extensively in Japan's war with China, from 1937.

The surprise event among this renewed thrust came from the Italians. Although a signatory to the Geneva Convention of 1925, Mussolini had been quietly producing large stocks of mustard gas and phosgene as he prepared his expansionist plans for the revival of an Italian Empire. On 3 October 1935, his long-expected invasion of Abyssinia began when thousands of young Italian troops charged across the border from Eritrea. Italian bombing planes roared overhead, unleashing their loads on the border towns as the ground troops began their march inland.

With the courageous Abyssinians digging in on terrain that was unfamiliar to Italian soldiers, Mussolini's invasion did not proceed as rapidly as he had hoped. Towards the end of the year, he ordered 1,000 tons of mustard gas to be shipped to the Italian bases. Soon bombs filled with the gas were being rained down indiscriminately on the unsuspecting Abyssinians. In January 1936, the Italians began using an aerial spray-bomb to achieve greater effectiveness. The gas was put into 500lb bombs equipped with a bursting charge timed to explode when each bomb reached 200 or 300 feet from the ground, causing the liquid gas to spray over a wide area.

Emperor Haile Selassie sought shelter in the West and at a meeting of the League of Nations international statesmen sat silent and glum as he made an emotional speech describing the attacks. The aircraft came in groups, one after the other, he said, spraying the liquid over the countryside. The liquid formed into a continuous fog enveloping all below it – men, women, children, animals – as well as polluting the rivers and lakes.

International news media reacted with horror. Reporters were soon describing scenes reminiscent of World War I. Hundreds of people were left to their own devices, too ill to walk, and miles from hospital facilities. The *New York Times* spoke of children screaming with agony through terrible injuries, their skin peeled away and hanging from their bodies, exposing blood-red tissue. Many were blinded. Men who had merely touched bushes carrying lingering mustard gas found their legs and genital areas burning with pain and the burned skin dropping away. There were at least 20,000 casualties of the Italian gas bombs, though the true number was never known. Many died later through gangrene and progressive wounds.

Chemical warfare was back on the international agenda. In America production at Edgewood was stepped up by a third. During that year of the Italian gas onslaught, the French opened a new phosgene-producing factory at Clamercy to add to two already geared for production. Stalin, already handsomely equipped and building a massive chemical armoury, ordered three more factories into production at Kuibyshev, Karaganda and Brandyuzhsky. The British government, which in theory had renounced its intention to accumulate stockpiles of gas, began building a new factory at Sutton Oak, Lancashire, and had plans prepared for two others.

A flurry of alarming intelligence reports detailed the known upsurge of CW research, with scientists and military advisers across the world feverishly working on gas warfare projects. Typically Porton Down became a place of high drama. Many field trials were started and realistic scenarios invented, which included 'the exposure of volunteers' to chemicals to test the performance, for example, of gun crews in conditions of war. On the Porton ranges, animals continued to be tethered in trenches and in the open as the Porton teams worked to perfect the most effective form of gas and its delivery to targets.

In other tests, mustard gas was being tested deep in the heart of Hampshire, at Tipner Pond, where its lingering effects on the qualities of sand and shingle were observed – experiments that would have particular relevance in the early months of World War II when Winston Churchill came to the very brink of ordering British beaches to be drenched with liquid mustard gas at the time of the threatened German invasion.

And Germany, in 1936, was the most worrying country of all to other European governments. While international attention was diverted by the Italian invasion of Abyssinia, Hitler invaded the Rhineland in March of that year, confirming what many had been warning for months. Germany's CW capacity was believed to be well beyond that of any other European nation, and matched only by the Soviets. It had at least six operational stations working on CB research and production, and was said to be heavily engaged in trial bombing sorties using low-flying aircraft to disseminate gas clouds.

British scientists had already observed that reports and analyses of many laboratory studies had disappeared from the pages of recently published scientific journals, normally the fount of all new knowledge. The true reason was missed by British and American intelligence, although it was picked up by the Soviets. In 1934, a team of German scientists had published a report of important work with organophosphorus compounds for use as a pesticide. It would turn out to be the precursor to what was singularly the most important discovery in the field of chemical warfare – one that would concentrate the minds of CW scientists for the rest of the century.

A year or so after the study had been published, commercial biochemist Dr Gerhard Schrader was using it as a model for his own work on a new pesticide for his employers, IG Farben. He was testing various combinations of chemicals to find a formula to kill leaf lice. He mixed minute concentrations of his liquid for spraying infected specimens. It was at that point he found it had some nasty side effects, on both himself and an assistant. First his eyesight began to deteriorate and a few days later he began to experience breathing difficulties. Within a week, both he and his aide were suffering from spasms and slight paralysis of the arm muscles. They could not work for nearly a month. Almost by accident, Professor Schrader had discovered what would become known as the nerve gas tabun.

Schrader wrote up a report on his findings, and the assessment of the substance reached higher ranks – and was eventually noticed by scientists running Germany's CW programme under the control of the Wehrmacht. He was called to Berlin to give an account of what he had found. Tests were ordered immediately, using a dozen assorted animals. They were dosed with minute quantities of the compound and fascinated observers watched in stunned silence as the animals dropped, one by one. Within half an hour, they were all dead.

The Wehrmacht commanders ordered a new series of tests using monkeys and baboons. Without exception, the animals lost control of their bodily movements and functions, excreting uncontrollably, vomiting, foaming at the mouth. Finally, they went into convulsive fits and died, all within 15 minutes of being administered droplets of Schrader's organophosphate. Its potential as a CW agent was quickly recognized. Wehrmacht scientists reported that it apparently had significant 'advantages' over the well-tried and tested mustard and phosgene gases.

It had virtually no smell, was colourless and, most important of all – as Schrader had personally discovered to his cost – its poisonous qualities were effective by mere contact with the skin, making it an ideal substance for aerial spraying. It was so strong that the corrosive effect on any metal container was found to be immediate.

Schrader was moved from his place of work to secret laboratories in the north to continue his research, with the oversight of leading figures in the German CW hierarchy. Within a year, he had made a further discovery, a compound related to tabun but that was found in tests on animals to be a dozen times more powerful in its effects. This, he called sarin – a name he made up by taking letters from the surnames of the four men who had worked on its discovery, himself and three others.

Another year of proving the substance finally convinced the Wehrmacht leaders of its lethal potential. Hitler was informed and he gave the go-ahead to the director of the Wehrmacht's Chemical Research headquarters at Spandau to build new laboratories to perfect the substance, for which animals by the score and eventually male prisoners from concentration camps were brought in and fell victim to the trials.

What the German scientists discovered was frightening – those working on the project described it in their notes as 'astonishing'. Little more than 1/1000 of a gram inhaled in one breath could kill a man in under 30 minutes. It was an agonizing death that resulted from chemical interference with the way the nerves transmit messages to the muscles of the body – hence the title of Nerve Gas. The whole muscular system of the body went into a state of irreversible vibration, even those muscles that controlled breathing and excretion, until the victim fell dead.

Germany, for the second time in a mere 30 years, had become the proud possessor of the most virulent chemical threat known to mankind. By the time Hitler ordered the invasion of Poland, sufficient stocks of sarin had been manufactured to be used in the attack if the military commanders so desired. The rout of Poland was so unhindered, however, that it did not become necessary. For the time being, sarin would remain Hitler's secret weapon and one that he merely hinted at in speeches he knew were being monitored by the British.

He ordered the building of a new German chemical factory that would be capable of producing upwards of 1,000 tons of nerve gas a month, miles away from the German population, in Silesia, western Poland. Its Wehrmacht code-name was 'Hochwerk', and to avoid any immediate clues to its true purpose even funds for its building and staffing were channelled through existing German chemical companies.

All of this remained beyond the knowledge of British intelligence. However, they were already alerted to Germany's expansion of its chemical facilities, especially in what the British believed was their development of arsenic-based gas, in which they had historically shown a keen interest. Their CW experts were reported to have a particular liking for arsine, or arseniuretted hydrogen (code-named 'Arthur' by Porton), which was an especially lethal agent capable of destroying the red blood cells of its victims.

In the two years before the outbreak of war, British intelligence had submitted a report on its concern that Germany was buying up all available arsenic on the world metal markets. A new respirator for use by its troops, produced as early as 1936, was also known to give particular protection against arsenical agents, and against the chemical particularly favoured by Russian scientists, hydrogen cyanide.

The Porton teams rushed ahead with research into the arsenic threat and produced what became known as Detector Paper Type A, which reacted to arsenic gas. Ironically, however, the intelligence reports of Germany's new weapon were well wide of the mark. Their cornering of the world arsenic market had been intended largely to meet their industrial use. But as soon as the German's learned that Porton had developed a detector paper for that chemical, its scientists assumed that this gas must have become a major part of the British chemical armoury – and they then rushed an arsenic gas into production.

Porton Down, like most chemical installations around the world, was now operating on an 'emergency' alert pretty well across all fronts of its operations. By the end of 1936, the British government had authorized the manufacture and issue of enough gas-masks for every member of the British public, a task that deeply involved Porton's proving expertise.

Although Porton's official history boasts that it had prepared a more efficient defence against chemical attack than any other similar centre in the world – at least as far as known weapons were concerned – this preparedness was not shared by the military. The Army's instruction literature and handbooks were so out of date that they still spoke of gas attacks being delivered by cylinders, as in World War I, rather than from bombs, aerial spraying and shell fire, as would now be the case.

Porton itself assessed that 'had Germany initiated chemical warfare at the outbreak, the immediate ability of the United Kingdom to retaliate in kind would have been negligible'. There were a few 250lb mustard gas bombs for the RAF and some spray tanks. Britain's total stockpile of mustard gas at that point was around 500 tons and about 5 tons of tear gas – a minuscule total compared with that available in Germany.

This state of affairs, Britain's almost total lack of capability to 'retaliate in kind', was being emphasized by military intelligence long before the war became a reality. In May 1939 intelligence reports drawn up to assess the CW preparedness of potential enemies proved devastating reading; it concluded with ominous forecast that if Hitler deemed it expedient to 'introduce gas warfare it will be pursued with the characteristic vigour, ingenuity and ruthlessness'.

The British and the French immediately began to discuss a joint effort, to pool their expertise and plan a collaborative effort on chemical warfare, but it was barely under way when Prime Minister Neville Chamberlain declared that Britain was at war with Germany. Two days later, the command team and intelligence unit of the Chemical Defence Research Department was moved *en bloc* from its headquarters in Grosvenor Gardens, London, to the Porton establishment. Leading scientists and academics were co-opted to the Chemical Defence Committee. Once again, some of the most distinguished scientists of the day were enlisted to head the various Porton research teams.

They included Professor (later Sir) Roy Cameron, the famed pathologist; Professor Sam Sugden, the English chemist and professor at Birkbeck College, London, and the University College of London, known for his outstanding work on molecular volumes; Sir Joseph Barcroft, the Irish-born professor of physiology at Cambridge and director of animal physiology for the Agricultural Research Council noted for devising appliances for blood-gas analysis; along with a host of other senior figures in the world of science, pathology and medicine.

Within a matter of weeks, both civilian and military personnel were piling into the Porton confines. The proverbial ring of steel was thrown around its perimeters and guards posted on its 'closed area' where secret experiments were performed. The Territorial Army sent an anti-aircraft gun battery and manned the perimeters with 24-hour patrols. Teams of men began camouflaging the buildings with paint and netting. Lines of new huts were appearing overnight to provide barracks and mess facilities for the influx of arrivals, and air-raid drill was performed as an almost daily task for the newcomers because of the fear that Porton would become an early target for German bombers.

All available factory production for military respirators and civilian gas-masks was working around the clock to meet the 'fully anticipated' fear that British Expeditionary Forces would be confronted by gas attacks in Europe and British cities would be subject to airborne gas bombing. Millions had already been manufactured to Porton-proved specifications. Up to and during World War II, 100 million gas-masks would be produced in Britain alone.

As in the World War I, there would be many false alarms, which Porton staff would be called upon to test out. Among the earliest was a mysterious, airborne cobweb-like substance, which was being reported by Home Guard and ARP wardens in various parts of the country, who saw it floating down into the countryside. The alert went up immediately, the theory being that the Germans had produced some unknown form of carrier for the mass poisoning of civilian populations. Porton scientists were drafted to collect samples, but it turned out to be no more sinister than a rare natural phenomenon, first identified in 1741 by the English clergyman and naturalist Gilbert White. He described a similar outbreak of 'airborne gossamer' in his *Natural History and Antiquities of Selborne* (1789), which, based upon a collection of letters, became an English classic.

Discovery of this past evidence of the suspected new weapon inspired a poem written by an unidentified member of the GHQ Home Forces in 1940:

> Security of home and health were shaking in their pants
> Till Colville quoted a piece from White of Selborne Hants.
> They sent it out on all the wires 'This matter's quite alright'
> For any references see letters, Gilbert White.

By the mid-1940s Porton was fully manned, running extensive field trials and overseeing the build-up of hefty stocks of the three major gases, mustard, phosgene and the tear gas, BBC (bromobenzyl cyanide), which were being produced at chemical factories commandeered by the Ministry of Supply under 'conditions of extreme secrecy and urgency'.

This hurried preparation was exacerbated by the fall of France and the threat of a German invasion of Britain, a possibility that moved Winston Churchill's War Cabinet to make one of the most significant decisions in the history of chemical warfare – that Britain would, in certain circumstances, be prepared to make the first strike with gas.

4

A MILLION TONS OF MUSTARD

IN JUNE 1940, with the Enigma decryption warning that Hitler's preparations for the invasion were actively under way, Winston Churchill urgently called for an assessment of defensive measures along all sections of the British coast through which a German invasion might be attempted. Seven weeks earlier, the very first letter he had received when he became prime minister was from the German-born physicist Professor Frederick Lindemann, the former director of the Royal Flying Corps Experimental Physics Station at Farnborough and one of the most senior advisers on gas warfare in 1914–18.

Twenty-two years on, he was personally still in no doubt of the importance of the chemical defence strategy and had written to Churchill on the subject of a Nazi invasion. Having experienced trench warfare first hand, he suggested in his letter of 12 May 1940 that enemy parachutists could not make a safe landing unless they were rapidly re-inforced with ground troops, whose arrival on British shores the parachutists would initially guard. Lindemann suggested that trenches should be dug across all potential landing areas, which would delay the German troops sufficiently until a British force arrived to 'deal with them'.

As the threat of invasion neared, Churchill asked Lindemann to draw up a draft proposal for the digging of trenches by voluntary labour, drawn from local communities. No mention is made in these early exchanges of any position on defensive gas, but very soon Lindemann would be appointed personal scientific adviser to Churchill. By 30 June 1940 it was being openly discussed at Cabinet level. Churchill's papers and those of his aide, Sir John Colville, record the sequence of events that put gas on the immediate agenda.

Churchill instructed General Hastings Ismay, head of his Defence Office, to report at once on the amount of mustard gas 'or other variants' in store. He also wanted to know Britain's capability of making airborne attacks with bombs charged with mustard gas as well as artillery. Whatever the output, Churchill added, it should be 'speeded up'.

He theorized on a possible scenario: 'Supposing lodgements were effected on our coast, there could be no better points for application of mustard gas than these beaches. In my view there would be no need to wait for the enemy to adopt such methods (i.e. their own use of gas). He will certainly adopt them if he thinks it will pay.' To Major-General Andrew Thorne, who was lunching with him that day, Churchill said of this prospect: 'I have no scruples, except not to do anything dishonourable.'

Churchill insisted: 'Everything should be brought to the highest pitch of readiness . . . but the actual deployment must be studied by the Cabinet.' The following day, as the Colville papers record, Churchill was actively considering the proposal that 'we must consider drenching the beaches with mustard gas if the enemy attempts a landing. In that event gas warfare would be entirely justified.'

Three days later, a reply from the War Office landed on his desk confirming that 'it is desirable to have Britain's preparations complete so that we may retaliate' against a gas attack or if the War Cabinet decided to initiate gas warfare. The new impetus towards building the gas stockpile was to begin at once, although when Herbert Morrison, the Minister of Supply, raised the question of purchasing large stocks of chemicals from America, Churchill replied it would be 'better to leave the United States out of this particular line . . .. Press on here.'

Britain, in the summer of 1940, was ready to bombard the invaders with its new gas-loaded weapons. The British Expeditionary Force in France also remained on full gas alert, especially when it was learned by British intelligence that the Axis had perfected the use of 'Substance S', a most deadly new form of nitrogen/mustard gas, although the Allies were still not aware of Germany's top-secret experiments with nerve gas.

As Britain's readiness to meet this threat became paramount in the eyes of both government and military commanders, Porton was at the forefront of the war strategy. From previously classified documents, it can be seen that 3,394,093 Porton-designed shells charged with mustard gas were produced in Britain between 1939 and 1945.

For the RAF, 1,862,643 bombs filled with mustard gas or phosgene and ranging from 30lb to 500lb were produced. And in accordance with Churchill's instructions to increase stocks to the maximum level, a total of 40,719 tons of mustard gas, charged into weapons or held in bulk storage, were manufactured, along with 14,042 tons of phosgene and tear gas at a cost of £24 million. In addition, chemical weapons for use by the Army and RAF and shells for naval guns were designed and tested. Substantial stockpiles of the shells charged with phosgene were laid in shore depots, though none was ever carried on active duty. They were to be reserved for 'naval use in bombardment of land targets before or in support of landings'.

These totals were frightening enough but they were a mere fraction of the stocks of chemical weaponry being prepared by the fighting nations in the early years of the war. A seemingly incalculable doomsday industry was growing, virtually out of control, a massive world-wide collection of often untried and unstable weaponry that the war lords and the politicians were preparing to hurl at each other if and when the need arose.

Undoubtedly, the Germans, by the mid-1940s, were the leaders of the race. They were pouring millions of reichmarks into a dozen chemical factories. The nerve gas factory in Silesia, manufacturing sarin and tabun, was one of the largest. Its covered production area alone was now over a mile long and half a mile wide above ground and below a massive underground network of separate units was being built to fill shells with the gas that was to be manufactured above. Vast areas of forest were cleared to make way for the barracks to house 3,000 workers engaged at the site. The manufacturing capability of this plant alone would account for the production of more than 3,000 tons of nerve agent a month.

It was daunted by problems, not least in the human cost. The manufacture of a gas whose effects were so insidious and that was lethal to the mere touch or airborne whiff brought many casualties. More than 1,000 workers at the plant suffered dire effects. Even those who were not directly exposed to the gas could not escape its effects. German documents captured after the war would show that there were few 'members of staff who were ever free from the effects . . . they could easily be recognized because of the contracted condition of their eyes.'

America had also begun its own substantial commitment to chemical weaponry, and suffered similar manufacturing problems. In April 1941, seven months before the US entered the war, the Army was given the go-ahead to build a new chemical warfare manufacturing plant, with a budget of $32 million. This decision was made a full month before President Franklin D. Roosevelt issued his historic proclamation 'declaring the existence of a state of unlimited emergency'. The Army Ordnance Department was ordered to expand its facilities in order to assure adequate 'production of ammunition in keeping with the time-objective requirements of the General Staff . . . and an immediate building of a chemical shell assembly plant'.

Until then, the Edgewood Arsenal, set up in 1917 in Maryland, was the only chemical manufacturing installation in America. About 30,000 acres of land were needed for the new plant. The location had to be inland, far enough from the seacoast to provide sufficient protection but with adequate access to rail, water, power and highways. On 24 July 1941, the War Department settled on Huntsville, Alabama, where by the end of the year, it began building stockpiles of mustard gas, phosgene, lewisite, white phosphorous, carbonyl iron and tear gas.

The now famous Redstone Arsenal, based at Huntsville, opens its official history by recording its initiation into chemical warfare as 'extremely important . . . marking the beginning of the arsenal's modern mission'. The Huntsville complex, once in full production, became the sole manufacturer of coloured smoke munitions and was 'noted' for gargantuan supplies of bombs charged with mustard and phosgene. 'During WWII more than 27 million items of chemical munitions, with a total value of more than $134.5 million, were produced,' the Redstone history proudly proclaims; 'Huntsville won the Army-Navy "E" Award four different times for their outstanding production record.'

In total, 45.2 million units of ammunition were loaded and assembled at Redstone – quite apart from production at Edgewood. The work included the arming and storage of mustard gas produced from five separate plants at the complex, which had caused some consternation among the local communities, not to mention the several thousand workers living or working at the site. The heavy output of M-16 coloured smoke grenades, which, at full capacity, Huntsville was turning out at the rate of 15,000 an hour, also caused problems.

The dye used in the grenades coloured workers' clothing and

stained their skin. 'It was common,' says the Redstone history somewhat casually, 'to see people of rainbow hues in the Huntsville area.' As at most other chemical-producing plants operating in various parts of the world by the mid-1940s, there were many accidents and injuries to personnel. Several explosions occurred at Huntsville mustard gas factories, resulting in the death of four people. The manufacture of a new drying and chlorinating agent used in the treatment of crude lewisite was considered so dangerous that it was discontinued within six months.

Behind this rush of chemical development, mirrored at similar plants built by the Soviet Union and Japan, lay another story, too; tales of horrific experiments on prisoners of war and concentration camp inmates would emerge at the end of the war.

Britain and American relied on 'volunteers' many of whom in later years fell victim to a variety of debilitating and sometimes fatal illnesses. Wartime experiments using human guinea-pigs began at Porton in 1940. By the following year, a series of tests was under way in which dozens of animals and a large number of humans were being used in trials. Many of the volunteers stepped forward simply for the honour of aiding king and country. Others saw it a chance for special leave; some were merely dispatched from the lines by an Army sergeant on a 'You, you and you!' basis. Most would later claim they were never made fully aware of the implications.

In the experimental laboratories and gas chambers of Porton, as in Edgewood in the US, men were being subjected to tests to study both their own bodily reactions to gas exposure and to the viability of protective gear. Reports of the first tests at Porton using humans are contained in scientific archives. They all emphasize that this was a very necessary step, because all data relating to the effects of mustard gas on the human body related to World War I, and were out of date.

Before the tests began, Porton scientists went back to the records of known cases of survivors injured by mustard gas in 1914–18. They called on hospitals to supply details of those recently treated and discovered 89 existing cases of delayed mustard gas injury. Their case histories were delivered to Porton ahead of the start of its own experiments using humans in 1939. It was clear from the records that there had been many severe cases of delayed reaction, resulting in chronic illness. Many of the men were totally disabled and receiving a modest pension. Even so, new trials were considered so vital that the War Office gave its unequivocal approval, regardless of the risks.

The first major batch of trials began in the spring of 1940 to 'assess the casualty producing value' of clouds of mustard gas. 'Men and animals were exposed to the artificially produced vapour to demonstrate the effects on man of transient clouds of minute droplets of mustard gas under temperate conditions,' the Porton reports relate, 'which showed that the effects on eyes were severe.'

Later, a Porton team travelled to India where tests were carried out by initiating '70 individual exposures on human subjects, both British and Indian' to varying concentrations of mustard gas in a hot climate. The reports of these experiments, now at the Public Record Office at Kew, gave no details of the ultimate effects. Another station was set up in Alberta, Canada, where similar tests were carried out.

Typical of research at Porton was a series of tests on men and rabbits to ascertain the recuperative period for damage to eyes through mustard gas exposure. In one series of tests in 1941, 64 rabbits had liquid mustard gas dropped into their eyes by scientists seeking to ascertain the level of permanent damage. A number of male volunteers underwent similar experiments, and their eyes were photographed at the various stages of recovery over a period of several weeks.

The report concluded: 'Exposure to mustard gas in the eyes produced no immediate sensation. Within two to six hours, there was a burning sensation . . . blood supply to eyes damaged . . . bleeding occurs . . . at eight hours, the eyes closed . . . unable to open them voluntarily . . . remained closed for period of minimum of five days . . . in very severe cases, the eyes remained closed for seven weeks . . . recurrent ulceration would occur.'

Porton also studied the case of sixteen men who were drenched with mustard gas during a training accident. The way in which the accident occurred is not recorded. Two men had both eyes splashed. One died the day after the accident; another would be blinded in one eye. Four men had one eye contaminated. Of the remaining ten, six had symptoms or signs of vapour burns of the eyes. They were all given treatment using an saline eyewash, but 'it was obviously impossible to irrigate 32 eyes sufficiently in the usually accepted period of three minutes.'

Following the accident, Porton conducted 43 separate sequences of experiments to test the effects of mustard gas on eyes, using human volunteers and rabbits. There were to be many similar tests, in relation to bodily effects, on the efficiency of protective gear. For many years, these experiments remained a closed book to the outside world.

Although Allied use of human trials was mild in comparison to what would be discovered in Germany and Japan, the denial of any long-term effects would cause considerable stress to many who took part. One of these World War II service volunteers, Harry Hogg, from Dumfermline, did not speak publicly of his experiences for almost 50 years until the 1990s when Gulf War Syndrome made the headlines. He began to consider that years of illness might have been caused by his wartime experiences at Porton.

Mr Hogg said he was sent to Porton in 1942 for what he thought was a training course in the use of chemical weapons. He recalled: 'I was put in a gas chamber along with several others. There was no ventilation . . . no windows, just a small light in the ceiling. And a thick door, of course, with a peep hole. I can't remember if it was an officer or not but he just put this canister on the floor and told us that no man would be let out until everyone was on his hands and knees.'

Hogg said the supervisor opened the canister and left the chamber as gas began to be released. He and the other men began choking. They were quickly reduced to a 'horrendous' state, distressed and with their lungs bursting. 'We were scrambling about on the floor with our heads at the door trying to get air. It seemed like an eternity.' Finally, the officer opened the door and the men 'just tumbled out . . . oh dear God, just tumbled out. One man in particular . . . was behaving like an animal, out of his mind.'

Harry Hogg suffered bouts of severe illness in the aftermath. There were many like him, and many more would follow with similar stories to tell. Much of his statement is borne out by Porton documents and contemporary classified reports on experiments using volunteers in that era, documents that dispassionately and clinically described the assessments by scientists of men's ability to withstand mustard gas in conditions of war. They wanted to know, for example, if a man would still be able to hold down a defensive position behind a machine gun, even though he might not be able to walk.

In America's twin establishment to Porton, the same tests were a daily occurrence. One young conscript, Russel O'Berry, claimed an officer had threatened him with imprisonment if he refused to take part in mustard gas tests. He said he was told it was merely a training exercise in the use of gas-masks. O'Berry, too, spoke of being herded with others into a little chamber, which he said terrified him. It was hot and crowded with a dozen 'volunteers' who all wore gas-masks.

He said he 'began to burn almost immediately' and felt sick. Some of the men vomited into their masks. He vomited as soon as he left the chamber. The tests were repeated every day for four days. On the last day, blisters appeared around his right eye and around his chest and genital area. Some years later, he lost the sight in that right eye, and during the 40 years after his gas chamber experience he suffered a number of skin cancers, had 40 separate growths removed from his colon, had more than half of one lung removed and was told by a specialist that the lower parts of his lungs were 'like stone – resulting from the mustard gas'. For years, O'Berry sought to get access to his military records; he was told repeatedly none existed and the burden of proof for any possible injury while in service fell upon himself. Unlike sufferers in Britain, he was able to use the Freedom of Information Act and, eventually, he was able to get the documents relating to the tests. 'I knew as soon as I saw them, I had a case,' he said. The battle for a pension would take years, as we will see in later chapters.

Nathan Schnurman from Charles City, Virginia, was a young US Navy rating when he volunteered for what he was told were experiments to test summer clothing at Edgewood. Instead, he was ordered into a gas chamber.

'I went in every day for six days, along with others. We were exposed to a mixture of mustard gas and lewisite while wearing gas-masks. On the sixth day, I just passed out. They carried me from the chamber and I was left unconscious at the side of the road. I was choking when I came to. I had thrown up inside my mask and I tried to remove it. They then carried me into a hut and took off my contaminated clothing. My nose and my eyes were burning. My throat was burning. I was throwing up, retching violently. I heard someone in the room ask the officer if they should call an ambulance. He replied, "No, let's wait and see what happens." Anyhow, I recovered slightly and the next day I was virtually carried to the rail station, put on a train and sent home.'

Schnurman finished his war in the Pacific. He had recurring bouts of illness but when he reported sick to the naval medical unit, he 'was accused of being a malinger'. In civilian life, he made many visits to his family doctor. He was told repeatedly that he appeared to have been poisoned but it was not until 1975 that he finally confided to his doctor that he had taken part in wartime tests. Almost 50 years after joining the tests, as we will see in the last chapter of this story, he finally won compensation.

There is a multitude of such wartime stories and testimony to draw upon, and many that Britain and the US would have preferred remained secret. Documents declassified in 1989 in Australia, but whose release in Britain is – in 1996 – still forbidden, show that between 1942 and 1945, British, American and Australian soldiers were used as guinea-pigs in a sustained programme of chemical warfare experiments in northern Queensland.

In 1943, a team of eleven scientists and two service officers were sent from Porton to conduct trials of mustard gas exposure in a hot climate and to test soldiers' ability to endure and withstand Japanese chemical attacks, thought to be imminent in Far Eastern positions. The researchers on this occasion went to great lengths to explain to volunteers why the experiments were necessary. The scientists believed that mustard gas of the potency that the Japanese were known to possess was thought to be up to ten times more effective in tropical climates than in the European war theatre.

One unit of 438 Australian volunteers was used in a series of tests for Porton-directed research on Brook Island, near Innisfail, Queensland, where their mock battlefield was bombed with mustard gas. Men were required to walk through the bush wearing anti-gas clothing. It was found to be defective, and many of them suffered immediate burns to the skin, some so severely that their skin simply peeled off. Other symptoms were very similar to those reported by other volunteers exposed to gas – vomiting, loss of appetite, confusion and a general malaise.

One of the veterans of that incident was a young Australian commando named Tommy Mitchell. He recalled: 'It was in December 1943, and the weather was scorching hot. We were decked out in heavy gas-protective clothing and masks and set off through the dusk. Six US aircraft, B-24 liberators, dropped bombs with mustard gas on Brook Island. Ten minutes later, we were charging through the bush in our sampling equipment. Several of us fell sick. Anyway, a few hours later, me and another soldier were ordered back on to the island, this time stripped of our respirators and protective clothing. We were forced to camp on the island from dusk till dawn. When they came and picked us up, the other soldier was badly burned. I don't know whether he lived or not. I had a burned face, burned hands and lungs full of gas.'

Porton documents set out the findings of the researchers testing mustard gas on humans, in cold, clinical terms. In one case the report stated: 'Seven hours after exposure there was severe nausea. At 24 hours, general erythema of the whole body. The penis, scrotum and popliteal fossae were oedematus. He was unable to walk because of pain in the scrotum . . . by day 17, complete destruction of the epithelium over the whole organ – thin greyish sloughs over the foreskin and glands.'

In defence of such experiments, the experts would insist that because it was war-time, and extreme situations not only seemed possible but highly probable as well, the discomfort and possible suffering of the few would in the fullness of time be of great benefit to the many. Indeed, a large number of the volunteers put themselves forward for that very reason.

There is no shortage of medical and scientific experts today, in analysing that situation, who agree that it would have been virtually impossible in the 1940s to predict what likely effects the exposure to gas and other chemicals might have on these men, other than the assessment that had been gleaned from gas victims of World War I. Some go as far as to say that at least the worst-case scenario ought to have been laid out before them – to prepare for the suffering that was to be endured by many veterans who willingly, and some not so willingly, gave their bodies for live experiments. Many survivors of those secret experiments, which, in Britain, if the Ministry of Defence had its way we could still not discuss, suffered debilitating illnesses in later life, including skin cancers, leukaemia, heart disease and respiratory problems.

As ever, 'necessity in time of war' underpinned the acceptability of such experiments. Whatever cost in terms of injury to personnel, or the suffering and 'sacrifice' of many thousands of animals, as the Allies strove to equip themselves with what they considered an adequate chemical and biological armoury to respond to whatever the Axis powers might have up their sleeves, the experiments would be excused away: the military wanted that capability, the government ordered it, and the scientists and chemists made it possible. But it was only part of the story.

5

KILLING THEM SOFTLY

RUNNING PARALLEL WITH the race for chemical supremacy was another quest that perhaps held far greater implications in its capacity for mass destruction: germ warfare. Dramatic discoveries on weaponry so insidiously devastating that their secrets were to be guarded by the Allies for decades to come were made by the Japanese under the guiding hand of General Shiro Ishii whose work was kept secret even from Emperor Hirohito. As the war approached, Western intelligence was alerted to BW work in south Manchuria where Ishii's experimental complex had grown to a large garrison of military technicians, with numerous offshoots in other establishments. They were producing vaccines for mass inoculation against a full range of diseases from typhoid to cholera as well as assembling a stockpile of bacteria for the Japanese offensive weapons programme.

The scale of it was only apparent to the West after the war. Ishii's plant at Pingfan was estimated to be capable of manufacturing 8 tons of bacteria a month. The key project, however, was his development of a bomb delivering anthrax, which Ishii had concluded was the most effective killer because of the agent's lingering qualities. He calculated that carefully targeted bombs could easily achieve a 90 per cent mortality rate in a town of 50,000. By the end of 1939, Pingfan had produced and stockpiled 4,000 anthrax bombs; each Japanese bomber could carry a payload of 12. The effectiveness had been meticulously worked out by bombing runs over isolated tracts of Manchurian countryside; 400 horses, 500 sheep and several thousand rats and mice were killed in the process.

Next, Japan was reported to have conducted bombing trials over China. A very large file of eye-witness accounts now lies in the Public Record Office. They give graphic descriptions of how a single light aircraft arrived over the town of Ch'angte, home for 50,000 people. It came in low and was seen to drop rice and wheat grain over fields and in the town. Within seven days, the town's rat population was dying in large numbers and soon its people were falling ill with the plague. Ninety deaths were recorded and the local Presbyterian Hospital was filled with victims. At least two other bombings were reported, with similar results, followed by an outbreak of plague in two separate Chinese provinces, affecting 600 people. There were suggestions that the reports were put out by the Chinese as a propaganda attack against its Japanese invaders. Winston Churchill, by all accounts, did not agree.

Britain's own move into biological warfare had taken on a note of urgency in the face of intelligence from Japan, Germany and Italy. In 1938, Sir Maurice Hankey's warnings were still tinged with restraint – that Britain should prepare a defence, work on the production of vaccines against disease and examine a defence system against sabotage, such as the poisoning of reservoirs.

Within a matter of months, however, the tone had changed. Hankey, by then a peer of the realm with the title of Minister without Portfolio, was given Cabinet approval to form what was initially called the Emergency Bacteriological Service, a name that in itself gave a clue to the fears of those who had proposed it – so much so that it was thought too 'disturbing' for public consumption. It was immediately changed to the Emergency Public Health Laboratory, a title that hid its true role – and the fact that it was under military control. And so Porton added another string to its bow.

In 1940, as reports of the Japanese raids in China intensified, along with intelligence assessments handed to the Chiefs of Staff that Germany itself 'would not be beyond deliberate and indiscriminate' use of bacteria, Britain was ready to move. Spearhead research was to be led by an anonymous group of less than a dozen men – eventually extending to around 50 – known collectively as the 'Biology Department'.

Arriving at Porton in October that year, the group was surrounded by what must have seemed like impenetrable security arrangements;

their mission was one of the most highly guarded secrets of Porton's already very secret war. Even their association with the Porton establishment was masked by the fact that their salaries were paid through the British Medical Research Council who were in turn reimbursed by the group's ultimate employers, the Ministry of Supply and the Chiefs of Staff Sub-Committee on Biological Warfare.

The team's key links to Churchill's War Cabinet, however, were Hankey himself and Duff Cooper, Chancellor of the Duchy of Lancaster. The team itself was led by Dr Paul Fildes, the strong-willed and autocratic surgeon who had risen to become director of the Medical Research Unit in Bacterial Chemistry at the Bland Sutton Institute of Pathology at Middlesex Hospital. Fildes, son of the Victorian artist Sir Luke Fildes, was a lifelong bachelor and wealthy in his own right. He did not take kindly to the 'fools in authority' and from the outset ran his operation in dictatorial style. Staff recruited from various universities and medical establishments were soon to be joined by a number of American and Canadian experts in the field of bacteriology to form a joint Allied investigation into the manufacture of vaccines and biological weapons.

From his first report to his superiors, Fildes' intentions were clear. His team would focus their experiments on airborne weapons and sprays as a means of releasing micro-organisms against the enemy. This, he argued, was the most effective form of attack. Biological agents could be 'carried through the air and thence deep into the lungs' if released from bursting munitions or by sprays. The research was on very similar lines to the work already proved to be effective by General Ishii in Manchuria.

The first step, according to Porton documents, was to identify the infectious diseases that were most suitable for disseminating in this manner and a series of experiments was carried out by the team, which had set up shop close to the Porton animal house. Using various kinds of animals for their tests, the BDP unit, as it was known, found most success with the use of anthrax, the highly contagious disease that kills animals, especially cattle and sheep, and is also fatal to man, in whom it develops as a hideous-looking cancer.

The team's early experiments discovered that several species of animal were rapidly and fatally infected with anthrax spores by inhalation but a larger test site was needed to calculate effective methods of disseminating the anthrax over potential enemy targets, in other words, German cities. The BDP unit began scouring the nation for a suitable site for tests, since it was far too dangerous to explode anthrax-charged munitions anywhere near a civilian population.

As most members of the team cautiously admitted, they were literally stepping into the unknown. No one could be certain of the ultimate effects. One small-scale trial was launched at an isolated cove, Penclawdd, on the Gower Coast but the major test site was to be the now infamous Gruinard Island, off the coast of Ross and Cromarty.

The story of Gruinard has gone into history, but a good deal of the background activity surrounding the poisoning of its landscape remains in the classified archives. Using simulants, the BDP team had calculated that anthrax spores could be delivered in aerosol particles from bomblets. They estimated that all animals and human beings within a range of 200 yards of the explosion of the bomblets would be infected, and would die. Those within 400 yards of the release of the aerosol particle would be 'seriously at risk' of fatal infection.

The most significant figures in the BDP reports, however, lay in the comparison with chemical weapons. On a weight-to-weight calculation, anthrax was up to 1,000 times more effective than any known chemical agent. All these theories needed to be tested, and the test site would be Gruinard, requisitioned by the Ministry of Supply in 1942 as the BDP team hurried towards the creation of the West's first biological weapon capable of mass killing.

Gruinard had been uninhabited since the deaths of the last crofters, although sheep farmers on the mainland community used to graze animals there in summer. The privately owned sheep were cleared off and forbidding notices were erected. Soon afterwards, Porton scientists arrived on the bleak and rugged island with its heather-covered cliffs dropping down to long beaches fronting Gruinard Bay, with a backdrop of the north-west Highlands and the shrouded hills of the Summer Isles.

Paul Fildes himself led the Porton team. They were billeted in Nissen huts at Mongasdale Farm on the mainland and their presence was the cause of much speculation, especially as they acquired their own animals, which they transported to this remote piece of British soil, now code-named 'X-Base'. Their mission was to put on trial prototypes for their projected 500lb cluster bombs, each carrying one hundred 4lb bomblets filled with anthrax spores. The security code-name for the BDP was 'N' and so the bomb would later be ascribed the title of the N-bomb – and early precursor of a far more devastating weapon of the same name.

Shepherd Kenneth MacLeod, who lived across the water at Little Gruinard and who used to go there before the arrival of the Porton scientists, kept a forbidden watch on the events there through a telescope he used to track his sheep. 'I saw them tethering sheep to posts on the slope beneath the black rock at the western end,' he would recall. 'When I looked again, there were rows of carcasses on the ground, and some were washed away on the tide and later reached the mainland.' A small outbreak of anthrax in the area followed, and it was the first real clue that the locals had of what might be going on at Gruinard.

Another contemporary observer was a local GP, Dr James Hunter, whose practice included the region of Gruinard Bay. 'There were a lot of explosions on the island at the time. We knew nothing then of what they were doing. Military exercises were the nearest we could guess at. It was all kept very secret, even from the likes of myself who were involved in community health and welfare. With the benefit of hindsight, we can conjecture that the bombing was to disseminate anthrax. They tried to bury the infected sheep carcasses by blasting rock on top of them. They didn't make a very good job of it. When the dead sheep were washed ashore, a horse and some farm animals became infected and died. The crofters linked the deaths to the goings-on over on the island and wrote to the Admiralty complaining. We were all astonished when they received compensation.'

The Ministry of Defence, in its eagerness to silence the complainants as quickly as possible, paid up virtually by return of post. The results of the Gruinard tests were judged 'highly promising'. The Porton team's findings were relayed to their opposite numbers in America and Canada who had joined them in the Allied programme to 'discover a retaliatory biological capability', which seemed to indicate it should only be used if Hitler himself brought CB weapons into play. Details of the Allied proposals remain classified, but the censors appeared to have overlooked an appendix attached to a report presented to the Joint Technical Warfare Committee at the end of the war, entitled 'Potentialities of Biological Warfare during the next ten years'.

The appendix contained the calculations prepared by Dr Fildes for an effective anthrax strike against Germany, apparently written in 1942. The anthrax bomb proposed was a 500lb 'cluster projectile' containing 106 bomblets of 4lbs. One of these bombs had been shown to produce contamination of more than 100 acres. Fildes estimated that 250,000 square metres of German countryside could be infected, or 50,000 square metres of populated area. Unprotected civilians who were unfortunate enough to be beneath the aerosol cloud of anthrax particles stood a 50 per cent chance of death, although the figures were soon revised drastically – to nearer 100 per cent. In typical precise and clinical manner, Fildes estimated that to achieve this 'kill rate' against the city of Stuttgart, which covered 53 square miles, the Allies would need to employ 268 Lincoln bombers loaded with approximately 4,000 cluster bombs. He pursued his theories to include six major German cites, for which the assumed area covered 538 square miles: 40,350 cluster bombs carried by 2,690 aircraft would be needed to make an 'effective strike'. The result of this bombing mission, he concluded, would mean that the German cities would be 'contaminated for many years to come and the danger from skin infection would enforce total evacuation'. Even Fildes admitted, however, that the weapons were so contrary to normal practice that 'appreciation may be liable to great error'.

Even so, the Allies put them into production. Britain had no factories or laboratories capable of large-scale production of anthrax spores, and it was planned that this should be done in America where a special factory was to be built by the US Chemical Warfare Service with the same urgency as those that went up at Huntsville. By the end of the war, America had built four biological plants under the command of its principal BW research unit at Camp Detrick, an hour's drive from Washington.

The field trials of anthrax-charged cluster bombs were to be conducted in a remote region of Canada, although, in the event, the war ended before the American plant had produced the large stocks needed to fulfill Fildes' strike force calculations. Assembling them, according to the Fildes appendix, had proved to be a 'major problem'.

Gruinard Island, of course, remained poisoned and contaminated and out of bounds to the public for decades. There was great fear in Scotland that birds would spread the organisms to the mainland. Indeed, many blamed Gruinard for three minor outbreaks of anthrax in 1954, 1961 and 1965.

The extent of the Gruinard problem could hardly have been predicted by the Porton research team and it remained with them for years to come. Reluctant Porton scientists, clad in protective clothing and masks, made irregular inspection visits to test the island for contamination levels. By 1978 there was still no sign of anthrax spores diminishing. Various ways of dealing with the contamination would be experimented with over the years, but it was not until 1986 that a suitable chemical was found to kill off the anthrax.

It was sprayed over the affected area in the summer of 1986 and a year later only a few pockets of anthrax were found to remain. After further treatment and new tests, sheep were moved on to Gruinard in 1987 and in May 1990 the island was finally returned by the Ministry of Defence to the heirs of the original owners – almost 50 years since it was originally taken over.

The use of anthrax had remained, almost to the last, a strong possibility with the Allies who were certain that Japan and Germany had greater capability. In fact, another more imaginative delivery plan had already been devised before the Gruinard trials were completed, to create 'mayhem among the enemy in the shortest possible time'. It was dreamed up specifically as a 'stopgap measure' until the anthrax bombs were built and perfected.

With Churchill's personal approval, the BDP team's work arose out of a memo from Lord Hankey to Winston Churchill outlining Porton's view that if 'we should desire for the purposes of retaliation, to take offensive action, the only method feasible at the moment would be the use of anthrax against cattle'. Hankey's close confidant, Dr Fildes, and his team devised a plan that would, as can now be seen with the benefit of hindsight, have devastated the German countryside, just as it had done at Gruinard.

It called for the manufacture of millions of cattle cakes, which were to be infected with anthrax spores. It was planned that these would be dropped by bombers over German fields to strike an 'effective blow at Germany's already weak agricultural sector' – not to mention its civilian population. A general outline of the plan was presented, and the entire operation was tested using dummy runs with uninfected cattle cakes over the British landscape, to determine weight, aircraft speed and height from which they should be dropped.

In his report submitted to the Chiefs of Staffs, entitled 'Distribution of Infected Cattle Tablets by Aircraft', Dr Fildes wrote: 'The object of this contemplated operation is to infect and kill the largest number of cattle as possible in enemy territory in a single effort by means of infected cattle cakes dropped from the air. From Ministry of Agriculture Records, the concentration of cattle per square kilometre has been obtained for Germany. The province of Oldenburgh is the most important district and contains 35 cattle per square kilometre. The most suitable cattle grazing areas would appear from a cursory glance to exist in the area bounded by a line joining Hamburg to Hanover in the east and the River Ems in the west.'

Dr Fildes and his team calculated that, assuming the cattle would be fairly evenly dispersed over the selected areas, 20 acres containing an estimated ten cattle could be targeted by bombers travelling at 200 miles an hour. The cakes would be packed in boxes of 400 tablets, which could be distributed every two minutes. Fildes continued: 'It is assumed that a stock of five million tablets contained in 12,500 boxes each weighing eight pounds three ounces can be carried as a supplementary weapon and disposed of to the best advantage during routine bombing operations beyond Oldenburgh. Maximum damage to cattle and complete dislocation of the enemy veterinary services may result from one single effort.'

The military commanders and the War Cabinet agreed that it was an 'entirely feasible' project and Operation Vegetarian swung into action. After several unsuccessful attempts at placing the contract through usual manufacturers, Fildes eventually reached agreement with the soap producers Lever Brothers and Unilever and production of the cattle cakes was assigned to one of its factories, Atkinsons of Bermondsey. They were supplied to Porton at the rate of 250,000 a week.

Meanwhile, creative technicians at the station had built a simple machine capable of charging and sealing the cattle cakes with their deadly poison. They estimated, with familiar scientific precision, that a team of 15 ladies could perform the task and pack them into boxes at the rate of 12,800 cakes a day.

Next, Fildes had to find the labour to perform this operation. Once again he turned to Unilever. He contacted one of the company's directors, Mr G. Hansard, to appeal for help in the project and suggested that the women might be sold the idea by treating it as a 'holiday'. In a letter to Hansard on 6 May 1942, Fildes wrote:

'The idea is that the girls would live in the camp. They would have a building which would be fixed up. There is already a sitting room in the camp. There are considerable social amenities, including cinema performances and so forth several times a week. There is a bus service to Salisbury and the local entertainment. They will be fed in the canteen situated in the camp. The work done will be in the closed area for which they will be provided with necessary security passes. I should think that if the project is looked upon as a holiday camp, it might be quite reasonably attractive for a few months.'

Fildes also emphasized that the whole project was to be regarded as 'top secret' and virtually no details of the work were to be discussed publicly. In fact, the soap company was given no more than a brief description of the work the women would be required to do. Anyhow, Hansard agreed to help and made inquiries in his factories for suitable volunteers. Shortly afterwards, he wrote back to Fildes to confirm the details:

> We are able to provide one supervisor and 25 girls. These will be employees of our soap factories in the London and Bristol areas. They will be girls who are reported upon by the managers as being reliable and it will be emphasized to them that they must not discuss this work outside of the station. We cannot of course give any further guarantee than this but we would do our best to choose reliable girls. They would be paid their present remuneration plus five shillings a week. This will cost approximately £2.10s and £2.15s per head and the supervisor £3.10s. In addition they should be provided with free board, this is to say accommodation in the building you described and free meals in the canteen. Working Hours: We understand they will be required to work from approximately 9 to 6 for five days a week and a half day on Saturday. For anything in excess of this overtime will have to be paid at the rate of time and a quarter for the first two hours and time and a half thereafter. Period of service: not to exceed three months. Travelling expenses will be paid for travel, third class, from their homes to the station. I understand you will provide us with a letter stating that this work is in the national interest and the Ministry of Labour are recommended by you to permit the transfer.

Unilever subsequently supplied a list of twenty-nine names – eight girls and a supervisor from Atkinsons, Bermondsey, ten girls from Christopher Thomas, Bristol, and ten girls from John Knights, Silvertown. He also arranged a reserve of seven girls. They would be sent to Porton on a rota basis, the first to arrive in the late summer. Hansard listed the twenty-nine names and, unknown to all concerned, they were immediately passed to Porton's security department and then on for vetting to the chief constables of the areas where the girls lived.

Any who were found to have dubious connections were to be rejected. In fact, all were approved although two subsequently dropped out; one discovered she was pregnant and another, by then already working at Porton, was found to be suffering from Scabies. Atkinsons began supplying the cattle cakes at the rate of 250,000 a week. The first batch of girls arrived in the late summer of 1942 to begin the task about which they still had little knowledge; nor did they appreciate that the end result would be the destruction of thousands of German cattle.

Travelling by rail from London and Bristol, they arrived nervous and chattering to be welcomed by the senior technicians who would oversee them and, once they had settled into the 'holiday camp' that would be their home for the next three months, they were given a security briefing.

There were a number of minor incidents. On one occasion the girls complained they had nowhere to hang their coats after walking in the rain between huts. The lack was immediately rectified with a row of hangers. One early problem among the chattering group was security. They were obviously being kept under observation when they travelled into Salisbury on their days off. An internal Porton memo from head of security to their unit chief reported that one of them 'has been heard talking about her work while travelling on a bus into Salisbury . . . she was overhead saying she had been burned by mustard . . . would you please address this problem.'

The memo seems to indicate that the girls believed they were probably working with a mustard gas product – not anthrax. Their work, however, was judged to be 'entirely satisfactory' and they were contaminating the cattle cakes at the required daily rate. Dr Fildes was so pleased that he recommended that the girls' supervisor, a Miss F.I. Hazell from Herne Hill, should be rewarded for her outstanding efforts. She was given an extra 5s above her special allowance.

The stockpile of five million cattle cakes was completed by April 1943 and Dr Fildes recorded his personal observation of the project. 'It was,' he wrote, 'developed as the quickest way in which we could make some retaliation at short notice.' The efforts of the soap factory women proved to be in vain. Operation Vegetarian was aborted. There are no documents in the files so far released that explain why it was called off, but by then the results of early tests on the use of anthrax by the Porton team were becoming known, proving the devastating possibilities of biological weapons.

Furthermore, in the year since the project was first discussed, masses of intelligence reports were being accumulated by the Allies on CB.W experiments in Germany, Italy and Japan. The British War Cabinet had authorized the cattle cake plan on the understanding that it would not be activated without their final approval. A first strike at a time when the Allies were already planning their invasion of Italy, through the Sicilian landings, may well have proved too risky.

The boxes of cattle cakes remained at Porton until the end of the war, when all but a few samples retained for the Porton archives were destroyed. The exercise was judged, however, to have been a total success and formed part of what Porton's official history would applaud: 'The apotheosis of research at BDP was to demonstrate the feasibility of biological warfare by all means short of actual use . . . besides these notable achievements, BDP pioneered several unique fields, notably in experimental airborne infection, biotechnology and aerobiology . . . in the future, successors to BDP were to become acknowledged leaders in such fields.'

And the soap-factory girls went away, unaware they had contributed to one of the most remarkable experiments in the annals of biological warfare.

6

THE UNFOUGHT BATTLE

AS THE WAR swung in favour of the Allies, the possibility that the Axis powers might yet unleash their CB weapons in a desperate bid to regain the initiative was constantly under review by the Allied Chiefs of Staff. A veritable mountain of intelligence reports, gathering up every snippet of information that might give a clue to the Axis intentions, was gathered and analysed. In readiness, the Allies had long before begun moving thousands of tons of chemical weapons by sea and air to strategic points of the war theatres both in Europe and the Pacific. The Axis did likewise. There was, to some degree, an element of cat and mouse, since both sides had an intelligence cover on the movement of arms.

At the end of October 1943, after the successful Allied landings in Italy through the island of Sicily, the US merchant vessel SS *John Harvey* pulled into Baltimore to take on a secret cargo. Under the supervision of First Lieutenant Howard Beckstrom, of the 701st Chemical Maintenance Company, 100 tons of mustard gas bombs were loaded aboard and the ship left immediately for Europe, with Beckstrom and a detachment from the Chemical Warfare Service. Their destination was southern Italy where the Allied armies had taken control. The mustard bombs were being sent as retaliatory back-up in the event that the Italian population and German troops retreating to the north resorted to chemical attacks in a last-ditch effort to halt the Allied advance through Italy.

The *John Harvey* reached its destination of Bari, towards the heel of the boot of Italy, at the end of November. The harbour was so heavily congested with Allied ships that the captain took orders to tie up at Pier 29 and wait for further instruction for unloading. They had been in the harbour for 48 hours when, on the night of 2 December, the air raid sirens sounded and the German bombers came roaring in from the north to inflict the worst sea damage the Americans had suffered since Pearl Harbour. Within half an hour, the Luftwaffe had sunk 17 ships, largely carrying supplies and equipment for the Allies, and another 8 ships were badly hit. Explosion after explosion ripped through the harbour as first a fuel tanker and then the *John Harvey* blew up with such force that buildings in the harbour 7 miles away shattered.

The disaster, bad enough, was heightened by the fact that no one knew what the *John Harvey* was carrying because Beckstrom and his party were travelling under orders of secrecy and they had all been killed. As the ship went down, the liquid mustard leaked out into the sea and mingled with oil from the fuel ship. Hundreds of sailors were in the water, some in lifeboats, clutching the sides, others swimming frantically. They all became engulfed by mustard fumes and many were completely immersed in the liquid gas itself. At least 1,000 men had been killed in the attack, and as the medical units ashore were inundated they simply did not know that hundreds of the wounded brought in had been contaminated by mustard gas. It was a chaotic catastrophe. By morning, the extent of the disaster had become very evident: many of the men were blinded, others badly burned; some had lost some 80 per cent of their skin, which hung from them in loose layers.

In the town itself, the effects of the mustard gas cloud were already appearing. At least 1,000 civilians were killed by the blast itself. Hundreds more were literally falling down, choking. General Eisenhower initially ordered a news black-out on the disaster, but it was too big to keep secret and, in any event, thousands of Italians fled in panic and confusion, claiming that their town had been hit by an enormous gas bomb attack. The deaths directly from mustard gas poisoning soon began to mount. Combined scientific teams from Porton and Edgewood were dashing to the scene to collect and record as much data as they could. The Bari explosion was the nearest they could possibly get to a true chemical warfare battle. The scientists selected 40 bodies; 20 were taken back to Porton Down and 20 to Edgewood Arsenal for post mortem examination and eventually dissection and microscopic investigation. The relatives were never told; they were merely informed that their menfolk had been killed in enemy action.

Later, in reflecting upon the situation and realizing the sensitivity of the gas issue, Eisenhower proposed that the death descriptions of the victims should be adjusted so that the classic symptoms of mustard gas poisoning – blocked windpipes – became 'bronchitis', and burns and eye injuries were ascribed to 'enemy action'. His 'most secret and most urgent' telegram, logged in War Office files, suggested that these descriptions would 'adequately support future claims by those injured for disability pensions'.

The Bari incident raised even further the massive anxiety about a chemical flare-up, apparently shared by Germans who believed that the Bari ship had been brought specifically to feed supplies for a CW attack. For months, intelligence reports had flooded in to both sides. The Allied sources seemed convinced that Hitler was on the brink of ordering both chemical and bacterial attacks on British cities – to such an extent in fact that on 15 June 1943 the Chiefs of Staff ordered a 'complete evaluation of the most significant readings to attempt to establish enemy intentions'. Examples from that evaluation, released into the public domain in Britain in 1996, reveal a series of seemingly trustworthy intelligence reports from both British agents and the US Office of Strategic Services (OSS) reports filed to London from the Pentagon. From among these the following digests have been made:

3 July 1943: 'Top secret' report from Tunisia describes the capture of a German army medical captain who had given first intimation of Hitler's experimental new gas, tabun, which could kill its victims in half an hour. He gave full description of a colourless gas and substantial clues as to the chemical compounds from which it was derived. The prisoner was interviewed several times and report was sent to Chiefs of Staff and to Porton.

11 December 1943: British intelligence reports the conversation with a senior Panzer general captured recently. He said he could not understand why the Germans, with all their talk of a new secret weapon, did not use it when 'everything is being smashed up nightly'. Germany had once initially held the advantage over its enemies in chemical weapons but she had lost it largely because senior scientists who had developed it, such as at Haber Laboratory in central Germany, 'are now in England'.

6 December 1943, Stockholm: A German naval officer reported that the Germans intended to spread disease in Britain with bacteria by dropping infected mice, rats and rabbits into the countryside and

in the cities. A relative of his in the Luftwaffe said he had dropped a quantity of rodents on several trips to England. This was in line with reports from scientists captured during the invasion of Italy, indicating that the Germans had perfected large cages that would open automatically when dropped by parachute over southern England, releasing 250,000 infected rodents 'sufficient to start an uncontrollable epidemic' of plague and typhus.

20 December 1943: The Dutch intelligence service had received several reports that the Germans were planning to attack Britain with airborne biological weapons 'out of sheer despair and revenge'.

March 1944: An OSS cable from Berne suggested that a Doctor Briault of the Pasteur Institute had received the following information from a German source: that the Germans were preparing a bacteriological mixture of which the largest element by percentage would be typhus, contained in breakable glass tubes, which will be dropped over Britain shortly. The Swiss press are full of speculation about Germany's secret weapon.

25 April 1944: 'Definite confirmation' of BW research at five named German medical research units.

3 July 1944: Report from the head of the Chemical Warfare Service, Intelligence Branch, Porton Down, on enemy intentions: 'Hitler's domination of the German High Command means that the use of BW becomes an imminent possibility. Although his aircraft have been neutralized, the use of robot bombers makes it possible to deliver chemical and biological weaponry to the heart of our cities . . . a leading scientist now in Allied territory personally heard Hitler state: "A nation which is denied the right to live has the right to use the most extreme methods of destruction, including germ warfare."'

10 July 1944: From OSS Technical Intelligence, Pentagon: 'The Germans carried out experiments with bacterial weapons which they intend to use against Great Britain. The main purpose was to establish the degree of efficiency and the size of the area which can be infected by a two ton missile projected by means of a rocket.'

Faced with this mountain of paper, from which the above is a small sample, Winston Churchill found himself confronted by having to make decisions on British intentions. In July 1944 Churchill made it plain that he would be prepared to order the use of chemical and biological weapons against Germany if two criteria were met: 1) that it was a life or death situation for Britain; or 2) that it would shorten the war by a year. On 3 July 1944 he dictated a memo for his Chiefs of Staff after they had told him they were against the use of the chemical bomb:

'I want you to think very seriously over this question. It is absurd to consider morality when everybody used it in the last war; on the other hand the bombing of open cities was regarded as forbidden. Now everybody does it as a matter of course.'

Churchill demanded that his military commanders made a 'cold-blooded calculation' as to how it would pay the Allies to use 'poison gas, by which I principally mean mustard. We want to gain more ground in Normandy . . . we could probably deliver twenty tons to their one.' He went on to ponder the mystery that had grown more puzzling to the war councils of the West as each year passed: Why had the Germans themselves not used it – especially then, as they began daily V-rocket attacks, firing 2,000 on London in the first two weeks of June 1944?

'Not certainly out of moral scruples or affection for us,' Churchill memoed.

> They have not used it because it does not pay them. The greatest temptation ever offered to them was the beaches of Normandy. That they thought about this is certain and that they prepared against our use of gas is also certain. But the only reason they have not used it against us is that they fear the retaliation. What is to their detriment is to our advantage. Although one sees how unpleasant it is to receive poison gas attacks from which *nearly everyone recovers* [author's italics] it is useless to protest that an equal amount of HE [mustard gas] will not inflict greater cruelties and sufferings on troops or civilians. One really must not be bound within silly conventions of mind whether they be those that ruled the last war or those in reverse which rule this.

It is an interesting side-element to the discussion that Churchill followed the notion put forward in the wake of the previous hostilities that chemical warfare did not necessarily cause lasting damage to those who were attacked by it – a theory that today finds few supporters. At the height of war, however, it was one that was readily, perhaps eagerly, grasped at as justification for the use of gas, demonstrated in the later paragraphs of Churchill's memo:

> If the bombardment of London really became a serious nuisance and great rockets with far-reaching and devastating effect fall on many centres of Government and labour, I should be prepared to do anything that would hit the enemy in a murderous place. I may certainly have to ask you to support me in the use of poison gas. We could drench the cities of the Ruhr and many other cities

> in Germany in such a way that most of the population would be requiring constant medical attention. We could stop all work at the flying bomb points. I do not see why we should always have all the disadvantages of being the gentlemen while they have all the advantages of being the cad. There are times when this may be so but not now.

Churchill was forthright in the final instructions to his commanders. He told them that if in the near or more distant future he gave instructions to use poison gas against Germany, it would have to be done wholeheartedly. Meanwhile, he wanted the whole matter considered sensibly and dispassionately, as befitted a serious question that could only be rejected for equally serious reasons. He added that he would have to get Stalin's acquiescence.

Ten days later, his initiative in the use of gas moved on, although by then one more element had been added, that of germ warfare, namely the use of anthrax. On 16 July the Joint Planning Staffs were issued with Churchill's personal directive, to undertake 'a comprehensive examination . . . of the military implications of an all-out use of gas, principally mustard, or any other method of warfare which we have hitherto refrained from using against the Germans'. And in the final paragraph of the directive, the issue was moved specifically a stage further, calling for the examination to include 'the use of biological warfare by us or by the enemy. It should take the form of a thorough and practical examination of the military factors involved and should ignore ethical and political considerations.'

Almost three weeks passed and Churchill had not received a reply. On 25 July, angry at not having had a response, he fired off another memo: 'I asked for a dispassionate report on the military aspects of threatening to use lethal gases on the enemy if they do not stop indiscriminate bombing . . . I now request this report within three days.'

Forty-eight hours later, the document that had the potential of adding a totally new dimension to the war, and especially to the way in which the attacks were delivered to cities on both sides, was presented to the War Cabinet.

The Joint Planning Staffs produced their assessment in a 14-page report. If chemicals were to be used, they said, they should be part of a combined, concerted attack by British and American bombers carrying a bomb cargo made up of 25 per cent high explosives, which would cause major damage to buildings and spread panic. The remainder would be made up of mustard gas and phosgene gas. There were sufficient stocks of mustard to bomb 1,500 tactical targets or 60 cities – and the 60 'most favourable' were listed.

There was sufficient phosgene to hit 1,000 targets or 20 cities. The likely effect would be to cause vapour burns 'on such a scale as to necessitate the wholesale evacuation thus paving the way to a subsequent incendiary attack. Speedy wholesale evacuation might well be impossible, in which case large casualties would follow.'

The war planners added a note of caution to Churchill in regard to his theory that gas attacks would speed up the Allied move through France. It might, they said, provide decisive local results 'allowing us to break through the German defences on a large scale' but warned that, on the other hand, 'gas on an unprotected population in the battle area would hamper operations . . . and might seriously impair our relations with the civilian populations.'

Above all, the planners said, there was little doubt that if the Allies used gas against the Japanese or the Germans they would undoubtedly retaliate in kind and added, with the classic understatement that regularly attaches itself to projections about chemical and biological warfare, that the public at large 'might be resentful' if they felt it could have been avoided.

As to biological weapons, the British strategists were less emphatic, indeed they seemed to favour their use over chemicals – although at the same time they were aware that the anthrax-charged N-bomb tested by Porton Down on Gruinard Island could still not be produced in sufficient quantities. Nevertheless, the report noted: 'The indications are that . . . "N" [the anthrax bomb] used on a large scale might have major effect on the course of the war . . . If extreme pressure were applied to the US enough "N" bombs might be accumulated towards the end of the year to make a very few token or demonstration attacks on selected objectives.'

The war planners' report made stark reading. There were sufficient stocks of chemicals for a massive and sustained attack against the Germans, though it would be several months before the biological warheads could be produced for an effective strike. On 28 July, the Chiefs of Staffs trooped into a meeting to discuss its contents and make their observations. They came out firmly against what they assessed would lead to a major chemical offensive by both sides – largely on the grounds of public opinion. They concluded that the British were capable of 'drenching the big German cities with an immeasurably greater weight of gas than the Germans could put down in this country'.

There was no reason to believe, however, that the German High Command would have 'any greater difficulty in holding down the cowed population if they were subjected to gas than they had during the past months of intensive high explosive and incendiary bombing . . . the same cannot be said for our own people who are in no such inarticulate condition.'

Churchill was still not persuaded, but with additional restraining pressure from Eisenhower and President Roosevelt, he grudgingly drew back, damning the report as 'negative' and adding: 'Clearly I cannot make head against the parsons and the warriors at the same time.'

At almost exactly the same time, similar discussions were taking place in Germany. The Nazis had already carried out a successful series of tests, charging their flying bombs and rockets with poison gas, just as Churchill had surmised. General Hermann Ochsner, commander of the Wehrmacht chemical division, presented a detailed report to the German High Command, recommending the immediate use of gas in bombing raids on British cities. It should be targeted at large industrial areas and at the major cities.

He painted a scenario that was almost identical to that put forward by the British war planners: 'There is no doubt that a city like London would be plunged into a state of unbearable turmoil which would bring enormous pressure to bear on the enemy Government.' With the V-rockets being despatched at the rate of 250 a day, Ochsner had the means to deliver swift and devastating attacks. As the Allies would later discover, his unit was ordered to prepare for the arming of V-rockets with both phosgene and the nerve gas, tabun. But, like their opposite numbers in Britain, the top brass held back from giving the 'Go' command.

The world was saved by a whisker from a chemical and biological bombardment on a scale largely incalculable at the time, but evident now with the benefit of hindsight. Apart from the mass killing and injuring of many thousand civilians and military personnel – bad enough with conventional bombing – biological weapons would have contaminated massive areas of both countries with disease and bacteria that would have taken decades to eliminate. Proof that that would have happened lay like a time bomb ticking away on Gruinard Island.

For all their knowledge and experiments, the scientists had been unable to predict such long-lasting effects. Nowhere in the archive reports is that possibility even discussed, and in many respects the outcome could have been almost as bad as that suffered by Japan after the dropping of the atom bombs on Hiroshima and Nagasaki in

August 1945. There was yet one further significant discovery, however, that would leave the British military commanders, and their scientific advisers, breathing a great sigh of relief that they had not launched an all-out attack against Germany. It came in the late spring of 1945. The war in Europe was virtually at an end. Staff at Porton Down were being stood down.

There was still the possibility of gas or germ attacks. Intelligence reports from France suggested that Germany had sent a detachment of agents to Paris to ensure one final strike against the city as its troops pulled out – by spreading thousands of glass containers filled with bacteria in the Metro. In the Far East, some isolated Pacific outposts of Japanese forces used chemicals. But, by and large, the threat was over.

Some of Porton's leading scientists and chemists were already drifting back to their pre-war jobs in the universities and medical faculties. Even the future of Porton itself was being discussed, amid speculation that the whole chemical and biological research effort might be scaled down to a minimal level.

That possibility was to be quickly dispelled.

On 25 March, the Allied armies thrust deep into the Ruhr, the industrial heart of Germany, after their stunning crossing of the Rhine and the capture of Cologne. To the north, Montgomery put up a massive smoke screen – another pioneering project from Porton Down – to move his huge assembly and troops, stores and munitions forward. It was during these advances that on 16 April 1945 British troops from the 21st Army, mopping up behind the advancing heavy guns, discovered a German munitions dump that contained shells marked with a white ring, previously identified by the Allies as being charged with chemicals. There were other shells, which carried green and yellow rings, a marking unknown to the explosives experts. Further investigation led them to one of the Germans' largest chemical warfare stations at Raubkammer bei Munster. There, 105 shells marked with green rings were discovered.

The shells were cautiously examined by a joint Porton and US team at a field laboratory. The white-ringed shells were found to contain a mustard gas mixture. The others carried a chemical that had never been previously identified. A report on the discovery states that 'the shells were found to contain a remarkably potent and hitherto unknown organophosphorus nerve agent' similar to a secret formula Porton was working at the time, codenamed 'PF3'.

The British had accidentally stumbled across the secret weapon that Hitler had never used – Dr Schrader's nerve gas. The shells were hastily transported back to England. That the Porton staff were 'open-mouthed and incredulous' at the potency of the chemical charging was putting it mildly. Immediate assessments were called for. A Porton report on the examination and tests on animals reported that the gas was 'rapidly toxic through skin or eye absorption . . . lethal dose of five grams through skin . . . lethal concentration by inhalation of same order and by injection . . . was ten times more toxic than PF3. On small animals after injection, death was rapid following tremors, convulsions and respiratory failure.'

Was it possible that Hitler had produced large stocks of this new and as yet unidentified gas? And if so, why had he not used it?

The answer to the latter question was now academic; the war with Germany was won, and it would be surmised later that the German High Command held back on blitzing London with its lethal new gas for exactly the same reasons that the British Chiefs of Staffs had rejected an all-out chemical attack on German cities: they were afraid of the consequences. Just as the development of nerve gas had remained unknown to the Allies, the Nazis themselves could never be certain whether or not the Allies themselves had similar weaponry among their chemical armoury and would retaliate in kind.

The same, incidentally, applied to the USSR. After the war, a defecting Soviet colonel confirmed that the Red Army had chemical weapons strategically placed ready for use, but Stalin had refused to agree to a wholesale attack on the Germans for fear of retaliation in kind. As to the question of stocks, that would remain for some months a mystery to all – all, that is, except the Soviets who, by then, were hurriedly transporting samples of the nerve agents sarin and tabun back to Moscow.

Unknown to the Allies in April 1945, the Soviet Army advancing south through Poland had discovered, and taken possession of, the largest of the German nerve gas production and scientific plants, the massive purpose-built compound in the Silesia region of Poland, forty miles from Breslau. They also found a new factory still being built at Falkenhagen. Between them, those two plants were capable of producing more than 10,000 tons of nerve gas a month. Even as the Soviet troops approached, the German High Command had given orders for everything at the plant to be destroyed but by then the Red Army had moved in, although most senior German scientists at the plant had fled.

Porton scientists had completed their analysis and tests on their sample of German shells and dramatic reports of the chemical potency were floated up the chain of command. With the help of a German scientist co-operating with the British, it was identified as tabun, or Trilon 83, one of the series of nerve gases that had evolved from Dr Schrader's initial experiments and code-named by the Germans as 'G-agents'. Although Germany was no longer a threat, the very discovery stirred considerable excitement in the Porton ranks and even its rather staid formal history records:

> Concern about possible chemical warfare in the Far East was immediately relegated and almost the whole of Porton activity was directed towards an investigation of the Germans' capability . . . a vast programme of work on the nerve agents was mounted, both within Porton and extramurally at the University of Cambridge.

Fifty years later it was still going on.

7

SPOILS OF WAR

AS THE MILITARY established its command across the defeated nation, it was followed by a smaller army of specialist personnel who, as we now know, were charged with identifying, assessing and evacuating the spoils of war. Hundreds of tons of documents and plans covering virtually every aspect of the Nazi regime, from foreign policy to industrial and scientific research, were captured and transported back to Britain and America and the USSR. The Soviets were doing the same in the sectors under their control and it had become clear to Western intelligence that the Red Army had, in one fell swoop, gathered up the secrets of the nerve gas factories. Fortunately for Porton, there were others in the territories that fell under British and American control, and the West also pulled off a significant coup by rounding up a greater number of scientists who would be prepared to co-operate. The renowned US Naval Technical Mission swept across Europe in search of every scrap of industrial material and scientific data that could be garnered from the fallen Reich. This mission set the stage for the wholesale importation of more than 600 top Nazi scientists under the auspices of Project Paperclip, which the CIA supervised during the early years of the Cold War.

Dozens were already in the US and Britain before the war ended, but by the same token the Soviets had gathered up their own quota of people and documents from which the secrets of sarin could be extracted. Even before Germany surrendered and, as the horrors of the concentration camps came tumbling forth, several scientific teams left England to join their US colleagues in pursuit of scientists and scientific records. Of particular early interest to Porton were the records at Natzweiler Concentration Camp, where allegations of experiments conducted on inmates by Professor Karl Wimmer, of Strasbourg University, and other leading chemists were to be studied under the direction of the Combined Intelligence Objectives Sub-Committee.

The camp was first inspected by a Porton-linked team of Captains W.J. Cromartie and Carlo Henze who had been assigned to examine the records of medical institutions in Strasbourg and in turn visited Natzweiler, one of the first Nazi concentration camps to be liberated. On 2 January 1945, Cromartie filed his first report to the head of intelligence at Porton:

'On the suggestion of an informant at the Institute of Hygiene in Strasbourg . . . visited Natzweiler Concentration camp . . . it is of the usual hutted style, surrounded by a barbed wire fence, electrically charged, with guard towers and powerful lighting. At the time, the camp was under the command of the French Army who were using it for the internment of German nationals rounded up in the Strasbourg area. As we were escorted through the camp, many stories of atrocities allegedly committed by the SS were recited . . . informant volunteered the information that doctors from medical research institutes in [Germany] had visited the camp in connection with experimental work on prisoners.'

The report, accompanied by a selection of photographs taken at the site, went on to describe in detail gas chambers, a morgue, autopsy room, incineration plant and associated installations. Outside, they made an inspection of a large dumping ground for ashes. There was also a collection of earthenware urns that were supposedly used by guards to sell ashes to relatives of camp victims, gassed and cremated.

The report inspired a further inspection, this time by another of the Porton team, Major D.C. Evans, who had been attached to the chemical and biological unit throughout the war. He was assigned the task of examining the gas chambers of the concentration camps, though not for any humanitarian reasons. His was a particular mission: to collect details of the gas used by the Nazis in their extermination programme, Zyklon B, cyanide gas.

One report on his findings noted in icily clinical terms that a great deal of time was spent 'trying to discover reliable data to calculate what concentrations of Zyklon were used for the extermination of victims. It would appear, however, that no controlled experiments were carried out on a scientific basis. The chief object was to kill the victims as quickly as possible so as to make room for the next batch.'

Major Evans, confronted by this disappointing lack of scientific data, tried to make his own calculations. His report to Porton recorded: 'Several witnesses have given measurements of the size of the gas chambers with which they were acquainted whilst others have stated the approximate numbers of Zyklon B canisters required for the extermination of given numbers of victims. Unfortunately, there were three sizes of Zyklon tins.'

Major Evans and others from Porton, along with many teams from the US, were also trying to retrieve as much information as possible on the nerve gas experiments, as well as the general chemical and biological weaponry developed by Germany during the war years. The pressure, according to one source at Porton, to bridge the gap in the knowledge of the Western Allies was intense and came from 'on high'. Evans was asked to examine the possibility that nerve gas had been tested using human guinea-pigs from the concentration camps.

His report spelled out unequivocally the intent: 'It is thought highly probable that such experiments have been carried out . . . and the results might provide invaluable data as to the lethal concentrations for man.'

Thousands of files on human experiments had already been destroyed by the Germans themselves in the last few months of the war. There was still enough to show that there had been masses of experiments on human beings in the cause of medical, scientific and chemical warfare research. At Natzweiler itself there were numerous experiments, on 'habitual criminals' interned there, into the lethal concentrations of mustard gas and nerve gas. Evans had several names on his file of scientists who had conducted experiments on humans, including Professor Karl Wimmer.

As soon as Wimmer was located, Evans contacted the military police and asked for him to be arrested at once. The major said in his report: 'He could be well worth interrogating . . . [he] is one of the few surviving individuals who might be able to provide such information.'

Wimmer was duly taken into custody – and then promptly disappeared. What happened to him thereafter remains a mystery. He was never summoned before any war crimes tribunal and there is no trace of his name in the British archives, at least not in those that have come into the public domain. If he was arrested and co-operated with Evans either in Germany or back at Porton, it remains classified information.

Other documents from Nazi sources, however, would confirm the fears of the Porton scientists of the mass suffering that a full-scale attack with sarin or tabun would have wrought on British cities. Among files in the hands of the Combined Intelligence Objectives Sub-Committee was a report retrieved from Spandau concerning industrial accidents at the Dyhernfurth plant where there had been at least 300 mishaps and a dozen deaths in under 24 months. In the worst case, seven men were squirted in the face with liquid tabun. Although they were all wearing masks, they fell ill instantly. The files described how they became giddy and began vomiting, so they removed their respirators only to inhale more gas. They all fell into a coma, their bodies convulsing violently even when unconscious. Their pulses became feeble, they had nasal discharge, contracted pupils and struggled to breathe. Involuntary urination and diarrhoea occurred. In spite of immediate injections of atropine and other drugs, along with artificial respiration and heart massage, only two of the seven survived. Even then, as they came out of the coma, they both suffered severe convulsions and had to be sedated for ten hours.

The bodies of the others were subjected to a rigorous post mortem. Their brains and lungs were so badly damaged and congested that the organs were despatched to Berlin for inspection by medical teams. This was the kind of evidence the British, the American and the Soviets were competing for in the months after the war. It made grim reading, but in many respects its importance seemed to have been superseded when the Americans unleashed the next generation of high explosives with their A-bomb attacks on Japan.

That, alone, was considered by some at the time to be sufficient to conclude all experiments on chemical and biological warfare – they should be scaled down to the point of snuffing them out. What was the use of anthrax and nerve gas now that one single bomb could wipe out a whole city?

That, however, could never become the rationale for the future. The Soviets had The Bomb, too. They also had possession of Germany's landmark nerve gas plant in Silesia and were the first to capture General Ishii's Japanese biological warfare stations in Manchuria. The huge Allied intelligence activity and a massive traffic, stunning in its quantity, in 'top secret' reports running to thousands of pages from every major centre of the war theatre, covering even the minutiae of chemical and biological discoveries, demonstrated an air of desperation.

A directive from the Pentagon, and matched by a similar edict from London, ensured that all available evidence would be collected up. At every location, any sign, any mention of chemicals and bacteria had to be pursued, and mere rumours from captives and prisoners of war would be followed up. Page upon page, file after file, poured into the various centres of CB technology for dissemination by a special assessment panel set up in 1945.

When Churchill made his famous Iron Curtain speech a year later, it merely confirmed the very obvious fears of the military establishment, that the Soviets had replaced the Germans and the Japanese as a future threat. Chemical and biological warfare was on the threshold of a new era, based to a large extent on Hitler's unused secret weapon – nerve gas – and the British and Japanese trials of bacteria-carrying bombs.

That probability was spelled out in an upwardly directed memo from Commanding Officer No. 1 Chemical Warfare Investigations Detachment, Porton, 13 October 1945: 'The chief IG chemists associated with sarin are now in British, American or French hands. They have talked freely on the subject and it is probable that any other chemists in Russian hands would talk as freely . . . much of the documentation on sarin had been stored at Spandau and was not thought to have fallen into Russian hands. However, a number of Spandau personnel have not been located in the West and can therefore be presumed to have been captured by the Russians. In conclusion, it would appear that it is more than probable that the Russians have followed up developments in this field. If they are producing tabun or sarin, or compounds very similar to them already, they have now probably learned enough about them in Germany to produce them in the near future.'

The scene was set . . . and as Porton's own history records: 'There was very little of the uncertainty about the future that had been evident at Porton after the Great War.' None, indeed. As the Porton records bluntly admit the post-war exploitation of German chemical weapons was 'particularly important'. Those engaged in CB research were placed on a new red alert – 'Red' being the operative word. The Soviets, it was commonly and correctly assumed, had equipped themselves with German knowledge. British and American teams spent months analysing every scrap of documentation relating to Nazi and Japanese research they could lay their hands on, along with a vast hoard of specimens, preserved organs, gas samples and thousands of photographs of experiments conducted on humans and animals. Leading scientists from both nations had been spirited away to secret hideaways in the West on the promise of immunity in exchange for their knowledge.

It was only then that the extent of the Japanese programme into biological research began to emerge. The pieces of the jigsaw were eventually put together from the interrogation of prisoners of war and Japanese scientists, along with a substantial cache of documents. They told a story that the Japanese themselves made attempts to hide in the last months of the war.

As the Soviet Army neared the Japanese biological plant at Pingfan in 1945, the military detachment within the institute's compound was ordered to begin a systematic destruction of everything of an incriminating nature – including all records of experiments, laboratory equipment and the contents of almost 1,000 tanks in which tons of bacteria had been stored. Its founder and the chief proponent of the Japanese BW capacity, General Shiro Ishii, was arrested five months later by the Americans and was imprisoned in Tokyo, where Allied intelligence officers, aided by scientists, began their interrogation.

For a long time Ishii simply denied all knowledge of the BW experiments. During the next 18 months, the Americans tried in vain to get him to talk about the work that the Japanese had attempted to eradicate from their history. Towards the beginning of 1946, a flurry of intelligence memos between the Pentagon in Washington and the Chiefs of Staff in London portrayed an air of high drama following the discovery that Ishii's BW plants in Manchuria had fallen into the hands of the USSR. Had the Soviets managed to retrieve all of the research material, accumulated over a dozen years, into biological weapons?

The question became a matter of top priority and the need to 'neutralize' any gains made by the Soviets in that respect became one of 'paramount importance'. In 1947 Ishii had been in the hands of the Allies for almost two years and was still refusing to confirm any details of the now notorious Unit 731 of the Japanese Army, which he controlled. In May that year, he apparently changed his mind after the Soviets had made a formal request to interview him, ostensibly to confirm claims that the Japanese had used biological weapons against China and the USSR.

Ishii, fearing he would be handed over, began to talk to the Americans. Two senior figures in the American BW team at Camp Detrick, Dr Edwin Hill and Dr Joe Victor, were despatched to Tokyo to assess the extent of Ishii's information. The evidence they collated had such implications as to inspire an immediate, panic-stricken security clampdown. Nothing from Ishii's interrogation should be allowed to leak out. Nor would it – and in the intervening years, very little has filtered into the public domain. Half a century later the reasons would become clear.

Classified US files pointed to the fact that the Americans wanted to mop up the Ishii intelligence and take it home, in part to deny the Soviets the key to the material they had already gathered in Manchuria, but more specifically to provide scientists in the West with an insight into Japanese research. The files provide graphic accounts alleging that Japanese doctors and scientists conducted experiments on prisoners at the Mukden PoW camp, located in Manchuria, about 300 miles south of the Pingfan BW institute.

The camp housed US, British and Australian PoWs as well as captives from regions in the Far East. The reports were suppressed as the US military officers arranged a secret deal granting certain Japanese immunity from prosecution in exchange for tissue samples and reports on experiments that might help give the US a germ warfare advantage over the USSR.

A 137-page counter-intelligence file, known as the Mukden Report, focused specifically on the operations of Unit 731 of the Japanese Imperial Army, which some historians have linked to the killing of 200,000 Chinese soldiers and civilians in 'field tests' of germ warfare. These included giving children chocolate laced with anthrax. Test subjects were injected with bubonic plague, typhoid, cholera, syphillis and other diseases. It has been claimed that some prisoners were dissected alive, after heavy injections of morphine, to see the effect of the diseases on their vital organs.

Both the US and Japanese governments have maintained there is no evidence to support the allegations or that there was any 'secret deal', a position they maintain today. Campaigners for relatives of the victims, however, claim that the files from the military's counter-intelligence corps of the Supreme Commander of the Allied Powers, headed by General Douglas MacArthur, confirm that US intelligence covered up war crimes against Western soldiers and gave safe-haven to General Ishii.

The Mukden files emanate in part from the findings of a counter-intelligence corps, which prepared a report on Ishii, just before the arrival of the Camp Detrick team in October 1947. Colonel Philip Bethune, a senior officer in US military intelligence, commandeered the report and declared that it was a 'top secret matter' on which nothing further should be written. The counter-intelligence officer, identified in the files only by the initials WSC, noted: 'Col Bethune desires no further action be taken in this case. No further action was taken.'

The colonel was merely following orders. On 17 April 1947, General MacArthur's headquarters, which was handling the investigation of Unit 731, issued a directive: 'The utmost secrecy is essential in order to protect the interests of the United States and to guard against embarrassment.'

Nor did the Americans give up Ishii for a 1949 war crimes trial in the USSR, in which 12 Japanese prisoners of war were sentenced to various terms of imprisonment for being involved with germ warfare against China. In typical propaganda, though it was undoubtedly true, the Soviets claimed that Americans were protecting Japanese war criminals to reap the benefits of their research. A clue to the Allies' dilemma over the Ishii material eventually emerged in 1985 when Dr Murray Sanders, who was enlisted as a lieutenant colonel to become BW adviser to General MacArthur, made a public confession. He claimed that the US military under personal orders from MacArthur agreed to exchange immunity to leaders of Unit 731 in exchange for details of their biological experiments.

Sanders, then 75 and with not long to live, admitted to newspaper reporters that he did not know at the time that the Japanese had experimented on humans. 'I feel terrible about it, that it should have been covered up all these years,' he admitted. His revelations were treated with scepticism in establishment quarters. Almost a decade later, they were to be confirmed in the Mukden files.

One of the PoWs, Greg Rodriguez, age 72, from Henryetta, Oklahoma, remembers how a Japanese doctor at the camp had passed a feather under his nose, which was a regular way of causing the inhalation of germs. Few years have passed since then when Rodriguez has not had to visit hospital with unidentifiable fevers. Ten years ago, he finally learned of his condition from a privately consulted doctor. He told him he had excessive levels of typhoid bacilli in his blood. Many similar stories are today emerging from survivors of Japanese PoW camps. And while few are now able to prove a direct link between illnesses in later life and what happened in the Japanese camps, suspicions remain. In 1986, a US House of Representatives sub-committee hearing was set up ostensibly to investigate the claims of Dr Sanders and others.

The only Mukden survivor to testify, Frank James, a Lockheed employee from Redwood, was able to give specific dates about his own experiences. He reported that captured American, British and

Australian soldiers in Mukden were examined on 11 November 1942 by a Japanese medical team, all wearing facial masks. Liquid was sprayed into the prisoners' faces and they were given injections.

James said that within 60 days, 200 or 300 had died and their bodies had been thrown outside, where they froze in the low winter temperatures, to be stacked 'like cordwood'. In the spring, said James, prisoners were ordered to bury some of them in a roughly hewn mass grave. The rest were allowed to thaw, and were then taken inside the laboratories for dissection. Their organs were placed in boxes, James testified, and each one was clearly labelled with PoW numbers, as if it had particular significance. Each of the bodies was photographed.

His claims are confirmed by other secret documents not produced at the hearing. They were part of a detailed report prepared by the Chief of the US Chemicals Corps, written on 17 December 1947. Headed 'Summary Report on BW Investigations', it concerned the examination of a number of bodies exhumed from mass graves. The report concluded that the remains showed that 31 deaths were due to anthrax, 60 to cholera, 12 from dysentery, 20 from mustard gas, 16 from tetanus, 106 from bubonic plague, 22 to typhoid, 41 to tuberculosis and 9 to typhus.

In 1996, there were an estimated 200 Mukden survivors in the US alone and several have come forward to make allegations of germ-warfare experiments. One remembers that he and his colleagues, skeletal from starvation and some on the brink of death, were made to brush their teeth every day with a particular powder. Another recalls how a group of them had to line up ever day to get oranges from the guards.

'They had a ledger with all the PoW numbers, and when you got your orange they checked it off,' said Jack Campbell, 75, a retired machinist from Rockwall, Texas. 'You just know there were germs in those oranges.' About a week later, he and eight of the camp's healthiest prisoners were put in a special ward where they were tended by a team from outside the camp. For three months, each was given an injection every third day. 'They told us it was horse urine that was high in vitamin B,' said Campbell.

In spite of known intelligence reports circulating in April 1945 alleging that the Japanese were experimenting on Allied and Chinese prisoners, both the British and the US authorities kept the lid firmly on General Ishii's activities for almost five decades. At least a dozen files in the British archives related to the Japanese experiments remain closed. Even the 1986 congressional committee to which Frank James gave evidence failed to unearth the truth. Indeed, it seemed to James that the intention was that it should not.

James was the only Mukden survivor called to testify and he was warned in advance that there were still matters of state secrecy, including references to General MacArthur, to which he could not refer. The US Army sent its chief archivist, John Hatcher, to say that there were no records proving that Americans had been the victims of wartime experiments. All relevant documents had been returned to the Japanese in 1959 and no copies had been kept in the US. The 'inquiry' lasted just four hours, and nothing more was heard of it.

Like Britain, Japan does not have a Freedom of Information Act, and in any event several leading scientists who had worked with Ishii became leading figures in the business, scientific and academic life of post-war Japan, including the founder of one of its largest pharmaceutical companies.

As for the Mukden files, there is one other reason why the Allies were reluctant to reveal their own hand. The British and Americans were well advanced in their own BW research, and they knew for certain that the Soviets now had the technology for developing two of the major CB elements – anthrax and nerve gas. That alone would ensure continued research on both sides of the Iron Curtain for the rest of the century.

8

THE VOLUNTEERS

PORTON'S OWN HISTORIANS admit frankly that there was among the military and scientific communities alike a 'desperate preoccupation' with nerve gas immediately after the war. Apart from their efforts to exploit the knowledge gleaned from German and Japanese sources by producing their own hoard of nerve gas and potential biological agents, Porton also began work 'as a matter or urgency' on producing the prototypes for new civilian and military gas-masks to protect against any possible attack using sarin or tabun. British and American factories that produced them were soon working flat out to fulfill the multi-million dollar orders.

The dash to re-arm and re-equip would lead to a massive new programme of experiments. In 1946, Sir Henry Tizard, charged with assessing the 'future potentialities' of weapons of war on behalf of the Chiefs of Staff, concluded that biological weapons would have little scope in future wars. Civilian populations could simply be vaccinated against them, although he conceded that the same could not be said of chemicals.

Meanwhile, Dr (now Sir) Paul Fildes, who had led the Porton BW team throughout the war and had been knighted as a reward, angrily defended the case for continued research on all fronts. In typically robust response, he insisted that Britain had to build and maintain an adequate defence against the possible future use of CB weapons – a view that was shared by many senior military figures, and certainly by the US top brass. Mass inoculations were impossible, said Fildes.

'Future possibilities' in CB.W were now so vast in potential that they could not be ignored. Fildes and his US counterparts were at one in maintaining that the only defence was to research and develop a comprehensive CB programme, both as a deterrent and as an offensive capability, should it be necessary. The question was quickly resolved. Research would go ahead. The Chiefs of Staff accepted Fildes' opinion on biological weaponry, just as they had on the development of chemical weapons on which the British, the Americans and the Canadians were already co-operating.

In 1947 the three nations concluded their Tripartite Agreement for joint research – scientists from each country would show the others everything they had, and go forward on co-operative research. Canada eventually dropped out, with its decision in 1950 to concentrate on defensive research. From the British standpoint, co-operation with the US was especially welcome because Porton, starved of cash, continued to operate among its dated surroundings.

The Americans had the modern facilities of the Edgewood Arsenal with 3,000 men employed in chemical research, along with the biological study areas of Camp Detrick and its associated laboratories. There would be a frequent exchange of both personnel and research.

Chemical research centred predominantly on the 'G-agents', or nerve gas. Porton was by then under the control of its first ever civilian director, A.E. Childs, a physical chemist who had held senior posts at the station successively since 1920. Dr J.M. Barnes, who had worked with Fildes' team with the rank of major during the war, and was among those assigned to inspect Nazi concentration camps, was promoted to head the physiological section. They had a combined staff of around 800 personnel, all working on a range of top-secret experiments ranging from potential weaponry to investigating new insecticides, the latter operating under the newly formed Colonial Office Pesticide Unit. Field trials began in Africa with eight Anson aircraft spraying pesticides across the Tanganyika landscape.

The sheer scale of the work at Porton required an equally massive inventory of suitable subjects on which the gas itself, antidotes to it and the newly ordered masks and protective clothing might be tested. By the end of the 1940s, extensive experiments with living creatures became a daily requirement. The problem confronting Porton, as identified and admitted in its own contemporary reports, was 'that unprotected men could not be put through gas chambers or allowed to see if nerve agents could be decontaminated swiftly from their skin'.

In spite that admission, it would not be long before men were being ushered through the security controlled gates of Porton (and the Edgewood Arsenal) by the lorry load. Initially, the bulk of the experimental work was done using animals, literally thousands of them. For this, the first major post-war animal-supply unit was set up. Its sole reason for being was to breed or obtain from other sources a large and continuous supply of animals, ranging from apes to mice. In wartime, the supply of animals over and above those self-bred at the establishment fell to the Royal Army Veterinary Corps. In 1949, this task was exclusively turned over to Porton's Orwellian-sounding 'Animal Farm'. In 1954, it became known rather more respectably as Allington Farm, which ran a complete agricultural operation, raising cereals, sheep and cattle.

Its brief was to handle the supply of animals for Porton Down and its brand new Cornwall outpost, Nancekuke, which became a prime centre for the production and storage of nerve gas during the next three decades. The place was carefully selected. It was set in beautiful countryside, like Porton, on the Cornish coast, well away from build-up areas and close enough to the sea so that any possible leaking gas would be carried away from the civilian population. It was to the remote Nancekuke site, surrounded by 9ft high perimeter fencing, that many pieces of plant and machinery stripped from German installations were brought in absolute secrecy.

At that time, there was virtually no public knowledge of the work, and the non-scientific labour employed to build the Nancekuke plant were not told of its intended use. Cornwall engineer Tom Griffiths, who began work at the plant in 1951 and remained there until 1965, recalled, 'They just told us it would be varied and interesting work in engineering. So I and my colleagues began building the nerve gas plant without the slightest knowledge of what it was for. We did not know for a long time what was going on there. It must have been one of the best kept secrets in the country, although the Americans knew, because their technicians were collaborating with the British. They were coming and going all the time.'

Nancekuke became Britain's first, and only, pilot plant for the production of nerve gas, a fact that remained another of the most closely guarded secrets within the nation's defence establishment. Porton's administrators viewed it as a sister plant under the control of their scientists. It was during this period of development of the British chemical capability and its defensive capacity that the demand for many species of animals was increased by the week: goats, sheep, pigs, rats, mice, rabbits, guinea-pigs, hamsters, primates, far more than Porton could breed itself.

Many were of a kind that could only be found in the tropics. Navy ships carrying supplies of animals, especially monkeys and apes, from the wilds of Africa and elsewhere were unloaded at the Portland naval dockyard and the animals were carried in special containers for delivery to Porton. Apart from laboratory experiments on thousands of rats, mice, guinea-pigs and rabbits, other animals would be tethered on the Porton ranges for open-air tests. Chimpanzees, goats, dogs tied to stakes and many smaller animals in cages would be placed outside while nerve gas shells were fired towards them, and above them to form gas clouds. They were then collected up and brought back inside for dissection. Most were already dead; the larger animals and those that did not get a heavy dose of the gas were kept alive to observe the effects of the chemicals on their bodies, their ears and eyes.

In many of the experiments, however, there could be no substitute for human guinea-pigs, and from the late 1940s onwards Porton began seeking an increasing number of volunteers from the three armed services on whom various tests were to be carried out. Most of the papers relating to human experiments are still secret today, and will remain so until well into the next century.

However, a number agreed to be interviewed for this book and their experiences are recounted in this and ensuing chapters. They are among approximately 3,000 men who volunteered in the decade of the 1950s for the most vital and early tests on sarin and its associated products. Gerald Beach, who now lives near Chester, was among the first exposed to nerve gas. Beach had been a regular serviceman in the RAF since 1946, having enlisted when he was 18. He explained:

> In 1950, I was an aircraft fitter stationed at RAF Valley, North Wales. I was 22 years old at the time. One morning, on parade, they asked for volunteers to take part in testing procedures at Porton Down research station. It was explained that a new chemical, a gas, was being studied and something similar was already in the hands of the Russians. They needed volunteers to take parts in experiments to discover an antidote. The experiments, they said, would be harmless and we would be paid one shilling – 5p in today's money – for each experiment we took part in. I stepped forward, obviously not for the money but simply because I felt I might be doing some good. No other reason than that. The way it was put, it sounded as if they needed help. So off I went to Porton.

> I was alone; there were no others from my unit. I was given a rail warrant to Salisbury where I was met by an Army truck. There were several others already there waiting to be picked up. When we arrived we were shown our billet, which was with the Army unit permanently stationed inside the Porton compound. It was explained that we would be there for a week. We could enjoy the facilities of the place, and would be required to take part in a few experiments. We were put in groups of ten.
>
> When we first went to the laboratories, they put a rubber patch on our arms. They said it was to test gas-mask rubber. Whether it was or not, I don't know, but it was to stay there for the whole week; we were not to remove it.

Although it is impossible to clarify the reason for the patch from such a distance in time, it is now known that many volunteers from this period had the liquid nerve agent, known through its code-name of 'GB', and antidotes to it applied in patches to test skin reaction. Other patches were indeed sited to test the strength of a particular fabric, or the protective powers of older suits that had already been worn. Beach continued:

> On the Tuesday, they called us to the laboratories where it was explained that we were required to go inside a gas chamber in which we would be exposed to a very mild dose of gas. They told us to just breathe normally and assured us there would be no ill effects. At the time, I noticed they were preparing dozens of rabbits. They had the fur shaved from their backs and there were patches of what looked like clay on them, through which they were giving them injections. It was all a bit puzzling to us laymen.
>
> Anyhow, that mystery would soon be resolved. When they asked us to go forward to the gas chamber, we were all given cages containing the rabbits to take in with us. Between us we must have taken in about 30 of these white rabbits. The senior man in charge, the laboratory supervisor, came in with us. He explained that the gas would be sprayed in through an electric fan on the far side, where there was also a glass partition through which we would be observed by the technicians in the laboratory.
>
> The supervisor stayed inside the chamber with us, but as soon as they closed the doors, he put on his gas-mask and stood right at the back. After a few seconds, the people on the other side of the glass window sprayed the gas, a liquid, from a large hypodermic needle into the fan, which in turn sprayed it into the

chamber. We were inside the chamber for about ten minutes. We didn't seem to suffer any ill effects at the time. We were all examined when we came out and they told us that we would be required again in a couple of days' time.

The following day we were not required but on the Thursday we were called again to go through the same process. This time, before we went in they examined our eyes and measured the pupils. Then we were taken back into the chamber carrying the rabbits with their shaven backs. The time we were in there was about the same as before, but I think they must have given us a larger dose. You could feel something happening to your eyes, almost straight away. I began to get really nervous when the rabbits started dying. When we came out, they were all dead. Not just from our group, either. I saw them bringing rabbits out by the score, all dead.

After that test, they examined us and paid special attention to our eyes. Everyone of us had trouble. We couldn't see in daylight for a good 48 hours, virtually blinded. The pupils of our eyes had gone right down to pinpoints. Throughout that day, our sight got worse. You couldn't see anything, because you had this kind of black blob in front of you. Oddly enough, at night you could see perfectly well. That condition lasted all Friday and although I could see pretty well on the Saturday, when I went home my wife said, 'You're eyes are like little spots.' By the evening, they were more or less back to normal.

I went back to camp on the Monday and not long afterwards I began to get spasms of breathlessness and reported sick. I reported to Doc Mason, the camp medic, who said I was probably suffering from asthma, which I had never had in my entire life, and he began treating me for that. But then I was walking around in a trance and could not do my work. So he gave me another drug to counteract the first one. After a few more visits, he downgraded my medical rating to A1G4. I was flying at the time, too, but this meant that although I was fit for aircrew, I could not go abroad because of my breathing difficulties.

I stayed at A1G4 for the rest of my service. The trouble seemed to clear up but about 18 months later, when I had been posted to Scotland, I had another attack; very bad this time. I just couldn't breathe. I reported sick and they put me into the sick bay. Again, they said it was asthma. I was in hospital for about a week and it cleared up and I was OK for the rest of my service.

> Not long after I left the RAF [1967], I had another attack and eventually had to go to see my own doctor. Now, the thing was, I could not tell her exactly what had happened because I had signed a declaration under the Official Secrets Act. Anyway, after two or three visits, I was given a complete check-up, at the end of which my doctor told me that I had damage to my lungs; my breathing capacity was down by a third and there was very little they could do. The condition was irreversible. It was quite debilitating; when I couldn't get the air I needed, I would sweat profusely and go dizzy.
>
> That's the way it has been ever since, year in, year out. When I left the RAF I worked as a fitter at a power station and for the last ten years before retiring early I took a desk job. My breathing never improved; I still have the problems and I know they date back to the time I went to Porton. In 1994, I wrote to the Ministry of Defence to inquire if I was eligible for any kind of pension. It took them 18 months to reply. They said my records had been lost in a fire at Porton and, as far as they were concerned, my presence there in 1950 could not be traced. They added that further inquiries were being made, and I would be contacted again in due course . . . I am still waiting.

Another RAF serviceman, Gerry Ashton, of Preston, Lancashire, had a similar experience. He was 20 when he went to Porton Down as a volunteer in the early 1950s, and he too was exposed to nerve gas. 'I went into the gas chamber and was told to breathe normally. Then after a few minutes, I was let out and told to go back to my billet. By the time I got there, I was almost blind. Everything was like . . . shadows.'

Ashton said he was 'just groping around' and was told by Porton staff that 'it would pass'. It took three days before he could see normally, and observed that the pupils of his eyes had become 'kidney shaped', rather than round. It was explained to him that he had been given a very mild dose of gas – although as far as he could remember, he was never told it was nerve gas. When he became ill, Ashton told his doctor about his experiences and asked him to write to the Ministry of Defence for his medical records. In their first reply, the MoD said they could find no record that Ashton had ever been to Porton. Ashton insisted that he had. His doctor wrote again, and the reply this time admitted he had taken part in experiments – but 'they were of a very innocuous nature'. In other words, they did not accept any responsibility for his condition and did not consider that it could have been caused by any exposure he had received there. And, they refused to deliver to Ashton's GP any of his medical records.

Some volunteers like Ashton and Beach were filmed while the experiments took place. A Ministry of Defence training film, shot in 1952 and entitled *Nerve Gas,* carried a commentary that described the situation the volunteers faced. 'We have a volunteer here to show you the effects of a mild trace of nerve gas . . . now this man is showing mild effects, tightness of the chest and throat and having a great deal of difficulty breathing.'

Next the film explained the results of a heavy exposure. 'You've seen the effects of a mild dose,' the commentary continued, and went on to describe the effects of a more severe dose. The casualty would suffer muscular twitching, followed by severe convulsions. After the convulsions, paralysis would begin in most of the muscles throughout the body. The breathing would stop. Shortly after, the heart would stop.

Part of the Porton experiments at the time involved the testing of an antidote to the nerve gas, called atropine. Although antidote tablets were to be produced later, at the time of the experiments the antidote was injected by syringe straight into a muscle.

One of those from that era who was treated with the antidote and exposed to two specific experiments was George Abbot (not his real name), who was coming up to 60 when interviewed for this book. He still lives near Salisbury, about 20 miles from Porton. At the very outset of the interview, he corrected the implication that he was a volunteer. 'It was Porton or guard duty – straightforward as that,' said Mr Abbot.

He is a game keeper by profession and in 1953 began his two years' obligatory National Service, as a regimental signaller with the Wiltshire, stationed at Warminster:

> No, I did not volunteer to go to Porton in the strict sense of the word. It was a case of 'Well, you can do this . . . or guard duty.' Plus, of course, we were offered a bribe of £1 and a 72-hour pass, which meant quite a lot to National Service conscripts, bearing in mind we only received about £1 a week and would jump at any chance to get home. So, off I went to Porton. There were quite a few of us, a lorry load at least. I had heard about the place, of course, because I was born and bred in the area – at the address I live at now. But there was never much written about it in those days. Nobody really knew what went on there. It was seen locally

> as some kind of Army camp and frankly I hadn't taken much interest.
>
> We weren't told very much about what was going to happen. But anyway, in the first experiment we were to be put into a cage where we would be exposed to gas. We were told we would suffer no lasting ill effects. Some of us were to be treated with antidotes, others weren't. I was one of those who had the antidote. After they gassed us, I did not feel anything or smell anything, and I seemed to suffer no ill effects, not straight away. Several of those who were not given the antidote suffered very, very severe problems with their eyes. Some of them were hospitalized and when they came back four days later they looked really terrible.
>
> In the second experiment we were each given a gas-mask and taken out to the Porton ranges. There we were told to run as fast as we could for about a quarter of a mile or so. We were told that if we felt ill, we had to get under a lorry on the way. I did actually feel rough then. I had trouble breathing in the gas-mask and I was going to take cover under the lorry when we came to it, but they told me to keep going, to go a bit further. They didn't take any notice of me.

This part of the experiment may well have been set up to test the efficiency of gas-masks under a light spraying of gas, although Abbot and his comrades did not know it at the time.

'We were never told quite what we were being exposed to, although I do remember the name sarin cropped up. I had no idea what it was. When it was all over, we went back to the camp and that was that.'

Mr Abbot had already left the Army and returned to civilian life when he began to suffer the first of a long sequence of health problems, starting with his hearing. He continued his story:

> It was about two years later when I first started having difficulties, not hearing very well. It progressively got worse, and eventually extremely painful. The pains got really bad; lasting half an hour and in ever increasing frequency; I just couldn't do anything. In the next four years, I saw seven different doctors and specialists, but none of them could find what exactly was wrong. Four of them said specifically it was a 'nerves' problem and I used to get annoyed with that. It was ridiculous. I had no problems in that direction at all. Once we were on holiday in

Jersey and the pain was so bad my wife called the doctor there. He too told me it was a nerve problem.

What was happening, as was discovered later, was that my ear was totally dry, rotting away inside. By the early 1960s, I was beginning to get quite ill, and very weak, and my boss telephoned a doctor. He took one look at me and sent me to hospital immediately and I had an operation the following day. He said that had it not been caught then, it could have gone to my brain and killed me. Even so, I lost my hearing totally in that ear.

Mr Abbot's ear problems were similar to the troubles experienced by many of the veterans of the Gulf War who, in their thousands, were to complain of a variety of unexplained illnesses. They, like him, had been injected with the antidote atropine. Ear problems were also one of the most common disabilities among the many children of Gulf War veterans born with deformities, a fact that has some significance. He continued his story:

I did improve after that, but over the years I have had so many problems, little things which were alien to me, such as when the skin came off my genital area. Five years ago, I began to have breathing problems. I had a respiratory attack and couldn't breathe. I was rushed into hospital and went through various tests, but the doctors told my wife that they just could not identify what was the matter with me and they didn't know what to treat me for; they took blood samples and then the hospital doctor came to my bed side and asked me if I had come into contact with organophosphates, of the kind that they put in sheep dip. I hadn't. I knew that, but they had obviously found traces of something in my blood that made them think of organophosphates. That night I became worse and went into a coma; at 3.20 in the morning the ward orderly was checking me and found my heart had stopped.

They pumped drugs into me and resuscitated me. They telephoned my wife and told her to prepare for the worst. If I survived, I might have brain damage. Fortunately, I was OK when I came round. I remained in hospital for two weeks, being treated with steroids and eventually it passed. Two years later, I collapsed with chest pains. They said the muscles around my heart were not working properly. I had to have a heart bypass . . . all of this and I had barely reached my mid-fifties. So many things, often little, mysterious illnesses. Looking back, I am

> certain that the start of my troubles was being gassed at Porton Down. They simply did not know what long-lasting effects it might have, I am sure.
>
> I have two children who were fine, although my two grandsons have both had problems. The eldest, a very bright lad, had serious ear problems and is very short-sighted. My youngest grandson was born with a slight ear defect. Obviously, there is nothing to link that to my experiences . . . but you can't help wondering, can you?

Abbot remains convinced that the experiments he joined at Porton were responsible for his own health problems. Certainly, he and many others like him, would not have gone there at all if the true facts about another of their number had been fully revealed at the time, instead of being covered by a blanket of secrecy.

The files on Leading Aircraftsman Ronald Maddison have never been made public, apart from scant records from an inquest in 1953, recording a verdict of accidental death. A bright, quiet 20 year old from Consett, Co. Durham, Maddison volunteered to go to Porton quite simply because he was homesick. He was serving in Northern Ireland at the time. He and others in his unit were told they would be awarded a 72-hour leave after the experiments – and Ronald stepped forward, apparently believing he would take part in medical tests related to influenza.

However, documents viewed from this book show that soon after his arrival at Porton, Ronnie Maddison took part in an experiment conducted to discover the evaporation rate of the nerve agent 'GB' when applied to the skin. A droplet of the liquid, said to be around 200mg, was applied on a patch to his forearm. He began suffering acute symptoms – similar to those described in the 1952 MoD training film – very quickly. Porton doctors, obviously shocked by the speed with which the nerve agent affected him, rushed to his aid. Four senior members of staff made desperate efforts to save him, giving him injections of antidote. They failed. Ronnie Maddison died an agonizing, convulsing death.

The blanket of secrecy thrown around the Maddison case prevented the publication of any real detail of what exactly happened. Senior officers from the Ministry of Defence descended upon Salisbury. The Wiltshire coroner charged with conducting the inquest into the death was informed that matters of 'national security' were involved and he took the highly unusual step of ordering a hearing 'in camera'. Only Ronnie's father was allowed to attend, and was sworn to secrecy. The press and public were excluded.

The death certificate, which even the MoD could not have hidden away, stated that he died from blockage of the bronchial passage, though did not add that this was a well-known symptom of nerve gas poisoning. The death was sufficient, however, to raise concern about the experiments. A formal MoD inquiry into Maddison's death agreed with Porton Down submissions that he was unusually sensitive to the liquid nerve gas. It recommended, however, that in future no more than 5mm, a fraction of the dose given to Maddison, should be applied in skin tests.

Today, many leading experts look back with horror upon these early trials and are mystified that in the mid-1990s it is thought necessary for them to continue in some form. Dr Alistair Hay, a leading chemical pathologist at Leeds University, went forcefully on record to say: 'A dreadful state of affairs . . . I think if you're asking someone to take part in a study that involves an agent that we know is lethal and could kill them, they have to be told.'

Concerns would also be expressed in many quarters about the possible long-term effects of exposure to Porton gases. The many volunteers from that period, interviewed for this book, all told a similar story. Those who have come forward suffered illnesses in later life, ranging from severe asthma to cancer. The response of the Ministry of Defence is, by and large, to deny that the Porton tests were in any way responsible.

Much the same attitude was adopted in cases of men who claimed to have been exposed to nerve gas while working at the Nancekuke manufacturing plant. At least two were to suffer serious repercussions, with illnesses and symptoms almost identical to those claimed by the volunteers, and incidentally quite similar to the accident recorded in Nazi documents relating to their gas plant in Poland.

Engineer Tom Griffiths' employment at Nancekuke, it will be recalled, dated to the time when the plant was first being built. For a long while afterwards he had no real idea of what it was they were actually producing, other than the notion that it was some kind of experimental chemical product. He discovered the secret first hand: in his case, the exposure was during the course of his work.

He had been called to check a cubicle in one of the Nancekuke bays. He says a technician told him it wasn't necessary to wear protective clothing because the cubicle had not been in use for a week. Then, Tom noticed a drop of liquid leaking from between two flanges, and almost immediately he had an uncontrollable coughing fit. He also noticed a damp area on the floor, where the pipe had been leaking. The technician told him 'to get out quick'.

'I could hardly breathe. My eyesight was badly affected. The pupils shut down to pinpoints,' Griffiths recalled. Outside, he recovered quite quickly, or so he thought. That night, at home in his modest council house, he became violently sick and his wife, Eileen, was preparing to call the doctor. Griffiths, an intensely patriotic and forthright man, stopped her. He said she would have to call the Medical Officer at Nancekuke, though did not say why. It would be another ten years before she learned the truth of his work at the plant, and that he was bound by the Official Secrets Act not to reveal the nature of his employment to anyone – including his wife.

Tom received treatment during the next few weeks and his condition seemed to improve. It was a mere respite from what would follow. His wife noticed the deterioration more than he did. He began to suffer breathing difficulties and fainting fits. He had muscle spasms and occasional lapses of memory. His condition became so bad that he was spending weeks off sick until finally, just before his 40th birthday, he was declared unfit to work. In effect, Tom Griffiths' working life was over, but the Ministry of Defence disclaimed any responsibility for that. They rejected out of hand his claims for compensation and it was 20 years from the time of the accident before he was finally awarded a modest disability pension.

Yet for his part, Tom Griffiths loyally maintained his commitment to the secrecy oath he had sworn when he joined the Nancekuke workforce. It would be 12 years before he even told his wife of the accident at work, a fact that she had difficulty in accepting.

'I couldn't understand it,' she would say. 'He was always so open and upstanding . . . yet he kept a secret like that from me for 12 years.' But Griffiths, like others who had sworn that oath, was even reluctant to tell his doctor what had happened at work and did not do so for many years.

An almost identical situation occurred with another Nancekuke fitter, Trevor Martin. His problems began in 1961 when he was ordered to dismantle a rusting old condenser, 5ft long. It was one of the spoils of war, brought back from a Nazi chemical plant in 1945. The condenser carried a label declaring it clean and so he wore no mask when he began the task of taking it apart, unbolting the flanges, which had asbestos seals. That evening, at home and after his meal, he went outside work on his car. It was then that he began to get his first attacks of dizziness and a tightening across his chest. His speech was also affected.

Within a week, he had suffered paralysis down the right side of his face and his body was subject to spasms, and a continual twitch in his right leg. A year later, Trevor Martin's working life was also at an end. At the age of 37, he began a long round of visits to doctors and hospitals for a succession of neuro-related illnesses, breathlessness and poor vision. He qualified for a modest pension but a 20-year campaign to achieve recognition that he had suffered nerve gas poisoning fell upon deaf ears at the MoD. As ever, the co-operation between the British and Americans in their efforts to maintain the utmost secrecy over their post-war dash to achieve world supremacy in chemical warfare remained an unassailable barrier to anyone and everyone who attempted to penetrate their clandestine domain and officialdom.

9

IT WOULDN'T HURT A MOUSE

OFFICIALLY, BRITAIN WAS no longer supporting a programme of offensive chemical weaponry. At the beginning of the 1960s all research, still extensive in its scope, was to be conducted in the name of defence and the protection of the civilian population and military personnel. It was, according to Porton's own directive – repeated by successive Defence Ministry spokesmen and politicians – 'in the business of saving lives'. The new direction barely had any effect on the work of Porton Down. The place continued just as before, inventing, testing, experimenting to provide a defence against every possible permutation of CB weaponry that any potential enemy might possess – and a good few others, besides.

Steps towards this worthy undertaking of 'saving lives' and withdrawing Britain from the chemical and biological arms race were begun in 1956. A year later, the Conservative Government of Harold Macmillan announced its decision to 'abandon all research on chemical and biological weapons for an offensive capacity'. This appeared to be a distinct change of government policy and although the Cabinet documents relating to all decisions concerning it are still unavailable for public inspection, it is now clear that it was never quite the magnanimous gesture towards saving mankind as it first appeared. The American government had made no such concession and the Porton team continued to maintain close links with its US counterparts, who were supervising the manufacture of very substantial stocks of everything.

While the British were said to be abandoning their offensive capability, the US was taking up a brand new and hugely more potent form of nerve gas: one more top-secret weapon, known as the 'V-agent', invented in Britain, pioneered by Porton and eventually manufactured in very substantial quantities in the United States. The V-agent, first discovered in the early 1950s, was so strong that one minute droplet absorbed through the skin could kill a man in minutes. First details of it were placed before the Offensive Evaluation Committee after proving trials at Porton. These confirmed that the V-agent showed 'considerable promise in the attack of personnel in the open, or in open trenches and for ground contamination'.

Further, those who might face it would require total head-to-toe protection, not just gas-masks. That requirement alone set Porton once again off into the realms of new discoveries and prototypes for combat suits that would provide the ultimate in protective battledress – research, it must be said, that would lead to the creation of the ultra-protective gear that was supplied to troops as they faced a possible chemical onslaught from Saddam Hussein's armies in the Gulf War.

Even as Britain publicly withdrew from its offensive position, Porton was already working on the next generation of the deadly V-agent. At the dawn of the 1960s, the research station came up with a far more potent version, coded as 'VX', which had the advantage of 'being absorbed more quickly through the skin'. Porton scientists took samples to their American colleagues at Edgewood where its significance was immediately recognized. Mass production was ordered by the top brass in the US military. Thousands of tons would soon be added to the vast stockpiles of CW agents.

Porton was, according to documents relating to the Offensive Evaluation Committee, also working on 'other variants' as well as the VX agent, and there was no let-up in research into the destructive qualities of the gas, and consequently the protection against these agents in the form of clothing and antidotes. The need for human guinea-pigs remained a priority, as it would down the remainder of this century, and among the new recruits for experiments was a then 24-year-old corporal in the Royal Engineers, Michael Roche.

Porton had taken steps to improve its relationship with volunteers and, in 1960, produced a recruitment film to persuade servicemen to come forward – once again propagating what amounted to the same 'holiday camp' theme that was so long before suggested by Dr Paul

Fildes when he sought to enlist girls from the soap factories for his anthrax project. The payment had also been increased from 1s per experiment to 2s 6d.

Roche was quite impressed, although not by the money, which was not a consideration for him. 'I volunteered out of – dare I say it? – patriotism. I remembered as a boy seeing grandfather slowly dying from the effects of gas in his war, and my father contracted pulmonary tuberculosis from exposure to asbestos. I did it because I wanted to help; it was as simple as that. And at the time, I was as strong as an ox. I could carry two bags of cement around on my shoulders. Now, I couldn't even lift two bags of sugar,' he recalled in 1996.

Roche volunteered twice. His first experience in 1962 threw up no particular problems for him, and he went again the following year:

> I didn't find the place particularly intimidating. Our quarters were very pleasant compared to army barracks. There was a club to relax in, with billiards and table tennis, and we were allowed to make trips into Salisbury to experience the nightlife. On arrival and leaving, all volunteers were given a cursory medical examination. I took part in about six tests on each visit. The first test was to establish if the gas protection suits in use at the time offered sufficient protection against chemical agents in liquid or droplet form. Various suits, having been worn for several days and subjected to wear and tear, were used. The most badly affected areas of the gear were those covering the elbows and the knees. These suspect sections were cut into one-inch squares and taped to the forearms of the volunteers. Each had three squares. We were then strapped in chairs with our forearms facing upwards and a small amount of a chemical agent was applied to each of the squares, which were left in place for six to eight hours, in a small, unventilated room exposed to mustard fumes.
>
> On removal, the skin was examined. If penetration had occurred, the amount of blistering or irritated skin was recorded.
>
> On the second occasion, I was exposed to nerve gas by inhalation. I was assured that the amount used would be minute and would not harm a mouse. We entered an airtight glass-partitioned cubicle, containing a face-mask similar to an oxygen mask. The mask was placed in position, the fitting being carefully checked by a technician, and the chamber was then sealed. A loudspeaker informed us that the dosage was about to be administered and to inhale normally. The immediate reaction was a tightening of the muscles and the lungs. For some volunteers, this

> lasted several seconds; others experienced it for several minutes. These symptoms quickly wore off and for the next 24 hours blood samples were taken hourly. From conversations and correspondence with others who attended Porton Down, many recall similar experiences and procedures, and, like so many others, I began to suffer ill health in later life.
>
> I was in my 40s when I developed extremely high blood pressure and breathing problems. My doctor, one day, casually inquired if I had ever been exposed to dangerous chemicals. I told him of my experiences at Porton Down and he remarked that it would be extremely useful to discover exactly what I had been exposed to, so that he could work out the best form of treatment.

It was at this point that Roche and his doctor ran up against the proverbial brick wall. Countless letters written to the MoD and Porton Down itself failed to produce any meaningful response. He says it took eight years just to get the details his doctor wanted. When his file was eventually retrieved, it carried the official stamp of secrecy, with the added instruction: 'Not to be shown to the patient'.

In effect, the instructions for confidentiality barred him from seeking assistance or advice from anyone other than the doctor to whom the file had been sent. For him, it was the beginning of a ten-year battle to achieve recognition of his increasingly debilitating health problems. He would come to discover there were many others in the same situation as himself, with a list of symptoms and health problems that was, he said, 'quite horrendous': severe headaches, skin and eye cancers, brain tumours, partial or full paralysis either temporary or permanent, severe respiratory difficulties, chronic bronchitis, asthma, nervous disorders, blistering; complaints involving ears, eyes and nose were especially common.

Another common thread among all of them was the persistent stone-walling of the Ministry of Defence. The high-handed tone of MoD correspondence was particularly galling to these men, just as it would be years later to Gulf War veterans. They were, without exception, made to feel guilty, as if they were malingerers or opportunists, and that they were the guilty ones. In many cases, volunteers were never allowed to see their medical records, and some were even told they had been lost or destroyed. Single-handedly, Roche began to put together his data, correlating all the information he could obtain. He planned to make it available to doctors or specialists as he campaigned to achieve an admission that exposure to chemicals at Porton Down may have seriously damaged the health of many of those involved.

He began lobbying for a long-term MoD study on the effects of chemical exposure on Porton volunteers. But Roche, as we will see in later chapters, was in for a long haul. The MoD and successive British governments refused even to acknowledge that a problem existed. This virtual blanket rejection of the volunteers' claims was in spite of the knowledge of numerous recorded cases of accidents and ill-health, even death.

The experiments, of course, were not merely limited to gas and gear tests. Porton conducted a wide range of trials on everything from poison techniques for the modern spy to experiments with LSD. Some of the files on its experiments with LSD were released into the Public Record Office in 1996 – 30 years after they had taken place. Although Porton's mandate was for 'defensive purposes only', the documents open with the proposals that the LSD tests were to discover the suitability of the drug to 'incapacitate a potential enemy'. What is equally interesting is that the Porton experiments on the manipulation of personnel with drugs ran alongside extensive research in America, often at Fort Detrick, on behalf of the CIA's so-called mind-control programme, which began under the code-name 'MKUltra' in 1951.

When details of the Porton LSD experiments were released in 1996 – or, at least, those that the MoD was prepared for the public to know about – they were treated rather light-heartedly in some sections of the media. It seemed, on the face of it, a huge joke that at the height of the Swinging Sixties, whole units of the British Army should be fed LSD tabs to go on hallucinatory trips – on the orders of Her Majesty's Government. The reality was rather different.

What Porton scientists, and the MoD, also knew very well at the time was that the substance had been extensively used in experiments under the guidance of their opposite numbers at Fort Detrick for the CIA – with fatal results. Once again, the LSD experiments were inspired by the fear that the Soviets were also testing the drug. It was likely, the CIA surmised, that they too had obtained data on similar studies found in captured German documents. The joint intelligence forces of Britain and the US had studied reports of mind-control experiments carried out on inmates of Dachau Concentration Camp. Nazi doctors had used mescaline as an interrogation agent. After administering the hallucinogen to 30 prisoners, the Nazis concluded that it was 'impossible to impose one's will on another person as in hypnosis even when the strongest dose of mescaline had been given'. But the drug still afforded certain advantages to SS interrogators, who were consistently able to draw 'even the most intimate secrets from the [subject] when questions were cleverly put'.

The mescaline experiments at Dachau were described in documents gathered up by the US Naval Intelligence Technical Mission after the war and were closely studied by the CIA when it launched its own intensive research on interrogation techniques that involved inducing a subject into a state of trance.

The CIA memorandum was precise in its intentions: 'Newer or more subtle techniques may be considered . . . a) psychosurgery, a surgical separation of the frontal lobes of the brain, b) shock method: electrical; drug (metrazol, cannabis, indica, insulin, cocaine); psycho-analysis, narcoanalysis or a combination of the foregoing'. It launched MKUltra, a multi-faceted project that was defined as 'The CIA's Program of Research into Behavioral Modifications', co-ordinated by Dr Sidney Gottleib, then deputy head of the CIA Technical Services Staff. The project moved into a wide range of sub-projects involving a variety of drugs, poisons and biological agents for which Gottleib enlisted the aid of Porton's good friends, the Army Chemical Corps, Special Operations Division at Fort Detrick.

Described in CIA documents as 'the twilight zone', LSD induced an ideal state for interrogation according to scientists. As in Britain, human guinea-pigs were used. Dr Harris Isbell, head of a drug treatment unit in Lexington, Kentucky, agreed to test various substances supplied by the CIA on addict patients – though he was careful to ensure they were informed of the risks and signed consent forms. The drug most widely used, on the instructions of the CIA, was LSD. Dr Isbell kept seven men tripping for 77 days while the CIA and Fort Detrick scientists maintained a check on this long-term high, regardless of the fact that they knew nothing about any residual effects the drug might have. They were, as the CIA documents clearly admit, venturing into the unknown.

In another series of tests, 12 men of 'limited intelligence' were used. They were given doses of between 100 and 150 micrograms, less than was used in later experiments at Porton.

The special interrogation research was strongly endorsed by Agency officials. A CIA document announced: 'We're now convinced that we can maintain a subject in a controlled state for a much longer period of time than we heretofore had believed possible. Furthermore, we feel that by use of certain chemicals or combinations, we can, in a very high percentage of cases, produce relevant information.'

The CIA brought the LSD trials together under the codename 'BLUEBIRD'. It was such a sensitive operation that details were withheld from the usual channels and approval came directly from Director Roscoe Hillenkoetter who authorized the use of undisclosed funds to finance it. The CIA's Office of Scientific Intelligence prepared a long thesis on the 'Potential New Agent for Unconventional Warfare'. It said LSD was useful 'for eliciting true and accurate statements from subjects under its influence during interrogation'. Even more promising was the fact that LSD might help in reviving memories of past experiences.

The CIA hierarchy concluded that at last they had found a drug that was capable of achieving all that they wanted from a subject, of unearthing secrets from the mind *and* causing amnesia during the effective period. Words like 'incredible' and 'astounding' were being bandied about. As one of their number put it, 'We truly believed we had found a drug that was going to unlock the universe.' The uses were seen as being universal. Apart from its value in interrogation, there were obvious advantages in the reverse situation. If CIA agents fell into enemy hands, they could simply swallow a minute acid tab and go off on a bizarre trip, leaving their interrogators mystified.

The CIA directorate wanted to know urgently if the Soviets had found the magical qualities of LSD. Almost certainly, came the reply. Its Officer of Scientific Intelligence discovered that the fungus from which LSD was derived flourished in the Soviet Union, yet there was no trade in it in the Eastern Bloc. This could only mean one thing: the Soviets, and probably Red China too, must be stockpiling LSD. The officer added in formal, scary language: 'It must be assumed that the scientists of the USSR are thoroughly cognizant of the strategic importance of this powerful new drug and are capable of producing it at any time.'

The CIA, by then under the direction of Allen Dulles, poured millions of dollars into research and into building its own LSD mountain – even after things started to go wrong. A temporary setback occurred when Dr Gottleib took two of his CIA aides and seven scientists from Fort Detrick working on the MKUltra and other US Army Chemical Corps projects to a log cabin in the Appalachians for an informal review of their work. During the evening, after their meal, Gottleib produced some LSD and put a small dose into a bottle of Cointreau to experiment on themselves. At least, that was the official story. A CIA inquiry into the incident after one of them had committed suicide recorded that there had existed, 'a conflict with respect to the administering of the LSD since a memorandum written by the then Inspector General of the Agency indicates that the individuals present were not told that the drug was LSD until 20 minutes after ingestion . . . when the group became boisterous and "happy". The civilian employed by the Army who later committed suicide complained of wakefulness that evening.'

The civilian was Frank Olson, a senior scientist working at Fort Detrick on Army and CIA biological projects. In the weeks following the experiment, he appeared depressed and his family complained of a personality change. Gottleib had kept them all under surveillance and realized there was something wrong with Olson. He arranged for him to travel to New York in the company of a CIA operative for psychiatric examination by an agency doctor. The psychiatrist was so concerned that he saw him six times in the course of a week. At that point he arranged for him to be admitted to a psychiatric ward at Rockville, Maryland.

Olson and the CIA man were staying at the Statler Hotel in New York, sharing a room on the tenth floor. At 3.20am, during the night before they were due to leave, Olson hurled himself at the closed window of his hotel room with such force that he crashed through the glass and fell to his death on the pavement below. The CIA man who was with him awoke only in time to see Olson's departure. Allen Dulles was immediately informed and, anticipating trouble, ordered an inquiry by his inspector general, Lyman Kirkpatrick. His report was highly critical, though for the wrong reasons:

'It is apparent that there is a strong possibility that the use of LSD was a trigger mechanism precipitating Olson's suicide. Uncontrolled experiments such as these could seriously affect the record and reputation of the agency . . . the Deputy Chief TSS [Gottleib] should be reprimanded for his poor judgement . . . the Chief TSS should be admonished to exercise tighter supervision and control of the use of this drug.'

The inspector general's report was never published, and Allen Dulles merely sent Gottleib a letter of reprimand. Olson was the first known case of LSD causing death, although there were many rumours that CIA double agents who had been given massive doses of it, and other substances to discover the extent of their treachery, had died during experiments.

Gottleib himself turned up in Africa seven years later, on a CIA mission to poison the Communist-inclined Congolese leader, Patrice

Lumumba, with a bacterium that would cause a fatal disease, again courtesy of Fort Detrick. Rebels beat him to it. The CIA officer was also involved in plots to assassinate Fidel Castro by having his food poisoned and to murder an Iraqi colonel with a germ-impregnated handkerchief.

By then, the CIA's enthusiasm for LSD had waned. They discovered that individuals tested had a distorted view of time, place, and body image, and suffered bizarre hallucinations. Self-administration would be even more precarious, it was discovered, because subjects simply could not remember exactly what they had said or done while high on LSD, at least not with accuracy. While the memory was not totally gone, it was distorted.

The CIA was steadily researching into other drugs and poisons in support of their various assassination plots to kill troublesome foreign leaders, which was itself the subject of a Senate Inquiry chaired by Senator Frank Church in 1975. He concluded that although the agency never actually killed any government head, it wasn't for the want of trying. 'It represented failure rather than a change of mind,' Church said.

So much effort had gone into the LSD project that the CIA would not give up. Their experiments extended over a decade. The military was still interested in LSD as an incapacitating agent and counter-intelligence wanted the experiments pursued as a defensive measure against possible LSD use by terrorists or saboteurs. A CIA officer who was involved in the LSD experiments testified at a secret government investigation into the MKUltra Project: 'It is awfully hard . . . to reproduce how frightening all of this was to us at the time, particularly after the drug scene became widespread. But we were literally terrified, because this was the one material of a kind that we had never been able to locate that really had potentially fantastic possibilities if used wrongly.'

Olson's death occurred in 1954. There is no doubt Porton knew about it, and all the other rumours swirling around the Maryland CB.W community. Even so, like the CIA and the US Chemical Corps, it continued its own experiments with LSD, using mass trials, which, incidentally, the CIA could no longer do, because of their mishaps.

Porton's own experiments using human guinea-pigs overlapped those of the CIA. The Porton volunteers were typically given 200 micrograms, whereas normal dosage is 50 to 100 micrograms.

The Porton files show that experiments did indeed prove that LSD could incapacitate normally fit and healthy men, in fact a whole detachment of highly disciplined soldiers. The tests involved each group of soldiers being put through routine drills and attack exercises after they had been administered LSD tablets. The 11 files described three operations, codenamed 'Moneybags', 'Recount' and 'Small Change'. None of the volunteers was told what drugs were being given, although they all received medical and psychiatric screening before the tests began. The men were placed in mocked-up surroundings and administered the LSD and other hallucinatory drugs.

Operation Recount was staged in September 1966 – 12 years after the death of Olson. Sixteen men from the 37th Heavy Air Defence Regiment were engaged for the experiment that involved an hallucinatory drug called 'T3456'. Half the men were given the drug, half were not. The trial was intended to assess the interaction between the two groups. The drugged soldiers became totally disorganized, and consumed with frequent bouts of uncontrollable laughter. The unit's commanding officer complained that one of his drugged men laughed even more wildly whenever he approached. The report stated: 'The officer found difficulty in controlling an entirely unjustified hilarity in spite of the presence of his commanding officer.'

The battery sergeant-major was so severely relaxed that after the exercise he removed most of his clothes and sat on his bed 'wearing only his underclothes and a seraphic smile'. Two-and-a-half hours later he complained of feeling tense and was sent to see a psychiatrist. The tests actually proved very little – except what Porton already knew from earlier trials: that the drug was a 'powerful incapacitator'.

Some of the tests, experimenting with LSD administered by aerosol sprays, were patently unsuccessful because of the low absorption rate. When only small doses of LSD were given, the soldiers were able to maintain reasonable discipline, although exposure over several days to low dosages gradually reduced their capabilities. With a dose of 200 micrograms, on the other hand, the soldiers became 'chaotic'. During one test, a drugged troop commander who was laughing and retching accused a radio operator of insubordination because he was talking gibberish and whistling down the handset – not realizing that the soldier's behaviour was due to the drugs. The commander cried out: 'This is getting too much. Why doesn't somebody who's sober take charge?'

In another sequence of tests, in November 1965, 13 Royal Marine commandos who, again, were given doses of 200 micrograms of LSD, were noticeably affected by it within three or four minutes. They became progressively more disorientated and refused to respond to orders.

Major J.L. Rickford, who monitored the exercise, reported that the whole unit would have been wiped out by modest enemy action within an hour. The men, he said, were 'out of touch' and unable to use equipment. They walked around aimlessly during exercises and, when given orders, could not remember what they were minutes later. The reports conclude that most men returned to normal within 48 hours. Many admitted to periods of depression but there had been 'no lasting damage' to any of the volunteers.

That, according to Porton, remains the case, although former Army corporal Bob Clarke, who took part in the LSD tests, will disagree. 'About two years after the tests,' he said, 'I began getting bad dreams and, during the day, these sort of flashbacks in my mind. I also suffered a lot with depression, which is really not me at all. I have had a good many problems in that regard and when I told my specialist about them, he more or less said right away that it was the cause of my troubles. We tried to get a more complete history of the dosages, but were told that individual records were no longer maintained for this experiment. But my doctor said that if, as he understood it, I had received particularly high doses of any hallucinatory drug, it had been known to cause long-term psychological effects.'

The irony was that these Porton tests, in the end, proved fairly worthless although they were no doubt part of a more diverse programme of research, which remains classified. It is known that both MI5 and MI6 explored the use of drugs and unidentifiable poisons for counter-intelligence missions from sabotage to assassination. The CIA, by the end of the 1970s, had stockpiled its own armoury of biological mini-weapons invented with the aid of Fort Detrick scientists under another code-named project, MKNaomi. The task of this project was to 'evaluate and obtain severely incapacitating and lethal materials for use by the TSD' – the Technical Services Division, which had been charged with assassinations and other deeply covert operations.

The interest in LSD continued throughout the decade, to the extent that it merited a particular mention in an important 1970 World Health Organization report by a panel of eminent scientists, warning of the potency of LSD and its particular dangers in the wrong hands. By then a whole generation of flower-power children could have told them that for nothing.

10

TESTING BUGS ON THE MASSES

THE LSD EXPERIENCE was just one of many excursions into the unknown being conducted in the name of the defence of mankind, but perhaps the most remarkable of all was a series of tests, also spanning more than a decade, conducted simultaneously on mass populations in Britain and American. Some were decidedly more risky to the health and wellbeing of tens of thousands of people unwittingly exposed to CB agents than anyone cared to admit at the time. They began as the Cold War slithered into deep-freeze. Intelligence models had been produced on both sides of the Atlantic on the possibility of a germ warfare attack on cities, that is by the Soviets, and by smaller clandestine saboteur or terrorist groups. Both scenarios had prompted much closed-door discussion among Western governments. NATO analysts conducted a number of studies, the Chiefs of Staff of Britain and the US kept the possibility of germ warfare under constant review and it was the subject of investigation by the World Health Organization.

One of the most likely targets of saboteurs was considered to be the underground rail systems of major cities, in which bacteria could be dispersed quite simply in the tunnels from the windows of a train and cause a huge death toll. This theory had been around for a long time. The Nazis had conducted trials with relatively harmless bacteria in the Paris Metro in 1943 and there had also been rumours that German agents planned to scatter glass tubes of cholera and anthrax in the underground system before they pulled out of the French capital and scampered back to Berlin.

A number of plans to test these theories in the London Underground were submitted to Britain's Biological Research Advisory Board by a joint committee of MI5 and military intelligence but the idea of conducting experiments on the public at large, without its knowledge, was obviously such a sensitive issue that five years of protracted discussion took place before it was approved. The board itself came out strongly against spreading live organisms in such confined public areas. One leading scientist on the panel went so far as to insist that the sabotage theory was 'a trivial hazard adequately predictable from existing knowledge'. Similar disquiet was heard in Washington when trials on the New York Subway were being discussed by the US Army in conjunction with the Chemical Corps and Fort Detrick staff.

London Transport was consulted on this 'most secret' matter and was given assurances that no harm would come to its passengers. The LT executive seemed more concerned about 'a suitable cover story to allay possible public suspicion'.

In fact, that was one of the main issues when the plan was finally presented to the British Cabinet for approval. The Secretary of State for War, John Profumo, spoke against it, although, according to the minutes of the Biological Research Advisory Board, he was more concerned about public reaction to the tests than any possible danger to health. This, ministers were assured, did not represent a great threat. Finally, the Cabinet gave the go-ahead. Porton Down biological experts were already standing by with supplies of bacillus *globigii*, a bacterium that they said would not cause disease, food spoilage or 'possess any other undesirable qualities'.

Preliminary tests were carried out in London Post Office cable tunnels. Then, during a busy lunchtime on 26 July 1963, the test controller boarded a London tube train on the Northern Line at Colliers Wood, carrying with him a small face powder tin, filled with the bacteria. At a point midway between Colliers Wood and Tooting Broadway, he opened the train window and dropped the tin on the track. The object was to discover how far the bugs could travel, so that estimates could be made of the number of people who might be affected by even this small container of bacteria, concealed virtually in one hand. During the next two weeks, Porton technicians examined air samples taken from the tunnels, the stations and from inside the actual trains. The results astounded even the battle-hardened BW experts of Porton. The bugs had travelled as far as ten miles north, with positive readings at Camden Town. The Porton report also said that trains became 'heavily contaminated internally'.

Based upon this information, a new set of tests was ordered using bacteria that more closely resembled pathogens, or disease-carrying bugs. The results of those are unknown. All documents relating to them remained classified when the 30-year rule expired, and so it is unlikely that they will be released for many years, if ever.

The same applies in America. There, the tests were conducted by the US Army, using a bacillus dispersed through the New York City Subway. They lasted for five days and, like those in London, were carried out at peak travel times. Scientists at Fort Detrick had filled ordinary light bulbs with bacteria, which were released into the subway system when the bulbs smashed as they were dropped from the train – exactly as the Nazis had planned to do when they left Paris. The dissemination rate was then measured in a series of air-sampling tests. The test results remain classified, although one source did comment that it was 'not considered necessary' to monitor any reactions among the travelling public to the bugs. 'We were assured there would be none,' he said, 'but we never really followed up on that.' As later tests would show, however, some members of the public did complain of health problems.

The experiments took place in an atmosphere of concern about biological warfare that verged on paranoia. Both the British and the Americans – matched as ever by the Soviets – earmarked a huge financial commitment to BW research. Although Britain dropped out of its 'offensive' work in the early 1960s, it was involved in a major testing programme through Porton and, of course, remained in partnership with America when the first production line of biological weapons was begun at a $100 million factory, built in a converted wartime arsenal of ten storeys, with three below ground, at Pine Bluff, Arkansas.

There were many on both sides of the Atlantic who supported the theory of Sir Owen Wansbrough Jones, a member of both the British Biological Research Advisory Board and the Chemical Defence Advisory Board, who maintained that within a decade biological weapons would be '100 times more powerful than now'.

The scientific community seemed intent on ensuring that that prediction was reached. A BW research programme started of such enormity and so potentially dangerous that human volunteers could not be allowed anywhere near it. Field trials had to be conducted well away from any population – even the already heavily polluted Gruinard Island, scene of the wartime anthrax trials, was now considered to be unsuitable for safety reasons, notably because of 'wind direction and its close proximity to the mainland'.

A search was made for another suitable island around the British coast, but finally it was decided to conduct the trials at sea, enlisting the aid of the Royal Navy in an operation generally code-named 'Pandora', although each specific 'field' trial was given its own title. They were to be conducted from floating laboratories, and for this two 4,000-ton tank landing ships – HMS *Ben Lomond* and HMS *Narvik* – were converted to house the Porton staff and fitted out with all necessary equipment required for a series of experiments over the next seven years. Apart from the crew, the scientists and technicians, the ships took on board a large stock of animals.

At the time, it was widely believed that the trials were a mere simulation to assess Britain's vulnerability to biological attack. Vague and unspecific press releases put out by Whitehall to ward off media inquiries gave no clue as to their real purpose, significance or scope.

Precise details are still classified, but information now to hand shows that after initial 'practicality' tests, real germs were used, including anthrax, brucellosis and tularaemia (a severe infectious disease). According to Porton's own reports, the trials were primarily aimed at perfecting methods of disseminating bacteria from bursting munitions and spraying equipment. They also had to establish whether the bacteria might be diminished by natural conditions, such as bright sunlight 'destroying infectivity'.

To achieve their assessments, the scientists devised a plan whereby bacteria would be released up-wind of an arc of dinghies and rafts. The dinghies would carry air-sampling devices to record the strength of infectivity. The animals, including goats, rabbits, rats and mice tethered or in cages on the rafts, were there to test 'inhalation and mortality factors'.

On board ship, the scientists and sailors would watch through binoculars as the bacteria was sprayed or exploded over the floating test equipment and livestock. Eventually the dinghies and rafts would be hauled in for data to be retrieved from the air samplers and for the animals to be dissected. Those not already dead were sacrificed and their carcasses were burned at sea.

These techniques were employed more or less throughout the seven-year period of the trials, which went under five separate codenames:

Operation Harness was conducted in waters off the Bahamas to 'determine the practicality of sea trials' using three bacterial agents, apart from anthrax.
Operation Cauldron was held off Stornaway in the Isles of Lewis with the 'aim of consolidating data from Operation Harness and to assess the use of a further bacterium'.
Operation Hesperus, also in Scottish waters, was to test, compare and report on the efficiency of 'several munitions, sprays and aerosols'.
Operation Ozone, a name that in itself held sinister implications, took the scientists back to a site 20 miles from Nassau, Bahamas, 'to acquire more data on spraying agents and, for the first time, on a virus'.
Operation Negation, also off the coast of the Bahamas in 1955, was staged 'to compare the loss of viability of three bacterial agents sprayed by aerosol – and a second virus'.

When the trials were completed, the two tank ships could not be used for any other purpose and were taken to a naval dockyard and broken up. The magnitude of these trials was such that the Porton hierarchy recorded it was 'very proud' that it had increased the establishment's 'international status not only in the biological warfare community, but as a centre of excellence in several areas of microbiology and allied disciplines'.

After almost a decade of intensive experiments in Porton labs and at sea, its scientists had determined 'the infectious levels of 15 species of micro-organisms' and made great advances in the discovery of 'the mechanisms of inhalation infection' and methods of airborne attack using germ-filled munitions and spraying devices. The sea trials, combined with many other simulated and live experiments with bacteria, demonstrated that while the pursuit of chemical technology had, on Porton's own admission, become a 'desperate preoccupation', the biological programme might be termed a dangerous obsession.

The same fear already gripped both the imagination and ambitions of military leaders in the US as they mapped out their own BW programme, which dwarfed the British trials. The CIA and military intelligence had already produced dozens of 'models' of possible attacks – such the New York city Subway experiment – by the Soviet Union against major US cities or by small terrorist groups, poisoning water, crops and animals. The Pentagon authorized a series of experiments that were to continue over the next 15 years.

One was to test the theory that a Soviet submarine could reach New York Harbor undetected and released a bacterial cloud, and then vanish before anyone knew it had happened. It proved to be a very viable idea. In another trial, two US Navy ships conducted six mock attacks on San Francisco, using what was said to be a harmless bacterium called *Serratia marcescens*, developed at Porton during the war.

Though secret at the time, reports filtered out years later that Fort Detrick scientists who monitored the mock attacks discovered that 117 square miles of the city had been contaminated by the bacteria, and it was estimated that at least 800,000 people had inhaled it. In 1977, the Archives of Internal Medicine noted the unusually high incidence of serratia pneumonia around the time of the attacks, from which one victim died. His relatives, on learning of this fact, unsuccessfully attempted to sue the US government. But the San Francisco experiment was only one of dozens carried out in the US, as the CIA and the Pentagon lobbied repeatedly for a viable capacity for both defence and attack, and of course for possible counter-measures in Vietnam.

There was, for example, the 'Mosquito Plan' – a scheme to breed a new strain of mosquitoes infected with yellow fever. The insects would then be installed in bursting air bombs for delivery into enemy lines. There, the mosquitoes would attack the opposing forces and they would all very quickly become infected; literally dropping like flies. The plan, worked out to the nth detail by Fort Detrick scientists, actually won approval from the military hierarchy, for a series of tests was carried out over an Army bombing range in Florida. Results of the tests, now hidden away in the archives of the US Army Chemical Centre in Maryland, record that within a day of the bombing mission, swarms of mosquitoes had spread up to two miles from the bombing run. 'Many people' were bitten and some fell ill. After each test, US Army personnel posing as public health officials photographed and tested the victims. The operation was judged so successful that the military placed an order with Fort Detrick: it should gear up to produce 100 million mosquitoes a month. The plant was built and there were later rumours – always denied – that the mosquitoes were used in US campaigns in the Far East, and in other irritating problem areas closer to home.

An outbreak of dengue haemorrhagic fever that afflicted 300,000 Cubans was linked to those experiments in an investigation by the magazine *Covert Action Information Bulletin,* which tracked the workings of intelligence agencies around the world. The magazine suggested that this outbreak was the result of a release of mosquitoes by

Above: A mother and baby lie where they fell during the gas attack on a Kurdish village by Saddam Hussein's air force in 1988. Up to 7000 died in agony; yet the international community took no action and continued to supply Saddam with arms.

Left: The US Army released a cloud of nerve gas during tests over the Utah desert; the lethal poison drifted on the wind towards the grasslands: 6000 sheep were killed.

Top: Eerie vision of the future if advanced Russian technology on genetically engineered anthrax weapons escapes into terrorist hands. These are Russian soldiers on a biological-warfare exercise.

Above: Proof of the devastating effects of anthrax lay on the remote Scottish island of Gruinard, bombed during Porton trials in 1942 to perfect an anthrax-charged weapon of war. It remained poisoned and unapproachable until Porton scientists finally succeeded in its decon tamination in 1987.

Overleaf: Jayce Hanson, son of a US army sergeant, and one of the many children of Gulf War veterans born with severe handicaps.

Left: The skull and cross-bones says it all – British troops drive into the smoke, fumes and chemical pollutants that filled the air in Kuwait.

Below: Coalition troops are unprotected from the poisoned atmosphere.

The scenes of battle are 75 years apart, but the enemy is the same – mustard gas

Above: Coalition troops in the Gulf War are masked up, ready for a possible chemical onslaught.

Below: An American solider rips off his flimsy mask and collapses choking from the German gas fumes in World War I.

Images of two conflicts

Above: World War I troops blinded by the 'Hun Stuff' – mustard gas – are led away from the medical tents.

Right: A German school had its picture taken for posterity, preparing for the Allied bombers to come at the beginning of World War II.

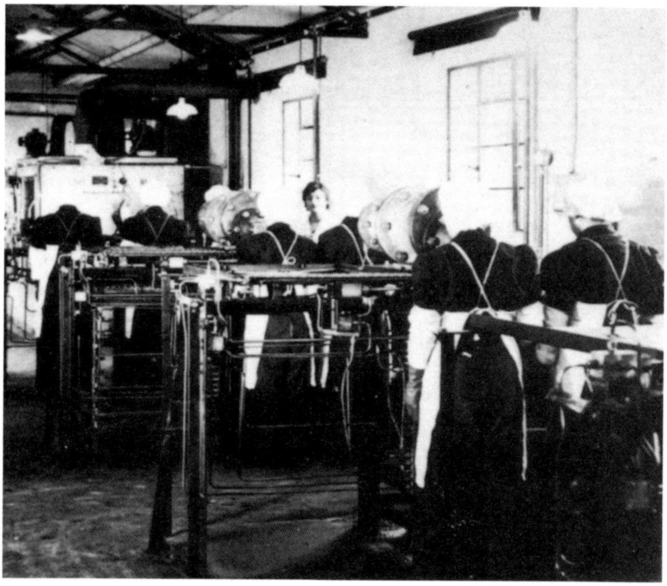

Above: The secret army of soap-factory girls was co-opted to Porton Down Chemical Defence Establishment in 1942 to pack five million cattle cakes into boxes. The cakes contained anthrax, which was to be dropped over German pastures.

Below: The RAF makes a dummy run over England

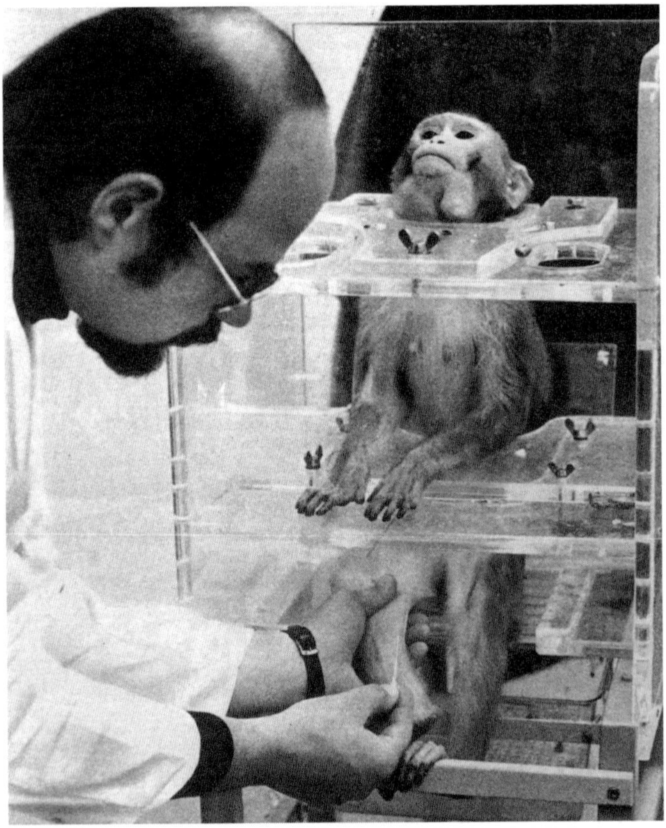

Emotive pictures of animal experiments have, over the years, drawn great protests and anguish over the dilemma posed by the needs of science. These scenes were pictured in a German laboratory. Porton carried out many experiments with monkeys; in one, 20 rhesus monkeys had their heads clamped, and they were then shot with metal balls to observe the damage.

Cuban counter-revolutionaries, masterminded by the CIA. During the last 30 years, Cuba has been subjected to a large number of human and crop diseases that are difficult to attribute to purely natural causes.

Coincidentally, an outbreak of dengue fever also hit Nicaragua in the 1980s. Observers said it came shortly after an increase in US aerial reconnaissance missions. Nearly half of the capital city's population was stricken with the disease, and several deaths have been attributed to the outbreak. The US vehemently denies any suggestion that it was involved.

By the turn of the 1970s, the Americans had produced no less than 35 'viable' and lethal combinations of BW agents and, like Porton, had advanced their work to produce antibiotic resistant types of pathogens capable of inducing diseases for which treatment was pretty well beyond hope. They were the first results of what would become a prime area of research in BW labs – genetically engineered strains of disease that would be completely untreatable by any known medicine, antibiotic or antidote.

Much of the work in this area centred around anthrax (fatal within 24 hours if it attacks the lungs), tularaemia, cholera and bubonic plague. Other less virulent but debilitating diseases investigated included Q-fever, brucellosis and even common influenza.

One of the most controversial tests among the US programme came to light when Dr D.M. McArthur, then Deputy Director of Research and Technology for the Department of Defense, appeared before the House Sub-Committee on Appropriations in 1969. He was seeking funding and approval for a research project 'to produce a synthetic biological agent, one that does not naturally exist and for which humans have no natural immunity'.

Dr McArthur won a $10 million grant for the study, lasting between five and ten years, at Fort Detrick. Congressional Records show that the most important characteristic of the research would be to attempt to invent a new infective micro-organism 'that might be refractory [resistant] to the immunological and therapeutic processes upon which we depend to maintain our relative freedom from infectious disease'.

Ten years after the study began, the first signs of the AIDS epidemic began to appear and the fact that the Pentagon had requested permission to research a synthetic AIDS-like virus in 1969 would become the subject of much speculation. This was advanced further when the respected East German scientist Professor Jakob Segal published a thesis suggesting that AIDS may have originated in a US biological warfare research laboratory. The theory was widely rejected, of course.

There was one devastating event, however, for which there was no doubt whatsoever that the US military had been the perpetrator. Aerial bombing trials using a highly toxic Porton-developed nerve agent had been conducted at the Dugway Proving Grounds, the main weapons testing centre for America's CB.W programme.

It was one of the most isolated of military bases ever built in the US: a million acres spreading across the Great Salt Lake Desert in western Utah. The only way to reach it was via an 80-mile drive from Salt Lake City through mountain ranges. The region was virtually uninhabited, except by sheep – run by ranchers controlling vast acreages.

Unlike the Nevada testing grounds for US atom-bomb research, few Americans even knew of the presence of the Dugway project, although it had been in existence since the mid-1940s. On Wednesday 13 March 1968, at 5.30 in the afternoon, a US Air Force jet swooped low over the most remote area of Dugway, spraying a colourless liquid as it went. The purpose of the flight was to test the effectiveness of a new high-pressure gas dispenser, which had been developed at Edgewood. The trial was 'live' and the contents of the chemical tanks on board the aircraft was the highly persistent VX nerve gas, which was held in large stockpiles at Edgewood Arsenal.

Military scientists had selected the site carefully, about 30 miles west from the nearest sheep-grazing land and about 35 miles south of the main autoroute linking the Midwest to California, the US40. With a multi-million investment at Dugway in wind gauges, meteorological equipment and air sampling devices the scientists believed that they could accurately calculate the dispersal area of gases discharged from aircraft, even on windy days. They had done it a thousand times.

On this occasion, something went wrong. Within 24 hours of the test flight with the VX agent, ranchers found that their sheep were in distress, coughing loudly and collapsing. By nightfall, they were going into convulsions, and dying by the hundred. The ranchers dashed to the military compound at Dugway and demanded to know what was happening. The Army sent in an emergency contingent of vets to begin inoculating the sheep with antidotes but they seemed to have little effect.

By Sunday morning, 17 March, the ranchers had counted 6,000 sheep dead, many put to death by the vets because they were so severely affected by the gas. The ranchers were told they would be fully compensated for the loss and implored them not to speak publicly about what had happened. The demise of 6,000 animals, however, was not something that would stay secret for long. The following week the Salt Lake City newspaper published a story about the mysterious death of sheep, linked to a poison of some kind.

A military spokesman at Dugway was quoted in the report as denying that there had been any tests at the base that could be linked to the death of the sheep. The Army spent three weeks repudiating the charge. Finally, on 18 April, after independent tests had shown the deaths were linked to organophosphates, the Army conceded 'a possible connection'. Pressure was brought to bear in the right places and the Utah sheep deaths passed into history without great public outcry. Nor were the exact details of another accident involving VX made public that year, 1968.

It was one that would prove beyond doubt that the American Chiefs of Staffs had already ordered stocks of the gas to be dispersed to strategic positions around the world – and in this particular case it was discovered at the vast US military base on Okinawa. A training accident led to a number of US troops being exposed to the gas and 23 were admitted to hospital. The lethal possibilities of VX were never revealed then, nor would they be for many years. The public would be given only scant details of 'this unfortunate occurrence'. The damage-limitation exercise was successfully completed, in accord with the established practice that was operated on both sides of the Atlantic.

By then it was known that at least a dozen other countries apart from the Soviet Union, the US and Britain were developing biological and chemical arsenals. They included Communist China, Nationalist China, France, West Germany, Poland, Sweden, Egypt, Cuba, Israel and South Africa.

America itself had still not ratified the 1925 Geneva Convention on CB.W, and Defence chief, Cyrus Vance, was unequivocal when questioned by a Senate Committee on Disarmament: 'As long as other nations, such as the Soviet Union, maintain large programmes, we believe we must maintain our defensive and retaliatory capability.' Britain concurred in terms of defence, and from its point of view America's non-ratification of the Geneva Convention meant that its foremost ally could continue to build hefty stocks of CB.W, while Porton itself went about its normal business under the banner of maintaining only a defensive role.

It was the syndrome of the vicious circle, as was pointed out in a report compiled for the World Health Organization in 1970 by 18 scientists from 11 countries, including two Nobel Prize winners, Professor J. Lederberg from the Stanford University School of Medicine and Professor A.M. Wolff, director of the Institute of Scientific Research on Cancer, Villejuif, France.

It was a damning report that condemned outright the continued research on CB.W, even for defensive purposes, and made particular mention of the wall of secrecy that surrounded the research itself. Even so, the report said, the fact that the panel had been unable to consult classified documents relating to experiments did not stop them from making 'realistic' assessments of the likely consequences of the use of CB.W. The WHO panel estimated that in a chemical attack, if 4 tons of the Porton-developed VX nerve gas was efficiently dispersed over a city,

'casualties of even a small attack in favourable conditions would affect an area about six square kilometres and cause anywhere between 50,000 and 180,000 deaths . . . but if a suitably stabilized fine aerosol of VX were developed, and four tons of VX employed, several hundred thousand deaths could result.'

A similar attack using biological weapons, weighing much less, could be even more devastating. The team suggested that:

'if a biological agent such as anthrax were used in an attack on a city by even a single aircraft disseminating just 50 kilograms of the dried agent in aerosol form . . . it would affect an area of 20 square kilometres, resulting in hundreds of thousands of deaths.'

Those calculations, the team pointed out, were based on small and limited attacks well 'within the capability of a number of nations'. And yet, for all that, those 18 most distinguished international scientists, in not so many words, concluded that the madness appeared unstoppable: 'With the real possibility of developing new and even more dangerous weapons, it is imperative to find ways of abolishing any presumed need for this military orientated research as soon as possible.'

With a forecast that would have particular relevance years later when the Gulf War troops returned home, the WHO team also added a gloomy forecast concerning experiments on gas and bacteria. The long-term risks of cancer, in some exposures, was high and there was clear evidence from breeding with rats and mice exposed to those chemicals that offspring were born with deformities.

11

AN EYEFUL OF CS GAS

A DECADE OF madcap schemes and experiments was followed, as the 1970s dawned, with an announcement by President Richard Nixon that he was planning to abandon the United States biological weapons offensive capability. He made bold statements decrying the 'massive, unpredictable and potentially uncontrollable consequences' of BW and there was plenty of evidence to back up that statement in the secret files of research establishments the world over. He planned, at last, to submit the Geneva Protocol for ratification by the US Senate, almost half a century after it was first adopted by most other leading nations, albeit without great regard.

All was not as rosy as first appeared. Waiting in the wings was another huge report resulting from a monumental study of CB.W launched by the Stockholm International Peace Research Institute. It would be published in six volumes, charting every development since the turn of the century. Not least among its contents would be some modern findings – the first precise details of some specific chemical weapons, harassing agents such as CS gas and anti-defoliants used by the American military during the Vietnam war. There was particular reference to defoliants, and the revelation that between September 1962 and March 1969 the US sprayed 13.8 million gallons of plant destruction agents over South Vietnam, covering around ten per cent of the surface of the country.

There would also be graphic accounts of the massive use of

harassing agents, CS, CN and DM gases, fired from 'a fantastic range of weapons'. Large quantities of tear gases were used to fire into the Vietcong system of underground shelters and tunnels where the US Army employed its 'normal procedure of blocking up all vents and exits' to achieve high levels of concentration. Reports of deaths from overdoses of tear gas were common. One claimed that '20 women and children did not make it out of the cave.'

Those stories would become more familiar in the years to come, as more of the American secret war in Vietnam became known. Nixon made his pronouncement of the abandonment of biological warfare ahead of them – and for all the wrong reasons. G.B. Carter's history of Porton reflected the anger and derision with which the Nixon statement was soon to be viewed, and exposed as something of a confidence trick. Porton apparently believed it was a political manoeuvre to draw attention away from the longer established and proven chemical capability recently displayed in Vietnam, to placate congressional, national and international concern, which, according to Carter, was 'a false rationale'. And the Nixon ban applied only to the production of biological weapons – not to the continued research into them, or indeed into the research and manufacture of chemical weapons.

The Portonian view of Nixon's statement, tempered as it was with anger and vested interest, was an interesting side element. Carter concluded that because of it, biological warfare became unmentionable and, as a threat, almost invisible, and he bemoaned the fact that 'this dangerous lack of perception' was almost fatal for the biological defence research programmes in several nations.

However, the whole Vietnam crisis and critical reaction to the methods employed by the American military turned the spotlight towards another controversial issue – CS gas, which had recently been accepted by the British government for use as a military training aid and for riot control by police as a replacement for some of the older forms of tear gas.

CS was first developed in America in 1928 and was used extensively by the Allies in World War II, but it did not fall into the domain of Porton scientists until the mid-1950s when the military began looking for a more modern tear gas. Porton began testing CS on volunteers and production studies began at Nancekuke in 1958. A decade later, after dozens of studies and reports, a British inquiry on the poisonous consequences of the gas vindicated the government's decision to adopt it for use in riot situations, notably and later in Northern Ireland.

The opposers claimed that CS gas came within the 1925 Geneva Protocol, which Britain had signed, preventing the 'use in war of asphyxiating, poisonous or other gases'. Ironically, however, the clause did not specifically preclude its use against a nation's own civilians or against individuals in a nation with whom she is not technically at war. Nixon had in fact deliberately excluded short-term harassing agents such as tear gas, herbicides and defoliants from the self-imposed restrictions on CB.W the US was prepared to adopt.

All of this flew in the face of the 1970 report by the World Health Organization's panel of experts, who were equally damning in their views on the over-zealous use of riot-control gases. It was clear, they said, that CN gas could cause serious lung damage when exposure occurred in enclosed spaces, and a number of deaths had been reported. CS gas was also known to be particularly harmful to people suffering from bronchial complaints. The controversy ran for many years and provided Porton and its US counterparts with hundreds of man-hours of study and experimentation.

At Porton, many human guinea-pigs and animals were used for trials of CS gas, and at the very time the controversy flared, a new version of the gas was being tested there. Among a group of servicemen who went to the research station for the trials was 23-year-old Able Seaman John Longden, from Lincoln, who was serving on HMS *Intrepid*.

In the summer of 1969, his ship was in dry-dock at Plymouth and Longden decided to apply to go on a course to achieve promotion. Initially, his request was refused, but he was told that if he volunteered for experiments at Porton, it would be reviewed. Longden agreed and checked into the research station for a two-week stay. Interviewed for this book, he gave this account of the experience:

> It was during Wimbledon fortnight, marked by the rare event of a British woman, Ann Jones, winning the ladies singles. I arrived at Porton along with a group of ten or twelve others. They allowed us to settle in, showed us around the social areas and explained that we could go into Salisbury in the evenings if we felt like it. They also gave us a briefing about the types of experiments we were to participate in and were quite open about the fact that we would be involved in tests for CS gas. There would be several experiments, averaging one a day I suppose. First of all, we went out on the Porton ranges where we did various exercises under gas conditions. We would have to fire a rifle, run for 100 yards or so through a light mist of CS gas, then fire again. It was

presumably to test reactions of soldiers or police in attack situations where CS was used. We also had patch tests on our arms.

Then there were a number of laboratory experiments. They described briefly what they entailed, that we would have gas sprayed towards our faces; but we needn't worry, they said, apart from an initial discomfort, there would be no ill effects. There would be doctors on hand for immediate treatment with antidotes. And, incidentally, the payment for each of these experiments was to be doubled to £2, although that was not a real consideration.

On the first day, we were taken from our barracks and led into the lab section where we lined up in the corridor and I noticed that they were closing all the connecting doors. When my turn came, I was led into a fairly ordinary room and found myself surrounded by chemists and doctors in white coats. I only began to get nervous when I saw the solitary piece of equipment – I can only describe it as resembling the electric chair you see in a James Cagney film.

It was exactly like that. I was strapped in, with my arms and legs buckled down and my head pushed back. Then a syringe, held by one of the technicians I think, came into view and liquid splashed into my face. I realized then why I had been tied down. I just had the urge to get up and claw myself out. A minute later, the syringe appeared again and the liquid was squirted directly into my right eye. The pain was excruciating. I shouted out, but of course at the same time you are thinking to yourself, don't let them see you are scared. It was absolutely traumatic.

They unstrapped me very quickly. The pain was bad, and my head was swirling. I could hardly walk, and certainly couldn't see properly. A doctor and a nurse helped me out and I was led down the corridor to a room where another doctor was waiting with what they said was the antidote. They looked at me and I can only describe their reaction as one of panic. They threw cold water straight on to my face and eyes. My face was red and burning, my right eye was completely closed and they had to sluice it out. They put a bandage over it and said it would have to stay on for a couple of days.

I wasn't alone in that, of course. At the billet, most of them that night were walking around with bandages over one eye. That night leave was cancelled. We were not supposed to leave the camp. We were told we would not be required the following day, and to rest. The pain and discomfort lasted a good two days, but the effects began to wear off and we went back on the ranges. At the end of the two weeks, I returned to my ship and went on my course.

My right eye occasionally gave me trouble, watering and so on. But it was not until some years later, after I had left the Navy and was working in the Middle East, as an electronics tutor in a university in Oman, when I consulted a doctor. She said my right eye was a good deal weaker than my left.

I had various eye tests over the years, intermittently during stays in Britain where I worked as a teacher and then a computer technician. In 1991, I finally wrote to the Ministry of Defence to raise the issue of compensation. It was my understanding that the tear gas used on me was one called Dibezoxa zepine and was of a type used in Northern Ireland but was later withdrawn.

The MoD reaction was, in a nutshell, to go away. As far as they were concerned, Porton Down did not exist. After various letters and contact with my local MP who also got nowhere, and incidentally didn't seem to care, I was eventually called to a medical at the Ministry of Defence. The upshot was that they wrote to say they could find nothing wrong with me. My claim was rejected. Which is where it still stands in 1996.

Today, CS remains one of the major tools of riot control the world over and was transferred to civilian production in the West in the 1980s. Back in 1969, when John Longden tested CS gas, it remained among the controversial elements of chemical weaponry, largely because of its visibility – in Vietnam, Northern Ireland, Paris . . . anywhere there was a riot.

It added to the growing unease. America had an appalling record of deploying chemicals in Vietnam, most notoriously Agent Orange. The chemical was a mixture of herbicides used between 1963 and 1971 and named for the orange-striped containers in which it was stored. It was employed to defoliate forest trees and destroy the enemy's crops. Agent Orange contained two highly potent herbicides: 2, 4, 5-T and 2, 4-D, which had first been used in the United States in the mid-1940s to control weeds in cereal fields, pastures, and turf.

By the mid-1970s, there was mounting concern over its use after the massive destruction caused in Vietnam, and amid public outcry Agent Orange and its associated civilian products were banned in 1983. Thousands of US military veterans who had been exposed to it were suffering the dire effects – a range of illnesses, and a large number had cancer. In what can now be seen as a preview for the veterans suffering from Gulf War Syndrome, they battled for years for compensation while long-term studies were ordered to discover whether they had a higher incidence of cancer than would be expected. They were in for a long wait.

The USSR faced similar accusations in the Yellow Rain saga. America, in the midst of the bad press over Agent Orange, openly accused the Soviets of supplying the fungal toxins for offensive use against the H'Mong tribes in Laos, and later in Kampuchea. The Soviets denied it. Eventually, environmental samples from the reported attack zones were retrieved and taken to Porton for analysis. The tests proved negative, but its scientists concluded that 'the epidemiological evidence led to the view that chemical attacks had occurred, albeit that the agent or agents used were unidentified'.

All this activity was against a backdrop of continuing negotiations around the Geneva Convention and international moves to reduce the world's stock of CB weaponry. America began its programme of unilaterally destroying its chemical arsenal – 7,000 tons of nerve gas alone during the next 15 years, although it still had ample stocks and an ever ready production capacity to turn Moscow into a massive graveyard if it felt so inclined.

The USSR also agreed to begin destruction of its chemical stockpile, although that was halted within a few years, allegedly and, if true, paradoxically, because of protests by environmentalists who accused the government of poisoning land and seas.

Britain meanwhile dumped its stocks of gas in the North Sea and the Atlantic, and trimmed back on research, especially on biological weapons. The old BW team was disbanded and a smaller unit remained under the direction of the more senior Chemical Defence Administration. A separate organization was formed for civilian research under the title of the Centre for Applied Microbiology and Research, answerable to the Ministry of Health, although some staff would retain links to defence projects.

For a time it seemed that the CB.W industry was in decline. But as on so many occasions in the past, it was a false dawn, a mirage. Very soon the whole Catch-22 of the international race once again moved back into top gear. Intelligence reports from the Soviet Union, reaching the ears of both British MI6 and the American CIA in the mid-1970s, suggested that far from halting its research in offensive BW, the Soviets had covertly stepped it up. Combined MI6/CIA reports confidently claimed that genetically engineered weapons were being researched in top-secret laboratories in the Soviet Union.

It would take more than 15 years before the claims could be proved, when two Porton intelligence experts finally gained access to a BW chamber of horrors. It was hidden deep in a pine forest 60 miles south of Moscow. With a single hand-held flashlight, they saw for themselves what had been built after the 1972 Convention was signed – a place to test a modern version of General Ishii's anthrax bomb and the Porton N-Bomb.

The story goes back to 1973. In that year, the USSR opened a brand new facility with the grand name of the All-Union Research Institute of Applied Microbiology at Obolensk, which was the newest of a network of supposedly civilian research institutes known as the Biopreparat. The truth, as would be revealed by a defector in the 1980s, was that Biopreparat was merely a cover for military work dating back to 1950. It employed 25,000 people at 18 separate active plants, had six mothballed production plants and a major storage facility deep in Siberia.

The work focused directly on the aims of its military masters: to create the ultimate doomsday weapon using genetically engineered agents that would be resistant to all Western antidotes. Work began in the autumn of 1973, bringing together all the previous research on bacteria-charged weaponry. A test chamber was built deep in the Obolensk compound. It would be one of the largest experimental chambers ever built: a cubed structure around 50 feet on each side with walls of steel and a viewing panel of bombproof glass. Most of the tests would be by aerosol dissemination.

Animals were tethered in its centre while a fine jet of bacteria-carrying mists would be sprayed through ceiling vents, which were then immediately sealed. All the diseases favoured by BW specialists, such as anthrax, various forms of plague, yellow fever and so on, were tried. Built-in sensors monitored the density of the deadly mist, and the animals were wired to machines recording their respiratory and heart rate as they sank slowly towards agonising death.

In 1979, a hushed-up explosion at the Institute of Microbiology and Biology near Sverdlovsk brought devastation to 200 square kilometres around the site. In the weeks following, more than 100 people died and many more fell ill. The Soviets blamed contaminated meat. The CIA and MI6 were quite certain of the cause: a release of a small quantity of anthrax spores carried upwind of the building and into the town. Although they were now convinced of the existence of an offensive germ warfare programme in violation of the 1972 accord, neither the Americans nor the British raised the issue through diplomatic channels through fear of revealing their intelligence sources.

There it rested in a kind of checkmate. In 1987, as pace gathered in the arms limitation talks between President Reagan and Mikhail Gorbachev, the Soviets made their first unequivocal admission that they possessed chemical weapons and were prepared to provide details to the international community. Still no mention was made of any biological weapons.

In June 1988, a party of MoD officials and scientists from Porton flew to the USSR to inspect its chemical plant at Shikhany and a return party of Soviets came to Porton. It was all very cosy, but not particularly revealing. There was no evidence of the feared biological bomb. Final proof of its existence did not emerge until 1989 when a senior Russian microbiologist, Vladimir Pasechnick, defected to the West, bringing with him first-hand knowledge of the Soviet BW work.

He confirmed the 'worst-case scenario' that the CIA and MI6 had suspected. Work on the super-generation of genetically engineered germs had been given 'top-priority' status by the mid-1980s. Scientists were working to a model predicting that if a single anthrax bomb were dropped on a city of 100,000, at least half the population would be wiped out. It was just as the WHO panel had predicted in 1970. By 1988 the Obolensk team had perfected strains of bacteria that were resistant to at least a dozen major antibiotics used in the West.

The information was of such quality that hotline telephone conversations buzzed between British Prime Minister Margaret Thatcher and US President George Bush. A new and delicate situation now existed. Mikhail Gorbachev was facing internal opposition to his moves for reform; Glasnost was under threat and Thatcher and Bush had no wish to disturb it further. On 11 April 1990, they quietly forced Gorbachev's hand by presenting a joint demand that he should end any remaining offensive BW research. Gorbachev's response was no more than a promise to investigate and question those at the helm. Bush was not satisfied.

In July, US Secretary of State James Baker met the Soviet Foreign Minister Eduard Shevardnadze and once again insisted upon assurances that the programme would be shut down. To back up his demands, Baker presented him with a 30-page report compiled by the joint MI6/CIA team, setting out chapter and verse of their knowledge of the Biopreparat programme and the work at Obolensk. Gorbachev's response came a month later. It was a virtual rejection of the intelligence claims. There was no current research and development on biological weapons (quite ignoring the previous two decades of work), and so the charges were groundless. The Soviets pointed to the fact that they had fully supported a new Chemical Weapons Convention and that exchange visits between scientists from the USSR chemical warfare facility at Shikhany and Britain's CDE at Porton Down had taken place in 1988.

The British MI6 knew that claims that the work had ceased were not true, and American intelligence agents with Pasechnick's help, were able to follow the Biopreparat's activities. Bush was furious that on the one hand the Soviets were attempting to finalize the START treaty on weapon controls and a new CW convention, while at the same time senior figures were 'lying through their teeth' about BW.

The USSR insisted that work had stopped and was prepared to allow a joint Anglo-America team of scientists to tour its establishments to prove it. The team was made up of seven US members and five from Britain; both parties included intelligence experts doubling as biochemists and Porton staff were also among the British contingent. The Soviets placed the visiting inspection team under the supervision of senior officials of the Foreign Ministry. They packed in a busy tour with several site visits, so many in fact that it was possible to stay only a short time at any one site. They were shown what appeared to be industrial and commercial chemical plants, along with a large number of 'not very active labs', according to one source who was on the trip. He recalled: 'We saw a few women messing around with beakers and bottles, but otherwise there was little sign of higher scientific work. Nor were we able to get any clue as to what biological material was being produced,' the source said.

One clue, however, came during a visit to the Obolensk facility. They were taken into a dimly lit labyrinth, which was clearly a test area. Two members of the British team, both linked to intelligence, stepped boldly inside a chamber where there were no lights at all; it was pitch black. One of them took a flashlight from his pockets and quickly trained it over the steel walls and the equipment inside. One of the Soviet officials intervened. 'Switch off the light,' he demanded. 'Or I will have to confiscate it. You agreed – no electronics.'

Those few seconds were sufficient for the British experts to identify the room as an aerosol chamber, the very heart of the biological experimental area on which so many intelligence reports had been centred. Other than that discovery, the Western investigation team came back with virtually no new information. Even so, they continued to pressurize Gorbachev on germ warfare, to the point that at a private meeting with him, following the 1991 G-7 summit in London, Major raised the issue again. He was angry, 'almost shouting', according to a US intelligence source who had seen a briefing report on the meeting. Major demanded that the programme be shut down. Four weeks later, he was told via the British Ambassador in Moscow that BW research would be halted. Gorbachev himself was on the verge of departure. Boris Yeltsin took over. The continuing priority that the West gave to the Russian BW capability, however, is demonstrated by the fact that it was among the topics raised by George Bush when Yeltsin visited the White House in February 1992.

At last it was admitted that the BW programme was indeed continuing. Yeltsin said: 'Some of our experts have done everything possible to hide the truth.' He promised to sign a decree to shut down the research, which he did in April 1992. In the mass of other problems that confronted him, it was one that would not command priority. The West remained unsure that the threat had been eliminated, and was even less convinced by Russian claims that it had made any great inroads into its CW capacity. Its experts had claimed, during the verification talks, that it had only 50,000 tons of chemical agents. Western intelligence believed the figure was nearer 300,000 tons, and there was no real evidence that the massive investment into plants during the late 1980s had been halted.

Worse still, as the military and scientific structures of the Russian hierarchy began to collapse in the economic reforms that Yeltsin imposed, wholesale leakage of technology and chemical weapons to smaller nations, notably Libya, was already under way.

12

SACRIFICIAL SLAUGHTER

MOUNTING INTERNATIONAL TENSIONS and local unease combined to turn an unprecedented spotlight on the activities of Porton Down, which came under closer public scrutiny than ever before as activists on several fronts were determinedly asking: 'What the hell is going on in that place?' Peace campaigners and animal rights activists joined forces to mount demonstrations outside the gates of the research centre.

The protests were ignored. Porton reacted with the words that there was 'undue concern' about the possible effects on adjacent villages of the release of chemicals or micro-organisms if there were to be an air crash on the Porton campus. Accidents and fatalities had always exacerbated public unease, wrote G.B. Carter with familiar understatement, and added: 'Suspicion and opprobrium . . . was of little concern to most at Porton. The tradition of heaping abuse on Porton and Portonians was after all well established; the press was an ever-ready means.'

Another accident added to the disquiet, even though full details of it were not revealed at the time. Porton was conducting experiments on the deadly 'Hot Zone' virus, ebola, shortly after its first recorded outbreak in Africa. It was untreatable and had the effect of turning human organs into liquid. The death rate was 80 per cent of those affected. Vivid proof of its continuing potential came in 1995 when it re-emerged in Zaire in February 1995, killing 200 people. Porton was, and remains, one of only a handful of laboratories in the world able safely to handle the virus.

The panic button was hit when, in 1976, Geoffrey Platt, then a 42-year-old laboratory technician in the microbiology unit, became accidentally exposed to the bug. He was working on a new exploratory research programme on ebola at the time, and was injecting guinea-pigs with the virus. He accidentally pricked his left thumb with a syringe as he was passing the samples from one animal to another. Mr Platt recalled: 'I knew straight away what the consequences could be but it was such a minute cut I hoped I had got away with it.' He quickly washed his thumb with disinfectant and squeezed the wound to make it bleed before reporting the accident to the Porton medical officer.

He was advised to check his temperature each day and call back if he began to feel ill. 'Five days later I had a temperature,' said Platt. 'I was vomiting and felt very much as if I had influenza. At the back of my mind I feared it could be ebola but I clung on to the hope that it was just a dose of flu.' He was taken to an isolation hospital in north London. All the other patients in rooms around him were evacuated. When tests showed he had ebola, he was moved to an isolation tent where he stayed alone for 40 days. More than 50 people with whom he had been in recent contact, including his wife Eileen and sons Richard and Graham, were put into quarantine. Platt, who retired from Porton Down in 1992 after 27 years' service, said: 'Fortunately, I had suffered only a mild attack. I lost a lot of hair but I was able to go back to work about three months later.'

In the aftermath of Platt's accident, the MoD held a formal inquiry into how it had occurred. The inquiry's findings were not revealed until almost a year after the accident. It recommended a tightening of laboratory procedures and the formalising of liaison between Porton medical staff and local public health officials. Locally, there was talk of a cover-up and some weight was added to that theory when the *Western Daily Press* revealed, in what it described as an 'exclusive' story, that Porton scientists were working on top-secret research into superbugs and genetic engineering.

The item was based upon information given by 'a senior scientist' at Porton, although the story had as much to do with scientists' fears of the future of biological research at Porton as with revealing the extent of recent discoveries. In his efforts to draw attention to the possible cutbacks in Porton's biological research and the fears about redundancy of his colleagues, the anonymous scientist revealed publicly for the first time details of the secret research work sanctioned by the government two years earlier.

It had given the go-ahead to work on the production of superbugs and genetic engineering. The link between civilian research and BW defence experiments was known only to those at the highest level. Certainly, too, a local reporter on the *Western Daily Press* would have no knowledge of the coincidental fact that government approval for the Porton superbug work came at a time when jointly the CIA and MI6 were receiving voluminous reports on the Soviets' genetic engineering project at Obolensk, which aimed at producing their bacteria bomb.

It was a highly sensitive issue. The *Western Daily Press* informant revealed to reporter David Humphrey that Porton scientists were on the verge of 'terrifying breakthroughs in the science-fiction world of gene manipulation and the creation of weird new life forms'. These included, said the informant, such bizarre hybrids as grass-eating lions and meat-eating cows. 'Anything is possible,' the scientist told Humphrey. 'These experiments could prove more dangerous than splitting the atom. We are in a minefield and sometimes we do not know what we are producing. These are totally new creations, hitherto unknown to man.'

In a follow-up article, Humphrey spelled out the dilemma facing scientists raised by new discoveries. He wrote:

'On the one hand they could be used to eliminate hereditary disease, prevent congenital deformities in babies and make common bacteria turn out insulin for diabetes. On the other hand, as many scientists have warned, if a bug escaped from a laboratory it might sweep the world, killing millions of people who would have no natural protection to it.'

The article, clearly from the mouth of the senior Porton scientist, brought swift results. The Porton establishment was so concerned at the leak that its security staff called in Scotland Yard's Special Branch to attempt to find the source. It also fuelled local concern about what was going on inside the establishment.

There had long been rumours of research work on animals that had produced some horrific results among Porton-bred specimens. One source interviewed for this book alleged that 'some terrible mutations were achieved. Animals were born with some pretty awful defects, peculiar bone structures and so on. I heard the usual horror stories – you know, a sheep with two heads, chickens with four legs – though I never saw the evidence myself. But in any event, there was a lot of stuff going on that was quite frankly stomach-churning, especially when these animals were kept alive for lab tests.'

That the Porton scientists required many animals for their experiments represented one of the great moral dilemmas of the age – sacrificing them in the name of science and the future protection of servicemen. Its 'own brand' of white rabbits, rats and mice were recognised as superior for experimental purposes.

Like laboratories the world over, Porton needed a continuous supply. This well-known and well-established practice was intermittently highlighted by newspaper exposés such as the Scandal of the Smoking Beagles, which revealed how laboratory dogs were being killed for research into the effects of cigarette smoke. The animal welfare organizations began marshalling their troops. The National Anti-Vivisection Society (NAVS) called a public meeting at Salisbury. Its then chairman, John Evans, described Porton as the 'sinister fringe on this beautiful city'. The NAVS produced a number of speakers in its campaign to outlaw vivisection and its demands for a government inquiry into the increasingly widespread use of animals for laboratory work. Porton itself, according to the NAVS' figures, had carried out an average of 200,00 experiments a year on animals in the 1970s. In the United Kingdom as a whole the total was peaking at around 5.5 million, in universities, medical and veterinary faculties, health laboratories and commercial research facilities for trials on a vast range of products ranging from cosmetics to flea collars for cats.

Yet, hundreds of thousands of people would not be alive today, says the Animals in Medicine Research Information Centre, without modern medicines, vaccines and treatments developed from research using animals. Set against those defenders of the practice are scores of animal welfare groups who can produce scientists and medical evidence to prove that there are alternatives, and to deplore the practice in modern society. The debate goes on.

Porton scientists have always attempted to distance themselves from the animal rights issue; they were special, a community apart. It is a view they have asserted, some would say, with a forthrightness that verges on arrogance. They were special inasmuch that for long periods of Porton's eight decades of history, they were inspired, promoted and defended by the *sotto* advisers of government: the counsellors of war, the Chiefs of Staff and the ambitions of the military. They had powerful, distinguished allies behind them and from the very beginning were surrounded by the protective arm of the security services, ever present to repel all attempted incursions into their secrecy. So 'suspicion and opprobrium . . . was of little concern to most at Porton'.

The anger of the animal welfare groups was further aroused when planning approval was sought to build four monkey breeding units at Porton's Allington Farm. Dennis Hobbs, in charge of procuring animals for the unit, was summoned by the local planning committee to explain the request. He said that monkeys had previously been imported from South East Asia, but increasingly they were disease ridden when they arrived and 30 per cent of an imported batch might die. The number of monkeys used in total by the Health Service had dropped from 20,000 a year in the 1960s to around 800 a year.

'The whole operation has sinister connotations,' said one councillor, Austin Underwood, who generally made a point of attempting to air Porton's secrets in the public sessions of his council. The world 'sinister' in connection with Porton had become common local usage, inspired by rumour and emotion. Occasionally, glimpses of the work could be gleaned from scientific journals and the writings of Portonians anxious, like all scientists, to have details of their research published. A large number of reports, routinely produced on a daily basis, have been viewed for this work and, as always, they highlight the difficulty in coming to terms with animal suffering in the face of the claimed benefits to mankind, especially as the latter do not always follow on specifically from any one set of particular experiments.

There are dozens of reports, running to thousands of pages, detailing decades of work. A brief excursion through them provides an adequate insight into both the nature of the work and the attitude of the scientists themselves. The more detailed scientific data and calculations will be omitted in the interests of brevity, and simplicity.

Typical in the mid-1970s were experiments at Porton on the discovery of pre-treatment antidotes for nerve gas. A number of trials had been conducted using guinea-pigs, dogs, rabbits, rats and mice, which were inconclusive in assessing their potential for use by man.

Female guinea-pigs were used as subjects in one series of tests. They were grouped into batches of six for trials to discover the level of protection from a combination of treatments both before and after poisoning, compared with animals that had been given no protection. The nerve agents used were sarin, soman and tabun at 95 per cent pure strength and VX at 90 per cent pure.

First, the pre-treatment drug being tested was injected into the right limb of each animals 30 minutes before the organophosphate was administered into the right groin. At the sign of the poison taking effect – when the animals began experiencing muscular convulsions and breathing difficulties – the antidote, atropine – later to be given extensively to Gulf War Troops – was injected into the right limbs of selected animals, and a further batch also received injections of diazepam into their left limbs.

This procedure was repeated for each of the four agents to test the effectiveness of the treatments. The results showed protection against sarin and VX, but overall the tests were inconclusive and were done again using different doses of the drug combinations. Even so, no precise comparison between the possible treatment of animals and of humans for protection against nerve agents was proved by the tests.

However, the results of another series of experiments were detailed in a report for the Procurement Executive of the MoD at Porton, this time using 28 rhesus monkeys and 15 marmosets. All the monkeys were tranquillized to enable easy handling while initial experiments were conducted. They were then injected with a pre-poisoning protective chemical, each was subjected to varying degrees of soman poisoning, and then given doses of the antidote atropine.

Under the heading 'Signs of poisoning produced under treatment', the report concluded that in low doses of soman, no deaths occurred; with medium doses, the death rate was 50 per cent and for high doses, 100 per cent. The following observations were made as the experiments proceeded:

Low doses: Signs of poisoning occurred within one to four minutes. The animals became prostrate with brief episodes of convulsions. They did not completely lose consciousness and only a low rate of respiratory depression occurred. After 15 minutes, the convulsions stopped, and the animals began to sit up about an hour after poisoning and were eating and drinking within 48 hours. During the period up to three days after poisoning, movements were co-ordinated but slow. All animals recovered after 3 to 4 days.

Medium doses: Animals became prostrate with violent convulsions within one minute and lost consciousness within ten minutes. Respiration became slow, shallow and laboured and the animals appeared close to death. The breathing of animals surviving at this stage gradually improved and they returned to consciousness within 30 minutes of poisoning. Within four hours, some were able to crawl about their cages but quickly showed signs of fatigue after a small amount of exertion. Some relapsed, but all the surviving 50 per cent of those tested at the medium dose recovered within four days.

High dose: All the animals collapsed into unconsciousness within one minute of soman poisoning, and all suffered violent convulsions. Those animals which survived this stage of the tests returned to consciousness within 30 minutes of poisoning and made attempts to crawl about their cages. Within one hour, all relapsed and subsequently died. 'It is worthy of note,' the report states, 'that 3 out of 4 animals regained consciousness and lived for 1–2 hours after poisoning.'

The test proved, said the scientists, that 'pretreatment with pyridostigmine combined with atropine therapeutically affords a high degree of protection in rhesus monkeys and marmosets poisoned with soman'.

A long series of experiments was conducted at Porton on a number of species to discover the effects on the eyes and respiratory tracts of gases, smoke and chemicals applied both directly to the pupils and through the bloodstream. The description of these experiments is long and complicated and can barely be reproduced in precis form for the purposes of a lay work. The preamble to the test reports, however, gives some notion of the form the experiments take and the imaginable consequences.

The tests were carried out using groups of six animals that had been allowed to acclimatize to their surroundings and permitted full recovery from the stress of travelling. They were housed in cages with wire mesh floors to make sure that particles such as wood chippings or sawdust did not accidentally enter the eyes. The day before the test both eyes of each animal were examined to ensure they were normal.

Next, the irritant materials were introduced directly to the eye by 'gently holding the lower eyelid away from the eyeball and dropping material into the sac, after which the lids were held together for a few seconds'. Liquids were introduced easily by automatic dispenser while solids were weighed and blown into the eye sac with a rubber teat. One eye for each animal was treated; the other eye remained unaffected for comparison. In some cases, it was important to know whether immediate irrigation of the eye a few minutes after contamination by the irritant was beneficial or – as in some cases – detrimental, and in those cases tapwater was sprayed into the eye. After the material had been introduced the animals were inspected several times during the first day of the test and daily thereafter. The process continued for one week, when the full effects of the irritant were apparent.

One important sequence of experiments was conducted by five senior Porton scientists to discover the effects of CS gas on laboratory animals. The experiments were clearly aimed at adding to international discussion on the effects that CS might have on humans. The scientists noted the warning about the use of the gas given by the 1970 report of a panel of experts commissioned by the World Health Organization.

This Porton report was significant in that it gave some clue as to the findings of experiments using humans in 1972 – information that has been repeatedly denied to those who have sought compensation. There were no 'authenticated' reports of death due to CS, it stated, and exposure of human volunteers to CS aerosols under controlled conditions produced 'no clinically significant changes in the electrocardiogram, chest radiograph or vital capacity that could be put down to CS'. However, there were notable rises in blood pressures and the report concluded that the use of CS in confined spaces might lead to prolonged and possibly damaging consequences.

Records concerning the use of CS in Northern Ireland were consulted for the tests. The Porton report drew from statistical evidence from Londonderry that had 'failed to show any evidence of association between CS gas and abortions, stillbirths or congenital abnormality in pregnancy' but pointed out 'long term animal tests are still the only ones capable of providing evidence' of the potential for cancer.

The team therefore began repeated-dose treatment to monitor the effects of CS aerosols on laboratory animals, using 300 mice, 200 rats and 200 guinea-pigs. The description of the experiments was similar to those recounted by human volunteers. The aerosol was directed through a glass entry port into a chamber 10 metres square with a small fan to ensure dispersal. Groups of animals were exposed to three different concentrations of CS for an hour each day. They were then removed to 'special accommodation next to the inhalation unit'. The experiments, however, produced results that evidently surprised the researchers.

Exposures to the mice in the two groups receiving lower concentrations of CS continued five days a week until they had received 55 exposures. Tests on the high-dose groups were stopped after only three exposures because of the large number of animals that 'succumbed'. The same happened with experiments using rats and guinea-pigs. Those in the two groups exposed to lower concentrations survived 120 exposures, while the high-concentration groups received only five exposures because of the large number of deaths among the guinea-pigs.

Surviving animals were examined daily to test the levels of toxicity and, the report added, 'debilitated animals were sacrificed' using nembutal. One of several problems encountered by the team was the high level of cannibalism, especially among mice. Another was the suddenness of the deaths of many of the animals – they collapsed often without warning at a time when toxic signs were not apparent. This was especially so among the guinea-pigs. During the first month of the tests, almost half of the high-dose groups had perished.

The surviving animals were kept under observation for six months following the completion of the exposure programme. All animals still live at the end of that period were killed with an injection of nembutal and dissected. Every one of their organs was then taken and fixed in a saline solution before being sectioned and examined independently by two pathologists.

The conclusion of this year-long study that had claimed the attention of some of Porton's leading scientific minds and the lives of 700 animals was a single sentence that recorded: 'Our findings suggest that inhaled CS is not harmful to the male mouse, rat or guinea-pig when the period of exposure is one hour per day for 120 days providing that the concentration is below [a given] level . . . somewhat more than eight times the concentration found to be intolerable to 50 per cent of an exposed population within one minute of the start of exposure.'

There would undoubtedly have been uproar outside the gates of Porton if the animal welfare activists had known about experiments on six dogs, poisoned with hydrogen cyanide (HCN) to test antidotes for this most lethal substance, which is a modern favourite of many chemical warfare experts, especially in Iraq and Libya. The work was a follow-up to several earlier studies elsewhere on the topic of discovering effective antidotes for the poison. Those already in existence had side effects that themselves could be life threatening.

The Porton tests were, for the specific purposes of this controlled experiment, conducted on nine Beagle bitches, bred at its own farm. In some earlier tests, a range of other dogs had been used, with varying results. The Beagles were considered to provide a more accurate test species.

The nine dogs were all injected with hydrogen cyanide over 20 seconds through the jugular vein. Six were protected by antidotes; three were not. They were kept under constant observation until 'death or recovery' and notes made of every visible reaction. If symptoms of poisoning were still evident after 210 minutes from the injection of the cyanide, the animal would be sacrificed by injection of a further chemical to prevent suffering.

The three unprotected dogs suffered spasms almost from the moment the injection was completed: 'respiration and pulse ceased within one and half minutes'. The six protected dogs appeared to be recovering from the injection. One of them, however, suffered two seizures and was 'terminated' by injection. Another died 44 minutes after the cyanide injection. The researchers saw the positive side of even this latter demise – that death was postponed for 44 minutes, which would have enabled other treatment to be tried out.

The scientists admitted that relating the findings to cyanide poisoning in humans was difficult because the antidote doses given to the Beagles had been carefully and individually tailored to each animal – which would be 'extremely inconvenient' if not near impossible for the treatment of humans.

Even a layman can spot the inadequacies, and many of those who press for an alternative to animals experiments believe that these tests, taking months of research at considerable cost, both financial and in animal life, are really not worth the paper they are written on. Not only do many of them duplicate earlier work dating back many years, and to which references are constantly made, but they often provide little data that is new enough and substantive enough to be worthy of the effort and pain that goes into the studies.

The view that results of experiments on animals cannot be universally applied to humans has been attracting increasing support in recent years. Comments typical of this view came in a paper produced jointly by Dr Howard Rogers, a senior lecturer in clinical pharmacology, and Professor Roy Spector, professor in applied pharmacology at Guy's Hospital, London.

Their doubts over the total reliance on animal experiments, so disastrously evident from the Thalidomide catastrophe of 1960, were pointedly demonstrated: 'Modern drug regulatory organizations demand that large numbers of tests be made on animals to predict the efficacy of new drugs in man. The drug industry is therefore required to kill many thousands of animals to submit "scientific" evidence. In practice, these tests have poor predictive value . . . many of the adverse drug reactions occurring in man have no animal counterpart.'

It was not an uncommon view, and one that would become all too relevant when the Gulf War troops arrived home after being given an array of drugs, some unlicensed. Other experiments – perhaps the most dramatic ever staged at Porton – had nothing to do with drugs.

They were set up to assess the damage likely to be caused to the human body by a range of modern weapons. The injuries were to be studied to provide insight into survival times, treatment and helmet designs.

A series of experiments was required, and were run by Ingrid V. Allen, of the Department of Pathology, Queen's University, Belfast, Colonel Robert Scott, a professor of military surgery at the Royal Army Medical College, and J.A. Tanner, a leading member of the Chemical Defence Establishment.

For tests under the heading 'Experimental High-Velocity Missile Head Injury', 29 rhesus monkeys were used as 'patients'. All the animals were anaesthetized with intravenous injection. Twenty were each clamped into a frame and shot in the head with steel balls to discover the damage caused by high-velocity rifle fire on the brain and skull. Five were used as control subjects for comparison and four were set aside for biochemical tests.

The test report describes the results: 'In the 20 experimental animals, a penetrating injury was inflicted by a steel ball of diameter 3.2mm, fired at a range of five and ten metres with an estimated impact velocity of 1,000 metres per second. The lesion was left-to-right trans-frontal wound, the head being held upright and the ball fired at the temple region.'

The test report goes on to explain the nature of the wounds and other experiments carried out on the 29 animals and includes a detailed assessment of the survival time of the shot monkeys. They remained alive for periods ranging from 2 to 169 minutes. The remaining 9 animals were destroyed separately, as part of the same controlled experiment. Brain sections were cut and photographed and other organs examined.

Other experiments by Colonel Scott were set up to compare the effect of bullet calibre using four standard types: a Lee Enfield 303, NATO 7.62mm, Russian 7.62mm and American 7.62mm. Two sheep were used to test each type of bullet. They were anaesthetized and then shot in the shaven upper parts of their back legs from a range between 13.7 and 18 metres. In each case, the femoral bone was shattered and the size of the wound varied according to the bullet used. The report concluded that hitting the bone greatly increased the destructiveness of the bullet, 'an effect which has long been described when animals were hit in the chest or pelvis'.

Two sheep were allowed to recover from wounds caused by standard NATO bullets fired from 13.7 metres to study healing. The experiment was to determine whether there were any blood-born indicators of the severity of the wounding. There were not. 'The animals were obviously not inaccommodated by this injury and quickly returned to grazing,' said Scott.

The potential for the wounding of living tissue from bullets fired at a particular distance from the target was also studied. Once again sheep were used for these trials. They were anaesthetized, shot in the thigh, the wounds were photographed, and then the sheep were injected by humane killer within one hour of being shot. The limbs were removed and deep frozen for 24 hours, before being sliced for sectional examination.

Pigs were used in another sequence of tests to find 'the effect of bullet velocity on living tissue'. Each pig was shot in the stomach 'from close range'. The pigs remained alive after the shooting. They were cut open and the damaged organs studied and photographed. On completion of the tests the pigs were put to death by humane injection. These kinds of experiments are justified, in Porton's own documentated assessment, as offering 'now considerable and valuable contributions to the treatment of British casualties – notably in Northern Ireland, during the Falklands War and elsewhere'.

Such self-congratulatory expressions were not, however, wholly supported by medical opinion. There are, for example, thousands of published papers on the treatment of contemporary war injuries, especially from the Vietnam era when more than 150,000 American troops were wounded. Britain, with its recent Falklands war and experiences in Northern Ireland, had also conducted many studies. As a senior professor of medicine in Belfast said: 'If they want to study bullet wounds, they should have come here. We have hundreds of real-life case histories. Today, there can be no justification for shooting animals; they aren't the same as humans, either in bone or tissue structure. Nothing they could have learned at Porton Down would help us here, in Belfast. Of that I am convinced.'

The tests continue, even as these words are being written, and almost 80 years after the invention of mustard gas, Porton is still testing its effects. It would seem that pigs will be in great demand there for the future. In the latest available annual report from the CBDE to the Ministry of Defence (for 1995), its director, Dr Graham Pearson, makes reference to the latest techniques for the treatment of mustard gas burns. The experiments are part of an on-going series over many years, but which were stepped up when casualties from the Iran/Iraq war, examined by Porton staff, were found to have large pendulous, fluid-filled blisters, which were difficult to heal. Porton experimented with many animals in an attempt to find the one that produced a wounding reaction closest to that of the human body. This entailed exposing animals to mustard gas, monitoring the effects and allowing the subjects to heal. They discovered a human likeness in a specially bred type of miniature pig. Dr Pearson explained:

'Research into mustard burns has been hampered by the absence of an appropriate animal model which reacts in the same way as human skin. Fur bearing animals do not blister . . . however research at the CBDE has successfully used mustard burns on the miniature pigs to develop and improve healing procedures. The burns develop rapidly . . . healing was slow and was not complete even at eight weeks after exposure. This is similar to injuries in man and suggests that the pig can be used to model aspects of human vesicant exposure.'

Research on the pigs enabled Porton scientists to develop a new form of battlefield treatment. They produced a hand-held cordless drill and grinding stone to remove the pendulous dead skin from the animals. They discovered that the technique, known as dermabrasion, reduced the healing time by up to two-thirds compared to the control group of mustard-burned pigs who were not treated in that way. The more rapid healing also reduced the threat of infection. The experiments, applauded by the Porton hierarchy, have been met with some scepticism out in the real world of daily hospital activity. Nicholas Parkhouse, director of the burns and plastic surgery unit at the Queen Victoria Hospital, East Grinstead, Britain's largest, commented: 'I don't think there is anyone in conventional burns practice who would use the dermabrasion technique. It is very messy.'

Pigs were also used in other recent experiments to find ways of protecting troops from the blast waves following explosions. While protection from missiles and heat was well advanced, conventional body-armour offered no protection against blast waves, which could travel, like sound, through most materials.

The blast wave, Dr Pearson explained, would normally result in limb fractures, head injuries, amputations and, most probably, death. Experiments were conducted on anaesthetized pigs. They were placed at varying distances from the site of an explosion to test the pressure of the waves as they entered the body. Those animals that were not killed by the blast were sacrificed without being allowed to recover.

There was one slight consolation to be gained from these particular experiments. It enabled technicians to construct computerised models, which will reduce the number of animals required. In the main, however, the slaughter – or 'sacrifice' as they call it – at Porton goes on. In the last available set of figures, for 1995, Porton claimed its use of animals had been 'reduced' to less than half of one per cent of the national total. It was using between 10,000 and 15,000 animals a year, although even that is not a true reflection, since a great deal of Porton's experimental work in recent years has been contracted out to universities. The true figure could be double Porton's own on-site tally.

13

THE ARMING OF SADDAM

PRESIDENT RONALD REAGAN'S sabre-rattling defence policy and his futuristic and, ultimately unachievable, Star Wars extravaganza brought a state of siege to Porton Down as peace campaigners surrounded sensitive defence installations in Britain. Reagan's 1984 defence budget included a $1 billion spend on chemical weapons. It included, specifically, $100 million for a new generation of nerve gas weapons – all of which appeared under the heading of 'defensive measures'. The knock-on effect in Britain was to trigger a new commitment to Porton. In the summer of 1983, a wide-ranging assessment of chemical warfare potential was presented to the British Cabinet.

Based upon MI6 reports, it listed specifically the chemical capability of more than a dozen nations, and another ten with embryo CB ambitions. Apart from the USSR, it focused particularly on the emerging 'new growth' chemical plants among nations in the most volatile regions, such as Iraq, Iran, Syria, Libya, North Korea, Taiwan, Burma and Israel.

Saddam Hussein was known, even then, to be building the largest and most sophisticated CW plant at the ancient city of Samarra, and intelligence reports identified at least four others. As early as 1975, he approached a New York company to build a factory to make pesticides – in other words, chemical weapons. The initial approach was for a small factory. When the company's architects arrived in Iraq, however, the Iraqis showed them plans for a plant capable of producing 1,200 tons of toxic material a year. The US company backed off, and diligently informed the CIA.

Iraq canvassed many other major companies including Britain's ICI before it turned to continental European companies in West Germany, Holland, Belgium and Italy. They were not so reticent, and the West German contact sold them the nucleus plant, which, as everyone well knew, was for CW manufacture. In 1983, a Belgium subsidiary of Phillipos Petroleum shipped 500 tons of thiodigycol, a key component of mustard gas, to Iraq but became suspicious when Saddam ordered another 500 tons the following year and pulled back. But it was already too late. With supplies from various undercover deals throughout Europe, Iraq was by the mid-1980s capable of producing 100 tons of nerve gas and 760 tons of mustard gas a year, along with its own brand of nerve gases from a new factory in the Baghdad suburb of Salman Park.

More worrying to the Americans were the intentions of Colonel Gaddafi. He was building a massive complex at Rabta, a desert location 50 miles south-west of Tripoli. More than half the site was to be devoted to chemical warfare research. The contract to build it was won by a Frankfurt-based company whose ultimate ownership could be traced back to an Iraqi-born civil engineer who had been living in Chelsea, London, since 1978, Dr Ibsen Barbouti, a gruff, mysterious multi-millionaire.

He ran a network of companies operating from London, Switzerland, Japan, West Germany and the United States. He introduced around 25 German-based firms to equip the centre with its infrastructure. Gaddafi's Rabta project occupied the minds of American intelligence for many months. The CIA produced a model scenario for the Pentagon. It would be possible, they said, for him to equip Russian-built Scud missiles with chemical warheads, capable of a range of at least 600 miles, well within reach of Middle Eastern cities as well as Europe. Political analysts added their conclusions: that Gaddafi might allow terrorist groups access to chemical weapons in the same way that he was known to be sending arms and explosives to the IRA.

But, as everyone now knows, the West should have been paying more attention to Saddam. The first real warning came with the discovery that led an American intelligence expert to coin the phrase: 'The genie is out of the bottle.' In March 1984, reports of the Iran–Iraq war had produced some intriguing developments for

Western analysts to mull over. Iranian troops had been making steady advances through Iraqi-held terroritory, effectively cutting a path through minefields and forcing an Iraqi retreat on two separate fronts. Suddenly, the Iranian forces began to scatter in panic. The reason would soon become clear. Saddam Hussein had ordered a chemical attack – bombarding and spraying his enemy with mustard gas.

Thousands of casualties were taken from the war zones to military hospitals. America gathered up its intelligence reports and physical evidence, some of which was sent to Porton for examination. These developments in the Middle East, along with the flurry of intelligence reports confirming Soviet work on genetically engineered anthrax, heightened anxieties in the West. As Porton's scientists recorded, the scene was set for yet another re-appraisal by Western military analysts. The new fear was that DNA-linked techniques and the latest advances in biotechnology would be 'misused to obtain an almost quantum leap in biological warfare'. The two elements of chemical and biological weaponry could no longer be viewed as separate entities. In all the latest assessments, they were being spoken of as forming a combined hazard representing a 'continuous spectre of proliferation'.

Largely in response to the Soviet threat, the British and Americans had secretly initiated a complete reversal of their BW defence policy. Less than five years after disbanding Porton's old Microbiological Research Establishment and turning it over to the Health Ministry, biological warfare research was resumed – for defensive purposes – and then 'energetically pursued'. A team of additional scientists was recruited to Porton to begin DNA-linked research. Although the exact nature of their work remains secret, it is possible through the US Freedom of Information Act to glean clues of the nature of British and American research, which was put in progress as 'a matter of priority'.

In 1984, America's premier BW team at Fort Detrick was working on isolating particular genes of bacillus *anthracis*, the anthrax organism that the Russians were researching. Officially, the explanation for the research was to discover a vaccine to be used in the event of a possible enemy attack. Three separate teams of researchers at the Walter Reed US Army Research Unit were working on the genes of trypanosomes (which cause sleeping sickness), and of the carriers of typhus and gonorrhoea, again with the stated role of discovering effective vaccines.

The US Defense Department had also contracted out a number of projects to universities for work on isolating the genes of a variety of lethal organisms. Porton was working along on similar lines. All the research had dual-use applications, for civilian protection by way of vaccines and for the military in the creation of defensive equipment, protective clothing, monitors and detectors for use in any theatre of war.

This rush of new activity in CB.W research can be judged from a few statistical facts. In the early 1980s, Porton recruited the largest number of human volunteers for almost a decade. Between 1980 and 1985, a total of 1,293 men from the three services took part in experiments, usually staying in the compound for a full two weeks. For that, they were paid up to £80, before tax. All, said Porton director Dr Graham Pearson, were 'carefully designed and controlled and great care was taken to ensure the health and wellbeing of the volunteers'.

The establishment was on the brink of one of the most vital eras of its existence and certainly the most controversial. The CB.W threat had never been higher. Dr Gordon Oehler, director of the Nonproliferation Centre of the CIA in Washington, has confirmed that by the mid-1980s the alarm bells were already ringing as far as Saddam Hussein was concerned. He had an aggressive chemical and biological programme. And, of course, the European nations were literally falling over themselves to sell their wares in the Baghdad market place – everything from chemicals to machine tools, with the full knowledge and absolute approval of their governments. Dr Oehler confirmed:

> Iraq's CB.W programme was developed gradually over the course of the 1980s, beginning from the time Israel bombed its nuclear plant. By the time of the invasion of Kuwait it had become deeply entrenched, flexible, and well orchestrated. Project managers for the weapons of mass destruction programmes went directly to European suppliers for the majority of their needs. Throughout the 1980s, German companies headed the list of preferred suppliers for machinery, technology, and chemical precursors.
>
> German construction companies usually won the contracts to build the CW facilities in Iraq and Iraqi procurement agents were sophisticated in exploiting local export laws by targeting countries for substances and technologies that were not locally controlled. In the pre-Gulf War years, the dual-use nature of many of these products made it easier for Iraq to claim that the chemical precursors, for example, were intended for agricultural industries. European firms, arguing that the facilities in Iraq were for the production of pesticides, built a chemical plant, including six separate chemical weapons manufacturing lines between

1983 and 1986. We were tracking it, even then, and these developments would have been reported also to the President, to the Secretary of Defense, and the Secretary of State as a matter of course.

European middlemen brokered chemical deals for Iraq under the pretext that the materials were intended for pesticide plants. A Dutch firm purchased supplies from major chemical firms around the world, supplying the Chemical Importation and Distribution State Enterprise in Baghdad in the 1970s, and in the 1980s supplying the Iraqi State Establishment for Pesticide Production, both cover names for the CW programme.

When the Iraqis requested phosphorous oxychloride, a nerve agent used for sarin, banned for export under Dutch law without explicit permission, the supplier balked. He drew this request to the attention of Dutch authorities. Subsequent Dutch investigations found that two other Dutch firms were involved in brokering purchases of chemicals. Iraq exploited businessmen and consortia willing to violate the export laws of their own countries. The Consen Group, a consortium of European missile designers, engineers, and businessmen, established a network of front companies to cover its role as project director of an Argentine, Egyptian, Iraqi sponsored Condor II ballistic missile programme.

By then, the Iraqis were already manufacturing their own Scud missile warheads. They had quite a missile refurbishment extension plant where they took the Scuds and added in extra lengths and the fuel tanks, changed the warheads to accommodate chemical or biological agents. The CIA [and MI6] was tracking this in real time as it was happening and had a great concern about it. In the US, the only concern was about the possibility of equipment being diverted to the Soviet Union or other communist countries. However, after evidence mounted in the mid-1980s about the use of chemical warfare in the Iran–Iraq war, the United States began to put into effect unilateral controls on exports of chemical precursors to Iraq and other countries suspected of having chemical warfare programmes. The US and several other industrialized nations joined what is called the Australia Group to establish more uniform licensing controls for the export of several chemical weapons precursors.

We saw Saddam Hussein, in a sense, go underground with some of his activities and the CIA predicted a real problem long

> before the outbreak of the Gulf War. We had it as a well-documented fact that Saddam had an advanced and dangerous CB.W capability underway and our intelligence reports increasingly pointed to the fact that he might use it.

That prophecy came disastrously true in March 1988 when Saddam Hussein launched his infamous genocidal assault on the unsuspecting Kurdish villages near the Iranian border and finally made the world realize the global threat in Iraq's recurrent breaches of international agreements against the use of chemical weapons. Soon, too, the world would see the horrific photographs resulting from the attack in which 4,000 men, women and children were killed by chemical weapons released in bombing raids by Iraqi aircraft. The weapons consisted of mustard gas, phosgene, nerve gas and hydrogen cyanide (HCN), a highly refined form of gas known in the trade as 'duty mustard'.

Survivors spoke of the foul-smelling yellow-grey cloud. First, the birds and the animals began dying, dropping from trees and falling dead in the fields. Then the villagers began screaming from the burning effects of the gas. Hundreds simply died where they stood, sat or lay. Others suffered a slow agonising death. Village streets were cluttered with corpses with blackened skin and with blood-tinged fluid oozing from noses and mouths – like a modern Pompeii without the volcano but just as catastrophic.

Fifty thousands Kurds fled into Turkish and Iranian refugee camps, leaving the bodies where they lay. Many thousands suffered eye problems, respiratory pain on breathing, blistering skin and persistent vomiting – all the signs well known to CB.W experts. By the time a United Nations investigations team arrived, the death toll had reached 5,500 and a further 7,000 were suffering dire effects from the gas, many with very visible signs of huge ulcerated blisters, muscle spasms, vomiting and diarrhoea.

Yet, as would be made clear in the worldwide protests that followed, Iraq had been able to carry out the attacks on its Kurdish minority with impunity. For all the professed outrage, there was no action taken against Saddam Hussein by the West. The British, a few weeks later, approved new trade credits that would build upon the £400 million a year in exports to Iraq from a dozen household-name companies. The French, one of Iraq's principal suppliers of arms after the Soviet Union, began 'friendly' talks over the re-scheduling of Iraq's £2.4 billion debt with them. It wasn't that the French especially wanted their money back – they wanted a repayment schedule in place so that the government could continue with its export guarantees and allow the military aircraft manufacturers to compete for an order for aircraft and supply 50 Mirage fighters worth 22 billion French francs.

The Italians were swimming around in even murkier waters after the discovery of a $3 billion loan to Iraq, mysteriously supplied by one of its leading banks, Banca Nationale del Lavoro, through a branch in Atlanta, Georgia. The US meanwhile continued to allow its own trading position with Iraq to continue.

In spite of the vivid proof that Saddam possessed chemical horrors and was prepared to use them – now appallingly evident for all to see – weapons that had been looked at, inquired into and warned about by countless humanitarian groups, which pleaded for action to halt Saddam, it was by and large business as usual. Quite apart from international outrage and the investigations of the UN, ample evidence of the effects of the attack on the Kurds was presented in a report by the Physicians for Human Rights (PHR). In October 1988, the group dispatched a medical fact-finding mission to refugee camps in Turkish Kurdistan and produced a graphic summary of the effects of the attack in a report entitled 'Winds of Death'.

Copies were sent to all Western governments, underscoring the global threat in Iraq's recurrent breach of international agreements against the use of chemical weapons. In February 1989, the evidence collected by this fact-finding mission was submitted to a US Senate Committee on Governmental Affairs, at which the PHR called for immediate action to stop the 'development, manufacture, deployment and use of chemical and biological weapons'. They urged all Western governments to apply immediate sanctions against Iraq for its 'assault on our common humanity'.

Nothing happened.

Impassioned though they were, the PHR team and other groups like Amnesty International presented nothing that Western intelligence, the military and the scientific community at large did not already know. Saddam Hussein had become the harbinger of the reality of CB.W – acting out the scenario forewarned in a thousand intelligence files. Yet, in the final days of the Reagan administration, the Pentagon still seemed more concerned about the connections of Colonel Gaddafi than the threat of Saddam Hussein.

Gaddafi's own Rabta industrial complex was always at the top of the White House worry list, to the point that Reagan and his advisers actually considered a bombing mission to destroy it. Their continuing ambivalence towards Saddam Hussein's expansive activities was matched by London where, as the Scott Report would reveal in 1996, the rules concerning exports were bent, twisted and modified with the full knowledge of government and with a deep involvement of MI6 agents. Dual-use material and equipment, which could ultimately be employed for the manufacture of weapons, continued to flow from factories in the West in the competitive dash for exports.

What amounted to a virtual blind-eye policy in dealings with Iraq continued after the departures of Ronald Reagan and Margaret Thatcher and into the administrations of George Bush and John Major. An abundance, mountains, of evidence of Saddam's acquisitions was piled high. As the CIA's Dr Oehler identified, the Iraqis had covertly bought their way into trading companies across the world, to ensure supplies of chemicals for Saddam's embryonic nuclear programme and for his notorious Supergun – all under the watchful eye of British and American intelligence.

Into the spotlight of this world stage, once again, stepped the ubiquitous Dr Ibsen Barbouti who, as was also well known, was the main contractor for Gaddafi's Rabta plant. In the autumn of 1988, the Reagan administration began feeding to the media reports about Gaddafi's efforts to acquire chemical supplies. They named names, companies in the West that had assisted him. The seemingly obsessive concern over Gaddafi was heightened by the December 1988 Lockerbie bomb disaster, for which they held him responsible.

The following month, January 1989, Dr Ibsen Barbouti was publicly named in one of the last proclamations of the Reagan administration as the man who had built Gaddafi's chemical warfare plant. No mention was made of the fact that Barbouti had established strong ties with Iraq. The CIA directorate was furious. By drawing attention to Barbouti, the Reagan administration had put at risk an 'asset' in the Iraqi/Libyan trading relationship – perhaps Barbouti himself.

By then Barbouti, who still lived in Britain, had extended his global network of companies into the US. Between 1986 and 1989, he had channelled $100 million into 50 holding companies based in America, with apparent access to funds that were certainly beyond even his well-endowed bank balances. They were a diversity of interests, but mostly dealing with dual-use products.

The CIA was well aware of Barbouti's interest in American companies. So was MI6. He was under constant surveillance from the early 1980s. In 1987, an executive of an Oaklahoma-based chemical company reported to the CIA that Barbouti wanted to buy into his company. He said Barbouti had talked openly about his dealings in the Middle East, and that Gaddafi was mad and wanted to build an atom bomb, sail it into New York on a civilian vessel and detonate it by remote control.

That prospect, incidentally, was not as far-fetched as it sounded. It was one of the very models of possible nuclear attack by an enemy or terrorist group that the Pentagon had explored years earlier and it remains 'live' to this day in the contingency plans that are constantly reviewed and updated. The Oklahoma executive was requested to keep the CIA informed of his contacts with Barbouti, which he did on an almost daily basis. It merely added to the CIA profile.

Barbouti's activities continued unassailed, even as one of his many partners in the Rabta project, Jurgen Hippenstiel-Imhausen of the German firm Imhausen-Chemie, had been arrested. He confessed to helping to build the Libyan chemical plant and at his trial in 1990 was sentenced to five years in jail.

But according to the CIA there were overriding reasons why Barbouti was not apprehended and questioned and, like many others, he was allowed to continue with dubious dual-use export deals. The reason was explained by Dr Oehler:

> In disseminating our intelligence, one of our primary duties is to protect the sources of the intelligence and the methods by which it was collected. Sources are most at risk when intelligence information is made public. The compromise of sources results in a diminished capacity to collect intelligence for the future. The most dramatic consequences of a compromise of intelligence information is the threat of the life of an asset [an informer or spy] but there are other significant consequences.
>
> For example, if we have intelligence indicating that a particular overseas company is actually, say a Libyan front company, we can often watch that company to learn more about Libya's programmes and its acquisition network. US Government action that publicly identifies the company will often result in the company shutting down and reopening elsewhere under a different name. Identifying this new company can be difficult. Meanwhile, we have lost a window.
>
> I'm not saying intelligence should dictate US Government action. But we have to stay flexible. And in some cases this may mean holding off on Government actions to protect sources. That is why sanctions became a difficult issue – nothing was that

> straightforward before the Gulf War. There was so much going on, that we had to let it run.

So the knowledge was there and the intelligence community was still tracking Barbouti – some say funding – when he began a new business operation from a nondescript, two-storey factory near Boca Raton, Florida, run under the name of Product Ingredient Technology in the autumn of 1988. It was supposedly the brainchild of one Louis Champon, inventor of a process for manufacturing natural food flavourings produced directly from fruit. He advertized for investors and Barbouti arrived, waving his cheque book. What was ostensibly an innocent-looking food additives plant had the potential for something much more sinister. The natural fruit flavouring process gave up a very useful by-product – hydrogen cyanide. Saddam was desperate for that particular chemical. Within a year, the factory was producing thousands of gallons of the stuff.

If there were any doubts about Barbouti's plans for the plant, they could have been intensified by the general atmosphere at the factory. He installed expensive security procedures, threw a 24-hour security patrol around the perimeters and installed electronic surveillance. Barbouti executives and personal aides came and went, driven in Jaguars and protected by armed bodyguards.

The CIA knew about that too. In the spring of 1989, they were contacted by a security consultant who told them he had been asked to quote for the installation of a system of video cameras, microphones and a cyanide detection system at the factory. Champon would tell investigators that he believed most of the cyanide was poured away.

It wasn't.

Barrels of it were loaded on to specially equipped lorries and transported through the night to Houston, Texas. There, they were crated and given a new identity and driven to Baltimore for shipment to Aqaba in Jordon and finally by road to Baghdad. The route was established and the export of cyanide to the Iraqis was running.

On 1 July 1990, however, Barbouti was found dead. The official cause of death was given as natural causes, from heart trouble. He was buried in a black marble tomb at the cemetery near his home in Brookwood, Woking, in Surrey, surrounded in death as in life by strong security in the shape of a large brick wall.

His death remains as mysterious as some aspects of his life. Rumours abound among his business associates, of whom there are still many around the world. One has claimed he had dealings with

MI6 and the CIA at the time of his death. Others say he was assassinated by Mossad, the Israeli intelligence service, which was also tracking him. There was an alternative theory that he did not die at all; that he faked his death with a substitute corpse because Saddam had discovered he had intelligence connections.

None of those possibilities should be discounted. A string of strange deaths and covered-up shenanigans among both intelligence and political circles was rife during those months and years immediately prior to the onset of the Gulf War. Dr Gerald Bull, inventor of the Supergun, was assassinated in Belgium in March 1990, probably by Mossad. British journalist Jonathan Moyle, editor of *Defence Helicopter World*, was murdered in his hotel room in Chile in the same month when he began asking too many questions about arms procurement for Iraq. Farzad Bazoft, a journalist working for *The Observer,* was arrested and executed in Iraq for spying – for revealing details of Saddam's nuclear weapons programme.

There was undisputed MI6 involvement with executives of the British engineering company Matrix Churchill, which had been taken over by an Iraqi front company with the full knowledge of the British government. The resultant inquiry, which saw ministers squirming their way through the howls of media derision, provided a view through a half-opened window on a particularly distasteful era in British politics, which has never been satisfactorily explained or resolved.

Edwin Dorn, Under-Secretary of Defense for Personnel and Readiness at the Department of Defense in Washington, explained with familiar understatement: 'Iraq clearly represented a case in which past efforts to prevent the proliferation of weapons of mass destruction had not been effective. We halted the Argentine Condor Programme that was aiding Iraq's weapons of mass destruction programme. And we spearheaded the effort to prevent Iraq from acquiring a more capable missile than the Scud. But it has to be remembered that all exports made to Iraq in the 1980s were completely consistent with the laws at that time, and Iraq was not considered a hostile country.'

Thus, most of the deals that Saddam Hussein had set up around the world had two things in common: they were, by and large, done with the full knowledge of the intelligence community and, second, with the exception of the Supergun confiscated by the British as it was about to be loaded on to a ship bound for the Middle East, and the shut-down of nuclear-linked technology from Argentina by the US, few of his arms and chemical deals were stopped before supplies reached Iraq.

By the summer of 1990, the importance of that truth was to concentrate the minds of Western political and military leaders like no other. On 2 August 1990 Iraq invaded Kuwait and, in the words of Senator Donald W. Riegle, who chaired a 1994 Senate Committee investigating pre-Gulf War exports to Iraq from the US, panic suddenly gripped those nations that had kept up their trade with Saddam Hussein virtually to the day of the invasion.

As Riegle recalled, a letter, which had a 'little bit of a frantic tone' to it, was sent from Secretary of State James Baker in the Bush administration. It demanded, said the senator, that the US immediately stop the shipments to Iraq of 'these kinds of items, things that could be either used in chemical weapons or biological weapons or nuclear weapons'. Riegle declared: 'Suddenly it dawned on people that we were going to have a real problem facing off against weapons that we had inadvertently, one presumes, helped create . . . because [Saddam Hussein] had not been on the bad guy list at the time.'

By then it was too late.

14

A DEADLY CHRISTMAS COCKTAIL

IN THAT SUMMER of the invasion of Kuwait, Michael Roche, the former Porton volunteer who stepped forward in 1963 to take part in nerve gas experiments for the future benefit of his colleagues in the British Armed Forces, was unemployable and unable to walk more than a few paces without pausing for breath. He was in a bad way. Nearly 30 years after he had allowed himself to become a human guinea-pig, the Ministry of Defence continued to deny any responsibility for him or his condition. His lonely campaign was slowly gathering weight and attention – not merely for himself, but also for the many like him who were beginning to believe that their declining health was linked to experiments at Porton all those years ago.

Roche's struggle had been so uphill that lesser men would have given up years before, which is obviously what the Ministry of Defence hoped would happen. Perhaps this nuisance of a man would eventually go away – or die. He spent eight years badgering them for his medical records and when he finally received them, discovered there was absolutely no mention of the two occasions he had attended Porton Down.

He spent another four years applying for – and being refused – the medical and laboratory records of those two visits to Porton. Finally, in 1989 he travelled from his home in Rochdale and staged a hunger strike outside the Porton compound. The media attention he received moved the MoD into action. Within four days, he was contacted and told the information he required would be released to his doctor.

It was a hollow victory. When the records finally arrived, they were incomplete and marked strictly private and confidential – for the doctor's eyes only, which meant Roche could not even see his own records. He began again. He launched an appeal for further information but, like most of the dozens of letters he had written in the past, it fell upon those well-known deaf ears. And, anyhow, events in Kuwait brought forth a state of siege at Porton that was impenetrable, certainly to the lone, unimportant figure of Michael Roche.

Wars and the threat of them have, over the years, kept Porton Down in business. Those periodic campaigners to have the place obliterated from the Wiltshire countryside have always been overshadowed by the reality that weapons of mass destruction, so easily made and readily available to even the small nations, were piled high in foreign lands.

In the early months of 1990, there had been a revival of the 'Stop Porton' campaign stirred in part by the attention Roche's hunger strike had brought. Conservative MP for Salisbury, Robert Key, reacted in his usual ardently supportive manner: 'Work at Porton is now more crucial than ever,' he announced in a public statement. 'When we are actually working towards international verification treaties designed to prevent the spread and use of chemical weapons, it would be ludicrous to call for the phasing out of Porton. We are still a long way from that position. The work must go on, and sadly animals continue to be a necessary part of achieving an effective defence.'

With spectacularly bad timing, extremist members of the Animal Liberation Front responded by launching a renewed terror campaign. They attempted to blow up one of Porton's senior veterinary officers, Margaret Baskerville. A bomb attached to her car exploded as she set off for work one morning in June 1990. Although the vehicle was wrecked, she escaped with minor injuries, though deeply shocked. Several of her colleagues and animal experiment researchers from other facilities were also known to be targets of the extremists. Security at Porton was stepped up. Every member of staff received warnings of possible attacks and senior members of the establishment were given added protection. Dr Graham Pearson was moved to write to the local newspaper: 'I wish to make clear that . . . the purposes, objectives and the benefits sought in animal experimentation must be fully justified. We only use animals when no effective alternative exists. Experiments are carried out by a few scientists who hold personal licences and Project Licences issued by the Home Office . . . it is a means of protecting life. The role of the CBDE is to protect the lives of our servicemen and women against the threat of chemical or biological weapons which might be used against them.'

Less than a month later, that threat finally presented itself, for the first time in almost half a century, when Saddam Hussein invaded Kuwait. Porton staff, along with their US colleagues, were placed on a new red alert. Ill-judged assessments by the CIA that Saddam would not invade, or, if he did, it would be a temporary incursion, proved disastrously wrong. President Bush was woken at 5am to sign orders freezing Iraq's assets in the US and, at last, banning all exports. Margaret Thatcher did the same in London. President Mitterand in France stated he would join them with comprehensive sanctions. West Germany, which had been the source of much of Iraq's CW technology, would agree only to control military exports and Japan, another major trading partner of Saddam, showed no immediate willingness to move towards any strong action.

US Defence Secretary Dick Cheney laid out the problems for the Western Allies if they were to move to free Kuwait. Saddam had one of the world's largest armies, although its fighting power was grossly exaggerated before the war by Saddam and after it by the Americans. He was also handsomely equipped, courtesy of the Russians and the West. Within the week, Bush flew to meet Margaret Thatcher at Aspen, Colorado, where she was delivering a lecture.

Predictably supportive, she promised that Britain would stand side by side with the US and called for a co-operative international action to get Iraq out of Kuwait. Pentagon military planners had already produced a stark assessment of the problems confronting them. They were presented to a meeting of the US National Security Council (NSC) when Bush returned to Washington. William Webster, director of the CIA, said the situation looked grim: 'The Iraqis are within eight-tenths of a mile of the Saudi border. If Saddam stays where he is, he'll own 20 per cent of the world's oil reserves, and he's within a few miles of seizing another 20 per cent. Jordan and Yemen will probably tilt towards him. We can expect Arab states to start cutting deals. Iran will be at Iraq's feet. Israel will be threatened.'

Mere sanctions against Iraq were unlikely to move Saddam Hussein. Nor was an immediate response-attack by bombing raids, similar to that on Libya during the Reagan administration, likely to succeed. There were also hundreds of Western expatriates living and working in Iraq and Kuwait – who in due course Saddam would infamously use as a human shield. Then, there were the wider implications of a possible Iraqi attack against Israel and the threat of an all-out explosion of hostilities in the Gulf. Even so, for the time being, Bush was telling his people, 'We're not discussing intervention.'

That position changed virtually overnight. The NSC reconvened at Camp David. On his return to Washington, Bush gave a running press conference as he made his way from his helicopter to the White House. With a delivery that General Colin Powell, chairman of his Chiefs of Staff, described as 'very Thatcheresque', Bush declared that Saddam's invasion of Kuwait 'will not stand'. Jabbing the air with his finger, he repeated, 'This aggression against Kuwait will not stand.'

From not even discussing intervention, Bush had made what Powell himself declared was a 'giant leap' towards sending a Falklands-style task force to the Middle East. At Camp David, the Pentagon analysts ran down their checklist of options and Saddam's ability to defend himself against a US attacking force. It was then that the question of Iraq's chemical and biological arsenal suddenly became one of the most contentious issues of the whole situation. The air began to turn blue as the Defense Intelligence Agency and the CIA laid out the realities of Iraq's CB.W potential. One source described the reaction of Bush and his advisers as one of astonishment, punctuated with 'a good many anguished expressions beginning with "What the . . . ?" and "How the . . . ?" and "Who the . . . ?" The realisation was upon them that the West had equipped this modern-day Hitler with an armoury for armageddon.'

As Senator Donald Riegle identified, quite apart from Saddam's massive array of conventional hardware, the knowledge and fear of his CB.W stockpile became the immediate focus of the American and British Chiefs of Staff when the prospect of Allied action loomed before them. With the benefit of hindsight, Riegle surmised: 'Now just think about this and think about it logically – 13,000 155-millimeter shells loaded with mustard gas; 6,200 rockets loaded with nerve agent; 800 nerve agent aerial bombs; 28 Scud warheads loaded with sarin; 75 tons of nerve agent sarin – that's what UN investigators recovered AFTER the war. There's no telling how much more was destroyed, or what was the total quantity of CB weapons of mass destruction that Saddam had squirrelled away.'

A United Nations investigation team later found more of it – stockpiles of 5,000 tons of chemical agents, 46,000 filled munitions and 30 chemical warheads for ballistic missiles, not counting some that had been buried during the bombing raids and were too dangerous to evacuate. Since the British MoD maintains its traditional stance of total secrecy on its pre-war assessments, even after the event, we must defer to sources in the US for a picture of what confronted political leaders and chiefs of staff that summer as they pondered the possibilities if they sent in the troops to 'face him down'.

According to Dr Gordon Oehler, the CIA had fairly accurately calculated that Iraq's main chemical plant was capable of producing more than 2,000 tons of mustard gas and sarin a year. They were also certain that Iraq had a stockpile of at least one metric ton of biological warfare agents, including anthrax and botulinum toxin. There were others, perhaps even more deadly. The CIA knew that, too.

As Senator Riegle himself was to reveal, the US had licensed the export of bacterial materials capable of being used to create genetically altered biological warfare agents to the Iraqi Atomic Energy Commission – the Iraqi governmental agency that conducted biological warfare-related research – prior to the war. One method of creating these genetically altered micro-organisms is by exposing them to radiation. The US had also licensed the export of several species of *Brucella* to Iraqi governmental agencies.

Bush wanted to know 'how in God's name' Saddam had managed to get his hands on American biological agents, which now might be used against their own troops. The Department of Defense could only excuse itself by saying: 'We're not a licensing agency. That responsibility falls on the Department of Commerce.' Records on the ultimate destination of dual-use biological, chemical, nuclear, or missile technology-related licenses were all issued by the Commerce Department. An inter-agency Subgroup on Nuclear Export Controls, which was in operation throughout the 1980s, kept close scrutiny for nuclear-related dual-use technology. As the Defense Department's Edwin Dorn described, it intervened only in certain dubious dual-use deals that had nuclear connections, but it claimed to have no jurisdiction over chemical or biological material until the invasion of Kuwait.

Lax laws and a general eagerness to trade with Iraq meant that few nations who would be called upon to support the Coalition action against Iraq could claim that they had not helped in some way or another to bolster the dictator's military strength; certainly, America was not alone in its embarrassment.

The question was what to do about it. Edwin Dorn recalled: 'I can tell you that American policymakers and military commanders were very concerned that Iraq would use chemical and/or biological weapons. We had the hard evidence that they had acquired a BW capability as well. From the outset, it became vital to find ways to protect our personnel against such weapons, through immunisation, through special training, equipment, and detection. The tension surrounding the possible use of CB.W was very evident.' Bush's defence secretary, Dick Cheney, flew to Saudi Arabia for talks with King Fahd. Bush wanted the ruler's co-operation and permission to base the invasion force in his country. At 3 in the afternoon of 6 August, Cheney called Colin Powell from Jidda: 'We've got his approval . . . start moving them out.'

Margaret Thatcher reaffirmed British support and a Coalition of Western military began moving tenuously towards its foundation under phase one of the operation, code-named 'Desert Shield', to establish a force in the Gulf to prevent any further advances by Iraq. Phase two would be 'Desert Storm' – to come into effect as and when Saddam Hussein refused to submit to United Nations' demands for withdrawal from Kuwait.

In London, the Chiefs of Staff mounted their own Operation Granby, a name that mystified the Americans. They were not familiar with that 18th-century piece of British history when the Marquess of Granby led the Battle of Minden during the Seven Years War. The name was among the operational titles reserved on the MoD computer for the next major troop movement. In this instance, according to the Thatcher Cabinet, Operation Granby was being launched as a deterrent to war, rather than to start one.

Porton scientists were at the forefront of the British effort from the beginning. A month before Margaret Thatcher's Cabinet agreed to dispatch the 7th Armoured Brigade to Saudi Arabia on 15 September, a team of its scientists was summoned to the Ministry of Defence to join discussions initiated by the Chiefs of Staff. They were required to provide a complete interpretation of intelligence reports on Iraq's CB capability. Armed with this appraisal, a British team of chemical warfare experts from the defence advisory establishment flew to the Gulf for on-the-spot briefings with their American counterparts, now gathering in Saudi Arabia in vast numbers.

General Norman Schwarzkopf, the US Commander-in-Chief, had already installed himself in the Ministry of Defence building in Riyadh, from which base the Saudis were themselves already preparing for the distribution of thousands of civilian gas-masks and protective suits. Schwarzkopf and Powell were more or less in agreement that although a chemical attack would be a public relations nightmare it was judged to be 'manageable' on the battlefield. 'What to do about Iraq's biological capability remained a more troubling question,' Powell admitted.

This particular aspect had caused something of a panic among the Americans. As a post-war assessment of the US defence capability by the Edgewood Arsenal revealed, major gaps existed. They were particularly lacking in the means of detection of CB agents in the climatic conditions within which they would have to operate. Porton faced similar demands. Towards the end of the summer, and with tens of thousands of troops already moving into the Gulf, two-thirds of Porton Down's senior staff were working around the clock to devise, test and perfect additional equipment and protective gear that would be necessary for those conditions.

Just as Edgewood claimed its own efficiency in meeting the challenge, Porton's readiness to react was pronounced in terms verging on Churchill's 'finest hour': an emergency in which years of work in troop protection would finally be put to the test. It provided, they would say, vindication of everything for which they had been criticized and villified in the past.

Dr Graham Pearson boasted that almost 75 years of research and development by the establishment's multi-disciplined teams provided the springboard for an immediate response. 'We are the experts,' Pearson declared. 'And priority was given to a number of questions raised by the Iraqi situation.'

The scientists produced a summary of the damage potential of Iraqi weapons based upon intelligence estimates of the CB stockpiles and the nature of agents most likely to be used. According to a Porton source, the military planners posed a great number of questions as they mapped out their strategy in the event of a war. The most crucial of them emphasized the planners' fears. They called for:

1) A complete scenario giving precise indications of the persistency of CB agents in the climatic conditions of the Gulf, based upon attacks at a number of fixed sites where troops might be deployed, and in mobile operations. It was known, for example, that the potency of mustard gas could increase dramatically in hot conditions and that all agents could penetrate a sweaty skin far more rapidly than a relatively dry skin.

2) The likely distance hazard to troops and civilian resulting from Allied attacks on Iraqi chemical and biological installations, many of which were already known by the intelligence communities and sited on the planners' maps. The planners had to be assured that by bombing BW installations they would not be unleashing, rather than

preventing, a catastrophe. That key question could not easily be resolved; the risks were virtually incalculable.
3) Estimates of the casualty potential of CB warheads delivered by Scud missiles, and the 'fall-out' possibilities that could result from Patriot interception of the Scuds, which were again 'desperately difficult' to forecast. High casualty figures were certain, especially if the Scuds landed in the highly populated areas of Saudi Arabia and Israel.
4) With the protection of troops to such attacks being of paramount importance, the military required confirmation that existing protective suits and clothing were adequate for anything that Saddam Hussein might throw at them.
5) Urgent trials were begun to evaluate the physical impact upon the soldiers themselves of wearing the protective gear in the extreme heat, or conversely the cold, in the Gulf and for the scientists to give an accurate calculation of the effects of the burden of protective clothing upon the fighting ability of the men who wore it.
6) While it would be intended that all troops posted to the Gulf would carry at least some form of external protection, a list of drugs and antidotes to combat any exposure to CB.W was required, and immediate steps should be taken to ensure that there were adequate supplies of those medicines by way of pills and injections, which it was planned to have available for every member of the task force.
7) Porton should advise on medical countermeasures for immediate treatment of troops injured by CB.W attacks in the field of operations. Porton should also advise on surgical techniques to increase the healing rate of wounds inflicted by chemical agents that were known to be particularly slow to heal, and to provide assistance and advice on the management of CB.W casualties in field hospitals, hospital ships and at civilian hospitals in the Gulf and in Britain.
8) It was necessary to consider the methods of warning of CB attacks and the detection of agents in the vicinity of troop positions. Urgent production of detectors and monitors was required to augment those already in service and an 'interim system' for the detection of biological agent aerosols was required immediately and teams trained in its use.

That equipment was designed, developed and dispatched to the Gulf within three months, along with service personnel hastily trained at Porton to use the BW detectors. Similarly, there had been no system in place for battlezone collection of samples in order to identify particular agents that might be dispersed, so that suitable treatment could be administered. Field laboratories were designed and ready for action by the time the war became a reality.

All these aspects were occupying the Porton establishment – and parallel teams in the US – as the prospect of a fight edged closer. There were endless meetings between military planners, medical faculties and drug producers and staff from Porton Down as new scenarios and possibilities emerged. General Sir Peter de la Billiere, who was appointed Commander of the British Forces in the Middle East, was among the military leaders who concluded that, even if the Iraqis' technology were primitive – and the CIA and MI6 knew it wasn't – it would have been quite possible for them to drop canisters upwind of troops in the desert, or even for them to drive a truck through Riyadh with an aerosol container spraying germs out of the back. 'All these probabilities were studied,' Sir Peter recalled. 'Far-fetched though it may sound, the possibility was a thoroughly uncomfortable one to have hanging over us. Because one of the simplest methods of delivering gas or biological agents was from the air.'

British troops were actually better off than the Americans in terms of protective gear. The British had more protective suits available per man than the Americans. Though they were immensely uncomfortable and psychologically caused the troops a good deal of worry, they provided excellent protection. Antitoxins against chemical or biological attack were, as General de la Billiere says, a 'more vexed question'. Large stocks of vaccines and tablets as pre-treatment and antidotes to gas and BW attack were produced for mass distribution. 'It seemed possible that Saddam might use anthrax,' Sir Peter wrote in his autobiography. 'My view was that if we had the vaccine, we should use it: to suffer casualties through not using it would have been quite wrong. Nevertheless, the issue raised a range of awkward and sensitive political questions. The decision to use the vaccine would also cause problems in the UK; in spite of our efforts to keep the matter quiet, the press were bound to get hold of it.'

The sensitivity towards public reaction indicated the concern among the generals about the extent and the volatile nature of some of the drugs that were to be prescribed. This one issue with its unpleasant overtones, said Sir Peter, gave rise to 'protracted discussion and debate'.

The reasons for their concerns were to become very evident. First, it was known that the drugs could have very unpleasant side-effects, which might affect the ability of the troops. More precisely, however, worries centred on the sheer scale of the programme. Never in any previous military action had such a large quantity of pre-treatment medicines been recommended for so many troops. There were acknowledged gaps in research on the combined effects of the drugs. And there were concerns that two of the treatments had received no formal licensing from the regulating authorities of either Britain or the US. Nonetheless, as war threatened, the Pentagon persuaded the US Food and Drug Administration (FDA) to waive its prohibition on testing a drug for new purposes without the subjects' 'informed consent'. FDA deputy commissioner Mary Pendergast defended that ruling: 'You can't have your troops being the ones to decide whether they'll take some step to keep themselves healthy.' Senator Alfonse D'Amato unearthed the use of unlicensed drugs while studying reports to the Riegle Senate Committee enquiry in Washington in May 1994. The discovery raised a number of issues:

'It is very illuminating . . . it takes us to the issue of the question of the effectiveness of the drugs that were administered to the veterans in an attempt to immunise them against possible CB attacks – and, of course, the long-term impact. Some of these drugs have not received the full approval of the FDA. How many and how often were these drugs used? Which of them were experimental in nature? What have we done in ascertaining the impact of the administration of these drugs on our veterans? Have we made or begun to make the kinds of studies that can lead us to the information and facts necessary?'

These were exactly the questions that faced the politicians and the military in the build-up to the war; in 1996 many of them remained unanswered and there was still grave disquiet about the possible side-effects, which, as thousands of troops fell ill, became one of the most contentious issues in the post-war debate. Only under pressure from action groups in the US would the Department of Defense and the Ministry of Defence in London finally reveal their cocktail of medicines. They had vaccines against: tetanus, malaria, hepatitis B, cholera, meningitis, yellow fever, two types of anthrax, bubonic plague, botulinus toxin, polio, typhoid and whooping cough. That against bubonic plague had not been licensed.

Then there were the pre-treatment tablets to combat the effects of CB agents. They were the NAPS (Nerve Anti Pre-treatment Sets) and BATS (Biological Agent Treatment Sets). The NAPS tablets, pyridostogmine bromide (PB), to counteract the effects of nerve gas, were also unlicensed. They were administered to nearly all US troops and to most UK service people. Doses of 30mg taken three times daily were considered to offer sufficient protection to troops against nerve gas when taken with the antidote atropine and 2-Pam chloride, which was to be administered immediately after a chemical attack.

Side-effects from PB caused the military most concern. Tests on civilians had shown that it could result in a neuromuscular disorder and a US medical investigation Task Force would later admit the likelihood of side-effects at the level of 1 per 1000 of those exposed to the drug but added that 'this hypothetical concern should be weighed against the hazards of unprotected exposure to chemical attack.'

The concern was hardly 'hypothetical'. A former senior scientific officer at Porton described the prospect of prolonged used of NAPS tablets as 'terrifying'. No one knew what happened when the drug was administered at low levels over a long period because there had been no such tests, but according to the Countess of Mar, the House of Lords campaigner against organophosphates in pesticides, it was 'suspected that the neuromuscular functions become modified and do not return to normal when the drug is no longer taken'.

Most of the troops took NAPS on a regular basis for around two months, although some members of the Coalition force, such as the Royal Fleet Auxiliary Services who arrived in the Gulf in September 1990, took them for much longer. Other warnings about the potency of NAPS were already in place. Senior officers across the whole spectrum of the Gulf Operations were in regular contact with medical authorities asking for advice. They received very little, simply because there was none to offer, said the Countess of Mar.

She maintains that no research had ever been conducted on the effects on the neurological and immune systems of the combination of NAPS and the vaccines administered. As the war edged closer, the Ministry of Defence was scrambling around for medical advice. Buried away in the files of the Department of Health is a document issued by the Royal College of Physicians, adding supplementary advice to the Gulf Contingency Planning, issued in February 1991, two weeks after the war began. It gave a clear warning in its detailed summary of the treatment of nerve agents:

'Experience . . . has shown that after apparently successful initial treatment, patients may deteriorate rapidly at any time . . . further respiratory failure, insomnia, psychiatric and myocardial problems may occur. These effects are not likely to be amenable to treatment with the combination of atropine and oxime and these drugs should not be given without the clearest clinical indication.'

The advice concludes with the following: 'Long term effects: muscle weakness, paraesthesiae, sensory loss, motor loss, tremors, glaucoma, depression, headaches, and ataxia have all been reported following organophosphate pesticide exposure . . . it *is not known* [author's italics] but believed unlikely that long term effects follow nerve agent poisoning.'

The same concerns applied to the effects of the anthrax vaccine widely given to troops in the war theatre, and the vaccine for botulinus, given to a lesser number who were considered most at risk. The vaccines were generally administered 'under orders'. This in itself raised another critical issue. The Countess of Mar said: 'I understand that fully informed consent was not obtained from the troops prior to the administration of the medication and that they were given no opportunity to refuse. They were simply marched into a room and ordered to roll up their sleeves. They were aware that refusal would result in disciplinary action.'

This was confirmed by a US military staff report prepared for a US Senate Committee on Veterans' Affairs after the war. It concluded that 'Gulf veterans were . . . ordered under threat of Article 15 for court-martial to take the treatment, to discuss their vaccinations with no one, not even with any medical professionals needing the information to treat adverse reactions from the vaccine.'

A survey of veterans who had taken the anthrax vaccine showed 85 per cent were told they could not refuse it, and 43 per cent experienced immediate side-effects. Only a quarter of the women to whom it was administered were warned of any risks to pregnancy. Of all surveyed personnel who had taken the antibotulism medicine, 88 per cent were told not to turn it down and 35 per cent suffered side-effects. 'Anthrax vaccine should continue to be considered as a potential cause of undiagnosed illnesses in military personnel,' said the US report, adding: 'The botulism vaccine's safety remains unknown.'

The US military was known to have been particularly deficient in antibodies for *botulinus,* which the CIA had noted was among Saddam's other likely biological weapons. Their production of a vaccine to counteract the lethal paralytic effects of *botulinus* had been largely derived, literally, from one old horse named First Flight stabled at the Veterinary College of Minnesota.

He alone had produced in total 300 litres of antibody plasma but it was a drop in the ocean compared to the amount needed for the mass inoculation of US troops. That, as it turned out, was one more gap in America's state of preparedness for BW attacks on its troops, and further heated exchanges ensued. General Colin Powell's head of CW defence, and in this instance aptly named, Brigadier General

Johnny Jumper, recruited the services of an additional 100 horses from which the antibody plasma was taken.

While many troops were already taking NAPS tablets, still no decision had been taken in London and Washington with regard to widespread inoculation of troops. Tension was mounting. Newspapers and television were full of stories of impending disaster. Casualties in a ground war had been estimated by the Pentagon planners as possibly reaching as many as 40,000. The field hospitals were in place; the ships and aircraft to carry casualties home were standing by; major hospitals throughout the United Kingdom were on alert.

Even the two key commanders in the Gulf, Generals Sir Peter de la Billiere and Norman Schwarzkopf, 'could not agree' when or where the anti-BW vaccines should be used. Sir Peter said he remained convinced that they would be 'entirely blameworthy' if they did not use the vaccine and then Saddam attacked with biological weapons. Some of their advisers felt that if Saddam did resort to a biological strike, he would most likely aim it at Riyadh to cause maximum panic. Others felt he would not deliver it directly into the Arab world but would hit the front-line of mainly US and British troops.

Eventually, word came down from on high. The risk of such an attack outweighed all other considerations. Soon after Christmas, thousands of doses were administered to troops, boosted by shots of whooping cough vaccine to make them work faster. The 700,000 men who had been kicking their heels in the heat and taking part in manoeuvres and training exercises since their arrival were already tense and bored. Now, many thousands of them would have the added discomfort of the side-effects of the jabs and pills.

As predicted, the jabs made them feel 'extremely ill', General Sir Peter de la Billiere would recall, and were one more cause of stress. Already, they were taking the anti-gas tablets, which gave many people diarrhoea, and even more worrying was the discovery that the NAPS were 85 per cent bromide. They were also given the biological vaccination at the same time as the whooping cough vaccine, which knocked them out for 24 hours. Then, it was widely rumoured they were going to be immunized against the plague, which no one had heard of since the Dark Ages. 'It was all too much,' wrote Sir Peter.

Meanwhile, General Colin Powell was agonising with his advisers over the two other key issues: 1) The consequences of Iraqi attacks using CB weapons and 2) the consequences of bombing Iraq's CB.W plants. Powell said he remained 'less concerned' over the chemical threat because his troops were relatively well protected and many would be in fast-moving shield vehicles. 'But the biologicals worried me,' he recalled, 'and the impact on the public the first time the first casualty keeled over to germ warfare would be terrifying.'

On the day the deadline for Saddam to quit Kuwait was due to expire, Powell sat in his office in the Pentagon drawing up a personal message to Saddam Hussein stating that as far as the Coalition was concerned, only conventional weapons would be used, in strict observance of the Geneva Convention. If Iraq, on the other hand, used chemical or biological weapons in violation of the treaty, they would have to suffer 'horrendous consequences'. The message was never sent. By the time it had passed through the Pentagon channels, war was a reality – and so was the need to decide on whether Iraqi CB.W plants should be bombed.

On that very day, Powell's opposite number in London, Sir David Craig, chairman of the British Chiefs of Staff, telephoned Powell and asked if he intended to bomb the chemical and biological installations. Powell said it was a gamble and admitted there was uncertainty as to whether the bombing would actually destroy any disease agents present or merely release them into the air. The decision was passed up the line to the President himself. The bombings would go ahead.

15

ATMOSPHERIC OVERLOAD

THE PSYCHOLOGICAL EFFECTS of the chemical threat on troops and civilians in the Gulf was immense when Saddam Hussein began firing his dreaded Scud missiles. Yards of speculation would be written: Would Saddam Hussein release the gas and the 'biologicals'? Yes, was the expert opinion of many observers. He had passed the psychological barrier with his gas attacks on the Iranians and the Kurds. Nothing would stop him now . . . especially if he were staring defeat in the face. And what of Israel? If the Scuds began exploding CB warheads over Tel Aviv, could the Israelis really be stopped from responding in kind? The possibilities were all too horrendous to contemplate as the Coalition launched its massive aerial bombardment of Iraq with high-tech missiles of extraordinary power and accuracy, viewed by hundreds of millions of armchair observers watching their television sets around the world. Tension among the troops mounted as they waited for Saddam's response.

When the Scuds started coming, all military and ancillary personnel within range were wearing their protective suits, gas-masks and respirators as a matter of course. After every raid, there was a 20-minute wait that seemed like a lifetime as detection teams checked the atmosphere with their sensors. Thousands of sensors and automatically activated alarm systems were in place to monitor possible CB attacks. The Americans alone had 14,000 alarms sited, most of which had to be tested at least twice a day. There were hundreds of occasions when they went off for reasons other than official tests.

General Sir Peter de la Billiere recounted one such scare that he himself witnessed on the very first night of the Scud attacks. As the second missile exploded, the sensors detected the presence of a chemical agent, but it was explained that it was merely 'a reaction to chemicals released by high explosive rather than to poison gas'. The progress and outcome of the war have now gone into history, and according to the official version the threat of widespread attacks using gas and biological agents did not materialize. That was the line adopted at the end of the war, and still aggressively maintained by the respective defence administrations in Britain and America as these words are being written in 1996:

'There is no evidence in any reports, classified or unclassified, that either chemical or biological agents were deployed at any level in the theatre of war or that there was any exposure of service members to chemical or biological warfare agents.'

Apart from the experiences of the thousands of Gulf War veterans who would claim differently, that statement can be actively challenged from the evidence of a large number of military and ancillary personnel who made on-the-spot reports of experiencing a chemical presence in the war zone, filed at the time with their operational NCOs and, in several cases, recounted under oath for the US Senate hearing chaired by Donald Riegle, 1992–4, and outlined at the beginning of this work. But quite apart from the claims and denials of the presence of chemical or biological agents in the battle zone, there were many other lethal pollutants around, which, combined with the effects of the anti-CB drugs, presented what has been admitted as an incalculable hazard to the troops.

Poisons of all kinds filled the air.

Gusting winds across the deserts of southern Iraq, through Kuwait and into Saudi Arabia carried literally dozens of other unknown and unseen dangers, swirling among the tents, through the bunkers, and across the troop emplacements and the medical villages.

According to a 1994 report by the US General Accounting Office, Gulf War troops were exposed to 21 potential 'reproductive toxicants', any of which might have harmed them as well as their future children. Similarly, another US report identified two dozen separate agents, micro-organisms and pollutants, which carried the potential for creating reproductive disorders. One investigations officer interviewed for this book described it as an atmospheric overload. 'The fumes and chemicals in an area intensely populated by troops began from day one of the build-up of the Coalition response force as they prepared for what Saddam Hussein promised would be the Mother of All Battles – and it just went on from there, uncontrollable, largely unaccountable . . . we were quite literally advancing into the unknown.'

The skies were filled with hundreds of aircraft, from the nimble jet fighters to the huge troop and equipment transporters, flying in and out, day and night, leaving their vapour trails behind them wafting down upon the troops below. On the ground were thousands of vehicles and hundreds of thousands of tons of diesel, which, apart from being used to fuel the hardware, was also spread on the ground to keep down sand. Lubricants and solvents along with the whole inventory of war weaponry all produced their own additives to the dusty, swirling air.

There was also widespread handling of a nerve-gas decontaminant, ethylene glycol monomethyl ether. As soon as equipment began arriving, highly toxic chemical agent resistant coating (CARC) was used to paint hundreds of combat vehicles and equipment. Post-war US investigations would show that civilian workers and several support units may have completed the painting without wearing the necessary respiratory protection.

This was confirmed by British Army corporal Robert Lake, who was 22 when he went to the Gulf. Five years later, he was bedridden, one of the thousands said to be suffering from Gulf War Syndrome. Lake had, like his colleagues, taken the full range of injections and tablets and, like many, had suffered bad reactions. He collapsed and fell into unconsciousness. When he came round, he recovered sufficiently for the medics to declare him fit for work. He was repairing chemical detection equipment. 'No one told me about the dangers. No one said anything about wearing gloves.' Today, Lake's life is hell: headaches, chest pains, continual vomiting and permanent fatigue. His marriage broke up and he now lives with his parents.

Another potential danger to troops lay in the chemicals used to control troublesome local insects and rodents. Common pesticides and organophosphates were used, including DEET, most of which contain elements that, in humans, cause headache, diarrhoea, dizziness, blurred vision, weakness, nausea, cramps, discomfort in the chest, nervousness, sweating, miosis (pinpoint pupils), salivation, pulmonary oedema, uncontrollable muscle twitches, convulsions, coma, and loss of reflexes and sphincter control.

There were virtually no serious, or at least public, studies in Britain of these additional chemical hazards by 1996, but a good deal of research was carried out in America. Studies by a US Medical Task Force concluded that in areas of high concentrations of troops, many may have suffered exposure to pesticides, although there were no reports of acute pesticide poisoning during the war itself. Again unlike the British, the US authorities would set up continued monitoring among veterans to establish the extent of neurophysical disorders, in spite of an apparent reluctance by certain government departments to do so.

James Moss, a scientist with the US Department of Agriculture, found that when cockroaches were exposed to the nerve gas pre-treatment, PB, with a common insect repellent containing DEET, the toxicity of both chemicals multiplied. Moss claimed he pursued his experiments in spite of orders to stop. His contract wasn't renewed when it expired in 1994 and he claims he was kicked out of the department for conducting the research. Since Moss's study, two others – one by the Pentagon itself, the second by Duke University – discovered neural damage in rats and chickens exposed to another chemical cocktail, this one a mixture of PB, DEET and permethrin, an insecticide.

Infectious diseases spread by insects, parasites and rodents were another hazard faced by the troops. Casualties were low but one insect-borne disease, leishmaniasis, was identified as a potential cause in later development of chronic illness. The leishmania species causes skin infections, severe visceral disease and chronic spreading infection that produces no outward signs of its potent effects.

Thirty-one cases of leishmaniasis were recorded by the end of the war. Many more suspected cases followed, but doctors found difficulty in identifying it. The reason, as US Army medical teams discovered in a later study, was that they were effected by a new and virulent strain of leishmania. The investigators noted this 'was a surprising new observation ... and that there may be many additional cases of cryptic infections causing chronic illness that cannot be diagnosed by current parasite isolation methods'.

The admission gave rise to rumours that the new strain may have been part of Iraq's biological effort, producing a new strain of germ that caused potentially fatal internal infections that were not only difficult to diagnose but also virtually untreatable by known medicines. After preliminary clinical studies, the US team concluded that 'more sensitive and less invasive diagnostic methods' were necessary to discover whether or not leishmaniasis was a significant contributor to the chronic unexplained illnesses suffered by many veterans.

With so many troops on the ground, water- and food-borne infections were anticipated to be high. Contaminated lettuce from local vendors, for example, was described as having led to outbreaks of severe diarrhoea. It was also caused by contaminated water, foods or utensils. In addition there were many cases of respiratory ailments that had begun with, or had been aggravated by, the living and working conditions for troops in Saudi Arabia.

Wind-blown sand embedding itself in respiratory tracts and lungs was a major cause. There were others. In one instance, troops occupying a long-vacant Saudi housing area in Al Eskan experienced 'significant rates' of respiratory disease due to the fine sand and dust from accumulated pigeon droppings.

As the war developed, other pollutants came into play. Not the least among them, said the US report, was flying steel, shrapnel and blast overpressures from conventional warfare munitions. But one of the most dangerous exposures came from extensive troop contact with depleted uranium (DU). Operation Desert Storm saw the first-ever battlefield use of armour-piercing weapons tipped with DU.

Munitions fired from tanks and A-10 aircraft consisted of DU kinetic energy penetrators, enabling US forces to 'engage and kill enemy vehicles at standoff ranges that enhanced their own safety'. Post-war concern centred around the possibility that expended DU projectiles, or the dust and fragments from them, posed a potential danger, a lingering hazard to troops on the battlefield. A number of Coalition soldiers came into direct contact with exploded DU shells when their vehicles were hit by friendly fire, resulting in DU shrapnel wounds. Nine soldiers in a British unit were killed in one such strike by a US A-10.

In other friendly fire incidents, 15 Bradley Fighting Vehicles and 9 Abrams tanks were mistakenly attacked and struck by DU munitions. Crew members who survived sustained wounds and retained fragments of presumed DU shrapnel. An initial survey by the Army Office of the Surgeon General revealed that 22 soldiers had imbedded fragments of DU.

Another 27 were given first aid for minor wounds in the battlefield and may also have experienced DU contamination of wounds. All the survivors were to become subject to a long-term follow-up study, to examine possible chronic effects from embedded DU fragments.

All these hazards were combined with the effects of the indisputable wind-borne fall-out from the bombing of Saddam's chemical and biological factories, for which clear evidence has been provided from numerous sources. Unlike the British, who continued to deny there was any such dangerous fall-out, this was finally accepted by the US Department of Defense after studying reports from a 180-strong Czech decontamination team, brought to the Gulf to aid Saudi Arabia.

To this huge array of poisons were added the airborne effects of the two ultimate catastrophes brought about as the war ended. Astonished television viewers across the world watched with horror as Iraqi troops made one last defiant gesture as they fled – setting fire to 700 Kuwaiti oil wells and sending choking smoke, flames and fumes into the air.

And then came the last great turkey-shoot of the war, as Allied aircraft bombed and shot up the thousands of lorries, cars and military wagons stolen and commandeered by panic-stricken Iraqi soldiers, a scene that remains one of the most vivid memories of Desert Storm. The incredible carnage of Matla Ridge added its own highly toxic pollutants to the already heavily laden air.

These final acts of the war merely augmented the vast array of harmful chemicals, fumes and naturally produced health hazards that had confronted the Coalition troops, and especially the British and American contingents, from the day they began arriving. Evidence of their effects on animal life lay all around, with thousands of dead birds and rodents, many camels and donkeys. Porton Down scientists know very well what dangers the troops faced by the simple act of breathing in during those months of build-up and in the aftermath of the war.

Along with their American counterparts, British scientists arranged for the collection of planeloads of material for testing. They included air sample test results, captured and discarded equipment, protective gear used by both Iraqi and Coalition forces – and even dead animals. In fact, anything from the war that would provide useful research data was gathered up and sent home. This detritus would form the basis of a wide-ranging programme of tests and experiments, combined with the need to find clues about what Saddam Hussein actually possessed., and may have used, in the way of CB weaponry. The hoard collected by the Porton-linked teams, moving anonymously among the carnage and the troop emplacements in unmarked desert suits, was flown back to Wiltshire for months of tests and experiments. The results remain secret in Britain.

Again, detailed analysis is only available in the US, where many separate studies were begun as the troops stood down and began to return home, bringing with them a host of mysterious ailments and chronic illnesses, the extent of which would take years to materialize. By then, it was abundantly clear that a large proportion of the Coalition troops had, from almost the very beginning, been encapsulated in an environmental nightmare, exposed daily to a diversity of pollutants that were, either individually or in combination with others, as lethal as any weapon and far more insidious.

As many have been heard to say: 'At least with a wound – you can see what the problem is.' Their wounds were not always visible, although they were not long in knocking down their victims, first with a trickle of reported 'unexplained' illness among veterans, building into a massive crescendo of complaints.

In the beginning, they were largely dismissed by the military and their examiners in the medical profession. It was probably some form of Desert Fever, they said, linked to exhaustion, psychological problems and even, in some cases, sheer malingering. Soon, the collective of illnesses would become universally known under the all-embracing and often misleading term of Gulf War Syndrome. The common thread that linked the veterans was denial by officialdom and authority that their troubles emanated from the war.

The many tragic case histories recorded in Britain and the US speak for themselves, and perhaps the only truth that the spokespersons for the various military authorities and government departments on both sides of the Atlantic continued to utter like a record stuck in a groove was that there was 'no single, identifiable disease that can be discerned among Gulf War veterans'.

That statement itself may be considered ridiculously immature, naive in the extreme, arrogant and irresponsible. All those words, punctuated with expletives born out of rage, would be used by the crippled and suffering multitude to describe the reaction of those in authority.

Insensitive comments from Britain's portly Armed Forces Minister, Nicholas Soames, would cause perhaps the greatest antagonism among sufferers. Without a hint of compassion, he declared, and repeated time and again, that the veterans' claims amounted to no more than a 'mixture of unsubstantiated rumour [and] incorrect information . . . there is no evidence of any medical condition peculiar to service in the Gulf.'

He deftly avoided the crucial issue. There was no single illness, simply because there could not be. The range of poisons, chemicals and drugs to which veterans were subjected made that virtually impossible. According to distinguished medical opinion emerging in the United States, these ailments resulted from a combination of pollutants and chemicals whose effects required precise medical study. It was not only a nonsense to dismiss them as a potential cause of illness, it was an insult to the sufferers to do so.

Hilary Jones was able to take a more precise view of her ailments than most. She had spent 16 years in the Queen Alexandra Royal Nursing Corps before she retired in 1988 at the age of 37 with the rank of major. Three years later, she volunteered to return to service when the Gulf War looked imminent. Her knowledge was welcomed. In the final days of her service she had been researching a manual for nursing aides in modern warfare situations. The reality, as she discovered on her arrival in the Gulf in January 1991, barely approached a 'modern' scenario. The British field hospital and medical facilities were old fashioned and out of date. Some of the beds had been saved from World War I and she had been given no prior warning that the facilities for treating casualties were woefully inadequate.

Like the others, she lined up for the course of injections against anthrax, hepatitis B, yellow fever and the rest and wondered how her immune system would cope with this onslaught. The vaccines were administered in a fairly haphazard way, and there was no question of 'informed consent'. Very soon there were queues of soldiers who were suffering from flu-like symptoms, high temperatures, headaches, chest infections and so on. 'It could have been a viral infection,' Major Jones concluded, 'or reaction to the injections, or even the result of biological agents released by Saddam Hussein.'

She suffered the effects herself. She was ill from the very first week of her arrival and her malaise never cleared up during the whole time she was there, which was for the duration. When she came home, she had a severe cough, which she couldn't shift. Within weeks, the effects became more severe. She began to suffer sleeplessness, and then slowly her general stamina grew weaker and weaker. The chest infection became worse, and she developed thrush, which she had never had before. Then, her speech became affected, and she developed a stammer. The fevers and the severe headaches came next; it was getting worse.

'I knew there was something wrong,' she said, 'and I got angry when my GP asked me if I had menopausal problems – a woman of a certain age. Eventually, he took some blood samples and discovered my white cells showed my immune system was reacting to something unknown.'

Worse, her whole life was falling apart. Her relationship with her boyfriend broke up. She was suffering memory lapses and taking time off work. Then the college where she taught made her redundant and she faced the prospect of perhaps never being able to work again. Her mortgage and the rest of her bills still needed paying and gradually, as her condition deteriorated, she cashed in most of her financial assets, such as several life assurance policies, simply to exist.

Within two years of her return from the Gulf, Hilary Jones was a virtual cripple, struck down by sheer fatigue. Even the daily household chores became a major undertaking. 'For a woman who was always bursting with energy and now supposedly at the prime of life, it was absolute hell. The utter bone-aching exhaustion left me no choice but to stay in bed days on end.'

The Ministry of Defence showed little sympathy, or even belief in her condition. She was undoubtedly assigned to the ranks of the Yuppie 'flu brigade about whom there had been so much misplaced malignity. For two years, she faced the brick-wall intransigence of the Ministry of Defence, and listened furiously to the repeated declarations of the Armed Forces Minister Nicholas Soames that there was no evidence of any such malady as Gulf War Syndrome.

In 1995, and by then confined to a wheelchair, she faced financially dire prospects, having cashed in her last insurance policy. She gave evidence to the first – and, to that point, the only – British government inquiry into Gulf War Syndrome, an all-party Defence Select Committee. Her articulate and moving speech convinced several among the inquiry team who admitted they had been sceptical about the claims of Major Jones and others like her. They were in agreement that the attitude of Mr Soames's ministry had been appalling, incredible and grossly inadequate. Major Jones, retiring to the privacy of the home that has become a virtual prison, was able to put it more succinctly: 'They are absolute bastards.'

Such words seemed to have little effect on Mr Soames and his colleagues at the MoD. Not long after the stinging reaction of the all-party committee, in November 1995, he continued to ignore the anger and the incredulity when he responded to a question in the House of Commons by Labour MP Angela Eagle. She had asked him why he had done nothing to counter criticism levelled at his ministry. He replied with a typically fatuous comment, aimed at scoring a party political point, which has made Gulf War victims spit with rage at the very mention of his name: 'The Honourable Lady is making mischief when she alleges in any way that there is any such thing as Gulf War Syndrome.'

Nigel Thompson, unlike some, could not exclaim his anger in loud voice. In fact, four years after completing his service in the Gulf he could not speak at all. At the time of the war, he fitted the 'average combatant' profile exactly when he went out there as a helicopter weapons officer with the Fleet Air Arm. He was fit, healthy, 34 years old – the average age of the 700,000 force – and eager to serve his country. Like most, doing his duty came above all else. He was in the Gulf for the duration, serving initially in Saudi Arabia and, after the Coalition offensive to reclaim Kuwait, saw service pretty well all over the theatre of operations.

He had all the jabs and as a weapons officer was in close contact with all the facets of the war. He returned home in the summer of 1991 and began complaining about problems down the left side of his body. He was seen by a Royal Navy doctor who could not pinpoint a specific illness. As the months passed, his condition deteriorated. He had difficulty in walking, suffered memory loss and soon signs of speech difficulties began to appear.

Almost two years after his service in the Gulf, he was diagnosed as suffering from motor neurone disease, after specialists examined him in January 1993. Within a year, he was virtually immobile without help, bound to a wheelchair and facing the agonising trauma of this progressive disease, which leads to chronic degeneration of muscle co-ordination. By the end of the year, his voice had gone completely. He had to substitute the act of speaking with a voice synthesizer, using a keyboard to activate the Americanised electronic speech.

By then his wife, Samantha, had given birth to their daughter Hannah who appears to be normal; stories of defects among Gulf War babies were just beginning to emerge. 'We had long ago decided we could not take the risk of having any more children,' says Samantha. 'The fact is, I know Nigel is going to die. We have been told that he cannot expect to survive more than two years. It is very traumatic for both of us to see him wasting away, especially when I remember how he was – a fine, active and handsome boy.'

As in the case of so many others, the MoD refused to accept that Nigel Thompson's condition was related to the Gulf War. The same applied to Edward Blench, who was a healthy 29-year-old physical training instructor and veteran of the Falklands War and of service in Northern Ireland. When he was shipped out to the Gulf, he was a lance corporal in the First Armoured Division HG. He had the jabs, and then became one of the team that did the jabbing.

He estimated he must have injected 25,000 troops for bubonic plague and anthrax, working 18 hours a day and travelling out to the encampments. He was told he might witness a few minor reactions, flu-like symptoms. In fact, he sawa great many bad reactions, with men collapsing and being evacuated as casualties.

Apart from his own responses to the NAPS and the local fumes, especially from the petro-chemical fires, Blench suffered an accident two days before he was due to leave the Gulf. He was burning some rubbish when it suddenly exploded. He was temporarily blinded and taken to hospital. Although his sight returned, he never fully recovered. He saw three specialists, one Norwegian, one American and one British. They all suggested that his eyes had been damaged by some form of toxin. When he came home, the breathlessness and respiratory problems began.

Asthma was diagnosed, although he had never suffered from it in his life. He failed the basic fitness test to be a physical training instructor. Blisters had begun appearing on his scalp, he experienced terrible perspiration, particularly at night, he lost the feeling in his legs. 'I began to get severe mood swings,' said Blench, 'and became aggressive. My family has to bear the brunt of that. I put it down to the NAPS, the vaccinations and the petro-chemical fires. I am also convinced that, in spite of MoD denials, Saddam used chemical warfare – that the Scud warheads were full of it.' Blench left the army and his £300-a-week job. He found himself to be virtually unemployable, and was reduced to delivering newspapers to make ends meet. In October 1993, he applied for a war pension. Two and a half years later, he was still awaiting a decision.

Paul Ash, who was with the Royal Fusiliers in the Gulf, read of Edward Blench's troubles in a newspaper. His own symptoms were very similar to Blench's and those of others he had heard about. He suffered joint pains, stomach problems, constant nausea, exhaustion. His wife complained he had become aggressive and forgetful. He was not the man he had been. Ash telephoned Eddie Blench and they had a long discussion. The upshot was that they formed the Gulf War Veterans Association and began to achieve increasing media interest until finally they were able to arrange a national conference in 1994. 'We received an enormous response,' said Blench. 'We had men and women from across the board – officers to privates – asking us for help. As we studied their symptoms, we discovered we all had at least three which were common to all of us, sometimes more. Above all, though, was the sheer anger at the way we had been subjected to all those drugs they pumped into us, often without telling the men what they were and, in the end, just ignored the very obvious effects. There have been many deaths among veterans, and suicides. I know of seven. But no follow-up studies were even contemplated in Britain – absolutely nothing. What it boiled down to was this: The Gulf War was a balls-up because we poisoned our own troops.'

In the early years after the war, individual cases of Gulf War Syndrome threw up a diversity of ailments. One of the first group studies to formulate some kind of pattern was conducted at the Veterans' Affairs Hospital in Allen Park, Michigan. There, doctors treating patients from a nearby military base began to discover many similarities among veterans and produced the most comprehensive findings to that point. Between them hospital doctors examined 250 Gulf veterans. More than half had muscular pain; skin rashes; and respiratory problems. A third had persistent diarrhoea, loss of memory, night sweats and many had lost their hair.

There was another aspect of the Michigan study. Military Police veterans had come into close contact with Iraqi troops, in addition to being exposed to oil-fire smoke and other chemical hazards. For four months, they had searched and herded thousands of Iraqi PoWs, hand-patting each up and down the trouser legs and across the back and sides. They escorted convoys of Iraqi prisoners from the front lines back 50 miles to a processing compound dubbed Log Base Nellie. The 1776th MP sometimes rounded up Iraqi stragglers behind the lines and flushed hold-outs from bunkers.

The prisoners were put into a barbed-wire compound and fed. Company medical officer Curtis Seaborn treated the sick among them. 'Many hadn't eaten for days,' he recalled. 'They had all kinds of ailments and were riddled with infestations like lice and fleas and rashes. Some clearly had nervous system problems before we got them. Some had hallucinations. Some twitched and shook. Others would go into convulsions.'

After treatment they would be sent to another camp at Hafr al Battin in Saudi Arabia, a tent-city three-quarters of a mile wide and a mile long, operated in part by the 301st MPs, housing almost 20,000 PoWs. Staff Sgt Bill Lickman often broke up fights between prisoners scrabbling for food. 'Every day, I had some type of physical contact,' said Lickman who, on his return to the US erupted in chronic skin rashes and diarrhoea.

The camp was also less than an hour downwind of the Kuwaiti oil fires and of bombed Iraqi chemical plants. Captain Tom Howko, the former commanding officer of the 1776th, recalls that after oil clouds had hung over Hafr al Battin for a day, oil began dripping from the lamp posts on the town's main street. On some days, the sun was completely obliterated and temperatures fell from 103°F to the 70s in minutes.

Sergeant Jim Combs of the same company said that when he landed back in Indiana in May 1991, he checked into a hotel in Indianapolis and he had to take three baths before he got clean. His wife, Kathleen, had to call room service to get the tub scrubbed out because black oil tar kept coming out of his pores and leaving a black film on the tub.

The Michigan study also revealed an increase in aggressive behaviour among returning veterans. One of them, John Copeman, who was living with his girlfriend, attacked her parents and beat them to death with a baseball bat at their home in South Rockwood, Michigan. Copeman then set the house on fire and ran from police. He got as far as the Ambassador Bridge. He jumped from the span into the freezing waters of Detroit River but survived when he was picked up by a passing mail boat. He is now serving life in prison for murder. 'When we talk about it, we talk about not wanting to do "The Copeman Thing",' Seaborn said.

By mid-1995, there were 30 separate studies under way in America, with teams of researchers looking into the effects of the pollutants of the Gulf War on the troops. In Britain, there was only one: a limited pilot study, funded by charity and initiated by Dr Goran Jamal, consultant at the Institute of Neurological Sciences at the Southern General Hospital, Glasgow. His team examined what he admitted was a small sample of 14 veterans, 12 men and 2 women, randomly selected from a computerized list of veterans from all over Britain.

In his first report, published in April 1996, Dr Jamal supported the view of researchers in America who had discovered that giving pyridostogmine bromide (PB) at the dose equivalent to that which the Gulf soldiers had been given had caused a breakdown of skeletal muscles after exercise in rats. Furthermore, although the toxic and biological effects of pesticides and other substances to which troops were exposed were well known, their combined effects were not.

The results of Dr Jamal's tests on the 14 veterans were compared with the results of tests on a control group of 13 healthy civilians.

Established procedures for assessing nerve function in the limbs, muscles, brain and spinal chord were carried out. In each of the 14 veterans, Dr Jamal's team discovered problems and dysfunction in the nervous system, particularly in the arms and legs. The results were more than adequate to provide the basis for 'urgent research' in a larger group of veterans.

16

STILLBIRTHS, MISCARRIAGES, DEFORMITIES

THOUSANDS OF GULF War veterans were falling ill and their medical ailments received widespread publicity. The authorities continued to dismiss them as unfortunate but coincidental to the war, even as more disturbing trends began to appear: sickness among the families of the veterans – their wives and then their children. Among those affected was Christine Turnbull whose husband, Richie, was an RAF corporal with 17 years' service behind him. He volunteered to go to the Gulf because he believed in the cause. He had three previous commendations to his credit. He was posted to Dharan in Saudi Arabia and joined the queue for the jabs and the tablets. He had both the NAPS and BATS, which he described as 'massive doses of antibiotics'.

He took the NAPS every 6 hours for 47 days, and he was 'totally shocked' when he heard Nicholas Soames admit to the House of Commons that they weren't even licensed. He wasn't sure of the complete list of vaccines that went into his arm; he knew they included vaccines for anthrax, bubonic plague and whooping cough. Dosage was supposed to depend on weight – except that he was never weighed. Nor was there informed consent. The reaction was immediate and it lasted ten days – fever and breathing difficulties.

Turnbull recalls vividly a Scud attack on the night of 20 January 1991 when the alarms for chemical agents went off. He is convinced the Scuds carried a chemical warhead. Soon after he returned from the

Gulf, he began getting chest infections, one after the other, accompanied by severe bouts of coughing. Then came short-term memory loss, and allergies to petrol fumes, brandy and perfume – most strong-smelling items. He was prescribed an inhaler permanently and can no longer swim one length of a swimming pool whereas once he used to complete a great number a day.

But then Richie's wife, Christine, became distressed. She discovered a lump in her armpit and though tests for breast cancer proved negative, the lump remained. It is caused by a swollen lymph gland, which doctors put down to some form of infection. Her periods began to become erratic and her ovulation became impaired. She was not alone in her experiences. Many others wives in Britain experienced the same problems and formed themselves into a support group.

Christine and Richard Turnbull were among three British couples who were included in a survey of Gulf War veterans and their partners by Dr Edward Hyman from New Orleans. Five hundred couples were studied. In almost all the cases, problems had arisen among the wives, many reporting excrutiatingly painful vaginal infections. Case histories in America reported by specialists who have treated Gulf veterans put the cause of the passed-on problems to a general overload of chemical pollutants, that the men's bodily fluids were actually toxic.

Several wives had complained that their husbands' semen caused their skin to blister. The study by Dr Hyman also identified abnormal bacteria in the urinary tracts of a large number of the veterans he studied. Similar findings have become widespread among the veteran community, said Dr Charles Jackson, staff physician for the Veterans Administration Medical Centre in Tuskegee, Alabama. There was also a large number of wives with mirror-image complaints of those of their husbands, such as fatigue and respiratory problems.

A high incidence of miscarried pregnancies and several stillbirths were recorded and then there began emerging one more terrible trend. Even as these studies on couples were beginning, children of the Gulf War veterans were being born with devastating and tragic deformities.

In the first major inquiry into the unexplained illnesses of Gulf War Veterans set up in 1993 by US Senator Donald Riegle for his Senate committee, his staff sent out questionnaires to a large number of US veterans. One question asked if there were any signs of birth defects among children born to veterans since the war. Of those who responded and had had children after the hostilities, a remarkable 65 per cent confirmed some form of birth defect or problems with their children's immune systems.

No similar inquiry had even been considered in Britain at that time. Instead the MoD was still adamant in its denial of pretty well anything and everything connected with Gulf War Syndrome, and this attitude was maintained even as the stories of severe birth defects and deformities, of stillbirths and miscarriages began to appear.

Kathryn and John Elliot had two children born after the war; both developed heart defects and suffer other problems. John, a corporal in the Royal Logistics Corps, was among the first to go to the Gulf. He arrived there in October 1990 and did not set foot back on British soil until the end of May 1991. What ill-effects he suffered from the vaccines and tablets were soon shrugged off and a year after his return Kathryn became pregnant. The birth of their daughter, Rebecca, was normal but at five weeks she began to have breathing problems.

Doctors diagnosed a hole in the heart and predicted that it would close. It did not. Rebecca's lungs also gave cause for concern, one of them persistently filling with fluid. Before she was a year old, she was operated on for the heart condition. It was then that Kathryn realized she was pregnant again. She was told she was having twins but one week after being given what should have been joyous news, she miscarried and lost one of them. The other survived and Jessica was born in 1994. Just before her birth, Rebecca fell ill again, and was rushed to hospital for an emergency operation for the removal of part of her bowel.

Jessica was quite jaundiced when she was born – 'very yellow,' said Kathryn. But she and John were told not to worry because Rebecca's condition was a one-in-a-million situation, which would never happen again in the same family. Sadly, that proved not to be the case. Jessica's yellow pigment did not decrease and she was admitted to hospital. Local doctors in Glasgow seemed unsure of what was wrong and she was taken to a specialist paediatric unit for a scan. The million-to-one chance that couldn't happen again, had happened again. Jessica had a hole in the heart and a narrowing of the main artery to the lungs. They operated immediately and Kathryn and John feared they were going to lose her.

Kathryn and John were both given blood tests but they were told their blood showed no abnormalities. They looked at the family history; nothing like it had occurred anywhere. Immediate relations had almost 20 children between them without defect. Kathryn has her own very positive theory: 'While Jessica was in hospital a young man approached me in the ward. He had a child in the same hospital. His baby had a heart condition similar to ours. He, it transpired, was also a soldier who had served in the Gulf. I am convinced there is a link. Definitely.'

Like many other veteran couples, Kathryn and John have decided to have no more children. To be certain of that, John has had a vasectomy. 'I don't think he will ever come to terms with what has happened,' said Kathryn.

Baby Kennedi Clark was born without a thyroid and without daily treatment of hormones would die. She was also seriously disfigured by another congenital condition called hemangiomas, benign tumors made of tangled blood vessels. They began appearing within a few weeks of her birth . . . on her face, in her throat and spinal canal; her speech was impaired and her life threatened. There is no permanent treatment for her condition. Laser surgery disposes of them temporarily but they grow back. What is worse, they attract the unwanted stares of strangers, some of whom stop and ask what is wrong.

Neither her mother Shana nor her father Darrell can answer that question.

Their baby was conceived after Darrell returned from the Gulf where he served as a US paratrooper. He came back with Gulf 'flu', which never went away. He has asthma and recurring pneumonia. He tested positive to radiation exposure, from the DU missile tips, but, like other parents, Shana and Darrell were told that there was no proof that their baby's defects are linked to Darrell's service in the Gulf. 'I know in my heart that was the cause of it,' said Darrell.

Support groups were soon being founded and what researchers call 'clusters' were being discovered. Melanie Ayers, 30, from Fort Bragg, North Carolina, started one informal group at the US Army base there when her five-month-old son, Michael, died of congestive heart failure in November 1993. Michael was conceived after his father, Glenn, returned from action as a battery commander in the Gulf. One night, the child woke screaming, his arms and legs ice-cold. He was found to be suffering from a mitral-valve defect.

Melanie soon began to learn of many other parents whose post-Gulf War children had been born with abnormalities; all were desperate for information and, crucially, wanted advice on whether they should ever again dare risk pregnancy. With Kim Sullivan, an artillery captain's wife whose infant son, Matthew, had died of a rare liver cancer, Melanie founded a group for fellow sufferers.

Among the many who joined was Connie Hanson, wife of an Army sergeant, Paul Hanson, also from Fort Bragg. Their son, Jayce, was an especially tragic case. He was born with multiple deformities: his hands were attached to his shoulders and his legs were deformed and twisted. he had a hole in the heart, ear problems and a blood condition similar to haemophilia. For all his problems, Jayce grew into a cheerful boy with a cherubic face and lively personality; but he required a daunting array of medical treatments.

In 1995, soon after Jayce's third birthday, his team of doctors decided that in order for him to walk, both his legs would have to be amputated so that they could fit artificial limbs. It was an agonising decision, but one for which there was virtually no alternative. The operation went ahead and within a few weeks Jayce was walking on his prosthetics. 'I think,' said Connie, 'the double amputation was the worst part of this nightmare that has befallen us. Afterwards he had night terrors and we wondered what would become of us all. But he pulled through it.'

Now, Jayce and his family face the years of agony that lie ahead, and the bitterness of it all comes in waves of indignation, especially when they hear people in authority denying that there is a connection between deformities in children and the Gulf War. Sergeant Hanson has no doubt that there is. He has his own problems, firstly from taking the NAPS tablets, which caused him severe headaches. He was also in the area of the oil fires. 'I still have my own troubles, with joint pains, bleeding gums and headaches. But my main concern is not for me but to discover what caused those terrible things in our son. I am sure it was because of the war. Whoever is at fault should at least accept the responsibility and make it right.'

Studies of clustering have produced strong evidence of previously rare illnesses and deformities among the children of Gulf War parents. One of the studies was undertaken by the Association of Birth Defect Children, which found many similarities among the children's deformities, especially among heart defects. Another was the very rare Goldenhar's Syndrome, a birth defect of internal organs that usually strikes 1 in 26,000. Two cases were found in Britain and 12 in America among the children of Gulf War veterans. The Association's study began tracking possible clusters and its director Betty Mekdeci found it significant that not one of the parents in the survey had a family history of those types of birth defects.

By mid-1995, the many studies of ailments affecting Gulf War veterans, their wives and their children under way in America were producing alarming data. The first one to report was that of the Senate Committee under the chairmanship of Donald Riegle, in 1994. His inquiry lasted almost two years, during which his team interviewed 600 veterans and called military and intelligence chiefs before them.

At the end of it, Riegle pulled no punches. His summary of the findings was music to the ears of veterans in Britain, America, Canada and France who had faced government stone-walling since Gulf War Syndrome first began to emerge. And while Britain, even then, continued to respond to the veterans with the same 'no evidence' reply, it is worth recording a few of Riegle's points, especially as there was no similar voice in Britain able to speak with the same informed authority.

> My inquiry began when a number of veterans contacted my office to complain that they were not receiving adequate attention to the myriad of medical symptoms that they were suffering from. Many of them were being treated symptomatically, with no long-lasting, positive effects on their health. Others were being referred for psychiatric evaluation because personnel in the Department of Veterans' Affairs were at a loss to explain their physical symptoms. These Gulf War veterans are reporting muscle and joint pain, memory loss, intestinal and heart problems, fatigue, nasal congestion, urinary urgency, diarrhoea, twitching, rashes, sores, and a number of other symptoms. They began experiencing these multiple symptoms during and after, often many months after, their tour of duty in the Gulf.
>
> I might say that, in virtually every case, these veterans were in excellent physical condition when they went over to the Gulf. In fact, under the voluntary Army arrangements, you have to be in exceptionally good condition today just to qualify for service in the Armed Forces, and that was particularly true for many who were asked to serve in the Gulf War. So we're talking about people with exceptionally strong health profiles before their service in the Gulf.

Riegle went on to explain how the Department of Defense, when first approached by his committee's investigators, contended that there was no evidence that forces were exposed to chemical warfare agents. However, on 7 September 1993, a Defense Department medical official admitted to Riegle's chief investigator, James Tuite, that the issue of CB.W agent exposure had not been explored because it was the position of 'military intelligence' that such exposures never occurred.

It was then they learned that the Pentagon had secretly accepted a report that a Czech chemical decontamination unit had detected the nerve gas sarin in areas of northern Saudi Arabia during the early phases of the Gulf War. They had attributed the detections to fall-out from Coalition bombing of Iraqi chemical warfare agent production facilities. After analysing the results of the Czech report, the Department of Defense concluded that the detections were unrelated to the mysterious health problems and produced a supporting view from Dr Graham Pearson, director of Porton Down, identified by the DoD as the 'world's leading authority' on chemical warfare. Riegle went on:

> We established that, contrary to the Department of Defense assertions, there is clear evidence that the chemical agents were detected at sufficient levels to harm troops. Second, the chemical agent detectors used by forces during the Gulf War were not sufficiently sensitive to detect sustained low levels of chemical agent and to monitor personnel for contamination.
>
> US Army Material Safety Data Sheets, called MSDS, indicate that chronic exposure to levels of over 1/10,000th milligram per cubic meter of sarin is hazardous and requires the use of protective equipment. The minimum amount of chemical agent required to activate the automatic chemical agent detection alarm that was commonly used during the war was 1,000 times greater than this amount.
>
> In other words, the levels for the alarms used in the war were set at a rate 1,000 times greater than the actual level that we know from other military records to be damaging and hazardous to people if they are exposed to them over a period of time. Next, we had detailed weather reports and information from satellite imagery which confirmed that during much of the war, the smoke plumes from the Coalition bombings were moving directly over troop positions.
>
> Our inquiries also revealed that the United States did not have effective biological agent detectors deployed with the capability to confirm whether or not troops were being exposed to biological agents. In response to direct questioning, a DoD official said that the department was withholding classified information on the exposure of forces to biological materials. We also discovered evidence that the United States shipped biological materials to Iraq which contributed to the Iraqi biological warfare programme.

Riegle uncovered other evidence that the Pentagon and the British MoD had not cared to make public at the time. In addition to the tens of thousands of other chemical munitions discovered by UN inspectors after the war, 28 Scud chemical warheads containing the chemical nerve agent sarin were found and destroyed. According to a Department of Defense official, these warheads had been obtained from the former Soviet Union.

With all the evidence that his investigators uncovered, and the testimony of veterans and defence chiefs, Riegle said there was an emerging pattern of information that required an 'immediate additional investigative effort' – especially on behalf of the thousands of veterans and their families who had suffered dire consequences from the war. Riegle called for the immediate release of all classified information relating to Iraqi chemical and biological warfare programmes and to the detection or discovery of chemical, chemical precursor, or biological warfare-related materials. 'It's time to put it all out into the light of day, make a thorough and detailed study on all Gulf War veterans – on all of them – to determine the origins and causes of the illnesses and the reports of transmission of the syndromes to family members. We have not had a situation like this before. We cannot have a situation where veterans, who have served their country, have come home and who are sick, and watch the military establishment, in effect, walk away from them. The story was always the same – veterans were challenged about their mental state. This is not a mental problem with the veterans. It may be a mental problem over at the Defense Department. It is not a mental problem with the veterans.'

By the time Riegle had concluded his investigation, more than 45,000 American veterans had come forward. The Clinton administration adopted most of his recommendations. They put up millions of dollars to fund research, ordered a full epidemiological study and set up helplines, support groups and therapy. Congress voted a system of *ex-gratia* payments in cases of hardship, pending the results of a full investigation. Meanwhile, teams of lawyers are preparing a mass of civil actions.

In Britain, the response was woefully tardy. Close to 1,500 veterans registered with lawyers as having had personal or family-related illness – including 40 cases of children born with defects. A group of British solicitors was formed to handle their cases, and pursue the Ministry of Defence and others for pensions and compensation. Hilary Meredith, from the Manchester solicitors involved in the bulk of the cases, made regular television appearances as the campaign for recognition progressed – yet seemingly failed to deflect the denials of Minister Soames and his department. Almost two years would pass from the time of Riegle's onslaught against the Pentagon before the British government reacted to stinging criticism from its own Commons sub-committee high level medical opinion. In February 1996, they announced a formal inquiry into 'so-called' Gulf War Syndrome – but it would be three years before any conclusions were to be reached.

What haunts the campaigners is the spectre of the Agent Orange. Litigation for compensation took almost ten years to come to court, and $184 million was won by the claimants, largely ex-servicemen, but the long-term health studies continued for more than two decades. Some observers concluded that the military on both sides of the Atlantic had no intention of making life easy for the present-day campaigners.

Pentagon reaction to Senator Riegle's demand for the de-classification of secret documents, for example, was somewhat cynical. It announced it was screening some 15.9 million pages of DoD documents and 2 million pages of intelligence reports to see what could be released. Of that number, the Pentagon estimated that around 1 million pages would eventually be released. But if the first 7,000 sheets posted by the beginning of 1996, and scanned for this book, are anything to go by it will be a fatuous exercise. Most of them amounted to nothing more significant than a note to the milkman.

Similarly, any British inquiry is unlikely to get access to secret documents, or the even more secret findings of Porton Down studies. As Hilary Meredith pointed out: 'It should not be allowed to drag on. Our people have already put up with years of anguish and pain. Some will not live to see the outcome. We have already had several deaths, and a suicide. The evidence is all around us. Deformed babies, a dozen reported miscarriages, two stillbirths that we know of in Britain.'

A central plank of any legal action the Gulf War veterans may take would be medical and scientific opinion as well as what happened in the theatre of operations. Porton Down's Dr Graham Pearson's view had already been made clear in a Department of Defense memo, that it was 'not useful to worry if Allied forces ever encountered chemical agents . . . because even if they did, such exposure would not have produced Gulf War disease.' The words 'no evidence' were repeated often by Pearson and others and angered the sick veterans like nothing else.

17

FORGOTTEN HEROES

THE BREATHLESS, SPLUTTERING voice on the answering machine that greets telephone callers to the home of Michael Roche, formerly of the Royal Engineers and now in ill-health and unemployed, is one of ironic, black humour: 'This is the Porton Down Division of British gas. Please leave a message . . . but don't make it too long, I might not last.' The words are tinged with bitterness.

As first reports of Gulf War Syndrome began to emerge, Roche was himself still fighting for Ministry of Defence recognition that he had been permanently disabled by the experiments he joined at Porton Down almost 30 years earlier. He noticed there were many similarities among the symptoms described by soldiers returning from the Gulf and those who had been exposed to chemicals at Porton and elsewhere. Apart from running his personal campaign, he had built up an archive on other examples.

By coincidence, the whole question of human guinea-pigs had come to public attention a year before the Gulf War began, when a hard-hitting documentary film, *Keen As Mustard*, was shown in Australia (but not in Britain, where documents relating to the incident are still classified). It focused on the Allied mustard gas trials on Brook Island, near Innisfail, Queensland, in December 1943, conducted by Allied scientists from Porton Down and Edgewood. As we have seen, Australian soldiers were recruited as 'observers' – as they were then called – to test respirators, protective clothing and ointments as the Allies prepared for the Nazi gas bombardment that never materialized.

One of those soldiers was Tommy Mitchell, the young commando who was in the Aussie unit sent back on to the island without masks and protective clothing a few hours after six American B-24 Liberators had dropped bombs charged with mustard gas. Years later, he began to suffer severe lung problems and then heart trouble. In 1981, Mitchell and a number of his surviving colleagues launched a series of claims for compensation against the Australian government. It took almost nine years to win their battle, aided by the prodding of the television documentary researchers.

In March 1989, Australia filed a little-noticed document at the Conference on Disarmament in Geneva, at which nations had been asked to declare their stocks of chemical weapons. The Australian government, though never a CW manufacturer, was forced to admit that it had 'become aware of a small stock of chemical weapons' in Central Queensland, which had been left over from World War II. Almost immediately, the government ordered its lawyers to settle the outstanding compensation claims by World War II veterans, including that of Tommy Mitchell, who received a payment of £18,000. The Australian government also relaxed its rules for all other claims. The Director of Compensation for the Department of Veteran Affairs announced that the burden of proof would fall on the department to disprove any claim, rather than the other way about.

Around the same time, the issue was raised by veterans in Canada who had taken part in similar experiments in that country – again, linked to Porton Down. Canada's stance was the same as that of Britain. Veterans who could demonstrate that they had been exposed to chemical weapons during tests and had become incapacitated as a result could claim disability benefit – but not compensation. They still had to prove they were involved in the tests and therein lay the problem – and the get-out clause for the authorities. Because they were conducted in secret, records had either not been kept or had been destroyed. And so it was virtually impossible for veterans to establish their claims.

The same applied in America, until four World War II veterans in Florida read of the Australian case and launched their own legal action. The response was predictably the same as it had been for the previous 50 years: no documents, no proof, no cash. They took their case to Congressman Porter Goss, of Florida. He attempted to introduce private legislation on behalf of the four veterans, and in the wake of the publicity many more who had remained silent began to come forward.

In June 1991, the US Department of Veterans' Affairs announced it would relax the burden of proof for certain conditions, including respiratory problems, chronic bronchitis, emphysema, asthma and various eye complaints. By then, the first indications of Gulf War Syndrome were already beginning, and the fight of the ageing US veterans was far from over. Still obstructed by the fence of secrecy and the lack of documentary evidence, they battled on. The National Academy of Sciences (NAS) took up their cause and investigated. A panel of eminent scientists produced a hard-hitting report castigating the Veterans' Affairs Department for dragging its heels, taking almost 50 years to acknowledge the problem even existed, failing to anticipate long-term health problems, and for ruthlessly threatening imprisonment to any one of them who broke the rule of secrecy.

The NAS report called on the US government to track down survivors of the thousands of men who had been exposed to chemical weapons from World War II and in post-war experiments, give each a medical assessment and pay compensation and benefits where necessary.

Not a lot happened until former Navy test veteran Nathan Schnurman from Charles City, Virginia, who had volunteered for six days of experiments with mustard gas in 1944, began his quest to find the records relating to his case. Until then, as required by his secrecy commitment, he had remained silent about the tests that brought him so much health trouble in later life.

At first, the Veterans' Affairs Department said they could not find any records relating to him. He went to the Department of Defense who offered to let him search their files provided he met the retrieval expenses of $25,000. He could not pay, and they offered him access to other documents in the Maryland National Archive collection. He agreed, gave 24 hours' notice of his arrival, as required, and when he turned up at the centre to examine the files, was told by a mystified clerk. 'That's odd. Those records are just being moved to Edgewood.'

Schnurman went to a national television programme, *60 Minutes*, which began making its own inquiries. Three days before he was due to appear on the show, he received a letter from the Department of Veteran Affairs stating he would be granted a full disability pension. Later that year, the Americans announced a benefits package for survivors of chemical weapon exposure. The NAS also continued its battle to discover the extent of experiments and was forced to use the terms of the US Freedom of Information Act. Even then, few documents were forthcoming and it was unable to establish a precise number of men who might have suffered long-term effects.

At best, the NAS could only estimate that 60,000 servicemen were exposed to mustard gas, lewisite and phosgene and perhaps as many as 90,000 military and civilian workers at chemical sites such as Edgewood might have been exposed to toxic fumes during its manufacture. The NAS tried one more assault on the attitude of the military, which has obvious relevance to the British experience with its demands that: 'Surviving family members of these veterans deserve to know about those testing programmes, the exposures and the potential damage they caused. For those veterans still living, diseases such as skin and lung cancer may still appear. Treating these ailments with the full knowledge of the likely causes should be the responsibility of the VA, and may be life-saving.'

Michael Roche could not agree more. While other nations were beginning to make amends to its CW victims, the British government remained steadfastly and resolutely unmoved.

Roche had made little headway. By 1993 he was severely restricted by his breathing difficulties, unable to work, unable to walk far and living from hand to mouth. Then he heard of Nathan Schnurman's similar battle in America, recounted on *60 Minutes.* He decided to attempt to contact other veterans in Britain, targeting specifically those like himself who had taken part in experiments at Porton. In January 1994, Roche formed the Porton Down Volunteers Association. Within a matter of months, he had been contacted by 250 other volunteers, and the widows of several others, all of whom had stories to tell of health problems. Nor could these be attributed to old age. Many ex-volunteers were still in their 40s and 50s.

Going through the returned questionnaires Roche had sent out to his members, he found the list of ailments was all too familiar to anyone who had been researching CB.W exposure for so long: throat and lung cancers, brain tumours, heart, asthma and other respiratory complaints, skin eruptions, nervous disorders, memory loss, eye and hearing failure, muscular and joint problems.

As Roche points out, he had reached out to a small percentage of potential victims in Britain. His membership was directed exclusively towards Porton Down volunteers, whereas experience in the US and Australia indicated that there might be many thousands of others who had suffered by some form of exposure in World War II. Even with the mass of new evidence obtained from his members, and the knowledge of a change of heart in Australia and America, all Roche's efforts still found no hint of any change in British policy.

The response of the Ministry of Defence and Porton executives remained the same: 'There has been no evidence available to suggest that service volunteers who participated in human studies at CBDE, Porton Down have suffered any long-term effects.'

Dr Graham Pearson, director of CBDE, added his own personal assessment in response to the mounting interest of the media and members of Parliament: 'There is no evidence to suggest that there is a need to call back volunteers on a regular basis . . . in addition, over the past 40 years there is no evidence that service volunteers have had any deterioration in their health as a result of their participating as a volunteer in a study at CBDE.'

The phrase 'no evidence' was as laughable to Roche as it was to Gulf War veterans, particularly in view of the recent acceptance by Australia of the Toyber dictum: 'Absence of evidence is not evidence of absence.' Undaunted by the continuing refusal to acknowledge any suffering among past volunteers, Michael Roche, now with the support of 250 others behind him, pressed on with his campaign and received backing from an influential source. The Countess of Mar had been a long-time campaigner in the House of Lords for action to limit the use of organophosphates in pesticides following deaths and injury to workers, especially farmers using sheep dip.

She began investigating Roche's situation, allied to that of the Gulf War veterans, and established one surprising association between the pesticides and nerve gas, apart from the fact that both were derived from the organophosphate group of chemicals. The only tests on the effects on humans of organophosphates had been carried out at the CBDE at Porton, using Service volunteers. Manufacturers of organophosphate pesticides regarded tests on humans as simply 'too dangerous'.

The Porton tests were classed as 'biomedical research' and they were ethically conducted. That in itself, for the countess, raised another vital issue: the probability that the British government had broken 'at least four' of the ten principles of the Nuremberg Code, cornerstone of the Helsinki Declaration on Human Rights. She said:

'After the discovery of the horrific experiments conducted by German physicians and professors during the Nazi regime, and the doctors' trial at Nuremberg, the judges, concerned that never again should humans endure such suffering in the name of science, wrote the code into their final judgement. I have established that the

Government accepts all of the principles . . . and that the scientists at Porton Down are bound by them . . . or are they?'

The countess contends that four of those principles were consistently broken:

1) that no medical research may be carried out without the informed, free, express and specific consent of the person undergoing it;

2) that each person should be given full information on the reason for the research and told of any foreseeable risks and inconvenience;

3) that those undergoing research should not be offered any inducement that compromises free consent; and

4) that volunteers or their dependants should be compensated for injury or loss caused by medical research.

There was no scope for doubt that all of those principles had been violated and that, said the countess, was the foundation of her concern: 'The organophosphates used in agriculture were developed first by the Germans prior to and during the war and later by the British and other nations for chemical warfare as nerve gases. These were tested on human volunteers at Porton Down. Some were exposed directly and others through protective clothing. There is a group of 300 men who underwent these experiments . . . some of whom had never volunteered, all were offered financial inducements very tempting to poorly paid Service conscripts . . . and many were misled to the extent that they believed they were merely testing a cure for the common cold and that any effects would be temporary and minor. In retrospect, many believe they have suffered the acute effects of exposure to nerve gas . . . in some cases, severe and prolonged. Yet not one of these men has been followed up by Porton Down or the Ministry of Defence and when they ask for help the shutters come down – as if they had never been to Porton. To me, there is no doubt that these men are chronically sick. And now we have another very large group of men and women from the Gulf War who are receiving very short shrift from the Ministry of Defence.'

Nor would there be any change in the policy of using human volunteers. In 1992 – the year in which the Gulf War Syndrome was becoming widely recognized – Porton more than doubled the number of service recruits used in experiments, compared with 1991. It continues today, and the tally since the end of the war now exceeds 12,000 men. The number of animals used in experiments, according to Porton's own figures, had been 'reduced' to less than half of one per cent of the national total – between 12,000 and 15,000 a year. Overall, however, Ministry of Defence experiments using animals increased by

51 per cent in 1994, compared with a general fall of 10 per cent in Britain as a whole.

Meanwhile the Porton establishment continues to advertize for volunteers in the Service journals in these terms: 'Volunteers for studies at Chemical and Biological Defence Establishment Porton Down – Volunteers could earn up to £250 (less tax) or in special cases more for a 3 week study and proportionately less for shorter studies.'

There is no mention in the advertisements that men are needed for tests in the £3.5 million containment building at Porton, opened in 1995, which houses a brand new gas chamber where the next generation of nerve agents and other insidious chemicals will be tested 'for defensive purposes', notwithstanding the fact that America banned nerve gas experiments on humans 20 years earlier. The new complex was built to replace four existing buildings consisting of two gas chambers, a respirator fitting and testing unit and bathhouse and store. Two of the buildings dated back to 1918, the others were built during World War II and it would have been too expensive to refurbish them.

The continuing need for these experiments was explained by Dr Graham Pearson in his last annual report, which he presented to the MoD before his retirement in 1995. Although the tone was one of haughty weariness at having to explain to the critics for the umpteenth time Porton's reason for existing, it highlighted the dilemma of scientists and the military. Porton's key aim was to ensure that British troops possessed the best possible protection against CB attack. That, said Pearson, could only be achieved by experimenting and modernizing, and that involved humans and animals, under the watchful eye of an independent Ethics Committee.

Over and above that, Pearson insisted, they had to scour the world, watch the marketplace, to make sure that no chemical or biological agents were developed by a potential aggressor that was beyond the scope of present protective equipment and drugs. The 1993 International Chemical Weapons Convention, which prohibits the development, production, stockpiling and use of chemical weapons, signed by 159 nations (but ratified by only 27), provided 'no grounds for complacency'.

Organophosphorus nerve agents, which Pearson described as the 'most potent of the classical CW agents', still represented the greatest threat. It remained the case – as Saddam Hussein, Colonel Gaddafi and the leaders of a host of other volatile nations have proved – that any despot legitimately acquiring chemicals for pesticide production could easily turn them into an effective chemical armoury. Porton's secret war was no longer about advising on a defence against nations building huge stockpiles of chemical weapons. Long storage life was no longer the main criterion.

Weapons could be created fast and effectively, especially by small terrorist units styled on the lines of the wartime Japanese saboteur groups. The Japanese religious fanatics demonstrated the simplicity of such a terrorist operation in the Tokyo underground in 1995. For the price of a few barrels of organophosphate compound and with the co-operation of a scientist with reasonable knowledge, anyone could make a bomb capable of killing thousands. The Tokyo subway attack with home-made sarin killed eight people and injured several thousand others.

More worrying to Porton's military masters, however, were apparently deliberate attempts by the Russians to find a loophole in the Chemical Weapons Convention. Pearson made an oblique reference to it in his final report. Recent intelligence, confirmed by two Russian scientists interviewed in the West, showed that Russia had developed three new nerve agents involving precursors not listed in the Chemical Convention schedules. One of them was similar to the Porton-developed VX agent. The other two were more disturbing. They were known to be five to eight times more effective than VX as a battlefield weapon.

Meanwhile, the Russian BW teams still maintained their research on genetically engineered biological agents, primarily using the military men's old favourite, anthrax – in spite of earlier undertakings to Western leaders. A meeting of 160 international scientists at St Alfred's College, Winchester, in September 1995 was told that the Russians had finally perfected their genetically engineered variation of the anthrax toxin, for which there was no known antidote. It is totally resistant to all known antibiotics. This merely confirmed what MI6 and CIA observers already knew. 'That one development alone is sufficient to create the absolute doomsday scenario,' said one intelligence source interviewed for this work, 'and the people at Porton know it only too well. They have been studying it themselves, just as they have in the US. The calculations of its effect speak for themselves. In theory, a thimbleful would be more than adequate to decimate the population of a city of a million people. In the wrong hands or with some madman in control . . . well, you can paint your own picture.'

Advanced Russian knowledge is already reaching those wrong hands. Tracking the leakage of nuclear and CB technology from the former Soviet Union has become one of the main pre-occupations of the intelligence community and the FBI. Hard-up or redundant scientists from its crumbling state enterprises are an easy target for those with foreign money. Former Soviet technology – and stolen equipment – is appearing in many parts of the Third World. China has a large commitment to CB research. So does North Korea. The CIA, however, has once again focused on Libya as one of the principal recipients of Soviet materials and knowledge.

In 1993, it discovered that Gaddafi was building a massive new underground factory carved out of the mountains at Tarhunah, 40 miles south of Tripoli. It acquired copies of the plans of the building, which covered a 6-acre land area and was estimated to be costing around $500 million. It was judged to be capable of producing 2,500 tons of chemical agents a year, sufficient for Gaddafi to go into the wholesaling business supplying stocks to his close allies.

In December 1995 a combined US intelligence assessment was presented to President Clinton, expressing fears that the old adversary who had haunted the Reagan administration had managed to build a plant that the US would find virtually impossible to 'neutralize' by bombing, should it become necessary. Work on the underground construction had begun alongside a fresh-water project Gaddafi's civil engineers had designed to divert river water to the desert. The complex included steel shelters supplied by Russia, making the site fairly impregnable, certainly by an aerial attack.

With their penchant for unveiling a model plan for every eventuality, US military intelligence had devised what they considered the only practicable way of knocking out the plant – a commando assault force. But the risks are so great that no such attack stands a chance of presidential approval. MI6 also pulled off something of a coup in 1996 when it blocked Gaddafi from obtaining biological technology from South Africa, though that news was offset by intelligence that Saddam Hussein was already rebuilding his BW plant, hidden away in a deep underground complex, 30 miles from Baghdad. In March 1996, six Gulf Arab states ended a two-day conference in Dubai with a communique accusing Iraq of resuming its production of germ and chemical warfare weapons and urged the world to keep the pressure up on Baghdad to comply fully with UN disarmament resolutions.

And so it goes on.

Critics of continued British and American counter-offensive research into CB.W are easily matched in number and in argument by those who support it. If Lady Thatcher is proved right in her warnings of impending doomsday, which she made in a speech at the beginning of 1996, CB warfare represents one of the greatest threats to world peace in the foreseeable future, quite simply because it is increasingly being seen as the poor man's answer to nuclear technology.

Porton Down CBDE, nurtured through eight decades by the military and successive governments of every political party, used and protected by the intelligence community, acquired a certain arrogance that was for years so evident among its senior staff. They were, and still are, The Untouchables of the Ministry of Defence, the Jewel in the Crown. Any hopes that its importance to the nation's defence strategy was being downgraded were ruled out in 1995, when it was relaunched as a subdivided government agency, retaining its title of Chemical and Biological Defence Establishment, but part of a wider group to be known as the Defence Evaluation and Research Agency. By the very nature of its business, its future is assured.

Michael Roche does not argue about the defence needs of the nation. What does concern him and his colleagues is the appalling, dismissive treatment that they – and many Gulf War veterans – have received. From Porton's claim that no long-term contact with volunteers was necessary, to what amounted to the brush-off from the minor tin gods who populate the corridors of the Ministry of Defence, and from ministers themselves, they have received no official recognition of their contribution to research. 'Many of the volunteers were frightened of ever mentioning the name of Porton Down,' said Roche. 'But I think the time has come to come out and say, "Look this happened to me, and these are the effects. Investigate please." Is that asking too much?'

Few in the seat of government have bothered with them or their health, although ten months after the Countess of Mar took up her cause in the House of Lords, Roche finally had some good news. On 3 August 1995, he received a letter signed by the Minister of State at the Department of Social Security. It read: 'Insofar as the personal injury of former Sapper Thomas Michael Roche of the Royal Corps of Engineers is due to anything suffered by him as a result of his service in the Army between February 16 1952 and April 2 1968, I hereby certify that his suffering that thing has been treated as attributable to service for the purpose of entitlement to an award under the Naval, Military and Air Forces Service Pension Order 1983.'

His disability had finally been recognized. The irony was that nothing had changed since he began his campaign – except that his condition had grown steadily worse. Lawyers see Roche's victory, modest though it is in financial terms, as a significant step as they begin to put together a case for the volunteers who have joined Roche's association. Alan Care, of the London firm Leigh, Day & Co. who have previously had dealings with Porton Down, launched an action against the MoD on behalf of six sample volunteers who have a long history of medical complaints. His quest was not dissimilar to that of Hilary Meredith as she pursued the Ministry on behalf of the Gulf War veterans. Care said: 'There is, finally, an admission in the case of Michael Roche that he was incapacitated by his experiences at Porton. There are many like him. They deserve recognition for the way they have suffered in performing what, after all, was a selfless act.'

As the lawyers gather for their separate confrontation with officialdom for what is expected to be a long battle to find justice, much will be made on behalf of both the Gulf War veterans and the Porton volunteers of article 3.1 of the Nuremberg Code, which declares that no medical research shall be carried out without the informed, free and specific consent of the person undergoing it.

Michael Roche will undoubtedly remind them of the second article of the code too: 'the interest and wellbeing of the person undergoing medical research must always prevail over the interests of science and society.'

In spite of their personal bitterness, however, Roche and his colleagues do not deny the importance of safeguarding troops and civilian populations from any chemical and biological incident. In a way, he says, they are living proof of the effects of even limited exposure and that the possibility of attacks on a mass scale are too horrific to contemplate. The threat is alive and well, and in the hands of a few unstable governments and dictators. The upsurge in terrorist activity in the 1990s has also reaffirmed a strong belief among the intelligence community that it is only a matter of time before chemical weapons, now so readily and cheaply manufactured, could enter this arena, too. That prospect was extensively explored at the G7 summit of leading industrial nations in Paris in July 1996, and one that was placed high on the agenda of new initiatives to counter such attacks.

If it ever happened, research from those simulated attacks on cities and underground rail networks, the years of study on protective and defensive measures, the search for antidotes and effective treatments, would all come into play. As ever in this highly emotive and exceedingly lethal issue, the moral dilemma becomes more complex with each passing year.

CHAPTER NOTES

Prologue

Descriptions of scenes in the theatre of operations as the Coalition forces switched from Desert Shield to Desert Storm, along with reports of suspected CB.W content of Iraqi Scud, and evidence of airborne agents from Iraqi chemical installations bombed by Allied aircraft, were drawn from personal interviews and the testimony of 600 servicemen to the US Senate Committee on Bank, Housing and Urban Affairs hearings 1992/94. The inquiry was set up under the chairmanship of Senator Donald Riegle to investigate the dual-use weapons exported to Iraq prior to the Gulf War and extended to the impact on the health of GW veterans.

The recollections of Dale Glover, Harold Edwards, Fred Willougby, Roy Morrow, William Brady were taken from sworn testimony to the senate committee or members of its staff; also *US Marines in the Persian Gulf, 1990–1991*, an official report published in 1993 by the History and Museums Division, Headquarters, United States Marine Corps, Washington, DC, and Richard Turnbull, in an interview, 1995, and quoted in *The Independent on Sunday*, 12 February 1995. Other sources: principally, 'The Tuite Reports' 1993–5, by James Tuite, chief investigator for Senator Riegle; Report of the Defense Science Board Task Force on Persian Gulf War Health Effects, Office of the Under-secretary of Defense for Acquisition and Technology (Washington, DC: DoD, June 1994); and DoD Press Release, June 23, 1994; suspect storage tank report prepared by Major J.P. Watkinson, Officer Commanding, 21st EOD Squadron Group, Royal Ordnance, August 7 1991, classified in Britain but the contents of which were publicly revealed at the US Senate Committee hearings staged by Donald Riegle; along with the report of Captain Michael Johnson, of US Chemical Munitions and NBC units, 4 January 1994. Other references were to be found in a memorandum to Lt Col. Vicki Merriman, Office of the Deputy Assistant to the Secretary of Defense for Chemical and Biological Matters, from Dr Graham S. Pearson, CBDE, Porton Down.

Czech Chemical Decontamination Unit reports of chemical detection in the theatre of operations, originally filed to the Saudi Arabian Defence Ministry, March 1991, and subsequently to the US Department of Defense in June 1993. DoD attempts to downplay the Czech report, quoting the view of CBDE director Graham Pearson, contained in DoD file No. 68360155.94d, headed 'British position on chemical agents in the Persian Gulf'; 'Tests on biological agents in samples from the Gulf', report to Senator Riegle, by the Lawrence Livermore National Laboratory Forensic Science Center, 15 April 1994. Sources for the summary of events in this preface are contained in notes to later chapters where these topics are dealt with in full.

Chapter One: The Haunted Garden

Life beside the Porton establishment was recalled in interviews with local residents, including former CND activist Richard Harvey, who also joined local archaeologists on a visit to the establishment. Porton's own literature catalogues the wealth of flora and fauna and sites of particular archaeological interest and it is also in G.B. Carter's *Porton: 75 Years of Chemical and Biological Research*. Early development of Porton as a research establishment was drawn from the reports of Lt Col.

Arthur Crossley, professor of organic chemistry at King's College London, secretary of the Scientific Advisory Committee of the Ministry of Munitions in 1916 and Porton commandant, who was a prolific writer on his establishment's early work. His 1919 account, known as 'The Crossley Report', was not released into the Public Record Office (WO142/265), along with an anonymous brief history of Porton (WO188/785), until 1981.

The description of the first use of gas in World War I was drawn principally from the accounts of Sir John French, Col. E.D. Swinton, and the Canadian Record Officer, which appear in *World's War Events*, Vols 1–3, and the archives of the British Trench Warfare Department, along with a vast collection of other files at the PRO, in WO142 series, WO35/5185 and Gas Shell Bombardment of Ypres, 12–13 July 1917, in WO32/5176. The diary of American surgeon Harvey Cushing is recorded in 'Gas: The Cry of Ypres' by Hanson W. Baldwin, *New York Times Magazine*, 18 April 1965.

The post mortem report by Lt McNee is in WO142/99. The story of the nucleus of experts is from *Gas: The Story of the Special Brigade* by Charles Foulkes and Robert Graves, *Goodbye to All That*, London, 1929.

Chapter Two: The Humane Killer

Early development of Porton is described in 'A history of Porton' by Lt Col. A.E. Kent, written in 1960, but which remained a restricted document for in-house use only until it was declassified in 1987. A vast collection of files amounting to several thousand pages relating to Porton work between 1916 and 1929, detailing experiments and trials, was lodged at the Public Record Office for viewing by historians between 1981 and 1987, along with the annual reports of the Chemical Warfare Research Department, under WO33/1014 through to WO233/1231. They contain the most detailed view of Porton's research and attitudes. J.B.S. Haldane's *Callinicus: A Defence of Chemical Warfare*, London, 1924, and a review in the *London Illustrated News* in the same year, underpins the 1920s' view of the pro-gas lobby that chemical warfare was the way of the future.

The experiment with cyanide gas by Sir Joseph Barcroft and the dog is described in WO188/373. Porton studies on delayed effects of WWI gassing, are in WO188/265 and also in the World Health Organization Report, 1970 (see bibliography).

Chapter Three: Hitler's Secret Agent

The initiation of the Japanese germ warfare project in south Manchuria after its invasion of that region in November 1929 is drawn from numerous reports and files from various sites, including more than a dozen at the PRO in the WO188 series and PREM 3/65 relating to suspected trial bombing raids on China using BW agents and from Combined Intelligence Operations papers, 1945–6, notably in the British Intelligence Objectives Sub-Committee (BIOS) reports Vols II–V; and Mukden files, National Archives, Washington.

The 'emergency' response to the threat of BW in Britain, led by Sir Maurice (later Lord) Hankey, is described in G.B. Carter's *Porton Down: 75 Years of Chemical and Biological Research*. Also consulted: *Hankey: Man of Secrets* by Stephen Roskill, London, 1974; and specifically the 1937 Committee for Imperial Defence reports, PRO CAB4/26.

Descriptions of the Italian gassing of Abyssinia were drawn from contemporary reports. The discovery of nerve gas by Professor Gerhard Schrader and discussion is contained variously in several files in the WO188 series, with precise details in Combined Intelligence Objectives Sub-committee reports Nos 30 and 31. The progressive development of Germany's overall CB.W capability is contained in numerous reports compiled after the war, notably from interviews with German scientific personalities, contained in BIOS reports Nos 9, 41, 138, and 542.

Chapter Four: A Million Tons of Mustard

Professor Frederick Lindemann, later Viscount Cherwell, was one of Winston Churchill's closest friends and wartime advisers on the use of poison gas. According to Martin Gilbert in *Finest Hour* (p. 593), he saw most confidential documents and many of his draft letters to Churchill were circulated unaltered above the premier's signature. His theories on anti-invasion plans were included in a letter to Churchill on 12 May 1940. Churchill himself began contemplation of drenching British beaches with mustard gas: 'I have no scruples, except not to do anything dishonourable,' from the Colville Papers, 1 July 1940, quoted by Gilbert (p. 618). His demand for a full state of chemical readiness is in PRO PREM 3/88/3, folio 250, and regarding involving the United States in PREM 3/88/1, folio 241. Stocks of CW weapons are listed in G.B. Carter's history of Porton, while the American output is contained in *The Redstone Complex: The Pre-missile Era* (1941–3), produced by the Redstone Arsenal, Maryland.

The sequence of experiments on humans, recounted by Harry Hogg, Russel O'Berry and Nathan Schnurman in interviews, 1994/95, with the author, newspaper articles in the US, Australia and Canada (see bibliography) and principally in two television programmes, *60 Minutes* in the US and the British Network First documentary, *The Secrets of Porton Down* (Observer Films in association with Ray Fitzwalter Associates, a Granada Television presentation for ITV, 1994). The Australian experiments were first revealed in the Australian television documentary *Keen as Mustard*, 1989, and subsequently in testimony by Tom Mitchell and others in claims for compensation. Confirmation of experiments in India, Canada and Porton, and descriptions of the latter, are contained in 29 PRO separate files relating to the human experience and experiments with animals in the WO188/189 series.

Chapter Five: Killing them Softly

A large number of eye-witness accounts of Japanese bombing raids over China, alleging the dropping of plague-infected rice and the Ch'angte incident are recorded in the PRO WO188/189 files. More precise details of General Ishii's Pingfan biological research station are included in a mass of intelligence documents, placed under the same reference at the PRO, and more extensively in the National Archives, Washington, and in the British Intelligence Objectives Sub-Committee *Scientific Intelligence Survey*, Vol. V, September 1945. Although most of the wartime documents on British experiments in biological warfare remain classified, details of the initial preparations to build an anthrax bomb seem to have been inadvertently attached as an appendix to a 1945 report to the Joint Technical Warfare Committee entitled 'Potentialities of Biological Warfare during the next ten years' (PRO DEFE2/1252). This related specifically to the calculations for a BW attack on German cities, leading to trials on Gruinard Island and the calamitous poisoning of its soil for almost half a century. Accounts of local reaction were taken from a *Daily Telegraph* report, 22 March 1967.

Original proposals to drop infected cattle cakes over Germany were drafted in a 'most secret' memo to Winston Churchill from Lord Hankey, dated 6 December 1941 (PRO/CAB120/782). A reply authorizing a more detailed projection demanding total secrecy is under the same reference. Details of the final plan, as delivered by Dr Paul Fildes, and his exchanges with Unilever, along with the selection of 29 soap factory workers, are contained in the WO188 lists. The conclusion of this story and an account of the decontamination of Gruinard Island is included in G.B. Carter's history of Porton.

Chapter Six: The Unfought Battle

In spite of a flurry of rumours, the Bari explosion of the US gas-carrying ship SS *John Harvey* (WO193/712): 'Most secret' report: 'Toxic Gas Burns Sustained in Bari Harbour Catastrophe' was kept under wraps for almost two months, which is why Eisenhower, in an attempt to halt news leaking, suggested 'coded' descriptions of the cause of death to be given to relatives (WO193/712 January 2 1944). It was not merely public sensitivity that the Chiefs of Staffs were concerned about (CAB79/77) but the German misreading of the gas being brought into the heart of operations. The rash of intelligence reports that followed, listed in this chapter, demonstrated the heightening tensions of a possible attack (WO188/189), culminating in Churchill's demand for consideration by the CoS for proposals for the use of CB weapons. The episode that followed and brought Churchill into conflict with his commanders and President Roosevelt, who urged him not to push for a chemical attack, are contained in PRO CAB84/64 and PREM 3/89. Germany's preparedness for CB attacks is covered in numerous files in the PRO WO188/189 series and in the BIOS final report on 'The Interrogation of Certain German Personalities Connected with Chemical Warfare', No. 542. The discovery of the nerve gas shells is also in WO188 and the impact of it in SIPRI, *The Rise of CB Weapons*, and G.B. Carter's history of Porton.

Chapter Seven: Spoils of War

Many tons of documents, photographs, laboratory samples and equipment were gathered up by Allied recovery missions in Europe and the Far East as the war ended, and a great deal of it was so sensitive that it was never released into the public domain. A number of specific missions by senior Porton officers, including those of the Captains W.J. Cromartie and Carlo Henze and Major Evans, and their visits to Natzweiler Concentration Camp are, however, recorded in WO188 files, which also include various photographs taken by the officers concerned. Other material on their discoveries was to be found in Report No. 30 of the Combined Intelligence Objectives Sub-Committee and the BIOS reports on the interrogation of personnel at German CW installations, and from files recovered from Spandau. The work of Major Barnes is also referred to in G.B. Carter's history of Porton. Many documents relating to General Ishii's experiments at Pingfan and the operations of the notorious Unit 731 of the Japanese Army remained classified until the 1990s.

The so-called Mukden files, counter-intelligence reports relating to the capture and interrogation of Ishii by General MacArthur, and experiments on Japanese prisoners of war were quietly released to a Japanese historian in 1994, and subsequently viewed at the National Archives by Washington-based researcher Greg Rodriguez, jnr, whose father was among the Mukden prisoners who had, for four decades, been suffering ill health. He had been campaigning for many years for information about the alleged atrocities at the Mukden PoW camp, which the Japanese and the US had always denied. The evidence of former PoW Frank James is included in a report of a House of Representatives Sub-Committee, 1986, in the National Archives, Washington, which was quietly dropped by the Reagan Administration and only brought into the public domain by persistent pressure from the US-based Alliance for the Preservation of Truth of the Sino-Japanese War.

In Britain, further insight was obtained from the BIOS Report on Scientific Intelligence Survey in Japan, Vol. V ('Biological Warfare', September 1945) and intelligence documents that flowed to Porton, located in PRO WO188/189.

Chapter Eight: The Volunteers

The post-war statement of intent to rush ahead with gas and germ warfare, in spite of the many causes for concern that had become evident in recent months, was demonstrated in the readiness of the Chiefs of Staff to accept without challenge the report of Sir Henry Tizard ('Future Developments in Weapons and Methods of War': PRO/COS [45]402 and WO189/2587). Chemical weaponry was on the agenda of the British government's military advisers almost continuously for the next decade (notable in COS/DEFE2-24; 2-433, 4-3 and onwards). The commitment of the US to its Edgewood and Fort Detrick establishments, with massive investment that had been ploughed into the American CB effort during the war, was in no way curtailed in the aftermath, in view of fears that the Soviets had acquired the same Nazi and Japanese technology in nerve gas and germ warfare. The 'desperate preoccupation' with nerve gas is admitted by G.B. Carter's history of Porton (p. 56) and, in the same discussion, is the difficulty of experimenting with 'unprotected men'. But men were used, as confirmed by the testimony in this chapter of two of the early volunteers to Porton's programme of testing agents and protective measures on servicemen. The descriptions of Gerald Beach and George Abbot were taped by the author in February 1996. For an account of the experiences of Tom Griffiths and the Nancekuke plant, the author is grateful to Elizabeth Sigmund whose own book, *Rage Against Dying*, was published in 1980 (pp. 28–40) and whose knowledge of CB.W admirably equipped her for a 1990s' role as adviser to the Gulf War Veteran Association. Trevor Martin told his story to the *Sunday Times*, 7 December 1969. The cloak of silence surrounding the Ronnie Maddison case has been maintained to this day; no documents relating to it have been published. Various contemporary newspaper accounts were consulted along with references in *A Higher Form of Killing* by Harris and Paxman.

Chapter Nine: It Wouldn't Hurt a Mouse

Michael Roche provided his extensive recollections of his visits to Porton for the author along with a good deal of his other personal research that appears at various points in this work, leading ultimately to his formation of the Porton Down Volunteers Association (detailed in the final chapter). Though much of the documentation on the CIA's LSD experiments remains classified, some details have emerged from various government inquiries over the past 20 years. The first real intimation of their scale came during the 1975 Church Senate Committee hearings on Alleged Assassination Plots Involving Foreign Leaders.

Among all the CIA's dirty linen that Senator Church hung out was an unconfirmed report that the President of Egypt Gamal Nasser was among the CIA targets, specifically at the request of British Prime Minister Sir Anthony Eden after the Suez crisis. It was also during these hearings that relatives of Frank Olson first discovered that his suicide came after he had taken LSD at Dr Gottleib's behest – a fact that had remained secret for 20 years. Although his widow, Alice, had been receiving a full pension since he died, lawyers took up the case and very quickly obtained $700,000 compensation from the government and a letter of personal apology from President Ford. Fuller details, though by no means all, of the projects that covered experiments with LSD emerged during 1976 joint Senate hearings before a Select Committee on Intelligence and a Sub-committee on Health and Scientific Research. Its report of the First Session, *Project MKUltra: The CIA's Program of Research in Behavioral Modification*, was published by the US Govt Printing Office, 1977 (pp. 122–6). The report also covered another CIA project, MKNaomi (in pp. 68–70), the object of which was to 'stockpile severely incapacitating and lethal materials for use by the TSD (Technical Services Division)'. Further references are to be found in John Ranelagh's *The Agency*.

The programme was halted in 1970 after President Nixon announced a ban on the use by any US agency and military of biological weapons that kill or incapacitate. The 11 files on Porton's experiments with LSD were contained in the 1996 new release folders at the Public Record Office, pending allocation to the usual class lists.

Chapter Ten: Testing Bugs on the Masses

The spreading of bacteria on the London Underground was first revealed in a brief summary of the experiments in PRO files opened under the 30-years rule in the DEFE class lists, although further releases of tests foreshadowed in the 1963 reports have not, at the time of writing, been made public. Similarly, the US Army tests on the New York City Subway remained classified, although the Pentagon has admitted that seven or eight such experiments were carried out. Details of the Porton experiments conducted at sea also remained restricted, and scant detail had been released into the public domain. They were first mentioned in *A Higher Form of Killing* by Harris and Paxman (pp. 155, 169). A brief summary was also included in G.B. Carter's history of Porton (pp. 65–6) and additional information has been obtained by the author from private sources. No full accounts of the San Francisco trials have been made public, either. However, doctors who treated a number of patients for serrartia in an outbreak at the time the city was sprayed (1977), felt it was such a rare occurrence they prepared an article for the *Archives of Internal Medicine*. They named one victim who died, one Edward Nevin who had gone into hospital for a routine prostate operation, then suddenly fell ill and died. He had the same organism that the US scientists had used in their spraying. Documents later unearthed by the *Washington Post*, in 1979, estimated 800,000 people had been sprayed with the bacteria. A young lawyer from San Francisco read of the story, and was amazed to discover that the Edward Nevin who died was his grandfather. The Nevin family sued the US government for compensation. The case was thrown out within two months, not because the government denied the experiments had been carried out, but because the judge ruled it was impossible to prove the basic elements of cause and effect after 27 years. Even so, one of the authors of the original report on the strange outbreak of illness in San

Francisco in the year of the US tests, Doctor Richard Wheat, remained adamant that the spraying of the bacteria on a mass population was 'not without some risk'. Meanwhile, the results of the mosquito experiments are contained in the archives of the US Army Chemical Center at Maryland.

Chapter Eleven: An Eyeful of CS Gas

Two major reports at the start of the 1970s highlighted the alarming spread of CB weaponry and the increased potency of a range of chemical and biological agents now proliferating around the world. The vastness of the two studies provided for the author a wealth of detail for this chapter and, indeed, the whole of this work. The first was the World Health Organization's report, *Health Aspects of Chemical and Biological Weapons* (1970), produced by a panel of international scientists of the highest calibre. As is detailed in this and other chapters, the panel was damning in its assessments of the continued race for CB supremacy by the major powers, and warned of the dangers of these new weapons reaching the hands of terrorists. More specifically, however, the WHO report concentrated on a seemingly appalling disregard for the human populations who might be subjected to CB agents, either accidentally or by intent. More wide-ranging was the series of volumes produced by the Stockholm International Peace Research Institute. The first, *The Problem of Chemical and Biological Warfare*, was a 361-page history of CB.W prepared by the British chemist Julian Perry Robinson, today one of the world's foremost authorities on the topic. His wealth of statistics noted that since 1914 there had been 23 conflicts in which chemicals had been used and 13 using biological weapons. Both the SIPRI and WHO reports made particular reference to the increasing use of anti-personnel agents, such as CS gas.

John Longden provided the author with his personal account of that material. His experiences as a Porton volunteer were described in a taped interview in February 1996. Details of the research and development of genetically engineered biological weapons is contained in a number of reports in the National Archives, Washington, and from the author's own research and interviews with private sources. See also 'Planning a Plague?' by John Barry, *Newsweek*, 1 February 1993, and 'The Red Death' by James Adams, *Sunday Times*, 23 February 1994.

Chapter Twelve: Sacrificial Slaughter

Porton's dismissal of public concern, suspicion and opprobrium is recorded by G.B. Carter (pp. 70–71), while details at last of Geoffrey Platt's accidental infection with the deadly virus ebola were revealed after the 1994 outbreak of the disease in Africa. Mr Platt, by then retired, had permission to speak about his own traumas at the time. Meanwhile, the public concern that Porton largely ignored was aroused by the series of articles leaked in the *Western Daily Press* on 'terrifying breakthroughs' in work behind the closed doors of the Porton experimental labs. The author was given excellent co-operation at the local offices of the *WDP* and the *Salisbury Journal*, which has dutifully kept its readers informed of Porton activities evidently without fear of upsetting the establishment, even if on occasions their stories have attracted the interest of the Special Branch.

The National Anti-Vivisection Society (NAVS) had increased its monitoring of Porton around this time, along with other animal welfare groups following the local rumours of quite terrifying experiments. Ongoing publicity concerning the role of Porton Down produced a reaction in the House of Commons on 23 March 1984, in answer to a written question by Mr Robert Key, Conservative MP for Salisbury, in the wake of protest demonstrations by the combined forces of peace campaigners and animal welfare groups. Mr Key asked the Secretary of State for Defence to make a statement on the 'particular contribution made by experiments involving animals and by service volunteers'. The long reply by the Defence Minister referred specifically to the wounding experiments on animals. He said that in 1983, 51 animals were used in wounding studies, but the work was vital to 'increase knowledge of the effects of wounds, contributing to the improvement of treatment'. CS gas experiments were staged to 'limit' the risk to humans in riot situations, and the use of service volunteers was required to ensure standards of protection for troops. They 'freely volunteered' and were well briefed. It was, however, impossible to give precise details of experiments and species of animals used because it would 'enable an informed observer to gain a useful insight into the scope of the establishment's work ... which must be protected in the interests of national security'.

Details of them could be obtained elsewhere. The series of experiments outlined in this chapter were to be found from the following sources: 'The Protection of Primates Against Soman Poisoning by Pretreatment with Pyridostigmine', *Journal of Pharmacology and Pharmology*, Vol. 31, pp. 295–9; 'The Efficacy of Bispyridinium Derivatives in the Treatment of Organophosphate Poisoning in the Guinea Pig', *Journal of Pharmacology and Pharmology*, Vol. 35 (pp. 427–33); 'Repeated Dose Study of the Toxicity of Inhaled 2-Chlorobenzylidene Malononitrile (CS) Aerosol in Three Species of Laboratory Animals', *Archives of Toxicology*, Vol. 52 (pp. 183–98); 'The Effect of Prior Treatment with 4-Dimethylaminophenol [DMAP] on Animals Experimentally Poisoned with Hydrogen Cyanide', *Archives of Toxicology*, Vol. 51 (pp. 247–53); 'Experimental High-Velocity Missile Head Injury', *Injury*, Vol. 14 (pp. 183–93); 'The use of miniature pigs to determine treatment in humans of mustard gas burns', and 'The use of pigs in the calculation of injury from blast waves', from statement by Dr Graham Pearson, director, in the 1995 annual report of the Chemical and Biological Defence Establishment.

Chapter Thirteen: The Arming of Saddam

Details of the activities of Dr Barbouti were obtained from intelligence sources and from contemporary reports (*Sunday Times*, *The Observer*, *New York Times*, variously published between 1985 and 1989). This information was further supplemented by the testimony of Dr Gordon Oehler, director of the Nonproliferation Centre of the CIA, who set out precise details of the CB material and installations acquired by Iraq and Libya in a long statement to the Senate Committee on Bank, Housing and Urban Affairs hearings, 1992/94. Also consulted for this chapter were the reports of the 1988 Report of Physicians for Human Rights on the massacre of the Kurds, and 'Abuse of Iraqi Children by Security Forces', a report by Amnesty International, 14 March 1989. Dr Barbouti's purchase of the Florida 'cyanide' factory was first reported in the *Financial Times* after a joint investigation with ABS's *News Nightline* in America, July 1991, and supplemented here with additional detail from intelligence sources interviewed for this work, and with Dr Oehler's own evidence on protecting intelligence 'assets'.

Secretary of State James Baker's frantic letter concerning exports to Iraq was revealed in evidence to the Senate Committee of Inquiry, and highlighted by the chairman, Senator Riegle.

Chapter Fourteen: A Deadly Christmas Cocktail

CIA assessments of Saddam Hussein's CB.W capability were provided by Dr Gordon Oehler, with additional information on the export of American and European products to Iraq in the years before the Gulf War from Edwin Dorn, of the US Department of Defense. His testimony to the Senate Committee on exports confirmed the tensions that existed within the Pentagon at the time troops were ordered to the Gulf. A fuller version of the US DoD/CIA calculations referring to what exactly Saddam Hussein possessed in both CB and conventional weaponry, along with the assessments of a possible 40,000 casualties in a ground war, were in the first 7,000 pages of documents declassified by the DoD in February 1996. The memoirs of four leading figures in the campaign were consulted: General Sir Peter de La Billiere, Commander of the British force, General Norman Schwarzkopf, overall Commander, General Colin Powell, chairman of the US Chiefs of Staff and HRH General Khaled Bin Sultan, Commander of Joint Forces and Theatre of Operations (see bibliography). Although their reflections on the extent of the CB.W threat are scant, they portray a pre-war scenario of uncertainty, anguish, delays, political considerations and high-level disagreements over the extensive use of pre-treatment vaccines and tablets among the Coalition forces. All carefully avoid the emotive issues of Gulf War Syndrome.

The preparedness of the Porton establishment to meet the challenge of the Gulf War was confirmed by Dr Graham Pearson in a statement to the *Salisbury Journal* in September 1990. Details of the vaccines and pre-treatment tablets against nerve gas attacks were contained in a report of the US Department of Defense Medical Task Force to the Pentagon, August 1994, and to the House of Commons Select Committee in Britain; confirmation that two of them were unlicensed was provided in evidence to both of those bodies. That point was also taken up by the Countess of Mar in a speech to the House of Lords, October 1994, when she asked the government to state 'whether the principles of the Nuremberg Code and the Declaration of Helsinki, 1964, have all been accepted by the Government of the United Kingdom, and whether these principles applied to members of HM Forces volunteers as well as civilian volunteers for research'. The answer from the government benches was, in a word: 'Yes.'

The warnings regarding nerve gas treatment were contained in a Royal College of Physicians report to the Health Minister, and for onward transmission to Gulf War medical officers in February 1991. The US deficiency in anti-bodies for botulinum toxin was mentioned in passing by General Colin Powell in his memoirs (pp. 494, 505 and 507) and confirmed during the Riegle Senate Committee hearings, while Sir Peter de la Billiere recalled the debilitating effect of the vaccines on his men (*Storm Command*, p. 174).

Chapter Fifteen: Atmospheric Overload

Details of the 'poisoned air' theme of this chapter were gleaned from numerous sources: from the statements and evidence of 600 Gulf War veterans interviewed by the staff of Senator Riegle and published in the final report of the committee in May 1994; from the report of James Tuite, chief investigator for the Riegle Committee, 'When science and politics collide', 1995; from the report of the US DoD Science Board Medical Task Force set up to investigate Gulf War Syndrome, published June 1994; from research completed by the

US General Accounting Office, reported upon in August 1995; from the report of James Moss, scientific researcher for the US Department of Agriculture, 1994; from a survey into injuries of Gulf War personnel involving fragments of depleted uranium by the Army Office of the Surgeon General, 1994; from the report of the Czech Chemical Decontamination Unit, presented to the US DoD and Porton Down in June 1993. The account of Corporal Robert Lake was given wide coverage after the War Pensions Agency recognized his condition and awarded him a small pension (see the *Guardian Weekend*, 27 May 1995, and *The Independent on Sunday*, 12 February 1995). The recollections of Nigel Thompson, Colin Blench and Paul Ash also received media attention, notably 'Something Nasty in the Gulf?' in *The Independent on Sunday* and 'MoD Insensitive Over Gulf Sickness', *Daily Telegraph* (see bibliography).

Chapter Sixteen: Stillbirths, Miscarriages, Deformities

In the absence of any major studies in Britain at time of writing, research on Gulf War Syndrome and its associated aspects was obtained almost entirely in America. Richard and Christine Turnbull were among the British couples who took part in the survey by Dr Edward Hyman, from New Orleans (see also *The Guardian*, 4 December 1995). Richard Turnbull also revealed his personal experiences in the Gulf (*Independent on Sunday*, 12 February 1995, and elsewhere). Other accounts recorded in this chapter are from interviews with the author, from evidence given to the Riegle hearing and collated published material (see bibliography).

Official reports consulted included: US Department of Health, 'Clinical Evaluation Programme for Gulf War Veterans'; 'Comprehensive Clinical Evaluation for Gulf War Victims', August 1995; 'Federal Activities Related to Gulf War Veterans', Department of Veterans' Affairs, June 1994; 'Unexplained Illnesses Among Desert Storm Victims', August 1994; investigations into Gulf War Syndrome by the staff of the Veterans' Affairs, Hospital, Allen Park, Michigan, 1994; Presidential Advisory Committee on Gulf War Veterans' Illnesses, and Declassification Briefing, October 1995; the report of the solitary British medical inquiry conducted by Dr Goran Jamal, at the Institute of Neurological Sciences of the Southern General Hospital Glasgow, published in the *Journal of Neurology, Neurosurgery and Psychiatry*, March 1996; interviews and assistance rendered to the author by Hilary Meredith, of the solicitors Donn & Co., Manchester, representing more than 1,000 Gulf War veterans and their families; from many personal accounts to the author, published interviews and from privately obtained information. The comments of Senator Riegle are included in the final report of his committee hearings, published in 1994.

Chapter Seventeen: Forgotten Heroes

The archives of Michael Roche, founder of the Porton Down Volunteers Association, provided much information, and interview with Alan Care, of Leigh, Day & Co., London, representing the volunteers in possible action against the Ministry of Defence. Statistics on the successful actions for compensation by former human guinea-pigs to World War II experiments with mustard gas in Australia were provided for Derek Fatchett, Labour MP for Leeds Central, by the International Affairs and Defence Section of the House of Commons Library. Other successful claims by WWII veterans obtained from reports and interviews with subjects in the US. Nathan Schnurman recounted his experiences on the US television programme *60 Minutes*, in 1993. (See also *The Bulletin of Economic Scientists*, March 1993, by Karen Freeman, assistant professor of Pennsylvania State University, report headed: 'The VA's Sorry, The Army's Silent'). The questions raised by the Countess of Mar in the House of Lords are taken from 'Parliamentary Question for Written Answer', House of Lords (1993/94) and her own comments and the subsequent debate appear in Hansard (pp. 1154–64).

Post-war estimates of the number of human volunteers used by Porton were contained in a letter from its former director Dr Graham Pearson, dated 20 March 1995, in response to a Commons question by Mr Fatchett. Latest statistics on animal experiments are contained in the 1995 Annual Report of the Director of Porton CBDE to the Ministry of Defence, and more detailed figures of general experiments in Britain from the annual tally prepared by the Department of Health.

BIBLIOGRAPHY

Books

Adams, James, *The New Spies*, London, 1994.

Allen, Thomas B., with F. Clifton Berry and Norman Polmar, *War in the Gulf*, London, 1991.

Benn, Tony, *Out of the Wilderness: Diaries 1963–1967; Office Without Power: Diaries 1968–1972; Against the Tide: Diaries 1973–1976; The Benn Diaries: Selected Abridged Edition*, London, 1995.

Billiere, General Sir Peter de la, *Storm Command: A Personal Account of the Gulf War*, London, 1992.

Bulloch, John, *The Gulf War: Its Origins, History and Consequences*, London, 1989.

Carter, G.B., *Porton Down: 75 Years of Chemical and Biological Research*, HMSO, 1992.

Collier, Basil, *The Battle of the V-Weapons, 1944–45*, London 1976.

—— *Hidden Weapons: Allied Secret or Undercover Services in World War II*, London, 1982.

Fitzsimons, Bernard (ed.), *Tanks and Weapons of World War I*, London, 1973.

Foulkes, C.H., *Gas: The Story of the Special Brigade*, London, 1936.

Gilbert, Martin *Finest Hour: Winston S. Churchill, 1939–1941*, London, 1983.

—— *Road to Victory: Winston S. Churchill, 1941–45*, London, 1986.

Haldane, J.B.S., *Callinicus: A Defence of Chemical Warfare*, London, 1924.

Harris, Paul, and Jeremy Paxman, *A Higher Form of Killing: The Secret Story of Gas and Germ Warfare*, London, 1982.

Hayward, James, *Shingle Street: Flame, Chemical and Psychological Warfare in 1940*, London, 1994.

Hersch, Seymour, *Chemical and Biological Warfare: America's Secret Arsenal*, London, 1968.

Hinsley, F.A., *British Intelligence in the Second World War*, Volume II, London, 1981.

Irving, David, *Goring: A Biography*, London, 1989.

Kent, Lt Col. A.E., *A History of Porton*, 1960, Public Record Office, London (declassified 1981).

Khaled, Sultan bin, *Desert Warrior: A Personal View of the Gulf War by the Joint Forces Commander*, London, 1993.

Lockhart, Sir Robert Bruce: *The Diaries, 1915–1938*, London, 1973.

Lusar, Rudolf, *German Secret Weapons of the Second World War* (trans.), London, 1959.

MacArthur, Brian (ed.), *Despatches from the Gulf War*, London, 1991.

Macksey, Terence, *Technology in War: The Impact of Science on Weapon Development* (Arms and Armour), 1986.

Mangold, Tom, *Cold Warrior*, London, 1991.

McCarthy, Richard D., *The Ultimate Folly: War by Pestilence, Asphyxiation and Defoliation*, London, 1970.

Moore, William, *Gas Attack: Chemical Warfare, 1915–18 and Afterwards*, London, 1987.

O'Neill, Richard, *Suicide Squads: Axis and Allied Special Attack Weapons of World War II*, London, 1981.

Pimlott, John, and Stephen Badsley (eds), *The Gulf War Assessed* (Arms and Armour), London, 1992.

Pincher, Chapman, *Too Secret Too Long: The Great Betrayal of Britain's Secrets and the Cover-up*, London, 1984.

Prentiss, A.M., *Chemicals in War*, New York, 1937.

Powell, General Colin, *A Soldier's War: An Autobiography*, London, 1995.

Ranelagh, John, *The Agency:L The Rise and Decline of the CIA*, New York, 1987.

Reynolds, Francis J., and Allen L. Churchill (eds), *World's War Events*, Vols 1–3, New York, 1919.

Robinson, Anthony, with Antony Preston, Ian V. Hogg, *Weapons of the Vietnam War*, London, 1983.

Robinson, Julian Perry, *The Rose of CB Weapons*, Stockholm International Peace Research Institute (SIPRI), Vol. 1, Stockholm, 1970.

Roskill, Stephen, *Hankey: Man of Secrets*, London, 1974.

Schwarzkopf, General H. Norman, *It Doesn't Take a Hero: An Autobiography*, London, 1993.

Sigmund, Elizabeth, *Rage Against Dying*, London, 1980.

Smith, Graham, *Weapons of the Gulf War*, London, 1991.

Speer, Albert, *Inside the Third Reich*, London, 1970.

Stanwood, Frederick, with L. Patrick Allen, *The Gulf War: A Day by Day Chronicle*, London, 1991.

Toland, John, *Adolf Hitler*, New York, 1976.

Wilkinson, Frederick, *A Source Book of World War One Weapons*, London, 1978.

Wright, Peter, *Spycatcher: The Candid Autobiography of a Senior Intelligence Officer*, Australia, 1987.

War and Weapons, text by the staff of the National Army Museum, Maidenhead, 1976.

Reports

'UK Policy on Weapons, Proliferation and Arms Control in the post-Cold War Era', House of Commons (Evidence to Foreign Affairs Committee) Vol. II, London 1994. 'Health Aspects of Chemical and Biological Weapons', Report of a World Health Organisation Group of Consultants, Geneva, 1970. 'Reduction of the Use of Animals in the Development and Control of Biological Products', Conference; *The Lancet*, 18 October 1985. Chemical and Biological Defence Research Establishment, *Annual Reports*, 1992, 1993, 1994, 1995.

Select press and other media articles consulted (in chronological order): 'Gas: The Cry of Ypres', Hanson W. Baldwin, *New York Times Magazine*, 18 April 1965. 'The Secret Arms Race', Robin Clarke, *Daily Telegraph*, 22 March 1967. 'CS Gas', Dr Robert N. Jones, *New Scientist*, 18 June 1970. 'Animal Experiments: Search for Understanding', Donald Gould, *World Medicine*, 21 April 1976. 'Elaborate Drug Tests on Animals Fall Short', Dr H.J. Roger and Professor R.G. Spector, *Pulse*, 10 February 1979.

'Letter from Baghdad', Joseph Kraft, *New Yorker*, 20 October, 1980. 'Harsh Realities of Biological Warfare, Professor A.P. Dharma, *Pulse*, 19 September 1981. 'GP's Damning Evidence', Dr Derek Bird, *Pulse*, 1 October 1983. 'Prolonged Active Life (Animal Experiments)', Robert Sharpe, *New Statesman*, 10 May 1985. 'The poisoned legacy', Leonard Doyle, *The Independent*, 2 August 1988.

'Putting the Genie Back in the Bottle', Shyam Bhatia, Simon Hoggart, Alan George, Nigel Hawkes and Robin Smith, *The Observer*, 8 January 1989. 'A Poisonous Prestige', Lawrence Freedman, *The Independent*, 13 January 1989. 'Russia Develops Genetic Weapons', James Adams, *Sunday Times*, 1 October 1989.

'Rape of the Gulf', Insight, *Sunday Times*, 5 August 1990. 'Scarred for Life', John Cropland, *Sunday Times*, 9 September 1990. 'The Night Watchman', John Simpson, *The Weekend Guardian*, 15 September, 1990. 'Sinister Alchemy', Alan Friedman, Lionel Barber, Jay LaMonica and Jimmy Burns, *Financial Times*, 3 July 1991. 'Planning a Plague?', John Barry, *Newsweek*, 1 February, 1993.

'The Red Death', James Adams, *Sunday Times*, 27 March 1994. 'Lethal Exposure', Martin Walker, *The Guardian*, 20 June 1994. 'Gulf War Syndrome', Peter Koenig, *GQ Magazine*, September, 1994. 'Iron Curtain goes up on Anthrax Offensive', Alastair Hay and Malcolm Dando, *The Guardian*, 24 November 1994. 'The Most Deadly Weapon of All', David Shukman, *The Spectator*, 26 November 1994. 'Something Nasty in the Gulf', Melanie McFadyean, *Independent on Sunday*, 12 February, 1995. 'We Must Know Why our Babies Died', *You Magazine*, 5 March, 1995. 'Soldier On', Melanie McFadyean, *The Guardian Weekend*, 27 May 1995. 'MoD Insensitive', Tim Butcher, *Daily Telegraph*, 8 November 1995. 'Why is the Government Lying?' Tim Sebastian, *Night and Day*, 12 November 1995. 'Children of the Storm', Russell Miller, *Sunday Times Magazine*, 14 January 1996.

INDEX

OKA:

A Convergence of Cultures and the Canadian Forces

Timothy C. Winegard

CANADIAN DEFENCE ACADEMY PRESS

Canadian Defence Academy Press
PO Box 17000 Stn Forces
Kingston, Ontario K7K 7B4

Produced for the Canadian Defence Academy Press
by 17 Wing Winnipeg Publishing Office.
WPO30375

Cover Photo: Cpl Colin A. Aitken, 17 Wing Imaging

Library and Archives Canada Cataloguing in Publication

Winegard, Timothy C. (Timothy Charles)
Oka : a convergence of cultures and the Canadian Forces / Timothy C. Winegard.

Produced for the Canadian Defence Academy Press by 17 Wing Winnipeg Publishing Office.
Issued by: Canadian Defence Academy.
Includes bibliographical references and index.
ISBN 978-1-100-10107-1 (bound) -- ISBN 978-1-100-10108-8 (pbk.).
Cat. no.: D2-227/1-2008E (bound)) -- Cat. no.: D2-227/2-2008E (pbk.)

1. Québec (Province)--History--Native Crisis, 1990. 2. Mohawk Indians--Québec (Province)--Kanesatake Indian Reserve--Claims. 3. Mohawk Indians--Québec (Province)--Kanesatake Indian Reserve-Government relations. 4. Indians of North America--Canada--Treaties. 5. Canada--Armed Forces. I. Canadian Defence Academy II. Canada. Canadian Armed Forces. Wing, 17 III. Title.

FC2924.9.O6W56 2008 971.4'04 C2008-980324-8

Printed in Canada.

1 3 5 7 9 10 8 6 4 2

For the leader of the band, my Dad.

ACKNOWLEDGEMENTS

There are so many people to thank that I regrettably cannot mention everyone individually. For starters, I would like to thank Dr. Sean M. Maloney for his help and guidance as a professor, but also by "urging" me to take my interest in the events and complications surrounding the Oka Crisis and run with it. I would also like to thank the late Dr. John Marteinson of the Royal Military College of Canada and Dr. David Murray at the University of Guelph for believing in and supporting me. A special thanks to Yves Raic for his continued friendship and enthusiasm in this project. I wish also to extend a warm appreciation to the staffs at the National Library and Archives of Canada, the library at RMC, the Access to Information Departments at the Department of National Defence, the Department of Indian and Northern Affairs and the Directorate of History and Heritage. Without your valuable help this endeavour would not have been possible. A final debt of gratitude must be extended to Colonel Bernd Horn and the staff of the Canadian Defence Academy Press.

In the process of researching the madness that was the spring and summer of 1990, numerous people provided me with their personal accounts, memorabilia and thoughts, often reliving traumatic experiences. Thank you all for your honesty and co-operation. Your pieces of history need to be recorded, remembered and most importantly taught. A special thank you to Waneek Horn-Miller for reminding me that the names in the books, papers and journals belong to human beings with thoughts, emotions and feelings. After all, this is what it is all about.

Finally, I would like to thank my family and friends for putting up with the endless stories and what must have been copious one-way "conversations!" To my parents Charles and Marian, and my sisters Casey and Kelly all I can say is: I love you all. Dad, thanks for your never-ending proofreading and support, and for dealing with my countless bouts of frustration! I am forever indebted.

Taleitha, everyday you make me realize that dreams come true. Your understanding during my long periods away from you on research trips, and my seeming absence even when at home while writing, has been limitless. I promise, no more Oka stories! Well maybe...

Thank you all,
Tim
Oxford, U.K., March 2008

TABLE OF CONTENTS

cont...

FOREWORD

I am delighted to introduce *Oka: A Convergence of Cultures and the Canadian Forces* by Timothy C. Winegard as the latest addition to the Canadian Defence Academy (CDA) Press collection. With its humble beginnings in January 2005, the CDA Press has published books of specific interest to the Canadian Forces (CF) and to those interested in the study of the profession of arms in Canada. Our aim has always been to create a distinct and unique body of Canadian military leadership literature and knowledge that will assist leaders at all levels of the CF prepare themselves for operations in a complex security environment, as well as to inform the public with respect to the contribution of CF personnel to Canadian society and international affairs.

As such, *Oka: A Convergence of Cultures and the Canadian Forces* is an important volume in the CDA Press collection. Aid to the civil power, particularly in cases of civil disobedience, is arguably one of the most difficult tasks the military may be called upon to perform. Although military forces represent the government's legitimate managers of violence, and often the government's last resort to re-establish law and order, the image of soldiers using violence against fellow citizens is one that everyone, particularly the nation's soldiers, would rather not see. Yet, in the spring/summer of 1990, the CF was called on to do exactly that. The CF was deployed to assist in the settlement of the emotionally-charged Oka crisis that had already cost the life of a Quebec provincial police officer.

The ensuing tense weeks were filled with conflict and potentially explosive situations, all in the glare of the ever-present media. Throughout the 78-day crisis, the potential for catastrophe was omnipresent. Yet, in the end, although mistakes were made and many lessons were learned, the CF and its leadership made the best of a terrible situation and earned the respect of Canadians. That story is told within these pages. Tim Winegard has written a well-researched study of Oka, which also focuses on the CF's participation during that aid to the civil power operation. As such, it provides the background and context to the major issues, as well as a detailed explanation of the struggle and eventual outcome. In sum it provides an excellent case study and is worthy of study by all military leaders and those interested in Canadian military affairs.

In closing, I wish to reiterate that *Oka: A Convergence of Cultures and the Canadian Forces* is an important new addition to the CDA Press list of titles. It adds to the sparse body of contemporary Canadian military operational leadership literature. As such, I believe that it will provide valuable insight to all those who serve in, and equally those who interact with, the profession of arms in Canada.

Colonel Bernd Horn
Chairman, CDA Press

INTRODUCTION

The sleepy town of Oka, Quebec, strategically positioned at the confluence of the Ottawa and St. Lawrence Rivers, existed in relative obscurity save for the production of a pungent semi-soft cheese made by the cloistered men of a local seminary. Located roughly 65 kilometres (km) northwest of Montreal, this one-stoplight village of 3,000 people hardly seemed the site to cultivate Canada's longest and most capricious internal rebellion since the late nineteenth century. Underneath what appeared to be the town's innocent atmosphere and playful outdoor demeanour lurked an ugly tenebrous reality that had plagued the region of the Lake of Two Mountains since the arrival of French missionaries in the early eighteenth century.

The protracted conflict between the Native inhabitants of Kanesatake ("On the Sandy Dunes") and the religious order of the Seminary of St-Sulpice had been seething for almost 300 years. On the surface, it took the proposed expansion of the Oka Golf Club to ignite the long-standing feud into an armed revolt, which spread to the neighbouring Mohawk Reserve of Kahnawake on the south shore of Montreal. The masked, gun-wielding Mohawk Warriors and the subsequent deployment of the Canadian Forces (CF) gripped the curiosity of a nation paralyzed with fear. This *was* happening in Canada.

The standoff during the spring and summer of 1990 between elements of the Mohawk Nation and various Canadian and American security agencies at Akwesasne, Ganienkeh, Kanesatake (Oka) and Kahnawake was not born in a vacuum. The federal government of Canada, the provincial governments of Quebec and Ontario, and the numerous factions within the Mohawk Nation had conflicting arguments to validate their own agendas. It is evident that the foundations of the violent events that transpired lie in none of the immediate or neighbouring factors on which the attention was focused.

To compound the confusion, the legal framework and the political understanding for the deployment of the Canadian Forces, 4,500 strong, in the function of *Aid to the Civil Power* were and are not understood. In reality, the CF deployment, dubbed Operation SALON, rivalled Canada's commitment to the 1st Commonwealth Division during the Korean War (1950-1953) and to NATO in West Germany during the Cold War. Currently, no more than 2,500 Canadian soldiers, at any given time, are in support of the International Security Assistance Force (ISAF) as part of Operation ATHENA in Afghanistan (2001—).

In contrast, the Canadian Forces deployment to Kanesatake and Kahnawake, under Operation SALON, peaked at 3,700 soldiers.[1]

The conflict at Kanesatake over the area locally known as "the Pines" appeared to stem from the decision of the Oka town council to expand the local golf course by nine holes, in conjunction with the erection of 60 luxury homes along the fairways of the proposed course. However, this pronouncement was preceded by numerous land claims dating back to the seventeenth and eighteenth centuries and what was perceived by the Aboriginal inhabitants to be a neglectful governmental policy towards Native issues. As the eventual 78-day standoff progressed, ulterior motives entered the Native agenda. Mohawk Nation sovereignty and self-determination became principal points of demand and debate, overshadowing the campaign to save the white pine forest.

The peaceful protests of the early spring were replaced with armed confrontations and violent blockades. Under the guise of Native rights, elements of the Mohawk Nation's Warrior Society sought to protect an illegal enterprise of gambling and a smuggling network for cigarettes, alcohol, weapons and human trafficking. Whether or not the Canadian public was aware of the deep-seated causes of the conflict, the ensuing media barrage that engulfed the standoff firmly entrenched Oka in the social consciousness of the Canadian public, and to some extent, of the international community.

Few would argue that the militant posture of a certain, relatively small, collective of Mohawks during the Oka Crisis amplified the nation's awareness of the plight of Indigenous Canadians and their struggles for cultural and territorial recognition. Standing alone then, this was indeed a positive attribute to the summer of 1990. However, this point, when coupled with the larger violent manifestation of Native frustrations cannot, in any rational thought, be considered a victory for the Mohawk Nation, Indigenous Canadians or the peoples and governments of Canada. The horribly frightening scenes of Canadians pointing guns at other Canadians cannot, and should not in the future, be seen as a viable solution to the divides of politics and ethnicity.

However, in openly criticizing the Warrior Society and its radical actions, the legitimate grievances of the Mohawk Nation and Canadian Aboriginals as an entirety might be detrimentally overlooked. In contrast, identifying the Warriors as the voice and ambassadors of the Mohawk people would be dangerous, disadvantageous and unequivocally unfounded and unwarranted.[2] Correspondingly, the Warrior Society was made up of a diverse collective with differing motivations and a large disparity in stance concerning illicit practices. The vast majority of Mohawks are proud, peaceful and law-abiding members of their communities.

What follows is neither a condemnation nor an accusation. The Oka Crisis was the product of two distinct cultures converging over 300 years to clash in the microcosm that was the spring and summer of 1990. Colonization and governmental regulations created an atmosphere of dissent and isolation within Native communities. Colonization, imperial warfare in North America, western religion and subsequent regal and Canadian policies created divisions in both the Iroquois Confederacy and the Mohawk Nation. This dissent and the long-standing religious and political factions of the Mohawk Nation, in combination with more recent neglectful governmental land claim policies, led to the violent manifestations of Mohawk frustrations. The original Warriors were highly idealistic and viewed themselves as the front-line defence to protect Mohawk land. With the continuation of neglectful governmental policies and a loss of economic stability, the Warrior Society transformed itself into a multi-facet organization, which included criminal elements.

In effect, the governments of Canada and Quebec helped create the Oka Crisis and the Warrior Society through a history of assimilation, neglect and non-negotiated policies. The creation of an *Indian Act* and land claim policies without any Native input or opinion left Aboriginal Canadians with little power to control or change the decisions made by governments that drastically affected their culture and communities negatively. Barricading roads and bridges with high traffic volume was seen as the only option to bring the governments to the negotiating table.

The Oka Crisis was about legitimate grievances over land rights at Kanesatake. There can be no doubting this. However, the longer it progressed through failed negotiations, the more members of the Warrior Society, aided by non-Mohawk corporate interests, were allowed to use these justifiable grievances of the Mohawk Nation to usurp power to protect a multi-million dollar gaming and smuggling network. The ultimate goal for certain Warriors was to intimidate both the Mohawks who opposed them, and also the governments of Canada and Quebec, so that control of the Reserves remained with them, unchallenged by internal or external police forces. The Oka Crisis originated from valid Mohawk frustrations over unheard and unheeded land claim submissions. It was a cause that all Mohawks could support. Unfortunately, this included elements of the Warrior Society which altered the methods for change using the classic revolutionary formula, ultimately transforming Akwesasne into a narco-parastate.[3]

The deployment of the CF was in many respects unavoidable. The Sûreté du Québec (SQ) was unprepared to confront the Warriors and their supporters and could not match the Warriors' weapon arsenal. When the SQ attempted to forcefully end the standoff on 11 July, they only escalated an already volatile situation. Secondly, the framework of *Aid to the Civil Power* left the CF with no choice but to intervene at the request of the Province of Quebec. The actions initiated by the CF ended the immediate crisis without any further loss of life. The deployment of the Canadian Forces in such magnitude within Canada warrants an explanation and an understanding, which is lacking in the historical record of the Oka Crisis.

The foundations of the Oka Crisis are extremely complex and embody many perspectives. The strife and violence that paralyzed Mohawk country were not a progression of isolated events but the radical culmination of many. In an attempt to reach a more comprehensive understanding of these viewpoints and to connect these events, the story must begin with an outline and synopsis of the Mohawk position within the framework of North American politics and history. Inextricably, their history is coupled with the history of European colonialism and western political thought, the evolution of which created long-standing feuds and disagreements over land claims and Native self-determination. The Oka Crisis represents the violent collision of the convergence of two distinct cultures.[4]

PART I
Converging Cultures

The Oka Crisis was not an isolated event in the history of the Mohawk Nation. It was the unfortunate manifestation of the convergence of Aboriginal culture and territorial holdings in connection with the arrival of Europeans and the posture, attitudes and policies of successive North American governments relating to Native rights and concerns. These are the two converging lines; the Indigenous peoples of Turtle Island in connection with Europeans. In relation, the story of the Oka Crisis must be written as such. The reasons for the Oka Crisis are equally as important as the events and approaches for resolution initiated by both sides during the crisis itself.

The converging lines narrowed during 300 years of precarious cohabitation to finally and violently meet in 1990 in the form of barricades and hostility within the territories of the Mohawk Nation. The introduction of these lines to form an uneasy relationship began with the arrival of European explorers and their contact with the Native nations of North America. When Jacques Cartier met the St. Lawrence Iroquois in 1534 the future of the Native population, more specifically the Iroquois Confederacy and its Mohawk Nation, became inseparably linked to the future of the colonizing nations. It is within this history that the origins of the Oka Crisis lie.

Included in this history are the political organizations, culture and practices of the Mohawk Nation as a microcosm of the larger Iroquois Confederacy. These characteristics were drastically altered by interaction with European settlers. The introduction of Christianity, European political thought, institutions, warfare and capitalism, in the form of the fur trade, all had a profound impact on the cohesion of the Five Nations Iroquois Confederacy and its Great Law of Peace.

The infusion of continental European wars into the landscape of North America, coupled with Native participation, forever altered the *status quo* and ultimately led to the downfall of the Iroquois Confederacy. Its position as the premier military power, not only among Native alliances but also among the rival European powers, was irreversibly lost. The inescapable onslaught of European culture unhinged the Iroquois Confederacy by creating political, religious and allegiance divisions within its member nations including the Mohawk. These divisions created through contact and fostered by consecutive governmental policies forged the atmosphere for future conflict within the Mohawk Nation culminating at Akwesasne, Kanesatake and Kahnawake during 1990.

The combination of these divisions and the failure of negotiated land claims created a dissident environment leading to the foundation of the archetype for militant Canadian Aboriginals in the form of the Mohawk Warrior Society. The Mohawk transition from loyal British ally to ward of Ottawa's paternalistic and assimilationist *Indian Act* was stubbornly resisted and the Mohawk actively took a lead role in the 1960s "red power movement." In the 20 years before the Oka Crisis, the Warrior Society was reintroduced into Mohawk culture, armed itself with a sophisticated weapon arsenal and subsequently grew corrupt.[5] To gain legitimacy, it connected the valid frustrations of Aboriginal communities with armed militancy and criminal activities. The Warriors implemented revolutionary tactics, and intimidated and attacked their brethren, creating further splits within the traditional Longhouse and the *Indian Act* Band Councils.

Given the numerous partitions within the Mohawk Nation and the struggle for power, the Reserves were left without any dominant form of governance. The Oka Crisis was an exercise of power. It was a struggle for power between the Mohawk Nation in its entirety against the land claims policies of the federal government. However, it also represented the struggle for power within the Mohawk Nation itself. While many Canadians view the Oka Crisis as a defining moment in Canadian-Native relations, this perspective is not shared by the Mohawk Nation. It is simply one more example of contention within the converging cultures throughout the past 300 years.

CHAPTER 1

The Iroquois Confederacy and the Great Law of Peace

In order to appreciate the complexities and causes for the Oka Crisis an examination of the remarkable, and at times confusing, history of the Iroquois Confederacy, or the Six Nations is paramount. This includes the culture, traditions and history of the Mohawk Nation and its people who still maintain the belief that they are a sovereign nation within the confines of North America; their historical record and oral history pre-date the "discovery" of the New World by Christopher Columbus. The Oka Crisis was simply another episode in a protracted conflict between their culture and that of the European powers. The European presence had profound impacts on the political, social and military systems of the Indigenous peoples of North America, the influences of which are still felt today.

Currently, more than two million Canadians can claim some Native ancestry, 650,000 under the bureaucratic decree of "Status Indian" living on one of more than 2,200 Reserves totalling roughly 600,000 square kilometres. The Canadian Assembly of First Nations estimates that at the time of European contact, some 20 million Natives were living in North America, organized in diverse and culturally distinct nations.[6] Although North American Native culture was less technologically developed than some Asian and European cultures, multifarious trade routes networking the entire continent had existed for centuries and great empires flourished.

The Mohawk or *Kanien'keha:ka* (People of the Flint) was one of five nations belonging to the Iroquois Confederacy or *Haudenosaunee*, an intricate political and cultural association of neolithic farmers and hunters centred in what is now upper New York State. The Iroquois nations migrated north from what is believed to be the Oklahoma-Missouri-Arkansas area in the fourteenth or fifteenth centuries, after being displaced by the more powerful Osage and Quapaw Nations.[7] Due to the relatively secure food supply in the north, the Iroquoian peoples lived a sedentary lifestyle resulting in greater population concentrations than those tribes of migratory hunter-gatherers. Some Iroquoian towns numbered 1,500 persons, while most consisted of 300-500 persons. This population density was responsible for the distinct architectural feature of the longhouse—multi-family dwellings, many of which were encircled by fortified palisade walls to create a defensible and guarded village. The Iroquois became known as "the people of the longhouse" or *Rotinonhesasha:ka*.[8]

The Mohawk were living in fortified villages along the Mohawk River near present-day Utica, Albany and Schenectady, New York State. The eastern-most nation of the Confederacy or "Keepers of the Eastern Gate," Mohawk territory stretched from the northern banks of the St. Lawrence River, including Montreal Island, to as far south as the Mohawk River, encompassing the Adirondack Mountains in Vermont, the Connecticut River Valley, and the lands surrounding Lake Champlain.

To the west were the villages and hunting grounds of the Oneida (*Hodenehiota*—People of the Standing Stone), Onondaga (*Onodahgeyga*—People of the Hills), and the Cayuga (*Gayogwenga*—People of the Swamp). The Seneca (*Donahguh*—People of the Great Hills) were the largest of the five nations and like their Mohawk brethren in the east, were the "Keepers of the Western Gate." Seneca lands bordered the shores of Lake Erie and Lake Ontario.[9] Farther west existed smaller groups of Iroquoian-speaking enemies: the Huron (*Wendat/Wyandot*), the Wenro, the Neutrals, the Tionontati and the Erie. To the south in present-day Pennsylvania lived the Susquehannock, another related enemy of the five nations. The Carolinas were home to the Tuscarora, who in the early eighteenth century fled settlers and rival Native nations, taking refuge in New York among the Iroquois. They entered the Confederacy as a non-voting member in 1722, thus creating the Six Nations Confederacy as it is still known today.[10]

The association of these initial five nations into an alliance predates European arrival. Iroquois tradition recounts that the formation of the coalition was due to the desires of Deganawida (Peace Maker) and Aionwatha (Hiawatha) to end the feuding, cannibalism and war that had long been present among the five nations, while also bringing a larger peace to the other Native nations in the surrounding regions.[11] Thus, by the creation of this powerful alliance, the five nations had the ability to defend themselves but also, if necessary, wage war in overwhelming numbers against their enemies. In a demonstration of solidarity, oral tradition recounts how the members of the five nations, under the influence of Deganawida, buried their hatchets and war clubs under the Tree of Peace. In short, the Iroquois Confederacy was an alliance predicated upon parallel cultural and clan associations for strategic military purposes.[12] Although the origin of the Confederacy has been dated as early as 1142, it is more likely, based on archaeological and historical evidence, that the

Confederacy was consolidated in the mid-fifteenth century, at which time the Iroquois numbered roughly 20,000.[13]

Based on the matrilineal clan system of the five nations and the fundamental tenet of resolutions by consensus, the Confederacy was a subdivided network of relations joining households to villages and in turn, connecting these villages to their respective nation councils. These national councils formed the basis for the Confederacy's Central Fire at Onondaga, the most central of the nations. The Onondaga also served as the "Keeper of the Wampum." Customary to Iroquois tradition, the Wampum—multi-coloured beads woven into a belt—served as an archival history of the treaties and important events of the Confederacy and its member nations.[14]

All nations followed the Longhouse traditions, in which 15 to 20 people lived in a longhouse, each represented by a head Clan Mother. In this complex political system, all 50 of the Confederacy Chiefs and the War Chiefs were men, and were chosen, based on matriarchal hereditary lineage, by the Clan Mothers at local councils. The Clan Mothers also had the ability to rescind a Chief's title and role. While the Chiefs had the power to make decisions based on consensus, their appointment resided with the women, giving all members of society a voice in the greater Iroquois political organizations.[15]

Table 1—Iroquois Clans[16]

Seneca	Cayuga	Onondaga	Tuscarora	Oneida	Mohawk
Wolf	Wolf	Wolf	Wolf	Wolf	Wolf
Bear	Bear	Bear	Bear	Bear	Bear
Turtle	Turtle	Turtle	Turtle	Turtle	Turtle
Snipe	Snipe	-	Snipe	-	-
Deer	-	Deer	Deer	-	-
Beaver	-	Beaver	Beaver	-	-
Heron	Heron	-	-	-	-
Hawk	-	Hawk	-	-	-
-	-	Eel	Eel	-	-

The clan arrangements also served to strengthen the ties between the nations themselves through singular clan allegiances. The Mohawk possessed only the Turtle, Wolf and Bear clans, however; other nations included the Heron,

Hawk, Eel, Snipe, Deer and Beaver clans. Correspondingly, a Mohawk of the Bear clan would inevitably be connected with a Seneca or Oneida of that same clan. Clan kinship and loyalties were as strong as kinship with and loyalty to a respective nation.[17]

The Great Law of Peace (*Kaianerakowa*), which is essentially the Iroquois Confederacy Constitution, ensured the autonomy of each nation over local interests, while jurisdiction over foreign and military policy remained at the Confederacy level. The Great Law provides the laws and doctrines that are the foundation of Iroquois life and culture. It consists of 117 articles, including the rights and duties of statesmen, ownership of land and animals, spiritual ceremonial customs and the rights of the people. In addition, as the Confederacy was formed for strategic military purposes, more than one-quarter of the articles refer to actions of war and to the role of "Warriors," known in Mohawk as *Rotisken'rake:ta*, or carriers of the burden of peace.[18]

These men who formed the war parties were guided by the Great Law of Peace and did not act independently of the wishes of the Clan Mothers and the Chiefs, although they were under the direct control of the War Chief of each nation making up the united Confederacy. The Great Law of Peace states: "If the War Chief acts contrary to the instructions or against the provisions of the Great Law of Peace...he shall be deposed by his woman relatives and by his male relatives.... The woman title holders shall then choose another candidate."[19] Again, it is clear that war itself was a democratic philosophy with all levels of society participating in the decision-making process.

Centuries before the arrival of Europeans the Mohawk developed their tradition of warfare. Its origins lie in a kind of masculine sport in which battles were relatively isolated and casualties low. Raiding parties were sent to settle scores, to avenge the deaths of clan members or simply to replace a deceased family member. In addition, the practice of taking prisoners and incorporating them into the tribe, sometimes after a period of torture or servitude, ensured the exchange of cultural traditions and information, the configuration of informal alliances, enhanced trading opportunities, and the dissemination of broader genetic traits. Although these practices perpetuated a chronic state of war, the bloodshed remained minimal.[20]

With the advent of the Confederacy in the mid-fifteenth century and the cessation of internal hostilities, the Mohawks emerged as the strongest and most militarily adept nation within the League of Iroquois. Although the Mohawk population (roughly 2,000 in 1580) was relatively small compared with other nations, their military prowess afforded them a prominent role within the Confederacy and so began an expansion of territory to bring peace and the justice of the Great Law to neighbouring Native nations. If these nations refused the requests of the Confederacy the Great Law authorized the use of force to conquer these objecting nations.[21]

While negating fighting within the Iroquois, the formation of the Confederacy broadened the scope and range of military excursions, and a more organized and disciplined method of warfare emerged from the Confederacy camps. War was now a tool used by the Confederacy to promote its own interests and policy within its sphere of influence. The Iroquois Confederacy was a military and political coalition unrivalled in North America. For the next 100 years, through proficient warfare and skilled diplomacy, the Confederacy expanded its territorial holdings and its population through the adoption of conquered peoples.[22] There were few tribes who avoided friction with this great power; in time this included the European nations.

Indigenous peoples warred, displaced one another and exterminated each other long before the European discovery of the New World. Military histories are marred by the often repetitious pattern of human behaviour; one culture's greater numbers and superior technology dominating another culture. However, the sophisticated political and military organization of the Iroquois Confederacy was drastically altered by the infusion of European culture, values and weapons into North America. Throughout the first two centuries after contact French, British, British colonials (Americans), Canadians and Native nations struggled for control of the continent. These wars, which pitted the world's two most dominant powers, Britain and France, against one another in a struggle for imperial domination left the Iroquois Confederacy in the uncertain position of attempting to promote its own policy and agenda in the face of a cultural upheaval.

CHAPTER 2

The Effects of Colonialism on the Shaping of North America

There can be no doubt that for all inhabitants of the Americas the arrival of Europeans was the most significant disturbance and threat to their populations, civilizations and futures. The clash of mores resulting from European settlement was composed of many contradicting features: a rapidly evolving modernity stemming from the Reformation and the Age of Reason against Native tradition relatively undisturbed by any equivalent social or intellectual revolution; Christianity versus a multiplicity of Shamanistic, animistic practices and rituals; paternalism in opposition to maternalism; European expansionism compared with relative changelessness and isolation in the Americas.[23] Furthermore, the literate European society contrasted with a creative Native oral tradition led to great misunderstandings and at times perfidious actions on the part of the Europeans.[24] With the arrival of Europeans also came modern weapons, deadly diseases, religion and alcohol. In addition, continental European wars were imported to North America and Aboriginals were enlisted to partake in them, which, in combination with the fur trade fractured long-standing Native alliances, including the Iroquois Confederacy. All would have a profound impact on the shaping of the Western hemisphere and its Native populations. It is within these initial years of European contact that the divisions within the Iroquois Confederacy and the Mohawk Nation, so prevalent during the 1990 crisis, were generated.

The Spanish, with the likes of Columbus, de Leon, Balboa and Cortes, had made contact with the Native inhabitants of Cuba, the Caribbean and Central and South America in the late fifteenth and early sixteenth centuries. Spanish greed for riches created more expeditions including those in North America by Coronado, de Vaca and de Soto in the mid-sixteenth century. Further north, representing England, John Cabot made voyages to Newfoundland-Labrador, continuing down the eastern seaboard in 1497/1498. The French-sponsored Verrazano retraced Cabot's voyage in 1524.[25] However, the Iroquois remained isolated from these early European expeditions. It was not until 1534 that Jacques Cartier, on a quest to find riches comparable to the Spaniards' sequestered Aztec and Inca plunder in the south (and a route to Asia), made contact with the Iroquoian people in the Gulf of St. Lawrence.[26]

While anchored off of the Gaspe Peninsula near Anticosti Island on 22 July 1534 one of Jacques Cartier's deck officers recorded the following statement in his log book: "Their heads are shaved all around in circles except for a tuft on the top...long like a horse's tail, tied in a knot with a leather thong."[27] What he was describing was a fishing party of St. Lawrence Iroquois. They occupied no fewer than 11 relatively small villages along the St. Lawrence River, with larger settlements at Stadacona and Hochelaga, near present-day Quebec City and Montreal. Further north and west were the communities of the Algonquian Nations, the primary enemies of the Iroquois.[28]

Cartier erected a large wooden cross on the Gaspe Peninsula, to the curiosity of Native onlookers, and claimed the land for his king and country. According to Cartier, "at length we bartered with them...for everything they possessed, so that nothing was left to them but their naked bodies; for they offered us everything they owned, which was, all told, of little value."[29] He returned to France with two sons of Chief Donnacona—Taignoagny and Domagaya—who held court with Francois I, King of France. Cartier was disappointed at having to tell the royal court that, "the whole lot of them had not anything above the value of five sous, their canoes and fishing-nets excepted," and that there were no great golden cities or vast empires similar to those in the south. Nevertheless, he was ordered back to the region the following year.[30]

In September 1535, Cartier returned to Stadacona with his two Native guides and proceeded upriver, passing several smaller Iroquoian villages until he reached the larger palisaded centre of Hochelaga on 3 October. Cartier numbered the population at roughly 1,500, living in 50 longhouses situated in the middle of corn fields at the foot of what he dubbed "le Mont Royal."[31] After climbing this mountain, one of Cartier's crewmembers noted: "We saw the river [St. Lawrence] extending beyond the place where we had left our longboats. At that point there is the most violent rapid [Lachine Rapids] it is possible to see."[32]

These Iroquois also told Cartier and his men that, "along the mountain to the north there is a big river [Ottawa River] that comes from the west...and that up there were the 'Agojuda,' which means bad people, who were armed to the teeth.... They also seemed to say that these 'Agojuda' waged war continually." The Iroquois were referring to the Algonquians, who had been embroiled in a perpetual state of war with the Iroquois Confederacy.[33]

While Basque whalers and French fisherman continued coming to North America, none ventured any farther upriver than present-day Tadoussac.

There it is believed the Montagnais traded furs with these visitors in exchange for metal wares including knives and axes. The Montagnais in turn traded these metallic weapons to the Algonquin for more furs. These metal weapons were far superior to the stone weapons of the St. Lawrence Iroquois, giving the Algonquian Warriors a clear advantage in the long-standing feud. Consequently, the people of Hochelaga and Stadacona were forced to abandon their villages and retreat south to live with other members of their nation, presumably the Mohawk.[34]

The diaries of Cartier and his crew are the only eyewitness accounts of the Iroquoian villages along the St. Lawrence. When Cartier returned for a third time in 1541 to establish the first French colony in the Americas under Roberval, there was a small village at Montreal but it was called Tutonaguy and was not Iroquoian. Later accounts by other explorers who traversed the Montreal region make no mention of any settlements in the area.[35] When Samuel de Champlain made his first visit in 1603, there were neither cornfields nor any remnants of human occupation where Hochelaga once stood. It was a no man's land in the protracted war between the Algonquian Nations to the northwest and northeast and the Iroquois to the south. Champlain recounted in 1603 that, "This region, although pleasant is not inhabited by Indians, on account of their wars; for they withdraw from the rivers as far as they can into the interior, in order not to be surprised."[36]

Despite the arrival of Europeans, the Iroquois possessed a unity and a purpose, in the form of the Great Law, which their enemies could not match. They continued to promote their interests through war on their traditional enemies. In the east, Mohawk war parties continuously harassed the Algonquin and Montagnais to the point of driving them from the Adirondack Mountains north back across the St. Lawrence. Threat of war with the Mohawk caused the smaller Pequot and Mohegan nations to simply migrate away from the potential confrontation, leaving their lands for new homes in southern New England around 1600. The Iroquois initiated war with the powerful Mahican Confederacy to the east, while Mohawk attacked the Poctumuc, a Mahican ally to the south in 1606.[37]

In 1608, Champlain was charged with setting up a settlement at Quebec to develop, promote and control the burgeoning fur trade with surrounding Native peoples. Champlain formed trade and military alliances with the Montagnais, Naskapi (Innu), the Algonquin and the Huron. This partnership obliged him to support and participate in their traditional wars against the Iroquois who were expropriating lands in all directions.[38] In July of 1609, Champlain accompanied a Huron, Montagnais and Algonquin war party which moved south along the Iroquois River (Richelieu River) and continued along the western shores of Lake Champlain: "We entered the lake [Champlain]...in which I saw four beautiful islands...which, like the Iroquois River, were formerly inhabited by Indians; but have been abandoned, since they have been at war with one another."[39] On the 29th, they encountered a group of roughly 200 Mohawk Warriors. In the ensuing battle, French arquebuses scattered the massed Mohawk formation while killing no fewer than 50 Warriors including two chiefs. The following year Champlain participated in another attack against a Mohawk palisade village on the Richelieu River.[40]

The Mohawks quickly adapted their tactics to combat this advanced weaponry. They began using small guerrilla forces instead of the previous mass formations, discarding their bulky wooden armour to achieve greater stealth and speed. If confronted directly by French muskets, Warriors learned to fall in a timely fashion to avoid the shots, quickly attacking before the shooter could reload. However, the French continued to push westward into Huron territory and subsequently began arming all Native nations opposed to the Iroquois, who were now in a predicament. In order to acquire these new technologically enhanced weapons and armour, the Iroquois needed a European trading partner. Thus far, the French fur trade was controlled by the Iroquois' enemies. The Iroquois continued to make the French traders pay dearly for their outside intervention by initiating raids along trading routes and by controlling Lake Ontario, forcing the French traders north to use the Ottawa River. Yet, they could not bring to bear the might of the Iroquois Confederacy without modern weapons.[41]

In 1610, Dutch traders arrived in the Hudson Valley of New York and the Iroquois began trading furs for firearms. However, the Iroquois were still being pressed by the Algonquin, Huron and Montagnais in the north and by 1615 were fighting the Susquehannock to the south. To make matters worse, the powerful Mahican Confederacy blocked Mohawk access to the majority of Dutch traders and outposts and the Mahicans soon became the primary Dutch ally and business associate. This situation inevitably led to war, with the Mohawks defeating the Mahicans and their western Abenaki allies, the Pocumtuc and the Sokoki, in 1628. Soon, the Mohawks became so dominant that their Dutch trading partners were forced to accept a Mohawk monopoly and a 1645 peace treaty using the two-row wampum belt.[42]

In order to secure more furs and trapping areas, the Iroquois (using Mohawk Warriors) turned their attention to their Algonquin, Huron and Montagnais enemies in the north, driving them well north of the St. Lawrence River. Expansion south was stymied for a time by a stubborn Susquehannock resistance created by an inexhaustible supply of weapons from the Swedes along the Delaware River. However, the Dutch expropriated the Swedish colonies in 1655. Now deprived of weapons, the Susquehannock quickly sued for peace with the Mohawk, who readily agreed. There were two outcomes of these actions. The first was the enlargement of Mohawk/Iroquois territory. The second was an increased hostility between the League of Iroquois, more specifically the easternmost Mohawk, and the French.[43]

The Iroquois used a combination of military might and skilled diplomacy to attain what can be termed an Empire. Through conquest and migration, at its height in 1680 this empire extended west from the Chesapeake Bay through Kentucky to the confluence of the Ohio and Mississippi Rivers, north along the Illinois River to Lake Michigan, across Michigan, southern Ontario and Quebec. To the south the Iroquois occupied northern New England, the Hudson and Delaware Valleys, across Pennsylvania back to the Chesapeake.[44] After having defeated the Susquehannock and the Mahicans, southern expansion remained stagnant at the Carolinas. One reason for this was that the fertile hunting grounds to the north were of greater importance. Another, probably more valid reason, was that the powerful Cherokee Nation blocked any potential expansion.[45]

Through the massive adoption of their conquered enemies, population also increased. However, the Iroquois never offered wholesale adoption to the non-Iroquoian-speaking nations, continuing to regard them as second-class citizens. Ethnocentricity was not the product of European contact. Equally important to future events was the fact that many of these new additions, the Huron in particular, had been indoctrinated with Christianity through French missionization.[46] Not only did these prisoners replace the Iroquois population that had been lost through disease and war, they also brought these religious facets into the Iroquoian culture contributing to the demise of the Confederacy and also to the factionalism and division within the Mohawk Nation itself.

By the mid-seventeenth century, the Native nations on the periphery of Iroquois land had been displaced, annihilated or absorbed and had surrendered their lands to the Iroquois Confederacy. The Potawatomi, Fox, Sauk and Mascouten had been driven from Michigan and were living in mixed camps in upper Wisconsin, while the Shawnee, Kickapoo and Miami had been forced from the Ohio Valley and lower Indiana. The Kickapoo and Miami relocated to Wisconsin, and the Shawnee scattered across Illinois, Tennessee, South Carolina, while smaller enclaves migrated into southern Michigan and Ontario. The Seneca drove the peoples of the Illinois Nation west of the Mississippi River after they had collaborated with the Huron in raiding parties. The Dhegiha Lakota (Sioux), a group of five sub-tribes, all moved west of the Missouri River, except for the Quapaw who ventured south to Arkansas. The Huron, Wenro, Tionontati, Neutrals and Erie were either close to extinction or incorporated into the Iroquois League. The Huron were virtually extinct after a series of battles along the south-eastern shores of Lake Huron and the Bruce Peninsula near present day Owen Sound. The Ottawa, Nipissing and Ojibwa moved north en mass, leaving only small groups behind in southern Ontario and Quebec. Most of these remnants were quickly absorbed into Iroquoian villages.[47]

Blessed with superb organization, modern European weapons and high numbers of skilled Warriors, the Five Nations swept to victory against their enemies. The Mohawk became the dominant power in the use of guerrilla warfare in the vast terrain east of the Mississippi River, and enjoyed the lucrative position of being located in the centre of the North American fur trade. However, Iroquoian supremacy was short-lived. The arrival of a new European power, the British, drastically altered the division of power and the relationships between the Iroquois nations and the European powers. The British had seized all Dutch assets in North America by 1664 and the Treaty of Westminster ten years later put an end to Dutch ambitions in the New World. In 1664, the British also revised the two-row wampum treaty originally cited by the Dutch. Again, the Iroquois viewed this wampum treaty as a sign that its nations and the British could both maintain political and territorial sovereignty in North America.[48] Both the British and the earlier Dutch wampum treaties would be referenced by the Mohawk in defence of their sovereignty and land claims throughout the twentieth century including the Oka Crisis itself.

British traders and officials quickly realized the importance the Iroquois could play as allies, and the negative repercussions of having such a powerful confederacy as an enemy.[49] The British sought to exploit the Mohawk enmity for the French to enhance their own position by forging trading opportunities and military alliance against the French. It should be noted that most Native nations fought for themselves and not for European powers. They pursued their own interests in both trade and war. As J.R. Miller accurately pointed out: "In other words, notions that one nation, or another took up arms to advance a commercial or strategic aim of the French or British were erroneous."[50]

For the Iroquois, their ambitions exceeded their power. During the 1660s, Mohawk Warriors engaged in a series of protracted wars against the French along the St. Lawrence while continuing their traditional hostilities with their Algonquian enemies. Worn down by these enduring conflicts and losing population to both war and disease, the Iroquois made a significant decision. Realizing that their geographical position between the French and the English made them targets of both powers and that they had little to gain from the victory of either state, the Iroquois Confederacy sought neutrality in 1665, against objections from the Mohawk.[51] This had numerous results. For the French, not only did it terminate the costly war between themselves, their Native allies, and the Iroquois, but it also robbed Britain of a powerful partner.[52] In turn, it isolated Mohawk interests and diminished the threat of an Iroquois military coalition. With no security offered by the Confederacy, the Mohawk initiated their own peace with the French in 1667.[53] Cracks began to appear in the once-cohesive structure and alliance of the Confederacy itself.

The divisions within the Five Nations caused by the incursion of European war, weapons and the capitalist fur trade would never be mended. While the convergence of Native culture and European culture continued, the League of Iroquois became progressively weakened. The presence of two European powers within the Iroquoian land base created shifting alliances. Individual Iroquois nations began to promote their own agendas, distinct from the greater Confederacy. The eastern most Mohawk were in the most difficult geographic position amidst the influx of European settlers and the front lines of the colonial wars. These unavoidable circumstances deepened the initial rifts between the Mohawk Nation and its Confederacy but also within the Mohawk Nation itself. By 1990 these separations were more numerous, complicated and complex.

CHAPTER 3

Deepening Divisions: Mohawk Communities in New France

The continuation of colonial wars and the intermittent periods of peace furthered the divisions within the nations of the Iroquois Confederacy. The wars created alliances between one nation and a European counterpart, while other nations remained neutral or sided with the opposite European counterpart, thus rejecting the principles of the Great Law of Peace. The cessation of hostilities allowed packets of the Iroquois population to migrate into once hostile territory and begin trading furs with traditional enemies. With the diffusion of the Iroquois population, different groups within its nations were exposed to different aspects of European culture, none more disruptive than religion and French missionization. Converted elements of the Mohawk Nation migrated north closer to their French religious benefactors, while other groups remained on their traditional lands in New York State and Vermont surrounded or occupied by the British. The religious Mohawk communities of New France, isolated both culturally and geographically from the Confederacy and the Great Law, promoted their own agenda and policy. Inevitably, the gaps in the Confederacy widened.

The fragile peace of 1667 had severe repercussions for the Mohawk and ultimately on the situations at Kanesatake and Kahnawake over the next 300 years. Having conquered their Native enemies and secured peaceful relations with the French, Mohawk families began moving north to the Montreal area to farm, live and trade furs with French settlers. In 1671, there was a sizable Native community (La Montagne) at the base of "le Mont Royal" and another on the south shore called Kahenta:ke. Both included families of Mohawk, Oneida, Onondaga, Nipissing, Abenaki and Huron.[54] The cultural diversity among these early settlements was enhanced as many of the Natives present were adopted war captives and converted Christians. This enabled French missionaries to cohabitate among these diverse Natives and to encourage the practices of Christianity.[55] The fact that these villages were not inhabited exclusively by Mohawk had severe repercussions on Mohawk claims to the land in subsequent centuries, including two formal land claims submitted to the Department of Indian Affairs in 1975 and 1977.

Many of the Natives came to settle these locations to avoid persecution within their own communities based on their religious conversion. In conjunction, the fertile farming and hunting grounds along the St. Lawrence, which had been vacant for over 100 years due to continuous warring with the Algonquian nations, began to be reoccupied by Iroquoian peoples. This included later settlements at Kanesatake/Oka and St. Regis/Akwesasne. These groupings became known as the "praying Indians" of New France.[56]

In 1676, the Native inhabitants of Kahenta:ke relocated roughly one mile upriver to a place astride the Lachine Rapids, known to them as Kahnawake or "At the Rapids." Before the move many of the non-Mohawk natives had left, leaving a dominant Mohawk population, which numbered 600 by 1680.[57] Shortly after this migration along the St. Lawrence, a priest from the Gentlemen of the Seminary of St-Sulpice in Paris began to visit Kahnawake. The Paris-based Father Superior of the Seminary of St-Sulpice was also the seigneur of the Island of Montreal. The territory of Kahnawake was composed of land that had been transferred to the Seminary of St-Sulpice by another religious order in 1663. Apart from the presence of Christianity, life in Kahnawake followed the Mohawk Longhouse traditions, language and clan affiliations.[58] A system was put in place whereby Chiefs representing each traditional Mohawk clan served as liaisons between the people of the community and the Jesuit hierarchy, thus preserving Mohawk traditions.[59]

The same can be said for the community of La Montagne, which was watched over by the energetic actions of the Seminary of St-Sulpice, who erected several European-style buildings, a chapel and schools for both boys and girls. By 1683, there were roughly 200 Native inhabitants from the Mohawk, Algonquin and Huron Nations, many of whom had been British or French prisoners of war.[60] Similarly, in 1676 during the relocation of Kahenta:ke, a small group of Christian Mohawk, Nipissing and Algonquin moved to Kanesatake (Oka) at the Lake of Two Mountains with no accompanying religious benefactor. The spot was known to the Mohawk, as it was previously used as a non-permanent wintering camp for Iroquois Warriors and had been witness to many confrontations between those Warriors and the French dating back to 1608.[61] The relative peace allowed for an interaction between once-hostile Native nations and with the introduction of Christianity, French mission settlements began to appear throughout New France (Quebec).

However, the uneasy peace would not last. With the advent of King William's War (1688-1697) between the British and French, the Iroquois found themselves in a precarious location between these warring nations. They had been trading furs with both countries; however, commercial ties with the British were strengthened, and it appeared to the French that the Confederacy had made a decision to support British interests.[62] The fact of the matter was that many Iroquois saw an alternative source of trade in the British, without the disruption of missionary activity. For the British, the religious agenda was not seen as a high priority, whereas the French regarded conversion of the Natives as not only a priority but a duty.

This newly created alliance with the British increased tensions within the Confederacy itself between non-Christian communities and the French mission communities, such as Kahnawake. The split within the Confederacy was so apparent that in 1684, the Confederacy indicated that it no longer recognized the communities and peoples of Kahnawake and La Montagne as part of the League of Iroquois.[63] Henceforth, these settlements became distinct entities, making independent decisions about their own interests and relations with European powers.

These Mohawk communities remained loyal to the French. Likewise, the Confederacy could not remain neutral. The French began to attack Seneca and Onondaga villages in 1687. The Iroquois retaliated with force, killing roughly 200 French settlers at Lachine across the river from Kahnawake in what has become known as the "Lachine Massacre."[64] The three-month siege that followed forced the Mohawk of Kahnawake, along with the French settlers of the region, to take refuge in Montreal.[65] This sanctuary only served to strengthen their political and military allegiance with the French. The Mohawks of Kahnawake had observed the Great Law of Peace up to this point and had remained neutral in the skirmishes between other Iroquois nations and the French; however, the massive Iroquois raid at Lachine altered the neutral position of Kahnawake with regard to the Great Law.

After a year-long refuge in Montreal, the people of Kahnawake established a new community west and upriver from the former site and renamed it Kahnawakon. Six years later it relocated again and was known as Kanatakwenke.[66] Continuing to grow due to migrants from Mohawk villages to the south, it moved for the last time in 1716, at which time the population of Kahnawake numbered roughly 1,000. Here Kahnawake has remained until the present day.[67]

Similarly, the collective at La Montagne was forced to move. It was ravaged by a great fire on 11 September 1694, which destroyed most of the dwellings and also the Sulpician Chapel. A drunken Mohawk was blamed by the missionaries for starting the fire. Serving their purpose, the Sulpicians used liquor as an excuse to move the community away from French settlers to a more remote location called Sault-au-Récollet on the north side of Montreal Island. The Priests of the Seminary of St-Sulpice cohabitated with and oversaw the religious education of this population.[68] Above all else, they deemed it necessary to isolate the Natives from alcohol and other vices, as they believed that the Natives were of weak character and were easily enticed into immoral behaviour: "Then the Priest settled among us and the other clergy of this Island [Montreal] represented in council the inconvenience arising...from our living so near a Town, particularly the disorders committed by some of our young men when they got Rum, and strenuously exhorted us to remove further off from the Town...and pointed out to us Sault-au-Récollet as the spot."[69] The vacated land at La Montagne reverted back to the Superior of the Seminary and was used as a summer retreat.[70]

These two communities of "Praying Indians" were markedly under French influence and 30 Warriors from Kahnawake joined the French and their Native allies in raids against British settlements in New York and Mohawk villages in the Mohawk River Valley throughout King Williams' War. They also served as guides during Louis de Frontenac's expeditions between 1693-1696 that laid waste numerous Oneida, Onondaga and Mohawk villages.[71] The Great Peace was broken as members of the Five Nations were now in direct conflict with one another.

Not only did the Iroquois population diminish from warfare, but smallpox emerged in 1690 and devastated populations in the interior for the next decade. In 1694, the Iroquois were sensing military pressure from both the east and west, while coping with a smallpox epidemic. The combination of these influences forced them to make overtures for a separate peace with the French. These peace offerings were ignored as the Iroquois refused to stop raiding the villages of France's native allies, in order to press their interests in the fur trade.[72]

A peace was finally struck between the British and the French with the Treaty of Ryswick in 1697. This did not include the Iroquois, yet it did place the League of Iroquois under British protectorate—an arrangement not wanted or requested by the Confederacy.[73] Fearing that continuing hostilities with the Confederacy might spawn another confrontation with the British, the French began to negotiate a separate peace with the Iroquois against the wishes of their Algonquian allies. Sensing the turmoil within the Confederacy and the devastation wrought by disease and war, the Algonquian nations and the

Ojibwa thought that by continuing the fighting they could secure the final collapse of the Iroquois Confederacy which continued to lose ground until the cessation of hostilities in 1701.

The Confederacy agreed to a peace with France's native allies, in exchange for a promise that the French would monitor and mediate any future disputes between the Iroquois and the Algonquian. In a rush to secure Iroquois neutrality, the French neglected to discuss claims to the Ohio Valley, and the British usurped the area, using Iroquois claims (as the latter was allegedly under British protection). Henceforth, Iroquois lands belonged to the Crown. The result was that any French attempts to expand westward into the Ohio Valley and the Mississippi River delta would be a violation of British territorial holdings. The Iroquois agreed to remain neutral in any future war between the two European powers.[74] That future war would break out the same year—Queen Anne's War (1701-1713).[75]

The Iroquois had been a British ally during King William's War only to the extent that it served their own interests. War was simply politics by other means. During Queen Anne's War, it served Iroquois interests to remain neutral.[76] The previous war, coupled with disease, had crippled the once-dominant Confederacy in both population and land, and left it vulnerable. While the British and French fought another war and enlisted whatever Native help they could, the Iroquois knew that they needed to recover and replenish their stocks. For the British, the Iroquois remained a useful buffer between themselves and French Canada. Although the Confederacy remained neutral, Kahnawake did not. It continued to support the French and participated in a number of raids on British settlements in New England and Lower Canada in conjunction with Warriors of the Abenaki Nation.[77]

Ending with the Treaty of Utrecht in 1713, Queen Anne's War saw the defeated French surrender their east coast territory, including Nova Scotia, to the British. What was also agreed upon, without the consultation of the Iroquois, was that the Confederacy would continue to be under the governing blanket of the British. Not having participated in the treaty, the Iroquois acknowledged neither empire's rule. They still maintained and regarded themselves as an independent, autonomous nation within the confines of North America and continued to pursue their own interests.[78]

By the end of Queen Anne's War, the Iroquois found themselves strong enough to exert their domination once again. The fur trade had flooded the European market and the price of beaver pelts plummeted drastically. The French, under pressure from their missionaries, renounced the fur trade in a royal proclamation and concentrated on the saving of Native souls through mission work. Still controlling access to British and Dutch traders, the Iroquois proceeded to attack the French/Native alliance, not through warfare but by using trade as a weapon.[79]

Sensing disaster, the Native tribes within the coalition of French allies, began to compete and fight one another for the limited fur trade that was still available. The Iroquois cleverly began trading British goods, which were not only superior in quality but also cheaper. One by one, French allies began trading with the British through the medium of the Iroquois. With the French alliance in disarray, the Confederacy realized that they held the balance of power between the two rival European nations.[80] Britain, fearing French influence among Native nations, supported the Covenant Chain—a loosely constructed alliance of Native nations led by the Iroquois—and pushed numerous tribes into joining the coalition. Membership included (at different times): Shawnee, Miami, Delaware, Susquehannock, Nanticoke, Munsee, Mahican, Cherokee, Creek, Choctaw and Chickasaw. However, the League's ability to represent some of the powerful nations was not absolute. The mighty Cherokee, Choctaw and Creek Nations refused to submit to the Confederacy's authority, often leading to war.[81]

The Iroquois often placed their own interests above those of the nations that they represented. This became a sore point for many non-Iroquoian nations within the Covenant Chain. The only exception would be the Confederacy's adoption of the Iroquoian-speaking Tuscarora, who joined them in western New York in 1714 or 1715 under Oneida sponsorship and became a subordinate member of the now Six Nations Confederacy in 1722.[82] The Confederacy even went so far as to send war parties to punish the Carolina colonists and their Catawba allies who drove the Tuscarora north during the Tuscarora War (1712-1713).[83]

Although outwardly it appeared that the Confederacy was strengthening its bonds by the addition of the Tuscarora and by leading the British-backed Covenant Chain, in reality all was not well. The demise of the Confederacy had already begun with the settlement of French influenced Christian Mohawks in Quebec and eastern Ontario. These communities, isolated from Confederacy support, began their struggles with the French colonial administration and the French religious orders over issues of culture and land. In reality, the Oka Crisis began in the early eighteenth century in the form of conflict over title to the land at the Lake of Two Mountains between the Natives occupants and their religious benefactor, the Seminary of St-Sulpice.

CHAPTER 4

Mohawk Settlement at the Lake of Two Mountains/Oka

The basis for the land claim at Kanesatake can be traced back to the early eighteenth century. Having settled within the influence of the Seminary of St-Sulpice, the Mohawks continuously struggled with this religious order over the propriety of the land they occupied at the Lake of Two Mountains. To compound this issue, the colonial wars continued and the Christian Mohawks at Kanesatake, Kahnawake and Akwesasne found themselves caught between the fragile Confederacy which supported the British, and the French with whom they were more closely associated. While the Mohawks at newly-settled Kanesatake were at odds with the Sulpician order over land rights, the divisions within the Iroquois Confederacy and the Mohawk Nation continued to expand.

By 1715, roughly 600 Natives were living on 400 acres of cleared land at the newly created location of Sault-au-Récollet, 14 kilometres north of Mont Royal.[84] In that year against their wishes these inhabitants were once again asked to move:

> Again our Priest, in conjunction with the clergy of the Seminary of Montreal, told us we should remove once more our families, for it was no longer proper that any Indians should live on this island [of Montreal]. If we would consent to go and settle at the Lake of Two Mountains we should have a large tract of land for which we should have a Deed from the King of France as our property, to be vested in us and our heirs forever, and that we should not be molested again in our habitations.[85]

Prior to this suggested relocation, the Superior of the Seminary (de Belmont) had met with the Governor of Montreal and New France (Marquis Philippe de Rigaud de Vaudreuil). De Belmont proposed that the mission be relocated to a tract of land at the Lake of Two Mountains.[86] The Superior also requested that the land be given in trust to the Seminary for the purpose of the religious education of the Natives. In addition, he applied for an adjacent piece of land solely for use by the missionaries.[87] Although there had been an earlier request by the Seminary for lands at the Lake of Two Mountains in 1712, it was not given serious consideration until this time.[88]

Reasoning that the temptations of liquor would be diminished by the establishment of a new mission isolated from Montreal, the Sulpicians propositioned the authorities of New France for these entitlements to land at the Lake of Two Mountains. However, the primary factor for moving the missionary settlement at Sault-au-Récollet to this suggested location was not out of moral or religious concerns for the Natives; rather, it was military in purpose. The creation of a settlement at the Lake of Two Mountains would provide security to the northwestern flank of Montreal and Quebec City against enemy Iroquois. As mentioned, the region of the Lake of Two Mountains had been a non-permanent camp for Iroquois war parties that frequently passed the north shore of the region to attack Montreal. With memories of the 1660 assault on Montreal and the Lachine Massacre still lingering, the French looked to their Native allies to alleviate this potential western threat:[89]

> It would be advantageous to the Mission of the Indians of the Sault-au-Récollet in the Island of Montreal, which is under their [Sulpicians] care, that it should be immediately transferred...on the north-west side of the Lake of Two Mountains, which said Mission would be advantageous not only for the conversion of the Indians...but also to the colony [of Montreal] which by these means would be protected against incursions of the Iroquois in times of war...[90]

The Governor of New France endorsed the idea, "for the good of the Island of Montreal and to cover it from attacks by other Indians,"[91] and insisted that the Sulpicians build a fort within two years and raise militia forces when needed.[92] On 15 June 1716, Philippe d'Orleans, Regent to the seven-year-old King of France, Louis XV, agreed that a concession at the Lake of Two Mountains be granted to the Seminary of St-Sulpice "in perpetuity" on condition that they would build a church, separate lodging for the missionaries and a stone fort within the previously proscribed two years.[93]

In October 1716, the Superior of the Seminary of St-Sulpice met again with the Governor to discuss not only the cost of relocation, but more importantly, the proprietorship of the land in question. He argued that if his organization was responsible for the expenditures related to the building of a church and fort, that the Seminary be given title to the land upon which they sat.[94]

The Governor agreed: "It seems there is some justice in granting the land to the Seminary in perpetuity."[95]

However, Governor Vaudreuil had no choice but to refer the matter to his superiors in France, as a moratorium on all seigneurial concessions in Quebec had been imposed by the French Crown in 1711.[96] He added that the new location would serve as a garrison protecting Montreal against attacks by other Natives. The military purpose of a missionary settlement at the Lake of Two Mountains was still seen as a priority.[97] It is important to note that Mohawk Chiefs from Sault-au-Récollet were not privy to these discussions and were not counselled on the motives of the Seminary or those of the administrators of New France.[98] On 17 October 1717, the French Crown officially granted the Seminary of St-Sulpice a land concession at the Lake of Two Mountains. The Sulpicians requested a time frame of seven years for the construction of the mandatory fort which was approved on 27 April 1718.[99]

In February 1721, the first families, mostly Mohawk with smaller numbers of Nipissing and Algonquin, arrived at their new home at the Lake of Two Mountains, which they called Kanesatake ("On the Sandy Dunes").[100] By this time there was relative peace in the area. The Iroquois had ceased attacking French settlements and there was no immediate cause for war with the British. The Chiefs, as was customary, proceeded to exchange a wampum belt at the time of the move. Not only did this symbolize a partnership, it also represented the Natives belief that the land they were to occupy belonged to them as originally promised. According to Chief Aghneetha:

> Although it was very inconvenient to us to be quitting our homes and small clearing, yet the desire of having a fixed property of our own induced us to comply, and we accordingly set out, and took possession of the land, and as was the custom of our forefathers we immediately set about making a [wampum] Belt...by which our children would see that the lands were to be theirs forever, and as was the custom of our ancestors we placed the figure of a dog at each end of the Belt to guard our property and to give notice when an enemy approached.[101]

This is the origin of the land claim dispute that led to hostilities between the Native inhabitants and the Seminary and in turn the governments of Quebec and Canada over the next 280 years. The 1990 Oka Crisis was the culmination of the deep-rooted problems associated with the ownership of this land.

After the Native occupation of the land at the Lake of Two Mountains, three more ratifications to the concession of the Seminary of St-Sulpice were approved by the King of France without any consultation with the Natives. In 1731, the Seminary received dispensation from the compulsion to construct any fortification in the area, in addition to compensation for the costs already incurred by the relocation of the settlement and the building of several small dwellings for the Native inhabitants.[102] In September 1733, the Seminary was granted additional land to the east of the existing seigneury. Following this endorsement, the Seminary built a stone church, three houses along with a watchtower. Three cannons were also purchased, which was the extent of any defensive fortifications on the Sulpician lands.[103]

Two years later, on 1 March 1735, King Louis XV signed an additional concession providing the Seminary with additional lands, "...to make the said land more profitable, it would therefore, be necessary to extend the said land further than the three leagues as set forth in the deed of one thousand seven hundred and eighteen."[104] Thus, between 1715 and 1735, the Seminary of St-Sulpice had increased their lands 15 fold from the original decree. Included in this land base was a three-square league tract granted to the Mohawk of the region in a 1716 letter which dubbed it "their land."[105]

The mission settlement at the Lake of Two Mountains remained as such for the next 30 years and the issue of proprietorship over the land did not arise. The Native populations of both the Lake of Two Mountains and Kahnawake remained loyal to the Roman Catholic Church and to the King of France, fighting on the French side in the wars against the British during the 1740s and 1750s. This further accentuated the split within the Mohawk Nation, the Iroquois Confederacy and its Great Law.

In fact, other religious native settlements administered by various French religious orders appeared throughout Quebec during these decades and became known as the Seven Nations of Canada centred at Kahnawake.[106] This Seven Nation alliance also included Kanesatake, which was constructed of the Mohawk, Nipissing and Algonquin, the Onondaga and Cayuga at Oswegatchie, the Huron of Lorette and the Abenaki of Odanak (St. Francis) and Becancour.[107]

The community of Oswegatchie was dispersed during the American Revolution (1775-1783) and after a brief stay at La Presentation (Ogdensburg, N.Y.), its members settled with the Mohawk of St. Regis/Akwesasne ("Where the Partridge Drums"). St. Regis/Akwesasne had been formed in 1755. During this year, the membership of Kahnawake split. One group remained, while another travelled upriver to Akwesasne, at the union of the St. Regis, Raquette, Grass, Salmon and St. Lawrence Rivers straddling present-day New York State, Ontario and Quebec near the city of Cornwall, Ontario.[108] Akwesasne also became a member of the Seven Nations Confederacy, which was thus composed of three groups of Mohawk, one of Algonquin, one of Nipissing, one of Huron and one of Abenaki. All loyal to the French for the next 50 years of colonial conflict, the British considered them formidable opponents and a pawn in French imperial strategy.[109]

When the French and British resumed hostilities with the outbreak of King George's War (1744-1748), Warriors from both Kahnawake and Kanesatake, along with Sokoki and Abenaki, joined in French raids against British posts in the New York frontier, southern Vermont and New Hampshire.[110] Although the Iroquois Confederacy remained neutral, the Mohawk sided with the British and the divisions within the Six Nations alliance became more apparent.[111] With the end of King George's War in October 1748 and the Treaty of Aix-la-Chapelle, the once-mighty Iroquois Empire was showing unmistakable signs of decay.

The Seven Years' War (1754-1763) would completely undermine the cohesive structure of the Six Nations Confederacy. Although the Confederacy initially supported the British, the Seneca, Onondaga and Cayuga shifted their allegiance to the French. Only the Oneida and Mohawk, thanks to Sir William Johnson, Superintendent for Indian Affairs, remained loyal to the British. Although Kahnawake and Kanesatake along with the other "praying Indians" initially sought neutrality, they eventually found themselves fighting alongside the French. Although the principles of the Great Law were now moot as members of the Confederacy were involved in direct military engagements against one another, its tenets were not wholly ignored. Iroquois on both sides were less active than they had been in past colonial wars.[112]

There were numerous examples whereby Iroquois refused to fight after realizing their brethren were part of the opposing force. During the Battle of Crown Point sometimes referred to as the Battle of Lake George on 8 September 1755, Mohawk loyal to the British under Chief Hendrick, accompanied by 13-year-old Joseph Brant, refused to fight when they saw Kahnawake Warriors within the French ranks. This was but one instance where the standards of the Great Law were loosely adhered to during the colonial wars.[113] However, the resulting British victory in the Seven Years' War would have tremendous implications for all Natives, especially for the "praying Indian" settlements of New France.

By August 1760, three British armies prepared to lay siege to Montreal, the last French stronghold in New France. Sensing the inevitable capitulation of Montreal, Sir William Johnson returned wampum belts to the Seven Nations of Canada, offering, "peace and protection" if they laid down their weapons in view of the advancing British forces:[114]

> We immediately called a Council...and determined to accept the protection held out to us. Accordingly the chief men of our village, as well as those from other villages, attended Sir William at Oswagatchie where he...granted us protection in the King's Name and confirmed to us our Lands and the free exercise of our Religion...in confirmation he delivered [back] to us the [wampum] Belt.[115]

On 8 September 1760, Pierre de Rigaud de Vaudreuil de Cavagnial, Governor of New France (and also son of the former Governor Vaudreuil who died in 1725), surrendered Montreal to the British. Eight days later on 16 September, Iroquois Chiefs met with William Johnson in Montreal. The Covenant Chain was renewed, friendship rekindled and the fur trade routes opened. However, the ethnic constitution of North America was changing at a dramatic rate against the favour of its Indigenous peoples. Inevitably, these alterations would further depreciate the value and cohesiveness of the Great Law. In addition, the peoples of the once-great Confederacy were displaced despite Article 40 of the *Articles of Capitulation* signed at Montreal:[116]

> The Indian allies of His Most Christian Majesty, Louis XV, shall be maintained in possession of the lands which they occupy, if they wish to remain thereon; they shall not be molested under any pretext whatsoever for having taken up arms and served His Most Christian Majesty, they will have, like the French, liberty of religion, and will keep their missionaries.[117]

According to an agent of British Indian Affairs, "The Caghnawageys [Kahnawake] and Caneghsadageys [Kanesatake] have lately been with me, and renewed their Engagements entered into last fall...they never again would take up the Hatchet against the English but would steadily mind their hunting."[118]

Although major military campaigns in Canada ended with the *Articles of Capitulation* in 1760, the war dragged on in other parts of the world until the final peace on 10 February 1763 with the Treaty of Paris. British colonial domination in North America was secured for the time being, as French and Spanish possessions were greatly reduced. It also ended the long-standing British-Iroquois military alliance against the French in North America. Although the peoples of Kahnawake and Kanesatake saw glimpses of a better future as partners with the British, not all nations trusted English motives. Ottawa Chief Pontiac's Rebellion (1763-1765), beginning on 7 May 1763 with a siege of Detroit, was an attempt to secure Native living space and drive out colonial nations, specifically the British. Pontiac's coalition distressed the British, and King George III quickly issued the *Royal Proclamation* on 7 October 1763 halting all new settlement west of the Appalachian Mountains.[119]

The *Royal Proclamation* was the first and most significant imperial regulation and is still seen by Canadian Natives as their equivalent to the Canadian *Charter of Rights and Freedoms*.[120] Its tenets have been used in Native land claims since its inception, including the land dispute at Kanesatake up to and including 1990. Former Grand Chief of Canada's First Nations Assembly Ovide Mercredi stated in 1993:

> A continuity in treaty relationships, from the pre-Confederation period to the present, reinforces the fact that our relationship with the Crown is one of equals. Despite this reality...the promises made in the treaties have been consistently breached by Canada's governments. We have been dispossessed of our homelands even though prerogative instruments like the Royal Proclamation of 1763 confirmed our pre-existing rights and committed governments to dealing with us on a consensual basis.[121]

The proclamation was intended to satisfy imperial and trading interests, in conjunction with limiting colonial expansionism into Native territory, thereby preserving an Anglo-Native alliance.[122] The most important section of this document for Natives was the provision concerning land rights:

> And whereas it is just and reasonable, and essential to our Interest, and the Security of our Colonies, that the several Nations and Tribes of Indians with whom We are connected, and who live under our Protection, should not be molested or disturbed in the Possession of such Parts of Our Dominions and Territories as...are reserved to them, or any of them, as their Hunting Grounds,... [any lands that had] not been ceded to or purchased by Us as aforesaid, are reserved to the said Indians.... We do hereby strictly forbid, on Pain of our Displeasure, all our loving Subjects from making any Purchases or Settlements whatever, or

> taking Possession of any of these Lands above reserved, without our especial leave and Licence for that Purpose first obtained... [N]o private Person [is allowed] to make any purchase from the said Indians of any Lands reserved to the said Indians...the same shall be Purchased only for Us, in our Name, at some public Meeting or assembly of the said Indians, to be held for the purpose by the Governor or Commander in Chief of our Colony.[123]

In short, the *Royal Proclamation* outlined the relationships between Natives, proprietorship of land and the responsibilities of the Crown. Most importantly, it forbade the purchase of Native land by anyone other than the Crown and the Crown alone had sole jurisdiction to negotiate all land claims and cessions.[124]

French subjects who would not proclaim fealty to the King of England were given notice of 18 months to liquidate their holdings and return to France. This was a reiteration of Article 35 of the *Articles of Capitulation* from 1760. For the Seminary of St-Sulpice, this created a problem. The seigneurial grants at both Kahnawake and Kanesatake had been entrusted to the head of the religious order in Paris by the French King, who could not sell the land under the constraints of the *Royal Proclamation* as Natives still occupied the land. However, four months before the deadline, the Seminary in Paris transferred all its holdings in British North America to the branch at Montreal, who in turn swore allegiance to King George III. Although the legality of this transfer was questioned in British courts, the Seminary was able to retain their rights to the land.[125]

For the inhabitants of Kahnawake and Kanesatake, the issue of land ownership had arisen prior to the declaration of the Proclamation. In 1761, Jesuits at Kahnawake attempted to sell portions of land to French settlers. The Native inhabitants took the matter to General Thomas Gage, the military Governor of Lower Canada, who proceeded to resolve the matter in their favour in 1762. He reasoned that the land at Kahnawake (Le Sault) was granted for the settlement of the Indians and was therefore retained by the British Crown for their use. Although the Natives at Kahnawake continued the practice of Christianity, Jesuit claims became invalidated and they were forced to vacate the premises.[126] This was the confirmation of Kahnawake as a Reserve. Earlier in 1759, the Mohawk Reserve at Akwesasne had been created.

Likewise, tenure of the land at the Lake of Two Mountains also came into question shortly after the decree of the proclamation. Aman, a Mohawk, believing that he was the title holder to land in the region, sold his house to an Englishman. The Superior of the Seminary immediately appealed the transaction to the British Governor in Montreal, citing the deeds of 1717, 1733 and 1735. The land transfer was annulled, "it having appeared to us the houses and fields of the village belong to them [the Sulpicians] as soon as the said Indians who hold the usufruct of them abandon them."[127] This argument and conflict of interest over land rights would be mirrored throughout the next 240 years, producing numerous violent clashes, none more so than in 1990.

While the Kanesatake Mohawks continued to protest the Sulpician's seigneurial claims, the American Revolution (1775-1783) unfolded, forever altering the Iroquois Confederacy. Kahnawake, Kanesatake and Akwesasne officially remained neutral, although a small number of Warriors fought for each side. The majority were Mohawk fighting for the British under Joseph Brant. However, the communities came out of the war relatively unchanged and unscathed.[128]

The Confederacy listened to the arguments of both combatants, and although recognizing the new United States of America in 1776, made the decision to remain neutral. However, Mohawk were raiding American settlements in the east and further west the Shawnee were ravaging frontier settlements in Kentucky. Likewise, other members of the Iroquois Covenant Chain actively took up arms in an attempt to stop American encroachment onto their lands. To the Americans then, the Iroquois and their subject tribes in the Covenant could hardly be perceived as neutral. Consequently, in 1777 American forces, with the help of allied Oneida, began extensive raids into Mohawk territory in New York, forcing most of the inhabitants to flee north to Canada. By 1783, their homeland had been completely overrun with settlement.[129]

At the end of the war, Joseph Brant crossed into Canada with 2,000 subjects—the majority Mohawk but also members of all Six Nations, as well as smaller numbers of Covenant allies. From a pre-war population of roughly 8,000, fewer than 5,000 Iroquois survived. Of these, roughly half migrated north to Canada. In 1784, they were given lands at the Bay of Quinte near Belleville, which became the Tyendinaga Reserve. A large number also settled at a site on the Grand River near Caledonia known as the Six Nations Reserve, under Joseph Brant.[130]

With little chance of victory and with poverty, hunger and disease flourishing in the communities, the Iroquois had no alternative other than to sign the Treaty of Fort Stanwix on 22 October 1784. In doing so, they ceded most of their ancient lands, including the rights to those located west and north of the Ohio River. Perhaps more importantly, the dissemination of the Iroquois not only led to the collapse of the Confederacy but also freed those nations who had been unwilling subjects of the Confederacy or the Covenant Chain, including the Algonquian tribes, the Shawnee and the smaller nations of the Ohio Valley.[131]

By the turn of the century the Mohawk and their Iroquois brethren were scattered remnants of a once-great Empire. Apart from the Reserves and praying villages in Canada, those who remained in the United States were confined to a series of small Reservations in central and western New York comprising 271,000 acres. Although Brant continued to attempt to pursue the resurrection of the Great Law and the Confederacy, both seemed confined to the ash heap of history.[132]

The Revolutionary War left the Six Nations Confederacy severely weakened, powerless and impoverished. The culture and traditions of the Iroquois were threatened by these factors and also by the development of American economic free enterprise, expansionism and alcohol abuse. Not surprisingly, a Seneca prophet, Handsome Lake, began preaching a social conduct that was peppered with many Euro-American principles after receiving prophetic visions in 1799. His teachings included the farming practices, gender roles and religious dogma of the Quakers.[133]

His teachings (known as the *karihwi:io* "Good Message" or the Code of Handsome Lake) were somewhat embraced by those Iroquois living in the United States. Canadian Iroquois were less enthusiastic as they were not experiencing the social or cultural disruption endured by their American counterparts. Moreover, they were predominantly Christianized already. According to Kahn-Tineta Horn, a Mohawk activist and participant in the 1990 standoff, "I think Handsome Lake was probably a well-meaning man who did see things, but the Quakers took that and tried to turn Mohawk society upside down."[134] The pacifism and mutual coexistence of the Code of Handsome Lake was never adopted by the Mohawk of Canada, who maintained the belief that they were an independent and sovereign nation not subject to the whims of any colonial administration or government.[135]

The 1794 *Jay Treaty* seemed to give credence to this claim. Following the American Revolution, the United States and Great Britain signed an agreement entitled the *Treaty of Amity, Commerce, and Navigation* (the *Jay Treaty*). In addition to postwar normalization of relations between the two countries, the treaty also extended and acknowledged various rights to Aboriginal nations occupying lands on or near the U.S.-Canadian border, such as Akwesasne: "...the Indians dwelling on either side of the said boundary line, freely to pass and repass by land or inland navigation, into the respective territories and countries of the two parties, on the continent of America...."[136] Like the *Royal Proclamation*, the *Jay Treaty* was used as a defence by the Mohawk who operated illegal smuggling enterprises primarily based in Akwesasne during the 1980s, through to the present day.[137]

Although Canadian Iroquois were not subjugated like those in the United States, following the Revolution they continued to battle for what they believed to be their ancestral lands. Since the inception of the *Proclamation Act* in 1763, the Natives of Kanesatake, which was now unofficially divided into two sections—the Mohawk and a minority of other Iroquois living west of the Mission church, and the Algonquin and a handful of Nipissing living east of the church—were at odds with both the colonial government and the Seminary. Problems persisted between these Native groups and the Seminary over the proprietorship of this land, its timber resources, and in particular the sale of this land to third parties—French settlers.[138]

Petitions were forwarded to the Legislature of Lower Canada by the Native inhabitants in 1781, 1787, 1795 and 1802, protesting the Seminary's transactions of land to settlers. Any answer given by colonial administrators favoured the rights of the Seminary.[139] By the 1780s non-Native families had settled on land leased or purchased from the Seminary, creating the origins of what became known as the "checkerboard" problem. Natives and non-Natives were living at the Lake of Two Mountains intermittently, with differing opinions about land use and ownership. The Mohawk still maintained that the seigneurial lands had been set aside for their use. The wave of intense settlement following the War of 1812 would further complicate the already fragile relationships at the Lake of Two Mountains.

The War of 1812 (1812-1815) dramatically modified Native relations in Canada. Although the Mohawk initially remained neutral, American incursions into the Montreal area threatened the lands of the Mohawk, who for their own interests took up arms with the British. Warriors from Kanesatake, Kahnawake, Akwesasne and the Six Nations at Grand River were instrumental in the victories at Chateauguay and Beaver Dam.[140] With the Rush-Bagot Treaty of 1817 came the demilitarization of the Great Lakes and nullification of future American threats. The Iroquois lost their importance as a military ally. The British began to initiate policies of assimilation rather than co-operation and understanding, thus shifting the status quo of Euro-Native relations in

Canada. This was exemplified in the disillusionment of Shawnee Chief Tecumseh's dream of an Indian State in the Ohio Valley.[141]

Following the war, the Natives of the Lake of Two Mountains continued to petition the government, submitting claims in 1818, 1828 and 1839. During this time, the Mohawks at Kanesatake prospered in the fur trade and a Hudson Bay Company fur post was opened in the area, handling roughly 5,000 pelts per year. By 1825, a steamboat from Lachine to Carillon was using the village of Oka as a regular stop, and the seeds of nature tourism in the region were sown. These circumstances only enticed French- speaking farmers to settle on the north shore and English traders on the south.[142] By 1837, the Native population of Kanesatake was reported to be, "300 Iroquois, 298 Algonquin, 264 Nipisin [sic]," occupying 260 acres of land while sharing what was deemed "common land" with non-Native farmers and cattle-ranchers.[143] Although the Seminary, French/English settlers and Natives were all in direct conflict over the land, the situation had remained relatively peaceful up to this point. This was not to last.

In 1841, the Legislature of Lower Canada enacted a statute confirming an 1840 legislation and the title of the disputed land to Seminary, while retaining a relatively vague clause of defined obligations to the Aboriginal population. It was also confirmed that the timber on the land belonged to the religious order.[144] Since the decline of the fur trade in the late 1830s and the rise of steamboats, Mohawks began selling timber to circumvent their loss of funds. By 1848, the Hudson Bay Company had vacated the area and closed its trading post.[145] This led to the migration of many Algonquin and Nipissing further north towards the Ottawa region, eventually settling on a parcel of land at Maniwaki provided for them in 1853. Kanesatake was now, more than ever, primarily Mohawk. Although the government had set aside 16,000 acres at Doncaster for the Mohawk of Kahnawake and Kanesatake in 1853, it was used for hunting and fishing, but very few actually relocated. Unlike the Algonquin, the Mohawks were farmers and the ground at Doncaster proved unfit for agricultural development.[146] The government's attempt at relocation as a solution proved futile.

Also in 1848, the Mohawks delivered another petition to Governor General Lord Elgin, asserting their right to the land and its natural resources. After an investigation by the Superintendent General of Indian Affairs, it was repeated that the Sulpician deeds had been approved by Her Majesty in 1841 and that the Mohawk had "no right to cut down and sell any of it [timber] without the consent of the missionary."[147] The Mohawk response was to cut down more wood and appeal the Seminary's attempts to stop them in another petition to the government. As a result, 12 law officials arrested an unknown number of Mohawk, jailing them in Montreal for eight days.[148]

To compound the Sulpician's anger, in 1851, Peter Jones, an Ojibwa and Methodist Minister, came to the Lake of Two Mountains on order of his church to convert the Natives to Protestantism. A mission was established in 1868, and many Mohawks simply joined as an act of defiance against the Catholic Sulpician order. This was contested in court by the Sulpicians and the Methodist chapel was torn down.[149]

Since the verdict in 1841, the Sulpicians continued to assert dominance over the land against a backdrop of constant feuding and tension. In 1859, the Seminary gained propriety over all of the ungranted land as the result of a bill abolishing seigneurial tenure and ownership. Attorney-General George-Étienne Cartier, former legal counsel for the Sulpicians, directed this bill through legislature, assuring the Seminary's right to parcel off and sell common lands.[150]

Mohawk resistance to the arrival of more settlers and the Sulpicians' increasingly dominant attitude was accelerated by Chief Joseph Onasakenrat, or Joseph Swan. Possessing a university education and knowledge of the Roman Catholic religion, he was hired by the Sulpicians for secretarial work at the age of 23 in 1868. Soon afterwards in July, he became one of three Chiefs of Kanesatake, and was hastily released by the Seminary. Mohawk resistance now had a leader literate in French, English and Mohawk, who quickly drew up a petition to the Governor General of Canada, signed by 122 other Mohawk. It was rejected and again the Sulpician ownership to the land was reaffirmed.[151]

Following the rejection of this petition, Chief Joseph proceeded to grant a large number of Mohawk land within the boundaries of the religious mission. Police entered the village and talked to the Natives and no arrests were made for the time being. Later on 26 February 1869, Chief Joseph and 40 Mohawk men appeared at the Seminary and served the priests a notice to leave.[152] On 5 March, Onasakenrat, two other Chiefs and a fourth man were arrested on charges of assault and trespassing. Sympathetic Montrealers posted the combined $400 bail. The prisoners were released on 22 March, acquitted of all charges.[153]

Over the next ten years, these episodes were repeated, with Mohawk being arrested and/or fined on many occasions for trespassing, cutting down trees, uttering threats and unlawfully carrying and discharging weapons. The Seminary also continued to sell land to settlers, so much so that Oka was made a municipality in 1875. By 1877, the scene at Kanesatake was becoming increasingly precarious. Those Mohawk who remained Catholic and did not embrace the arrival of the Protestant Methodists were threatened with death by anti-Catholic Mohawk. Local settlers were complaining to the Lieutenant-Governor of Quebec that armed Mohawks were roaming the streets, discharging their weapons and threatening to remove them from their property. In May, the Seminarians erected a fence around the sandy grass dunes behind the village (later becoming the Pines). These dunes were part of the common lands where Mohawk grazed their cattle. The Mohawk removed the fence and burned the wooden posts. Subsequently, on 19 May, the missionaries who had posted armed guards at the site were met by armed Mohawk men, including Chief Joseph. A firefight ensued, resulting in no serious casualties to either side.[154]

Warrants were issued against 46 Mohawk and on 14 June 1877, eight men were arrested, indicted on charges of inciting a riot as a result of the armed engagement. On the morning of 15 June, cannon blasts were heard and the Roman Catholic church and presbytery were set ablaze. 14 Mohawk men were subsequently arrested, including Onasakenrat. Even more foreshadowing was the fact that Colonel Amyot and 15 of his police officers stayed in Kanesatake from 15 June to the end of August—76 days in total.[155]

News of the violence was reported to Ottawa and a remedy was sought to negate any future confrontation and violence. Having witnessed failed attempts to mollify the Natives by litigation, relocation now became the primary governmental solution to the "Oka Question." A land deal had been brokered with the Algonquin and Nipissing, as mentioned, and almost all had relocated to Maniwaki by 1868. With this in mind, a tract of land, 12,000 acres, was offered to the Kanesatake Mohawk south of Lake Temiscaming in northern Ontario in 1871. The Mohawk declined, citing that the land was too far north, the soil quality poor and the tract too small.[156]

In June 1881, the Government of Ontario passed an order-in-council authorizing the sale of 25,582 acres at Gibson in Muskoka to the federal government for the creation of a Reserve for the Mohawk of Kanesatake. On 22 October 1881, the first families arrived at their new location courtesy of the steamer *Dagmar*. A year later, only 22 families had relocated, some to Gibson (Wahta) but also others to Kahnawake and Tyendinaga. For those who did settle at Gibson (roughly 175 or one-third of the Mohawk at Kanesatake), the agreed provisions were never delivered by the government and most returned to Kanesatake to find their houses sold by the Sulpicians.[157] The Superintendent General of Indian Affairs, Hayter Reed, offered this response in 1894: "A reserve...was provided for your people at Gibson.... If they prefer to live at Oka they must take the consequences. The Department has done all in its power for your people and has gone out of its way to help them and guard their interests."[158]

Thus far, both pre-Confederation colonial administrations sided with the Seminary of St-Sulpice in any ruling concerning the land base at the Lake of Two Mountains. Without the support of the Confederacy, which was in tatters, the Mohawk of Kanesatake were left to fend for themselves in a political, religious and social environment that did not recognize the inherent rights of the Native population to the land. Yet the Mohawks still refused to accept the decisions made by both the French and subsequently the British in favour of the Sulpicians when the land claim was submitted to the colonial administration. With the 1867 *British North America Act (BNA Act),* the land claim issues were inherited by the newly created Government of Canada.

CHAPTER 5

The Oka Land Claim Post-Confederation

The Government of Canada recognized its responsibilities to the Indigenous population of Canada through the BNA Act which assigned jurisdiction for Native affairs to the federal level. However, the two decades prior to Confederation were marred by British attempts to assimilate the Native population by undermining Native links to the land and traditional political organizations through enforced laws and regulations. These programs were expanded by the federal government of Canada which continued the practice of usurping power from traditional Chiefs through the *Indian Act*, which was awash with assimilationist protocols. These policies reduced the control all Natives in Canada retained over the administration of their Reserves and lives. The Mohawk communities were equally affected and government policies seemed to further agitate the already existing fractures of religion and politics apparent in the Mohawk Nation. The government directives in the *Indian Act* directly affected the issue of land ownership at Kanesatake.

Trying to relocate the dissident Mohawk of Kanesatake to Gibson was consistent with the evolution of Canadian Indian policies during the mid-nineteenth century. Indian Reserves, which were born into Crown protocol during the 1830s, served two strategic purposes: they opened up land for unhindered settlement and industry, and established a framework by which the Natives could be integrated or, if not, easily monitored. The names of governmental aboriginal programs reflect this not-uncommon ethnocentric view of the Victorian era.[159] In 1857, the *Gradual Civilization Act* was passed, allowing enfranchisement for certain Natives who passed a test, after which they would be granted 20 acres of Reserve land. It was a furtive ploy on behalf of the Department of Indian Affairs to remove communal ownership of and attitudes to the land. One Mohawk was granted citizenship under this policy, but his community of Six Nations on the Grand River refused the granting and partitioning of the proscribed land.[160]

The *BNA Act* of 1867 introduced a clause assigning jurisdiction for, "Indians and lands reserved for the Indians" to the federal government of the newly created Dominion of Canada. In 1869, the *Gradual Enfranchisement Act* was conceded, allowing Natives to live as distinct "Municipalities." However, under this act, their traditional laws were subject to governmental scrutiny, further undermining the role and power of the traditional Chiefs and Clan Mothers. An additional criterion for "Status" was having genetic Native blood of a minimum of 25 per cent. Likewise, the 1869 Act removed "Status" from any Native female who married a non-Native, a penalty procured by their kin regardless of blood quantum.[161]

The Canadian Department of Indian Affairs (DIA) was unofficially formed in conjunction with the 1876 *Indian Act*, which after several revisions remains in force to this day. The core features of this policy included the resettlement of Natives to federally controlled Reserves owned by the Crown, the creation of residential schools, the banning of certain Native rituals such as the Potlatch and sun dance, and federal control over membership and enfranchisement of and in Aboriginal political organizations. More importantly, it maintained the principles for elected band councils in keeping with the 1869 Act, but did so on a voluntary basis.[162]

The Department of Indian Affairs was formally established in conjunction with the 1880 *Indian Act*. The electoral system for Native councils was amended yet again, giving the federal government powers to impose elected councils regardless of whether the Natives in question preferred it to traditional forms of non-elected leadership, such as the Iroquois Longhouse. The 1884 *Indian Advancement Act* supplemented this clause whereby Ottawa had power, through the medium of the Superintendent General of DIA, to depose any Chief who was considered unfit.[163]

With the dawn of these policies and the destabilization of the Iroquois Confederacy and Longhouse traditions, a tense and unfamiliar environment for the Native populace of Canada emerged. By the turn of the century, the divisions within the Iroquois Confederacy and the microcosm of the Mohawk Nation were quite apparent. Members of the now-divided Confederacy were scattered throughout Canada and the United States, making any revival of the Iroquois League extremely difficult. In addition, some Mohawk had been Christianized while others had not. Large portions of the Mohawk population had followed the teaching of Handsome Lake and continued to adopt Canadian and American practices, including the democratic electoral system and Christianity. Others remained devout to the traditional Longhouse culture and band councils. Furthermore, many of the Iroquois Reserves were not homogenous. These factors created distrust within Native councils and communities.

These divergent attitudes within the Mohawk Nation manifested themselves during 1990. The same suspicions and conflicting agendas created an atmosphere of mutual distrust leading to violence, not only with the Canadian state, but also between the factions present within the Mohawk Nation territories of Akwesasne, Kanesatake and Kahnawake. For those who follow the Longhouse, a fundamental principle of the Great Law is that any members of the Confederacy who cease to follow the traditional customs in favour of a foreign system of governance, religion and beliefs forfeit their position within the social and political spheres of the Confederacy.[164] This dichotomy caused a deep rift among the Mohawk people. Those who had converted to Christianity and those who had lost matriarchal clan ties due to intermarriage with non-Mohawk seemed to support the elected Chiefs, while others still practised the Great Law and refused to recognize the jurisdiction of the *Indian Act* over their lives.

Under the provisions of the *Indian Act*, elected band councils had been created at Akwesasne and Kahnawake in 1898 and 1889 respectively. By order-in-council of 16 May 1899 an elective system was applied to all bands in Ontario, Quebec and the Maritimes. There is no indication that the decision to initiate this policy was the expressed choice of the Natives concerned. In fact, it was actively resisted. At Akwesasne in 1899, traditional Chiefs were arrested with five being held in prison for one year. Similarly in 1924 at Oshweken, "the elected council system was summarily introduced...when Lieutenant-Colonel C.E. Morgan, flanked by RCMP officers, dismissed the traditional chiefs from the Council House, confiscated the Council's Wampum belts...and organized the election of a Band Council."[165]

The Kanesatake Mohawk were included in this sweeping reform even though there was doubt as to whether the lands they occupied at Oka constituted a Reserve under definition of the *Indian Act*. The people of Kanesatake are in an anomalous situation under the jurisdiction of Canadian law and the interpretation of the *Indian Act*. Although they are "Indians" under the clauses of the *Indian Act* and have an *Indian Act* Band Council, they do not live on an official Reserve. They live on federal Crown lands reserved for their use under Section 91(24) of the 1867 *BNA Act*.[166] In the early part of the twentieth century a court action was initiated to determine the legal rights and obligations of the Seminary to the indigenous population of Kanesatake. This included the clarification of land rights, the ability to sell land to third parties, as well as determining if indeed a Reserve could be created.

After much deliberation in February 1909, the case of *Corinthe vs. the Ecclesiastics of the Seminary of Sulpice* was heard by the Superior Court in Montreal. This case was initiated by Chief Angus Corinthe who had personally met with Prime Minster Wilfrid Laurier and the Superintendent of Indian Affairs, Clifford Sifton, in 1905: "What I told the Government when I went up there was, 'They [Seminary] are going to put up a fence on our common, and the first man who comes to stick up a post there I will smash his head.'"[167]

Under the protection of Quebec Provincial Police in the summer of 1907, municipal workers erected the fence without any violent occurrences. Early in 1909, former Chief Joseph Gabriel ventured to England to bring the Mohawk grievances before British authorities in person: "We now lay to the Government of the throne our complaints to have justice be done, to place us in the employment and full possession of our land…."[168] Although King Edward VII did not humour the petition, Laurier did. The land dispute was already before the Superior Court in Montreal. The court's verdict pleased neither side. After several appeals from both parties, the case was finally heard by the Judicial Committee of the Privy Council (JCPC), then the highest court of appeal in Canada, at London, England in July 1912.[169]

The JCPC ruled that the Seminary of St-Sulpice maintained full title to the disputed lands and "to place beyond question the title of the respondents [Seminary] to the Seigniory; and to make it impossible for the appellants to establish an independent title to possession or control in the administration." More importantly, the Privy Council ruled that the Mohawk could not assert any claim to the land by virtue of Aboriginal title, nor by way of land held in trust by the Seminary. The basis for the verdict was that the legislation of 1841 had already confirmed the Seminary's right to that land. In short, the court ruled that the Mohawk people had a right to occupy and use the land until that point in time when the Sulpicians exercised their tangential right to sell it.[170] The Mohawk refused to accept this decision and continued to lobby both the courts and the government for recognition to their entitlement of the land in question.

Problems arose again in 1936 when a large tract of land, including portions of the common land was sold to a Belgian syndicate, Belgo-Canadian Real Estate Company. The following year, the company laid charges against Mohawk for cutting timber, which were followed by a series of arrests by the Quebec Provincial Police. The Seminary continued to liquidate parcels of land throughout the Second World War, prompting the federal government to act.

On 31 May 1945, the federal government procured the remaining land owned by the Sulpicians, which included 51 or 52 lots in the village of Oka, plus 1,556 acres of land to the northwest "outside the town." Title to these lands was vested in the Crown, which also assumed all the Sulpician's fiduciary obligations to the Mohawk, save for spiritual care of the minority Catholic Mohawk.[171]

This was the origin of the process (which continues today) of assembling land under federal jurisdiction for an official Reserve at Kanesatake under the *Indian Act*. The main obstacle to assembling a Reserve is that the land purchased in 1945 consists of a series of blocks interspersed with privately owned land and also land held by the Municipality of Oka. This has been referred to in the literature of Oka as the "checkerboard problem." Both the municipality and the community of Kanesatake faced the quandary of making decisions regarding land management that could in turn affect the other community. The predicament of coordinating land-use policies became a source of friction.[172] This was heightened in 1947 when parcels of land not occupied by the Native people but used by them for community purposes—the Commons—was sold by the Seminary to the Municipality of Oka for the creation of a municipal park.[173]

Over the next 15 years, the Chiefs of Kanesatake continued to press the government for an explanation regarding the legal status of their people and their title to the lands they now occupied. The Mohawks did not view the 1912 decision as a final settlement and maintained the opinion that the Seigneury land had been given to them initially in 1717 and that the religious authorities had no legal right to sell or dispose of any portions of these original lands. Nevertheless, Oka was never given official "Reserve" status as defined by Subsection (1), Section 2 of the *Indian Act*, C. 149 (1952).[174]

The disagreement was further escalated in 1959 when the Seminary transferred lot 69 of the parish to the Municipality of Oka without consulting the Mohawk. Lot 69 was part of the Commons, but was not acquired by the Crown in 1945 as no one resided on it. In September 1959, Paul Sauve, Member of the Quebec Legislative Assembly for the Deux Montagnes region, became Premier of Quebec. On 18 December, a private member's bill was passed in the Assembly authorizing the Corporation of Oka to acquire the lot and lease it for "sporting or commercial purposes." Again, the Mohawk were not consulted about the transaction and the Council petitioned the Joint Committee of the Senate and the House of Commons on Indian Affairs to no avail. Soon after, construction of the nine-hole Oka Golf Club began in the Pines.[175]

The record of the white pine forest at Oka is worth mentioning, as it relates directly to the larger land claim issue. Originally, the area of the Pines (west of the village of Oka) was a large sandbank some 30 metres high, which was unstable and prone to slides and shifts. It had been deforested for lumber and for the grazing of livestock throughout the nineteenth century. These lands were referred to as the "Commons," and were used by all area residents. With deforestation and progressive grazing removing the grass coating, sand slides became more frequent. By the 1880s, damage to properties and roads below became common.[176]

Between 1886 and 1897, 100,000 trees were planted by the Mohawk under the watchful eye of Oka village priest Joseph-Daniel Lefebvre. White pine (70,000) was planted on the slopes, while hemlock and red pine (30,000) were planted on the flat surfaces. Although the Sulpicians paid for the reforestation project ($1700), most saplings were obtained by the Natives and transported in canoes from the north before being planted in rows at Oka. Careful selective cutting of white pine allowed those that took root to flourish. By 1920, roughly 80 per cent of the saplings had been cut to provide space and light to the fittest trees, thus halting the erosion completely.[177]

It was also during the 1920s that the Sulpicians allowed local residents to construct a crude golf course of sand and gravel on the last remaining common grazing grounds that had not been reforested. With the Sulpicians parcelling and selling land, which included areas of the reforested Commons, the new owners cleared land for development. By 1947, only 18 per cent of the white pine remained and fewer than nine per cent of the hemlock. With the construction of the golf club in the early 1960s, more trees were felled to enlarge the fairways, the borders of which came extremely close to a traditional Mohawk cemetery.[178]

While the Oka Golf Club was being built around Kanesatake, all was not well in neighbouring Kahnawake, either. Construction of the St. Lawrence Seaway from 1955 to 1959 to circumvent the Lachine Rapids had a negative affect on the village of Kahnawake. Besides the hundreds of acres lost to construction, the seaway robbed the community of its riverfront shoreline. According to Johansen in his work, *Life and Death in Mohawk Country*:

> Without loss of land and the way of life that Mohawks had based on it, the nationalistic Warrior Society, a Mohawk paramilitary group whose image mesmerized headline writers in northeastern United States and most of Canada during that violent

> summer of 1990, might never have arisen. Had the construction of the Saint Lawrence Seaway shortly after World War II and subsequent industrialization of the area not destroyed traditional ways of making a living in Mohawk Country, gambling and smuggling may never have emerged... [179]

To what measure the smuggling and gambling can be attributed to this cause and effect duality is unknown. However, as Johansen correctly points out, the rise in illegal activities, gaming and Mohawk nationalism, including the Warrior Society, corresponds to the time period of the 1960s and 1970s, shortly after the construction of the seaway.

To further Native Canadian irritation and alienation, in 1969, the Minister of Indian Affairs, Jean Chrétien, under Prime Minister Pierre Trudeau, released the federal government's vision of Native-Canadian relations in a *White Paper.* In summary, it promulgated that Natives were at a social and economic disadvantage because they enjoyed unique legal status and considerations under Canadian law. The solution was to change the direction to "a road that would lead gradually away from different status to full social, economic and political participation in Canadian life."[180]

Not all Mohawk were prepared to assimilate or accept the direction of the federal government without a fight. The social upheaval during the 1960s spawned the creation of the American Indian Movement (AIM) which was the forerunner to many smaller activist or militant native groups. The Mohawk Warrior Society was reborn in the tumultuous era of social conscience of the 1960s. With the destabilization of the Iroquois Confederacy, the divisive politics within the Mohawk Nation which was left without concrete leadership and the refusal of the governments of Canada and Quebec to appreciate, legislate or negotiate Mohawk land grievances, the rise of a militant faction of Mohawks was quite understandable and, given the history, predictable. These factors, in conjunction with the radical social movements of the 1960s, solidified the rise, recruitment and actions of the Mohawk Warrior Society which initially sought to protect the land and culture of its communities.

CHAPTER 6

The Rebirth of the Warrior Society

The decades of the 1960s and 1970s were a cataclysmic time for social reform, protest and movements of every kind. It is not surprising that Native rights organizations and Native political lobbyists also appeared alongside anti-Vietnam War groups, African-American civil rights assemblies and women's rights supporters. However, not all organizations sought to change the consciousness, values and laws of the United States and Canada by peaceful means. In this atmosphere of political ferment, Dennis Banks and George Mitchell, two Anishinabe, founded the American Indian Movement (AIM) in Minneapolis, Minnesota in 1968.

According to the FBI, the American Indian Movement was "self-consciously patterned after the Black Panther Party's community of self-defense model pioneered by Huey P. Newton and Bobby Seale two years earlier in Oakland."[181] AIM chapters quickly sprang up in urban centres throughout the country, attracting tough young Natives. Within two years, AIM's agenda smartly shifted from the roots of its urban background to rural Reservations, creating a direct link between itself and the issues of treaty rights and lands claims, giving the movement a degree of legitimacy.[182]

In November 1969, members of the radical coalition called Indians of All Tribes (IAT), headed by Mohawk Richard Oakes of Akwesasne, occupied the island of Alcatraz, citing an 1882 statute (22 Stat. 181) which mandates that all abandoned federal facilities be used for Native schools. The occupation of Alcatraz ended after a 19-month standoff, when a joint task force of U.S. Marshals launched an assault and arrested the occupiers. This episode demonstrated an extremely important strategic lesson. Effective public support could be garnered through the media attention afforded to militant Native actions. AIM continued to gain considerable media attention through numerous seizures of U.S. military facilities, hydro and gas plants, and through high-profile demonstrations throughout the early 1970s.[183]

Actions such as these were not restricted to the more dissident population of the United States. On 18 December 1968, 48 Mohawk, including Kahn-Tineta Horn, blocked the International Bridge at Cornwall to protest the decision of Canada Border Services Agency to charge duty on goods carried across the border by Mohawks. The 1794 *Jay Treaty* was used to support the Mohawk argument that the border did not apply nor did they recognize its division of their own land.[184] It was this same argument that is being used by casino operators and cigarette/alcohol bootleggers to defend their operations. The smuggling of weapons and other illicit drugs is an illegal activity in both the United States and Canada. The *Jay Treaty* cannot be used to defend these activities. The blockade of the bridge ended when RCMP and Ontario Provincial Police (OPP) retook the bridge and made arrests. This was not an isolated event. By the mid-1970s, at least five armed blockades had occurred in Canada, the best known being the Ojibwa occupation of a park near Kenora, Ontario.[185]

In the United States, the most publicized AIM action occurred in 1973 at the Oglala Lakota (Sioux) Pine Ridge Reservation, South Dakota, better known as Wounded Knee. The eventual 71-day armed standoff between AIM and joint U.S. security and military agencies parallels the Oka Crisis in numerous facets. The struggle originated over land issues, treaty rights and the prospect of uranium mines on disputed territory. It also involved numerous factions of Native groups and band councils, which U.S. agents tried to pit against each other. AIM leaders called it, "the old divide-and-conquer tactic: they are trying to pit Indian against Indian."[186] The corrupt band council led by Dick Wilson and his "goons" were being funded and bribed by the FBI to intimidate AIM and those opposed to the mines. Lawyer William Kunstler represented the grievances of AIM. He would also be present behind the barricades at Kanesatake in 1990.[187]

In addition, members of the 82nd Airborne and the U.S. 6th Army were deployed: "It is significant in some of these AIM centers the residents have built bunkers which would literally require military assault forces if it were necessary to overcome resistance emanating from the bunkers."[188] In the first instance since the Civil War, the U.S. Army (not to be confused with the National Guard) was dispatched in a domestic operation. In all, 17 APCs, 200,000 rounds of various calibre ammunition, flares and explosives, 12 M-79 Grenade Launchers, 600 cases of C-S Gas, F-4 Phantom jets, helicopters and personnel were deployed under the direction of General Alexander Haig.[189] The Oka Crisis would later mirror many of the events which transpired at Wounded Knee.

It was within this dissident environment of Native North America that the Mohawk Warrior Society began a resurrection of sorts after years of relative dormancy. Members of the Warrior Society identified with AIM and the militant trend and began to take action against what it perceived to be elements of Native and non-Native society in conflict with the Longhouse traditions and a sovereign Mohawk Nation. One instrumental figure in the rejuvenation of the Warrior Society was Louis Hall of the Kahnawake Reserve. During the 1970s, Hall, widely regarded by Warriors as the founder of the movement, produced several bodies of literature calling for the resurgence of Mohawk sovereignty and the Six Nations Confederacy through whatever means necessary, including the use of armed force: "Legal extermination of the Indians as a distinct people is an act of aggression. Oppression is an act of war against the people. Legislating Indians into extinction is an act of war."[190]

Hall's most militant works are his fanatical manifestos *Rebuilding the Iroquois Confederacy* and *Warrior's Handbook*. In both booklets, Hall cites wampums of the Great Law calling for active resistance against the invasion of Mohawk territory and the protection of its interests. According to Hall: "What can the Warrior Societies do? They can dump bridges into the rivers which are now sewers and into the [St. Lawrence] seaway cancelling all traffic, knockout powerhouses, high tension power lines, punch holes in the reactors of nuclear powerhouses."[191]

Using an ideology of nationalism and the argument that Mohawks were the victims of systematic oppression, the militant movement began to recruit members from Mohawk territories. The Warrior Society at Kahnawake received official sanction from the Longhouse members in 1972. However, the Warrior Society itself further accentuates the divisions of opinion over the governance of the Mohawk Nation, the support for its various Band Councils and the means by which sovereignty should be addressed and procured. The traditionalists who support the Longhouse were divided over the role of the Society and were not as unified as they may have appeared.

This divisive atmosphere among these groups helped fuel the violence of 1990. One person's freedom fighter is another person's terrorist. Accordingly, when members of a society are oppressed and feel isolated and alienated, they turn to violence to protect what remains of their land, culture and religion with a view that there is nothing left to lose. Mohawk activists and the Warrior Society developed through this system of oppression and isolation. Leaders fed on these fears, resentments and traumas to recruit members. According to Mike Mitchell, former Grand Chief of the elected Canadian government sponsored Mohawk Council of Akwesasne: "It was a movement for cultural survival. It was commonly known as the warriors."[192]

An ex-Warrior nicknamed "Cartoon" who served in Vietnam and initially trained the original Warriors in military tactics during the 1970s and 1980s surmised that the society, "took the garbage and the throwaways and put pride into them. What they [Warriors] set out to be is not what they are." He renounced the Warrior movement when he was asked in 1989 to go to Ganienkeh "to train children to act as hit squads." He was also deeply concerned that the movement had lost its social credibility and was now a front for illegal activities where the "expendables" or "unstable expendables such as Lasagna" who were floundering in life were put in the front lines "to hold the fort" and protect the multi-million dollar illegal enterprises of a few "Silks or Silk-shirt." This is derogatory Mohawk slang used to describe the business men or entrepreneurs behind the gaming and smuggling network who use the Warriors to protect their "investments."[193]

There remains much debate over Hall (who died on 9 December 1993) and his recruitment and methods of motivation. The pro-Warrior Longhouses of Kahnawake and Ganienkeh (Mohawk Nation Councils) and the pro-Warrior factions of the Longhouses at Akwesasne and Kanesatake support its legitimacy. These Longhouse members view his interpretation of the Great Law as correct and subscribe to his belief that, "We shall resist by every means, any aggression, any violation of the treaties, any disturbances of our people in the free use and enjoyment of our land, any usurpation of our sovereignty, any encroachment and oppression. We pledge that the noise will be heard from one end of the world to the other."[194]

In contrast, other members of the various Longhouses vehemently reject this call to arms viewing Hall's militant theories and rhetoric as a bastardization of the wampums of the Great Law, which have been twisted in meaning to promote and mobilize for his radical agenda. These traditionalists relate more to the Code of Handsome Lake.[195] The Warrior Society does not have blanketing endorsement throughout the Mohawk Nation.[196] Also, in opposition are the elected councils at Akwesasne, Kanesatake and the Iroquois Grand Council. To Hall and his followers, this faction of the Longhouse and those who support the governmental electoral system are traitors who have subscribed to the "peace-oriented path" and to the "hallucinations of a drunk [Handsome Lake]."[197]

Hall's works are bursting with racial slurs, ethnocentrism and fanatical fascist psychological manipulation and ideologies. Throughout 1990, *Indian Time* produced an anonymously written dissection of Hall's ideology and found frightening comparisons to Nazism and the "Big Lie" techniques of Rudolph Hess and Joseph Goebbels:

> Hall appeals to the young in the same fashion Hitler appealed and won over young Germans to enlist as Cadets and soldiers. Those in society who have been labelled as 'rejects' are actively recruited...and are made to sense oneness with others, and a sense of 'false love.'... Hall bases his army on the insecurities, social isolation, and low self-worth of its recruits. It's this false sense of nationalism which, in the mind of Hall and his followers justifies their actions..... Terrorism is advocated in the name of nationalism.[198]

Hall makes numerous allusions to Hitler and the Nazis within his works including a claim that Hitler admitted to adopting the concept of *Blitzkrieg* from the Iroquois practice of warfare.[199] However, despite the influences of a fascist style doctrine, Hall also repeatedly singles out Jews as a source of inspiration: "Look at the Jews who have survived 3,000 years of inhuman persecutions.... Behold the meek and humble Jew suddenly turned tiger and even killed a lot of Arabs to set up Israel."[200]

The rise of the Warrior Society also corresponded to a time when the economies of Mohawk territories were in decline. Throughout the nineteenth century, a disproportionate number of Mohawks had made a living in high steel, building bridges and skyscrapers throughout the larger centres of northeast North America. By the 1970s, the demand for this brave skill was dissolving, deteriorating the economic conditions by producing higher unemployment rates among Mohawk men: "It came at a time when, in Mohawk country, the economy of the average ironworker, who had long been prosperous and respected, had shrunk and collapsed."[201]

As a result, illegal enterprises began to compensate for this loss of income. Since the 1970s, and the introduction of Canadian "sin-taxes" on tobacco and alcohol certain Mohawks have used their tax-free status to earn a profitable living selling cigarettes at discount prices. A complex business and administrative system was put in place connecting all of the Mohawk territories. Also, as gasoline prices soared during the 1972 Oil Crisis, these Mohawks opened up various petrol stations, where motorists could fill up at a lesser cost. Soon this underground pipeline included in its inventory liquor, drugs, alien citizens and a vast array of weapons. The 1794 *Jay Treaty* was used as a legal argument to defend the right of Mohawks to freely carry goods across the U.S/Canada border without penalty of duty.[202]

In addition, bingo parlours and casinos began to appear on Reserves throughout North America, including those of the Mohawk. Akwesasne became the largest proprietor of the lucrative gambling enterprise in the Mohawk territories. The gambling war can be traced back to 1983, when the St. Regis Tribal Council, made up of pro-gaming members, licensed the first high stakes gambling venue—Mohawk Bingo Palace. By 1989, six other facilities located on tribal land were in operation under independent owners without agreements from either the tribal council or the State of New York.[203]

These "Bingo Chiefs" gained support as they injected new sources of income into the struggling Akwesasne economy. Inevitably, a connection emerged between the illegal smuggling, the gaming industry and the militant Warrior Societies, who quickly gained financial resources from these activities. A Warrior on the casino's payroll could earn upwards of $60,000 a year. Organized crime syndicates, including the Hell's Angels, became increasingly connected to the activities of the Warrior Societies, which helps to explain why the Reserves themselves did not financially benefit from the gambling industries. Casinos and bingo halls also provided a medium for laundering money earned from smuggling operations.[204]

It did not take long for the Warrior Society to act in a manner which they deemed as protecting Mohawk interests. In 1973, the Kahnawake Warriors embarked on a campaign to remove all non-Native "trespassers" from the Reserve and served these families with eviction notices of two weeks. Included were Natives who met the government requirement for status, but were not Mohawk through the traditional lines of descent. Members of AIM came to Kahnawake to aid in the cleansing of the Reserve. Under this pressure most families did leave peacefully; however, some did not, resulting in the forceful and physical occupation of their homes by members of the Warrior Society. This induced the Quebec Provincial Police to intervene and patrols began in Kahnawake. After a riot at the police station on 15 October and a brief armed standoff at the Longhouse, the police agreed to leave Kahnawake on the premise that the AIM activists leave Canada.[205]

Shortly after this episode, a more radical agenda was planned. The Kahnawake Warriors would "repossess" traditional lands in New York or Vermont. This was not necessarily a new idea. In 1970, Stanley and Loon Islands in the St. Lawrence River had been reclaimed. It was decided that the 612 acre state-owned abandoned Girl Scout Camp at Moss Lake, New York would be the intended target. On 13 May 1974, a convoy of cars and buses left

Akwesasne and travelled to Moss Lake, named Ganienkeh ("Land of Flint") by the Mohawk.[206] Although governmental authorities were slow to react, exchanges of gunfire between resentful local residents and the Warriors became all too common. On 28 October, a firefight resulted in the wounding of two non-Natives; a 22-year-old man and a nine-year-old girl.[207]

Soon, Ganienkeh was surrounded by law enforcement authorities and an armed standoff ensued. To defend the territory, the Warriors took advantage of their members with Vietnam experience and military service, including "Cartoon," and constructed bunkers, trench fortifications and booby-traps.[208] No raid was ever mounted, no search was ever conducted by authorities and no arrests were made. Eventually in May 1977 an agreement was reached whereby the Mohawks would abandon Moss Lake and be given two parcels of land near Altona, New York, some 60 miles southeast of Akwesasne. These lands (600 acres) are still known as Ganienkeh, and are used as a Warrior training camp.[209]

The burgeoning cigarette trade at Akwesasne and Kahnawake had produced violent clashes between Warriors, those supporters of gaming, and U.S. and Canadian security agencies. After the 1973 standoff at the Longhouse, although maintaining jurisdiction over Kahnawake, the SQ was reluctant to enforce the law on the Reserve. The unofficial creation of "no-go zones" on Mohawk Reserves occurred gradually since the late 1970s. Regular police almost never enforced jurisdiction over the Reserves and policing duties were left in the hands of the Band Council appointed Mohawk Police Forces or "Peacekeepers." The rise in smuggling and gaming can be correlated to this lack of policing and the intimidation practices of the Warriors on the Native police and the Band Councils.[210]

This uneasy relationship came to a head in 1979 on both Kahnawake and Akwesasne. At the former, David Cross, a 28-year-old Mohawk, was shot and killed by the SQ on the Reserve. At Akwesasne, a dispute over the erection of a fence prompted a violent takeover of the St. Regis/Akwesasne Police Station and Band Council office. This created the Racquette Point siege. Roughly 70 Warriors avoiding arrest took refuge for a year on land owned by Loran Thompson. Thompson is an unofficial leader of the Akwesasne Warrior Society, a former Band Chief of the Mohawk Nation Council, and a casino owner: "We have been taken for suckers long enough.... As a nation we have decided we are going to fight for our rights.... And if it takes armed confrontation, we have no choice but to do what the other side is doing.... There is nothing Canada can say or do to convince me that armed resistance is neither necessary nor worthwhile for us."[211] Accordingly, the Warriors entrenched themselves for a standoff building bunkers and trenches, while carrying AK-47s and other weapons. The siege ended with the police protecting the Warriors from other vigilante Mohawks and then maintaining them in protective custody after their surrender. All charges, including those against Thompson were dismissed.[212]

By this time the Longhouse was split into two distinct camps; those who supported gaming and those who did not. The anti-gambling side was made up of the elected Council Chiefs, those who supported the electoral process and those who resented the Warrior movement. The pro-gaming faction consisted of casino owners (and those who worked for them, including 'private security'), the Warriors, and those who rejected the elected councils believing them to be an adjunct to the governments of Canada and the United States.

This produced sporadic violence throughout the 1980s between the Mohawk factions and also incited raids by Canadian and American security agencies. On 16 December 1987, the New York State Police launched a raid confiscating 293 slot machines. The office of *Akwesasne Notes* was set ablaze in January of 1988 and again in 1989. Its editor, Doug George, was an outspoken opponent of gaming. On 6 June 1989, a brawl involving 400 people erupted between the opposing gambling factions. Five Mohawks were arrested and 200 slot machines were confiscated as a result of state police and FBI intervention. According to Johansen, by 1987, the New York State Police estimated that the owners of six casino establishments at Akwesasne were profiting $7 million tax-free per year. By 1989 this figure had swelled to more than $100 million (annually) in unreported income generated by seven gaming facilities operating without tribal consent, supervision or sanction.[213]

Given the geography of Akwesasne, which is located in Ontario, Quebec and New York State, raids had to be carefully conducted with co-operation from both countries law enforcement agencies. If a raid was attempted by one country without the co-operation of the other, Mohawks could simply cross the border to evade law officers whose jurisdiction was limited to their own side of the Reserve. Although many Mohawks do not recognize the border, this was a convenient loophole used to avoid arrest and prosecution.

In Kahnawake, Canadian authorities were making incursions into the Reserve to seize smuggled cigarettes, cash and drugs, much of which had been filtered through Akwesasne. On 1 June 1988, 200 RCMP personnel with helicopter support raided Kahnawake, sequestering $450,000 worth of contraband and another $284,000 in cash while arresting 17 Mohawks. The cigarette trade was costing the Canadian Government an estimated $25 million a year in lost revenue. The Warrior Society brandishing rifles and bats responded by blocking the Mercier Bridge, connecting Kahnawake to Montreal, for 29 hours until it was agreed that negotiations take place over the cigarette issue.[214] The Warriors had exercised power and achieved their desired results.

The raids only intensified the Warriors' resolve to rid their territories of government interference. There was a growing militancy between both the pro- and anti-gambling and smuggling camps. Warrior patrols were set up on both Kahnawake and Akwesasne to give notice of raids and possible police intervention. Guns, protests and odd angry shots during nights became common place on Akwesasne, which was undergoing a gradual metamorphosis into a narco-parasitic state (Narco-Parastate): "We patrol our land as the Mohawk Sovereignty Security Patrol, and we will persist like the people of Vietnam or Afghanistan until outside intervention is stopped. Just like Afghanistan was to the Soviet Union and Vietnam to the United States, Akwesasne will be to New York State and the United States. Our patrol is just the beginning."[215] The violence spawned by smuggling, casinos and armed intimidation was spreading to the other Mohawk territories. In April 1988, an RCMP raid of a home at Kanesatake yielded a methamphetamine laboratory, chemicals and three kg of 70% pure methamphetamine. The RCMP estimated that the drug laboratory had the ability to produce two kg per day or a street worth of $200,000.[216]

Monies from illegal enterprises could support the instruments of revolution and provide the economic base for political independence: "...a member of the Akwesasne Warrior Society, who asked not to be identified, revealed that the various Mohawk Warrior societies and the Mohawk Warrior Movement itself has been funded by the cigarette and gambling trade..."[217] The Warrior Societies and their leaders followed the classic revolutionary formula. Phase one is typified by the rejection of all existing authority and the parallel construction of their own hierarchies—provisional governments, police forces, army, courts. They then demand their legitimacy as an autonomous nation. However, in order to accomplish this, loyalty from their own peoples must be demonstrated. Acquiring this allegiance can be done through schools, community groups, political organizations or intimidation. Once accomplished, the coercion or conversion of the larger audience must occur. In this case it would appear to be the Canadian public. Next, negotiations with the host government(s) must occur to acquire recognition and finally victory. Pressure can be put on the host nation through employing broader international organizations or non-governmental organizations (NGOs) such as the United Nations, the Red Cross and the International Federation of Human Rights. This process can be called phase two.[218]

However, allegiance to such a militant ideology requires credibility and legitimacy. People will only commit to such movements if there is a belief or sense of accomplishment and victory. Hence, there is a vital need for action. The establishment of Ganienkeh, the blockades of the bridges and the cleansing of Kahnawake all demonstrate the willpower and the ability of those revolutionaries to exercise this power and achieve positive results. These actions can also be predicated on legitimate grievances, such as land claims and treaty rights in the case of the Mohawk. Thus, action and the enhancement of powers is phase three.

As AIM had quickly learned, one action can serve a greater function than one hundred petitions and protests. If these militant actions are met with authority and force from the host nation, the insurgents or revolutionaries are quickly turned into martyrs, thus the mobilization of a nation and the sympathies of the larger audience are completed. Inaction on the part of the host government implies an acceptance of sovereignty of the revolutionary or Narco-Parastate. For the host nation, it appears to be a lose-lose situation.[219] In the case of the Mohawk Warrior movement, all three phases form a joint relationship and were no doubt occurring in unison. However, no stage was complete by any means. The Oka Crisis was another step in this revolutionary process.

This revolutionary process is by no means isolated or original to the Mohawk Warrior Society. The combination of illegal activities and revolutionary movements is widespread. In Ireland, both the IRA and the Protestant Ulster Volunteer Force funded their activities with bootlegging and smuggling. In Sri Lanka, the Tamil Tigers are widespread heroin smugglers and currency counterfeiters. South American Maoist guerrillas have strong connections with the cocaine lords. In Afghanistan, the Taliban and Al-Qaeda had economic links to heroin production. The criminal elements and power struggle survives the often fleeting legitimate grievances and original directions of revolutionary organizations and movements.[220]

The Mohawk Warrior Society was originally formed as a social movement. However, leadership elements quickly realized that the divisions within the Mohawk Nation left the Reserves in a state of lawlessness. Using their tax-free status to circumvent the government's "sin-taxes" on tobacco and cigarettes, the agenda of the Warrior Society slowly shifted its emphasis from protectors of Mohawk sovereignty and land, to smuggling and gaming. Intimidation was used to quell opposition within Mohawk territory. The Oka Crisis afforded the Warrior Society a situation to persuade the government that policing on the Reserves by outside law enforcement agencies (LEAs) would have immense political ramifications and that the Reserves and the Warriors were better left alone. In the years immediately preceding Oka, government raids had intensified in Akwesasne, Kanesatake and Kahnawake. The Warriors wanted a return to the earlier "no-go zones." The Oka Crisis under the guise of legitimate grievances could serve just such a purpose.

The Oka Crisis, rooted in the uneasy convergence of two distinct cultures over 300 years, found its breaking point for the Mohawk Nation at Kanesatake in 1990. Colonialism with all its European aspects created divides within the military, political and religious institutions and of Iroquois Confederacy and the Mohawk Nation. Successive governmental policies created an atmosphere of opposition and hopelessness within the native communities. The dawn of the assimilationist and paternalistic *Indian Act* shortly after Canadian Confederation furthered the divisions within the Mohawk Nation as federal policy shook the foundations of Mohawk Longhouse government. Band Councils were created in conjunction with the Department of Indian Affairs accentuating the already uneasy state on Mohawk Reserves.

The land claim at Kanesatake between the Mohawks and the Seminary of St-Sulpice was only a segment of the larger frustrations brewing within the Mohawk Nation concerning sovereignty, land rights and a return to the traditional Longhouse administration over their land and lives. Many Mohawks tried to settle their complaints with the federal government over land rights and self-determination peacefully through the judicial process. However, by the 1960s, in connection with the many other social movements, a militant trend appeared in the Mohawk framework of resisting government policy and encroachment.

Not all Mohawks agreed with or supported the Warrior Society and its militant actions. As the rifts within the Mohawk Nation continued to fester throughout the 1960s and 1970s, a change in governmental policies in regard to land claims offered the Mohawk of Kanesatake a legal and peaceful means to finally settle the historic land claim at the Lake of Two Mountains. The Comprehensive Land Claim system was introduced in 1975. By this time many members of the Aboriginal community had been educated in Canadian institutions and Canadian law schools. They used this knowledge to combat the federal government, not with guns and barriers, but by using Canada's own laws and regulations in favour of their arguments.

PART II

From Convergence to Confrontation

The situation within the Mohawk Nation, and more specifically at Kanesatake, had been steering towards confrontation since colonization. The divisions within the Mohawk Nation caused by colonial administration and Canadian policies left the Mohawk with little control over the affairs of their own lives and communities. The subsequent power vacuum allowed for the rise of a militant posture, in the form of the Warrior Society, to plant its roots and expand from a social protectorate to a Narco-Parastate. The power struggle heightened by the political divides generated an atmosphere of lawlessness on Mohawk Reserves.

While militant resistance became an option for the radical elements, the vast majority of Mohawks still adhered to the belief that the differences between the Mohawk people and the governments of Canada could be resolved peacefully through negotiation. By the mid-1970s a newly-developed framework for land claim disputes gave new hope to resolving the land contentions at Kanesatake and Kahnawake without the use of revolutionary tactics. The promulgation of Comprehensive Land Claims and Specific Land Claims by the federal government was the framework through which resolution could be achieved.

However, while these claims were drafted and submitted, the Warrior Society continued to expropriate power from the moderate elements of the Mohawk Nation in an effort to promote their own agenda and safeguard the lucrative gaming and smuggling operations which had previously been established. Nowhere in Mohawk country were the divides of politics and opinions on the Warriors and their activities more prevalent than at Akwesasne. The power struggle at Akwesasne had been raging since the late 1970s with the introduction of high-stakes bingo and casinos and the continuation of the discount cigarette and alcohol trade. The violence between the disputing factions intensified to the point of civil war.

The troubled situation at Akwesasne left the governments of Canada and the United States with little choice. By 1990, state intervention was not only necessary but also unavoidable. The Canadian Forces was called upon to support LEAs under the legislation of *Provision of Armed Assistance* in an attempt to detain and suppress the violence in Akwesasne. Under this legislation, the CF had to comply with the federal government's demand to deploy and intervene.

While the circumstances at Akwesasne remained mercurial, the general uneasiness was exported to Kahnawake and Kanesatake. The land claims at Kanesatake had not produced the desired results for the Mohawk inhabitants and their frustrations soon took the form of barricades to defend the Pines against the Municipality of Oka, which threatened their destruction by the enhancement of the local golf course. The convergence of cultures at Kanesatake was heading towards confrontation. Although the Canadian public and media agencies were not yet focused on the impending clash at Kanesatake, Native rights were receiving top media billing in the form of the *Meech Lake Accord*.

CHAPTER 7

Kanesatake and the Modern Land Claims Process

Although there was a trend during the 1970s to get results through increasingly militant diplomacy, shifting avenues within the framework of government land claims opened peaceful possibilities for the Mohawk, most notably at Kanesatake. The 1973 *Calder* or *Delgamuukw* case produced drastic ramifications and set a precedent for future land claims. It stated that Aboriginal title was more than a simple right of usage and that the claimants must prove to be descendants from a society that occupied the land in question to the exclusion of all other peoples at the time of contact. It also stated that oral stories recorded in tradition, song and dance are admissible as court evidence.[221] In light of the Supreme Court ruling, Prime Minster Pierre Trudeau allegedly responded: "Perhaps you had more legal rights than we thought you had when we did the *White Paper.*"[222]

With the advent of this new policy, a joint Comprehensive Land Claim was submitted by the Mohawks of Kanesatake, Kahnawake and Akwesasne in January 1975. According to the Department of Indian Affairs, the general description of the land involved in the Mohawk claim was as follows:

> The southwest part of the Province of Quebec encompassing the area along and adjacent the St. Lawrence and Ottawa Rivers stretching south and east to the U.S. border and north to a point near the Saguenay River and including the areas north and west of the St. Lawrence and Ottawa Rivers. This territory would include the disputed lands in The Pines...[223]

Comprehensive Land Claims are accepted by the federal government for negotiation based on the following criteria:

1. The claimant group is and has historically been an organized society able to exercise authority over human use of land;

2. The claimant group has occupied the claimed territory since time immemorial. Their use and occupancy of the land must have been an established fact prior to European arrival;

3. The group historically occupied and used the land essentially to the exclusion of other aboriginal people;

4. The claimant group can demonstrate that many of its members continue to follow traditional pursuits within the claim area; and

5. The claimant group's aboriginal rights to use the resources have not been extinguished by treaty or other direct actions of the Crown.[224]

After reviewing the claim, the Department of Indian Affairs and Northern Development (DIAND) under Judd Buchanan dismissed the claim on the following grounds: Firstly, the Mohawk could not assert aboriginal title as they had not solely maintained possession since time immemorial. The land had been occupied by both Iroquois and Algonquian Nations during their protracted war before and after colonization. During the eighteenth and nineteenth centuries, the land had been occupied concurrently by Mohawk, Nipissing and Algonquin peoples. Furthermore, the department argued that the current Natives at Kanesatake are descendants of Nipissing, Algonquin and Mohawk; not solely Mohawk.[225]

Secondly, any aboriginal title that may have existed was extinguished by the successive Kings of France in the form of land grants, including the seigneurial grant(s) to the Sulpicians, and subsequently through the British Crown.[226] The Mohawk accepted none of these arguments and produced archaeological evidence, in the form of carbon-dated artifacts from Oka, oral histories and Cartier's documentation of the St. Lawrence Iroquois, to support the fact that the land had been occupied since time immemorial.[227]

With the rejection of the Comprehensive Land Claim, the Kanesatake Mohawk, (on advice from the Department of Justice), argued that the Sulpician land grant was for the benefit of the Indigenous people in their religious care and therefore was intended for use by the Natives. Thus in June 1977, the Kanesatake Mohawk submitted a Specific Land Claim for title to the land at Oka. Essentially, a Specific Land Claim refers to claims made by a Native group or nation against the federal government which relate to the administration of the land and other Native assets and to fulfilling the obligations made in treaties. The pursuit of such a claim has to be made with evidence supporting the government's failure to fulfill treaty rights or to administer those Native lands in question.[228]

This claim was rejected verbally in April 1986 by the Minister of Indian and Northern Affairs, David Crombie in a meeting with the Band Council. It was put to paper in October of the same year. His department concluded that the Kanesatake Mohawk did not meet the criteria for a Specific Claim, while taking the position that the 1912 decision of the Privy Council was a justifiable and complete answer to the question of any unresolved outstanding legal obligations of the federal government.[229] Again, Kanesatake was not a Reserve under the definition of the *Indian Act;* therefore, it was not subject to the same considerations under the land claims policies.

In summary, Mohawk claims have been advanced on a number of grounds. Although each represents a distinct legal argument, they are all no doubt related:

1. Territorial sovereignty stemming from status as a sovereign nation;
2. Treaty Rights;
3. The *Royal Proclamation Act* of 1763;
4. Unextinguished aboriginal title under common law and Indian Affairs statutes;
5. Land rights flowing from the obligation imposed on the Sulpicians in the successive eighteenth century land grants by the King of France.[230]

Based on these viewpoints, the federal, provincial and municipal governments held a position that these issues were decided, against the Mohawk, in the 1912 ruling of the Privy Council. Even with the advent of the new claims policy, these matters had, in the government's view, been previously settled. The issue of sovereignty has never been applied in court. Therefore, during 1990 this claim was repeatedly tabled by the Mohawk during negotiations. The Longhouse faction at Kanesatake stated that these past land claims had been submitted by the *Indian Act* Band Council and not by the traditional Longhouse representatives, which were negotiating their own grievances during 1990.[231]

Table 2—Mohawk Territory, 1990[232]

Territory	Acres	Population	DIAND Funding 1989-1990 ($Cdn.)
Kahnawake	12,477	6,000	17,071,078
Akwesasne	28,460 (14,460 U.S. and 14,000 Canada)	9,000 (Canada) 3,000 (U.S.)	14,226,580
Kanesatake	2,100	1,500	2,608,835
Tyendinaga	17,448	2,000	
Gibson (Wahta)	14,058	500	
Six Nations--Brantford	44,914	2,000	
Ganienkeh	7,500 (U.S.)	?	
Doncaster	19,000	None	

Until 1985, the land claim issue at Kanesatake had been tabled primarily to the federal government. Local interest and confrontation over the land had been relatively quiet over the past few decades. However, in September 1985, the Band Council at Kanesatake informed the Municipality of Oka of a project to build a drug and alcohol rehabilitation centre for Native peoples. The project was sponsored by Kahnawake, the Department of Indian and Northern Affairs and Health and Welfare Canada. This proposal was rejected by the municipality, and it urged the federal government not to purchase these lands within Oka for the intended use of a treatment centre.[233]

Nevertheless, on 21 January 1986, the proposal received confirmation of funding by the Treasury Board of Canada. Immediately, local residents protested and formed the Regroupement des Citoyens d'Oka (RCO). They argued that such a facility would depreciate the value of their lands. There was concern for the safety of their families, although a non-Native treatment centre, Maisonnée d'Oka, had been operating in the area since 1982 under no such fears or protest. The Onen'to:kon Treatment Centre opened in 1987, although the land it was situated on was never transferred to the Mohawk.[234] The allegations of bigotry, racial tension and ethnic fear surrounding the construction of the treatment centre weakened the mutual respect and cohabitation between Native and non-Native residents at Oka and the ill will was not forgotten.

Although relationships at Kanesatake and Oka were unstable, issues surrounding ownership of the Commons had been relatively peaceful over the past years. In 1987 this changed irreversibly when the Oka Golf Club tabled the possibility of expanding the existing nine-hole course to the standard 18 holes. Accordingly, in early March 1988, Mohawks began interrupting workers and surveyors from the Municipality of Oka in the areas perceived to be reserved for Native use.

On 12 April, a foreboding telex was sent by Chief Kanawato Gabriel of the Five Nations Longhouse People of Kanesatake (Longhouse Council) to the Minister of Indian Affairs, William McKnight:

> You are no doubt aware of the problem that now exists here in Kanesatake pertaining to the land situation and more specifically the area of 'our' lands we call 'The Pines....' Even now our young men have vowed that no work will be carried out in this area even to the extent of a possible usage of violence. Violence breeds more violence. The viscous circle will not end.... We request a meeting with you...to halt the threat of this grave situation that faces both our peoples.[235]

The municipality filed for an injunction against the peoples of Kanesatake to allow the workers to complete appointed tasks; the injunction was granted on 14 April.[236]

Coinciding with these problems, was the release of the findings by Pluritec-Environnement, a private firm hired by the Kanesatake Band Council, to examine and report on the land base required by the community to ensure its proper growth and development over the next decade (1986-1996). The final report, *Kanehsatake Indian Reserve – Land Needs Evaluation for Community Expansion*, no doubt frightened the Mohawks as it suggested that both population and the subsequent housing needs would double over this time period. Concurrently, a legal battle was raging over the right of Mohawk Jean-Roch Simon to erect an apartment building on lands within the town of Oka; both sides claiming title to the land.[237] With the possibility of a golf course usurping the Commons and excluded from Reserve status, the people of Kanesatake felt that their grievances were being ignored and their demands over the land sacrificed in the name of progress.

Nevertheless, on 8 March 1989, the Oka Golf Club unveiled its grand expansion project estimated at $1.35 million dollars. Included in its blueprint were an additional nine holes and "about 50 luxury houses" along the fairways just north of highway 344, straddling the tiny Mohawk cemetery. In light of this, Mohawks protested at the clubhouse. The Municipality of Oka argued that

Figure 1: Blueprint for the expansion of the Oka Golf Club.[238]

the land in question belonged to Mr. Maurice Rousseau and is not part of the Commons or the Pines. In contrast, the Mohawk argued that the land, including the existing nine-hole course, was part of the original seigneury and included the Commons and the hand-planted forest of white pine and hemlock and accordingly was reserved to them under the land grants and the *Proclamation Act*.

By 13 March, the Municipality had accepted an offer by Mr. Rousseau of 45 acres in exchange for $70,000, on condition that it be used for the golf course and that an additional 30 acres be afforded to the planned subdivision. Grand Chief Clarence Simon wrote to the municipality soon afterwards strongly advising that the construction of the course be delayed, citing unextinguished Aboriginal title to the land. Simon also made clear that any incursion would be seen as a violation of Mohawk territory. Likewise, on 1 April, 300 Mohawks, in addition to other non-Natives and environmentalists, marched peacefully through the town of Oka in opposition to the expansion of the golf links.[239]

On 27 April, facing increasing Mohawk opposition, representatives from the governments of Canada and Quebec, the Kanesatake Band Council and the Municipality of Oka partook in a meeting whereby the federal government announced a land purchase program, in which the land of the proposed extension was identified. This proposal stagnated and nothing was resolved. However, a moratorium on construction was put into effect on August 21 after Chief Simon, Oka-Village Mayor Jean Ouellette, and Oka Parish Mayor Yvan Patry started negotiations. In addition, the federal government initiated a framework agreement in July in conjunction with the provincial and municipal governments involved and the *Indian Act* Band Council at Kanesatake with the view to creating a Reserve under the *Indian Act* in the area of the disputed lands. This was not a new prospect as the federal government had tried this avenue in the past, most recently in 1987.[240]

The volatile situation was made worse by a high profile SQ raid. On 29 September 1989, during negotiations over the golf course expansion, between 50-75 SQ members, with the aid of a helicopter, forcefully raided the Kanesatake Riverside Bingo. The raid resulted in seven arrests and eight more searches. In the past, Mohawks had had run-ins with the SQ over hunting, fishing and traffic laws and distrusted them immensely. The SQ was seen by the Mohawks to be a racist adjunct arm of an oppressive Government of Quebec. Following the incident at the Bingo Hall, the Kanesatake Joint Services Council sent a letter to the Human Rights Commissions of Canada and Quebec condemning the use of excessive force used by the SQ. Another peaceful demonstration was held in October protesting not only the golf course but also the SQ intervention on Mohawk Territory.[241]

Although the moratorium on the expansion of the golf course was renewed until December, the situation within the community of Kanesatake was fragile. On 26 January 1990, Grand Chief Clarence Simon of the Six Nations Traditional Hereditary Chiefs (Indian Act Council) was dismissed by the Clan Mothers over allegations of conflict of interest. He was replaced by Grand Chief George Martin, who was not able to move into the Band Council office until 19 February as it was being picketed by Simon supporters. They argued that the Clan Mothers did not follow proper procedure under band custom. Martin only gained entrance to the Band Council office under protection of the SQ.[242]

In 1969, the Department of Indian Affairs had used a clause in the *Indian Act* to create a hybrid (Longhouse customs and *Indian Act* regulations) council which was unique to Kanesatake as it was not an official Reserve. The hereditary system was used to select a council of eight Chiefs headed by a Grand Chief from the Turtle Clan, all appointed by the Clan Mothers in consultation with the three Mohawk clans: Turtle, Bear and Wolf. While still having to comply with administrative rules set by *Indian Affairs*, the council's leaders were appointed not elected. Still, there was friction over the unique council. Two rival groups—Kanesatakeron League for Democracy and the Group of Change—wanted a return to band elections. Between 1987 and 1990, the Clan Mothers had appointed new chiefs six times. Those who wanted the electoral process were made up of those who had lost clan ties due to intermarriage with non-Mohawks; therefore, they had no clan to voice an opinion. Others who belonged to a clan argued that they were seldom consulted of Clan Mother decisions. This went against the principles of the Great Law.[243]

In addition to the Band Council, there was also a Kanesatake Longhouse. The Longhouse followers had their own Clan Mothers and their own Chief, Samson Gabriel. The followers of the Longhouse did not recognize the hybrid Band Council or any outside intervention from the Department of Indian Affairs and the *Indian Act*. Many Mohawks at Kanesatake belonged to many of these groups and were not unilateral in support for one or another, confusing the political framework of Kanesatake even more.[244] A repercussion of the political instability at Kanesatake was that the ongoing negotiations concerning the golf course and more importantly, the Reserve framework agreement stalled and a breakdown in communication between the conflicting parties ensued.

With the infighting over council appointments and political issues, for a time, the golf course expansion had been forgotten. However, the moratorium on the golf course expansion was lifted on 9 March 1990. DIAND and the Kanesatake Band Council convinced Oka Mayor, Jean Ouellette to postpone expansion for two weeks. That night many Mohawks, mostly from the Longhouse, held a peaceful demonstration at the club house under the direction of Allen Gabriel. The following morning, a fishing shack was dragged into the Pines and a make-shift camp was erected complete with a banner reading, "Are you aware that this is Mohawk land?" A petition bearing the signatures of 1,276 people opposed to the expansion was also sent to the Municipality of Oka. According to Ellen Gabriel of the Turtle Clan and head spokesperson for the people of Kanesatake during the standoff: "It was actually March 8th. That is when the fishing shack went up. There was no barricade, but the fishing shack and observations on whether workers were going to come in and start cutting trees. I don't know where they got March 11th maybe that was when the media started paying attention."[245] Nevertheless, the Oka Crisis had begun.

The rejection of Kanesatake's federal land claims in association with the proposed expansion of the Oka Golf Club left the Mohawks of the Lake of Two Mountains with little forum in which to voice their concerns and disagreements. In reality, after negotiations concerning the Pines failed they saw little recourse other than to peacefully occupy the land in question. The original barricades were weapons free. Although the initial protest was peaceful, its backdrop of Kanesatake was not. The divides of politics, the appointment of a new Grand Chief and the intervention of the SQ had created violence within the community. With the SQ monitoring the Pines and court injunctions being served to forcefully remove the protestors from the land, the Mohawk territory of Kanesatake and the Province of Quebec were on a collision course to confrontation. However, the clash would begin at Akwesasne.

CHAPTER 8

Akwesasne: Gambling and Civil War

While the Mohawk at Kanesatake were negotiating with governmental authorities and trying to resolve matters without the use of violence, the situation at Akwesasne had deteriorated and evolved somewhat differently, forcing the governments of Canada and the United States to intervene. The divisions of government at Akwesasne and their sponsors created complications unique to Akwesasne and a power vacuum, leaving the Reserve with no consensus on policy or governance. In this atmosphere, it became the hotbed for Warrior presence and operations. This struggle for power, in a lawless Reserve, forged the conditions for civil war.

Within the Reserve, there were three disparate councils which exercised functions of government. The Mohawk Nation Council operated as part of the greater Iroquois Confederacy under the traditional system of the Great Law of Peace incorporating the teachings of Handsome Lake. The oldest of all governing bodies, it claims to represent Mohawk on both sides of the international border. However, it is not recognized by federal, provincial or state authorities. This right is bestowed upon two other councils. In the New York State sector of the Reservation, three elected tribal chiefs operate under the laws of New York State and the federal laws of the United States within the St. Regis Tribal Council formed in 1802. The third council, the Mohawk Council of Akwesasne, was created in 1898 under the *Indian Act*. It represents the districts of Akwesasne in Ontario and Quebec.[246]

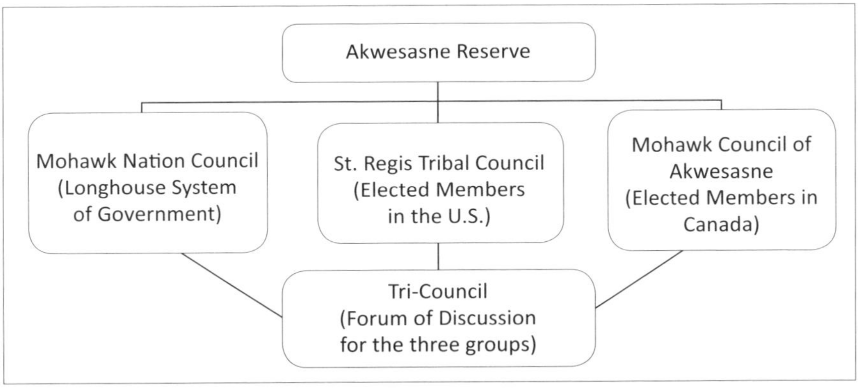

Figure 2: Band Council hierarchy of the Akwesasne Reserve.

On 6 June 1988, the DIAND received a request from the Akwesasne Councils to revert to a custom electoral system, to be put in place for the upcoming election scheduled for 25 June. The request met the criteria of DIAND policy and it was decided to revoke section 74 of the *Indian Act* in relation to Akwesasne. These consolidating orders were signed on 14 and 21 December 1989. Although not received in time for the election, Akwesasne held the 25 June election pursuant to the newly-adopted custom electoral system (Akwesasne Election Regulations) whereby a Grand Chief and 12 sub-Chiefs were selected for a three-year term.[247]

However, this decision and these appointments were not supported by all members of the Akwesasne community. On the surface, Mohawk Council of Akwesasne Grand Chief, Mike Mitchell, opposed the influx of gaming as did the Chief of Akwesasne Police Force, Ernest King. Within the American St. Regis Tribal Council, only Head Chief Harold Tarbell contested the gambling culture so prevalent in the community: "I wanted the police, the governor, the FBI, the federal bureaucracy, the BIA—anyone—to come in and restore order. If they didn't want to come in then I said give us the power, deputize us.... We couldn't have gamblers walking around proclaiming sovereignty. We had to have the rule of law."[248] This view was shared by Tom Porter, Jake Swamp and Ron LaFrance, all sub-Chiefs of the Mohawk Nation Council.

In an interview with CBC, Tarbell reaffirmed the framework of revolution within the Warrior movement:

> It's basically a paramilitary standing group which has taken unilateral authority onto itself.... It's a group...that understands political goals that we [Mohawks] have...but have formed a philosophy of force to achieve those goals. I think it is a group of people who are sincere in their belief...but are young and caught up in the machoism of it all. Then I think there are a number of others who are on the fringes of our society and are involved in different things and are either the outcasts or have vested interest in there being a lack of a regulatory and enforcement capacity in Indian communities so that they can capitalize on that for their personal gain.... Without an alternative to replace it [gambling and smuggling], it's a hard thing to battle against.[249]

The violence at Akwesasne between the pro- and anti-gambling factions intensified throughout 1989 and 1990, the specifics of which are depicted by Johansen and Hornung with accurate detail. The 8,500 Mohawks living on the

Reserve began to fight one another, the SQ, the New York State Police, the OPP, the RCMP and the FBI. Roving bands of gun-wielding Mohawks, armed law enforcers, barricades, frequent outbursts of gunfire and widespread arson became commonplace within the amplifying violence of the "Civil War." School boards refused to send in buses to take children to school, businesses were shut down, postal services interrupted, cars and houses became burnt-out carcasses, and many families fled to shelters set up in Cornwall by the Ontario Department of Transport. It is estimated that 2,000-4,000 Mohawks had left the Reserve by April 1990.[250]

As the "Civil War" in Akwesasne was raging, another Mohawk Reservation became embroiled in scandal and violence. On 30 March 1990, a Vermont National Guard helicopter was hit by three rounds of AK-47 ammunition over Ganienkeh. A passenger, Dr. James Kirk, was struck by a bullet and another bullet punctured the hydraulic line forcing the helicopter to land just outside the Mohawk territory. The Mohawks refused to allow investigators into Ganienkeh. Since the formation of the Reservation in 1977, after the Moss Park incident in 1974, the Warrior occupants were resolved that no foreign agencies were allowed to set foot on this territory. To prevent police forces from entering, Warriors set up barricades on in-routes and patrolled the forested perimeter. Finally, after an 11-day standoff, the police were allowed in for two hours to search one building. A Warrior by the code name "Omega Man" was arrested later in September for the helicopter shooting incident after participating at the barricades at Kahnawake.[251]

By April, violence in Akwesasne became increasingly common. Throughout April, barricades set up by both sides had been repeatedly dismantled, attacked and rebuilt. On 23 April, the North American Indian Travelling College was one of three buildings set on fire, destroying cultural and archival material of Reserve history. That night numerous gas bombs were thrown at anti-gaming blockades. A grenade was thrown into the Canadian Akwesasne Police Station, injuring three people. Several private homes were damaged by fire bombs. The following night, anti-gambling blockades were attacked with hundreds of rounds of automatic weapons fire and Molotov Cocktails. This assault was videotaped by Mike Francis and was shown on news stations across North America. Throughout the night, scuffles ensued between the opposing sides. By morning, the burnt out hulls of 20 cars lined Route 37. Indicative of the anarchy unfolding, no one was arrested and fortunately no one was seriously injured.[252]

All rational law and order, whether imposed by Mohawk means or governmental means, had melted away. Akwesasne was in chaos and the head Chiefs for both the American and Canadian Councils urged the governments to act, while encouraging residents to seek safety off of the Reserve. Harold Tarbell pleaded with New York Governor Mario Cuomo to order in the National Guard, as did Canadian Minister of Indian Affairs, Tom Siddon. On 25 April, a letter was sent to Major-General L.P. Flynn, commander of the New York Division of Military and Naval Affairs, from "all three of the governing Councils, acting on behalf of the Mohawk people of Akwesasne (Saint Regis Tribal Council, Mohawk Nation Council of Chiefs and the Mohawk Council of Akwesasne) urgently request emergency law enforcement assistance to restore peace and order...Immediate action is needed by appropriate law enforcement or military agencies."[253] Grand Chief Mike Mitchell wrote a similar letter to Prime Minister Brian Mulroney and Tom Siddon asking for "assistance in restoring Peace, Safety and Security for all citizens of Akwesasne by sending in Canada's equivalent of the National Guard."[254]

Governor Cuomo, who was making provisions to legalize gaming on the U.S. side of the Reserve, refused to activate the National Guard, believing that the reports of violence were overblown and exaggerated. Finally on 28 April, Cuomo, "directed the New York state Division of Military and Naval Affairs... to take steps to be prepared for that type of action" and the National Guard was readied for possible intervention. Cuomo added that, "There is a time for the use of military force but only after we have done everything in our power first to bring about a peaceful resolution."[255] According to Tarbell, "It was very clear that the Canadian government understood the threat to public safety, while Cuomo just shrugged."[256] Tarbell's Canadian counterpart, Mike Mitchell, agreed: "The Warriors are terrorists and if they are going to have control of Akwesasne, then our land is not safe for anybody who wants gambling to stop and our people to lead normal lives."[257] Even George Erasmus, Chief of the Assembly of First Nations publicly, condemned the Warriors.[258]

Although criticism towards the governments of both countries from Mohawk Chiefs was mounting, political negotiations were taking place and there was an understanding that multi-national coordination was vital before implementing any operational components. Action on each side of the border required cooperation at all levels of policing and governance. On 30 April, representatives from the police forces of Ontario, Quebec, New York State and the RCMP met to discuss tactical options in an undisclosed destination in New York State. On 1 May, Canadian and American mediators met at the U.S. Embassy in Ottawa with a view to forming an agreement and a unified political stance. Tom Siddon and Governor Cuomo were in constant communication, as were James A. Baker III, U.S. Secretary of State and Joe Clark, Canadian Minister of External Affairs. These occurrences were never made public.[259]

The solution offered by American representatives was to legalize gambling with the protection of state police forces. The apparent flaw in this plan was that the Warrior Society was not to be included in negotiations and that gaming would still not be under community control. Even gambling opponents, such as Mike Mitchell, were willing to allowing gaming on Akwesasne if it was controlled by the entire Akwesasne Council (both U.S. and Canada), that the profits be used for the entire well-being of the territory and that these concepts were enforced. The obvious impediment to this arrangement was wrestling the monopoly on gaming and its profits away from the Warriors and their supporters. Governor Cuomo secretly admitted that he wished to maintain a distance from the issue for political reasons and in his opinion the worst case scenario was to disarm the Warriors by force, including the use of military personnel, a solution he would not endorse.[260]

Although military resources had yet to be deployed, police raids continued throughout the growing violence. During March and April, U.S. agents seized $1.9 million in cash and 19 pounds of cocaine. Estimates reveal that the cocaine ring through Akwesasne to Montreal and Toronto was worth $40 million per month.[261] On the Canadian side, teams of SQ, OPP and RCMP patrolled the roads, while the American side was curiously absent of any significant law enforcement. The editor of *Akwesasne Notes*, Doug George concurred: "It's a real good strategy to stick to the Canadian side, where our police have the authority and the provincial and federal governments have said they would support our police."[262]

Indeed the provincial and federal governments were preparing a military response to aid police forces if required. Contingency planning was initiated by National Defence Headquarters (NDHQ) on 25 April and three options were evaluated, complete with a needs assessment. The first option was simply to support police forces in their attempt to impose law and order by supplying equipment and military resources. This was seen as the most likely option. The second was the evacuation of innocent persons, should violence occur in the process of option one. The last option, regarded as the least likely, was a military intervention. All options were limited to the sovereignty of national borders and co-operation with U.S. forces.[263]

Interestingly, contained in the original assessment was a clause to specifically "avoid, if possible, using 5 BM du CA...." It was 5 Brigade that was ultimately deployed to Kanesatake and Kahnawake for Operation SALON. There is no concrete evidence to suggest that NDHQ was withholding this brigade as a reserve force for Oka. However, with the construction of barricades on 11 March, the suspicion of weapons and with the situation and negotiations at Kanesatake deteriorating, it is feasible that NDHQ was aware that CF assistance might be requested.[264]

On 27 April, elements of 2nd Combat Engineer Regiment (2 CER) from CFB Petawawa and 450 Squadron (Ottawa), dressed in civilian clothing, conducted a reconnaissance of the Canadian portions of the Akwesasne Reserve. In addition, the Special Investigations Unit (SIU) was conducting its own intelligence gathering. The goal was to identify resource requirements and armoured personnel carrier (APC) fording sites between the mainland and Cornwall Island (Akwesasne) and helicopter landing zones on the Islands of St. Regis and Cornwall. Authority was also given to take aerial photographs and imagery of the Reserve with CF-5s in synchronization with U.S. forces and government satellites. Aerial imagery was considered of paramount importance.[265] In addition, the RCMP emergency response team was scheduled for familiarization training with CF equipment including AVGPs and service weapons at CFB Petawawa.[266]

The following day, 28 April, Prime Minster Brian Mulroney secretly alerted Bill McKnight, previous Minister of Indian Affairs and now Minister of National Defence (MND), to prepare contingency plans to support operations by the RCMP, OPP and SQ, with the RCMP being the lead agency. It was stressed that no military intervention would occur unless these agencies could not handle the situation.[267]

Facing the prospect of a possible CF insertion on Akwesasne, thorough intelligence and threat assessments were conducted and liaison was established with OPP, SQ and the RCMP to determine the nature and extent of potential involvement. A summary of all gathered intelligence revealed that the number of Warriors and sympathizers at Akwesasne fluctuated between 300-500, as both Warriors and supporters seemed to come and go, including many from Kahnawake. Many were identified to have U.S. Marine Corps or Vietnam experience.[268]

It was known by Canadian and American security agencies that the Warrior Society was heavily armed. As of 27 April, the following weapons had been seen and identified (although at this point the quantity was unknown): reactivated grenades (inert grenades which had been refilled with black powder, rearmed resulting in the explosion of larger fragments), semi-automatic rifles (AR-15, M-16 and shotguns with 30-round barrel magazines), automatic rifles (AK-47 and 9mm Uzi) and revolvers (.357 Smith and Wesson and .223 Mini 14 Ruger). Ammunition was plentiful. 25,000 rounds of various calibres had been purchased through Canadian commercial sources and American commercial purchases were estimated at four times that amount. It was known that 500-800 rounds were fired daily, another indication that the Warrior's ammunition reserve was large. In addition to these weapons, the Warriors were in possession of, or could acquire on short notice, two .50 calibre heavy machine guns and M-72 light anti-tank weapons (LAW).[269]

Other equipment in the Warrior arsenal included a very sophisticated and expensive communications network. They were monitoring police frequencies and conducted successful jamming operations using white noise, Native music and threats. They also were in possession of at least two high-powered speedboats (Pride and Joy) outfitted with 265 hp inboard/outboard engines. There was a concern that if police or military intervention by force occurred that the use of these weapons by young men (ages 14-18) would be unpredictable, as would the reaction of the Native population.[270] However, as of 30 April any CF involvement was still considered "unlikely" by NDHQ.[271] This changed literally overnight.

On 30 April-1 May, incidents on Akwesasne prompted the Canadian Government to act. Over the course of these two days, a nine-hour gun battle raged, marking the zenith of the Civil War. The principles of the Great Law were in tatters. Mohawks were fighting Mohawks. During the battle Doug George called a radio talk show, the guest of which was Governor Cuomo. After describing the violent situation, George got into an argument with Cuomo, who promptly hung up.[272]

In addition to superficial injuries, two Mohawks—Matthew Pike, an anti-gamer (22) and Harold "Junior" Edwards, a pro-gamer (30)—were killed by gun shots both on the Snye, Quebec land base of Akwesasne. Numerous houses were set ablaze and an estimated 3,000-4,000 rounds of ammunition were expended. An RCMP patrol boat also received direct fire from a high-speed power boat.[273] Between 1-3 May, 500 police officers from six individual organizations converged on Akwesasne from both borders in a well-coordinated joint operation and sealed off all access to the Reserve. With their presence, an eerie calm descended over Mohawk country.[274] This battle prompted the federal government to act and military resources were mobilized under the *National Defence Act* (NDA).

At 2045 hours (hrs), 1 May 1990, the Solicitor-General of Canada, Pierre Cadieux, asked the Minister of National Defence, Bill McKnight, to provide military assistance to the RCMP in and around Akwesasne. The request loosely hinted at amphibious armoured vehicles, secure communication systems and engineering assets (totalling roughly 100 personnel) to be in readiness for RCMP operations. However, this was not done under the traditional clause of *Aid to the Civil Power*. This request was done under *Provision of Armed Assistance*.[275]

A province can request, if necessary, the assistance of the Canadian Forces in managing riots and domestic disturbances without invoking *Aid to the Civil Power* under Part XI of the *National Defence Act*. The Solicitor-General of Canada can request armed assistance from the Minister of National Defence. The latter's response is discretionary. He/She can direct the Chief of the Defence Staff (CDS) to order deployment; however, control remains with the federal government.[276] This was the scenario for the CF implementation and deployment of Operation FEATHER (renamed Operation AKWESASNE for obvious politically sensitive reasons) to Cornwall and Akwesasne. The creation and legality of this operation differs immensely from what would be labelled Operation SALON at Kanesatake/Oka and Kahnawake which followed the traditional *Aid to the Civil Power* skeleton.

The federal government could no longer ignore the violence plaguing Akwesasne and the Cornwall area. The Grand Chiefs of both the American and Canadian Band Councils requested intervention. They knew that the situation was well beyond the control of internal police forces and the band councils. The RCMP and OPP did not have the required equipment to carry out operations without the support of the Canadian Forces. Gathered intelligence also revealed that these LEAs did not have the capacity or weapon systems to suppress the Warriors if direct confrontation occurred. The result was the request for CF support under *Provision of Armed Assistance*. This legislation forced the CF to participate in operations in and around Akwesasne through the planning, initiation and deployment of Operation FEATHER. Although CF intervention at Akwesasne differed in both form and function from the future deployments to Kanesatake and Kahnawake, it no doubt served as an example and warning to the federal government, the Government of Quebec and the Canadian Forces to begin preparing for another possible request for *Aid to the Civil Power* for other domestic operations in Mohawk territory.

CHAPTER 9

The History and Framework of *Aid to the Civil Power* and Domestic Operation Legislations

In order to understand the deployment of the Canadian Forces to Akwesasne, Kanesatake and Kahnawake the framework of legislations relating to domestic operations must be detailed. In Canada there is only one "Armed Force," this being the Canadian Forces controlled at the federal level. There are no provincial "armies" and municipal governments do not have the right, as the provinces do, to requisition the sole federal force under *Aid to the Civil Power.* Desmond Morton has written numerous articles on the history of *Aid to the Civil Power* in Canada. Briefly summarized, Canadian Militia was used on a frequent basis to enforce law in the period before regular or effective police organizations. The first appearance of the phrase "Aid to the Civil Power" appeared in the *1855 Militia Act*. The first post-Confederation *Militia Act* of 1868 clearly identified the requirement of a local militia commander to take action when a request in writing was promulgated by a local official such as a city mayor or a warden. The regular force replaced the militia in this function in an amendment of the 1904 act.[277]

According to Morton, there were 145 episodes of *Aid to the Civil Power* in Canada during the first century of Confederation. These served a broad range of functions from preventing boxing matches, guarding hangings, encouraging people to pay taxes, guarding the Welland Canal from Fenian threats, to quelling strikes and prison riots. Apart from the Riel Rebellions of 1870 and 1885 and the dispatch of troops to the Yukon in 1898 during the Gold Rush most circumstances were brief and relatively peaceful.[278] In fact, 80 of these occurred before the Second World War. With the advent of modern and properly trained police forces, the involvement of the military in domestic affairs became relatively moot. Between 1933 and 1969, there were no requests for troops made during peace time (seven were made during WWII). The basis for the decline can be found in a 1924 amendment to the *Militia Act* whereby the authority to requisition federal troops rested with the attorney general of a province, thus reducing the potential for the application of military force.[279] According to Morton, "The emergence of the 'urban-guerrilla' and the search for acceptable Army roles revived an old role in two new guises: low-intensity warfare and domestic peacekeeping."[280]

Accordingly, the most recent cases of *Aid to the Civil Power* are the 1969 Montreal police strike, the 1970 October Crisis, and the 1976 Olympic Games in Montreal. The FLQ or October Crisis illustrates the various levels of domestic operations and their implementation, including the *War Measures Act*. The Front de la Libération du Québec (FLQ) embarked on a terror campaign to ignite ethnic revolution in Quebec. Formed in 1963, the FLQ followed a five-step Maoist revolutionary war doctrine which had been successful in Cuba and Algeria in the recent past: mass organization, political mobilization, armed resistance, preparations for mobile warfare and finally national liberation. Evidence also showed that members were trained and backed by the *Front de Libération nationale* (FLN) in Algeria, and had a broad-based network of terrorist support and perhaps affiliation to internationally recognized countries such as France.[281]

Although the FLQ conducted 34 attacks in 1963, the pinnacle of activity occurred between 1968-1970, in the form of 137 attacks using increasingly sophisticated weapons on higher profile targets, including National Defence Headquarters in Ottawa. On 5 October 1970, British trade commissioner James Cross was kidnapped in Montreal by an FLQ cell (He remained in custody until December when a cordon and search operation stumbled upon his location). In exchange for Cross, the FLQ wanted their manifesto broadcast on national television. Prime Minister Pierre Trudeau refused. Similarly, on 10 October Pierre Laporte, Minister of Labour and Immigration for Quebec was kidnapped by another cell (He was eventually murdered on 17 October and his body found in the trunk of a car).[282]

After the Laporte abduction, newly elected Quebec Premier Robert Bourassa asked Trudeau to "send in the army [and] think about invoking the *War Measures Act*." Trudeau directed the Vice Chief of the Defence Staff (VCDS) Lieutenant-General Michael Dare, who was in command at that point, to establish liaison with the Attorney-General of Quebec to develop a plan for *Aid to the Civil Power* when and if it was requested. This was called Operation ESSAY. Concurrently, the VCDS authorized Operation GINGER, which unlike ESSAY was not an *Aid to the Civil Power* deployment. Similar to Operation FEATHER in Akwesasne, the Solicitor-General of Canada was urged to request assistance to the civil authority. The 9,000 troops of Force Mobile Command (FMC) were tasked to assist the RCMP in guarding federal buildings, escorting dignitaries and government officials and if necessary provide a rapid reaction force.

Both operations were authorized on 15 October 1970 when the formal request for *Aid to the Civil Power* was submitted by the Attorney-General of Quebec.[283]

Provincial Premiers do not possess their own military forces in the way that Governors in the United States have state-controlled National Guard units at their disposal. The legalities for *Aid to the Civil Power* operations are found in Part XI of the *National Defence Act*. Section 275 reads:

> 275. The Canadian Forces, any unit or other element thereof and any officer or man, with material, are liable to be called out for service in aid of the civil power in any case in which riot or disturbance of the peace, beyond the powers of the civil authorities to suppress, prevent or deal with and requiring that service, occurs or is, in the opinion of an attorney general, considered likely to occur.[284]

Thus, an Attorney-General of a province or territory has the right to request members and equipment of the Canadian Forces if they deem necessary. It is important to note that this request is a right and cannot be denied according to Section 277:

> 277. Where a riot or disturbance occurs or is likely to occur, the attorney general of the province in which the place where the riot or disturbance occurs or is considered as likely to occur is situated, on the initiative of the attorney general,...may, by requisition in writing addressed to the Chief of the Defence Staff, require the Canadian Forces, or such part thereof as the Chief of the Defence Staff or such officer as the Chief of the Defence Staff may designate considers necessary, to be called out on service in *Aid to the Civil Power*.[285]

Again it should be noted that the request circumvents all political authority such as the Prime Minister or the Minister of Defence and is submitted directly to the CDS. Once such a request is tabled in writing, it is at the discretion of the CDS or a designate to decide the weight and scope of the military force on loan to provincial police forces as formulated in Section 278:

> 278. On receiving a requisition in writing made by an attorney general under section 277, the Chief of the Defence Staff, or such an officer as the Chief of the Defence Staff may designate,

> shall call out such part of the Canadian Forces as the Chief of the Defence Staff or that officer considers necessary for the purpose of suppressing or preventing any actual riot or disturbance that is considered likely to occur.
>
> 280(4). A statement of fact contained in a requisition made under this Part is not open to dispute by the Chief of the Defence Staff.
>
> 283. The Canadian Forces...called out in Aid to the Civil Power shall remain on duty...until notification that the Canadian Forces are no longer required...is received from the Attorney General of the province concerned and, from time to time as in the opinion of the Chief of the Defence Staff the exigencies of the situation require, the Chief of the Defence Staff may increase or diminish the number of officers and non-commissioned members called out.[286]

Following this premise then, there is no discretion as to whether or not elements of the CF are deployed. Where there is discretion is in the number and amount of materials to be deployed. This is redundantly stated in 23.09(2) of the *Queen's Regulations and Orders* (QR&Os): "The composition of a force employed in *Aid to the Civil Power* shall be at the discretion of the Chief of the Defence Staff or of an officer designated by him for that purpose."[287] The QR&O's also makes clear reference to the conduct of soldiers deployed in such a mission. Chapter 23, entitled, "Duties in Aid to the Civil Power" outlines the rules and orders that govern the behaviour of CF members:

> Section 23.15, Note D: The law, that no more force may be used than is necessary, applies at all times; lethal weapons must not be used to prevent or suppress minor disorders or offences which are not serious, and in no case shall firearms be discharged if less extreme measures will suffice.[288]

With the formal 15 October request for *Aid to the Civil Power*, the Canadian Forces prepared to implement the previously constructed contingency plan. However, the following day Prime Minister Trudeau invoked the *War Measures Act*, which unlike *Aid to the Civil Power*, had jurisdiction across Canada and most importantly in Ontario which was also an FLQ target. Before 1988, aside from a special legislation for the federal government to assert dictatorial powers after a nuclear attack, the *War Measures Act* was the only mechanism by which the federal government could authorize the use of the military within Canada.[289] Created in 1914 by Prime Minister Sir Robert Borden to meet the demands and turbulence spawned by the First World War, the act is applied nationwide and cannot be confined to a single province:

> 3.(1) The Governor in Council may do and authorize such acts and things, and take from time to time such orders and regulations, as he may by reason of real or apprehended war, invasion or insurrection deem necessary or advisable for the security, defence, peace, order and welfare of Canada; and for greater certainty, but not so as to restrict the generality of the foregoing terms, it is hereby declared that the powers of the Governor in Council extend to all matters coming within the classes of subjects hereinafter enumerated... [290]

These subjects named in the act include the deployment of military forces, imposing censorship, undeterred arrest and detention, banning subversive organizations, the expropriation of private and public property, and control of all transportation and trade. In short the *War Measures Act* imposed draconian principles and afforded the Prime Minister dictatorial powers.[291]

In conjunction with the *War Measures Act*, the *Public Order Regulations* was also passed. Although not superseding either the *War Measures Act* or Part XI of the *National Defence Act*, these regulations gave CF personnel status as Peace Officers, and further rights to exercise greater functions: 1) maintenance or restoration of law and order; 2) the protection of property; 3) the protection of persons; 4) the arrest and custody of persons; 5) the apprehension of persons who have escaped from lawful custody or confinement; 6) the enforcement of warrants issued by the Minister pursuant to section 218 of the NDA; 7) enforcement of the Customs Act and regulations there under; and 8) the enforcement of the Boating Restriction Regulations and the Small Vessel Regulations.[292]

Due to the national nature of the *War Measures Act*, in theory, police in British Columbia could have used these extraordinary powers, even though the province faced no threat. In actuality, some police chiefs in western Canada used the suspension of civil liberties afforded by the War Measures Act to arrest and harass inoffensive left-wing hippie groups.[293] It became obvious that the *War Measures Act* was too extreme. Therefore, in early December the *Temporary Measures Act* was introduced, nullifying both the *War Measures Act* and the *Public Order Regulations*. The enhanced powers did not change and were equally draconian, but were now limited to the Province of Quebec.[294]

What cannot be overlooked is that by invoking the *War Measures Act* and the subsequent *Temporary Measures Act*, Prime Minister Trudeau ensured that the federal government held the balance of power, removing it from the hands of Premier Robert Bourassa. The request for *Aid to the Civil Power* was nullified the day after it was received by Trudeau's actions. Both the military and police forces conducted operations that seriously deterred any further violence and the FLQ has not conducted any terrorist operations since. The military commitment which totalled 12,500 troops over the period of events was stood down in January 1971.[295] Operation ESSAY was carried out so successfully that NDP leader T.C. Douglas compared it to "using a sledgehammer to crush a peanut."[296]

In 1973, a review was conducted on the provisions of internal security (IS) operations in light of the FLQ Crisis. It concluded that the system and legislative provisions were competent based on the fact that the federal government had means to limit the powers of requisition by provinces but also had the ability to act if the provinces did not. The *War Measures Act* and the *Temporary Measures Act* were the means in which to do so. However, a closer look at the legislation for domestic operations reveals both advantages and disadvantages.

The first advantage is that due to the circumvention of political organizations, *Aid to the Civil Power* reduces delay in deployment thus minimizing possible threats to life and property. Secondly, for the federal government, the responsibility for *Aid to the Civil Power* operations and possible negative impacts and repercussions rests solely with the requesting province negating any blame on the federal government.[297] This scenario would play out in the Oka Crisis.

The disadvantage of *Aid to the Civil Power* is that a large scale CF deployment can be made without any federal decision or judgement. An Attorney-General of a province could promulgate political, military and policing policies which may be unacceptable to the federal government. Second, the CDS may be forced to make a military commitment without formal support of political figures. However, there is nothing in any law which prohibits the CDS from consulting with politicians either before or after a request for *Aid to the Civil Power*. It would be professional suicide not to do so. The only contradiction can be found in section 18 of the NDA which states that the CDS is subject to the direction of the Minister of National Defence. In part XI of the same act, the CDS is given exclusive authority. The latter seems more reliable for if a decision was left to the Minister, the inevitable delay in deployment due to political discourse could endanger lives.[298]

However, the nature of *Aid to the Civil Power* was drastically altered in 1988 when the *War Measures Act* was replaced with the *Emergencies Act*. The 1987 *Defence White Paper* had concluded that the *War Measures Act* was "too broad and too sweeping" and did not include enough "safeguards against abuse" in domestic operations. The new act identified four types of national emergency: 1) public welfare; 2) public order; 3) international; and 4) war.[299] A national emergency is defined as:

> 3. For the purposes of this Act, a "national emergency" is an urgent and critical situation of a temporary nature that...
>
> (b) seriously threatens the ability of the Government of Canada to preserve the sovereignty, security and territorial integrity of Canada and that cannot be effectively dealt with under any other law of Canada.[300]

However, by leaving in Part XI of the NDA, legislators consciously made it virtually impossible for a Prime Minister to invoke the *Emergencies Act* for any Oka-type scenario. More importantly, Section 25(3) of the act specifically renders the federal government impotent in the ability to override a province determined to use Part XI, *Aid to the Civil Power*:[301]

> 25.(3) The Governor in Council may not issue a declaration of a public order emergency where the effects of the emergency are confined to one province, unless the lieutenant governor in council of the province has indicated to the Governor in Council that the emergency exceeds the capacity or authority of the province to deal with it.[302]

In effect, during the Oka Crisis Prime Minister Brian Mulroney did not have the options that were available to Prime Minister Trudeau under the *War Measures Act* during the FLQ Crisis. Although the violence of Oka had the potential to spread and ignite Indigenous peoples across the country, the wording specifies that the "effects of the emergency are," meaning current to the time. Future predictions or possible effects cannot be legally taken into consideration.[303] These legal factors surrounding Oka will be dealt with later, but were no doubt influential to the decision-making process surrounding the events at Kanesatake and Kahnawake in 1990 which highlighted serious flaws within the *Emergencies Act* and IS legislation.

Most significantly, if Bourassa, who was the Premier of Quebec during the Oka Crisis, had ordered the CF to take direct lethal action against the Warriors at Kanesatake and Kahnawake the result could have been horrendous bloodshed. It could have sparked violent retaliation from Natives across Canada and the United States. It appears logical that the Prime Minister should have executive powers to intervene and legally commandeer control of the CF. This is not the case under the *Emergencies Act*.[304]

Another noteworthy amendment to the *Emergencies Act* according to Morton was that the new framework transformed the cost and payment attributes of *Aid to the Civil Power*. Under the new legislation all Canadians would bear the cost burden through the Consolidated Revenue Fund, which until 1988 had rested with the municipalities and the provinces. In Morton's words: "A free service is likely to be used."[305]

Therefore, by 1990, there were three circumstances which afforded the use of domestic military deployments. The first and most relevant to the topic is *Aid to the Civil Power*, which fundamentally had not changed since the FLQ Crisis. This is limited to a single province. The second is through the decree of the *Emergencies Act*, but as shown, this nationwide framework has serious flaws. The third instance, *Provision of Armed Assistance*, usually implies that the CF will be called out for non-combat or non-confrontational duties. These are usually for short time periods and follow pre-existing contingency plans. Operations include relief of natural disasters, fisheries and narcotic-trafficking surveillance, pollution monitoring and ice flow reconnaissance. However, this can also be used to request armed intervention.[306]

The deployment of the Canadian Forces in support of LEAs at Akwesasne was only guaranteed so long as an official request for *Provision of Armed Assistance* was submitted. The federal government was handcuffed in the sense that the violent situation at Akwesasne did not constitute a national emergency; therefore, the newly created *Emergencies Act* could not be invoked. Once requested, the CF had the ability to independently determine the commitment of resources necessary to fulfill its mandate and function in consultation with LEAs and as outlined in the formal request under *Provision of Armed Assistance.*

CHAPTER 10

Operation FEATHER/Operation AKWESASNE

The deployment of Operation FEATHER in May 1990 to Akwesasne was unique as it did not fit the typical *Aid to the Civil Power* construction; nevertheless, it was still an *Aid to the Civil Power* type operation. On 1 May, the request from Solicitor-General Pierre Cadieux for CF assistance to the RCMP was a shock to Lieutenant-Colonel Derald Prosser who coordinated the operation from the Regional Direction Centre in the Long Sault, Ontario detachment of the OPP: "Although I had met with the police the same day, there was no indication that the military would be called in to assist."[307]

By the morning of 2 May, with the exception of certain service and support elements, all CF personnel and equipment were in their designated locations with the intent to complete this mission:

> CF to provide armed assistance to RCMP to restore law and order on Canadian portion of St Regis Akwesasne Indian Reserve. CF assistance to be confined to provision of armoured vehicles for transport and protection of police personnel, mobile VHF/FM secure communications for LEA use and any non lethal operational support requested to ensure success and safety of personnel involved. Duration of Operation undetermined however commitment made for seven days. Contingency planning must take place to cater for any increase in scope of operations.[308]

The operation was strategically commanded by Force Mobile Command (FMC) with sub-command elements at HQ Central Region and HQ Eastern Region. Major-General Bob Stewart was the designated commander, while Lieutenant-Colonel Norris Pettis, commanding officer (CO) of 1st Battalion, The Royal Canadian Regiment (1 RCR) was appointed tactical commander. He was well aware of the jurisdictional intricacies of his command: "I can't imagine a more complicated problem. We're dealing with three police forces [SQ, OPP and RCMP], two provinces and two national governments. It has taken days to develop mutual trust and understanding."[309] To assuage miscommunication concerns between the various forces, a Joint Operations Centre (JOC) was set up at the OPP station at Long Sault, 19 km west of Cornwall. As of 2 May under command of Pettis, was the Special Service Force (SSF) made up of

248 personnel, 81 vehicles, 3 rafts, various boats and 2 CH-135 helicopters. The deployment to Akwesasne reached its peak on 9 May after which time there were continuous reductions in both men and materials:[310]

Table 3—Operation FEATHER—Peak Deployment, 09 MAY 1990[311]

Unit/Home Location	Officers	NCMs	Vehicles/Equipment
1RCR (1st Battalion, The Royal Canadian Regiment) London	10	150	14 x AVGP (Grizzly) 2 x APC Dozer 1 x APC (ARVL) 2 x Husky 5 x Iltis (all equipped with VINSON Comms.) 33 x Support Vehicles
2 CER (Combat Engineer Regiment) Petawawa	2	41	20 x Support Vehicles 5 x Kenworth 4 x Assault Boat 2 x Power Boat 2 x Sealander Jetboat 8 x Dive Team Equipment 2 x Class 16 Raft 1 x Class 60 Raft
2 SVC BN (Service Battalion) Petawawa	1	14	8 x Support Vehicles
2 MP PL (Military Police Platoon) Petawawa		4	2 x Support Vehicles
2 FD AMB (Field Ambulance) Petawawa, Ontario	1	4	2 x Ambulances 6 x Support Vehicles
SSF HQ and SIGS (Headquarters and Signals)	14	17	10 x Support Vehicles
2 EW Sqn (Electronic Warfare Squadron) 1 Can. Div. Kingston	3	34	12 x Support Vehicles
1 Int Coy (1 Intelligence Company) 1 Can. Div. Kingston	1	6	2 x Support Vehicles
427 Sqn Petawawa	6	11	2 x CH-135 3 x CH-135 (8 hrs Notice to Move or NTM) 4 x CH-136 (8 hrs NTM) 1 X FARP (for refuelling)

cont...

Unit/Home Location	Officers	NCMs	Vehicles/Equipment
430 Sqn Valcartier			3 x CH-135 (8 hrs NTM) 4 x CH-136 (8 hrs NTM)
450 Sqn Borden			1 x CH-147 (4 hrs NTM)
Other	2	18	
Total	40	299	161
Cornwall Armouries: Base Security Force		20-30 Reserve Pers.	All assistance was unarmed. Units: 28 Ottawa Service Bn, Stormont, Dundas & Glengarry Highlanders, Cameron Highlanders of Ottawa and the Brockville Rifles.

CF personnel had authority to carry weapons only when participating in active operations with deployed police forces. These soldiers did carry live ammunition; however, the magazines could only be loaded into the weapon on order or in self-defence and in accordance with the use of force guidelines provided in the QR&Os. Body armour and helmets were also mandatory. In addition, due to the Operation FEATHER mandate as an internal security mission, no foreign exchange officers were allowed to participate. This would hold true for Operation SALON (military operations at Kanesatake and Kahnawake) as well.[312]

Having completed preliminary reconnaissance patrols and intelligence gathering in late April, in conjunction with intelligence reports from LEAs, Operation FEATHER commanders knew the capabilities of the Warriors. Bursts of gunfire continued to be discharged throughout 2-4 May and were identified as semi-automatic weapons. In addition, receipts from gun stores in New York and Vermont recorded Warrior purchases of many heavier machine-guns and RPGs (rocket-propelled grenades). However, no weapons were visible during joint police/military patrols and with no visual confirmation, the extent of the Warrior arsenal remained inconclusive. Two boat loads of weapons were seen being transported from Cornwall Island to St. Regis Island on 2 May. It was also ascertained that the Warriors had a mobile detection unit, which had the ability to intercept and jam the radio communications of LEAs.[313]

To alleviate this concern, secure CF communications equipment was requested by LEAs. The CF acquiesced to the demand by deploying elements of 706 Communication Squadron from Borden. The CF thought it was also necessary to monitor Warrior message traffic (most of which was on cellular phones), to locate base stations and mobile parties, and if need be, jam Warrior communication in the event of hostile activity. Recent Warrior phone traffic had revealed an intention to resume armed operations once the CF and police effort declined. In addition, the Warriors were successful in short length jamming of RCMP and OPP communications.[314]

To satisfy their perceived needs, 1st Canadian Division (Kingston) deployed 2 Electronic Warfare Squadron (2 EW Sqn) and 1 Intelligence Company (1 Int Coy) on 6 May, "to be kept to lowest profile possible." However, due to complications over legality only radio transmission could be intercepted. Cellular communication was a new phenomena in 1990 and although intercepting and jamming radio communications did not contravene Part IV of the *Canadian Criminal Code* (under which the CF must operate), there was a question as to whether cellular phones were included in "radio communication." As such, information from cellular phones was not divulged to third parties including LEAs. All lawful Signal Intelligence (SIGINT) was for use of the CF and LEAs with the "understanding that CF pers would under no circumstances be called upon to testify in a court of law nor would the source of product be used in formal court proceedings. Good Hunting!"[315]

With the arrival of police and the ensuing CF deployment the situation at Akwesasne remained relatively quiet. Police presence on both sides of the Reserve seemed to have soothed the violence. The funerals of both Pike and Edwards passed without incident on 5 and 7 May respectively. This is not surprising as it is customary in Native culture to cease hostilities during periods of mourning. Those Mohawks who had fled Akwesasne in the wake of the gaming violence slowly began to return to their homes with support from governmental agencies and LEAs. As of 6 May it was estimated that only 215 Mohawks remained in the Cornwall shelters, the number lessening to 125 the following day. All schools reopened on 9 May.[316]

Human intelligence sources (HUMINT) also reported that the police presence on the Reserve, "is deeply felt by the Warriors as it has cut their main sources of income, which are the gambling and traffic of cigarettes across the border to Canada. This lack of money gain is also felt severely at Kahnawake Reserve by Warriors there, as this police presence has curtailed many main source of income...forcing many Kahnawake Mohawks to close their illegal tobacco stores." Canada Border Services Agency at Cornwall required the use of the

Cornwall Armouries in order to store an estimated $3.1 million worth of cigarettes sequestered at the border crossing over the past two months.[317]

It also appeared that the Warriors were using the influx of media to Akwesasne to convey the message that they believed the police presence was a form of occupation of their territory. They also indicated that they were the victims of a disinformation campaign portraying them as oppressors to the Mohawk Nation and terrorists to the Canadian and American public. According to a 6 May intelligence report: "The request for withdrawal of all white police from Akwesasne Reserve by Warriors and their supporters will soon become the main topic in this conflict."[318]

Up to this point, the primary functions of the CF were limited to service and support elements such as the feeding and canvas tent housing of LEA personnel. The CF also supplied secure communication assets, intelligence cells and night vision equipment. 2 CER had ferried police and military vehicles, including a helicopter from Cornwall to Cornwall Island and St. Regis on rafts in order to conduct joint mobile patrols on the islands and main land of Canadian Akwesasne. Each military patrol was accompanied by one or more police officers, to avoid a situation where CF personnel were required to make arrests. Concurrently, the New York State Police and the FBI conducted patrols and searches in American Akwesasne.[319]

Having already been deployed with no foreseen extraction in the near future, and facing a relatively low immediate threat, elements of the CF took advantage of the situation to conduct training. Joint infantry/engineer rafting and amphibious insertion training were conducted throughout the operation, including night movements and the recovery of a sunken OPP patrol boat. Between 6-8 May, float tests and swim tests were conducted with the Grizzly AVGPs. After completing successful float tests with the aid of a cable, the AVGPs were loaded with troops to conduct swim tests. These were accomplished with various successes, with at least one Grizzly sinking almost immediately after entering the frigid St. Lawrence River.[320]

As CF training continued, a joint patrol on Cornwall Island raided a home in the early morning of 10 May seizing over $1 million worth of cocaine (4 lbs) and 12 weapons. With the arrests stemming from this raid, the total for the operation was 14.[321] On 13 May, five more arrests were made in conjunction with the murder of Harold Edwards. Those arrested were: Ken Lazore, Roger Mitchell, Steve Lazore, David George and Doug George, with the latter two being formally charged. A truck rented in the U.S. was intercepted illegally crossing the border near Sutton, Quebec carrying 350 cases of cigarettes headed for Kahnawake.[322] (It should be noted that on 16 May, Operation FEATHER was renamed Operation AKWESASNE by the CF and will now be referred to as such).

As the overall threat to LEAs was believed to be reduced through patrolling and checkpoints, the supporting role of CF commitment was reduced. By 25 May the CF commitment at Akwesasne consisted of 89 personnel (all trades), 35 vehicles (all models) and 9 marine vessels.[323] All but three personnel from 2 EW Sqn and 1 Int Coy returned to Kingston between 13-16 May, and most of the secure communications equipment was withdrawn on 18 May. However, the threats to both LEA personnel and the Mohawk inhabitants was not completely negligible thus, "the continued requirement for CF SP [support] was confirmed...However, in view of the current comparatively quiet situation on the Reserve...it is appropriate that a prudent and gradual thinning out of CF resources be undertaken. Strength has now reached bare minimum to meet mandate." It was felt that the CF was still required to provide immediate armed assistance resources, in addition to, offering operational equipment and administrative support.[324]

Although the overall atmosphere at Akwesasne was calm, there were still instances of violent episodes. Gunshots were still heard during the nights and unmanned roadblocks were frequently erected to impede police activity. Cars raced towards police roadblocks with the intention of ramming them and quickly braked before skidding to a halt and racing away. On 19 and 22 May, Molotov Cocktails were hurled at New York Police checkpoints. Another box of 10 Molotov Cocktails was discovered on Cornwall Island and 6 more were found in a parked car. There were two reported incidents of bomb threats in Hogansburg, New York. On another occasion, a cache of weapons was seen being thrown overboard into the river. 2 CER conducted combat dive training in the area of the drop but did not recover the weapons. An OPP raid on 24 May uncovered, "6 misc. weapons and ammo including an AK-47." On 28 May a hostage-taking incident occurred, which ended without injury.[325]

Information for conducting searches and raids came from the joint intelligence cell operating out of the Long Sault HQ, and mobile command post units made up of three members of 2 EW Sqn and 1 Int Coy as well as RCMP, OPP intelligence officers, DND analysts and SIU agents. They received and analyzed information from numerous sources including intercepted communications, visual observations by forces in the field, aerial and maritime observation, media reports and imbedded human intelligence agents. After compiling the data, field operations were planned or adjusted accordingly.[326]

During a 24-hour period, this cell intercepted an average of 21 Warrior transmissions citing that on certain occasions "net [radio network] discipline seemed to be poor. There were indications that those participants [Warriors] were intoxicated and this could explain the lapse in discipline." As the police and CF posture became more relaxed and numbers began to diminish, the intelligence cell reported an increasing number of smuggling related incidents. Warriors and smugglers were still monitoring police frequencies and had determined the pattern of police presence and movements and consequently changed their routes. Smugglers and Warriors also used wooded area and holes in fences to bypass police checkpoints.[327]

Compounding the already volatile environment in Akwesasne was the fact that an election for Grand Chief of the American St. Regis tribal council was scheduled for 2 June. Anti-gambling supporter and incumbent Grand Chief Harold Tarbell was being challenged for leadership by a pro-gambling Norman Tarbell (no relation). Harold was the only anti-gamer on the council and if he was defeated, the St. Regis Tribal Council would be made up of all pro-gambling supporters. Demonstrations of support for both men were frequent throughout late May. The outcome of the election would no doubt have an effect on Warrior intentions. Also, the Akwesasne Police Force (APF) returned to active duty on 28 May under protest from groups of Mohawks who believed them to be corrupted by pro-gaming supporters.[328]

Norman Tarbell won the election over Harold Tarbell 637 votes to 538 votes. The only eligible voters for the election were American Mohawks (roughly 3,500 eligible) as ruled by a New York State judge. Anti-gambling factions were quick to begin protesting the manner in which the election was conducted and also its outcome. In relation, threats to LEA officers and damage to police vehicles increased as pro-gamers wanted to rid Akwesasne of outside forces. In fact, Norman Tarbell who was to take office on 2 July made campaign promises to reopen the casinos and remove non-Native police forces from Akwesasne.[329]

On 18 June, the Bingo Halls of Akwesasne reopened without incident. The casinos remained closed. Governor Cuomo and the New York State Legislature were negotiating the legalities of gaming on tribal land. While Cuomo sought to legalize gaming, most members of the Legislature were of the opinion that keeping the casinos closed was essential to a continuing peace on Akwesasne in conjunction with continual police patrols.[330]

Although elements of the OPP, SQ and RCMP remained in Mohawk territory, they all agreed that CF support was no longer required provided that the personnel and equipment as of 6 June (87 soldiers, 33 vehicles, and 11 marine vehicles) could be redeployed within six hours. As a result, on 7 June Operation AKWESASNE was withdrawn leaving behind a small rear party and 9 intelligence personnel. By 25 June the CF commitment was limited to 12 personnel (two from 2 EW Sqn), eight vehicles, and seven marine vessels.[331] If the operation was prolonged, 2 Royal Canadian Horse Artillery (2 RCHA) was to provide relief in place on 3 July.

The lack of CF support had a negative effect on policing operations and violent activities increased almost immediately. On 11 June the Warriors held a meeting at The Bears Den as was observed by the SQ and OPP. Most if not all casino owners were present. Use of electronic communication devices by the Warriors ceased almost completely, cutting off a vital supply of information to LEAs. The Warriors also continued to monitor police movements and numbers.[332]

On 15 June, 42 rounds were fired at an RCMP roadblock, with ten near misses reported. This incident was repeated at an SQ checkpoint on 17 June. This was believed to be in retaliation for the arrest of prominent Warrior spokesperson Christine King for impaired driving on 15 June. Sporadic gunfire still plagued the Reserve and counts of petty crimes and vandalism were rising. This was attributed to the beginning of summer vacation for school students. On the nights of 15, 16 and 19 June, police responded to shots fired. Upon investigation, members of the Warrior Society were conducting target practice.[333] An intercept by elements of 2 EW Sqn revealed the following conversation:

> Navajo: One of them state troopers that were out yesterday said well if he's in his own yard he said we can't do a damn thing about it and they went over there and I guess he couldn't do nothing.
>
> UM1: Who was shooting around?
>
> Navajo: ...My young Warriors were testing out the new machines that what it was...They were checking out the new artillery... probably start again tomorrow....
>
> UM1: Probably get a new lot tomorrow.

UM2: Save your ammo.

Navajo: We've got about 75,000 rounds just waiting to be used.

During the same conversation, a bazooka was also mentioned.[334] Analysts were cautious with the information received from monitoring Warrior communication. The Warriors surely knew that they were being screened and conversations could be phoney as part of an overall disinformation campaign. Another furtive action of the Warriors was to handsomely pay non-Natives to smuggle weapons over the border.[335]

Nevertheless, police presence continued to deter any escalation of violence and patrols frequently uncovered caches of cigarettes, weapons and other contraband. LEAs all cited the CF existence and support had a positive impact on their mandate. In view of the LEA's protracted commitment, they agreed that CF men and materials could be withdrawn completely, provided assistance could be quickly redeployed. Accordingly, as of 5 July, only three CF members remained: a liaison officer and 2 members of 2 EW Sqn. Equipment was reduced to three vehicles and one raft.[336]

The involvement of the Canadian Forces in support of LEAs appeared to have a calming effect on the condition of Akwesasne. The violence had subsided and for the CF, Operation AKWESASNE was thought to be nearing completion. However, the circumstances that transpired at Kanesatake and Kahnawake throughout the month of July prolonged CF intervention at Akwesasne. The negotiations concerning the land dispute at Kanesatake were at a standstill. Neither side was willing to compromise their positions. As Akwesasne was continuously monitored and patrolled by police forces, the Warriors slowly began to infiltrate the peaceful Mohawk camp at Kanesatake. Warriors and weapons began to appear behind the barricade in the Pines creating divisions between all elements in the Pines but also between the members and organizations in the community itself. Frustrated by the Mohawk position, the Municipality of Oka secured court injunctions for the forceful removal of these Mohawk elements by the SQ, which had been closely observing the situation; one that was heading towards confrontation.

CHAPTER 11

Protest in the Pines at Kanesatake

Although CF involvement at Akwesasne was diminishing due to a decrease in overall violence, NDHQ was keeping a close watch on the events at Oka knowing that, "concerns about the situation at Oka could make its way to Akwesasne Reserve."[337] The environment at Oka was becoming increasingly hostile and negotiations over the expansion of the golf course were floundering. With the advent of the Mohawk's watch and picketing of the Pines beginning 8 March, the relationship between the Municipality of Oka and those Mohawks who supported the action weakened. The Regroupement des Citoyens d'Oka (RCO), which had protested the construction of the drug rehabilitation facility, also began to protest the actions of the Mohawk. In addition, with the influx of Warriors and radical elements, the Pines were transformed into a defensive fortification.

However, not all Mohawks agreed with the decisions of those protesting in the Pines and the fishing shack was set ablaze in early April. There were continuous disagreements among the Kanesatake Mohawks over the course of action to be taken to protect the Pines and the Mohawk cemetery. Thus far, no barricades had been erected and although weapons were at the camp, none were visible. Dan Gaspé, Kanesatake band administrator from January to 9 March 1990 suggested in his evidence to the Standing Committee on Aboriginal Affairs that, "On March 8, I co-chaired a meeting. About 10 people decided that there would be an occupation of the territory.... We tried to set some rules about how this project was going to go forward, we lost the argument as to whether or not arms were going to be used."[338] Having no official Warrior Society of its own and unfamiliar with confrontational tactics, these demonstrators sought advice from the leadership of the Kahnawake and Akwesasne Warriors on how to best patrol, construct barricades and maintain surveillance on the Pines. It appeared that certain members of the Kanesatake community were prepared to use weapons to defend their land and agenda.

According to Ellen Gabriel, "The barricades didn't start going up until the snow melted, maybe the end of March, the beginning of April, so that the non-Native people of Oka would understand that your Mayor is doing this to us, so we are not letting you come through. We are not holding this against you but this is the principle of the claim, we don't want our trees to be cut so we are only allowing our people to go through."[339] Although the exact date differs according to sources, during the time period mentioned, a barricade was erected blocking access to Chemin du Milieu, a dirt road heading north off of Highway 344, running along the western boundary of the golf course. Gabriel insists that it was not, "344, but on a dirt road that nobody uses, but they made an excuse that the ambulance needed to be able to go through, but it never went through because the road is so bumpy and they always use the highway or the paved roads. There was a lot of propaganda going on against us. The closing of the highway was after we were attacked on July 11th."[340]

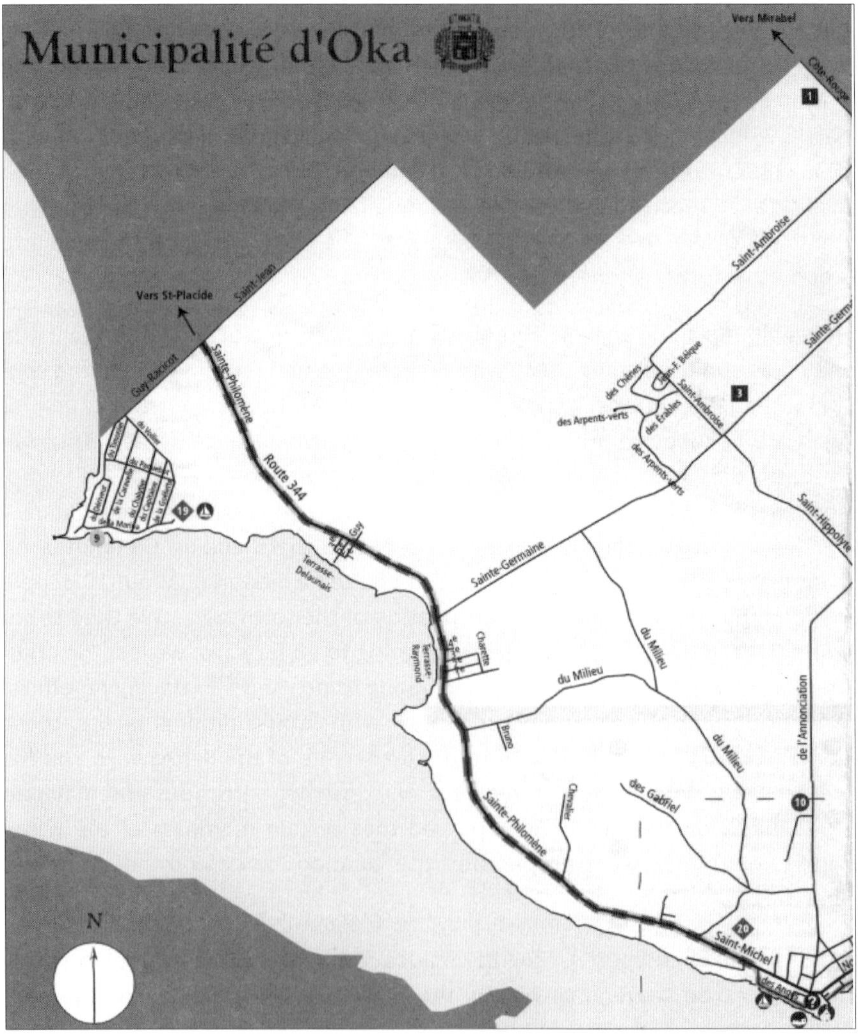

Figure 3: Map of Oka. The Oka Golf Club is marked by the gray (20) diamond. The original barricade was immediately to the left at the junction of du Milieu and Highway 344. (Information touristique d'Oka).

On 26 April, the Superior Court of the district of St-Jérôme issued a provisional injunction as requested by the Municipality of Oka forbidding Mohawk demonstrators from impeding the movement of any traffic, including the Chemin du Milieu, and from posting signs on neighbouring properties. Failure to comply could result in forceful intervention by the SQ. The month of April had already seen members of the SQ in Kanesatake. On 6 April, supporters of dehorned Chief George Martin occupied the Band Council office. Acting Chief Clarence Simon called in the SQ, which forcibly removed the crowd.[341]

The serving of the injunction changed the representation of the Mohawks manning the barricades on the north and south entrances to the Pines along Chemin du Milieu. During late April continuing into early May, the RCMP and SQ tracked the movements of many Warriors from Ganienkeh, Kahnawake and Akwesasne to Kanesatake. Warriors from the three sister territories began to pour into Kanesatake armed with their support but also with truckloads of camping equipment, food, communication devices and weapons. During this time period CF intelligence at Akwesasne noted that the Warriors were "conspicuous by their absence."[342] When asked if he saw the Warrior Society taking over the legitimate land claim grievances at Kanesatake for their own interests, Harold Tarbell replied:

> I see that happening. For example, this started over a land claim dispute in Oka, in Kanesatake, and I think every Indian and probably most of the people in North America agree with the Kanesatake Mohawks on their land dispute. But clearly with this promotion of a trans-Mohawk agenda that's coming forward about, for example, one of the demands in Kanesatake being the removal of the police from Akwesasne. It's clear that somebody else is promoting a different agenda, and it's clear that that agenda is beyond, I think, the desires of the Kanesatake people. I would encourage the Canadian federal government to actively engage in that process. I think that it's important that they do it, but if they do that and do that with the Warrior Society, they will in effect give the Warrior Society recognition as being the de facto Mohawk nation....My view on this has always been that the Mohawk people...can win this situation in Parliament, in court, in political and public relations issues...I don't think we gain with the long term philosophy that is promoted in our culture by force of arms or by having everything resolved at roadblocks.[343]

Since the Natives refused to co-operate and adhere to the injunction, on 1 May the municipality asked a contractor to remove the barricades consisting of cement blocks, trees and other materials. The SQ detachment in Oka was monitoring the situation very closely and was ready to intervene if necessary. On 1 May SQ patrol cars made frequent passes along Highway 344 and a helicopter made routine passes over the area of the Pines. On 2 May a planned SQ raid was called off on the advice of Quebec Minister of Affairs John Ciaccia. The barricades remained.

On 2 May, representatives of the municipal, provincial and federal governments met with the two rival Chiefs, Allan Gabriel (who had been the unofficial leader of the movement) and other Longhouse members at the Kanesatake Longhouse roughly one kilometre northwest of the Pines. According to Mayor Ouellette:

> The Indians raised issues that went beyond the question of the barricades and local territorial claims to include the vast issue of self-government for the Mohawks in Canada. It should be said that the representatives of the Department of Indian Affairs and the Native Affairs Secretariat were duped by the radical natives and the Warriors, who had virtually carried out a coup d'état by neutralizing the Band Council and its Chief as well as the great majority of right-thinking Natives....They [Warriors] quickly realized that with the co-operation of the media, they could successfully destabilize the status quo so as to have a chance of achieving there objectives.[344]

The talks were broken off when two Mohawks riding an all-terrain vehicle (ATV) burst into the Longhouse claiming that they had witnessed police trucks dropping off wooden boxes in a shed behind the clubhouse signalling a potential police raid. Although both negotiating teams went to investigate, nothing was ever found to substantiate this claim. Mayor Ouellette and others later testified that this was a ploy by militant Mohawks to sabotage negotiations. Afterwards, roughly 100 Mohawk, including armed Warriors descended on the Pines. Distress calls were made to the Warrior Societies of Kahnawake and Akwesasne. Although it was the wishes of the Clan Mothers to have the weapons remain hidden, many were visible to onlookers and the media.[345]

Included in the crowd of onlookers were SQ personnel. The rotation of SQ members at Akwesasne in early May was perceived by the CF liaison elements, "as a step towards a future intervention at Oka. The troops used presently at

Akwesasne are trained members of the Unité d'urgence who would be used for any type of intervention at Oka. It is therefore logical to conclude that concrete plans are being made for a future intervention." It was also addressed that any small incident at the two roadblocks could rapidly degenerate into a conflict, "so the Quebec Provincial Police (SQ) is monitoring the situation very closely."[346] The CF unit FMC Headquarters located in St-Hubert was also concerned with the prospect of violence at Oka and on 4 May requested, "air photos of the Oka and Kahnawake Indian Reserves for possible contingency plan.... This HQ considers that some disturbance might occur...."[347] Canadian Forces contingency planning for Operation SALON occurred much earlier than previously thought or recorded.

While negotiations continued on the political front with meetings held on 7 and 8 May, the Warriors and their supporters began digging trenches and fortifications in preparation for a raid. Even though John Ciaccia had convinced Mayor Ouellette to postpone the development of the golf course indefinitely, the Oka Town Council refused to endorse this idea unless the barricades were removed.[348] The barricades remained. Mayor Ouellette made a second request for SQ intervention on the 7th. Correspondence received from human intelligence sources revealed that 60-100 Warriors were conducting training at both Ganienkeh and Kahnawake. This was confirmed by both the SQ and the NYSP.[349]

Although the Six Nations Traditional Hereditary Chiefs supported the picketing of the Pines, those in the Pines began to distrust Chief Martin and his non-Native lawyer Jacques Lacaille. They thought he was trying to usurp their role, even though they knew that the federal government recognized only this council as being legitimate. There was also growing discord between the members of the Longhouse. Longhouse Chief Samson Gabriel had asked Allen Gabriel, Curtis Nelson and Marshall Nicholas to represent the Longhouse, in conjunction with Linda Cree, Ellen Gabriel and Debbie Étienne.[350]

However, on 14 June the women publicly severed their ties from the other members of the Longhouse, citing the Great Law, believing that they were not being consulted on key decisions and meetings: "Women shall be considered the progenitors of the Nation. They shall own the land and the soil." Although an uneasy peace was restored and an effort was made to adhere to decisions by consensus, this example demonstrates the divisions within the community despite the public façade of a "unified front." Marshall Nicholas also began to remove himself from the situation after weapons and armed confrontation entered the agenda. The disparate groups within the Longhouse were the traditionalists and the moderates; those in favour of the principles of the Great Law and those who skewed them to promote their advantage and agenda.[351]

There was a clear difference in opinion within the Longhouse over the critical issue of bearing arms. While some occupants of the Pines supported the use of arms, Ellen Gabriel and others did not:

> We really felt like we were set up by people from our community, who knows maybe Kahnawake, but I know there was. Allen Gabriel was working with the RCMP without our information. He was one of three men that originally brought in weapons and shouted and decided that this is what they wanted. We said we don't want weapons here, take them out, take them out, and yet they walk around with their guns. They had already created in the public sense that there were people there with weapons, when the perspective of the group was no weapons. He was one that we suspect helped set us up. The Longhouse people stand in the way of the moderates and these moderates are now the ones that control the community.... There was someone working on the inside to set us up, to de-legitimize our claims to the land.[352]

By this time there were over 100 people in the Pines and cars bearing licence plates from various American states and Ontario. With the attitudes of the Mohawks becoming more militant and with an increase in Warrior participation, Longhouse Chief Samson Gabriel, his wife Ida, Curtis Nelson and others left the Pines. Allen Gabriel claimed that it was never intended to become a Warrior action and denied any link to the presence of arms. The departure of Chief Gabriel was significant in that as leader of the Longhouse, this institution did not support the extremists' concept of "stand and fight."[353] The confusion of politics within the Pines was clarified by Ellen Gabriel:

> Allen, Samson Gabriel and his son David, Curtis Nelson and some women who followed Samson, came to us in early July to say that we should bring the blockade down and that they disagreed with what was going on even though it was they who officially invited the 'Warriors' and it was Marshall Nicholas, Curtis and Allen who encouraged and carried guns early on in the movement. The 'People of the Pines' were a group of people in the community of Kanesatake who decided that all members made

up of Longhouse and Christian members would put away our differences and that we would unite to fight the expansion of the golf course. I include myself in this group.

The remaining occupants described themselves as traditionalists but were in effect acting contrary to the "be of one mind" principle of the Great Law. The departure of those who brought in the weapons and Warriors, but now were seemingly opposed to the use of weapons, made it more difficult for the remainder to make unanimous decisions over the course of the Oka Crisis. In fact, partially based on the fact that support from their own Longhouse Council was withdrawn, the occupants gave themselves the name "The Longhouse People of the Pines," creating further divisions within the political community of Kanesatake.

Although there was disagreement among the Mohawk themselves about weapon use and armed resistance, negotiations were still taking place. On 21 June members of the Longhouse and the Band Council met with Tom Siddon in Ottawa. The meeting did not go well. Siddon concentrated on the unification proposal to grant the Mohawk a land base and Reserve at Kanesatake, the same proposal which had been rejected by the Mohawk in 1989. In addition, he focused his delivery on the Band Council representatives and refused to acknowledge the Longhouse People. He, in keeping with government protocol, did not recognize them as the legitimate voice of Kanesatake. Had he negotiated with them, he would have indirectly legitimized their claims and those of the Warrior Society. After talks stalled, the Mohawks tabled their own agenda, the points of which all involved implicit assumptions of Mohawk Nation sovereignty. Again, Siddon, as a representative of the Canadian Government, would not endorse a sovereign Mohawk Nation within Canada. These refusals were taken as insults by the Longhouse Mohawks who left Ottawa even more disillusioned about reaching an agreement.[354] When asked if the government's refusal to recognize and negotiate with the Longhouse hindered a settlement, Ellen Gabriel simply replied, "It hindered everything."[355]

On 28 June Siddon met with Mayor Ouellette and the Oka Town Council. Siddon assured them that mediation was still possible and that he would never negotiate with "terrorists" and that the Band Council was the only representative in his opinion. His advice was not heeded as the following day, another injunction requested by the Municipality of Oka for the removal of the barricades was granted by Judge Anthime Bergeron of the Quebec Superior Court in St-Jérôme. While Bergeron described the situation at Oka as anarchy, he also advised the municipality against using his judgment as a means to promote the golf course expansion: "No golf project is valuable enough to necessitate the wiping out of an important forest, especially in the context of the evidence I've heard."[356]

The injunction was served to Chief Martin in the Band Council office. However, he admitted that he was powerless to order the barricades down, even if he wanted to. The Longhouse People did not recognize his authority and he refused to do the "dirty work" of the municipality. Although Martin made a feeble attempt to order the removal of the barricades, this was a gesture of lip-service to DIAND, as he knew full well that his voice would be ignored by the people of the Longhouse.[357]

On 5 July, Sam Elkas, Quebec Minister of Public Security, issued public statements that the injunction would be enforced warning the Mohawks to remove the barricades by 9 July (expiry date of the injunction) or face the possibility of an SQ intervention. On the expiration day, John Ciaccia sent a letter to Ouellette to suspend the golf course construction indefinitely to allow the barricades to be dismantled and negotiations to resume. Ciaccia argued that this particular situation involved many more facets than strictly legal rights. The Municipality of Oka interpreted this plea as evidence that Ciaccia had been influenced by the radical Mohawks.[358]

On 10 July, The Oka Municipal Council requested the assistance of the Sûreté du Québec by addressing the Director-General of the SQ, Robert Lavigne:

> We ask you...to put a stop to the various criminal activities currently taking place on the Chemin du Milieu and to arrest the authors of the crimes so that we can proceed with the re-establishing the recreational use of the occupied lands... but we will not be able to do so until you have restored public safety in the occupied territory. We are counting on you to settle the issue without further delay and without further requests from us.[359]

Upon receiving this letter, Lavigne sent a requisition for equipment to NDHQ/FMC on 10 July. This application was not considered *Aid to the Civil Power* since it was limited to equipment and not CF personnel (save for vehicle drivers). According to Brigadier-General Armand Roy, Commander of 5 Canadian Mechanized Brigade Group (5 CMBG or 5 GBMC):

> [The] assistance was a technical one which means that we provided them with C-7 type weapons that the Sûreté du Québec did not possess and that they thought they would need to counter the arms that the Warriors had turned on to them. We lent them some equipment that allowed them to see by night.... We lent them bullet-proof jackets...and provided them with 18 armoured vehicles...that were never used, but they were...in Longue-Pointe during the month of July, so that the Sûreté du Québec could use them if need be.[360]

With these requests, it appeared that the SQ was ready to act.

With increased numbers of Warriors and supporters in the Pines, the defensive perimeter became more complex. The strategic organization of the site relied on two barricades and fences along the north-south axis, strategically located surveillance posts along the east-west axis, a communications post and rendezvous points (RV). Along the north-south axis (from Highway 344 and the intersections of Chemin des Gabriel and the Chemin du Milieu) the only two passable approaches by vehicle were heavily barricaded and under constant surveillance. Roughly 25m from the southern barricade a fence was built out of logs.[361]

The defensive organization along the east-west axis of approach was less evident; however, it was no less developed. The plan to guard this axis of advance was one pertaining to specific reference points and a functional defensive arrangement from these locations for the purpose of observation, resistance and retaliation. The Mohawks dubbed the western edge of the Pines "Flower Pot." A covered trail connected this point to the intersection of Chemin des Gabriel and Chemin du Milieu dubbed Sector 5 by the Mohawks. Discreet movement along this trail "Ho Chi Minh" could be conducted. Another fence was erected near the lacrosse field to serve as an obstacle and observation post (OP). In the centre of the Pines were rendezvous locations called "AB" and "MP". At AB, a communication post (CP) was set up by Dennis Nicholas, nicknamed "Transformer." According to Mohawk testimony, the radio system was used for communications between Kanesatake and Kahnawake. From this post, Warriors were also able to intercept SQ communications. Moreover, walkie-talkies were used to communicate between the respective defensive positions.[362]

Further to the east, a trench dubbed "China Beach" was dug in a tactically sound position to monitor the golf course. Another trench at the extreme right (east) of the Pines was constructed and given the name "Hell Hole." In addition to the defensive fortifications mentioned, other trenches and low walls had been constructed using sand bags and logs. It is quite evident that the Mohawks concerned had constructed a tactically competent defensive perimeter from "Sector 5" in the north to "Sector 4" in the south. The Pines had been transformed into an armed fortress in anticipation of a police raid.[363] On the night of the 10th, barbed wire was added to the perimeter and the number of masked Warriors increased. To combat the wire, the SQ received 20 pairs of wire gloves and five wire cutters from Force Mobile Command that same night. Intelligence also revealed that on this night a large number of weapons were smuggled into the Pines disguised as a load of gravel.[364] CF intelligence revealed that Warrior meetings at Akwesasne and Kahnawake occurred simultaneously on the night of the 10th.[365] According to testimony and as stated by York and Pindera, the Mohawks had been tipped off that evening about the raid which came the next morning.[366]

The Warrior influence had increased and those in the Pines were prepared to take a hard stance. The stance taken by the Municipality of Oka was no less firm. The SQ had been keeping close watch on the protest in the Pines and was being pushed to forcefully intervene through court injunctions. The first violent episode in the clash of cultures at Kanesatake took place on 11 July.

CHAPTER 12

The Sûreté du Québec Raid at Kanesatake

Shortly before 0530hrs on the morning of 11 July members of the SQ emergency service unit and three SQ SWAT team groups (five men each) assembled at the edge of the Pines in order to conduct Operation DORE 90-4. They quickly realized that the occupants of the Pines were armed and proceeded to negotiate, thus deviating from the planned intervention mandate as was presented the day before. However, the log book revealed that shots were heard around 0545hrs and were not fired by SQ members. Confusion prevailed as to who was speaking on behalf on the Mohawks; nevertheless, it was made clear that the occupants of the Pines were not prepared to leave and that they would remain past the SQ deadline to evacuate the premises.[367]

At 0755hrs a message was received from Assistant Director General Lizotte for "intervention with chemical irritants or otherwise as quickly as possible." Two canisters of tear gas were fired into the southern barricade in order to disperse the large crowd which had been amassing along the southern perimeter. This process was mirrored at "Hell Hole." At 0847hrs, more gas was released along the southern barrier, in addition to a stun grenade. As SWAT teams entered the Pines, shots rang out at 0853hrs and a 20-24 second shoot-out ensued during which an estimated 93 rounds were expended (51 by the SWAT teams and 42 by the Mohawks).[368]

There has been much debate concerning the events of 11 July. Who fired the fatal bullet that killed SQ Corporal Marcel Lemay? Which side fired the first shot? The coroner's report was made public in 1995; hence, "facts" written in books prior to this date were pure speculation. There are two points worth mentioning. The first is that forensic experts and investigators could not enter the Pines to conduct research until September 1990, as it was continuously occupied by the Mohawks until 3 September. This no doubt hindered the eventual investigation. Secondly, although policy, curiously, SQ radio transmissions were not recorded for the events of 11 July. Nevertheless, the coroner's report is incredibly detailed and included 22,000 pages of stenographic notes from video and audio testimonies of journalists, witnesses and both SQ and Mohawk participants, all under oath. The shoot-out was in fact video taped by Guy Cote of CBC and recorded on three other audio devices.[369]

Based on the entirety of the evidence coroner Guy Gilbert came to the following conclusions:

1. Corporal Lemay was struck by a 5.56mm (.223Rem.) full metal jacket projectile equipped with a penetrator. It was an American made round manufactured specifically for military purposes.

2. The Mohawks in The Pines had armour piercing and tracer rounds confirmed by forensics and audio tape: "I got armour piercers and tracers, can I whip at them?"

3. On 11 July 1990, the SQ was not using such projectiles.

4. Corporal Lemay could not have been struck by a round from members of his own SWAT team or his own weapons (as the Mohawks claim).

5. The pathology of the lesion caused at the point of entry excludes all possibility of a ricochet or a stray bullet (as Mohawks claim).

6. Corporal Lemay was the victim of an intentional shot fired by someone who was aiming at him.

7. The fatal shot was fired from the weapons of one of four unidentified Mohawks located near the lacrosse field.[370]

Although nowhere in his report does Gilbert actually state who killed Lemay, the implications are obvious. Corporal Marcel Lemay was killed by a projectile fired from a weapon in possession of one of four Mohawks near the lacrosse field, one of which can be heard on audio recording shouting, "We've got one, we've got one...."[371] As no single shooter could be delineated, no charges were ever laid in connection with the shooting of Lemay who left behind a wife and two daughters. The report also revealed, "beyond a shadow of a doubt that the first shot was fired by the occupants [Mohawks]," at the request of Warrior, Dennis "Psycho" Nicholas.[372] Gilbert concluded in his report that, "it was a mistake to intervene on the morning of July 11, 1990."[373] In the words of a CF intelligence liaison to the SQ at the time, who wished not to be named, "The SQ raid turned into a comic opera farce. It is one thing for a police SWAT team to corner a couple of punks in the corner grocery. It is another thing to take on determined men who are fully armed and prepared to defend themselves. The Mohawks routed the police, there is no question."[374]

The consequences of the raid were immediate and multiple. By roughly 0915hrs, the wind had changed direction blowing the tear gas towards SQ lines as Corporal Lemay was being evacuated by ambulance. The SQ unprepared for and staggered by the violence and resistance, retreated down Highway 344 to the village of Oka. The Mohawks had commandeered three SQ patrol cars. The SQ front-end loader that had been brought up to dismantle the barricades was now being used to construct a barrier out of the abandoned SQ cruisers, logs and stones at the top of the hill along Highway 344. Two more barricades were hastily constructed. One was erected on the western portion of Highway 344 leading into Kanesatake and another at the northern entrance on Sainte-Germaine. All three paved roads leading into Kanesatake were now under armed control of the Warriors and their supporters.[375] The SQ responded by assembling barricades opposite those of the Mohawk.

Support for the defiant action had also filtered into Kahnawake. At 0545hrs, the Mercier Bridge, a vital lifeline connecting the suburbs of the south shore to Montreal, had been blocked at the intersection of Highways 132 and 138 at the base of the bridge by Mohawk sympathizers. The Mercier Bridge was the commuting link for over 60,000 vehicles per day, amounting to roughly 200,000 passengers.[376] According to participant Cookie McComber, the action was done without the consent of the Kahnawake Warrior Society or the Band Council: "We did it on our own. We figured on taking the bridge to protest the SQ attacks and tell them that they had to deal with us as well...."[377]

Immediately after the raising of the initial barricade, Warriors assembled barriers at Highway 138 directly opposite the town of Chateauguay, at the southern entrance to the Reserve on Highway 221 and a third at the eastern entrance at Highway 132. According to Kahnawake Warrior Society spokesperson Kenneth Deer: "There was no plan, no coordination.... We had to stand behind them, but we didn't have any idea what it would mean."[378] Many residents of Kahnawake immediately challenged the Warriors actions and vocally condemned the operations. These dissident voices were ignored and many revealed publicly after the crisis that they had been threatened with their lives.[379]

Although the radical Mohawk of Kahnawake claim that the barricades were a reaction to the SQ raid at Kanesatake, there are considerable flaws in this explanation. The most striking is that SQ intervention at Kanesatake did not begin until 0755-0800hrs. The original barricade blocking the Mercier Bridge occurred at or shortly before 0545hrs. News stations were reporting this incident as early as 0600hrs.[380] In addition, there were direct communication links open between those in the Pines and their supporters at Kahnawake, including the Warriors. Lastly, by all accounts the occupants of the Pines knew of and expected the SQ raid on 11 July and that negotiations in the early morning of the 11th had been hindered and delayed for as long as possible. Given this information, the seizure of the bridge was not a reaction to the events of 11 July. Rather, it was a stratagem and an action designed to support Kanesatake, while providing more negotiation leverage through the importance of the bridge itself.

Inexorably, these actions affected the already tumultuous state at Akwesasne. Intelligence from 2 EW Sqn elements still present in Akwesasne revealed that, "Akwesasne Reserve is being used as a rear supply/support base for activities taking place on other Reserves. There is evidence of communication between Oka and Akwesasne. Information is passed on and assistance is requested." In addition, it was noted that a "deliberate yet disorganized psyops campaign is being waged against authorities."[381]

Warrior activity increased immediately after the raid. A meeting was held at the residence of War Chief Francis Boots at 0930hrs on 11 July. Threats were made about occupying the International Bridge. Warriors were observed purchasing large amounts of canned goods in Cornwall and eight VHF marine radios in Messena, New York. Two cars driven by Akwesasne residents were stopped near Kahnawake carrying hundreds of pounds of food. Gunfire and protests occurred throughout the week following the SQ raid on Kanesatake. In addition to supplies, Warriors from Akwesasne were routinely observed travelling to and from Kahnawake and Oka. As a precautionary measure and due to increased movements within and from Akwesasne, CF commitment to Operation AKWESASNE was increased in both men and material in order to facilitate the evacuation of LEA personnel if necessary. The extraction was dubbed Operation CROSSBELT.[382] However, the focus of Warrior activity had shifted from police patrolled Akwesasne to its sister Reserves near Montreal.

The effects of the July raid went well beyond the Kahnawake blockades and a potential escalation at Akwesasne where CF numbers fluctuated between 15-25 in support of LEAs. For those Mohawks who believed in the use of force to promote their agendas, it united them in resistance, but also fuelled the belief that the governments would if necessary use excessive force to end the standoff, especially since Lemay had been killed. CF intelligence revealed that, "There was a lot of resistance to the Warriors within the Mohawk Nation, and they needed some kind of catalyst to get the support they did get and were able to hold on to for a certain period. 11 July was that catalyst. We had found evidence that the closure of the bridge was already planned and 11 July hastened it or was the perfect excuse."[383] The raid helped the Warrior Society garner support for, and promote, its revolutionary doctrine.

The intention of the governments was not to show signs of weakness or allow the insurgency to remain or spread to other Native groups in Canada. Even more eye opening for the government negotiators, who had already attempted to diffuse the situation, was the realization that the Oka Crisis could result in serious bloodshed if confrontational tactics were solely adhered to.[384] For the moment, it appeared that the first action was to seal off Kanesatake and Kahnawake and hope negotiations could produce a peaceful solution.

The failure of the 11 July SQ raid was a victory for the Mohawks involved and hardened their stance against government incursion onto Mohawk territory. It stimulated a renewal of violence at Akwesasne and spawned resistance at Kahnawake in the form of barricades. More importantly for the Mohawks it brought their concerns over the land claim at Kanesatake to the forefront of media consideration. Canadian and international media began to report on the protracted conflict over the Pines. In actuality, apart from the meetings at Oka, national negotiations and contention between the federal and provincial governments and Native groups had been at the forefront of federal politics and media coverage throughout the spring and summer of 1990 in the form of the *Meech Lake Accord*.

CHAPTER 13

The *Meech Lake Accord* and Elijah Harper

Shortly before Oka received national media attention, Canada's Indigenous peoples were receiving notice across the country within the context of the *Meech Lake Accord*. The new attitude and innovative tactics of the Native movement were illustrated in the spring of 1990 during the Meech Lake constitutional negotiations. This constitutional document signed by Prime Minister Brian Mulroney and ten Provincial Premiers in 1987, perpetuated the national myth that Canada had two founding cultures—French and English—and promulgated undefined "distinct-society" status for Quebec. Native leaders viewed this as another indication of the federal government's continuous refusal to address the concerns of Aboriginal Canadians and were adamantly opposed the principles of the Accord. Native leaders were also worried that Quebec could use its "distinct-society" clause as a guise to override Native rights within that Province.[385]

The three-year period for final approval of the Accord had dwindled down to a few precious days in June 1990, the Provincial Governments of Manitoba and Newfoundland had not yet voted on a decision.[386] However, the Accord could only pass the Manitoba Provincial Legislature if it had the unanimous approval of its members. One member of the Manitoba Legislative Assembly was not prepared to endorse. Elijah Harper, a member from the riding of Rupertsland in northern Manitoba and a former Chief of the Ojibwa-Cree community of Red Sucker Lake was an obscure member when the controversy began. However, he became the spokesperson for all Native Canadians as the negotiations progressed. Armed with only an eagle feather and the staunch support of Native Chiefs, Harper quietly shook his head every time the council asked for undisputed consent to introduce the Accord into the legislature.

The *Meech Lake Accord* collapsed in the face of one man who instantly became a national hero to the Aboriginal population of Canada.[387] Harper later said that, "We blocked the accord because it posed a threat to aboriginal people. Aboriginal people have no quarrel with Quebec. But we are a distinct society too, and we've fought for many years for the basic rights that Quebec takes for granted, such as participating in constitutional talks."[388] The death of *Meech Lake* was hailed as a major victory by Aboriginal Canadians and strengthened their unity and militancy. Harper and his dismissal of the Accord laid the foundation for the national support the Oka Mohawks would receive from Native Canadians throughout the summer of 1990. Phil Fontaine, leader of the Manitoba Chiefs remarked that, "Harper represents the collective will of the Indian peoples of Manitoba and Canada...There is greater unity among us since Meech Lake."[389]

The Native opposition to the Accord represented resounding frustration and anger over a neglectful governmental policy toward Native rights. This frustration would manifest into violence in Quebec but also in and around Native communities throughout Canada shortly thereafter. Ovide Mercredi commented on this scenario: "Had our issues been dealt with then, we would not have seen the defeat of the *Meech Lake Accord* and we would not find ourselves in the position we are in now with the Province of Quebec."[390] Less than one month after the quashing of *Meech Lake*, the world would again be reminded of Canada's unsettled business. In turn, the Oka Mohawks used the international coverage which *Meech Lake* attracted, to bring the same global coverage to their own plight.

With Harper and *Meech Lake* already attracting journalistic consideration to Native rights in Canada, the violence and barricades of 11 July only intensified media interest. The earlier events at Akwesasne and Ganienkeh received little press attention outside of local media publications. The Oka Crisis did not dominate the Canadian and international media until after the 11 July shootout with the SQ.[391] As the SQ continued to tighten the perimeter around Kanesatake and Kahnawake the media presence intensified. Pressure on the Province of Quebec to end the standoff and reopen major traffic routes including the Mercier Bridge also escalated.

CHAPTER 14

The Cordoning of Kanesatake and Kahnawake

Following the events of 11 July, the SQ quickly sealed off both Kanesatake and Kahnawake by erecting their own barricades. Checkpoints for both cars and pedestrians were maintained on a 24-hour basis to ensure no contraband and weapons were entering to resupply the armed Mohawks. As mentioned, the SQ had already secured CF resources from the 10 July request. These 37 vehicles, 151 personnel, 113 C-7s (22,000 rounds 5.56mm), NVGs, vests and helmets from the 3rd Battalion, Royal 22e Régiment (3 R22eR) arrived at Longue-Pointe on 12 July, under command of Lieutenant-Colonel Robin Gagnon. His superior was Lieutenant-General Kent Foster, commander of Eastern Region and also commander of FMC. At the same time, 515 RCMP officers were involved with operations in Mohawk territories and the SIU was rigorously, yet secretly, taking pictures of Mohawk defensive positions on all three Reserves. A CF liaison officer was immediately dispatched to plan for joint operations with the SQ and RCMP.[392]

On 19 July most of the equipment and personnel, save for 25 soldiers, were withdrawn to CFB Valcartier and placed on 4 hours NTM. That same morning elements of 2 EW Sqn and 1 Int Coy arrived at CFB Montreal to begin compiling an intelligence portfolio for Kanesatake and Kahnawake in support of Operation SALON. With another 2 EW Sqn/1 Int Coy post still involved at Akwesasne, a complete representation of Warrior movements and communications could be obtained and shared. Later that day, Lieutenant-General Kent Foster, commander of Force Mobile Command, met with Brigadier-General Armand Roy, commander of 5 CMBG, to discuss contingency plans for future operations.[393]

The SQ established and maintained a perimeter around both Kanesatake and Kahnawake. In the course of isolating both territories, the SQ came under scrutiny for allegedly denying the entrance of food stuffs, clothing and medicines. The Canadian Red Cross had analysts and medical teams on the ground in both Kanesatake and Kahnawake by 17 July. The first Red Cross report from 23 July states that there were "major gaps in certain basic food groups and sanitary articles" at Kanesatake. At Kahnawake, the food banks, commercial stores and the Kateri Hospital were all found to have adequate resources.[394]

Interestingly, Francine Chartrand, Director General of the Quebec Division, wrote to Grand Chief George Martin at Kanesatake complaining that the Red Cross office had been contacted by at least five other individuals claiming to be the spokesperson for the Mohawks: "We have also been told that Ellen Gabriel has been identified as the spokesperson for the Mohawk Warriors Society. We would appreciate your assistance in identifying the respective roles of these parties...should we need to enter into discussions...we will know who will be the spokesperson(s) for the native community."[395] The Red Cross, like governmental negotiating teams, was also at a loss to identify a clear structure and voice within the Mohawk Nation.

In addition to the Red Cross, the Commission des droits de la personne du Québec had representatives behind the barricades at Kanesatake as of 5 July. However, the Commission states that it had "been following the situation in the region since 1986." The Commission's findings outline numerous examples of Mohawks citing incidents of racial slurs and allegations of the denial of the entrance of food and other materials while the SQ was monitoring the perimeters.[396] However, the commission also received numerous calls from Chateauguay residents upset by the closure of the Mercier Bridge which they deemed to be a violation of their human rights. Two-hundred such calls were received on 25 July alone.[397]

The situations at Chateauguay and Sainte-Cathérine were becoming volatile. Residents upset by the long commute, due to the closure of the bridge, began to gather at the barricades and protest against the Warriors by taunting and jeering. Throughout July and into early August, nightly riots broke out between angry residents, supremacy groups, including members of the Ku Klux Klan, and the SQ. On numerous occasions, the SQ were pelted with bricks, rocks, bottles and vegetables, in addition to the odd Molotov Cocktail. They responded with tear gas and clubs, donning full riot gear.[398] Although no one was seriously injured in these frequent exchanges, the racial tension was obvious to all. During one such riot, a Mohawk effigy was hung from a traffic light and burned. The validity of the Warrior's claims was only strengthened in the eye of the public by the loutish behaviour of a minority of hate-mongers. In relation, the actions of the SQ and the decisions of the Quebec Provincial Legislature were coming into question.

The tactic by the SQ of using limited resupply was overcome with great determination on the part of all supporters of the Mohawk. Food and water were smuggled in using a variety of different techniques. Women and men walked through the bush at night to deliver parcels. Native and non-Native supporters dropped off care packages at the barricades. Vehicles smuggled in supplies, the drivers hiding goods in various places in their automobiles, to avoid detection at SQ checkpoints. Red Cross and Salvation Army workers transporting supplies in trucks pleaded with the officers and were allowed to deliver their goods.[399]

The "Mohawk Navy" operating in small crafts would venture out at night amidst police patrol boats and ferry provisions from Hudson, on the south shore. They knew the shoals and rocky coves and safely navigated around them delivering much needed supplies. The Six Nations Reserve also secretly sent two boatloads of camping equipment.[400] Even the leader of the New Democratic Party, Audrey McLaughlin came to Oka with a boat load of food-stuffs:[401] According to the Director of the Kateri Hospital at Kahnawake: "We have been getting food by boats.... Most of us are stunned that this could happen in this day and age. I used to think Canada was a good country, now it is no better than South Africa."[402] John Ciaccia agreed, later admitting that, "I still could not believe that an agency of the government, the SQ, would actually attempt to starve an entire community into submission, and refuse them medical necessities...the world was watching."[403] Furthermore, the Mohawks even obtained permission from Ciaccia's son to use the family dock at Dorval as a landing site for boats trafficking food, medical supplies and aid workers to Kahnawake: "I didn't want politics to rob him of his ideals. I didn't have the heart to say no. 'You're doing the right thing,' I told him."[404]

Although tension undoubtedly increased after the 11 July raid and the ensuing barricades, negotiation was still seen as a viable solution. On 12 July, John Ciaccia was sent to Kanesatake. He assured the Native community that there would be no more police attacks as long as the lines of negotiation remained a possibility. On the following day, he again met with members of the Warrior Society led by Loran Thompson and appointed spokesperson for the Mohawk at Kanesatake, Ellen Gabriel. The Mohawks demanded amnesty in the death of Corporal Lemay and refused to negotiate so long as the heavy police presence remained.[405]

The radical elements at Kahnawake refused to open the bridge until the situation at Kanesatake was resolved. The bridge was seen as the top bargaining chip. Throughout July, talks stalled as demands were rejected by both sides. Though DIAND had been asked to intervene, Tom Siddon believed that federal mediation would only complicate the matter. However, by the end of July, the

Mohawks demanded that negotiations only take place between the Mohawk Nation as a sovereign entity and the federal government as outlined in the *Proclamation Act*.[406]

By 24 July a political framework had been developed at both the provincial and federal levels. Both were based on a three tiered approach. Tier one for the province of Quebec (Cabinet Crisis Committee) was primarily made up of Sam Elkas, Minister of Public Safety and Security, Chairman Claude Ryan, and John Ciaccia, Minister of Native Affairs. The second tier was headed by Alex Patterson, chief Provincial negotiator. Lastly, the third rung within Quebec was the tactical level, involving the SQ director, Robert Lavigne.[407]

The hierarchy of the federal government was headed by an Ad Hoc Ministerial Committee. Its membership reflected the responsibilities of the Ministers most directly concerned with the crisis: Tom Siddon (Indian and Northern Affairs), Kim Campbell (Justice), Bill McKnight (Defence), the Solicitor-General Pierre Cadieux, and in the Chair, Deputy Prime Minister Don Mazankowski. The second level was invariably connected to the first and consisted of the Privy Council Office, the Prime Minister's Office and head negotiator Bernard Roy. Lastly, the administrative level rested with the RCMP and DND which was required to call federal level one at 1100hrs daily for updates on policy and operations and again at 1400hrs daily for communication/public information matters.[408]

The first meeting of the federal level one committee took place on 24 July. It concluded that the first order of stratagem was to brief all foreign embassies in Ottawa to get the "international word out," as well as communicating with the United Nations Committee on Indigenous Population in Geneva. The occurrence of information leaks was also addressed, urging all levels to treat information as "very sensitive." There was confirmation from CF and RCMP intelligence sources that an unidentified mole existed within the circles of Ottawa. On 27 July, the first federal Cabinet meeting took place, the details of which are still classified.[409]

By 25 July, DIAND was in final negotiations in a bid to buy the private land from Mr. Rousseau and the Municipality of Oka. Although Mr. Rousseau who owned most of the land in question agreed, the municipality tabled a counter offer that was judged to be too high by governmental representatives. The following day DIAND submitted a subsequent counter offer. Rousseau, who had been flown to Ottawa from France, sold 18 hectares of land for $70,000 to the town of Oka as had been previously arranged. DIAND then purchased the remaining land in his possession (12 hectares), which was to be used for the condominium development, for an inflated $1.44 million. Mayor Ouellette and the town of Oka were offered $1.34 million for the remaining 28 hectares (including the land it had just purchased from Rousseau) by DIAND. This offer was rejected on 31 July after a town council meeting. In early August, DIAND made it very clear that the land would be expropriated if a deal was not reached in the near future. On 8 August, the town council begrudgingly accepted a deal for the land worth $3.84 million, including $2.5 million in compensation for foregone taxes and lost revenue from the expansion of the golf course. The tiny Mohawk cemetery directly west of the parking lot was also purchased for one dollar.[410]

The purchase of land did not placate the Kanesatake Mohawk. They insisted that it was rightfully their land and it was impossible for the government to purchase land that already belonged to the Mohawk Nation. Negotiations were suspended on 27 July and the barricades remained. While the arrangements for the purchase of the land were being settled in early August, the SQ was realizing that the situation at Kahnawake and Kanesatake was more than they could handle. With rumours of the sophisticated Mohawk weapon arsenal, the SQ could not and was not trained to counter such resistance.[411]

In light of failed negotiations and the presence of barriers, the SQ advised the provincial government that it did not have the resources necessary to achieve the forcible dismantling of the barricades, given the weapons visibly available to the Warriors, and the muscle of the fortified defensive positions which they had developed. According to General John de Chastelain, Chief of the Defence Staff, "In this assessment they were supported by the RCMP."[412]

The events leading to the deployment of the Canadian Forces at Kanesatake and Kahnawake were numerous. The failed SQ raid of 11 July strengthened Mohawk resolve to resist forceful attempts to remove them from the Pines. Not only did they maintain a presence in the Pines, Kanesatake and Kahnawake had been transformed into fortified positions. Secondly, the long-standing animosity between the Mohawk population and the SQ, made worse by the alleged denial of foodstuffs, would be a severe detriment if another SQ operation was undertaken. Moreover, the SQ did not possess the firepower needed to confront the Warriors if a firefight resulted from any further encroachment onto Mohawk land or any attempt to remove the barricades by force. Hence, the employment of the Canadian Forces to terminate the standoff was seen by the Government of Quebec as the court of last resort.

PART III
The Clash of Cultures

With the erection of barricades at Kahnawake and the violence in the communities surrounding the Reserve, the Province of Quebec was forced to act. The SQ had been accused of human rights violations and unnecessary aggression and provocation. With the ingress of more Warriors and highly sophisticated weapons behind the barricades at Kahnawake and Kanesatake, the SQ was in no position to attempt another operation. The already unstable situation was made worse by an accumulating presence of media and non-governmental organizations. The scenes of Oka were being broadcast nationally and internationally.

The Province of Quebec needed to act and find a way to end the crisis. Accordingly, a request for *Aid to the Civil Power* was submitted to the Chief of the Defence Staff for assistance in ending the standoff. Although CF elements were still active in Akwesasne, the mission at Kanesatake and Kahnawake was more extensive and precarious. There was jurisdictional confusion between the levels of government, law enforcement agencies and the CF. Military operations were limited by an absence of rules of engagement (ROEs) and the inability to use force against Mohawk positions. In addition, the continual negotiations between Mohawk representatives and all levels of the federal and provincial governments curbed what the CF wanted to show as an initial strong show of force and its psychological impact upon deployment.

As the crisis wore on, and with CF initiative hampered by negotiations and jurisdictional confusion, the radical remnants of the dwindling collective of Mohawk supporters were content to remain behind the reduced perimeters, continuing to draw media attention to their plight. They bought time by continuously changing their demands and agenda, the most stubborn of which was that they would not lay down their weapons unless they were given criminal amnesty. They also insisted that the Mohawk Nation be given sovereignty. Neither demand was acceptable to the federal government.

In attempts to end the crisis, reopen traffic routes and reintroduce an environment of security to the areas, the CF thought it necessary to conduct numerous operations and raids with varying degrees of success and instances of violent repercussions. Yet in doing so, the CF, most notably at Kahnawake, in a sense replaced the civil authority. 2 RCR and 3 R22eR found themselves performing the role of a police force by having to conduct crowd control operations and cordon and searches. The CF was not equipped or trained for such tasks. Nonetheless, the 4,500 soldiers deployed in Operation SALON under *Aid to the Civil Power* ended the crisis without any further loss of life. However, the clash of cultures did not end with the conclusion of the Oka Crisis.

CHAPTER 15

Operation SALON

The Province of Quebec invoked Part XI of the *National Defence Act* on 6 August. Sam Elkas, acting as Attorney-General, issued a requisition for the assistance of the CF in *Aid to the Civil Power* to, "repress the troubles which subsist at this moment in Oka and Kahnawake to secure the protection of works, public and private, which are essential to the general welfare and to the security of the population of Quebec."[413] The official written demand was received the following day by the VCDS, Vice-Admiral C.M. Thomas, as General de Chastelain, the CDS, was in Russia. The VCDS immediately informed FMC commander, Lieutenant-General Kent Foster, to identify the CF allocations needed for this task.

FMC had previously been tasked to maintain three battalion-sized units (600 personnel each) on 12 hours notice to respond to any defence or civil emergency. Each of these units maintained a company-sized (100 personnel) subunit on eight hours notice as a vanguard or advance force. Thus in an emergency, FMC could quickly muster 1,800 personnel for tasks within Canada. In extreme emergency, it had been designed for 5,000 personnel to be committed if required. Air, maritime and other CF resources had similar frameworks in place.[414] On 8 August, Foster met with Premier Robert Bourassa to discuss possible approaches and to ensure that the Premier was aware of the extent of the operational capabilities of the CF. Bourassa was fully cognizant of the CF's role and abilities. After all, he had requested *Aid to the Civil Power* for the FLQ Crisis in 1970.[415]

The following day, Foster, in consultation with Brigadier-General Armand Roy, issued orders to begin the preliminary stages of battle procedure to include briefings, reconnaissance, and the establishment of liaisons with all cells of the SQ and RCMP currently deployed. He also authorized the use of Primary Reserve personnel within the CF. Lastly, all individuals of 5 CMBG were recalled from leave to begin unit briefings, training and full scale rehearsals with the strategic mission to:

1. Remove all barricades in the affected areas;

2. Restore freedom of movement on all roads and bridges;

3. Remove all strong points;

4. Restore normal conditions of public order and security.[416]

For his part, the VCDS sat in on daily meetings with the Privy Council Office and the Prime Minister's Office from 6-10 August until de Chastelain's home-coming.[417]

Upon his early return from Leningrad, the CDS was given a private briefing by Foster at 1300hrs on 10 August. Later that night a special briefing was given by Foster to a larger audience. In attendance at this meeting were 21 officers representing the highest appointments in the CF, in addition to the Deputy Minister of National Defence, Mr. R.R. Fowler. Foster briefed his audience on the situation and his analysis of the requirements. Planning was deduced for a maximum 30-day operation.[418]

The CF chain of command for what they termed Operation SALON was as follows: The Chief of the Defence Staff, General John de Chastelain, was the strategic commander. His immediate subordinate and operational commander was Lieutenant-General Kent Foster, commander of Eastern Region and also Force Mobile Command. Brigadier-General Armand Roy, commander of 5 CMBG, was charged to carry out the tactical scenario.[419] Once assigned this role, one of Brigadier-General Roy's first actions was to talk to the equivalent commander during the 1970 FLQ Crisis to obtain the lessons learned from those operations and, where relevant, apply them directly to Operation SALON.[420]

During the 10 August meeting, the political/military fellowships were also generated. For the CDS, his political counterpart was Premier Bourassa, although it was specifically stated that Foster would maintain contact on his behalf. De Chastelain himself was to sit in on Cabinet meetings and the assemblies of the Privy Council Office and the Prime Minister's Office. This circumvented the traditional *Aid to the Civil Power* relationship whereby the CDS was under the chain of command of the Attorney-General of the province, in this case Sam Elkas. Although acting as the medium between Bourassa and de Chastelain, Lieutenant-General Foster's political contact was Sam Elkas. At the tactical level Brigadier-General Roy's equivalent was Robert Lavigne, Director of the SQ.[421]

On 8 August, Prime Minister Brian Mulroney publicly announced that he had personally appointed Alan Gold, Chief Justice of the Superior Court of

Quebec, as the federal negotiator and mediator between all parties concerned. Mulroney also made reference to the possible intervention of the CF. Chief Justice Gold was to liaise with both de Chastelain and Foster, as the events which transpired during negotiations would have direct influence on military operations.[422] This was reiterated to the public in the first CF press conference held by Lieutenant-General Foster on 9 August: "The army's deployment is contingent upon the state of negotiations between Chief Justice Alan Gold and the Mohawk negotiators... If Mr. Gold would feel that the military presence would be necessary to help...we would immediately respond."[423]

On the evening of 10 August, de Chastelain spoke with Premier Bourassa. As Foster had done two days earlier, the CDS confirmed that the Premier was aware of the tasks at hand, the actions the CF was prepared to take to accomplish this mission and the political ramifications inherent to IS deployments:

> I have instructed General Foster to commence his actions with an open and frank discussion with the Mohawk leadership of his plan to restore normalcy. This is to be followed by the interposition of the Canadian Forces between the SQ and the Mohawks and, hopefully, the peaceful dismantling of all barricades and associated strong points. The final stage will see...the restoration of a normal, peaceful state. Each stage will be preceded, as necessary, with public statements of our intentions... Once the Canadian Forces have declared publicly the intention, for example, to dismantle the barricades, precisely that will be done—with or without the agreement of the Mohawks..... Accompanying this authorization will be firm instructions that the use of these weapons...will be the minimum necessary and will be used only in the event that the Mohawks open fire on my troops first.[424]

Although in principle, the CF commanders were constructing their concept of operations, deployment of their forces to the actual areas of operation was not yet solidified. On 12 August, Justice Gold met with Foster and, as a result, the restriction on military deployment was maintained. The same day, both Foster and Roy met with Premier Bourassa, who agreed that if CF intervention was required, the inter-position option was the best approach.[425]

Prior to the dialogue with Foster, Justice Gold had met with Mohawk negotiators on 10 August under a media blackout. Both sides appeared pleased with the discussions. The Mohawks contented that by extension of Gold, the federal government was involved in the efforts to end the standoff with the

Mohawk Nation on a nation to nation basis. However, the Mohawk representatives were displeased by the apparent connection between Gold and the CF. He had the ability to empower military intervention if he deemed the negotiations futile. This was seen as a furtive threat by the Mohawks not to disagree or argue with him.

On 12 August, the situation appeared to be nearing an end. Tom Siddon, Alan Gold and John Ciaccia met with Ellen Gabriel and other negotiators, in the Pines, to sign a three point precondition agreement to expedite negotiations for a peaceful resolution. The government negotiators conceded to the Mohawk demands that unhindered passage of food, medicine and other essential materials take place at Kahnawake and Kanesatake. Secondly, that spiritual and legal advisors have free passage through the barricades. Finally, the Mohawks proposed that an international observer force made up of non-Canadians be present as created by the Paris based International Federation of Human Rights. These observers arrived at both locations on 15 August. Mohawk representatives from each territory (Akwesasne, Kahnawake, and Kanesatake) were to sign the documents. Among the onlookers were many unarmed, masked Warriors.[426]

While the documents were being signed, a masked Warrior unexpectedly sat down and proceeded to sign his traditional Mohawk name on behalf of Akwesasne. Although Loran Thompson was present, 17-year-old Akwesasne Warrior "4-20" signed on behalf of his Reserve. After the ceremony, "4-20" handed a properly folded Warrior flag to Alan Gold.[427] According to Ellen Gabriel, someone, who was never identified, wanted to make a point to show Canada that they had to legitimize the Warrior Society: "The presence of the masked Warrior, that didn't help us, but that was not our intention either. We had our elder there and he was signing for us." She also still maintains that someone on the inside was purposely trying to sabotage negotiations.[428] Furthermore, there was also division within the Mohawk communities as to who had the right to sign on their behalf.

As a result of the ceremony, roughly 2,000 angry residents of Chateauguay and other supporters brawled with SQ police and riot squads throughout the afternoon and evening of 12 August. The mob smashed police cruisers, lit fires and opened fire hydrants. They threw golf balls, bricks and Molotov Cocktails at the outnumbered SQ personnel, many of whom were injured. RCMP reinforcements were called in and tear gas canisters were released in an attempt to disperse the crowd. Nevertheless, rioting continued until the night of 15 August, when local Chateauguay police officers, acquaintances of many of the rioters, wandered through the protestors chatting and diffusing the hostilities.[429] The pressure for CF intervention was mounting.

Thus far, no direct CF intervention had occurred; however, the CF elements tasked to carry out the mission were by no means dormant. 5 CMBG consisted of three infantry battalions: 2 R22eR, 3 R22eR and 2 RCR. Intense training was conducted from 7-14 August at both Valcartier and Gagetown CF bases. As Colonel (then Major) Alain Tremblay, Commander of "C" Coy, 2R22eR remembered:

> At that time we believed that if we were called upon it would be as the force of last resort, so all of the training was done at the upper end of the spectrum. Training for an assault using all military means available on the barricade in a non-permissive type of environment...focusing on assaults on barricades in the live-fire mode. From there we went through Platoon and Company attacks on mock-up barricades using the full fledged spectrum of military weapons.[430]

According to Lieutenant-Colonel (then Major) Colin Magee, Operations Officer for 2 RCR, this training was repeated within his battalion:

> We had the Engineers and some of the intelligence community with photos and reports as to their [Mohawk] positions and barricades. We had information on how they were manned, what they were made with and how they were booby-trapped. We set up barricades to those specification, had the Engineers booby-trap them and then practiced various live-fire scenarios, including the use of Leopard Main Battle tanks, 105mm artillery in a direct fire role. The companies practiced mounted, dismounted, combined arms, by day, by night, noisy, stealthily, on the various barricades just to get our skills down.[431]

Training throughout the Brigade was very similar to the accounts described above. The training was conducted at the highest level of the tactical and operational scale, with the idea that as a force of last resort. Failure was not an option. Training was conducted in order to be prepared for the worst case scenario: a conventional assault on the barricades during an armed confrontation. Consistent with this preparation Lieutenant-Colonel R. Landry, a Captain at 5 CMBG HQ during the crisis, recalled: "General Roy used to say, 'We will deploy but we won't go there in shorts; all or nothing.' I think that was a surprise to the politicians. I don't think they realized until we were on the ground what they had signed up for."[432]

Conspicuously absent in the pre-deployment training was riot control and crowd confrontation techniques. No previous training had been conducted for IS operations since the Canadian Army eliminated this scenario from its mandate in 1985 and equipment for such operations was obsolete. Accordingly, very few soldiers were knowledgeable in tactics for crowd confrontation and the procedures of riot control. Those who had experience in these operations were veterans of the FLQ Crisis and those who had received training prior to 1985; however, these were, for the most part, senior NCOs and officers who would not make up the bulk of the force being deployed. The average private or corporal had no training in riot and crowd control operations. In addition, the CF's equipment for such tasks was generally in non-serviceable condition. This lack of knowledge, equipment and training would be costly during the events which transpired during Operation SALON.[433]

What was also lacking was a clear concept of the ROE for those soldiers involved. The framework for ROEs was in its infancy. The men and women of 5 CMBG did get a 45-minute briefing, by a lawyer, on the legal construct of the *Criminal Code of Canada* under which the troops were operating during Operation SALON.[434] Simply put, there were no ROEs for Operation SALON other than two guiding principles: the use of minimum force and the much publicized directive that the CF would in no case fire the first shot. This declaration was modified during operations to include the disclaimer that the CF would take the first casualty. The concepts of ROEs did not evolve until after the Oka Crisis in subsequent CF deployments, most notably, those to Bosnia-Herzegovina and Croatia (1992-1995).

The insufficiency of ROEs during Operation SALON had three significant consequences. Firstly, it prolonged the crisis. Although it put the onus on the Native side not to initiate hostilities, the CF promise not to be the first to engage unarguably raised the bravado of the Warriors and their confidence was heightened by the removal of what usually is an unknown factor in military operations. As explained by Colonel (then Major) Jacques Morneau a staff officer at 5 BMC HQ: "There was [sic] never ROEs. When you have an unknown factor, the level of courage is impacted by that unknown. When you take away the unknown, people get more confident. So that psychological factor was never there. It makes your job more difficult to neutralize their [Warriors] will to fight because they don't feel threatened and their will to resist is preserved."[435]

The second outcome was that the soldiers were unclear of what actions they were allowed to take when being physically assaulted or pelted with debris and objects. The definition of the use of minimum force was very vague which compounded the confusion. A senior CF intelligence agent mused over this predicament: "It was really quite an experience. We did not want to hurt anybody and we didn't want our guys to get hurt. But we were told that we have to take casualties before we can shoot back which is a pretty grim thing to say and have to do. We are supposed to have the inalienable right to self-defence. There we did not. That is a hell of a thing to ask soldiers to do, but they did it."[436]

Lastly, the tactics on the ground during operations were transformed into a reverse advance to contact structure. Due to the premise that the CF would take the first casualty before opening fire, instead of the section moving forward with the commander behind, the opposite actually occurred. Colonel Tremblay made reference to this point during his movements at Kanesatake with "C" Coy 2 R22eR:

> We were moving forward with the section commander up front contrary to all of our basic principles. That is why at Oka you see the company commanders up front, the platoon commanders and the crowd behind—almost a reverse wedge, mainly because of the lack of ROEs and the high constrain that you cannot open fire until you have a confirmed kill or casualty on your [CF] side. The Sergeant is not keen on this coming from Germany and the Cold War ideals. So we moved forward in a follow me approach which sometimes made things on the ground awkward. Somebody had to fall first—the leadership. But that was the consequence of the ROEs we were dealing with—not even written.[437]

Although the lack of ROEs and crowd control training certainly had negative repercussions on the actual manoeuvres, valuable training was conducted prior to the deployment of 5 CMBG to the two distinct areas of operation.

All 5 CMBG training was conducted in secrecy so as not to give away CF intentions and contingency planning. For meticulous field exercises, the CF even quietly procured the use of two White Pine forests, hand planted in rows, identical to the Pines at Oka, from the Ministry of Natural Resources, which owned and operated both locations. The first near Eganville, Ontario roughly 40 km south of CFB Petawawa, with the second hugging the southwest border of CFB Borden near Barrie, Ontario.[438]

Even more secretly, Lieutenant-General Foster had authorized the Canadian Airborne Regiment (CAR) to begin training for a possible deployment to Kanesatake. The paratroopers, like their counterparts, conducted training on mock-barricades in all possible scenarios. Foster was vehement that CAR's activities remain secret as he considered this elite unit his "ace in the hole."[439] CAR members trained for six weeks during the Oka Crisis, but to their frustration, were never deployed.[440]

In addition to practical training, CF members also received cultural awareness and threat briefings on the state of affairs. For 2 RCR, the entire battalion sat in on a two-hour seminar: "We brought in one or two people to talk about the history of the Mohawk Nation, what was the Warrior Society, what were its ties to the community, how they viewed themselves and how the police saw them. They saw themselves as protectors of the Mohawk Nation. The police saw them as organized crime. We got into that piece of it."[441]

While the combat soldiers of 5 CMBG were conducting exercises and receiving briefings, the intelligence community was assiduously amassing information and photographs on the threat possessed by the Warriors, their fortifications and positions. Intelligence was gathered through a variety of modes before and during CF deployments. Highly effective EW was used to intercept Mohawk transmissions on radios and cellphones. Aerial imagery was acquired by helicopters, CF-5s, and a jet ranger equipped with a WestCam system which monitored events on a 24-hour basis. Daily covert RCMP flights, at approximately 7,000 feet, gave updates on defensive fortifications, as well as CF locations. These flights also featured a real-time downlink, feeding analysis to the various CF headquarters as it was happening.[442] 5 CMBG signal squadron, with the aid of Bell Canada, also installed 211 regular telephone lines, 25 secure lines, several hotlines and land lines linking the command posts and intelligence cells.[443]

HumInt personnel from the CF, the RCMP, the SQ, the SIU and CSIS were also very active. A joint intelligence cell (JIC), or Intelligence Collection and Analysis Centre (ICAC), was created at FMC HQ in St-Hubert, where members of the aforementioned intelligence agencies could report and conference. At least three highly trained intelligence members fluent in Mohawk dialect posed as journalists and were behind Warrior lines at both Kanesatake and Kahnawake. Mohawks at all three territories opposed to the Warriors' motives also supplied the CF with leads and tips on weapons caches and Warrior activities and plans.[444] According to an intelligence agent:

> It is very interesting to compare the Mohawk Warrior Society and the people associated with the smuggling and Bingo Halls with somebody like Hamas or the PLO because they were business men but were also fairly radically politically motivated and they used the Native revival movement as a mask. Certainly not everyone on their side agreed with this confrontation and these people provided us with very useful inside information.[445]

However, dealing with so-called "insurgents" with no set doctrine or fixed military organizations but rather blended into a civilian population in a domestic setting, was new for the CF and the intelligence cells. Thankfully, many senior officers and intelligence agents had previously worked with the British Army and devised intelligence operations based on British doctrine from Northern Ireland. 2 RCR intelligence officer Major (then Lieutenant) David Lambert correctly pointed out that at that time, "Focus was very much on the Cold War, insurgency operations were not on the radar screen. Oka was an insurgency. What General Frank Kitson wrote in the 1970s after Malaya and Kenya applies to this scenario in varying degrees."[446] Kitson described guerrilla warfare as, "A weapon of protest employed to rectify real or imagined wrongs levied on a people either by a foreign invader or by the ruling government."[447] The Oka Crisis certainly adhered to this definition.

Lambert also stated that the intelligence assets were quite aware of the danger of the CF being used by Natives as a tool to do "their dirty work." The threat existed that Mohawk sources would leak information to set the CF up or to get at someone within their own community: "We had to be careful that it wasn't a set-up or ambush or that it wasn't someone hacked off at a neighbour. That threat is always there."[448] Nevertheless, intelligence cells were able to get a fairly lucid picture of Warrior strengths and positions.

Original CF estimates placed Warrior/supporter strengths between 150-250 at Kanesatake, with another 300-500 at Kahnawake. It was assessed that the more radical members were prepared to stand their ground to oppose any military action. Among the insurgents, there were at least 20 who had seen combat action in Vietnam. Another six were ex-members of the CF. In addition, there were between 10-20 Mohawks who had more recently received military training with U.S. forces, most significantly the U.S. Marines. There were also confirmed reports that many Mohawks with no professional experience had been pseudo-trained in basic military skills at Ganienkeh.[449]

According to York and Pindera, active Mohawk members of U.S. military forces took their annual leave to return to Kahnawake, where they helped man the barricades, initially still wearing U.S. service camouflage uniforms. This was confirmed by an SIU intelligence report that revealed, "10 x U.S. Marines home on leave in Akwesasne on 17 July. Have contacted U.S. Consulate Montreal for help in getting them RTU [Returned to Unit]." Another 12 Mohawks quit their CF Reserve training in Longue-Pointe to return home. York and Pindera also make reference to 100 Oneida Warriors arriving in Kahnawake in the middle of July after a "request for assistance" was sent to Oneidas in Ontario, New York and Wisconsin by the Kahnawake Longhouse.[450] What was clear is that the Mohawks relied on those with military background to design the extensive defensive fortifications and positions in both territories. The defensive perimeter at Kanesatake has already been described. However, after the 11 July raid aerial imagery revealed that the fortifications, trench systems, anti-tank ditches and obstacles had all been enhanced.

At Kahnawake, the defensive perimeter was designed in three concentric rings (consisting of 10 sectors) of field fortifications from the outer edge of the Reserve back into the inner core. In addition, there were barricades on all roads leading into Kahnawake, an OP on the permanently raised railway bridge, in conjunction with trenches and positions along the railway itself and patrols along the north bank of the canal. Essentially, all likely approaches into Kahnawake were covered. 5 CMBG had created a detailed target list of 42 individual targets. Each individual target had its own comprehensive brief or "analysis of area of operation" including numerous aerial and ground level photographs.[451]

Like neighbouring Kanesatake, the defensive perimeter at Kahnawake included 14 bunkers, trenches, anti-tank ditches and other obstacles including booby-traps both homemade and commercial.[452] Cans filled with rocks were strung through the bush acting as early warning devices, fish hooks were hung from trees and large latex balloons were placed in areas perceived to be probable landing zones for helicopter insertions. The Warriors also possessed trip flares and flare guns and constructed homemade mines. Colonel Tremblay summarized the arrangement at Kanesatake:

> Nasty booby-traps. Fish hooks hanging from trees, holes and spikes. Soldiers were injured by kneeling on nails in planks of wood and getting fish hooks in their face at night. Basic booby-traps, no different from unconventional war anywhere else. There is no doubt that they had some level of military

> expertise when you look at the trenches they dug, mutual support, mutual firing positions and firing ports. Some of the systems they built were well planned. They built an entire defensive posture on a wedge from the golf course to the club house to the junction of the roads, with extensive trench networks, bunkers with overhead cover and so on. Too long and difficult to man but well done; they did very well from that perspective. Some of them had training. You could see it in their personal movements and how a soldier would behave on the ground, handling weapons and so on. Despite all their planning and training, and the ex-militaries that came up from Akwesasne and that they had a decent array of weapons, they were no match.[453]

The Mohawks had also established an excellent command and control network at both Kanesatake and Kahnawake. Both territories were divided into sectors or areas of operation. They created squads of 12-20 men with a leader to maintain tactical control. They had a shift schedule and rotated squads through the barriers on 8 to 12-hr intervals, to allow for rest and personal maintenance. Never more than 38 armed Warriors were seen at one specific occasion, excluding major operations. The Warriors and supporters also maintained constant surveillance at the barricades, were intercepting police transmissions with some success, and had scouts outside of the Reserves reporting on police and CF movements.[454]

The Warriors also had a sophisticated communication network consisting of cellular phones, band radios, very high frequency marine band radios and a secure fax link. The presence of an ICOM Receiver was confirmed at the Warrior command post (CP) at Kanesatake, which permitted the Warriors to eavesdrop on unsecure military communication networks. They also possessed commercial encryption devices and used low level codes on air. Their radio nets were generally operated in a professional manner.[455] They had code names and code words for different sectors, RVs and locations and often transmitted in Mohawk thinking the CF and other intelligence agencies could not decipher. This assumption was wrong; the intelligence HQ had members who were adept in the Mohawk tongue.[456]

SECRET

OP SALON TARGET LIST

KAHNAWAKE

AS OF 2609[illegible] AUG 90

1	WF08802821	JOHNSON BEACH
2	WF988[illegible]624	CHEMIN OLD CHATEAUGUAY
3	XF00102565	OP
4	WF99682609	RAILROAD STRONG PT
5	XF012290	MARINA
6	WF99702649	OP
7	XF01302530	PROB CP
8	XF01082484	STRONG PT HWY 132/138
9	XF02732969	CANOE CLUB
10	XF02412815	STRONG PT INTERCHANGE
11	XF01072466	BARRICADE
12	XF03322380	OP
13	XF03412974	WARRIOR OFFICE
14	XF044275	LONG HOUSE
15	XF04082951	RADIO STATION/BOSS CP
16	XF04432919	FILTRATION PLANT
17	XF047293	LIFT BRIDGE
18	XF049291	MERCIER BRIDGE
19	XF032280	BINGO HALL
20	XF04952583	BARRICADE
[illegible]	XF05752319	BARRICADE
[illegible]	XF04802883	MERCIER BRIDGE APPROACHES
23	XF070281	BARRICADE
24	XF064282	STRONG PT
25	XF05802303	BARRICADE
26	XF05862282	BARRICADE
27	XF076282	BARRICADE
28	XF07102810	STRONG PT
29	XF09062815	BARRICADE
30	XF08552664	BARRICADE
31	XF09232865	BARRICADE
32	XF08802760	BARRICADE
33	XF09272860	BARRICADE
34	XF09232860	BARRICADE
35	XF08922759	BARRICADE
36	XF00902505	PYLON OP
37	XF00922911	CHINA BEACH
38	XF069243	OP
39	XF094289	UNMANNED ROADBLOCK ON ISLAND
40	XF071279	FLEA MARKET
41	XF 022 286	Barricade
42	XF 038 285	Barricade

TE: KAHN 24 WAS TEMP GIVEN NEW TGT # KW 3,THIS IS NOW CANCELLED.

SECRET

000489

Figure 4: Kahnawake Target List, 26 August 1990. (Canada. DND ATI).

Figure 5: 2 RCR/3 R22eR tactical map of Kahnawake showing Mohawk barricades, observation posts, strong points and command centres, 20 August 1990. (Private Collection).

Communication was frequent between the triangle of Akwesasne, Kahnawake and Kanesatake. All three territories were on a coloured alert system devised to designate threat levels and possible actions: "You could tell there was a high level of planning and knowledge. They did have a great information processing capability. The Warrior Society was able to surge people into locations very quickly, until their influence started to decline."[457]

Completing the Warriors defensive perimeter was a vast array of weapon systems which were transported between all Mohawk territories. Both Canadian and American security agencies had long been monitoring the weapons purchases made by Mohawks, most notably at Akwesasne. Between January 1988 and December 1990, over 800 weapons had been legally purchased by Mohawks. On the other hand, the international transport of certain weapons was by no means legal. Fifty per cent of these weapons were military assault rifle variants (21 different models), including many semi-automatic weapons that could easily be converted to fully automatic weapons with little skill or resources.[458]

Included in the list of weapons purchased by Warriors were: at least 164 variants of the AK-47 (7.62mm), 82 Mini-14 Ruger Rifles (5.56mm), 6 Uzi Ingram M9-M10-M11 submachine guns, 5 Barrett 82A1 .50 calibre long-range sniping rifles (bipod) and one .50 calibre HMG (heavy machine gun, tripod). Other assault weapons included: AR 15/M-16s, RPKs (7.62mm, bipod), Ruger Mini-30s (7.62mm) and FN Browning 125Ss among others. The Warriors also possessed 87 hunting rifles, 109 shotguns and 203 handguns of various makes and models. They had also legally purchased over 50,000 rounds of various calibre ammunition and 400 magazines during this time period. Warrior acquisitions prior to 1988 were unknown.[459]

In addition, to weapons, the Warrior arsenal also boasted over 400 grenades, dynamite, homemade Molotov Cocktails and pipe bombs. Other equipment included night-vision devices and police scanners. Unconfirmed weapons included: mines, Claymore mines, M-60 General Purpose Machine Guns (GPMG, 7.62mm bipod), M-72 LAW, RPG 7 and 8s and light and-or medium mortars.[460] The purchase of these weapons was explained by a federal intelligence officer:

> A lot of things were illegal on the Canadian side but not on the American side. All you had to do was get it across the border. Now at Akwesasne that is not hard. They had a real smuggling network. Everything came down that net. When the wars in

Latin America shut down in the 80s the place was awash with sophisticated weapon systems, people willing to sell them for a little money. It is not hard to get these. For these guys [Warriors] it is almost a free run with boat loads, car loads of cigarettes, weapons, drugs, illegal immigrants, you name it.[461]

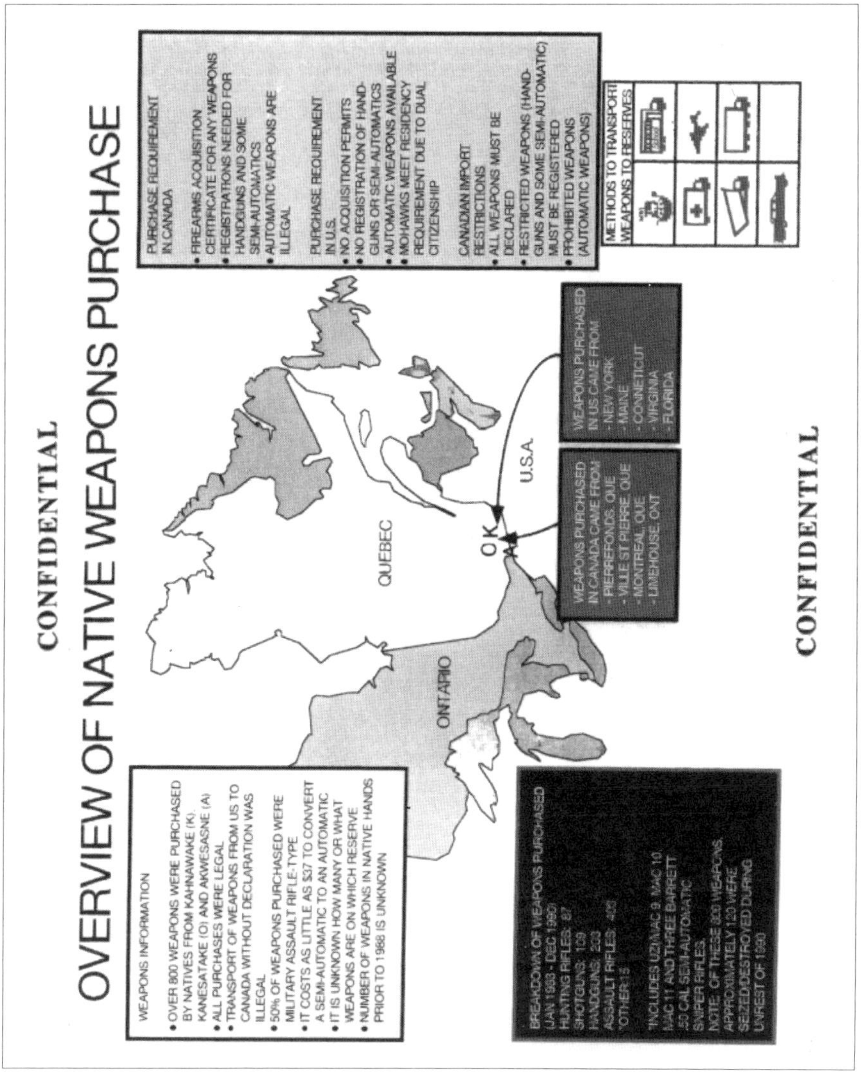

Figure 6: Joint Intelligence Summary of Weapons. (Private Collection).

LIST OF WEAPONS PURCHASED BY WARRIORS

WEAPON	KNOWN
NORINCO 565 7.62 mm	11
A semi-automatic rifle manufactured in China. It is a civilian pattern of the Type 56 assault rifle, which is a copy of the Soviet AK-47.	
AK-47 7.62 mm	160
The AK-47 assault rifle is a Soviet-designed automatic weapon firing 7.62 mm rounds. It has an effective range of 300 metres and a rate of fire of 600 rounds/minute. It has become the weapon of all the Eastern Bloc countries and most communist countries elsewhere.	
.45 automatic	7
.45 calibre automatic pistol	
7.62 mm Ruger Mini 30 rifle	2
The Ruger Mini 30 is an American-produced semi-automatic rifle capable of firing a 7.62 mm round.	
5.56 mm Mini-14 Ruger rifle	82
The Mini-14 is an American-produced semi-automatic rifle capable of firing a 5.56 mm round.	
Mossberg 500	4
An American-produced, civilian-pattern 12 gauge shotgun.	
Rossi 44 Magnum	40
Handgun	
Uzi B 9 mm	3
An Uzi pistol, which is a modification of the Uzi sub-machine gun, capable of semi-automatic fire, using a 9 mm round.	
Luigi Frenchi 12 ga.	5
An Italian, civilian-pattern 12-gauge shotgun.	
AR-15 5.56	2
A semi-automatic, civilian pattern weapon, similar to the American M-16, which fires 5.56 mm rounds.	
Remington 870	1
A civilian pattern shotgun firing a 12 gauge cartridge.	
Galil .308	2
An Israeli-produced assault rifle, capable of automatic fire using a 7.62 mm round.	
Polytech AK-47 7.62	2
Similar to the AK-47 noted above	
AK-M47	2
Similar to the AK-47 noted above	
.44 Magnum revolver	5
An American-produced double-action revolver firing a 44 Magnum cartridge	
.22 semi-automatic pistol	1
A civilian pattern semi-automatic pistol, which may have been manufactured by one of many manufacturers in various countries. American producers include Colt and Smith and Wesson.	
Uzi submachine gun	6
An Israeli-produced submachine gun firing a 9 mm round, capable of automatic fire up to 600 rounds per minute	
9 mm automatic	5
Automatic pistol firing a 9 mm round, manufactured by several manufacturers in various countries.	
.25 cal automatic	1
Civilian pattern pistol firing a .25 calibre round.	

.22 cal Ruger Civilian pattern revolver.	1
Barrett 82A1.50 cal An American-produced semi-automatic rifle firing the .50 inch (12.7 mm) Browning heavy machine gun cartridge. It is intended as a sniping and long-range interdiction weapon.	5
31,000 rounds of 5.56 mm ammunition	
10,000 rounds of 7.62 mm ammunition (AK-47)	
magazines (banana style)	300
magazines (drum style)	75

Figure 7: List of Weapons Purchased by Warriors. (Private Collection).

With the perceived threat of Warrior motives and the known positions and sophisticated collection of weapon systems, the situation in Mohawk country was above the scope of the SQ. On 14 August, CF movements began to replace the SQ at the barricades in a situation described by Lieutenant-General Foster as, "completely different from any peacekeeping mission the Canadian Forces has participated in."[462] According to de Chastelain, "The taking up of arms by an individual or any group to right their causes or to settle their perceived wrongs must be countered by the forces of law and order or else anarchy in this country will prevail."[463] The CF was, in the view of the Province of Quebec, the court of last resort in an effort to restore law and order.

In order to achieve the missions previously outlined, Foster, in consultation with both the CDS and Brigadier-General Roy, intended to deploy resources exceeding 4,400 soldiers accompanied by all the resources available to them. The strong CF representation was deemed necessary for two reasons. The first and most obvious to all three commanders in the words of the CDS was that, "If we failed, what next? It is anarchy. If we failed there was no one left to call. Armed Forces are only called out in the last instance, and at the last resort."[464] By virtue of the overwhelming numbers the impression was given to both the Warriors and the Canadian public that CF was there to do its job and was prepared for such a task. In addition, the psychological impact on the Warriors of having to face such a large force was also a conscious factor in the initial concept of operations.[465] Colonel (Major) Jacques Morneau, an officer with 5 CMBG G3 (Operations), outlined: "As history shows, when you have overwhelming force you don't need to use that force, but when you have more or less equal force, the other side believes that they have a chance and they will try you on. Also, basic tactical doctrine states that if you attack you should have a 3:1 ratio."[466] Secondly, the perimeter at Kahnawake was roughly 20km and that of Kanesatake was in the region of 15km. In Foster's words, "What would it take me to put a net around both these areas?" A certain amount of waterfront also had to be included. Relief in place of front-line soldiers on a 24-hour basis at what was estimated to be 75 soldiers per kilometre was not an option: "The number of troops we used was smaller than that required to put entire nets around the entire area at those distances."[467]

On the night of 14 August, the entire 5 CMBG moved from their locations, predominantly from Valcartier, to their designated staging areas. Again, the move was designed to show overwhelming force; to induce an element of shock on the Warriors who were monitoring CF movements and deployments.

Table 4—Operation SALON, 14 August 1990[468]

UNIT	LOCATION
FMC HQ	St-Hubert
QGET 5 BMC (Headquarters and Signals Squadron)	Longue-Pointe
2 R22eR	St-Benoît
3 R22eR	St-Rémi
2 RCR	Farnham then Delson
5 RALC (Light Artillery)	Blainville
5 BSC (Service Battalion)	St-Hubert
430 ETAH (Tactical Helicopter Squadron)	St-Hubert
5 AC (Field Ambulance)	St-Hubert
5 PPM (Military Police)	Longue-Pointe
W Battery and Cougar Troop	Farnham

By the morning of 15 August, all elements had completed initial deployment. Reconnoitring began on all SQ locations to be relieved by CF elements. 2 R22eR quickly realized at Kanesatake that the SQ-controlled perimeter was not tactically sound and could not hermetically seal off Mohawk movement through the perimeter. Battalion and Company Commanders also met with Mohawk leaders at both locations to relay the intentions of CF operations at the barriers, as previously promised. Lieutenant-Colonel Robin Gagnon, CO of 3 R22eR at Kahnawake recalled his first meeting on the night of 18 August:

> I brought along my three rifle company commanders and met with three Warriors...Red Turtle, Skywalker and Omega Man, as well as a political representative of the Band Council Irwin Goodleaf. The aim of the first meeting was to lower tension, in order to allow a situation of dialogue and progress to develop. The aim of our first meeting was achieved.[469]

Also from this meeting came the agreement that neither side would point weapons at the other. A phone line running directly from Mohawk spokespersons to FMC HQ in St- Hubert was installed as well.[470]

While both R22eR battalions were planning for the occupation of the barricades at their respective locations, 2 RCR, the designated reserve battalion, arrived from CFB Gagetown to Camp Farnham on 17 August, some 40km southeast of Chateauguay. Indication was given to the Mohawk negotiators that 2 RCR would be called in to assist 3 R22eR at Kahnawake if all of the barricades were not removed.[471]

General de Chastelain released a statement on 17 August declaring the blanket intentions of the CF to replace the SQ at the barriers, with emphasis placed on the concept of minimum force.[472] At 0800hrs on 20 August, the 12 main SQ barricades at both Kanesatake (2 R22eR) and Kahnawake (3 R22eR) were manned by CF personnel in unison. Immediately, soldiers began to transform the barricades into military positions. Vehicles were tactically placed for observation and cover, trenches were dug and wire was strung along the perimeter "to protect both soldiers and civilians."[473] These first stage positions were completed by 2000hrs that evening. SQ officers and liaison officers remained behind the CF barricades. It is important to note that the CF did not replace the civil authority (SQ) but was there to aid the civil authority.

At many barricades, Warriors and Platoon Commanders exchanged pleasantries and introductions and relayed intentions and possible approaches to their immediate tactical situation. No CF movement past the existing SQ barricades took place. At one barricade at Kahnawake, Warriors became aggressive as they believed the CF advanced past the line agreed upon. The CF withdrew to a position of mutual satisfaction. The replacement of the SQ by the CF occurred without any violent incidents.[474]

Initially, the involvement of the CF was seen as a positive step by the Mohawk community. They possessed a severe hate and distrust for the SQ and the military was seen to be more disciplined and professional. The cordial handshakes at barricades and the open dialogue between the Warriors and CF commanders, which had not existed with the SQ seemed initially to de-escalate the volatile situations and allow governmental negotiations to transpire.[475]

Although negotiations had been ongoing and resolution was in sight, meetings on 21 August severely hampered a final arrangement. The Mohawk negotiators at Oka tabled a three-point proposal and greatly extended their bargaining demands. The first point was the acquisition of the disputed lands at Kanesatake. This was not an issue as the federal government was already buying up the land in the hopes of creating a Reserve for the Mohawks in the region. The second was that the governments of Canada and Quebec recognize a unified Mohawk Nation consisting of six Mohawk territories in Quebec, Ontario and New York State. All future negotiations and land claim issues would be negotiated by this nation to be known as *Kanienkahaka*. To the governmental negotiators, this was an untenable proposition and went well beyond the issues at hand. Mohawk concerns about the expansion of the Oka Golf Club had now evolved to demands and recognition of sovereign nationhood within North America. How could the negotiators from Ottawa and Quebec possibly have jurisdiction and authority to negotiate such a claim without consultation with Ontario and the United States? This demand was viewed by governmental negotiators as absurd, prompting Prime Minister Mulroney to openly declare this demand to be "bizarre." The third demand was for a guarantee that the SQ and other Quebec authorities not to interfere with gamblers and occupants of the high-stakes bingo facility at Kahnawake.[476]

Obviously those trying to protect the Pines were no longer formulating the Mohawk agenda and were relegated to the background. The Oka Crisis was now about sovereignty whereby outside police forces could not disrupt the lucrative smuggling and gaming operations. The Oka Crisis was now about securing the right to operate bingo parlours and casinos without any form of government reprisal. The Oka Crisis was now about power and money and a struggle for those in possession to maintain and increase their shares. The crisis was no longer about saving a small patch of White Pines on the western edge of a tiny golf club at Oka, Quebec. The Warriors felled 155 of these sacred trees to build barricades and bunkers.[477] The Pines were being used to protect profit.

Immediately after the meetings of 21 August, Premier Bourassa hinted at other options and wanted to put pressure on the Mohawks to remove the barricades, specifically the ones impeding movement over the Mercier Bridge.

Sam Elkas insisted that the Mohawks were negotiating in "bad faith," and regarded military pressure as a means to ensure that the Mohawks did not alter negotiating demands even further. On 22 August, detailed aerial reconnaissance was conducted over both territories revealing remarkable improvements to Warrior trench systems, anti-armour ditches and route obstacles which would force infantry to dismount. This intelligence and the drastic alteration of negotiations on 21 August were the catalysts for direct CF operations in Kanesatake and Kahnawake.[478]

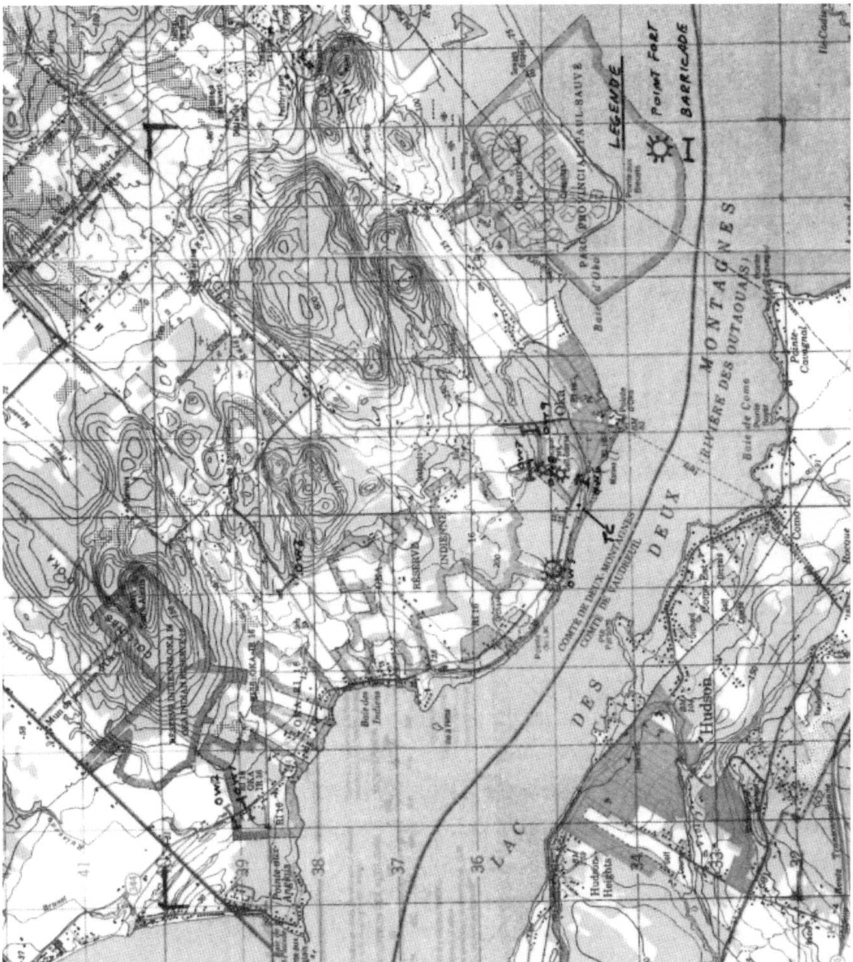

Figure 8: Tactical Map Kanesatake and Surrounding Area, 2 R22eR. (Private Collection).

At 0800hrs on the morning of the 23rd, elements of "C" Company, 2 R22eR moved to establish a forward position in front of the previous SQ barricade along Rang Sainte-Germaine. Soldiers advanced 1,500m until reaching the vacated Warrior barricade, which was soon dismantled. Although not intending to advance this far, the commander pushed onward to gain a more tactically advantageous position where a CF barricade was erected.[479] According to Colonel Tremblay, who commanded the operation: "One lesson we learned following this first gain on the ground highlights certain principles of war; surprise and force concentration. The massed arrival of the 14 Grizzlys armed with two machine guns was the best deterrent. While uttering their death threats, the Warriors nevertheless realized that they would never come out on top in an exchange."[480]

Following the first military advance, General de Chastelain initially briefed the Minister of National Defence, Bill McKnight. At 1800hrs on the 23rd, the CDS held a private briefing for Prime Minister Mulroney. The Prime Minister held a press conference later that night urging patience but was adamant that the "situation would be resolved at all costs." During the following two days of negotiations, optimistic talks resumed. However, the situation broke down again when the Mohawk negotiation team insisted that the Warriors had to have criminal amnesty and would not lay down their weapons or remove the barricades until the CF and police presence dispersed.

This was not an option for either the government of Canada or Quebec, as seen through the medium of negotiators Bernard Roy and Alex Paterson respectively. In their opinion everyone was equal under the laws of Canada, despite the fact that the Warriors believed these laws did not apply to them. On 27 August, Premier Bourassa ordered all negotiations to be terminated in light of the increased and unreasonable Mohawk demands and an impulsive agenda that seemed to change with every progressive negotiation.[481] General de Chastelain publicly stated that, "Premier Bourassa has now directed the Canadian Forces to proceed with the mandate [four points] given to them by the Quebec Government.... The Canadian troops will not use force unless obliged to do so by the Warriors."[482]

While negotiations were stalling, FMC HQ was increasing military resources throughout the areas of operation. SQ and RCMP naval vessels had been active on the river systems, as aquatic reinforcement was known to be the Warriors main network. However, on 27 August, the HMCS *Acadia*, a 65-foot patrol boat belonging to the HMCS *Donnaconna* began patrolling the waters of the St. Lawrence, specifically in the Lac Saint-Louis area near Kahnawake.[483] To compliment marine surveillance, covert shore-based SIU detachments were deployed along the St. Lawrence River. To aid aerial reconnaissance 10 sets of "14- power gyro-stabilized binoculars for the use of G2 Intelligence and G3 Aviation staffs," were acquired from Fuji Photofilm Canada at a price-tag of $89,000.[484]

The increased low level flights of helicopters and CF-5s not only enhanced CF presence but also provided daily intelligence of Mohawk positions. Reconnaissance patrols increased at both Kahnawake and Kanesatake, where 2 R22eR employed a squadron of soldiers on horseback to patrol areas where military vehicles could not venture, due to thick vegetation, thus countering the Warriors' extensive use of ATVs.[485]

In preparation for military intervention, 2 RCR moved from Farnham to the train museum grounds in Delson, east of Kahnawake on 28 August. Three Leopard main battle tanks (MBT) equipped with dozer blades were also brought under command of FMC HQ at St-Hubert after being authorized directly by the CDS. These were to be kept under "low profile to give negotiations every possible chance." These tanks did not have 105mm ammunition on board although rounds were stored for use at ammunition points.[486] They were equipped with two 7.62mm machine guns, as was the standard, and were to be used as mobile strong points and, if needed, to take down the barricades by force.

On 28 August, news conferences were held by Lieutenant-General Foster and Brigadier-General Roy, in keeping with the CF's policy to disclose operational plans. This transparent approach did not include statements which would jeopardize tactical operations or essential elements of tactical doctrine such as concentration of force, surprise and security. Both Foster and Roy relayed to the Mohawk Nation and the population of Canada that the CF would fulfill its mandate and the barricades would come down either through co-operation or through force. Foster then pleaded for the Warriors and supporters, "not to force my soldiers to resort to the use of force as the army moves to carry out its orders. We will not fire the first shot."[487] He closed his press conference with the statement that "the consequences of an attack are unthinkable...the implications of our actions are grave indeed." However, forebodingly, he mentioned that those civilians in the affected areas may be evacuated and those "within a danger area will be asked to remain indoors, away from windows and preferably in their cellars."[488]

Immediately following the briefings by Foster and Roy, DND, under direction of spokesperson Colonel Alain Forand, released a videotape complete with aerial photos, television footage and still photos highlighting Warrior positions, fortifications and weapon systems to justify the forthcoming intervention to the Canadian public. Included in this video were RPGs, M-72 LAWs, .50 calibre heavy machine guns and mortars.[489] The Warriors denied having any of these heavier weapons.

They claim that they made homemade devices out of sheet metal, pipes and plumbing tubes to imitate the weapons the CF thought they had. These mock weapons included the aforementioned heavy weapon systems. They also climbed the rafters of the Mercier Bridge with packs on their back to simulate the planting of explosives. They used welding torches on scrap iron to simulate cutting the bridges bolt pins. At both Kahnawake and Kanesatake, Warriors tiptoed through fields looking at maps to insinuate that they were weaving their way through minefields. The Warriors claim this was all part of their psychological manipulation against the CF which included references to those weapons over their communication means hoping the CF would be listening. When the 28 August video was released, according to York and Pindera, the Warriors roared with laughter.[490] Cookie McComber relayed this tactic: "We played on their fears and let their imaginations play games with them. It was paranoia. They took themselves so seriously."[491]

There can be an argument that not all Warriors, Band Council members and Mohawk negotiators knew what weapons were actually at their disposal. However, there were confirmed sightings of an M203S Grenade Launcher, an M-60 machine gun and RPKs. In addition, at Kahnawake, visual contact and HUMINT confirmed one M-72 at the barricade along Highway 132 (KW35) and also a .50 calibre HMG at the barricade along Highway 207/221 (KW26). Furthermore, a HUMINT source within Warrior circles confirmed that, "Warriors in Oka/Kahnawake have 500 to 1000 weapons including AK-47s, 2,000 grenades, 300 Mini-14 Ruger rifles, and a large quantity of mines."[492] Aerial photographs and covert patrols also revealed mortar plate positions and "the likelihood of explosives, with remote detonation devices, having been placed on the Mercier Bridge." While the wiring of the Mercier Bridge was unconfirmed, trip wired booby-traps were confirmed underneath the bridge and on the railway bridge. None of this information was ever made public.[493]

As shown, the Warriors were in possession of most of these weapons or these arms were close enough for immediate employment. In affect, it does not matter if they had them or simply made mock replicas to dupe authorities into believing they possessed them. Both scenarios ultimately hurt their attempts to persuade the larger audience to sympathize with their cause and gain credibility in accordance with the revolutionary model. The threat of these weapons was real and the public was made aware that they were in the hands of radical insurgents, thereby legitimizing the involvement and future actions of the CF and the governments instead of the Warriors. The CF could have knowingly allowed the Warrior disinformation campaign to achieve this exact result.

2 RCR Intelligence Officer, Major David Lambert recalled that, "Air photos showed mortar positions. When we actually got there they were stovepipes in spare tires, so had they originally been there or replaced with dummy positions we really don't know conclusively, but it isn't really important. The perceived threat was there, so you must plan for that on the tactical level."[494] Realistically then, one could hypothesize that had the Warriors not showcased their weapon systems or feigned to have them the CF deployment might have not been as substantial and extensive.

Later on the night of 28 August after the briefings by the CF commanders and the showcasing of the Warriors' arsenal, Prime Minster Mulroney held a national press conference on CBC to solidify the CF's justification to intervene: "They [Mohawks] have put on the table a series of totally unacceptable claims, including immunity from criminal law.... In short, they have sought to give themselves the status of an independent nation within the boundaries of Canada.... Obviously there will be no pleasure in this task but the Canadian Forces will do their duty and the barricades will come down."[495] Prime Minister Mulroney also methodically reiterated the quantity and types of weapons in the Warriors possession, their illegal smuggling enterprises and the fact that many Mohawks did not condone the rhetoric and violence of the Warrior Society.

The Canadian Forces was collecting intelligence and delivering press conferences to validate their operations by detailing the threat to the Canadian public. Although they had officially taken over responsibility from the SQ, no major operations had been conducted. The CF wanted time to construct positions and gather intelligence before actively engaging the Warriors at the barricades. Another reason for the delay was to give negotiations every chance to diffuse the situation. However, the CF commanders at the strategic, operational and tactical levels had announced, after failing negotiations, that operations would commence and that the barricades would come down.

This point was corroborated by Prime Minister Mulroney during his 28 August press conference. Although Mulroney was directly addressing the Mohawk communities and the front-line radicals at Kahnawake and Kanesatake, he also appealed to the larger Aboriginal population of Canada not to view the Warriors as the rightful voice of the Mohawk Nation. In reality, the Prime Minister was worried that the violence of Oka could spread to other Native communities across Canada and also about the subsequent national and international reactions.[496]

CHAPTER 16

The Oka Crisis: Native Nationalism, Internationalism and the Media War

The Canadian Prime Minister called upon Natives across the country for calm and understanding and not to take Warrior rhetoric as a legitimate voice for national Aboriginal grievances and rights. He was worried, as were his top Ministers, that the situation at Oka could ignite the frustrations of Natives across North America producing continental pockets of resistance and violence. If this not unlikely scenario occurred, the Prime Minister could not avoid taking responsibility and would have to invoke the *National Emergencies Act*. As it stood, under *Aid to the Civil Power*, the responsibility rested with the Province of Quebec and Premier Bourassa. Mulroney could avoid getting "egg on his face" and any repercussions for Operation SALON could legally be passed to Quebec's use of *Aid to the Civil Power*.[497] Mulroney had a reason to be worried.

The shock waves from Oka had reverberated across Canada, even trickling into the United States. Marches, protests and pickets were just as common as violence and vandalism. Numerous Reserves produced "copycat" barriers across bridges, roads and rail lines, the majority occurring after the 11 July raid. Many also threatened the use of arms. It went so far that Natives incarcerated at Headingley Prison in Winnipeg went on a fast. A group of 250 Natives, with help from AIM members protested in Belleville and then proceeded to block the Causeway leading to the Royal Military College of Canada and CFB Kingston. They were removed with force by OPP and Kingston Police.[498]

In late July demonstrations took place near Nipigon, Thunder Bay and Longlac, Ontario. A main railway blockade and a barrier across the Trans-Canada Highway were established by Ojibwas of the Longlac, Pays Plat and Pic Mobert bands in northern Ontario. They were removed only after local negotiations on 20 August. Canadian National Railway estimated losses at $2.6 million per day in commercial backlog due to the Longlac barricade. Natives near Matepedia, Quebec blocked a rail line and began digging up portions of the track with a hydraulic shovel. Five hydro towers were toppled outside of London, Ontario and a bridge was set on fire nearby.[499]

Protestors picketed the provincial legislatures in Regina, Winnipeg, Edmonton, Yellowknife and Vancouver. Demonstrations also took place in front of CF bases in Saskatoon, Moose Jaw, Calgary and Oromocto. A bridge was set on fire near CFB Cold Lake in protest of CF involvement. On 23 July, 200 Micmacs from the Indian Brook Reserve marched in Shubenacadie, Nova Scotia. Micmacs in Halifax organized a food bank for the residents of Kanesatake and Kahnawake. A similar event took place on Manitoulin Island. At least 30 Micmacs from the Atlantic Provinces travelled to Kahnawake on 26 July. The Mohawks at Tyendinaga were actively recruiting men to go to Oka and blocked three routes into their Reserve. Oka Park became the rallying point for over 2,000 Native and non-Native protestors.[500]

The most significant demonstrations and actions transpired in British Columbia, which refused to negotiate Aboriginal land claims. It was the only government in Canada that rejected any concept of land title, as outlined in the comprehensive land claims process. In July, blockades set up on seven roads and railway lines across the province created commercial losses in forestry, tourism and transportation. British Columbia Rail was losing $750,000 per day. Originally designed in support of the Mohawks, these barricades were soon used as a tool to force the provincial government to recognize land rights.[501]

Carter Camp, an original AIM member and AIM chairman at the time of the crisis, released a statement on 30 August revealing that Natives from Oklahoma were on their way to Oka: "Canada must realize that an attack on Oka will engulf the entire country in flames. Our people are going to fight alongside the Mohawks...they joined us at Wounded Knee and we're going to reciprocate."[502] Other supporters came from inside the political arenas of Canada. Both George Erasmus, National Chief of the Assembly of First Nations and Dene Liberal MP Ethel Blondin now refused to denounce the Warriors.[503]

The federal government was so gravely concerned with the national situation that they had initiated steps to monitor Reserves and Natives across the country. Airlines were required to submit passenger lists directly to federal intelligence agencies in order to monitor patterns and movements of the Native population. Arms and ammunition dealers in Canada were also obliged to contact authorities about any irregular or large purchases by Natives and non-Natives. The VCDS questioned banning the sale of weapons and ammunition indefinitely but could not do so under the current gun control legislation. However, many retailers in Montreal and Quebec voluntarily restricted these purchases. In addition, Reserves in "critical locations" were being examined and the CF was ordered to conduct "overall plans for military involvement in expanded Indian disruption in Central Region."[504]

The federal government and the CF were both worried about the control of public perception. They, like the Warriors, needed to control the media in order to draw sympathy and support for their actions. In the war of words, the media was an important propaganda tool. Both the Natives and the CF learned to appreciate the significance of the media in the formulation of public opinion and support, and tried to use it to their advantage. The Warriors and their supporters, both Native and non-Native, presented the actions at the barricades as the last resort of a systematically oppressed nation rebelling against a political system based on a legacy of broken promises and bad faith; the Mohawk David against the governmental Goliath. This was a propaganda ploy to bring the Mohawk plight to the attention of the media, the peoples of Canada and the rest of the world. A plan to embarrass a government and country which prided itself on the cultural mosaic ideal, human rights, socialist policies, democracy and peacekeeping. To further the embarrassment, the Mohawk used the fact that Canada pledged a fledging force of 800 personnel to Operation FRICTION as part of the UN-sanctioned, U.S-led coalition in the First Gulf War, while it deployed over 4,000 troops, armour and air support to quell an uprising on its own soil.[505]

The manipulation of the media was directed by a network within the Mohawk community and the Mohawk Nation Office in Kahnawake. These Mohawks understood the politics, impact and power of television and newspapers. Journalists remained with the Warriors and Mohawks behind the barricades, often presenting biased reports which were printed in leading newspapers across the country. These reporters were often criticized by their peers for less than impartial journalism.[506] An example of the less than honourable tactics and reporting used to defame the CF occurred on 23 September when a man dressed in a CF uniform with 2 RCR insignias, claiming to be an active member, addressed a demonstration and journalists criticizing the actions of the CF.[507]

In addition, in order to put greater pressure on the Canadian government, the Mohawk control group also systematically tried to acquire the help of international lobby and legal groups and support from countries around the world. Believing they were a separate sovereign nation, the Mohawks sought the help of the World Court at The Hague and also the United Nations.[508] As the number of educated Native Canadians increased, a new generation of activists emerged, well-versed in the tactics of modern political warfare, legal principles and the land claims process.[509] While the Warriors manned the barricades with guns, these activists tried to use the legal system to authenticate the Mohawk grievances.

With this in mind, the Mohawks drafted a demand to the Canadian government that current and all future land claims be referred to the Permanent Court of Arbitration at the World Court. What started as a disagreement over a tiny patch of land had transformed into a question of sovereignty or the creation of a "nation within a state." On 21 August, Mohawk negotiators met with government officials and submitted a six-page report citing their position on sovereignty. It included quotes from the Great Law, colonial era treaties, the UN Declaration of Human Rights, The Hague Conventions, and the Geneva Convention.[510]

The international public was already being inundated with media reports coming out of Oka. The Mohawks used the SQ's blockade of food and aid, and the accusations that the CF continued this practice, as a means to expose to the world the slow, relentless genocide that was being inflicted upon them in order to gain global support and humiliate the Canadian government. While there is evidence that the SQ did deny the entrance of foodstuffs, the same cannot be said for the CF. Putting pressure on the Warriors and Mohawk communities by denying food and other requirements was never mentioned by any level as part of the strategic, operational or tactical planning of the CF.[511]

News of the events sped around the globe and the Oka Crisis received front-page coverage in newspapers as far away as China, Italy, England and France.[512] Even the master of the "Photo-Op," Reverend Jesse Jackson, came to Kanesatake to film a documentary on the Mohawk Crisis.[513] The world was indeed watching and listening as demonstrators marched in such places as Oslo, Sydney, Berlin and Rome.[514] In Washington D.C., Natives picketed the Canadian Embassy and in Minneapolis, 40 AIM members invaded the Canadian Consulate, seized the official flag and burned it on the street.[515]

Despite the worldwide attention, the Mohawk media group still communicated their situation directly to leaders of countries and organizations around the world. Among the organizations that sent observers after being contacted by the Mohawks were: the Paris-based International Federation of Human Rights, which is recognized by the UN, the Red Cross, S.O.S. Racism, the Quebec Human Rights Commission as well as dozens of smaller church and human rights lobbyists.[516] Ed Broadbent, former head of the New Democratic Party, and the director of the Canadian Human Rights Commission urged the government to act, insisting that the deliveries of the Red Cross were not enough.[517] He was worried that Canada would lose international credibility when trying to raise human rights issues abroad: "Countries will be saying to me, 'What about aboriginal rights in Canada?'"[518]

In addition to these organizations, numerous countries and factions granted their support after being summoned by the Mohawks. The Canadian office of the African National Congress, representing Nelson Mandela, acknowledged a letter sent to them and assured the Mohawks that "Your struggle is our Struggle..." Nobel Peace Prize winner Desmond Tutu, who was on a visit to Toronto trying to bring the apartheid in South Africa to the attention of the world, was also summoned for support by the Mohawks. The possibility of a meeting with the Mohawks was raised but never arranged.[519]

The Mohawk Nation Council of Kahnawake also invited the World Health Organization in Geneva to send observers and summoned the Secretary-General of the UN through a letter, requesting that he "stop Canada's genocidal war against the People of the Mohawk Nation.... At the moment our people are penned up behind barbed wire, like animals. The army has already fired shots at our people there."[520] This greatly exaggerated letter with false accusations toward the CF and the federal government also made allusions to the massacres of Shabra and Chatilla Palestinian Refugee Camps, Soweto in South Africa and Mai Lai in Vietnam. The Mohawks urged the UN to send peacekeepers and observers but it immediately declined, insisting that only recognized member nations could request such a force. The UN Sub-Commission on Human Rights did however communicate that "non-violent negotiations will continue" and closely monitored the situation but asked only the Canadian government for situation reports. Obviously, both decisions illustrated that the United Nations did not view the Mohawk Nation as a sovereign nation and rejected this claim.[521]

On 30 July, Oren R. Lyons, a Mohawk who had been behind the barricades, went to Geneva and addressed the 8th Session of the Working Group on Indigenous Populations of the UN. He made reference to other injustices taking place around the world, including the Navajo and the Indigenous populations of Australia, Central and South America.[522] On 13 September, the European Parliament adopted a resolution and criticized the governments of Canada and Quebec, asking them to initiate 10 steps to end the conflict. This communication was voiced in unusually harsh diplomatic language. After the crisis, between 13-18 January 1991, a group of Members of the European

Parliament (MEPs) carried out a "fact-finding mission on the situation of the indigenous peoples of Canada." The final report noted little of significance.[523]

Like the Mohawks, the governments concerned and the CF realized the importance of the media. While the CF realized that the presence of reporters on the "front-lines" reduced the likelihood of violence and the use of arms, the media presence also contributed to prolonging the crisis since the Warriors could use these mediums to advance their agendas. While the media certainly gave the Mohawks the avenue to garner First Nation support across Canada, it also had consequences.

Decima Research, an independent survey organization, conducted polling across Canada throughout the months of July, August and September. Its findings revealed that public support for the Mohawks in Canada progressively decreased as the crisis dragged on. Support for the Mohawks fell by 20 per cent over the course of the three months while support for the federal government increased by 17 per cent over the same time period. By 12 September, 73 per cent of those polled thought the CF was performing a helpful role in decreasing tensions. The study also concluded that although most Canadians sympathized with the Mohawks and the land claim issue, most Canadians did not support the actions of the Warrior Society.[524]

In an attempt to destroy the Mohawk's credibility government officials repeatedly referred to the Warriors as terrorists or insurgents. On CBC Tom Siddon announced that, "as a matter of principle we cannot negotiate behind barricades, and we cannot negotiate under threats of intimidation by people carrying guns."[525] Harry Swain, the Federal Deputy Minister for Indian Affairs, in an interview with the *Globe and Mail*, referred to the Warriors as, "a criminal organization...it is a potent combination of guns, cash, and ideology. They are pretty successful in cloaking themselves in the guise of Indian Rights."[526] By portraying the Warriors as terrorists breaking the rule of law, the Canadian government was successful in gaining the support of the Canadian public.

In reality, the Warriors were terrorists according to the FBI's definition of the term. Indeed, they were guilty of "the unlawful use of force or violence against persons or property to intimidate or coerce the government, civilian population, or any segment thereof, in furtherance of political or social goals."[527] There was also proof that they were funded by, supported or had communicated with other international terrorist organizations such as AIM, the IRA, Libya and numerous black activist groups, most notably the All African People's Revolutionary Party.[528]

For the CF, the large media representation so close to the areas of operation was a hindrance. However, it was realized early on that it was in the CF's best interests to remain as transparent as possible and to provide the media with information good or bad rather than have them "digging around for it." It was also ascertained that timely correspondence with the media was essential and by releasing information before the Warriors, credibility and support was heightened for the CF.[529]

In fact, the concept of embedding reporters, which received so much acclaim during the 2003 U.S.-led invasion of Iraq, was actually initiated by 2 RCR during Operation SALON. The Regiment's Deputy Commander, Lieutenant-Colonel (then Major) Rusty Bassarab, articulated this novel idea: "Did we have the idea of embedded? Absolutely. 2 RCR took an embedded reporter from the *Fredericton Gleaner* and he stayed with us all that time we were in Farnham training and awaiting deployment. Unfortunately he left four days before we got called out. Was the concept there? Yes. Did we encourage it? Yes. We would have been happy to have one because then you get someone who sees your perspective."[530]

Media centres were established at Oka and Chateauguay under control of FMC HQ. These facilities, operating 24 hours a day, were responsible for all media queries, briefing CF commanders of aspects of public affairs, and developing news releases. In accordance, operational components of the CF's planning were always relayed to the media. The CF held briefings by operational commanders twice a day and arranged for interviews with tactical officers. The information and press releases would be coordinated at these media centres and then passed to NDHQ for approval. They would then be disseminated across the entire operation to ensure that all CF spokespersons and commanders presented unified opinions and statements. The CF also provided transportation to journalists, media tentage and telephone lines to facilitate reporting.[531]

In terms of impact on military command and control, print media played less of a role than television. In fact, although the live feed from the WestCam, Skyguard and television news reports had advantageous qualities as far as tracking movements of weapons and Warriors, they also had repercussions on the command and control integrity of Operation SALON. It was also the first operation in which the CF used cellphones. According to Colonel Tremblay:

> You have to remember there were company commanders on the ground that chose orders. I am the senior commander on the ground; it is my call, my decision. I am fully aware of company

> commanders on the ground refusing orders from FMC commanders. You had FMC commanders calling company commanders on the ground short circuiting the entire chain of command. We were learning on the fly some very important lessons. Because of the news and all of those T.V. cameras it was almost real time. FMC commanders could sit in HQ and see actions on T.V. and pick up a cellphone and call any commander on the ground, involved, and say, 'What the hell are you doing? Move that vehicle.'[532]

Field Marshall Bernard Montgomery's dictum, "Do your estimate, make your plan, give your orders and go to bed," became during Operation SALON, "Do your estimate, make your plan, give your orders and then watch T.V."[533]

Television reports also played a key role in discrediting the Warriors. Average Canadians saw first-hand the weapons in possession by the masked Warriors. These frightening scenes, in conjunction with timely CF releases detailing the quantity and capacity of the Warriors' arsenal, successfully damaged the public standing of the Warrior Society. Under the scrutinizing eye of the media, numerous reports and video clips showed the Warriors hurling insults, rocks or pieces of wood at the soldiers, who remained calm and poised. Television reports and pictures also discounted the Mohawk claim that the CF was withholding food and supplies. Soldiers were frequently videotaped or photographed passing boxes of food and supplies across the barricades. The reputation of the Canadian Forces was enhanced in the public eye through its calm and methodical intervention in a highly volatile situation.

Throughout August, negotiations were given priority to rectify the standoff. However, both sides accused one another of negotiating in bad faith and talks were broken off. In light of the unsuccessful negotiations, the CF was directed by the Province of Quebec, on 27 August, to initiate operations to force the barriers and restore law and order on the Reserves and their surrounding areas. On 28 August, through numerous press conferences both the CF and the governments involved stated firmly that direct CF intervention was to occur and that the barricades would be removed. The standoff needed to be settled. The longer it dragged on, the more the Warriors could use the media to support their agenda and retain the status quo that thus far secured their positions. It was also worried that this in turn could ignite other Native communities to take militant action. In addition, the stagnant situation did not favour the CF. Although the discipline of soldiers had been commendable but the likelihood of soldiers retaliating in the face of provocation would no doubt increase. The barricades needed to come down.

CHAPTER 17

The Canadian Forces: Operations in Kanesatake and Kahnawake

On 28 August, all political and military echelons had publicly declared that the CF would satisfy its four point mission through operations beginning the following day. An event on the night of the 28th solidified the need for a quick solution to the closure of the Mercier Bridge at Kahnawake. After hearing the CF's intentions, roughly 100 Mohawks—mostly women, children, the elderly and those requiring advanced medical attention—scared for their safety evacuated Kahnawake crossing the Mercier Bridge in a mobile convoy. Arrangements had been previously designed with the SQ, RCMP and the CF.

When the convoy reached the northern side of the bridge (Montreal side), there were not enough police officers to hold back the angry mob that had collected to protest the closure of the bridge. Bricks, rocks and other objects were hurled at the cars crawling along amongst the swarming crowd. At least six Mohawks were injured in the scuffle. A soldier who wished to remain anonymous remembered: "Something went through a windshield and hit an old man [71 year old Joe Armstrong a WWII veteran] in the chest and he subsequently died. The cops didn't do anything or wouldn't do anything. The amount of hatred was just incredible. Once a cycle of conflict starts it is hard to dampen it. You need to use more force to end it and it was strange to do it in our own country."[534]

The tension over the closure of the Mercier Bridge was at a breaking point. Groups of angry residents from the communities of Chateauguay and Sainte-Cathérine, straddling the Reserve, were becoming increasingly hostile toward, not only the Mohawks, but police and CF members. These dissident citizens thought the CF was moving too slowly and could not understand why they had not already forcefully advanced on the barricades. In reality, CF action was limited in order to protect these people and their fellow inhabitants of the surrounding communities as well as the Mohawks.

In his initial evaluation Lieutenant-General Foster assessed the level of weaponry possessed by the Warriors and the CF resources needed to neutralize these weapons with as little loss of life as possible in the event of a firefight.

This analysis included the civilian population of Kahnawake and surrounding suburbia. Foster concluded that:

> A 50-calibre bullet's effective range is two kilometres, but it can travel nine kilometres. So if you are talking about the possibility of someone firing those kinds of rounds at you, you must take appropriate action .... But if you take a 10-kilometre circle and draw it around the end of Mercier Bridge, there are many thousands of people who would be in that danger area.... That brings you very quickly to the price you would have to pay to execute whatever wishes you desired and how fast you wanted to end a circumstance like that...we were not ready to do that, and as it turned out it was not necessary.... [I]t is absolutely essential that everybody in the country understand that is the kind of weaponry we are talking about at play on the streets of Canada.[535]

This statement does not take into account larger projectiles fired from APCs, Leopard tanks or artillery pieces. Even firing smoke-based extraction rounds from artillery guns could be hazardous as the canisters could end up in civilian neighbourhoods.

Daunted by the prospect of a military invasion, the Warriors took action to avoid legal repercussions. On the night of the 28 August low level flights of light planes were observed by 3 R22eR Observation Posts flying in and out of Kahnawake, the first flight occurring at 2015hrs. These flights were also tracked by ADATS (anti-aircraft missile defence system) located at St-Hubert and by U.S. Customs in New York State.[536] The Warriors and Mohawks emphatically deny that any such flights took place claiming that it was a hoax to create the impression that Warriors had fled Kahnawake.[537] However, these flights were confirmed by a senior level intelligence agent:

> It is not a rumour. It occurred. People tried to play it down. The Canadian Government will always try to wait to dissipate things. I remember when the reports came in. They were light planes; they flew at tree-top levels and were easy to see. There were eye witness accounts from Vandoo outposts. We believe that they got out the crew served and heavy weapons as well as a number of Warriors, mostly to New York State. How many flights were there? The reports varied but there were multiple flights, no more than 12. We knew at Akwesasne there were a couple of sea planes and we linked one to a retired Canadian

> Forces Captain who was a Mohawk. There was a link that this plane was used. After that we deployed the Skyguard, but the horses had already bolted.[538]

Other CF personnel interviewed also confirmed the existence of these flights. In the words of Lieutenant-Colonel (Captain) Landry a Staff Officer at 5 CMBG HQ: "They were reported because they happened."[539] On 3 September, the 5 CMBG issued a press release describing, "an unknown number of light aircraft made 15 landings and takeoffs on a roadway in Kahnawake between 8:15 p.m. and 9:35 p.m.... The aircraft were not using instruments which would have allowed the Dorval or Saint-Hubert airports to record the flight path of planes flying at such a low altitude."[540]

Regardless of the removal of heavy weapon systems and a number of Warriors, the barricades were required to come down. On the morning of 29 August, APCs and soldiers approached the Mohawk barriers as negotiations were taking place at all levels. On the ground the commanders of 3 R22eR, led by Lieutenant-Colonel Robin Gagnon, talked to their Warrior counterparts and discussed the appropriate actions for the removal of the barricades:

> It took nine days, from the 20th to the 29th...to convince them to co-operate in lifting the barricades. We gave, in return, our word that we would: first respect the Mohawk people; and, secondly, that we would not use the press or make statements to place them in a situation where they would lose face. They gave credibility to our engagement and, on the afternoon of the 29th, we lifted the first row of barricades. By 1 September, the Mercier Bridge was in our hands.[541]

Negotiations had stalled during the morning at Kahnawake. In order to increase the pressure, 2 RCR relieved 3 R22eR positions on the eastern portion of the perimeter around Kahnawake supported by artillery ("W" Battery). Having already publicly stated that 2 RCR would only be moved forward in the need for direct action, many reporters and Warriors believed that the swelling in CF numbers signalled an assault. The movement of 2 RCR put pressure on Mohawk negotiators and Band Council Chief Joseph Norton to co-operate in hopes of resolving the problem. By 1900hrs, the blockades on Highways 132 and 138 were peacefully removed in a joint effort.[542] That night, Lieutenant-General Foster announced that, "Army units, in co-operation with the Mohawks, will open the principle routes leading to, and including the Mercier Bridge.... The situation at Oka remains unchanged."[543]

The following morning Lieutenant-Colonel Gagnon met with Mohawk representative Jack LeClerc to solidify the arrangement which included:

1. No more than groups of 10 military personnel on Reserve;
2. All barricades to be inspected for booby-traps and military engineers will supervise all road work;
3. Routes will be patrolled by military personnel including unarmed Mohawks;
4. APCs less .50 calibre machine guns can move onto Reserve;
5. No SQ on Reserve; and
6. Supplies must be allowed to pass through freely.[544]

By the morning of 31 August, all barricades had been removed or were in the process of being dismantled save for the Mercier Bridge. The Warriors were reluctant to give it up. They knew that once vacated, their comrades at Kanesatake would be in a drastically different situation and would have no leverage in further negotiations. However, the population of Kahnawake was suffering emotionally and economically. CF intelligence received message traffic from the Kahnawake Peacekeepers (Reserve Police Force) suggesting Warriors were threatening those Mohawks who wished to leave the Reserve until normalcy returned. The Warriors said they would allow women and children to leave but threatened to burn the houses of all Mohawk men who evacuated.[545]

The hard stance taken at Kahnawake over the clearing of the bridge affected operations at Kanesatake. To put pressure on both locations and to send a message that CF operations did not revolve around the Warrior agenda, Brigadier-General Roy authorized the movement of 2 R22eR to capture and dismantle both western Mohawk barricades on Highway 344 (there were two: OW1 and OW2) and also the northwest barrier at the junction of Rang Sainte-Germaine and Chemin du Milieu (OW3).[546]

Although Warriors were still present, most of the Mohawks at the barricades were women and children. This replacement of personnel had been progressively taking place at Kanesatake and Kahnawake since the CF announced its intentions to remove the barricades on 28 August. At this time, 10 per cent of the population of Oka and Kanesatake had been evacuated.[547] Lieutenant-Colonel (then Lieutenant) John Fife had an explanation for the withering support: "The people manning the barricades were not always the same, most of them were teenagers, 15-19 years of age. It was summer employment. Believe it or not they were getting paid. When the school year started up and the weather began to change things changed. It was no longer fun to sit up at night at a barricade when it is freezing cold. Much of the enthusiasm went."[548]

At 1300hrs on 1 September 2 R22eR initiated its encirclement operation. "A" Coy was to maintain a blocking position starting at the golf grounds to the eastern barricade along Highway 344 (OW6), while "B" and "C" Coys advanced supported by reconnaissance platoons, APCs and helicopters. "B" Coy's objective was to advance on the two western blockades along Highway 344 (OW1 and OW2), while "C" Coy was given the most difficult task of clearing the Pines while advancing to the rear of the original barricade on Chemin du Milieu. Upon completion, the perimeter and Warrior positions would be greatly reduced.[549]

The advance was rapid and on site commanders decided to maintain pressure, taking advantage of the element of surprise and the confusion among Warrior ranks. "B" Coy advanced in unison with six APCs and found a solitary Warrior manning the barricades in a camouflaged golf cart. Robert "Mad Jap" Skidder—whom Colonel (then Major) Tremblay described as the rather rational leader of the Warriors at Kanesatake—and lawyer Stanley Cohen were soon on the scene. After negotiation and the realization that "B" Coy intended to advance, the Warriors vacated these positions. "B" Coy pushed east along 344.[550]

Major Tremblay was leading "C" Coy through the Pines along the back roads with APC support. Warrior resistance was first encountered at a bunker at the edge of the golf course in "Sector 5." In spite of Warrior threats and the discharge of warning shots, "C" Coy pushed forward to "exploit the situation and terrain," as remembered by Tremblay:

> Mad Jap was basically commanding their troops, he was the one calling the shots. There were a lot of youngsters in the armed Mohawks at Oka and it was very difficult for them to maintain control. By using some of the elder women which were very well placed, and they are key from the Mohawk point of view, they always managed to diffuse the situation before it reached the point of no return. When we closed in we went much farther than forecasted. We decided to maintain pressure and ended up pushing them back to the lacrosse arena.[551]

By 2030hrs 2 R22eR was in control of all barricades less one (OW6), the eastern barricade atop the hill on 344 facing down towards the village of Oka. A temporary perimeter was fabricated around the last Warrior position and "C" Coy remained at stand-to. At 2230hrs three gun shots were heard coming from the woods south of 344 towards the Treatment Centre. Three hours later a Warrior message requesting advice from Akwesasne as what to do with weapons was intercepted. The answer was to burn or bury them. The CF took this as a sign that at least a portion of the Warriors were "fading into the woodwork to fight another day."[552]

When dawn broke on 2 September, elements of "C" Coy 2 R22eR, including three APCs advanced slowly toward the last barricade on 344 and began to seal it off using razor wire. Although 20-30 Warriors were actively shouting and yelling, they retreated to the Rehabilitation Treatment Centre (TC) in the woods south of Highway 344 towards the river. The soldiers quickly began checking the overturned cars, logs and debris for booby traps and explosives. This final barricade at Kanesatake was completely dismantled by 1800hrs that night.[553] By 0800hrs on the morning of the 3rd, a perimeter had been established by 2 R22eR around the TC. On 3 September the perimeter of some 500 square metres was tightened around the TC with "B" Coy to the west, "C" Coy at the centre—to the north of Highway 344, and "A" Coy to the east. Here the perimeter would remain until the final stand on 26 September.[554]

The situation had Kahnawake was no less volatile during the removal of the barricades. All had been removed save for the barricades blocking the entrances and the south side of the Mercier Bridge. Major routes were being patrolled by mounted and dismounted elements of 3 R22eR in the western area of operation and 2 RCR on the eastern sector of the perimeter. CF and SQ roadblocks were maintained to control movement on these axis routes in and out of the Reserve. A WestCam was mounted on the bridge and was used as a standing OP by 3 R22eR.[555]

At 1530hrs on 1 September with 2 R22eR advancing on the barricades in Kanesatake, an urgent message was sent to the Kahnawake Warriors ordering them to blow the bridge. This did not happen and it is still not known if the Mercier Bridge was wired for demolition. The Warriors certainly had enough explosives and the expertise to do so (steel workers experience). No wiring or explosives were ever found on or adjacent to the bridge, except for minor trip wires and booby-traps.[556]

After lengthy negotiations between Lieutenant-Colonel Robin Gagnon and Chief Joe Norton, the bridge was vacated by the Warriors and their supporters 20 minutes after midnight on the night/morning of 1-2 September. "A" Coy of 3 R22eR secured the bridge and waited for demolition experts and engineers to begin the arduous task of clearing the bridge of any suspected mines, wires and explosives.[557] Although the bridge was not open to the public just yet, both 2 R22eR at Kanesatake and 3 R22eR and 2 RCR at Kahnawake had completed the first task of their four point mission statement—remove all barricades in the affected areas—without the use of extreme measures.

The realization of the second assignment, to restore freedom of movement on all roads and bridges, was within grasp. The closing two charges would be more difficult to accomplish: remove all strong points and restore normal conditions of public order and security. In order to achieve these goals entrance onto the Reserve was necessary, as many weapon caches and "strong points" were well into the heart of Kahnawake.

Entrance into the Reserve itself did not take long to manifest and was reactionary on the part of the CF. As the perimeter at Kanesatake was tautened on 3 September, a group of roughly 30-50 Mohawks including Warriors, women and children in addition to vehicles, erected a makeshift sandbag blockade at the southern end of the Mercier Bridge as a show of support for their kin at Kanesatake. The Kahnawake Mohawks claimed that it was intended to be peaceful and was hijacked by the Warriors who showed up bearing arms including a .50 Calibre machine gun. The initial Warrior blocking moves occurred at 1042hrs. These quick reaction barricades were all removed by 1420hrs.[558] During this attempt to retake the Mercier Bridge, most armed Warriors fled when 3 R22eR quickly redeployed APCs and soldiers across the bridge. On the authority of a senior intelligence officer:

> We received a tip-off that they were going to re-occupy the bridge on EW. The intercept was simply, 'Deploy five security teams.' We put the WestCam over it and caught them in the act. It came close to confrontation in my opinion but the internal politics within the Mohawk diffused it. No matter who was in front of the camera, unless the women backed it, it didn't go. When the women shut it down, they shut it down. When they dismantled everything we followed the armed Warriors with a WestCam both in a school bus and in a van to the Longhouse on Highway 207 which we knew to be the location of their communications

> network. There was one lad that went into the bush with a long, heavy barrelled system which resembled a .50 calibre.[559]

Brigadier-General Roy ordered 2 RCR and 3 R22eR to enter the Reserve to control the main access points. Thus far no CF personnel had actually entered Kahnawake proper. "G" Coy (2 RCR) commanded by Major Lawrence O'Neill moved forward toward the Longhouse expecting resistance from armed Warriors. "K" Coy (2 RCR) moved into a reserve position to support "G" Coy. "G" Coy was met by 30 women who blocked the progress of the APCs. The forward Platoon dismounted and struggled forward on foot. At this point 50-60 more Mohawk women arrived. Pushing forward "G" Coy reached the Longhouse by 1750hrs and was met by a hostile crowd of roughly 100 Mohawks, mostly women.[560]

Although SQ members were present they could not be used for crowd control under Brigade orders. As "G" Coy and elements of "K" Coy set up a cordon around the Longhouse, 5 SQ officers, with a legal search warrant were "assisted into the Longhouse by rugby-style tactics." The crowd was held back and slowly dispersed as SQ and CF personnel began to uncover numerous weapons and ammunition. While the search was conducted, a vehicle with two armed passengers trying to transport additional weapons out of the area was intercepted. One passenger pulled a knife and was quickly subdued by a soldier and subsequently arrested with his fellow traveller by the SQ. The operation was completed by 2230hrs.[561] Weapons sequestered during the Longhouse search included: three AK-47's, a Ruger Mini-14 Assault rifle, an FNCI, an M-16 and a .50 Calibre 82A1 Barrett sniper rifle.[562]

Brigadier-General Roy stated that the new barricade temporarily erected violated, "Our understanding with the Mohawks.... In response to this, I ordered that patrols be increased."[563] These increasing patrols entered the Reserve. "H" Coy (2 RCR) Commander Lieutenant-Colonel (Major) Bradley Boswell recalled the events of 3 September and his advance into Mohawk territory:

> Rock Bass and War Pig rushed up to me and said, 'You can't do this, don't do this.' I told him that we had our own job and that these routes had to remain clear. Things were getting tense and you were not sure if the heavy weapons were being placed again. Luckily Lieutenant-Colonel Mitchell [2 RCR Battalion Commander] arrived by Kiowa helicopter and walked over calmly to Rock Bass and War Pig and he pointed at me and said, 'This man is going onto the Reserve today.' Colonel Mitchell left after

> giving me some direction and I then chatted to Rock Bass. He told me to wait for awhile until he could go talk. Obviously there was a chain of command. He came back 20 minutes later and said that we could move as long as they could escort. I agreed. We moved our four vehicles onto the onramp of the Highway inside the Reserve. When my vehicle was in position, Rock Bass came up and tapped on the hull and said, "Yeah we can't get through that!' At that point he took off his mask and we talked for 45 minutes sitting on the guard rail. He told me that he was coerced into taking a leadership role by the Warriors. We had our .50 calibres mounted and part of the original agreement was that they would not be seen as they said they were scaring the children! We covered them but had a quick release system so that they could be effective in seconds.[564]

The tightening of the TC perimeter also affected the relative peace at Akwesasne where elements of the Royal Canadian Dragoons (RCD) were now part of the CF contingent of 40 persons and nine aquatic vessels. On 3 September, a group of Natives led by four Warriors attempted to block the Cornwall Bridge to no avail. Later that day two SQ patrol cars were overturned and damaged by 80 Mohawk demonstrators. That night over 100 rounds of gunfire were heard throughout Akwesasne.[565]

At Kahnawake, the ongoing inspections of the Mercier Bridge were nearing completion. Lieutenant-Colonel (then Major) Boswell recalled this tedious task:

> It took a long time because of the amount of garbage under that bridge. After awhile we were still at it, the Warriors who were escorting/watching us got fed up and I can quote them saying, 'There is nothing fucking here! It is just a pop can! It is just a piece of wood!' as they were kicking at all of the garbage. I said that we had a job to do and they seemed to understand that we had to take this seriously and I think they respected that professionalism.[566]

At 2115hrs on 3 September the Mercier Bridge was declared safe and devoid of any explosive devices.[567]

For the Mohawks of Kahnawake the incursion of the CF onto their land, accompanied by SQ members contravened the earlier principles established between Lieutenant-Colonel Gagnon and Grand Chief Joe Norton and his negotiators: "White man speak with forked tongue."[568] As far as CF commanders were concerned this agreement in trust was violated by the attempt to recapture the bridge and thus all points became moot.

Despite Mohawk objections, the CF had begun active operations to fulfill its four-point mandate. At Kahnawake, all major traffic routes had been cleared by 2 RCR and 3 R22eR. Although the raid of the Longhouse was a reaction to the re-barricading of the Mercier Bridge and the sight of heavy weapons, it did send a signal to everyone involved that the presence of weapons would not be tolerated and that the rule of law would be restored. At Kanesatake, all barricades had been removed and the remaining demonstrators had been cordoned in the TC.

CHAPTER 18

The Treatment Centre at Kanesatake

At Kanesatake, 2 R22eR continued to seal off the TC in an attempt to corral the last holdouts and force an end to the standoff. However, with the inability to use military means to solve the crisis, alternative methods were needed. The use of psychological techniques in combination with negotiations was the solution implemented by the CF and performed by 2 R22eR around the TC perimeter. However, this would take time and the longer it took the more likely an incident or escalation could occur whether instigated by the CF or the Warriors. The close proximity of soldiers, Warriors and the general population of Kanesatake produced frequent exchanges of verbal and physical confrontation.

After several shoving matches between soldiers, Warriors and Mohawk women, a second layer of concertina wire was ordered around the entire perimeter. In reality, after the erection of this second line, Operation SALON and Operation AKWESASNE had completely depleted the supply of concertina wire across the entire CF. Colonel Tremblay remembered using, "the entire barbed wire supply in the CF at the time. There was no more left anywhere in Canada. I have never put up so much barbed wire in my life; not in Bosnia or even Afghanistan. It was truly amazing."[569] In addition, the access to the river behind the TC was encircled by a log-boom placed by marine elements of the SQ on 5 September.[570]

In the background, negotiations continued. Tom Siddon met with the Chiefs from the Six Nations Confederacy. They told him that the military pressure was being felt by those remaining in the TC and that this could compromise a peaceful resolve. General de Chastelain and Premier Bourassa offered a settlement to those inside. If they laid down their weapons and exited the perimeter peacefully, they would be taken into military custody at Camp Farnham rather than be arrested on site by the SQ, whom the Mohawks despised. The legal framework for a detention centre at Farnham had been authorised by the CDS on 5 September. Those encircled in the TC refused this offer and submitted a counter offer insinuating that if the military withdrew they would vacate their position. This was flatly rejected.[571]

The government response centred around three important issues. The first was that all long-term subjects revolving around sovereignty and extended land claim issues would no longer be discussed. The second assured that all military and police forces involved had the powers to enforce the *Criminal Code of Canada* and that its statutes apply to all persons including the Warriors. This was a reminder not a new initiative as soldiers in *Aid to the Civil Power* operations are given the powers of a Peace Officer. Lastly, it was made known that both the federal and provincial governments were ready to discuss the possibility of a Native police force at Kanesatake similar to those already in operation on Kahnawake and Akwesasne.[572] On 9 September Minister of Justice Kim Campbell issued the following statement:

> I'm making this statement today because I'm concerned that the Canadian people and the media misunderstand what is happening at Oka and the events involving the Canadian Forces and the Warriors.... But, let me be clear,--we must not confuse the highly legitimate concerns of the Indian people with the resistance of armed Warriors at Oka due to the due enforcement of law. The Warriors at Oka do not represent legitimate Native grievances. They carry guns...and we will not negotiate with them. They blatantly use the words of normal Indian claims to mask their true intent, just as they mask their faces... The Army's offer has been turned down...The Governments of Canada and Quebec cannot and will not accept that the Warriors are not governed by the laws of this country, including the Criminal Code. They receive full protection of our laws, including the Charter [of Rights and Freedoms]. Neither they nor anyone else in Canada can pick which laws to obey.[573]

In the event of these points and the Warriors' intransigence in rejecting the proposal, 2 R22eR proceeded to find a solution to end the crisis. The military operation at Kanesatake after reducing the perimeter on 3 September was fairly simple. Due to the resounding statement that the CF would not fire the first shot, it would have been difficult and precarious to remove those holed-up in the TC by force. There were reports in early September that the Warriors were ready to lay down their arms but changed their mind after Lieutenant-General Foster personally appeared at Oka to assure the Mohawk population, including the Warriors, that the CF would not initiate a conflict. The impact of this was that the standoff was prolonged indefinitely.

It was clear that the environment around the TC could only be shaped with limited military means, so psychological operations using light and sound to induce sleep deprivation, thus unnerving the opponents, were used to put pressure on those inside. Three towers mounted with high powered search lights and speakers were built around the TC. Helicopters made continuous low level flights over the area. CF observation posts with TOW weapon systems were erected across the river near Hudson and 2 R22eR patrols were ever prevalent to unnerve the Warriors. Only the resupply of essential resources was allowed to the TC by outside agencies. Colonel (Major) Tremblay recalled the situation:

> Then it became more of a PA game than anything else, by trying to paint us as the bad guy and how ill-treated they were. I think at that point they were more interested in gaining visibility with the entire crisis with the media to promote their agenda, to stretch it to maintain as many visibilities on their claims and issues. It was a matter of keeping them off balance and maintaining pressure without going to the point of somebody firing shots. They had a network of communication and we were never able to completely sever that line. They were still able to go into discussions with Kahnawake, Akwesasne and the States. They were resupplied by daily/nightly boat runs, speed boats. The spectrum of military resources we had, short of using fire arms, was limited, so psychological operations were conducted with light and sound and so on, to limit their sleeping time. Actually we were losing the sound battle because they had bigger speakers than us.[574]

Intelligence reports reveal that even though the TC was completely surrounded, the Warriors used the river with great adroitness to resupply the TC throughout the first two weeks of September. Interceptions of cellphone calls and radio traffic also indicate that the communications network, although limited, was still quite active. Warrior patrols outside of the contained area were reporting military movements and activity to the TC.[575] They were also identifying military personnel, units and unit strengths through name tags, unit insignias and vehicle markings. Lieutenant-Colonel Rusty Bassarab, Deputy Commander for 2 RCR made reference to this point:

> Lasagna, his brother was in 3 RCR in Germany. We had three Natives that were part of our battalion, one was a Cree. He had

> an awful hard time, including a woman who threw hot coffee in his face. I think that the Velcro name tags we have now is a direct result of that operation. We all had to put tape over our name tags, in order to protect all troops from being identified. They [Mohawks] viewed it as hiding our names so we could commit illegal acts. No we just don't think it wise to advertise their names, except for the officers, who wore berets not helmets like everyone else. Pretty good target indication. You can throw a rock pretty hard with a lacrosse stick. They were also driving golf balls at the helicopters, which is pretty ironic.[576]

As the pressure inside the TC mounted, troublesome occurrences began to take place along the wire perimeter. On 6 September a soldier accidentally shot himself in the foot. The Warriors responded by firing six high calibre rounds into the air. Three more shots were fired from inside the TC boundary later that night. The military moved the media centre established by the CF back 300m from the wire perimeter to stop interference with soldiers and also for the safety of the journalists. On the night of the 7th, Warriors in the Oka enclave erected a canvas screen behind which they proceeded to carry out a number of unknown activities. At 2154hrs, they adopted firing positions, aimed their weapons at the opposing soldiers and placed their front-end loader in a position to effect a breakout. 2 R22eR countered this move by blocking the exit with a D-6 Dozer. Later that night a breach in the wire was created by the Warriors which was quickly sealed off. Tempers flared as Warriors pelted soldiers with rocks. The situation was brought under control after the on-site commander ordered the troops to fix bayonets.[577]

Although threats and intimidation were ubiquitous from both sides, thus far no major injuries had been incurred. This changed on the night of 8 September during a situation that tarnished the reputation of the CF. In an attempt to unnerve the Warriors guarding the perimeter and to prevent them from sleeping, 2 R22eR conducted aggressive patrols along both sides of the wire perimeter. There were very few Warriors left and by conducting extensive patrolling, these Warriors were forced to remain in their positions for extremely long intervals. The CF believed that only 24 Warriors remained in the TC compound in addition to 10 women, 11 children and 23 journalists.[578]

At 0500hrs on the morning of the 8th, a four-man reconnaissance patrol crossed the perimeter to investigate the nature of work which had been taking place behind the large canvas screen during the past two days. A single soldier from the patrol met a Warrior, Randy "Spudwrench" Horne, and informed him of the nature of the patrol and that no weapons would be used. At this point a second soldier joined his comrade as "Spudwrench" appeared to be aggressive. This prompted Horne to draw a knife and slash one soldier across the face. While attempting to restrain Horne, the other soldier was stabbed in the abdomen four times. The soldiers retaliated using their rifle-buts to subdue "Spudwrench." The situation concluded when the two other members of the patrol appeared along with four other Warriors. The patrol withdrew immediately.[579]

Horne was taken into the TC and using the "hotline" that had been established between the TC and 2 R22eR HQ, medical assistance was offered by the CF and was refused. Eventually a paramedic entered the TC to provide assistance. The Warriors called their own doctor, David Gorman in Malone, New York. He reached Oka at 0830hrs and was allowed inside the TC to see to the injuries of Horne. The Warriors distrusted the CF and thought that if he was put in the care of the CF or the SQ he would be arrested.[580]

At 1630hrs a private ambulance carried Mr. Horne out of Oka towards Montreal. On route to Notre-Dame Hospital in Montreal, the convoy of the ambulance, army and SQ vehicles and reporters was detoured as a bomb threat was called in to that hospital. After some deliberation the convoy, less reporters who had been lost in the trail, ended up at Hotel Dieu in the north end of Montreal. From there they proceeded to Montreal General Hospital. The injuries to the two soldiers were superficial as were those to Mr. Horne contrary to media reports.[581]

On 12 September, Horne was taken into military custody at Farnham and was arrested by the SQ on five charges including possession of a dangerous weapon. After an investigation no charges were laid against any members of the patrol. "C" Coy commander, Colonel (then Major) Tremblay, who ordered the patrol insists that, "the soldiers on that patrol showed great restraint, because from a Criminal Code point of view they could have shot him [Spudwrench] right there. Obviously the guy was injured but this was not a game and the military was not there to play a game."[582]

The version of the story forwarded by the Warriors differs immensely from that of the CF. They insisted that Mr. Horne was attacked unprovoked, that he was asleep in his sleeping bag. They are also very sceptical about the manner in which he was taken to the hospital.[583] The CF press release concluded that, "The facts have been stated and obviously either side is going to interpret those facts as they see fit."[584] Like many other aspects of the Oka Crisis the unfortunate incident on the morning of 8 September is a matter of perspective. On 9 September, "A" Coy replaced "C" Coy at the perimeter at Kanesatake. This was seen by the Warriors as the CF saving face for being too aggressive when in reality it was the scheduled standard rotation of CF troop allocations.[585]

The potentially confrontational environment at Kanesatake did not dissipate after the events surrounding Randy Horne. A gap in the wire perimeter was found on 10 September that had possibly been exploited by the Warriors to transport weapons and persons in and out of the TC complex. A "journalist" inside the TC reported to CF intelligence that they had positively identified numerous cellphones, two RPK weapons, at least a dozen operational gas masks and a quantity of grenades. It was also relayed that Orders Groups were always carried out on the second floor balcony and during inclement weather in an office facing the water. From this he deduced that Robert "Mad Jap" Skidders seemed to be in charge of those inside the TC.[586]

On numerous occasions, Warriors aimed their weapons at soldiers and simulated firing. The Warriors were contacted through the "hotline" and made aware of the seriousness of these actions. By 13 September, only one "hotline" remained. On that day the other two telephone lines were cut to further pressure the Warriors into negotiating a peaceful settlement. It was also done to minimize the amount of communication afforded to the Warriors inside the TC. On the night of the 9th, 12th and 13th mysterious planes were again spotted near Kahnawake, with an OP from "H" Coy (2 RCR) confirming at least one successful landing on 9 September. Correspondingly, intercepted Warrior communications disclosed information about a possible helicopter extraction of those inside the TC.[587]

Giving credence to this message traffic, on 14 September, the FBI forwarded a receipt of and information about the purchase of two helicopters at an army surplus store in New York, New York by a reputed member of the Kahnawake Warrior Society. However, not much other information was forwarded except that the helicopters were black in colour and that the procurer had a pilot licence.[588] FMC immediately implemented local measures to address this situation. Additional helicopters were ordered to patrol and AIRCOM (Air Command) provided the "necessary sources to allow for 24/7 radar surveillance and tracking." These resources and personnel were deployed and operational by 1400hrs on 14 September. 1 Commando was also placed on 24 hours

NTM.[589] With the Warriors' aerial escape route cordoned off, a tunnel feasibility reconnaissance was conducted along the perimeter of the TC.

On 15 September, 2 R22eR personnel and all OPs were questioned about any unusual tunnelling activity or suspicious patches or colours of earth. There were no reports of these activities. FMC went so far as to remove soil samples from likely tunnelling routes around the perimeter at a depth of 15 metres. The test results from the soil plugs deduced that the ground around the TC was primarily made up of fine sand overlaid by roughly 10-20cm of organic soil and decaying materials bound by small unstable roots. Due to the soil's composition, tunnelling in the area was possible yet highly unlikely as a large amount of bracing was needed to make any tunnel solid enough to be utilized.[590]

2 R22eR at Kanesatake had thus far removed all barricades and restored freedom of movement on traffic routes. The only "strongpoint" and immediate threat to "normal conditions of public order and security" that remained was the TC. Elements of 2 R22eR continued to deny the Warriors any escape route other than leaving through CF lines. Psychological manipulation in connection with "hotline" negotiations was being used in an attempt to resolve the standoff at Kanesatake without violent confrontation. The situation at Kahnawake was quite different. Here, there were many more highly used traffic routes, a much larger Mohawk population, a larger land base and correspondingly a greater perimeter, which was still flanked by hostile Québécois and other radical groups.

CHAPTER 19

Raids, Retaliation and Relationships

The Mercier Bridge and its on routes officially opened to traffic on the morning of 6 September. The bridge had been closed for 55 days. 3 R22eR and 2 RCR continued to patrol and maintain checkpoints on the major routes. They also began conducting patrols and weapon searches in Kahnawake to remove threats to themselves, LEAs and the Mohawk. Although the bridge was open, the angry protestors surrounding the Reserve continued to hold rallies and intimidate soldiers, Warriors and the Mohawk population.

Lieutenant-Colonel (then Major) Boswell will never forget episodes of racial hatred that serve as only two examples of the chaos surrounding Kahnawake:

> The local population had erected a barricade and they used 40 gallon drums, lit fires and they also used a road chain to break tires. I never ran over it but I had the tires on my Iltis slashed on a daily basis. They were actually more abusive towards the soldiers than the Natives or the Warriors. They wanted us to get in there and clean it up, but it wasn't that simple from a political sense. I will never forget two events. One day, the first weekend after the barricades had been removed, a car, a little Omni full of Mohawk women were coming back after grocery shopping. The crowd was overpowering, they smashed out the back and rear windows and ripped out all of the groceries and terrified these three women inside. We managed to get them inside. One soldier began picking up the groceries and the local population started yelling and swearing at him for helping these women. I'll never forget his reaction and quote. He simply smiled and said, 'I do not speak French. Have a nice day.' He picked up the rest of the food and gave it back to the females there and off they went on foot.

He vividly recalled another frightening scene:

> It was 2:30 in the morning and I was out visiting an OP of Lieutenant Fife's Platoon on the railway line entering the Reserve. It was 400m parallel to Highway 132. We heard a terrible noise

> and it was an old '77 T-Bird screaming down the railway line. It got to the wire and two young Mohawk guys jumped out and we lifted the wire to get them under it into the Reserve just as the local population got to the car and torched it on the spot with a Molotov Cocktail. The crowd had blocked 132 and chased them, so they had to use the rail line. It was scary stuff.[591]

At another barricade on the night of 3 September locals were stopping vehicles before they reached the RCR checkpoint leading into the Reserve. Seemingly out of the blue, the RCR Regimental Piper began playing "Vive la Canadienne" and it completely distressed the civilian crowd. He then proceeded to cross the barrier and play for the Warriors. Lieutenant-Colonel (Major) Bassarab fondly remembers one of the Mohawks saying to him, "Yeah, the Jesuits used to do that to us too, but then we had to listen to them preach for two hours!"[592]

There were moments when tensions at the barricades relented and the soldiers and Warriors or civilians facing each other often communicated. Such was the case in a story told by Lieutenant-Colonel (Major) Brad Boswell: "'H' Coy had a tall, thick unmistakable black Sergeant in its ranks, Sergeant Welsh who was a terrific soldier. He went on leave for 3 days. When he wasn't at his usual barricade position, the kids in the house across the street put a huge sign up in their window reading, 'Where's Buckwheat?' The folks at those barricades got to know who each other were."[593]

The CF elements at Kahnawake had accomplished the first two objectives. All barricades had been removed and by 6 September all traffic routes and bridges were open to traffic. However, as the prior anecdotes illustrate, by no means were "normal conditions of public order and security" restored and a plethora of different intelligence sources revealed the existence of "strong points" and weapons caches on the Reserve. Over the next two weeks 3 R22eR and 2 RCR intended to fulfill the remaining two tasks to which they had been assigned.

At 1700hrs on 12 September, "G" Coy (2 RCR) had seen some weapons in a barn whilst setting up for dinner. The area was cordoned and the SQ was informed. "K" Coy was moved forward as a reserve. 60 SQ officers arrived to conduct the search but would not enter unless the building was cleared. Rather than wait for the SQ SWAT team, fearing that inaction might lead to confrontation with Mohawks, "G" Coy cleared the building by knocking out windows and hung glow sticks to report that the room was clear.

The house owned by Peter Diome, one of the negotiators at Kahnawake, was searched and only two weapons and a small quantity of ammunition were found.[594] However, what was also found was interesting and puzzling. Numerous boxes of recently dated governmental and CF paperwork was confiscated from the house corresponding to a variety of organizations and functions. Federal Cabinet documents were recovered. CF intelligence reports, unit strengths and fan-out sheets, some of which were stamped with confidential and secret classifications, were also recovered. The suspected mole and pipeline to Ottawa was confirmed, although no one was identified as a primary suspect.[595]

The CF and SQ efforts to restore safety and security to Kahnawake and the surrounding communities through cordon and searches for weapons and contraband continued two days later. Having received a tip from a Mohawk informant, cordon and searches were carried out by 2 RCR and the SQ at the Flea Market and the residence of Dan Delisle on 14 September. Several cases of cigarettes were seized at the Flea Market. The search of the Delisle house located on route 207 in Kahnawake was the result of "G" Coy (2 RCR) conducting a routine patrol and finding weapons in an orchard outside of the house. The SQ conducted a search of the house at 2000hrs under an official warrant, while "G" Coy provided the cordon. The result was the confiscation of $500,000 worth of illegal tobacco products, eight boxes of various calibre ammunition, magazines for multiple weapons, including AK-47s, and 24 weapons including: revolvers, shotguns and semi-automatic machine guns.[596]

The following day another raid on an unidentified private home yielded 60 boxes of assorted calibre ammunition, stolen golf equipment, 1.75lbs of packaged marijuana and 58 marijuana plants.[597] On 16-17 September patrols involving dismounted CF and SQ personnel, the SQ scuba diving squad and SQ canine units produced seven more weapons and 15 Molotov Cocktails as well as the positive identification of several reported stolen motorcycles and vehicles.[598]

The largest raid of the Oka Crisis occurred on 18 September at Tekakwitha Island which is adjoined to the northern boundary of Kahnawake by a single bridge at the east end. At 0800hrs, the SQ intelligence liaison to 2 RCR reported receiving a tip from a reliable source about a large weapons cache on Tekakwitha Island. 2 RCR HQ surmised that there were only three possible approaches to the Island: by land through the town (not an option), by sea (lacking the resources to do so) and by air.[599]

Air-mobile planning was conducted and 5 BMC HQ gave its approval. The plan was as follows: one platoon would be inserted at the bridge in a single Chinook Helicopter lift. Another platoon would be dropped in a similar fashion at the western end of the island as there were reports of bunkers. Once the east-west axis was secure, two platoons would be inserted to conduct the sweep. The SQ SWAT Team would be inserted by SQ boats to gain entry and secure the marina buildings at the south-western tip. The boats would remain in the vicinity to block the aquatic escape route. Two CF sniper groups were inserted on a tiny island roughly 1 km west of Tekakwitha.[600]

Due to lack of helicopters the original plan was amended. The only change made was that a section would be inserted at the bridge (instead of a full platoon) and the remainder of the platoon would be dropped 300m to the west to secure the western perimeter. The remainder of the plan was unchanged. With battle procedure moving extremely fast, the original H-Hour (initiation of operations) was moved from 1330hrs to 1430hrs. In keeping with the policy of informing the Mohawks prior to any movement or operation on the Reserve, Lieutenant-Colonel Gagnon informed the Band Council, specifically Jack Leclair, at 1420hrs of what was taking place. Brigadier-General Roy contacted Elvin Delisle five minutes later. Therefore, the residents and Warriors of Kahnawake had knowledge of what was happening and 15 minutes warning before "G," "H", and "K" Coys of 2 RCR deployed. Obviously, they could also see and hear the Chinook Helicopters. The first detailed elements of 2RCR landed at 1433hrs after one pass over the island to gain a bearing of the ground and surroundings.[601]

The reaction of the Natives who assembled at the bridge head was exceedingly quick and aggressive. In a short period of time a group of 300 Mohawks had amassed at the wire cordon of the bridge and violence quickly ensued. A truck was driven through the wire at the end of the bridge and the angry crowd spilled over pelting the 30 soldiers protecting the bridge with rocks and golf balls.[602] Several soldiers were knocked down and were being beaten by numerous Mohawks. The soldiers responded by shoving the crowd and using rifle butts to fend off the protestors. Six grenades of CS gas were released by the RCR which temporarily stunned most of the angry crowd; however, a certain portion appeared not to be affected and continued forward. A single warning shot was fired into the air by Private Pellecchia which halted the advance momentarily.[603]

The situation was made worse when soldiers in riot gear and SQ helmets arrived. The Mohawks, believing these were actually SQ officers, became even more enraged. Shortly thereafter, a 2 RCR reconnaissance platoon commander attached a Warrior flag upside down on his radio antenna which further infuriated the throng of Natives. He was charged by the CF the next day, left the mission and was released from the Army.[604]

What followed can best be described by those who were there. Lieutenant-Colonel (then Captain) Pat McAdam:

> I was back at HQ being the Adjutant and I got a phone call telling me to prepare everybody I had and that we were needed on the Island immediately. So I grabbed all of the cooks, clerks, truck drivers and everyone lying around and the Regimental Sergeant-Major (RSM) jumped in to be my Platoon Warrant. We flew into the island and tried to give as much help to keep that bridge route shut. I started talking to Chief Joe Norton and tried to get him and the Peacekeepers to control the crowd. By then the weapons on the island had been confirmed. One of the Natives caught me looking the other way and hit me on the head with a large rock, the size of a basketball and I went unconscious. I actually have pictures of it. I went down and Captain Shayne McArthur, a platoon commander ordered another round of gas. John Fife who was south of me came up with some soldiers in a reinforcement role same as me. He was the one shown on television being dragged by his binoculars and being beaten. I then got Medivaced. I ended up with 15 stitches.[605]

Lieutenant-Colonel (then Lieutenant) John Fife also shared his story:

> The first person I saw was the RSM, CWO Irving. He told me that we were needed to help evacuate the Adjutant [McAdam]. The crowd came face to face with me and a few of my soldiers. There was spitting and punching and then a riot broke out. I was in front and got pulled into the crowd and took some kicks and punches. I fell and that is when one of my soldiers fired a burst of C-9 [Light Machine Gun] ammunition which caught the attention of the crowd and they were able to come in and drag me out. I was not Medivaced but a few of my soldiers were. They were beaten quite badly. When we fired the C-9 burst we also moved back creating a larger buffer zone.[606]

While Lieutenant Fife was being beaten on the ground, Private M.L. Tilley released a 4-6 round burst from his C-9 over the heads of the crowd. At roughly the same time, Private M.P. Robertson fired five rounds into the air. Correspondingly another round of CS gas was volleyed at the crowd.[607]

During the melee, two C-7 rifles were taken; one from Lieutenant Fife and the other from Master-Corporal Corrigal who was knocked down and beaten after being pelted with rocks. The sniper groups tracked those weapons and were given permission to shoot if those weapons were even pointed in the direction of the RCR soldiers: "Had the Natives who took those weapons turned with them, even inadvertently, that was it, they were dead. That would have been really bad. That was not their intent in taking them though; they were scoring a coup of sorts. If one of them had been foolish enough, even pretending, pointed and turned, the snipers would not have waited to see if he was kidding. That was their ROE. It was close there," as explained by a confidential source.[608]

Eventually, Mohawk leaders and the Peacekeepers were able to subdue the crowd. The extraction of the troops began at 2100hrs and was completed an hour later in a total of eight airlifts using CH-147 Chinooks and CH-135 Twin-Hueys, while two CH-136 Kiowas provided overhead surveillance. In all 244 soldiers and 78 SQ members (in a secondary role) participated in the raid. Many of the soldiers who were flown in as reinforcements were the service and support elements of 2 RCR including cooks, clerks, mechanics and soldiers fresh off their QL3 infantry course. 22 soldiers were injured in total, nine of which had to be evacuated. One soldier was beaten unconscious with his own helmet while another had to have his ear surgically reattached. 75 Mohawks were treated for minor injuries, broken bones and gas inhalation.[609]

In total 48 weapons were seized in five different caches. Although all were illegally stored, only three were illegal including a six shot Striker Automatic Grenade Launcher. 6,000 rounds of ammunition were also found as well as a crossbow, knives, communications equipment and other military clothing and kit. Small amounts of alcohol and tobacco products were also confiscated.[610]

Afterwards many of those involved in the raid questioned what went wrong. The first point was that the CF was not well-versed in crowd confrontation techniques, including confrontation with women and children, nor was the proper equipment available. Although crowd confrontation training was conducted during Operation SALON itself in coordination with SQ officers, none had been done before hand. Compounding this problem, no effects-based planning had been done at an operational level. The raid occurred after the barricades had come down. The mission now was to restore normal conditions to the area. Were weapon raids an implied task? Obviously Brigadier-General Roy and Lieutenant-Colonels Gagnon and Mitchell believed so. Fifteen years later, this is how Lieutenant-Colonel (then Major) Bassarab analysed the raid on Tekakwitha Island:

> One of the biggest shortfalls of that operation was the lack of what we now call effects based planning. Our official mission was to stay in place and monitor and control those routes and the area in general. One of the mistakes we made during the control and stabilization was going after weapons. The reason I say mistake is because if you check with British experiences in Northern Ireland, and a few other places, going after weapons in that type of environment is not easy and due to the nature of that particular job it gets back to cause and effect. Is the capture of weapons worth all of the other aspects that you have now influenced?[611]

Although soldiers with shields and batons taken from the SQ were eventually inserted on Tekakwitha, it occurred after the riot had subsided. Another aspect of this was that officers were wearing berets not helmets in order to be recognized by both their own soldiers and the Mohawks. Had Captain McAdam been wearing a helmet he might not have sustained any injury.[612] Correspondingly, having no previous experience in this type of confrontational environment the soldiers were all wearing webbing which with all the buckles and straps was very easy to grab and was used to pull soldiers to the ground.[613] There was also strong evidence to suggest that those Mohawks not affected by the CS gas were on pills to negate its symptoms: "Some of them were not affected in the least bit by the gas, which is another interesting story, as that gas usually affects people. They had pills against the gas," recalled Lieutenant-Colonel (then Major) Bassarab.[614]

Three days after the raid, a Mohawk informant, who was an active member of the Kahnawake Warrior Society, explained how such a large crowd accrued so quickly at the bridge. He explained that the Band Council, the Mohawk Nation Council and the Warrior Society did not operate as distinct entities. There was coordination and council between these groups. Hence, when 2 RCR telegraphed the raid by informing Mr. Leclair and Delisle, this information was made communal. Secondly, Kahnawake had a number of systems in place to alert the people of the town. These systems included the air raid/tornado siren, the fire hall bell, a telephone fan-out sheet, patrols, handheld radios and the Kahnawake radio station (103.5FM). This was confirmed by soldiers on the ground who reported that when Mohawks and Warriors arrived at a confrontation they were effectively directed where to go.[615] On 20 September Lieutenant-General Foster stated that future search operations would continue but may not in all cases be announced before hand.[616]

The informant also mentioned, which was confirmed by EW, that those Mohawks with Vietnam and other military experience had a great deal of input into operations and decisions. They were instrumental in organizing the Reserve into sectors and coordinating squad leaders and squad rotations. In addition, the informant revealed that most of the heavy weapons had previously been taken out and were now in the U.S. at Akwesasne and Ganienkeh. A smaller amount had also been buried. This man also reported that the LAWs had been transported elsewhere as they were, "too valuable to lose." He concluded that these were the reasons why so few illegal weapons were found on Tekakwitha.[617]

However, the major point of contention existed in the premise that the CF was carrying out the function of the civil power, the SQ. On many occasions during the aforementioned raids, the SQ refused or neglected to perform its functions. In a sense it was not a traditional *Aid to the Civil Power* operation; rather, replacement of the civil power. Jurisdiction was oft times convoluted and confused. Protocol for cordon and search operations was that CF elements provide the cordon and the SQ conduct the search as they have the warrant. However, this did not happen in the case of the Diome raid or at Tekakwitha Island. In both instances the SQ refused to co-operate and 2 RCR was left to execute both functions. Secondly, those CF personnel involved quickly realized that the involvement of the SQ was counterproductive as the Mohawks had a severe hatred for them at both Kahnawake and Kanesatake. Lieutenant-Colonel (then Captain) Pat McAdam:

> The Mohawks complained a lot about the SQ. We only worried about how it would affect our operations. We knew that if we went in with the SQ beside us the Natives would respond very poorly. Instances like the Diome house and Tekakwitha Island, they said they would not come in. We lost faith in their ability to support us and carry out their functions. So we were forced to because they would not react.[618]

The situation for 2 R22eR at Kanesatake was quite different. They were not involved in cordon and search operations in conjunction with the SQ. Nor were they ever in situations where crowd confrontation became an issue for the soldiers where warning shots would have to be fired. Unlike Kahnawake, there was no arrangement at Kanesatake whereby the CF would have to declare its intentions before acting. The tactical scenarios at both locations were completely different as the environment dictated the courses of action to be taken. Colonel Tremblay highlighted these differences:

> Apart from accidental discharges there was never a single weapon fired by the CF at Kanesatake. There was never warning shots because we always managed the situation and never got into that crowd control situation. We used pure military tactics, no shields, no batons, no CS gas. The modus operandi at the battalion level between the RCR and 3 R22eR in Kahnawake and 2 R22eR at Oka was very different. The tactical situations were also different. The area of operations around Kahnawake and Chateauguay was much more problematic, higher risk of collateral damage, where in Oka we managed to sanitize a small area which gave us more flexibility as there were no civilians and less Mohawk population. The two different operations cannot be compared as they were very different in scope and nature. We never gave them notification. Surprise is a principle of war.[619]

The relationship with the civilian population was also drastically different. At Kanesatake, only a handful of people had to be evacuated from their houses. Many others chose to leave the area voluntarily. There were numerous instances where these displaced people gave their house keys to senior CF commanders stating that they could use the houses for sleeping quarters or for other administerial purposes. Unfortunately, there were confirmed reports of both Mohawks and CF personnel stealing electronic equipment from these vacated homes or lounging in the backyard swimming pools. The CF members were charged in military court.[620]

The Warriors also committed arson on two houses, looted and extensively vandalized another owned by Mohawks sympathizers Dr. Réjean Mongeon and his wife Andrea on 31 August. Later that night, they severely beat Francis Jacobs and his son Cory with baseball bats. It was this incident which prompted the first military action the following morning on 1 September throughout the Kanesatake area of operation.[621]

Problems with the SQ went beyond the jurisdictional impediments. Most CF members interviewed admitted that the professionalism of the SQ was marginal and they were able to pick up elements of racism. Also, some SQ members complained about the meals and sleeping quarters provided for them by the CF service and support battalions during both Operation AKWESASNE and Operation SALON. At the expense of the taxpayer, many SQ members chose to stay in hotels instead of the military modular tents provided for them.[622] An NCO who wished to remain anonymous shared his feelings and those of his peers:

> The soldiers were frustrated with fact that the SQ got to stay in hotels and they also resented the fact that the SQ worked shift work, could go home, see their families and then come back three or four days later. Yet they [SQ] still complained about rations and quarters when the soldiers were in tents and working 24/7, not on shifts. Some members of the CF viewed it as a situation where they were called in to clean up the mess left by the SQ, who seemed to shirk responsibility.[623]

The SQ was seen as a corrupt force by the Mohawks even before they deployed. The raid of 11 July only enhanced this reputation. For the CF, any loss of neutrality would compromise their effectiveness and legitimacy. In addition, the soldiers were under close public scrutiny and acts of racism or intolerance would be highly visible. More troublesome, was the realization that the initial psychological impact of the massive deployment was lost. This factor coupled with the inability of the CF to use force undermined the actions and capacity of the CF to perform its duties quickly. The longer the crisis dragged on the more the CF was seen by the Mohawk communities in the classic definition of an occupying army.

This resentment and the political constraints, in conjunction with the raids on Kahnawake, tainted the role and neutrality of the CF so much that legal actions were being taken to remove the CF from its role in *Aid to the Civil Power*. As it stood under the legislation, the CF had to remain until released of its duties by the Province of Quebec. On the night of 14 September a court injunction was served to the Federal Court of Canada in order to transfer the control of the CF from the Government of Quebec to the Attorney-General of Canada and that the CDS and CF refrain from any further activities under the *National Defence Act*. These requests were denied as no current legislation could be used to overturn Quebec's request for *Aid to the Civil Power*.[624]

The complex relationship between the CF and its role in an IS operation such as Operation SALON was not inherent to only the CF. Most western military forces were also clinging to the Cold War paradigm. Training was equivalent to the threat; mass formations of Russian forces attacking Western Europe and the ever-present prospect of nuclear attack. The qualities required for fighting a conventional war are different from those required to quell subversion, insurgency or "peacekeeping" for that matter. When soldiers endowed with the skills and training to be courageous, aggressive and proactive become involved in counter-insurgency operations these good qualities can be exploited by a clever enemy, nowhere more so that in an IS operation. According to Frank Kitson: "For example firm reaction in the face of provocation may be twisted by clever propaganda in such a way that soldiers find the civilian population regarding their strength as brutality, and their direct and honest efforts by helping to restore order as the ridiculous blunderings of a herd of elephants."[625]

Many Oka veterans recalled a single episode on 12 September which epitomized this fragile status of neutrality and the problems associated with domestic operations. One of the initial rules at Kahnawake was that no weapons would be allowed to be transported in or out of the Reserve. The Kahnawake Peacekeepers possessed legal jurisdiction to carry service weapons and uphold law on the Reserve as afforded to them through the Band Council by the Ministry of Indian Affairs. On the 12th, three members of the Kahnawake Peacekeepers crossed a barricade with their service weapons. The soldiers at the barricade arrested and handcuffed them in plain view of all the Mohawk onlookers. They were to be handed over to the SQ to face charges; however, Major Bassarab delayed this action. Instead they were brought to a private location nearby, the handcuffs were removed and discussions ensued.[626]

Eventually, they were taken by the SQ accompanied by a military police officer. Lieutenant-Colonel (Major) Bassarab explained: "In the end we sent one of our MPs with them. Is that a lack of trust? No, it was a measure to answer that you could claim that you provided full assurance that you [CF] are not turning these guys [Peacekeepers] over to the enemy [SQ]. They were not hiding their weapons, they were their service weapons. In the end we established good relations with these guys."[627]

The relationship between the Peacekeepers and 2 RCR and 3 R22eR was by all accounts well-natured and co-operative. They often accompanied soldiers on patrol on the Reserve and frequently calmed angry crowds of Mohawks at barricades. They even went so far as to borrow mine detectors and equipment from 2 RCR in attempts to locate buried weapons caches. Although the arrest angered the Band Council and Grand Chief Norton, and was seen as provocative by the community of Kahnawake, it did not erode the working, professional relationship between the Peacekeepers and the CF. In fact, it was the Peacekeepers who recovered the two C-7 rifles purloined during the actions on Tekakwitha Island. They were given back to 2 RCR the day after the troubled raid.[628] Lieutenant-Colonel Boswell captured the awkward position the Mohawk Peacekeepers were in:

> We dealt with the Native police regularly and I must admit all in all they were pretty darn good. They were stuck between a dog and a fire-hydrant and they were doing the best they could to enforce the law within their own community but also became a buffering factor between their community and the military which was not a welcomed or easy task. But they did it and I suspect they probably paid a price for it personally.[629]

The presence of the Peacekeepers was a positive attribute to the mission at Kahnawake. Acting as a go-between for the CF, the Band Council and the population led to greater lucidity during negotiations. With the help of the Peacekeepers, the situation at Kahnawake seemingly settled down after the Tekakwitha Island incident. The worries were now the return of the SQ to the Reserve, the loss of status by the Peacekeepers as sole police force in the community and the realization that, "Chief Joe Norton is trying to establish himself as an authority as Band Chief but he is a Warrior promoter and has shown time and again that he cannot be trusted."[630] Kanesatake had no Peacekeeping force as they were not an official Reserve and although a small difference, the absence of this force did have an impact on the military operations and the disclosure of plans as previously described by Colonel Tremblay.

The relationships at Kahnawake were threatened by the numerous raids within the village itself. 2 RCR and 3 R22eR were carrying out the role of a police force, in the form of crowd control and searches, for which they were not equipped or trained. The grudging acceptance by the Mohawks to CF presence turned violent as the cordon and searches intensified. Although the Mohawks accepted CF and LEA security around the perimeter and even agreed to dismantle the barricades, the raids nullified negotiated settlements that had been previously arranged. However, the raids did produce numerous weapons, including a .50 calibre sniping rifle as well as large deposits of contraband

and shocking government and military documents. On the surface the raids were a success. They helped restore security to the area in one sense, but in another sense created more animosity.

Without effects-based planning and surprised by the violent resistance mounted by the general Mohawk population, not just the Warriors, to the incursions into Kahnawake, the raids also had negative repercussions. The relationship between the CF and the peoples of Kahnawake worsened. The longer the Oka Crisis dragged on, the more the CF was seen by the Mohawk population as an occupying force. The uneasy relationship between the Canadian Forces and the citizens and leadership of Kahnawake was ameliorated by the mediation of the Kahnawake Peacekeepers. From all accounts, they performed their role diligently in a very precarious position. Nevertheless, with all traffic routes open in and around Kahnawake, the withdrawal of 2 RCR and 3 R22eR from this area of operation was contingent on the outcome at Kanesatake where the last radical elements were confined to the compound of the Treatment Centre.

At Kanesatake, the remaining protestors holed up in the TC refused to surrender themselves to the whims of the Canadian justice system. On 14 September, they stated that they would no longer use the one remaining telephone hotline, increasing the unknowns at the perimeter. The CF continued to promise that those who laid down their arms and vacated the TC would be placed under military control and custody and not under that of the SQ. The remaining Warriors continued to refuse this proposal.[631] Lieutenant-General Foster ordered 5 CMBG to, "continue to exercise progressive pressure to obtain the surrender of the Warriors entrenched at Oka and to restore public law and order in the areas of Oka and Kahnawake."[632]

CHAPTER 20

Exodus from the Treatment Centre

The prolongation of the standoff at Kanesatake was having implications on operations at Kahnawake. 2 R22eR was applying more pressure through patrols, lights, sound and by limiting communication and media access. However, negotiations were still ongoing. Most of the Mohawk community thought that the Oka Crisis had served their purpose. It brought governmental and national attention to their land claim of the Pines which had already been purchased by the federal government. Still, the Warriors inside knew that they would be arrested upon vacating the compound and when they did finally exit on the night of 26 September they did so according to their design, not in the framework which had been agreed upon.

Lieutenant-General Foster publicly stated on 20 September that no other negotiation points from the Warriors would be entertained other than the matter of disengagement. Further to the point, Foster announced that he had been advised that no transfer of the land obtained earlier by the federal government at Oka would take place until the Warriors laid down their weapons and were treated in accordance with the laws of Canada.[633] Behind the scenes, Foster proposed a number of measures to resolve the situation which were acquiesced to by his political peers.

It was agreed that no one outside of the TC could negotiate for the Warriors and that no one should answer their "never-ending list of questions." It was also stressed that neither the CF nor governments should confer on those inside the perimeter the status or belief that they were speaking on behalf of the Mohawk Nation: "The Warriors speak for themselves." Foster proceeded to give three courses open to end the crisis in considerable detail. The first was a "Final Assault." This, he believed would lead to bloodshed while putting the children inside the TC at grave risk: "THIS OPTION CONSIDERING THE PRESENT SITUATION IS BEYOND MINIMUM FORCE." The second course of action was dramatically "Increasing the Pressure." This amounted to cutting off food, water, clothing, electricity, heating oil and clothes to the TC: "Such a decision would reverse our position that food and other necessities would not be used as a weapon. THIS OPTION CONSIDERING THE PRESENT SITUATION IS BEYOND MINIMUM FORCE." It was assessed that while not resorting to the denial of food and essential resources, pressure tactics would increase in scope to include the media as well.[634]

The CF was becoming increasingly concerned and agitated with the journalists still inside the TC. The reports coming from inside were often misrepresented and it appeared to the CF and other external journalists that those inside were suffering from what was known as "Stockholm Syndrome." Although no journalists were held against their will, "Stockholm Syndrome" describes the behaviour of kidnapped victims who, over time, become sympathetic to and identify with their captors or guards in close contact stressful situations.[635]

In order to alleviate this problem and the perceived biased reports originating from inside the TC, which evidently incorporated Warrior rhetoric and propaganda, the CF legally secured the right to deactivate the known cellphones of Warriors and journalists operating in the Oka area. Through EW, the CF also restricted the ability for any cellphone to effectively operate in the area. Both were initiated on 14 September. However, the most proactive recourse was the CF decision on 16 September to stop the flow of all tapes, films, text and copy to or from reporters within the Detoxification Centre. Many journalists were furious, citing the *Charter of Rights and Freedoms* and calling the tactic "war-like censorship." The CF released a statement countering these claims using legal documentation and court approvals.[636]

With the increasing pressure put on those inside the TC by 2 R22eR and other branches of the CF, the mood at the perimeter became increasingly tense. The Warriors crept out of the perimeter and stole flares and other military devices. On two occasions they discharged red flares, trying to hit a helicopter on one occasion. At one point they threw a smoke grenade at the soldiers opposite their position and cocked their weapons. The soldiers responded alike.[637]

After the raid on Tekakwitha, "Lasagna" from inside the TC went on the air of the Kahnawake radio station and exclaimed that the people inside the TC were disappointed with the lack of support from their brethren. He told the people of Kahnawake to take a stand against the Army and that all of the men in the TC were prepared to fight.[638] The fact that "Lasagna" successfully transmitted his message revealed the holes in the CF's jamming network.

Warriors frequently probed the perimeter, trying to cut or jump the wire and test the likelihood of escape by these means. Each attempt was thwarted by the reaction of soldiers. On 23 September the Warriors pelted the soldiers with bottles, rocks and pieces of wood which they had been stockpiling. The scene was repeated on the night of the 25th and the soldiers responded by using a high powered water hose to push the Warriors back from the wire with mixed results.[639] As dawn broke on the morning of the 26th off-duty soldiers played hide and go seek with a group of Mohawk children. This relaxed atmosphere was not indicative of the situation inside the TC.[640]

Inside the TC the mood and relations had become argumentative. Many believed that the original goal of saving the Pines and bringing the government to the negotiating table had been fulfilled. Canada, and to some extent the world, had taken notice of the Kanesatake Mohawk and prolonging the crisis served no further purpose. However, many of the more radical Warriors still maintained the belief that they were willing to die for the cause and in effect become martyrs. They also distrusted the authorities and knew that they would be arrested upon exiting the perimeter. What little freedom they had inside the perimeter and confines of the TC was better than no freedom in a penal institution. Many of the journalists and supporters had already left including lawyer Stanley Cohen and reporter Geoffrey York.[641]

After some coaxing, the radical Warriors inside the TC agreed to leave in what they described as a "unilateral cessation of hostilities," not a surrender.[642] Arrangements for the exit of those in the TC had been agreed upon two days earlier in the presence of Stanley Cohen. Colonel Tremblay recounted the plan and eventual happenings:

> We had three companies around the perimeter short of the water. Everything was put in place for an orderly extradition to the east of the TC along 344. The entire plan was to have them exit in an orderly fashion to the main gate, separated into groups of men and women and children get on the awaiting buses and move out to Farnham. But these were clever people and that would not make the case and would be discrete without media attention [the media had been moved further east], so that is not what happened.[643]

Before exiting, those inside the TC destroyed their weapons, equipment and documents in a fire or dumped them into a cesspool. They held a traditional Mohawk ceremony, packed their belongings and said their goodbyes. At 1855hrs, the column of children, women and Warriors slowly approached the main gate towards the awaiting soldiers and buses. At the halfway point the unarmed parade took a sharp right turn towards the northeast corner of the perimeter where the media was gathered. Stretcher boards were laid over the wire and the massed group began to scatter creating a chaotic scene. CF representation was scant as most of 2 R22eR had been deployed to the centre at the arranged departing area.[644]

The Mohawks and their supporters in the TC breached the wire in the location of Colonel (then Major) Tremblay's "C" Coy:

> We managed to contain 99 per cent of them, some managed to escape and squeeze out. It was quite nasty, because there were no weapons so we got into hand to hand trying to control and restrain people. But it gave them a lot of visibility again so their final moment was extensively covered by the press. I was hand to hand fighting with Mad Jap. They breached the wire and walked out women and children first and they were pushing very hard and that woman [Waneek Horn-Miller] got the bayonet wound. I was standing right there and saw it. The two soldiers said, 'Stop moving, stop moving,' and she basically impaled herself on the bayonet. They were trying to force their way out but our orders were very clear—to contain them. It was a great lesson on how to set up wire though. People can breach it easier than we thought.[645]

One of those who snuck down the road towards Oka was Loran Thompson. After breaking clean of the rabble, he managed to hitch a ride in town and made his way to U.S. Akwesasne. On 2 October he turned himself in at the RCMP station at Westmount and was handed over to the SQ.[646] CF intelligence had previously done psychological appreciations on everyone present in the TC and also collected all legal and financial records relating to the more radical holdouts:

> Loran Thompson was an extremely clever individual. He got out. A very resourceful man. We got a financial profile on him. He was managing these bingo halls and although his salary wasn't large he was taking 4 per cent of the gross take, tax free. Imagine the money this guy had. I have to say I was surprised by the amount of wealth a few people were accumulating through gambling, smuggling and other questionable activities.[647]

Waneek Horn-Miller was indeed stabbed in her sternum by a bayonet. She remembered the unfortunate events with vivid recollection:

> They put us in front to protect us, so that we were not mistaken as adults when the fights broke out. I had all of the children and I'll never forget my sister screaming. It was something no one should ever have to hear. The soldier in front of me froze and I pushed him backwards and walked by him. I think he was as scared as I was. We originally didn't go out the way we were supposed to because the media wasn't there and we wanted them there for our safety. Everyone was afraid that even if by accident a shot was fired, there had been enough tension that summer that we would be blown away. I had my sister by my side and I was carrying a lot of stuff. I was trying to make my way to the media barricade and a soldier kept pushing me back. I was not going backwards because I thought my safety zone was ahead towards the media. I don't really remember what happened but I just couldn't breath but I got stabbed and I fell forward and someone kicked my feet out from under me and I was pulled backwards. I was in such a state of hysteria and fear that I don't really remember. I was scared and angry. I only realized on the bus that I had actually been stabbed. On the bus the women MP actually kicked me back as I approached her to get medical attention. Being totally at the mercy of someone else was scary. We didn't know what was going to happen.[648]

By 1955hrs, with an influx of 2 R22eR reinforcements, the situation was under control. The Mohawks and their supporters were loaded onto two buses for transportation to Farnham. In all 26 men, 16 women, 10 journalists and six children arrived at Farnham in military custody at 2215hrs. They were processed and photographed in the drill hall and then placed in a guarded section behind a large burlap screen all under authorization of the service custody regulations section 277 of the *National Defence Act*. Eight others including Ronald "Lasagna" Cross were arrested by the SQ during the exodus and were in SQ custody at St. Eustache.[649] The standoff which had lasted 78 days was over.

The final stand at Kanesatake had immediate repercussions on the uneasy peace at Kahnawake and Akwesasne. Based on the events that occurred at Kahnawake it was obvious that communication lines existed between those in the TC and their Kahnawake brethren until the final moments. In addition, a weapons sweep of St. Nicolas Island by 3 R22eR earlier in the day angered many Kahnawake residents. Similar to past raids, they viewed this as an incursion into Mohawk territory by a foreign force. Although some Mohawks did harass the soldiers performing the search, they left on the recommendation of the Peacekeepers.

On 26 September at 1942hrs, a Warrior dispatch was intercepted. This message summoned all Warriors and supporters to the Legion Hall. Ten minutes later the alarm was rung at the Kahnawake fire station. At 2025hrs a group of 200 Mohawks armed with bats and axe handles removed the barbed wire and attacked an EW installation and set its tent on fire. New wire was erected, "B" Coy 3 R22eR was deployed to reinforce the position and the group withdrew quickly. However, they moved to strike another CF location.[650]

Correspondingly, between 2000hrs and 2020hrs physical altercations took place between 2 RCR and a growing group of 100 Mohawks. Warrior radio traffic continued to request that more supporters advance to the 2 RCR barricade at Highway 138. By 2030hrs, the angry mob had swelled to roughly 300 and overran 2 RCR's forward position and continued to press forward pelting the soldiers with rocks and bottles. Many were carrying bats, batons, shields and gas masks which had been purchased after the Tekakwitha Island raid. One soldier was struck with a stone and beaten. A section of troops was ordered forward and after hand to hand fighting they retrieved the injured soldier and withdrew. Yet, the crowd continued to surge forward and the requests of platoon commander Lieutenant Dave Selhaney to stop, fell of deaf ears.[651]

He then ordered his soldiers to fix bayonets and form a defensive line. The crowd surged forward. Three canisters of CS gas were fired into the crowd with little result. Six rounds of M38 were fired as a warning but the Mohawks continued to advance. Another three shots from a C-7 were fired at the ground. Only after Lieutenant Selhaney ordered his soldiers to load their weapons and gave direct fire orders to aim at the ring leaders did the crowd stop. At this time another platoon arrived in reinforcement and a negotiated withdrawal of the Mohawks took place. Two Mohawks were injured and one soldier was treated with 45 stitches after being beaten over the head with a lead pipe. He also suffered a fractured skull.[652] The incident became known as the "Riot at K3B." The Mercier Bridge was closed by the SQ for three hours during the melee and was reopened shortly after midnight. As a result of the events of 26 September, the Canadian Airborne Regiment was placed on three hours standby as a quick reaction force. Fortunately, they were not needed.[653]

Akwesasne was also more active on the night of 26-27 September due to the finality at the TC. Several RCMP cars were vandalized. LEA personnel were threatened on numerous occasions. They were also pelted with a wide variety of objects ranging from tomatoes to large stones. Three reported cases of shooting incidents during the early morning were also reported. The 37 CF personnel were placed in alert to extract police forces. However, this did not occur.[654]

The following morning a joint SQ/CF team conducted an extensive search in and around the TC. The sweep revealed trench positions and also the remains of 54 weapons in the smouldering fire. The breakdown of the weapons was: 12 shotguns, 4 handguns, 10 rifles and 28 semi-automatic assault rifles.[655] Inside the TC itself there was overwhelming evidence of fortified positions, boxes of ammunition and in the words of the CDS himself, "There was an awful lot of frozen food in the freezers. There were loads of food: canned food, frozen meat, etc. There were also cars inside."[656] Colonel Tremblay was part of the initial search:

> The human rights violations that were reported were never the case. Basic human needs were provided. When we searched the TC, they had food, water and reserves for still a while. To say it was against the Geneva Convention or human rights that would not be true. It could be perceived that way but there was no way we were going to allow beer, alcohol and those types of thing to enter. There is a difference between basic needs and things that could be potentially dangerous. But perception can be made into what ever people want to believe is reality. There was plenty of food and water and diapers for a while. It is a question of perspectives.[657]

Reports regarding the denial of food and basic resources by the CF had been published throughout the standoff at the TC. Many of these reports came from journalists inside the TC. This was generally not the case. The CF actively participated in the resupply of those inside the TC delivering packages and boxes over the wire perimeter.

However, certain soldiers did make independent decisions to damage food packages with bayonets or urinate on parcels of food and clothing. Waneek Horn-Miller's school books sent by her teacher and principal from Glebe Collegiate in Ottawa never found their way into her hands inside the TC. Rotten food parcels were also delivered to the TC. These actions and denials were not CF policy and these soldiers were charged in military court if they were caught in the act or if enough evidence against them was accrued. Another soldier who tried to cross the perimeter shortly before the exit from the TC, wanting to steal a Warrior flag was also punished. In actuality, there was not one CF unit that did not terminate an officer for incompetence or malfeasance. At one point during the middle of the crisis, the entire administrative staff of the Farnham Base Security Company was fired and replaced.[658]

With the final search of the TC, it appeared that 2 R22eR had accomplished its four-point mandate. Lieutenant-Colonel Pierre Daigle, commander of 2 R22eR, initiated preparations for the withdrawal of his battalion in a handover of responsibilities to the SQ. By 29 September, only the 2 R22eR rear party remained in Oka. The remainder had relocated to Saint-Benoît and then to Farnham on 1 October. The SQ was now responsible for all operations in Kanesatake. At Kahnawake, the military presence continued although the CF elements gradually began to thin out. The last weapons search was conducted by 3 R22eR on 7 October. A cave was searched for weapons with no results.[659]

On 2 October, General de Chastelain sent a letter to Premier Bourassa outlining the decrease in CF manning and the transition plan to hand over all operations to the SQ. It was made clear that a battalion would remain on standby until the Premier, through the medium of the Attorney-General of Quebec, cancelled the request for Aid to the Civil Power. On the 3rd, Lieutenant-General Foster publicly announced the timeline for the withdrawal of 5 CMBG. By 9 October, 1,582 CF personnel remained active in Operation SALON. Overall, 4,500 soldiers had been deployed throughout the crisis. At any one time the peak deployment was 3,700. Included in the total numbers were almost 700 Reservists and 180 females.[660]

5 CMBG continued to reduce its numbers. The Canadian Airborne Regiment was released from its Operation SALON reaction force tasking on 3 October. By 5 October, all detainees at the military custody area at Farnham had either been released or handed over to the Quebec judicial system; therefore, the custody area was closed. By 15 October, only 2 EW Sqn and 3 R22eR remained in Farnham as a rapid reaction force (RRF) to support LEAs. The remainder of 5 CMBG elements had returned to their home bases at Valcartier and Gagetown. 2 EW Sqn returned to Kingston on 26 October. By 31 October, all remaining CF participation was removed from the Kahnawake/Montreal area. 3 R22eR continued to be tasked as the RRF on 12 hours NTM from Valcartier.[661]

The Government of Quebec still refused to withdrawal its request for CF assistance. With the questionable legislation of *Aid to the Civil Power*, Quebec could maintain the assurances of CF participation for as long as it desired. However, the amount of CF participation was left in the hands of the FMC commander Lieutenant-General Foster having been appointed by the CDS. On 2 November, Foster told Claude Ryan that one company from 3 R22eR was now on 36 hours NTM as the RRF. Ryan responded by stating that a withdrawal of the request has not yet been discussed and it was the intention of the Province of Quebec to maintain the request until it deemed that the situations at Kanesatake and Kahnawake had proven stable. The Government of Quebec officially withdrew its request for *Aid to the Civil Power* in writing on 30 May 1991.[662] Operation SALON was finally terminated after 10 months.

The direct participation of CF personnel actually lasted longer for Operation AKWESASNE. On 14 November LEAs reported that CF support to their operations was no longer required. As a result, all CF personnel and stores were returned to their home units by 23 November. On 1 December, DND sent a letter to the Solicitor-General of Canada indicating the military's intention to be released from its role of *Provision of Armed Assistance.* Operation AKWESASNE was officially concluded by Pierre Cadieux, the Solicitor-General, on 5 December 1990. The deployment, reaching its zenith at 373 CF personnel, had lasted just over seven months.[663]

Although the standoff ended on 26 September and all CF forces were removed from the various areas of operation by November, the strife in Mohawk territory did not end. After the withdrawal of the CF and LEAs, the Reserves reverted back to no-go zones. The internal violence, factionalism and smuggling continued. The convergence of cultures had reached its breaking point in Mohawk country, but was by no means over.

CONCLUSION

Section I: The Canadian Forces

Although the soldiers accomplished their tasks without any loss of life and 5 CMBG met its objectives, the standoff illuminated inherent problems associated with IS operations. These problems existed not only in the political arenas but also throughout the strategic and operational doctrines originating at NDHQ for domestic operations. The most obvious lesson learned was that a review of the *National Defence Act* and the principles of *Aid to the Civil Power* in conjunction with the *Emergencies Act* needed to be analyzed and subjected to scrutiny in light of the crisis. This included not only the power of requisition but also the chain of command and an override clause within the current legislation to include the role of the CDS, the Minister of National Defence, the requisitioning province and finally the Prime Minister. In addition, the cost capture for *Aid to the Civil Power* needed to be re-examined.

The cost for Operation FEATHER/AKWESASNE totalled $840,000.[664] The cost of Operation SALON for the Canadian Forces was $120 million, of which 80 per cent would have been incurred on exercises, training and other previously planned activities had the operation not taken place.[665] The cost for the RCMP was an additional $25 million.[666] In relation, the Oka Crisis cost the Province of Quebec $108 million of which $71 million was paid by the federal government in compensation.[667] The financial burden to the federal government, and in relation to the taxpayer nationwide, was consistent with Part 7 of the *Emergencies Act*, which states that such military activities are a federal responsibility in accordance with Section 91(7) of the *Constitution Act*.[668]

Other agencies incurred costs as a result of the events during the summer of 1990. The Province of Ontario provided transportation and accommodation in Cornwall to Mohawk refugees fleeing Akwesasne in the midst of the violence. The OPP also incurred inflated costs due to its involvement in Akwesasne.[669] The Canadian Red Cross' bill totalled $144,275 for its humanitarian efforts in Kanesatake and Kahnawake.[670]

On a strategic level, military intervention cannot constitute an end in itself. Any intervention by the CF must at most be one step in a governmental plan which should be followed by a settlement or, at the least, political negotiations. Political decisions cannot be derived on the spot from the actions of the CF on the ground. For the CF itself, both the Oka Crisis and the Gulf War led to the development of the J-Staff system within NDHQ contributing to greater overall organization and efficiency.[671]

Lack of military knowledge in the general population, the absence of recent IS operations and the lack of familiarity of military culture at the political level resulted in poor mutual understanding between military and civil authorities during Operation SALON. Politicians, government officials and LEAs had limited knowledge of military capabilities, weapons effects, planning, deployment procedures, reaction times and control methods. The implications of ordering a military assault on the barricades in the presence of civilians were not understood.

What is for certain is that had the Oka Crisis deteriorated to the point of engagement, the outcome would have been disastrous. Given the parameters of the Canadian Forces' mandate and the weapons present within Warrior circles, the CF would have, had it been deemed necessary, used appropriate military means to end the impasse. As General de Chastelain noted upon Quebec's request for the CF under *Aid to the Civil Power*, "The government has now gone to the court of last resort, which is us. We cannot fail, because we are all that is left."[672] Given this realization and the disparate margin between the CF and the Warriors with regards to weapon systems, number of personnel and professional military training, there can be no question as to what the outcome would have been. Thankfully, all parties involved maintained enough dialogue and discipline to avoid such an unthinkable outcome to resolve the immediate elements of the Oka Crisis.

In addition, the civil authority (Quebec) was astounded and frustrated by the time it took the CF to plan operations. Considerable time and discussion were required to arrive at a consensus between military and civilian agencies.[673] If called out in the role of *Aid to the Civil Power*, CF commanders need freedom of action. Concomitant with this freedom, bureaucratic and political interference in CF operations should be eliminated or minimized.[674]

Accordingly, contingency plans must be maintained and developed through intensified and more focused liaison between political leaders, government officials and police forces to improve planning for future operations. A closer and more structured civil/military relationship is also required at all levels. Joint training of CF personnel, including Reservists, and LEAs is necessary to avoid confusion with jurisdiction, command and control and equipment when deployed in combined operations.[675] This includes the sharing of all intelligence materials.

During Operation SALON, the media played a large factor in the shaping of the public perception and demonstrated that relations with the public, including the media, must be an integral part of the operational plan. It was noted that a technical network of public affairs staff should have a representative at every level of the chain of command, thus avoiding confusion of facts and statements while providing the media with a unified CF front. Furthermore, the approach to the media should be proactive, not reactive. It was also noted that the requirement for legal advisors at all levels existed. Due to the delicate nature of IS operations, it is vital that the legal framework of the operation be understood at all levels.

This legal jurisdiction also includes a better understanding of the ROEs. The concept of "use of minimum force" cannot be narrowly defined. This principle and the legality that it never be violated were paramount. Since the Oka Crisis, ROEs have become extremely intricate, complex and lengthy. They are not blanket statements; rather, mission orientated. This evolution occurred after the Oka Crisis during subsequent CF missions to the Balkans throughout the 1990s. This was lacking during the operations in Mohawk country in 1990, the result of which was confusion amongst soldiers on the ground as to what they could and could not do.

The lack of ROEs during Operation SALON and Operation AKWESASNE was accentuated by the lack of training for IS operations including crowd confrontation. Had soldiers been trained for the riot scenarios they encountered and had the proper equipment—shields and batons—the volatile situations, including the use of warning shots on many occasions, might have been less violent and confrontational. Although warning shots seemed to quell the violence on most occasions, they also could have sparked the opposite reaction.

In accordance, better effects-based planning was needed. Even though the Mercier Bridge had reopened, unsure of its mission, 5 CMBG ordered a series of raids aimed at seizing contraband and weapons. Although many weapons were confiscated, these raids presented some of the uglier images of the crisis, undermining the overall performance of the CF. These raids also heightened tensions and stirred up the resentment of the Mohawk population at large, not just its more radical members. By taking up "offensive operations", the CF gave the Mohawk media and propaganda opportunities they would not have had.[676]

The raids also intensified the general resolve of the Mohawk population to achieve sovereignty and resist the encroachment of government agencies onto their land. The consequences of this resentment made its way into CF recruitment policy. In 1999, the CF recruitment guide, *Strengthening Relationships Between the Canadian Forces and Aboriginal People (Recruitment Guide)* directed CF personnel to, "Avoid the following references: the conflict at Oka, Quebec, the dispute at Ipperwash, Ontario... The 1990 incident is still an emotional topic with many First Nations. It invokes negative images of the CF and any reference to Oka should be avoided in a First Nations setting."[677]

Despite these infrequent tarnishes, the CF did maintain a positive and professional outward appearance to the Canadian public. One reason for the actions of the soldiers on the ground was the familiarity of working and training together within the regimental structure. This concept was stressed by numerous CF personnel that were interviewed. Major Lambert asserted that, "The thing we wouldn't be as good at now is the stability and the discipline from our sections having been together for a long time, what you get with formed Regiments and sub-units having been in garrison and the messes as opposed to a group coming together just a few months before deploying operationally. The Regimental style works."[678] Prime Minister Mulroney lauded the CF's performance: "The Canadian Forces...are to be commended for the level of professionalism that has been evident throughout.... All the personnel of 5 Brigade showed great courage and almost superhuman self-control in the face of extraordinary provocation. They have earned Canadians' respect and gratitude for a difficult job well done."[679]

As both Operation AKWESASNE and Operation SALON were domestic, no CF individuals were awarded decorations and no campaign medal was issued, although 5 CMBG was awarded the Canadian Forces' Unit Commendation (which is not worn on uniforms).[680] Both Operation SALON and Operation AKWESASNE illustrated the high level of professionalism within the ranks of the CF but also the flaws associated with IS operations and planning. Over a year after the crisis, Lieutenant-General Foster made these observations:

> The possibility exists that we could be faced with a number of similar incidents across Canada, in which case our limited trained resources would be quickly exhausted.... We must not hold back from early discussion with civil authorities at the outset of any potential crisis...and increase early warning. At the same time we must look closely at our own...organizations to fit them as

> best we can for the simultaneous conduct of operations similar to Operation Salon in more than one region.[681]

It is also a little known fact that during Operation SALON, the CF evacuated 850 Native Canadians using CC-130 Hercules transport aircraft and CC-115 Buffalo aircraft on two separate occasions from Webequie, Ontario in the face of spreading forest fires. Although information regarding these airlifts of July and August was relayed to public media agencies through the CF Defence Media Liaison Office, neither humanitarian assistance airlift was reported. In light of Oka, the media seemed to be focused on guns and golf courses and not the positive disaster-relief operations concurrently being undertaken by the CF.[682]

In actuality, the Oka Crisis was not be the first time the CF was tasked to quell Native violence and insurgency. In 1989, local Innu protesting the decision to make CFB Goose Bay a NATO aerial training range began camping on the runway and range area. They claimed that the low level flights of fighter planes and the subsequent live-fire training disrupted the migratory patterns of the Caribou. CF Reservists from the Atlantic region were tasked to guard the base and remove protestors in what was dubbed Operation UNIQUE. The affair ended peacefully and the Innu took their complaint to the judicial system.[683]

If the governments of Canada are not prepared to tackle the larger issues and roots of the problems plaguing Aboriginal communities the CF could be called upon in the future to quell Native uprisings. The Canadian Forces must be adequately equipped and trained, as given the current legislation they cannot refuse a request for military intervention. Unless alterations in the political arenas occur in consultation with Aboriginal leaders, the convergence of cultures towards violent clashes will continue.

Section II: Native-Government Relations

The outcome of the Oka Crisis for the Mohawk Nation was varied. The federal government did procure the disputed land and turn it over to the Mohawk of Kanesatake. The tiny cemetery was also purchased for one dollar. However, all of the land belongs to the Crown, reserved for the use of the Aboriginal population. In 2001 Bill *S-24: The Kanesatake Interim Land Base Governance Act* was passed detailing the rules and regulations between the territory of Kanesatake and the governments of Canada and Quebec. This legislation is unique to Kanesatake, as it still does not fall under the *Indian Act* and is not a Reserve.[684]

Another positive aspect which resulted from Oka was that the federal government abolished the regulation to only examine six comprehensive land claims at one time. In conjunction, the province of British Columbia finally recognized that Native Canadians had land rights and agreed to the principles of land claim issues.[685] Aside from these issues, the Oka Crisis did little to change the policies of DIAND and the federal government, while it broadened the divides already present within the Mohawk Nation.

For the communities of Akwesasne, Kahnawake and Kanesatake the cleaves of internal politics remained after the crisis. The Warrior Society stayed active and the influence of their activities continued to plague the communities. Only two of the 37 Mohawks charged were ever convicted: Ronald "Lasagna" Cross and Gordon "Noriega" Lazore. Neither served a full sentence. These communities still suffer from degradation and from violence derived from their internal political divides. Once again the Mohawk territories have become no-go zones for LEAs. Both Kahnawake and Akwesasne continue to have their own Peacekeeper police forces and Kanesatake was granted the same in 1997.[686] Certain members of the Mohawk Nation continue to expound the belief that they are a sovereign nation not subject to outside governance and laws. While certain traditionalists contend that they are not subject to the laws of a foreign government, they have been quick to take advantage of the legislation that these governments accord them. They do not hesitate to use the *Jay Treaty* or to invoke the Canadian Constitutional Charter. At the Oka inquest, many Mohawks also invoked the protection of section 5 of the *Evidence Act* so that they were not compelled to testify.[687]

It is apparent that the Warrior Society and its sect of followers are using this duality to gain on all fronts to promote their radical agendas. They use litigation to enhance these agendas but also do not hesitate to borrow the tactics of revolutionary insurgency in order to intimidate the opposition within their own communities and also the governments of Canada. After the Oka Crisis, the Government of Canada was reluctant to become embroiled in another standoff and took a hands-off approach to dealing with the continuing smuggling, intimidation and revolutionary upheaval spawned by the Warrior Society. Correspondingly, lawlessness and the influence of the Warrior Society increased in Mohawk territories, nowhere more prevalenty than in Akwesasne. In this sense, the Warriors won the Oka Crisis and same situation of pre-1990 was continued.

As smuggling activity increased, the violence between the Native factions increased as well. By 1993, the smuggling and violence was reaching epidemic proportions and gunfire became a common sound to the residents of Akwesasne and neighbouring Cornwall. As of 1993, "sin-taxes" on tobacco and alcohol had grown enormously. The price of a pack of cigarettes in Canada was double that of the same brand in the United States. These costs and the increased demand created unparalleled profit margins for the "Silks" and the Warriors. At Akwesasne, $3.6 billion worth of tobacco products were flowing south to north through the Reserve, in addition to alcohol and weapons. In exchange, the Warriors shuttled counterfeit money, illegal aliens and narcotics south. Before 1990, loose ties had existed between the Warrior Society and organized crime. By 1993, these connections had grown stronger and larger to include the Chinese triads, the Russian Mafia, Jamaican Posses and other ethnic mafia organizations. A senior police officer in Cornwall described the area as the, "Klondike of organized crime [and] multiculturalism's finest hour."[688]

Ottawa was finally ready to act. Throughout December 1993 and January 1994, strategies were discussed and preparations and training were conducted for joint operations in all three Mohawk territories by CSIS personnel, elite members of Joint Task Force 2 (or JTF 2, Canada's Special Forces), 800 RCMP officers and over 2,000 CF members. The operation was given two names: Operation CAMPUS and Operation SCORPION-SAXON. The first was used in reference to the actual operation. The second was a decoy used to describe a "training exercise" in order to deceive the media about the real actions. Members of JTF 2 and the CF conducted training exercises similar to those of 5 CMBG leading up to deployment during Operation SALON. Stories were concocted and released to the media to mislead journalists about the movements of CF personnel and equipment throughout the country during January and February 1994.[689]

The operation was eventually called off eight days prior to its scheduled start. Intelligence revealed that the element of surprise had been lost and that the actions would lead to bloodshed and the possibility of a nationwide indigenous uprising. Instead, the government took notice of the reduced sales and tax revenue from alcohol and tobacco and lessened "sin-taxes." Although never disappearing, the cigarette industry in Mohawk territory took a hard hit.[690] Nevertheless, JTF 2 members were covertly inserted on the Reserves to conduct surveillance on smuggling personnel and routes. This information was relayed to other LEAs.[691]

To placate the different political elements present at Kanesatake and attempt to find common ground, the structure of the band council was changed to combine the traditional and electoral systems. Before the Oka Crisis, Chiefs were appointed by Clan Mothers. The council consisted of three Chiefs from each clan (Turtle, Bear, Wolf) including one Grand Chief. After the crisis, the council was amended to consist of six Chiefs and one Grand Chief (instead of eight) all elected by the people. However, most of the Longhouse followers refuse to vote, deeming the electoral system to be a bastardization of the Great Law of Peace.

The political divides remain as evidenced as recent as 2004. Grand Chief James Gabriel, with the help of DIAND, gathered a group of Aboriginal police officers from other regions of Quebec in a large anti-crime raid on Kanesatake targeting cigarette dealers and the mounting number of drug growers and operators. In order to do this Gabriel bypassed the Kanesatake Police Commission and also secured a $900,000 emergency loan from DIAND. This compounded the already rising debt of the band council. Gabriel had also negotiated and agreed to the controversial Bill S-24 in 2001, which angered many Longhouse supporters.

The police raid went ahead on 12 January 2004, causing violence within Kanesatake. In light of the resistance, Gabriel requested SQ intervention. The provincial authorities refused. Soon after the conglomeration of police forces left the community, Gabriel was forced to flee to Laval after his house was set ablaze. He was later defeated in an election, losing to Steven Bonspille on 26 June 2005. However, the six band members elected with Bonspille are Gabriel supporters. The political stalemate continues and the divisions in the community are far from reaching a consensus. Ellen Gabriel recognized the inherent problems in Kanesatake:

> The Longhouse people stand in the way of the moderates who are now the ones that really control the community, like last year when they burned James Gabriel's house down. These are the moderates who have been able to do what ever they want in the community without any prosecution by the SQ or anyone else. We know they [SQ] have surveillance and the means to come in and to get rid of these criminal elements within the community. I think 15 years ago up to now it is still in place; the undermining. Also in land claims the government sets all the rules and the conditions for negotiations. There is no flexibility or consultation for the Aboriginal people to say, 'No this is not what we wanted and we want to approach it this way.' If you say that then they replace you with someone else through the department [DIAND] who will perform their agenda. The impact of colonization

> throughout the Americas has created a lot of dysfunction and I told Prime Minister Martin that when we had our meeting.... You may think that you are not responsible because these things happened before you were born, but no, the perpetuation of colonization, institutional racism, these are the things hampering our people. As long as this trend continues there is going to be difficulties, problems, unrest and all the high incidents of 'the whatever' in our communities.[692]

If the legacy of Oka is represented by any single facet within the community of indigenous peoples of Canada, it is that the trend of violent insurgency has not diminished. Young radical Natives respect neither the laws of Canada nor the traditional authority of the First Nations peoples. Using the assertion of legitimate Aboriginal grievances, they undermine the peaceful intentions and negotiations of the people they purportedly represent. For the Government of Canada, the legacy of Oka is that Mohawk threats and frustrations went unheeded by successive governments for 300 years. Although certain amendments were made to the framework of land claim policies and governmental influence at Kanesatake, little has actually changed. Ipperwash, Gustafsen Lake and the current barricade at the Six Nations Reserve near Caledonia demonstrate that the dissatisfaction of Canada's Native population has not been mollified. In relation, the militant trend within Aboriginal communities continues. According to Mohawk Waneek Horn-Miller, "It is alive and well."[693]

The revival of Native traditions and Aboriginal rights through peaceful means is understandable and extremely necessary for the future of both Native territories and Canada as a whole. Unless the Government of Canada and those of its Provinces find alternative and compromising ways of dealing with the complex problems associated with indigenous Canadians and their legitimate demands, there can be no doubt that extreme Native factions will continue to usurp power and promote an atmosphere of violence. DIAND must incorporate Native concerns into its policies for land claims. Aboriginal contributions into the legislation and mechanisms which influence their communities and lives must be recognized. To avoid future violence, Canadians must also learn new views about Native peoples and their cultures and reassess our own duties and responsibilities to these proud people and provide the respect they deserve. Confrontational tactics should not be the court of last resort.

However, the onus for a more co-operative and harmonious existence does not rest solely with the non-Native population and governments of Canada. Native Canadians must come to some unified consensus and contingency plan as to the direction they see themselves progressing. Simply claiming to be a sovereign nation and clinging to an isolationist policy is not the answer. They must understand and accept the constraints imposed by the historical record of events which has influenced their nations.

Promoting legitimate grievances through the use of violence and insurgency tactics is also not an option. The violent manifestations of a select few Mohawks who wish to maintain the power and money of their communities to the detriment of sincere and legitimate grievances must cease. The Reserves must somehow rid themselves of the presence of the violent radicals and unify themselves to peacefully promote their justifiable and valid voice of complaints. When this occurs, the governments involved must listen and co-operate to find a solution that both parties can agree upon and live with by incorporating the Native voice and concerns. To achieve this end, Mohawk territories cannot remain "no-go zones" for LEAs. The "un-policing" of the Reserve in the past left them to the mercy of corrupt elements. That was and should not remain Canada's failure to those undeserving of such communities.

The RCMP reported in May 2006 that seizures of contraband cigarettes at Akwesasne were on the rise, confiscating 100,000 more cases of cigarettes in 2005 than in 1994, when they began keeping inventory. The year 2005 saw a 20 per cent increase in confiscated contraband compared to the year before. Currently, 10 factories are operating on the Akwesasne Reserve with only four having official licence.[694] In addition, a 1996 *Globe and Mail* report cited that U.S. Border Security had intercepted 299 "deportable aliens" moving across the border through Akwesasne between October 1995 and October 1996. Another report connected Akwesasne with international human smuggling networks transporting "thousands of illegal immigrants into Canada...a new breed of global outlaws."[695] There is also evidence linking Akwesasne to the movement of Al-Qaeda operatives shortly before 9/11.[696]

As it stands, the process of alienation and mutual distrust continue to plague Native-government relations. The Oka Crisis did little to solve the larger problems of corruption within the administration of Native communities. Nor did the Oka Crisis remove the hard stance of the government to accept the radical agenda or to negotiate with Natives carrying weapons or threatening to use them to achieve their revolutionary goals. The use of weapons and violence does not follow the Great Law of Peace. Alternatively, the use of the CF cannot be used to solve problems that should be negotiated by all parties involved in a room at Parliament and around a sacred fire. As tactical commander Brigadier-General Roy aptly stated at the end of the crisis, "There is no glory in conducting an operation like this in your own country against your fellow citizens."[697] Confrontational tactics to remedy the convergence of cultures should not be the court of last resort. When asked if another Oka was likely, Ellen Gabriel replied:

> It is possible because you have the same situation happening. But the likelihood is not as great as 15 years ago. I think people are trying to use words; however, the government is learning that they cannot only pay attention to the deep-rooted concerns and the long-standing issues of Aboriginal people only if you put up a barricade. Still before 1990 the government only recognized the Band Councils which they imposed on the communities, a system created by them and it is still continuing today. They put a lot of things in the disguise of self-government but it is still not self-determination.[698]

EPILOGUE

From Oka to Caledonia—The Clash Continues

The historical record since Oka illustrates that little has changed and that certain elements of the Native Canadian population perceive the erection of barricades or occupation of lands as the only means by which to bring governments to the negotiating table. In reality, the Government of Canada was assessing future Native "hot-spots" during the Oka Crisis itself. Ipperwash eventually became the setting for another violent confrontation between Native activists and the Ontario Provincial Police (OPP) in 1995. During the Oka Crisis, in response to the national support for the Mohawks given by other First Nation communities, the CF, in conjunction with other security agencies, was tasked to complete a threat assessment of areas and Reserves where potential violence was likely.

The final document was called "The Next Oka." Heading the list of 118 locations was Ipperwash, Ontario, 35km northeast of Sarnia on shores of Lake Huron.[699] Not only was Ipperwash home to a CF training facility, it was also Reserve residence to the Kettle and Stoney Point Natives. Between 02-16 September 1990, during the Oka Crisis, 50 Natives had camped inside the perimeter of CF Camp Ipperwash in support of the Mohawks. CF contingency planning was done for the possibility of armed confrontation with the local Natives. However, after negotiation with local CF personnel stationed at Ipperwash they peacefully withdrew.[700]

Tempers over the transfer of Camp Ipperwash back to the local Natives, as had been promised, flared in 1995 when a group of Stoney Point Chippewa/Ojibwa occupied the base and nearby Ipperwash Provincial Park (which contained a Native Burial Ground) in protest. The OPP tactical response unit, flanked by snipers, was called in on 6 September and during a brief shootout unarmed Native Dudley George was shot and killed. Although the CF was not involved, the OPP did submit a request for a Bison APC to transport its personnel, which never materialized. CF contingency planning to move 1 RCR from Petawawa was also promulgated in what was dubbed Operation MAPLE and Operation PANDA. However, there was no direct CF intervention at Ipperwash.[701]

The Natives maintain that no arms were present and neither police officers nor police equipment showed signs of gunfire. Although there is no indication that Mohawk Warriors were present, the pattern of the leaders doing the talking and offering up "expendables" to confront police appeared to have played itself out again at Ipperwash. An observer inside the Native camp asserted that George was exhorted into "proving himself" by the protest leaders consisting of Buck Doxtater and Oneida Peacekeepers (Warriors).[702]

The protest was not backed by the Stoney Point Band Council but the attraction of free housing and the lack of band council regulation, in conjunction with an ambiguous treaty over the land, prompted the occupation to continue.[703] The disparate views concerning the land at Ipperwash dated back to June 1942, when the Government of Canada appropriated the land under the War Measures Act against the wishes of its Native occupants.[704]

The CF land was given back to the Stoney Point Band and the findings of the long awaited Ipperwash Inquiry were released on 31 May 2007. Great controversy and conspiracy surrounded the use of force by the OPP, a subsequent cover-up and perjury on the stand by its members and also the role of Premier Mike Harris in the decision-making processes.[705] Since the Native occupation, the area has become a centre for criminal activities and narcotic trafficking. One only needs to drive by the old Army barracks or "sacred healing place" along Highway 21 to see the state of disrepair, the clutter of burnt-out automobiles and the signs warning of unexploded ordnance left by the CF. In addition, the once thriving deer population has been hunted out of existence.[706]

Following the release of the final report and findings of the Ipperwash Inquiry, negotiations between the Province of Ontario and members of the Chippewa of Kettle and Stoney Point First Nation took place regarding the Ipperwash Provincial Park. On 20 December 2007, the Ontario government announced its intention of returning the 56 hectare Provincial Park to its original Native owners. The park, formed in 1936, will be co-managed by the province and the Natives, with consultation from the surrounding communities, for an unspecified time period before complete control is given to the Kettle and Stoney Point Chippewa.

Although the CF was not directly involved in the altercation at Ipperwash, 1 Canadian Mechanized Brigade Group (1 CMBG) assisted the RCMP in countering another armed Native movement in 1995 at Gustafsen Lake, British Columbia near the Nautley Reserve some 130km west of Prince George.

It allegedly started over protest concerning the non-Native use of a "Sundance site." The Plains Native tradition was never practiced in the British Columbia interior before 1989.[707] This uprising of Shuswap Natives transpired at the same time as the occupation in Ipperwash, although there is no evidence to suggest that they were linked. The CF contributed a platoon of Bison APCs and drivers to what was dubbed Operation WALLABY in support of the RCMP around Gustafsen Lake. Elements of JTF 2 were also present. On 11 September 1995, a tense firefight erupted between the RCMP backed by CF elements and the armed Natives. The siege ended on 17 September when the Natives peacefully surrendered. 18 Natives were charged in connection to what the locals called Wolverine's War named after the ring-leader code named "Wolverine."[708]

The convergence of cultures continues. While in the process of writing this work, barricades were erected on 28 February 2006 near the Six Nations Reserve south of Caledonia, Ontario along Highway 6. This author was allowed behind the barricades on 23-24 March 2006. The script is identically frightening to that of the beginning of the Oka Crisis almost 16 years earlier. Natives of the Reserve, mostly Mohawk, were joined by others from Akwesasne and New York State to protest the construction of a new subdivision of nine to 10 houses called Douglas Creek Estates by the local firm of Henco Industries Limited. Although not supported by the Band Council, the original spokesperson Dawn Smith stated that the council did not have jurisdiction over land issues and that, "It doesn't matter if they support us or not." The following day, she was replaced by Janie Jamieson. The confusion of politics and leadership was evident when speaking to those behind the barricade, although no weapons were visible.[709]

The protestors are arguing that a 385,000 hectare tract of land along the Grand River, with six miles on either side from its source to Lake Erie, was granted in title to the Six Nations under Joseph Brant in the *Haldimand Proclamation* of 1784 after the exodus from the United States following the American Revolution. In 1792, Lieutenant-Governor John Graves Simcoe reduced the land grant to 111,000 hectares. Four years later, Six Nations granted Chief Joseph Brant the power of attorney to sell off parcels of the land in question and invest the proceeds for the benefit of the entire Reserve. The Crown opposed this decision but eventually conceded to the Native's demand. Six Nations maintains that although Brant did sell off large tracts of the original land grant, this parcel was never transferred to non-Natives.[710]

To compound the complications of land ownership, in 1840, the Crown recommended that a Reserve of 8,000 hectares be established on the south side of the Grand River and the remaining land be sold or leased. The following year Six Nations Chiefs agreed to this proposal on the stipulation that the government sell the land and invest the revenue into the Reserve. At this point, a faction of the Reserve protested the Chiefs' decision believing that they were deceived and intimidated into the arrangement. This decision became the basis for a lawsuit in 1995.[711]

The specific tract of land which is currently being disputed was sold on 15 May 1848 to George Marlot Ryckman for 57 pounds and 10 shillings and a Crown land deed was issued to him upon finality of the sale. Henco Industries argues that the land in question was originally granted to the Natives in the form of a licence to occupy the land, but that the ownership was still vested with the Crown. The Natives dispute this claim. In 1850, the Crown and Six Nations Chiefs agreed to a proclamation detailing the extent of the Reserve lands totalling roughly 19,000 hectares (an Indian Act Band Council was not established at Six Nations until 1924 under RCMP enforcement).[712]

It was not until 1992 that Henco Industries Ltd. purchased a company that owned the 40 hectares of what would later be called Douglas Creek Estates. Native opposition to this sale occurred in 1995. In March 1995, Six Nations sued the federal and provincial governments citing 14 specific allegations and claims, one of which included the Douglas Estate land. Prior to this litigation, the Six Nations filed 29 claims with Canada between 1976-1994. Henco Industries insists that this legal action was for, "all assets which were not received but ought to have been received, managed or held by the Crown for the benefit of the Six Nations," which would negate this private land. In 1999, the Six Nations Reserve filed a land claims suit over the area known as the Haldimand Tract. Although the governments of Canada and Ontario met with Six Nations representative in 1999, 2000 and 2001, it remained unsettled.[713]

In July 2005, the blueprint for the planned Douglas Creek Estates received registered approval with title to the property guaranteed by the Province of Ontario. When dealing with non-Native land, the provinces of Canada have exclusive rights to legislate concerns of property and civil rights, including land transaction, under Section 91 (13) of the *Constitution Act, 1867*. While it is law that Natives can only surrender their land to the Crown, once transferred, full title of the land then passes to the province.[714]

On 26 October, Six Nations Chief David General wrote a letter to Henco Industries warning the company of the probable dangers of developing the Douglas Creek Estates. On 28 February 2006, Natives began to occupy Douglas Creek Estates area and prevented construction workers from entering the subdivision building zone. Soon after an RV was brought forward, tents erected and a small barricade complete with Six Nations and Mohawk Warrior flags was constructed on the access road to the west of Highway 6. Signs reading: "Canada, your home on Native Land," "Thou shall not steal, including Land," and "This country needs a true history lesson" among others were visible along the highway. Another large banner reading "Six Nations Land" straddled the northern boundary of the Iroquois camp.[715]

The Iroquois asked for a moratorium on the building of the subdivision but nothing was ever negotiated or granted. On 3 March, Ontario Superior Court Justice David Marshall issued an injunction (submitted by Henco Industries): "This court issued an order requiring the occupiers to clear the site by March 10, 2006 at 10:00am. The protestors did not leave...and burned the court order." On 17 March, Marshall issued another injunction against the Natives and their supporters that by 1400 hrs on 22 March they must vacate the site or be arrested by the Ontario Provincial Police on contempt of court charges.[716] As the deadline approached there was no indication that the Natives were prepared to break camp. Shortly before the deadline, the OPP stated that they did not intend to arrest or remove the Natives by force. Instead they parked patrol cars along the northern and southern boundaries of the barricade and monitored the situation. Also present that day was a throng of journalists and media, including the CBC. The barricade at Caledonia had gone national.[717]

The Natives were asking for negotiations to begin with the federal government and the Department of Indian Affairs on a nation to nation level, citing the *Royal Proclamation Act*. Developer Don Henning of Henco Industries said the he was sympathetic to some of the Native causes but also told the *Hamilton Spectator* that, "We have done nothing wrong or illegal. The real problem is with the federal government. It has nothing to do with us. We are caught in the middle. We'd like to see a quick and peaceful resolution to this." He has repeatedly appealed to the Minister of Indian Affairs, Jim Prentice, to help resolve the protest and land dispute. Thus far, the only response from the Ministry of Indian Affairs was to send an emissary on a "fact finding mission" which was not cordially welcomed by those at the barricade.[718] The resounding statement from the Natives at the barricade was: "We are here for the long haul until it is recognized as Six Nations territory."[719]

The "fact finding mission" Henning referred to was that of Michael Coyle, a law professor from the University of Western Ontario. On 24 March 2006, Indian Affairs stated that Coyle, was assigned "to undertake a fact-finding initiative related to the ongoing situation involving members of the Six Nations of the Grand River, to investigate the nature of the grievances, identify the jurisdictional implications and explore the possibility for mediation." According to Indian Affairs, the dossier on Six Nations' claims already contained some 70,000 pages of materials dating back to the 17th century.[720]

On 29 March, the OPP met with the Six Nations Chiefs and the Clan Mothers and hinted that they would remove protestors by force. This was met by a challenge from Michael "Sahtakaientes" Laughing of Akwesasne, one of about two dozen Natives behind the barricade. He repeated that he was ordered to the barricade by his own Clan Mothers of Akwesasne to protect the people and the land: "If I have to die here that's what I'm going to do. They will have to kill me to take me out of here." In a lengthy interview with the *Hamilton Spectator,* he made reference to the Great Law of Peace and the Two-Row Wampum Belt stating that they govern his way of life and that his orders from his Clan Mothers supersede those of the OPP from the Ontario Court. Laughing also alluded to the fact that many believe the Band Councils to be an arm of the federal government. He made numerous references to the Oka Crisis and the military tactic game played by the governments: "I hope the world sees this... We are here ready for a confrontation again." Jeff Hawk, a resident of the Six Nations Reserve, added that they will only deal with the Attorney-General of Canada, the Governor General, the Queen or her delegates on a "nation to nation" basis.[721] Deirdre McCracken, a spokesperson for Minister of Indian Affairs Jim Prentice, has stated that the blockade, "has nothing to do with the federal government. This isn't a land-claims matter. The actual root of the problem is not a land claim."[722]

On 5 April another incident eerily mirrored the Oka Crisis. With the barricade still in place, 300 to 400 angry Caledonians gathered in front of the OPP station to protest the in action of both the police force and the federal government. The Caledonia OPP detachment released a public statement stressing that they had no intention to forcibly remove the Iroquois protestors from the site stating that they had learned their lesson at Ipperwash in connection with the fatal shooting of Dudley George.[723] Although the OPP were reluctant to use force to solve the dispute, the court order compelled them to act. At roughly 0430hrs on 20 April, OPP officers conducted a raid on the Native protest lines using tear gas, pepper spray and tasers. After violent skirmishes,

16 Native protesters were arrested. However, the remainder of the protesters refused to vacate the site and the barricade remained.[724]

Similarly to the Oka Crisis, the repercussions of the raid extended beyond the Six Nations Reserve. Mohawks in Kahnawake responded by raising Warrior flags and temporarily blocking the Mercier Bridge for 30 minutes. Mohawks from Tyendinaga lit bonfires on a CN railway line suspending cargo and passenger rail service for two days. The situation at Caledonia was also made worse by the OPP raid. A railway bridge near Caledonia was set ablaze. A van was hurled over a bypass on Highway 6 and a new barricade was erected on the highway using burning tires and gravel. On Argyle Street South in Caledonia two more barricades were erected using a dump truck, tires and gravel, blocking the road to both the north and south of the original barricade on the service road leading into the subdivision.[725]

As a result of the escalating unrest, the Grand Erie School Board and the Brant-Haldimand School Board closed their schools for the two days following the 20 April raid. In addition to the swelling number of OPP officers, RCMP members began to form a presence at the barricades. Police forces were not the only groups growing. The Native numbers at the multiple barricades increased as support was filtering in from Ontario and parts of the U.S., including members of various Warrior Societies. This was met by an increasingly larger and more hostile crowd of local Caledonia residents backed by outside radical group members including the Ku Klux Klan.[726]

As in 1990, the police now found themselves in the precarious position of keeping these two factions apart. On 24 April, roughly 3,000 area residents marched toward the police lines. During the ensuing violence police vehicles were smashed, sporadic fights erupted between Natives, non-Natives and the police forces, before order was restored and the angry crowd melted away. This ugly scene was repeated on 29 April and non-Native protesters became regular at the barricades, as Caledonia businesses were suffering from the blockade of the two major north-south axis of the town (Highway 6 and Argyle Street).[727]

While the tension over the land claim mounted, political negotiations were ongoing between the Natives, Henco Industries and the Province of Ontario. Although federal Minister of Indian Affairs, Jim Prentice, was monitoring the situation and was in communication with his subordinates in the provincial and municipal governments, most notably Ontario Aboriginal Affairs Minister David Ramsey and local MP Diane Finley, both he and Prime Minister

Stephen Harper maintained their stance that the dispute remained a provincial matter.[728] On 30 April, the Government of Ontario responded by appointing former Liberal Ontario Premier David Peterson as chief arbitrator. Peterson publicly stated that he is aware of the complexities of the situation: "The genius here is to find common ground.... The reality is this has been going on for 200 years, so we have to find something that everybody wins with... What you fear is something like the permanent stain of an Oka." Peterson also contradicted Prime Minster Harper by insisting that Ottawa has the biggest role "by a long-shot" in solving the Six Nations standoff.[729] The Native leaders agreed, still upholding their argument that it is a Crown issue as set forth in the Royal Proclamation Act. Clan Mother Doreen Silversmith relayed this and other grievances to the United Nations Committee on Aboriginal Affairs in Geneva, Switzerland on 3 May.[730]

Growing frustrations over the political impasse and the barricades heightened the tensions in Caledonia itself. On 16 May, Native protestors removed part of the barricade on Highway 6, allowing traffic on one lane of the road, stopping each vehicle that passed through. They went so far as to issue I.D. cards to those living behind the barrier. Non-Native residents responded by erecting their own barricade, thus preventing Natives from entering the protest site. In what was described as a "gesture of good will," Native protestors removed the barricade on Highway 6 at 0800hrs on 22 May after the government announced an indefinite moratorium on construction the day before.[731] This did not mollify the non-Native protestors.

At roughly noon on the 22nd, non-Natives formed a human barricade across Highway 6, preventing Six Nations members from passing through. Shortly thereafter, Aboriginal protestors re-established their barricade using an electrical transmission tower. In addition, two backhoes were used to tear a trench across the road. Soon Native and non-Native protestors began trading punches and racial slurs. The OPP quickly formed a buffer between the hostile groups. During the violent exchanges, vandals shut down a transformer in Caledonia cutting power to 8,000 of residents in the surrounding Norfolk and Haldimand counties. The OPP Emergency Response Team arrived later that night in riot gear to shore up the police buffer zone and calm was restored.[732]

The following day, 23 May, 17 schools were closed due to the ongoing power disruption which was eventually restored on 24 May. Also on 23 May, the barricade on Highway 6 was removed and the trench was filled in; however, barricades still remained on Argyle Street and at the original site. Following a week of relative calm, Ontario Superior Court Justice David Marshall ordered all parties involved in the dispute to a special court session in order to explain why his initial court order for the Aboriginal protestors to be evicted was not enforced. The session appeared to be futile and nothing was resolved.[733]

The situation at the barricades escalated on 9 June with a series of violent events all occurring within the period of one hour. The first incident involved a couple in their 70s from Simcoe, Ontario who pulled their car over to the side of the road near the protest site. Native demonstrators quickly surrounded the car, forcibly removed the occupants and stole the vehicle. A short time later, two news reporters from Hamilton's CH approached the couple who were standing in front of the nearby Canadian Tire for an interview. They were attacked by Native protestors, who demanded the footage and stole their cameras. Both reporters were taken to hospital for treatment and stitches. The third incident involved an unmarked U.S. Border Patrol car, which was studying the methods used by the OPP in dealing with the standoff. The car was swarmed, the officers inside dragged out. The car was stolen and the driver proceeded to try to run down an OPP officer, who was subsequently injured. During this incident classified police documents, including the identities of undercover agents and information from Native informants, were taken from the vehicle.[734]

The violence ended the ongoing negotiations between the Six Nations and the Province of Ontario. The OPP issued warrants for seven Natives believed to be involved in the violent events. The OPP suspected that they were taking refuge on the Reserve but did not enter as they have a protocol not to enter the land base of the actual Reserve. Ontario Premier Dalton McGuinty stated that negotiations would only resume once the barricades had been dismantled. Native protestors responded by using heavy machinery to remove the Argyle Street barricade made of tires and twisted metal. However, the original barricade into the construction site still remained intact. In another effort to resume the negotiations, the stolen documents were returned to the OPP, but not before being photocopied.[735]

On June 15, negotiations resumed between the Natives and the Province of Ontario. The following day, the province buys the land in question from Henco Industries for an undisclosed amount. On 23 June, David Ramsey finally revealed the amount paid out for the piece of land; $12.3 million. The McGuinty government also announced that it will offer $1 million, in addition to the already proposed $760,000, to compensate Caledonia businesses affected by the barricades and road blocks on 15 June.[736] Despite these events, the barricade remained at the construction site, with Natives conducting an archaeological dig of the site, claiming that it is a Native burial ground. An archaeological survey done during Henco Industries' initial layout of the subdivision revealed Native artifacts but showed no evidence of burials.[737] On 5 July, the Henco lands in question were officially transferred to Government of Ontario not to the Government of Canada as Crown lands "reserved for the use of Indians" as stipulated in the *Royal Proclamation Act.* The land was privately owned before the transfer and was not, in the eyes of the government, Native land. The land was not transferred to the Six Nations.[738]

Although the land was now in the possession of the Government of Ontario, neither the Natives nor elements of the Caledonia community were assuaged. Protests continued from both parties, one resulting in a violent clash on 7 August. Many citizens of Caledonia were questioning why the OPP had not enforced the injunction to remove the protestors, citing a two-tier judicial system and that the rule of law applies equally to all Canadian citizens regardless of ethnicity. The following day, Judge Marshall stated that, "in the court's view, after much deliberation, there should be no further negotiations till the blockades are lifted and the occupation is ended...these reasons be send to the Attorney General who has the responsibility for enforcing the criminal law...in regard to the criminal contempt." He also ordered the province/OPP to arrest and charge the protestors with contempt of court for not obeying his previous court injunctions.[739]

The following day, after another violent confrontation between residents, Natives and police, Ontario's Attorney General Michael Bryant stated that while the province would comply with the ruling that all negotiations cease, the province will appeal the decision. On the ground, the OPP continued to separate the crowds but did not make the arrests demanded by Judge Marshall. The appeal was heard on 25 August in The Court of Appeal for Ontario which granted a stay on the injunction: "[I]n our view, the maintenance of the rule of law favours a stay." Moreover, the court gave instructions to the OPP to proceed cautiously: "The uncontradicted evidence of the O.P.P. is that a stay of the injunction order will reduce the risk of harm to the community. The Province should be permitted to determine what level of occupation and what use of its own property best promote the public interest in these difficult times... and negotiations will continue."[740]

Table 5—Six Nations (Caledonia) Negotiation Structure, August 2006[741]

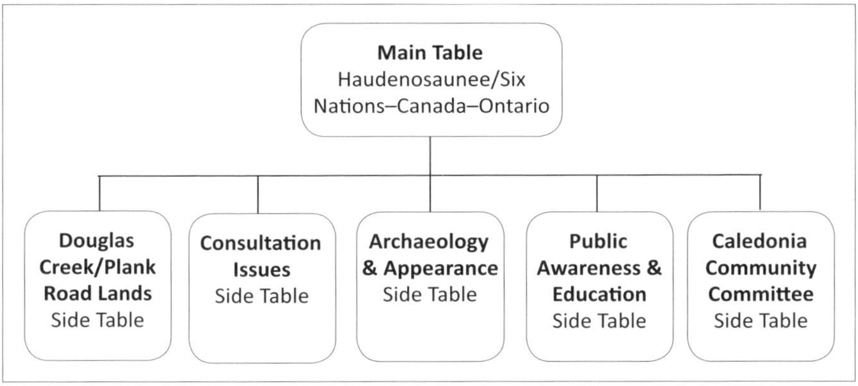

Although negotiations were ongoing, increased civil unrest prompted a consensus with the Six Nations and the Ontario government to form a 100-foot buffer-zone on the north end of the disputed lands on 25 September "intended to facilitate a better sense of privacy and security for both the people living in close proximity...and the Haudenosaunee/Six Nations." Signage and yellow police tape were used to cordon off the area. According to the agreement only the OPP and other authorized persons, such as the archaeological teams, were permitted in the buffer-zone with the OPP monitoring the area "as operational requirements necessitate."[742]

Despite the buffer-zone, on 15 October, more than 300 Caledonia residents and their supporters staged a rally headed by Gary McHale of Richmond Hill, while the native protestors and their advocates staged a "potluck dinner for peace." Dozens of police officers formed a protective barrier between the two factions and although there were three arrests, the feared violence did not manifest. The frustration of some Caledonia residents was voiced over the duality of the law while "Caledonia is held hostage." Conservative MPP of Haldimand-Norfolk-Brant, Toby Barrett took the opportunity to criticize the McGuinty government for their inaction: "There does appear to be a double standard. People see a different application of the law depending on which side of the barricade you stand."[743]

Although Barrett may have used the opportunity for political grandstanding, the political situation was far from cooperative. On his first day as newly appointed Commissioner of the Ontario Provincial Police, former Toronto Police Chief Julian Fantino stated on 30 October that the OPP's job is to "preserve the peace, deal with offences and bring those who transgress the laws of the land to justice. Beyond that, the resolution of this is beyond the police doings, beyond any scope that I could have." He also alluded to the fact that the drain on his force's manpower cannot continue.[744] The following day, Federal Indian Affairs Minister Jim Prentice canceled a scheduled meeting with his Ontario counterpart David Ramsey, his office stating that he was "disturbed [by the] political grandstanding" of both Ramsey and McGuinty. Ramsey was planning on asking the federal government for $25 million to cover some of the provincial costs while McGuinty publicly stated that the crisis and land claims at Caledonia were, "If you check the Constitution, it'll make it perfectly clear that when it comes to these land claims issues, that is solely the responsibility of the federal government." Ramsey echoed his leader's disapproval: "This is another example of the federal government failing to live up to its obligations to the people of Ontario."[745]

This political manoeuvring came on the heels of Michael Coyle's submission and presentation to the Senate Committee on 3 October detailing his investigation into the Six Nations standoff. In his findings, he stressed that the governments of Canada and Ontario must co-operate: "Each takes the position that it is confident that if the Crown is liable for wrongdoing in relation to Six Nations' land claims, that it is the other government that is legally responsible. It is difficult to see how the Crown will be able to reach a settlement of Six Nations' land claims unless Canada and Ontario can agree on a reasonable sharing between them." Among his recommendations were the following:

1. Recommendation: The government should significantly increase the number of personnel devoted to the historical and legal review of claims.

2. Recommendation: Canada should establish an independent body with the power to resolve disagreements over the validity of all Specific Claims, and where negotiations reach impasse, on the extent of Canada's liability in accordance with legal principles.

3. Recommendation: The same body, or a related independent body, should be established to supervise the adherence to agreed time frames in claims negotiations and to offer mediation where requested by one party.[746]

Despite these suggested reforms, the barricades remained at Caledonia and negotiations continued as did local protests. On 16 December another rally was headed by Gary McHale, who maintains a website called "Caledonia Wake Up Call," dedicated to those who oppose the occupation. He was arrested, along with another man, although the OPP said that he would not face criminal charges. However, negotiations between the Main Table occurred on 11 January 2007, with Side Table meetings sitting for the week of 15-19 January.[747]

During these discussions, Ontario's Ministry of Culture stated that stones discarded by nomadic hunting groups dating back to 9,000 years ago were found on the disputed land. Spokesperson Gary Lepage also stated that remains of an 800-year-old Longhouse, complete with pottery and waste refuse pits, was also unearthed. However, despite vast media documentation claiming the contrary, these artifacts were discovered in digs during 2002 and 2005, not by the Native archaeological dig conducted after the occupation of the disputed lands which was overseen by the Ministry. Neither a burial site nor human remains have ever been unearthed. Six Nations spokesperson Janie Jamieson said the findings strengthen their claims and connection to the land: "It just goes to show you how far back our connection to that territory goes. Our connection stems back to our very existence, our creation."[748]

In reality, the evidence found in the digs has minimal influence. Firstly, it needs to be determined if the land was legally and willingly sold or given back to the Crown. Within this context of the dispute, the artifacts bring no weight to bear. Secondly, given that the Six Nations people occupied the land under Joseph Brant in 1784, the artifacts could belong to another Native Nation, albeit an Iroquoian (Longhouse) Nation, and does it show occupation to the exclusion of all other peoples as outlined in a comprehensive land claim? For this type of claim, the artifacts become relevant. However, this criterion is not part of a specific land claim which makes up the bulk of the 29 claims made by the Six Nations as of 1995, all of which are unanswered.

As of writing, the barricades remain at Caledonia, negotiations are ongoing as is the convergence of cultures. Although the violence has subsided for the time being, the clash of cultures continues and by no means is the standoff at Caledonia over. As of 1 February 2007, the Government of Ontario released the figures of expenditures thus far for the standoff:

Table 6—Six Nations Negotiations Costs as of February 2007.[749]

Item	Cost (in millions)
Purchase of Douglas Creek Estates Property	15.8
Other costs paid to Henco	1.1
Acquisition of interests of other builders to Douglas Creek lands	4.0
Other costs paid to builders	1.8
Financial Assistance Recovery Program to businesses of Caledonia	1.4
Support for Haldimand County economic recovery activities (including charities affected by lower business contributions)	0.56
Policing Operations (to date)	21.6
Other Ongoing Costs	TBD
Total	$46.26 million

While the occupation of the disputed lands at Caledonia/Six Nations continues, another little known standoff is occurring at the Mohawk Reserve of Tyendinaga (Mohawks of the Bay of Quinte) near Belleville, Ontario. Similar to the Six Nations Reserve, Tyendinaga was established by Captain John Deserontyon, a Mohawk serving in the British Army during the American Revolution. Tyendinaga was named after Deserontyon's superior Joseph Brant or Thayendanegea. On the 22 May 1784, Deserontyon and about 20 families arrived on the shores of the Bay of Quinte, Lake Ontario. On 1 April 1793, a tract of land was granted to the Six Nations people by the Lieutenant-Governor of Upper Canada, John Graves Simcoe, in a document known as the *Simcoe Deed* (also referred to as Treaty 3½). The original area of the territory was approximately 92,700 acres and currently stands at 18,191 acres with a population of roughly 7,600 both on and off the Reserve.

The land in question in the current claim, the 923-acre Culbertson Tract, runs along the eastern boundary of the Reserve. The federal government procured the land in 1837 and it is this transaction which is under dispute. The Mohawks claim that they never surrendered title. Similar to both Oka and Caledonia, the land in question was the proposed site of a $35 million, 140-home subdivision of developer Intergroup Financing AG headed by Tim Letch. Construction was slated to begin on 15 November 2006. With letters of protest coming from Chief Don Maracle and members of the community, talks began with the federal government, including federal Minister Jim Prentice in early

November. Chief Maracle outlined his community's stance: "We believe it is absolutely imperative that the developer should not proceed with the development unless there's some sort of arrangement made that's agreeable to our people," and must be brokered by the federal government. Letch, who agreed to meet with Maracle, stated that he believes, "the federal government should resolve the matter properly with the Native people. But I don't think it is my responsibility to resolve it." Similar to Caledonia, and to some extent Oka/Kanesatake, Native and non-Native communities had been living harmoniously for decades in what Marcale described as a "tight-knit community." He added that, "I don't believe any of the citizens want to see any kind of quarrel among neighbours [like Caledonia] over the property, and I think we would like to see that harmony continue."[750]

Tyendinaga Chief Don Maracle was optimistic after a meeting on 10 November with Minister of Indian Affairs Jim Prentice: "I think the minister made a very positive gesture. It was one we appreciate. I'm very hopeful there's an opportunity to work out something." Deseronto Mayor Clarence Ziemen hoped the meeting resulted in the postponement of construction: "I'm not in favour of proceeding with this at all at this time until we get some of this land claim issue out of the way." The federal government also confirmed to all parties that there is a claim involving 827 acres of land, including the contested site, accepted under Canada's Specific Claims Policy in November of 2003.[751]

However, on the proposed day of construction, 15 November 2006, roughly 20-30 Mohawk protestors, claiming that they only intended to post signs, blocked a section of Highway 2 using two vans, as five Canadian Forces vehicles approached: "It was not a planned blockade, it was just posting of the land to let people know that it is Mohawk land. Coincidently, the army drove through Deseronto [town] today. They were stopped and asked why they were there, what they were doing in the area. They were detained for...maybe half an hour, then they were allowed to go through." While the CF vehicles were stopped and blocked from both sides, tempers flared but there was no violence. The OPP arrived on site shortly after to supervise the demonstration and to divert traffic around the roadblock. In reality, according to CF Captain Dan Madryga, the convoy was travelling from CFB Borden to CFB Trenton, near Tyendinaga, as part of a long road move for a driver training course and inadvertently encountered the protestors. The vehicles were all marked with yellow signs reading, "Student Driver."[752]

Activist Shawn Brant, who is also involved in the Tyendinaga tobacco industry, claimed that he did not, "necessarily agree with the notion that they

[CF] just happened to be passing through." He also stated that the community of Deseronto has been supportive and there were no plans to occupy the land on a full-time basis, but would continue to monitor the situation and gather again in protest if need: "People know what we have here. We have the 401, [rail] tracks, bridges, highways and a lot of infrastructure to manipulate if negotiations get stalled. It was only through the co-operative efforts of the band council, Native peoples and other support parties that it did not happen [today]."[753]

Construction was delayed on the housing development while talks ensued between the Tyendinaga Band Council and Indian Affairs. Another protest was held on the disputed land on 17 November. Initially, the land claim dispute raised fears that the situation could escalate into one similar to that in Caledonia. However, the Tyendinaga Territory's chief of police, Larry Hay, stated that peace will likely continue in Deseronto, provided the federal government works quickly toward a resolution. Norm Clarke, the incoming mayor of Deseronto, also said that he hoped the negotiations will resolve the situation quickly.[754]

On 9 January 2007, Minister Jim Prentice announced the appointment of Sean Kennedy as chief federal negotiator to the Tyendinaga Mohawks' Culbertson Tract specific claim: "I have full confidence in Mr. Kennedy's abilities to advance the work to resolve the First Nation's specific claim and related issues."[755] Despite this announcement, the following day, 20 protestors blocked a county road off of Highway 2, barring access to Thurlow Aggregates quarry, which is also on disputed land. The protestors handed out information pamphlets to passing motorists. The protest was not sanctioned by Maracle or his council, which believed it to be, "premature considering a federal negotiator has been appointed to settle the land dispute."[756]

On 12 January, an OPP officer, exercising existing warrants arrested Shawn Hill and Mario Baptiste in connection with the confrontation with the CF on 15 November 2006. Hill was charged with three counts of uttering death threats, while Baptiste was charged with two counts of assault and one count of mischief. OPP Spokesperson Sergeant Kristine Rae issued a statement to "ensure that everyone is aware that the OPP respects lawful protests, but will not tolerate criminal activity."[757] On 24 January, Tim Letch, the developer, announced that he had hired a lawyer and planned to bring his grievances to court as the landowner. The ongoing protests and barricades at both Caledonia (now entering its second year) and Tyendinaga remind Canadians of the grievances and frustrations of today's First Nations Peoples and the ongoing convergence of cultures.

As of 31 December 2006, Indian Affairs had settled 277 specific land claims with another 123 in negotiation. Likewise, there have been 29 final agreements for comprehensive land claims, with a further 18 negotiated in principle or subject to a framework agreement. However, there remain roughly 800 outstanding comprehensive and specific Native land claims lodged with Indian Affairs.[758] Hopefully, these and future claims are resolved satisfactorily for all concerned parties without resorting to violence or barricades as were witnessed at Akwesasne, Kanesatake, Kahnawake, Ipperwash, Gustafsen Lake, Caledonia and Tyendinaga. The convergence of cultures must be mutually beneficial for both Canada and its Indigenous Peoples.

ABOUT THE AUTHOR

Timothy Charles William Winegard was raised in Sarnia, Ontario. He was awarded a Bachelor of Arts (Honours) in 1998 from the University of Western Ontario and proceeded to gain a Bachelor of Education from Nipissing University the following year. In 2006, he completed his Master or Arts in War Studies at the Royal Military College of Canada. Currently, he is pursuing his Doctorate at the University of Oxford in military history under the direction of Professor Hew Strachan. His thesis is a comparative study on the use and treatment of Indigenous peoples from Canada, Australia, New Zealand and South Africa during the First World War. Tim is also a serving officer with the 1st Hussars in the Canadian Forces Reserves.

BIBLIOGRAPHY

Canada Access to Information Act (ATI) Documents Department of National Defence

A98/1501 After Action Reports./Post Deployment Analysis Conducted by the 12e Régiment blindé du Canada (12 RBC) for Operations Conducted during OP SALON (The Oka Crisis of 1990).

96/27 J3 Operations and Plans, the J-Staff System and National Defence Operations.

97 A 0916 Oka Crisis, OP SALON, Political and Military Objectives and Deployment of CF, and Ministerial Level Discussions.

99/30 General A.J.G.D. de Chastelain Fonds.

94/184 OP SALON War Diaries. Series: 1-14.

97 A 00200 Record that Analyses, Assesses or Reviews the CF's Ability to Respond to Civil Emergencies.

97 A 00524 All Documents, Notes of Operation Pertaining to the Deployment of Troops in Quebec since 1976.

EPC/J3 The Role of the CF in Major Civil Disasters, Summary Record, Canadian Emergency Preparedness.

Complete Records: OP FEATHER/OP AKWESASNE

Maps

Natural Resources Canada—Canada Map Office/National Defence Headquarters—Mapping and Charting Establishment

031G02 Cornwall, Ed.: 00-07

031G08 Vaudreuil, Ed.: 00-07, Loc.: J44

031G09 Lachute, Ed.: 00-08, Loc.: D42

031H05 Lachine, Ed.: 03-10

031H12 Laval, Ed.: 00-10, Loc.: J56

031G Ottawa, Ed.: 96-05, Loc.: A18

Government Publications

Begin, Patricia, Wendy Moss and Peter Niemczak. *The Land Claims Dispute at Oka.* Ottawa: Minister of Supply and Services Canada, 1992.

Campbell, Kim (Minister of Justice). *The Warriors and the Criminal Law.* Ottawa: Ministry of Justice and the Attorney General of Canada, 9 September 1990.

Court of Appeal for Ontario. *Ontario Reports, 82 O.R. (3d).* Toronto: Law Society of Upper Canada, February 2007.

Coyle, Michael. *Report Senate Committee Submission on Specific Land Claims.* Ottawa: 3 October 2006.

European Parliament. *Resolution on Indigenous Peoples: For Relations with Canada.* EU: Directorate General for Committees and Delegations, January 1991.

Gilbert, Guy (Coroner). *Rapport d'enquête du Coroner: Guy Gilbert sur les Causes et Circonstances du Décès de Monsieur Marcel Lemay.* (English Version). Quebec: Province of Quebec, 1995.

Gilmore-Dickson, E.J. and Chris Whitehead. *Aboriginal Organized Crime in Canada: Developing Typology for Understanding and Strategizing Responses.* Ottawa: Research and Evaluation Branch, Royal Canadian Mounted Police, 2005.

Gilmore-Dickson, E.J. *Communities, Contraband and Conflict: Considering Restorative Responses to Repairing the Harms Implicit in Smuggling in the Akwesasne Mohawk Nation.* Ottawa: Research and Evaluation Branch, Royal Canadian Mounted Police, 2002.

Government of Canada. *Emergencies Act R.S. 1988, c. 29.* Ottawa: Minister of Public Works and Government Services Canada, 1988.

______*National Defence Act, Administrative Code.* Ottawa: Minister of Public Works and Government Services Canada, 1987.

______*National Defence Act R.S. c. n-5.* Ottawa: Minister of Public Works and Government Services Canada, 1987.

______*War Measures Act R.S.C. c. w-2.* Ottawa: Minister of Public Works and Government Services Canada, 1985.

Grant, T.J. Colonel. *Training on Rules of Engagement Domestic Operations*. Ottawa: Department of National Defence, 1998.

Hurley, Mary C. (Law and Government Division). *Bill S-24: The Kanesatake Interim Land Base Governance Act*. Ottawa: Law and Government Division, 2001.

Jaenen, Cornelius J. *Historical Background of Kanesatake (Oka)*. Ottawa, 1990.

Ministry of Indian and Northern Affairs Canada. *Agreement with Respect to Kanesatake Governance of the Interim Land Base.* Ottawa: Department of Indian Affairs and Northern Development, 2001.

______*Backgrounder on the Claims of the Six Nations of the Grand River Band of Indians.* Ottawa: April 2006.

______*Comprehensive Land Claim of Kanesatake Indians.* Ottawa: Department of Indian Affairs and Northern Development, July 1990.

______*Federal Policy Guide: Aboriginal Self-Government*. Ottawa: Minister of Public Works and Government Services Canada, 1995.

______*How DIAND Programs are Administered at Akwesasne, Kahnawake and Kanesatake.* Ottawa: Department of Indian Affairs and Northern Development, July 1990.

______*Land Claims Policy.* Ottawa: Department of Indian Affairs and Northern Development, July 1990.

______*Mohawk Band Government*. Ottawa: Department of Indian Affairs and Northern Development, July 1990.

______*An Overview of the Oka Issue.* Ottawa: Department of Indian Affairs and Northern Development, July 1990.

______*Various Press Releases*. March 2006-February 2007.

Ministry of National Defence. *Military Operation in Unique Environments Domestic Operations: Précis.* Toronto: Canadian Land Force Command and Staff College, 1995.

______ *Queen's Regulations and Orders, Vol. I* (Administration), (1968): Chapter 23, Section 5, Article 23.15, Note D.

Mohawk Council of Kahnawake. *Institutions of Mohawk Government in Kahnawake: An Overview.* Ottawa: Ministry of Indian Affairs and Northern Development, 1990.

Mulroney, Brian P.M. *Notes for an Address to the House of Commons on the House Resolution with Respect to Oka, 25 September 1990*. Ottawa: Office of the Prime Minister, 1990.

Nicholson, G.W.L. *The Official History of the Canadian Army in the First World War: Canadian Expeditionary Force, 1914-1919.* Ottawa: Queen's Printer, 1962.

Office of the Auditor General of Canada. *Review of the Request by the Province of Quebec for Financial Assistance Related to the Emergency in July 1990 Affecting Oka, Kahnawake and Chateauguay.* 1995.

Ontario Executive Council, Order in Council. *Establishment of Inquiry—Ipperwash.* Toronto: Executive Council, 12 November 2003.

Ontario Secretariat for Aboriginal Affairs. *Six Nations (Caledonia) Negotiations.* Toronto, February 2006.

Report of the Somalia Commission of Inquiry Vol. 2, Chap. 10. Ottawa: Minister of Public Works and Government Services Canada, 1997.

Royal Commission on Aboriginal Peoples. *Aboriginal Self Government: Legal and Constitutional Issues.* Ottawa: Canada Communication Group, 1995.

______*Canada's Fiduciary Obligation to Aboriginal Peoples in the Context of Accession to Sovereignty by Quebec: Vol. 2 Domestic Dimensions.* Ottawa: Canada Communication Group, 1995.

______*Treaty Making in the Spirit of Co-existence: An Alternative to Extinguishment.* Ottawa: Canada Communication Group, 1993.

Stacey, C.P. *Official History of the Canadian Army in the Second World War: Six Years of War, Vol. I.* Ottawa: Queen's Printer, 1955.

Standing Committee on Aboriginal Affairs. *Minutes of Proceedings, 19 March 1991, Issue No. 55.* Ottawa: House of Commons, Aboriginal Affairs, 1991.

______*The Summer of 1990: Fifth Report of the Standing Committee on Aboriginal Affairs, 9,10,17,18 April 1991, Issue No. 59.* Ottawa: House of Commons, Aboriginal Affairs, May 1991.

Standing Committee on National Defence and Veterans Affairs. *Evidence, 10 May 2001.* Ottawa, 2001.

______*Evidence, 27 May 2002*. Ottawa, 2002.

Thompson, John. *Materials Relating to the History of the Land Dispute at Kanesatake.* Ottawa: Claims and Historical Research Centre, Department of Indian and Northern Affairs, 1993.

Primary Sources

An Historical Notice on the Difficulties Arisen between the Seminary of St-Sulpice of Montreal and certain Indians, at Oka, Lake of Two Mountains: A Mere Case of Right of Property. "By No Means a Religious Question." Montreal: La Minerve Steam Printing Job Office, 1876.

"Beta." *A Contribution to a Proper Understanding of the Oka Question.* Montréal: Witness Printing House, 1879.

Borland, John Reverend. *An Appeal to the Montreal Conference and Methodist Church Generally, from a charge by Rev. William Scott, in which is shown his charge to be invalid, and his defence of the Seminary of St-Sulpice against the Indians of Oka to be baseless – a fact in proof of which he has himself largely contributed.* Montreal: Witness Printing House, 1883.

Canadian Red Cross Society. *Report on the Intervention by the Canadian Red Cross Society at Kanesatake, Kahnawake, Oka and Châteauguay during the Indian Crisis in the Summer of 1990*. Ottawa: Communications Department, 1991.

de Champlain, Samuel. H.P. Biggar ed. *The Works of Samuel de Champlain, Vol. 2: 1608-1613*. Toronto: 1925.

Ciaccia, John. *The Oka Crisis: A Mirror of the Soul*. Canada: Maren Publications, 2000.

Cross, Ronald and Helene Sevigny. *Lasagna: The Man Behind the Mask*. Vancouver: Talon Books, 1994.

Gagnon, Reginald. *Fait d'armes à Oka.* Quebec: Arion, 1994.

Hall, Louis Karoniaktajeh. *Rebuilding the Iroquois Confederacy*. U.S.A.: Louise Leclaire, Kahnawake, 1985.

______*Warrior's Handbook*. U.S.A.: Louise Leclaire, Kahnawake, 1985.

Mercredi, Ovide and Mary Ellen Turpel. *In the Rapids: Navigating the Future of First Nations*. Toronto: Viking Books Ltd., 1993.

Murray, Norman. *The Oka Question: Containing the Original Title, and a Brief Account of the Feudal System of Seigniorial Tenure in Canada, and its Abolition in 1854 with a general review of The Oka Question in Particular and Roman Aggression in General.* Quebec: E. Frechette, 1852.

Protestant Defence Alliance of Canada. *The Indians of the Lake of Two Mountains and the Seminary of St. Sulpice.* Montreal: Witness Printing House, 1876.

Scott, William Reverend. *Report relating to the Affairs of the Oka Indians made to the Superintendent General of Indian Affairs.* Ottawa: MacLean, Roger & Co., 1883.

Secondary Sources

Allen, Robert S. *His Majesty's Indian Allies: British Indian Policy in the Defence of Canada, 1774-1815*. Toronto: Dundurn Press, 1992.

Atlas of American History. Illinois: Rand McNally, 1993.

Baigent, Michael. *Ancient Traces: Mysteries in Ancient and Early Societies.* England: Viking, 1998.

Bauhn, Per, Christer Lindberg and Svante Lundberg. *Multiculturalism and Nationhood in Canada: The Cases of First Nations and Quebec*. Sweden: Lund University Press, 1995.

Belisle Guy Maitre and Helene Thibault. *Oka After the Crisis: Final Report*. Quebec: The Oka Advisory Group, 1991.

Berkowitz, Bruce. *The New Face of War: How War will be Fought in the 21st Century*. Toronto: The Free Press, 2003.

Bland, Douglas L., ed. *Canada's National Defence Volume 1: Defence Policy*. Kingston: Queen's University School of Policy Studies, 1997.

______ed. *Canada's National Defence Volume 2: Defence Organization*. Kingston: Queen's University School of Policy Studies, 1998.

Bland, Douglas L. and Sean M. Maloney. *Campaigns for International Security: Canada's Defence Policy at the Turn of the Century*. Kingston: McGill-Queen's University Press, 2004.

Beauchamp, William M. *A History of the New York Iroquois.* New York: New York State Museum, University of the State of New York, 1905.

Beauvais, Johnny. *Kahnawake: A Mohawk Look at Canada and Adventures of Big John Canadian, 1840-1919.* Canada, 1985.

Churchill, Ward and Jim Vander Wall. *Agents of Repression: The FBI's Secret Wars Against the Black Panther Party and the American Indian Movement.* Boston: South End Press, 1990.

______*The Cointelpro Papers: Documents from the FBI's Secret Wars Against Dissent in the United States.* Boston: South End Press, 1990.

Clarke, T. Wood. *The Bloody Mohawk.* New York: Ira J. Friedman Inc., 1941.

Coates, Ken and Robin Fisher ed. *Out of the Background: Readings on Native Canadian History.* Toronto: Copp, Clark Ltd., 1996.

Decima Research. *A Report on Public Opinion Surrounding the Events at Oka, Quebec.* Ottawa: Decima Research, 1990.

Deloria Jr., Vine. *Custer Died for Your Sins: An Indian Manifesto.* New York: Macmillian, 1969.

Diamond, Jared. *Guns, Germs and Steel: The Fates of Human Societies.* New York: W. W. Norton & Co., 1999.

Edwards, Peter. *One Dead Indian: The Premier, the Police and the Ipperwash Crisis.* Toronto: McClelland and Stewart, 2003.

Engelstad, Diane and John Bird, ed. *Nation to Nation: Aboriginal Sovereignty and the Future of Canada.* Ontario: The House of Anansi Press, 1992.

Facey-Crowther, David. *Better than the Best: The Story of the Royal Newfoundland Regiment, 1795-1995*. Newfoundland: RNR Advisory Council, 1995.

Farwell, Byron. *Encyclopaedia of Nineteenth-Century Land Warfare*. New York: W. W. Norton & Co., 2001.

Fowler, William M. *Empires at War: The Seven Years' War and the Struggle for North America, 1754-1763*. Toronto: Douglas & McIntyre, 2005.

Frideres, James S. *Canada's Indians: Contemporary Conflicts*. Canada: Prentice-Hall Ltd., 1993.

Gabriel-Doxtator, Brenda Katlatont and Arlette Kawanatatie Van Den Hende. *At the Woods' Edge: An Anthology of the History of the People of Kanehsata:ke*. Quebec: Kanesatake Education Center, 1995.

Goldstein, Robert A. *French-Iroquois Diplomatic and Military Relations 1609-1701.* Paris: Mouton, 1969.

Goodleaf, Donna. *Entering the War Zone: A Mohawk Perspective on Resisting Invasions.* Canada: Theytus Books Ltd., 1995.

Granatstein, J.L. *Canada's Army: Waging War and Keeping the Peace*. Toronto: University of Toronto Press, 2002.

Green, Magnus and Jonas Stier. *"The Oka-Conflict" a case study of Mohawks in Canada.* Sweden: Vaxjo University, 1991.

Horn, Bernd. *Bastard Sons: An Examination of Canada's Airborne Experience, 1942-1995*. Ontario: Vanwell Publishing Ltd., 2001.

Horn, Kahn-Tineta. *Mohawk Warriors Three: The Trial of Lasagna, Noriega & 20-20.* Kahnawake: Owera Books, 1994.

Hornung, Rick. *One Nation Under the Gun*. Toronto: Stoddart Publishing Ltd., 1991.

Hunt, George T. *The Wars of the Iroquois: A Study in Intertribal Trade Relations.* Madison: University of Wisconsin Press, 1960.

Johansen, Bruce E. *Life and Death in Mohawk Country*. Colorado: North American Press, 1993.

Kennedy, Paul. *Preparing for the Twenty-First Century*. Toronto: HarperCollins Publishers Ltd., 1993.

Kitson, Frank. *Low Intensity Operations: Subversion, Insurgency & Peacekeeping.* India: Natraj Publishers, Dehra Dun, 1992.

Klare, Michael T. and Peter Kornbluh ed. *Low-Intensity Warfare: Counterinsurgency, Proinsurgency, and Antiterrorism in the Eighties.* New York: Pantheon Books, 1988.

Krotz, Larry. *Indian Country: Inside Another Canada*. Toronto: McClelland & Stewart Inc., 1992.

Landsman, Gail H. *Sovereignty and Symbol: Indian-White Conflict at Ganienkeh.* New Mexico: University of New Mexico Press, 1988.

MacLaine, Craig and Michael Baxendale. *This Land is Our Land: The Mohawk Revolt at Oka*. Toronto: Optimum Publishing International Inc., 1990.

MacMillan, Margaret. *Paris 1919*. New York: Random House, 2003.

Matthiessen, Peter. *In the Spirit of Crazy Horse.* Toronto: Penguin Books, 1991.

Miller, J.R. *Skyscrapers Hide the Heavens: A History of Indian-White Relations in Canada.* Toronto: University Press, 2001.

Morgan, Lewis H. *Ancient Society.* U.S.A.: The University of Arizona Press, 1985.

______*League of the Ho-de-no-sau-nee or Iroquois.* U.S.A.: Reprint Services Corp., 1922.

______*Systems of Consanguinity and Affinity of the Human Family*. U.S.A.: The University of Nebraska Press, 1997.

Morrison, Andrea P. ed. *Justice for Natives: Searching for Common Ground.* Kingston: McGill-Queen's Press, 1997.

Morton, Desmond. *Understanding Canadian Defence*. Toronto: Penguin Books, 2003.

Newman, Peter C. *The Secret Mulroney Tapes: Unguarded Confessions of a Prime Minister*. Canada: Random House, 2005.

Parker, Arthur C. *Parker on the Iroquois*. New York: Syracuse University Press, 1968.

Pasquaretta, Paul. *Gambling and Survival in Native North America.* Tucson: University of Arizona Press, 2003.

Perrett, Bryan. *The Battle Book: Crucial Conflicts in History from 1469 BC to the Present*. London: Arms and Armour Press, 1992.

Pertusati, Linda. *In Defense of Mohawk Land: Ethnopolitical Conflict in Native North America.* New York: State University of New York Press, 1997.

Pugliese, David. *Canada's Secret Commandos: The Unauthorized Story of Joint Task Force Two.* Canada: Esprit de Corps Books, 2002.

Reid, Gerald F. *Kahnawa:ke: Factionalism, Traditionalism, and Nationalism in a Mohawk Community.* U.S.A.: University of Nebraska Press, 2004.

______*Mohawk Territory: A Cultural Geography.* Kahnawake: Center for Curriculum Development, Kahnawake Survival School, 1981.

Richter, Daniel K. *The Ordeal of the Longhouse.* U.S.A.: University of North Carolina Press, 1992.

Rochon, Monique and Pierre Lepage. *Oka-Kanesatake-Summer 1990. A Collective Shock: Report of the Commission des droits de la personne du Québec.* Québec: Commission des droits de la personne du Québec, 1991.

Ross, Rupert. *Dancing with a Ghost: Exploring Indian Reality.* Ontario: Octopus Publishing Group, 1992.

Scheele, Raymond. *Warfare of the Iroquois and their Northern Neighbors.* U.S.A.: Columbia University, 1950.

Smith, Dan. *The Seventh Fire: The Struggle for Aboriginal Government*. Toronto: Key Porter Books, 1993.

Smith, Trefor. *Bridges and Barricades: In Defense of Mohawk Land.* Montreal: Kanienkehaka Solidarity Group, McGill University, 1991.

Snyder, Ross B. *Algonkian Warfare in Canada and Southern New England 1600-1680.* Ottawa: University of Ottawa Press, 1972.

St-Denis, Guy. *Tecumseh's Bones.* Montreal: McGill Queen's Press, 2005.

Tait, George E. *Breastplate and Buckskin: A Story of Exploration and Discovery in the Americas.* Toronto: Ryerson Press, 1953.

Thompson, John. *Ipperwash...Again*. Toronto: The Mackenzie Institute, 2003.

______*Sin-Tax Failure: The Market in Contraband Tobacco and Public Safety*. Toronto: The Mackenzie Institute, 1994.

______*The Long Fall of the Mohawk Warriors.* Toronto: The Mackenzie Institute, 1996.

Tugwell, Maurice and John Thompson. *The Legacy of Oka*. Toronto: The Mackenzie Institute, 1991.

Van Creveld, Martin. *The Transformation of War.* Toronto: The Free Press, 1991.

Watt, Gavin K. *Rebellion in the Mohawk Valley: The St. Leger Expedition of 1777.* Toronto: The Dundurn Group, 2002.

Wilson, Edmund. *Apologies to the Iroquois*. New York: Farrar, Straus and Giroux, 1970.

York, Geoffrey. *The Dispossessed: Life and Death in Native Canada.* Toronto: Little, Brown and Company Ltd., 1989.

York, Geoffrey and Loreen Pindera. *People of the Pines: The Warriors and The Legacy of Oka.* Toronto: Little, Brown & Co., 1991.

Journal Articles

Austin, Lisa and Christina Boyd. "The Oka Crisis," Peace Research Reviews Vol. XIII, No. 1 (October 1993): pp. 1-70.

Baril, Gerald Major. "Mission Accomplished," Sentinel: Magazine of the Canadian Forces 1990/6, Vol. 26, no.6, pp. 2-8.

Beauregard, Claude. "The Military Intervention in Oka." Canadian Military History 2, 1 (Spring 1993): 23-47.

Cape, Lois. "Oka: 1990 and Beyond," contained in Diane Engelstad and John Bird ed., *Nation to Nation: Aboriginal Sovereignty and the Future of Canada.* Canada: The House of Anansi Press, 1992: 215-220.

Charters, David A. "From October to Oka: Peacekeeping in Canada, 1970-1990," contained in Marc Milner ed., *Canadian Military History: Selected Readings.* Toronto: Copp Clark Pitman, 1993.

David, Dan. "Anarchy at Kanehsatake: Drug trade, child porn, death threats," THIS Magazine Vol. 29, no. 5 (January 1996): 11-15.

de Chastelain, A.J.G.D. General. "The Art of Prudent Wing-Walking: Coming to Grips with Détente – an Update from a Canadian Military Perspective," Canadian Defence Quarterly (June 1990): 11-14.

Fitzgerald, Todd and Michael A. Hennessy. "An Expedient Reorganization: The NDHQ J-Staff System in the Gulf War," Canadian Military Journal (Spring 2003): 23-28.

Gabriel, Ellen. "Kanesatake: The Summer of 1990," contained in Diane Engelstad and John Bird ed., *Nation to Nation: Aboriginal Sovereignty and the Future of Canada.* Canada: The House of Anansi Press, 1992: 165-172.

Girard, Michael F. "The Oka Crisis from an Environmental History Perspective, 1870-1990," contained in R. Douglas Francis and Donald B. Smith ed., *Readings in Canadian History: Post Confederation*. Toronto: Harcourt Brace & Co., 1994: 578-596.

Grenier, Marc. "Native Indians in the English-Canada Press: The Case of the Oka Crisis," *Media, Culture & Society* Vol. 16, no. 2 (April 1994): 313-336.

Horn, Kahn-Tineta. "Beyond Oka: Dimensions of Mohawk Sovereignty," Studies in Political Economy 35 (Summer 1991): 29-40.

Johansen, Bruce E. "Dating the Iroquois Confederacy," Akwesasne Notes Vol. 1, no. 3 & 4 (Fall 1995): 62-63.

Keene, Tony Captain. "Guns Among the Mohawks," Sentinel: Magazine of the Canadian Forces 1990/4, Vol. 26, no. 4, pp. 2-4.

Lackenbauer, P. Whitney. "Combined Operation: The Appropriation of Stoney Point Reserve and the Creation of Camp Ipperwash," Journal of Military and Strategic Studies 2/1 (Fall 1999): pp. 1-38.

Lavoie, Roland Lieutenant. "Behind the Scenes at Op Salon," Sentinel: Magazine of the Canadian Forces 1991/1, Vol. 27, no. 1, pp. 8-10.

Lerhe, Eric Commodore. "Civil Military Relations and Aid to the Civil Power in Canada: Implications for the War on Terror," CDIA-CDFIA 7th Annual Graduate Student Symposium, RMC (October 2004): PhD Paper, Dalhousie University.

Leslie, Andrew Major-General. "The 2004 Haycock Lecture: Boots on the Ground: Thoughts on the Future of the Canadian Forces," Canadian Military Journal (Spring 2005): 18-24.

MacFarlane, John and John Moses. "Different Drummers: Aboriginal Culture and the Canadian Armed Forces, 1939-2002," Canadian Military Journal (Spring 2005): 25-32.

Maloney, Sean M. "Domestic Operations: The Canadian Approach," Parameters, US Army War College (Autumn 1997): 135-152.

______"Force Structure or Forced Structure? The 1994 White Paper on Defence and the Canadian Forces in the 1990's," Choices Vol. 10, no. 5 (May 2004): 1-30.

Miller, J.R. "Great White Father Knows Best: Oka and the Land Claims Process," Native Studies Review 32, no. 64 (1991): 23-45.

______"Owen Glendower, Hotspur, and Canadian Indian Policy," contained in R. Douglas Francis and Donald B. Smith ed., *Readings in Canadian History: Post Confederation.* Toronto: Harcourt Brace & Co., 1994: 161-184.

Morris, Martin J. "Overcoming the Barricades: The Crisis at Oka as a Case Study in Political Communication," Journal of Canadian Studies 30, no.2 (Summer 1995): 74-90.

Morton, Desmond. "Bayonets in the Streets: The Canadian Experience of Aid to the Civil Power 1867-1990," Canadian Defence Quarterly Vol. 20, no. 5 (Spring 1991): 30-36.

Naylor, R.T. "Loose Cannons: Covert Commerce and Underground Finance in the Modern Arms Black Market," Crime, Law and Social Change Vol. 22, no. 1 (March 1994): 1-57.

Purich, Donald. "The Future of Native Rights," contained in J.R. Miller ed., *Sweet Promises: A Reader on Indian-White Relations in Canada*. Toronto: University Press, 1991: 421-437.

Roy, J.A. Brigadier-General. "Operation Salon," Canadian Defence Quarterly Vol. 20, no. 5 (Spring 1991): 15-19.

Skea, Warren H. "The Canadian Newspaper Industry's Portrayal of the Oka Crisis," Native Studies Review 9, no. 1 (1993-1994): 15-29.

Thompson, Loran. "Fighting Back," contained in Diane Engelstad and John Bird ed., *Nation to Nation: Aboriginal Sovereignty and the Future of Canada*. Canada: The House of Anansi Press, 1992: 173-178.

Tobias, John L. "Protection, Civilization, Assimilation," contained in J.R. Miller ed., *Sweet Promises: A Reader on Indian-White Relations in Canada*. Toronto: University Press, 1991: 127-144.

Vachon, Robert. "The Mohawk Nation and its Communities," INTER culture Vol. XXIV, no. 4 (Fall 1991): 10-18.

Westra, Laura. "Environmental Racism and the First Nations of Canada: Terrorism at Oka," Journal of Social Philosophy Vol. 30, no. 1 (Spring 1999): 103-124.

White, Tony Captain. "Drug-Net," Sentinel: Magazine of the Canadian Forces 1992/2, Vol. 28, no. 2, pp. 7-9.

Media Sources

Ashley, Jeremy. "Mohawk protestors charged," Belleville Intelligencer, 10 January 2007.

Bergman, Brian. "Drumbeats of Anger," Maclean's Magazine, 2 July 1990: 28-29.

Burke, Dan. "Higher Stakes," Maclean's Magazine, 20 August 1990: 12-13.

______"Law and Disorder," Maclean's Magazine, 27 August 1990: 12.

Came, Barry. "Tear Gas and Fury," Maclean's Magazine, 1 October 1990: 18.

______"The Fury of Oka," Maclean's Magazine, 10 September 1990: 16-19.

Canadian Press. "Natives block rail line in eastern Ont.," 21 April 2006.

______"Natives Hit Gaming Jackpot," The Hamilton Spectator, 30 March 2006.

______ "Native Protestor Prepared to Die Over Rights to Land," The Hamilton Spectator, 30 March 2006.

______"Que. Mohawks raise banner in support of Ont. Native dispute," 20 April 2006.

______"Trial of the Warriors." 23 January 1992.

______Various Articles. February 2006-February 2007.

CBC News. "Cigarette smuggling on the rise, Mounties say," 05 May 2006.

______ "Indepth: Caledonia Land Claim, Historical Timeline," 21 April 2006.

______ "Indepth: Caledonia Land Claim, Timeline of Recent Events," 20 June 2006

______"Native protestors expect police will evict them," 23 12:30hrs March 2006.

______"Native protestors face deadline to leave subdivision," 22 11:00hrs March 2006.

______ CBC News, Various Articles, 1990-2007.

Craggs, Samantha. "Heated confrontation with Mohawks at development," Belleville Intelligencer, 15 November 2006.

Fragomeni, Carmela. "Native Standoff is a Provincial Matter: Ottawa," The Hamilton Spectator, 07 April 2006.

Fulton, E. Kay. "Looking for Lost Dignity: Oka's Mohawks are not Alone," Maclean's Magazine, 23 July 1990: 22-23.

Hamilton Spectator. Various Articles. February 2006-February 2007.

Howard, Robert, "Standoff needs a time-out," The Hamilton Spectator, 01 April 2006.

Howse, John. "A new native hero," Maclean's Magazine, 16 July 1990: 13.

Katz, Signe. "CBC: The National." 05 April 2006.

Kopvillem, Peeter. "Summer Faceoffs," Maclean's Magazine, 6 August 1990: 25.

Legall, Paul. "Natives Vow to Stand their Ground," The Hamilton Spectator. 31 March 2006.

______"Six Nations protestors say land 'stolen.' Developer says it's the federal government's problem," The Hamilton Spectator. March 2006.

McDonald, Marci. "Following the Oka Example," Maclean's Magazine, 8 October 1990: 34.

McLaughlin, Ann. "Under Siege: Slipping Behind the Warrior Lines," Maclean's Magazine, 23 July 1990: 19.

Nelson, Marissa, "Clan Mothers seek UN's help," The Hamilton Spectator, 03 May 2006.

______"Harper rapped on Caledonia issue," The Hamilton Spectator, 26 May 2006.

Nolan, Daniel. "Natives Build Cookhouse on Protest Site in One Day," The Hamilton Spectator, 08 April 2006.

Ottawa Citizen. Various Articles. June 2006-August 2006.

Siblin, Eric. "Mohawk Factions Fight Nine-hour Gun Battle," The Globe and Mail, 2 May 1990.

"Standoff—Native protestor prepared to die over rights to land," The Hamilton Spectator. 30 March 2006.

Taylor, Greg W. "Rough Justice," Maclean's Magazine, 6 August 1990: 18-20.

______"The Battle of Oka," Maclean's Magazine, 23 July 1990: 16-21.

Various Reporters. "Akwesasne Gambling Dispute," The London Free Press, 3 May 1990.

Walters, Joan, "An Angry Generation: Aboriginal young people full of pride—and fury," The Hamilton Spectator, 22 April 2006.

______"Peterson fears another Oka," The Hamilton Spectator, 23 May 2006.

Westaway, Jennifer. "Oka: Are Mohawks Criminals?" CBC Radio: The House, 28 July 1990. Ottawa: Bowdens, 1990.

Wilson-Smith Anthony and Nancy Wood. "Starting Over," Maclean's Magazine, 8 October 1990: 28-30.

Wood, Chris. "Sending in the Troops," Maclean's Magazine, 3 September 1990: 16-18.

Unpublished Materials

Boswell, M.B. Lieutenant-Colonel *Internal Security Rules of Engagement: The Need for Clarity.* Toronto: Canadian Forces Command and Staff College, 1993.

Edwards, Victoria. *Don't Mention It! The Oka Crisis and the Recruitment of Aboriginal Peoples.* Ottawa: Department of National Defence, 2002.

Interviews

Allen, John. Office of Archbishop Desmond Tutu. 11 July 2005, Johannesburg, S.A. via e-mail.

Bassarab, Rusty Lieutenant-Colonel (Major). Deputy Commanding Officer, 2RCR. Interview with Author. 06 September 2005, Kingston, Ontario.

Boswell, Martin Bradley Lieutenant-Colonel (Major). H Company Commander, 2RCR. Interview with Author. 08 September 2005, Kingston, Ontario.

Chafe, Howard Captain (Lieutenant). Platoon Commander, Base Defence Force, Longue-Pointe. Interview with Author. 14 September 2005, Ottawa, Ontario.

Dorau, Peter Master-Corporal. Interview with Author. 08 December 2005, London, Ontario. With 1 RCR in the Signal Squadron at Akwesasne.

Fife, John Lieutenant-Colonel (Lieutenant). Platoon Commander, H Company, 2RCR. Interview with Author. 05 October 2005, Gagetown, N.B. via telephone.

Gabriel, Ellen. Spokesperson and Clan Mother, Kanesatake Mohawks. Interview with Author. 01 September 2005, Kahnawake, Mohawk Territory, Quebec.

Goodleaf, Donna Dr. Author of *Entering the War Zone: A Mohawk Perspective on Resisting Invasions.* 14 June 2005 via e-mail.

Horn-Miller, Waneek. Daughter of activist Kahn-Tineta Horn and occupant of TC. Stabbed with a bayonet on 26 September while leaving TC. Interview with author. 26, 30 January 2006, Montreal, Quebec.

Johansen, Bruce E. Dr. Author of *Life and Death in Mohawk Country.* 18 July 2005, Nebraska via e-mail.

Lamarre, Bruno (Corporal). Interview with Author. 16 July 2005. Bright's Grove, Ontario. Reservist attached to 12 RBC at Kahnawake.

Lambert, David Major (Lieutenant). Intelligence Officer, 2RCR. Interview with Author. 08 September 2005, Kingston, Ontario.

Landry, R. Lieutenant-Colonel (Captain). Staff Officer, 5 BMC Head Quarters. Interview with Author. 22 September 2005, Valcartier, Quebec via telephone.

Magee, Colin Lieutenant-Colonel (Major). Operations Officer, 2RCR. Interview with Author. 25 October 2005, Leavenworth, Kansas via telephone.

McAdam, Pat Lieutenant-Colonel (Captain). Adjutant, 2RCR. Interview with Author. 29 September 2005, Gagetown, N.B. via telephone.

Morneau, Jacques Colonel (Major). Operations Officer (G3), Chief of Staff, Deputy Commander, 5 BMC. Interview with Author. 19 September 2005, Toronto, Ontario.

Pertusati, Linda Dr. Author of *In Defense of Mohawk Land: Ethnopolitical Conflict in Native North America.* 18 July 2005, Ohio via e-mail.

Tremblay, Alain Colonel (Major). C Company Commander 2R22eR. Interview with Author. 15 September 2005, Ottawa, Ontario.

York, Geoffrey. Reporter for the *Globe and Mail* behind the Mohawk barricades at Kanesatake and co-author of *People of the Pines: The Warriors and The Legacy of Oka.* 11 July 2005, Beijing, China via e-mail.

Various interviews conducted with Natives behind the barricade at Caledonia, Ontario, 23 March 2006.

Confidential Interviews held by author with members of the Canadian, Ontario and Quebec Intelligence Communities and Canadian Forces Intelligence personnel.

Private Collections

Electronic Sources/Internet Sites

<www.answers.com/topic/lewis-henry-morgan> Lewis H. Morgan. 07 November 2005.

<sisis.nativeweb.org/sov/oh11oka> Voices from Oka: transcripts from speeches delivered at a defence benefit held in Vancouver, B.C., 10 December 1991. 14 June 2005.

<sixnations.buffnet.net/Threats_to_Traditional_Governments/> Haudenosaunee: Threats to Traditional Governments. 14 June 2005.

<sixnations.buffnet.net?Grand_Council/?article=ganienkeh> Letter: Grand Council of Six Nations Confederacy to President Gerald Ford, 24 November 1974. 14 June 2005.

<users.resist.ca/~wiinimkiikaa/issue1/mohawkwarriortradition> The Mohawk Warrior Tradition. 26 May 2005.

<www.ainc-inac.gc.ca/qc/gui/kanesatake_e> Indian and Northern Affairs Canada. Settlement of Kanesatake and Reserve of Doncaster. 01 June 2005.

<www.ainc-inac.gc.ca/pr/pub/sg/plcy_e> Indian and Northern Affairs Canada. Federal Policy Guide: Aboriginal Self-Government. 01 June 2005.

<www.crystalinks.com/iroquois> Iroquois Nation Maps. 07 November 2005.

Persons/Organizations Contacted

Akwesasne Cultural Centre.

Broadbent, Ed.

Canadian Human Rights Commission—Secretary General, Ottawa, Ontario.

Canadian Red Cross Society, Ottawa, Ontario.

Canadian Security Intelligence Service (CSIS), Ottawa, Ontario.

Comité Québec-Irlande, Montréal, Québec.

Department of History and Heritage, Ottawa, Ontario.

Department of Indian and Northern Affairs Canada, Ottawa, Ontario.

Department of National Defence, Ottawa, Ontario.

European Union—Parliament.

International Federation of Human Rights, Paris, France.

Kahnawake Cultural Centre.

Library and Archives Canada, Ottawa, Ontario.

McKnight, Bill Hon. Minister of Defence during the Oka Crisis and former Minister of Indian Affairs.

McLaughlin, Audrey.

Ministère de la Sécurité publique du Québec—Sûreté du Québec (SQ), Sainte-Foy, Québec.

Ministry of Natural Resources Canada, Ottawa, Ontario.

Ministry of Public Safety and Emergency Preparedness Canada—Office of the Inspector General of CSIS, Ottawa, Ontario.

Mohawk Council of Akwesasne.

Mohawk Council of Kahnawake.

Mohawk Council of Kanesatake.

Mohawk Nation Council, Akwesasne.

National Defence Headquarters, Ottawa.

New York State Police (NYSP), Albany, New York.

Ontario Ministry of Community Safety and Correctional Services—Ontario Provincial Police (OPP), North Bay, Ontario.

Quebec Superior Court, Montreal, Quebec.

Rideau Hall—The Chancellery of Honours, Ottawa, Ontario.

Royal Canadian Mounted Police, Ottawa, Ontario.

Sevigny, Helene. Co-author of *Lasagna: The Man Behind the Mask.*

Siddon, Tom Hon. Minister of Indian Affairs during the Oka Crisis.

The United Nations Economic and Social Council, New York, New York and Geneva, Switzerland.

U.S Department of Justice—Federal Bureau of Investigation (FBI), Washington, D.C.

Endnotes

Introduction

1 Canada. DND ATI, "NDHQ Command and Control Volume 3: A Case Study Operation SALON (The Oka Crisis), December 1993."

2 Maurice Tugwell and John Thompson, *The Legacy of Oka* (Toronto: The Mackenzie Institute, 1991), pp. 1-5.

3 Term coined by Sean M. Maloney, "Domestic Operations: The Canadian Approach," *Parameters*, US Army War College (Autumn 1997), p. 135. A "narco-parastate" is an unrecognized "nation" within a legitimate host nation, which survives on the trafficking of drugs and other illicit materials in order to further political independence. The drug cartels of South America are examples.

4 Note on Sources: In this effort to embody a historically complete representation of the Oka Crisis, primary sources were used as much as possible, many referenced for the first time. Interviews were also conducted with numerous military personnel who had been involved. Many also graciously volunteered their own personal collections of documents, maps and photographs. For obvious reasons, certain members of the military and intelligence communities who provided information cannot be named. In addition, interviews were held with government officials, Mohawk representatives and other participants. Efforts were made to corroborate statements with documented evidence, admittedly at certain times to no avail. All interviews were conducted in accordance with the approval and protocols of the Research Ethics Board at the Royal Military College of Canada. Ranks for those military personnel interviewed are listed as current title at the time of interview with rank during the Oka Crisis following in parentheses, e.g. Major (Lieutenant) John Smith. Tens of thousands of pages of materials have been consulted from governmental agencies in both Canada and the United States, including the Canadian National Library and Archives, the Department of Indian and Northern Affairs, the Department of National Defence, the Canadian Security Intelligence Service (CSIS), the Office of the Secretary to the Governor General, the Royal Canadian Mounted Police (RCMP), the Canadian Red Cross, the Canadian Human Rights Commission, the Canadian Public Safety and Emergency Preparedness Office of the Inspector General, the Ontario Ministry of Community Safety and Correctional Services (the Ontario Provincial Police or OPP), the Quebec Ministry of Public Security, the Sûreté du Québec (SQ), the New York State Police (NYSP) and the Federal Bureau of Investigation U.S. Department of Justice (FBI). Other materials include *Canadian Access to Information Act* (ATI) and American *Freedom of Information Act* (FIA) requests to the institutions mentioned above. Although the Oka Crisis is now 17 years passed, many requested documents were denied under the stipulations of both Acts, as they are still regarded as sensitive to national security. Many other documents received were censored, with information removed or blocked out. Nevertheless, many of the referenced documents were at one time classified with "secret" denotations and are being made public for the first time. In addition, the United Nations, the European Parliament, the International Federation of Human Rights (Paris), and the Office of Archbishop Desmond Tutu were contacted as they were involved at the higher levels of the crisis.

Part I

5 John Thompson, *The Long Fall of the Mohawk Warriors* (Toronto: The Mackenzie Institute, 1996), p. 1.

Chapter 1

6 Ovide Mercredi and Mary Ellen Turpel, *In the Rapids: Navigating the Future of the First Nations* (Toronto: Penguin Books, 1993), p. 18. In Canada they are called Reserves. In the United States they are referred to as Reservations. Both of these terms will be used based on the location of the actual Native land base. Also, the terms Native, Aboriginal, Indigenous and First Nations will be used interchangeably.

7 T. Wood Clarke, *The Bloody Mohawk* (New York: Ira J. Freidman Inc., 1941), pp. 2-3; George T. Hunt, *The Wars of the Iroquois: A Study in Intertribal Trade Relations* (Madison: University of Wisconsin Press, 1960), pp. 151-16; Vine Deloria Jr., *Custer Died for Your Sins: An Indian Manifesto* (U.S.A.: University of Oklahoma Press, 1988), p. 203; Kahn-Tineta Horn, "Beyond Oka: Dimensions of Mohawk Sovereignty," Studies in Political Economy 35 (Summer 1991): pp. 36-37. Evidently, a Mohawk/Seneca/Cayuga settlement still exists in Oklahoma. There is also an Oneida settlement in Wisconsin.

8 J.R. Miller, *Skyscrapers Hide the Heavens: A History of Indian-White Relations in Canada* (Toronto: University of Toronto Press, 2001), pp. 8-9.

9 Gerald F. Reid, *Kahnawa:ke: Factionalism, Traditionalism, and Nationalism in a Mohawk Community* (U.S.A.: University of Nebraska Press, 2004), p. 1; Brenda Katlatont Gabriel-Doxtator and Arlette Kawanatatie Van den Hende, *At the Woods' Edge: An Anthology of the History of the People of Kanehsata:ke* (Quebec: Kanesatake Education Centre, 1995), p. 6.

10 Miller, *Skyscrapers Hide the Heavens: A History of Indian-White Relations in Canada*, p. 8.

11 Miller, *Skyscrapers Hide the Heavens: A History of Indian-White Relations in Canada*, pp. 13, 75; York and Pindera, *People of the Pines: The Warriors and The Legacy of Oka*, pp. 145-147; Gabriel-Doxtator and Van den Hende, *At the Woods' Edge: An Anthology of the History of the People of Kanehsata:ke*, pp. 8-10; Robert S. Allen, *His Majesty's Indian Allies: British Indian Policy on the Defence of Canada, 1774-1815* (Toronto: Dundurn Press, 1992), pp. 13-14. Archaeological records indicate that the practice of cannibalism existed among the Iroquois nations from the fourteenth to sixteenth centuries.

12 William M. Fowler Jr., *Empires at War: The Seven Years' War and the Struggle for North America, 1754-1763* (Toronto: Douglas & McIntyre, 2005), pp. 7-9; Reid, *Kahnawa:ke: Factionalism, Traditionalism, and Nationalism in a Mohawk Community*, pp. 1-2.

13 Bruce E. Johansen, "Dating the Iroquois Confederacy," Akwesasne Notes, Vol. 1, no. 3 & 4 (Fall 1995): pp. 62-63; Reid, *Kahnawa:ke: Factionalism, Traditionalism, and Nationalism in a Mohawk Community*, pp. 1-2; York and Pindera, *People of the Pines: The Warriors and The Legacy of Oka*, p. 147; Gabriel-Doxtator and Van den Hende, *At the Woods' Edge: An Anthology of the History of the People of Kanehsata:ke*, pp. 8-10. The Confederacy was initiated at Onondaga, located near present-day Syracuse, New York. Based on oral traditions and the solar calendar, certain scholars insist that the Confederacy was formed on 31 August 1142, during a solar eclipse at what is now a football field in Victor, New York. However, they also mention that there was another eclipse in 1451, which seems to be a more accurate date. Most archaeologists and scholars tend to believe that the Confederacy was ratified in the mid-fifteenth century. What is important and relatively undisputed is that the Confederacy was formed before the arrival of Europeans.

14 Allen, *His Majesty's Indian Allies: British Indian Policy in the Defence of Canada, 1774-1815,* pp. 14-15; Trefor Smith, *Bridges and Barricades: In Defense of Mohawk Land* (Montreal: McGill University, 1991), p. 19; Gabriel-Doxtator and Van den Hende, *At the Woods' Edge: An Anthology of the History of the People of Kanehsata:ke*, p. 12.

15 Robert A. Goldstein, *French-Iroquois Diplomatic and Military Relations 1609-1701* (Paris: Mouton, 1969), pp. 35-37. See: *The Great Law of Peace* (U.S.A.: Syracuse University

Press, 1992); MacLaine and Baxendale, *This Land is Our Land: The Mohawk Revolt at Oka,* pp. 99-121.

16 Daniel K. Richter, *The Ordeal of the Longhouse* (U.S.A.: University of North Carolina Press, 1992).

17 James S. Frideres, *Native Peoples in Canada: Contemporary Conflicts* (Canada: Prentice Hall Inc., 1993), pp. 385-386; Larry Krotz, *Indian Country: Inside Another Canada* (Toronto: McClelland & Stewart Inc., 1992), pp. 73-74; Indian and Northern Affairs Canada, *An Overview of the Oka Issue* (DIAND: 1990), p. 8. The representation of nations was as follows: Onondaga 14; Cayuga 10; Oneida 9; Mohawk 9; and Seneca 8. From the Mohawk there were three from each clan (Turtle, Bear and Wolf), which is also the order of nobility within the Mohawk. There was a hierarchy within the Confederacy. Mohawk, Onondaga and Seneca were the "elder brothers," while the Oneida, Cayuga and later the Tuscarora were "younger brother."

18 Mohawk Council of Kahnawake, *Institutions of Mohawk Government in Kahnawake: An Overview* (Ottawa: Ministry of Indian and Northern Affairs, 1990), p. 3; MacLaine and Baxendale, *This Land is Our Land: The Mohawk Revolt at Oka*, pp. 99-121; York and Pindera, *People of the Pines: The Warriors and The Legacy of Oka,* pp. 147-149; Lewis H. Morgan, *League of the Ho-de-no-sau-nee or Iroquois* (1851), (U.S.A.: Reprint Services Corp., 1922); Lewis H. Morgan, *Systems of Consanguinity and Affinity of the Human Family* (1870), (U.S.A.: University of Nebraska Press, 1997); Lewis H. Morgan, *Ancient Society* (1877), (U.S.A.: University of Arizona Press, 1985).

19 The Great Law of Peace, Wampum 19 as quoted in MacLaine and Baxendale, *This Land is Our Land: The Mohawk Revolt at Oka*, p. 108; Gabriel-Doxtator and Van den Hende, *At the Woods' Edge: An Anthology of the History of the People of Kanehsata:ke,* pp. 10-12; Louis Karoniaktajeh Hall, *Rebuilding the Iroquois Confederacy* (U.S.A.: Louise Leclaire); Louis Karoniaktajeh Hall, *Warrior's Handbook* (U.S.A.: Louise Leclaire).

20 Miller, *Skyscrapers Hide the Heavens: A History of Indian-White Relations in Canada,* pp. 7-14; York and Pindera, *People of the Pines: The Warriors and The Legacy of Oka,* pp. 145-149.

21 Goldstein, *French-Iroquois Diplomatic and Military Relations 1609-1701*, pp. 38-40; Reid, *Kahnawa:ke: Factionalism, Traditionalism, and Nationalism in a Mohawk Community,* pp. 2-3.

22 Raymond Scheele, *Warfare of the Iroquois and their Northern Neighbors* (U.S.A.: Columbia University Press, 1950), pp. 61-75; Gabriel-Doxtator and Van den Hende, *At the Woods' Edge: An Anthology of the History of the People of Kanehsata:ke*, pp. 10-12.

Chapter 2

23 Tugwell and Thompson, *The Legacy of Oka*, p. 5.

24 *Ibid,* p. 5.

25 *Atlas of American History* (Illinois: Rand McNally, 1993), pp. 7-11; George E. Tait, Breastplate and Buckskin: A Story of Exploration and Discovery in the Americas (Toronto: Ryerson Press, 1953), pp. 7-42.

26 Gerald F. Reid, *Mohawk Territory: A Cultural Geography* (Quebec: Kahnawake Survival School, 1981), p. 109; Goldstein, French-Iroquois Diplomatic and Military Relations 1609-1701, pp. 14-15.

27 As quoted in Thompson, *Materials Relating to the History of the Land Dispute at Kanesatake*, p. 1.

28 Reid, *Mohawk Territory: A Cultural Geography,* pp. 109-111; Miller, *Skyscrapers Hide the Heavens: A History of Indian-White Relations in Canada*, pp. 28-30. The most

probable location of Hochelaga is an archaeological site discovered just south of Sherbrooke Street opposite McGill University in Montreal.

29 As quoted in Goldstein, *French-Iroquois Diplomatic and Military Relations 1609-1701*, p. 21.

30 *Ibid*, pp. 19-21.

31 Hunt, *The Wars of the Iroquois: A Study in Intertribal Trade Relations*, pp. 24-26; Reid, *Mohawk Territory: A Cultural Geography*, pp. 109-110; Thompson, *Materials Relating to the History of the Land Dispute at Kanesatake*, pp. 2-4. Archeological records and oral traditions put the number somewhere between 1,500 and 2,500, so Cartier's estimation was relatively correct.

32 As quoted in Thompson, *Materials Relating to the History of the Land Dispute at Kanesatake*, pp. 2-3; Miller, *Skyscrapers Hide the Heavens: A History of Indian-White Relations in Canada*, p. 30. La Chine (China) was what Cartier called the impassible rapids, as he was looking for a route to the Orient.

33 As quoted in Thompson, *Materials Relating to the History of the Land Dispute at Kanesatake*, p. 3.

34 Hunt, *The Wars of the Iroquois: A Study in Intertribal Trade Relations*, pp. 16-17; Miller, *Skyscrapers Hide the Heavens: A History of Indian-White Relations in Canada*, pp. 26-27, 34-35; Reid, *Mohawk Territory: A Cultural Geography*, pp. 111-112; Thompson, *Materials Relating to the History of the Land Dispute at Kanesatake*, p. 3. There are many theories concerning the disappearance of the St. Lawrence Iroquois. Reid provides an explanation for most theories and concludes—as do the other sources referenced—that these Iroquois, who were probably most closely related to the Mohawk, were driven out of the area as a consequence of war caused by the burgeoning fur trade and the superiority of the Algonquian weapons. They most likely migrated south and were incorporated into the larger Mohawk communities along the Mohawk River and the southern part of what would be named Lake Champlain. The only metal known to North American Natives was copper which came from Lake Superior. It was ornamental and not strong enough to be used in weapon production.

35 William M. Beauchamp, *A History of the New York Iroquois* (New York: State Museum and University of the State of New York, 1905), pp. 149-152; Clarke, *The Bloody Mohawk*, p. 4.

36 Samuel de Champlain, H.P. Biggar ed., *The Works of Samuel de Champlain, Vol. 2: 1608-1613* (Toronto, 1925), pp. 90-96.

37 Fowler Jr., *Empires at War: The Seven Years' War and the Struggle for North America, 1754-1763*, p. 4.

38 Champlain, *The Works of Samuel de Champlain, Vol. 2: 1608-1613*, pp. 90-99.

39 *Ibid*, pp. 90-91.

40 Ross B. Snyder, *Algonkian Warfare in Canada and Southern New England 1600-1680* (Ottawa: University Press, 1972), pp. 33-60; Clarke, *The Bloody Mohawk*, pp. 17-20.

41 Goldstein, *French-Iroquois Diplomatic and Military Relations 1609-1701*, pp. 43-45; Reid, *Mohawk Territory: A Cultural Geography*, p. 120.

42 Reid, *Kahnawa:ke: Factionalism, Traditionalism, and Nationalism in a Mohawk Community*, pp. 2-4; Gabriel-Doxtator and Van den Hende, *At the Woods' Edge: An Anthology of the History of the People of Kanehsata:ke*, pp. 23-24.

43 Goldstein, *French-Iroquois Diplomatic and Military Relations 1609-1701*, pp. 43-45.

44 Fowler Jr., *Empires at War: The Seven Years' War and the Struggle for North America, 1754-1763*, pp. 8-9; Deloria Jr., *Custer Died for Your Sins: An Indian Manifesto*, p. 203.

45 Fowler Jr., *Empires at War: The Seven Years' War and the Struggle for North America, 1754-1763*, p. 8.

46 Miller, *Skyscrapers Hide the Heavens: A History of Indian-White Relations in Canada*, pp. 65-68.

47 Hunt, *The Wars of the Iroquois: A Study in Intertribal Trade Relations*, pp. 87-130; Miller, *Skyscrapers Hide the Heavens: A History of Indian-White Relations in Canada*, pp. 1-22, 62-81.

48 Goldstein, *French-Iroquois Diplomatic and Military Relations 1609-1701*, p. 99.

49 Allen, *His Majesty's Indian Allies: British Indian Policy in the Defence of Canada, 1774-1815*, pp. 15-16.

50 Miller, *Skyscrapers Hide the Heavens: A History of Indian-White Relations in Canada*, p. 76.

51 Reid, *Kahnawa:ke: Factionalism, Traditionalism, and Nationalism in a Mohawk Community*, p. 5; Goldstein, *French-Iroquois Diplomatic and Military Relations 1609-1701*, p. 98.

52 Allen, *His Majesty's Indian Allies: British Indian Policy in the Defence of Canada, 1774-1815*, pp. 161-17.

53 Hunt, *The Wars of the Iroquois: A Study in Intertribal Trade Relations*, pp. 100-101.

Chapter 3

54 Thompson, *Materials Relating to the History of the Land Dispute at Kanesatake*, p. 5.

55 Clarke, *The Bloody Mohawk*, pp. 77-78.

56 Miller, *Skyscrapers Hide the Heavens: A History of Indian-White Relations in Canada*, pp. 67-68.

57 Reid, *Kahnawa:ke: Factionalism, Traditionalism, and Nationalism in a Mohawk Community*, pp. 6-7.

58 *Ibid*, p. 9.

59 Mohawk Council of Kahnawake, *Institutions of Mohawk Government in Kahnawake: An Overview*, p. 4.

60 Thompson, *Materials Relating to the History of the Land Dispute at Kanesatake*, p. 5.

61 Gabriel-Doxtator and Van den Hende, *At the Woods' Edge: An Anthology of the History of the People of Kanehsata:ke*, pp. 24-25.

62 Clarke, *The Bloody Mohawk*, pp. 93-94; Fowler Jr., *Empires at War: The Seven Years' War and the Struggle for North America, 1754-1763*, p. 2. In 1689, the War of the League of Augsburg began in Europe when it reached North America, it was known as King William's War.

63 Reid, *Kahnawa:ke: Factionalism, Traditionalism, and Nationalism in a Mohawk Community*, p. 10.

64 York and Pindera, *People of the Pines: The Warriors and The Legacy of Oka*, p. 156

65 Thompson, *Materials Relating to the History of the Land Dispute at Kanesatake*, p. 6; York and Pindera, *People of the Pines: The Warriors and The Legacy of Oka*, p. 156; Reid, *Kahnawa:ke: Factionalism, Traditionalism, and Nationalism in a Mohawk Community*, p. 10.

66 Smith, *Bridges and Barricades: In Defense of Mohawk Land*, p. 20.

67 Reid, *Kahnawa:ke: Factionalism, Traditionalism, and Nationalism in a Mohawk Community*, pp. 10-11.

68 Thompson, *Materials Relating to the History of the Land Dispute at Kanesatake*, pp. 6-7.

69 Chief Aghneetha as quoted in *Ibid*, p. 6.

70 Protestant Defence Alliance of Canada. *The Indians of the Lake of Two Mountains and the Seminary of St-Sulpice* (Montreal: Witness Printing House, 1876), p. 2; *An Historical Notice on the Difficulties Arisen between the Seminary of St. Sulpice of Montreal and certain Indians, at Oka, Lake of Two Mountains: A Mere Case of Right of Property.* "By No Means a Religious Question." (Montreal: La Minerve Steam Printing Job Office, 1876), p. 7.

71 Clarke, *The Bloody Mohawk*, pp. 101-102; Reid, *Kahnawa:ke: Factionalism, Traditionalism, and Nationalism in a Mohawk Community*, pp. 10-13.

72 Goldstein, *French-Iroquois Diplomatic and Military Relations 1609-1701*, pp. 181-182; Clarke, *The Bloody Mohawk*, pp. 104-109.

73 Clarke, *The Bloody Mohawk*, p. 108.

74 Goldstein, *French-Iroquois Diplomatic and Military Relations 1609-1701*, pp. 195-197; Reid, *Kahnawa:ke: Factionalism, Traditionalism, and Nationalism in a Mohawk Community*, p. 11; Allen, *His Majesty's Indian Allies: British Indian Policy in the Defence of Canada, 1774-1815*, pp. 18-19.

75 In Europe this was known as the War of Spanish Succession.

76 Clarke, *The Bloody Mohawk*, p. 110.

77 Beauchamp, *A History of the New York Iroquois*, pp. 261-262; Reid, *Kahnawa:ke: Factionalism, Traditionalism, and Nationalism in a Mohawk Community*, p. 12.

78 Allen, *His Majesty's Indian Allies: British Indian Policy in the Defence of Canada, 1774-1815*, p. 16; Fowler Jr., *Empires at War: The Seven Years' War and the Struggle for North America, 1754-1763*, pp. 8-9.

79 Miller, *Skyscrapers Hide the Heavens: A History of Indian-White Relations in Canada*, pp. 78-80; Clarke, *The Bloody Mohawk*, pp. 119-121.

80 Fowler Jr., *Empires at War: The Seven Years' War and the Struggle for North America, 1754-1763*, pp. 9-10.

81 Allen, *His Majesty's Indian Allies: British Indian Policy in the Defence of Canada, 1774-1815*, pp. 15-16. This Silver Covenant Chain was established in 1677. The Covenant Chain included most nations of the Great Lakes and eastern seaboard. It served Britain, from its conception until 1763, as a defence against New France, after which time it served as a protective measure for British North America/Canada against the United States.

82 Edmund Wilson, *Apologies to the Iroquois* (New York: Farrar, Straus and Giroux, 1970), p. 126.

83 Beauchamp, *A History of the New York Iroquois*, pp. 263-266.

Chapter 4

84 Thompson, *Materials Relating to the History of the Land Dispute at Kanesatake*, p. 7; Gabriel-Doxtator and Van den Hende, *At the Woods' Edge: An Anthology of the History of the People of Kanehsata:ke*, p. 31.

85 Chief Aghneetha as quoted in Thompson, *Materials Relating to the History of the Land Dispute at Kanesatake*, p. 8.

86 *An Historical Notice on the Difficulties Arisen between the Seminary of St. Sulpice of Montreal and certain Indians, at Oka, Lake of Two Mountains: A Mere Case of Right of Property. "By No Means a Religious Question,"* pp. 7-8. One league is approximately 4.8 km or three miles.

87 Thompson, *Materials Relating to the History of the Land Dispute at Kanesatake*, p. 8.

88 Gabriel-Doxtator and Van den Hende, *At the Woods' Edge: An Anthology of the History of the People of Kanehsata:ke*, p. 32.

89 *Ibid*, p. 33.

90 Concession of 1717 as quoted in *Ibid*, p. 35.

91 Dispatch from Vaudreuil and Begon, November 1714 as quoted in Thompson, *Materials Relating to the History of the Land Dispute at Kanesatake*, p. 8.

92 *An Historical Notice on the Difficulties Arisen between the Seminary of St. Sulpice of Montreal and certain Indians, at Oka, Lake of Two Mountains: A Mere Case of Right of Property. "By No Means a Religious Question,"* p. 8.

93 Beta, *A Contribution to a Proper Understanding of the Oka Question; and a Help to its Equitable and Speedy Settlement* (Montreal, 1879), p. 78; *An Historical Notice on the Difficulties Arisen between the Seminary of St. Sulpice of Montreal and certain Indians, at Oka, Lake of Two Mountains: A Mere Case of Right of Property. "By No Means a Religious Question,"* p. 8.

94 *Ibid*, p. 9.

95 Vaudreuil and Begon to Council of Marine France, 14 October 1716 as quoted in Thompson, *Materials Relating to the History of the Land Dispute at Kanesatake*, p. 9

96 Gabriel-Doxtator and Van den Hende, *At the Woods' Edge: An Anthology of the History of the People of Kanehsata:ke*, p. 33. This moratorium lasted until 1732.

97 Vaudreuil and Begon to Council of Marine France, 14 October 1716 as quoted in Thompson, *Materials Relating to the History of the Land Dispute at Kanesatake*, p. 9

98 Norman Murray, *The Oka Question: Containing the Original Title, and a Brief Account of the Feudal System of Seigniorial Tenure in Canada, and its Abolition in 1854, with a General Review of the Oka Question in Particular and Roman Agression [sic] in General* (Quebec: E. Frechette, 1852), p. 4; Gabriel-Doxtator and Van den Hende, *At the Woods' Edge: An Anthology of the History of the People of Kanehsata:ke*, pp. 30-33; Thompson, *Materials Relating to the History of the Land Dispute at Kanesatake*, p. 9

99 *An Historical Notice on the Difficulties Arisen between the Seminary of St. Sulpice of Montreal and certain Indians, at Oka, Lake of Two Mountains: A Mere Case of Right of Property. "By No Means a Religious Question,"* pp. 7-8.

100 Smith, *Bridges and Barricades: In Defense of Mohawk Land*, p. 21; Thompson, *Materials Relating to the History of the Land Dispute at Kanesatake*, p. 10.

101 Chief Aghneetha as quoted in Thompson, *Materials Relating to the History of the Land Dispute at Kanesatake*, p. 10.

102 Thompson, *Materials Relating to the History of the Land Dispute at Kanesatake*, p. 11.

103 *An Historical Notice on the Difficulties Arisen between the Seminary of St. Sulpice of Montreal and certain Indians, at Oka, Lake of Two Mountains: A Mere Case of Right of Property. "By No Means a Religious Question,"* pp. 9-11; Gabriel-Doxtator and Van den Hende, *At the Woods' Edge: An Anthology of the History of the People of Kanehsata:ke*, p. 34.

104 Deed of Concession, 1 March 1735 as quoted in Beta, *A Contribution to a Proper Understanding of the Oka Question; and a Help to its Equitable and Speedy Settlement*,

p. 81; Protestant Defence Alliance of Canada, *The Indians of the Lake of Two Mountains and the Seminary of St. Sulpice*, p. 2.

105 As quoted in Thompson, *Materials Relating to the History of the Land Dispute at Kanesatake*, p. 12.

106 Sir William Johnson as quoted in Allen, *His Majesty's Indian Allies: British Indian Policy in the Defence of Canada, 1774-1815*, p. 30.

107 Reid, *Kahnawa:ke: Factionalism, Traditionalism, and Nationalism in a Mohawk Community*, pp. 12-13.

108 Reid, *Mohawk Territory: A Cultural Geography*, p. 118.

109 Allen, *His Majesty's Indian Allies: British Indian Policy in the Defence of Canada, 1774-1815*, p. 31.

110 Clarke, *The Bloody Mohawk*, pp. 123-134. The King George's War was an extension of the War of Austrian Succession (1740-1748).

111 See: Allen, *His Majesty's Indian Allies: British Indian Policy in the Defence of Canada, 1774-1815*, Ch. 2; Fowler Jr., *Empires at War: The Seven Years' War and the Struggle for North America, 1754-1763*, Ch. 4. William Johnson, was first a military commander and then Superintendent of Indian Affairs for the British. He was well accustomed in Iroquois traditions and culture and married Molly Brant, the sister of Mohawk Chief Joseph Brant.

112 Reid, *Kahnawa:ke: Factionalism, Traditionalism, and Nationalism in a Mohawk Community*, p. 13; Fowler Jr., *Empires at War: The Seven Years' War and the Struggle for North America, 1754-1763*, p. 1. The Seven Years' War is referred to by Americans as the French and Indian War and by some Canadians as the War of Conquest. Fowler Jr. calls it the "first world war."

113 See: Allen, *His Majesty's Indian Allies: British Indian Policy in the Defence of Canada, 1774-1815*, Ch. 2; Fowler Jr., *Empires at War: The Seven Years' War and the Struggle for North America, 1754-1763*, Ch. 4; Gavin K. Watt, *Rebellion in the Mohawk Valley: The St. Leger Expedition of 1777* (Toronto: The Dundurn Group, 2002).

114 Gabriel-Doxtator and Van den Hende, *At the Woods' Edge: An Anthology of the History of the People of Kanehsata:ke*, p. 50.

115 Chief Aghneetha as quoted in Thompson, *Materials Relating to the History of the Land Dispute at Kanesatake*, p. 13.

116 Fowler Jr., *Empires at War: The Seven Years' War and the Struggle for North America, 1754-1763*, pp. 240-241.

117 Article 40 of Articles of Capitulation, Montreal 1760 as quoted in Thompson, *Materials Relating to the History of the Land Dispute at Kanesatake*, p. 14.

118 As quoted in Thompson, *Materials Relating to the History of the Land Dispute at Kanesatake*, p. 14; Gabriel-Doxtator and Van den Hende, *At the Woods' Edge: An Anthology of the History of the People of Kanehsata:ke*, p. 45. The Natives of Kanesatake and Kahnawake were also eager to settle for peace as outbreaks of smallpox had decimated the communities in 1748, 1755 and again in 1760, 1761 and 1765.

119 Watt, *Rebellion in the Mohawk Valley: The St. Leger Expedition of 1777*, p. 49; Allen, *His Majesty's Indian Allies: British Indian Policy in the Defence of Canada, 1774-1815*, pp. 33-34; Fowler Jr., *Empires at War: The Seven Years' War and the Struggle for North America, 1754-1763*, pp. 277, 283. On numerous occasions, the British knowingly presented members of Pontiac's force with parting gifts of smallpox-laden blankets, clothing and handkerchiefs after truce meetings.

120 Allen, *His Majesty's Indian Allies: British Indian Policy in the Defence of Canada, 1774-1815*, p. 193. Allen refers to it as the Magna Carta of Native Rights in Canada.

121 Mercredi and Turpel, *In the Rapids: Navigating the Future of First Nations*, p. 33.

122 Allen, *His Majesty's Indian Allies: British Indian Policy in the Defence of Canada, 1774-1815*, pp. 34-35.

123 The Royal Proclamation, 1763 as quoted in Miller, *Skyscrapers Hide the Heavens: A History of Indian-White Relations in Canada*, p. 88.

124 Royal Commission on Aboriginal Peoples, *Treaty Making in the Spirit of Co-existence* (Canada: Communication Group Publishing, 1995), pp. 24-25. It is a little known fact that the British rescinded the Proclamation in 1768. With fear of a revolution, which inevitably came, the British under Johnson negotiated a treaty with the Iroquois for Ohio dubbed the Treaty of Fort Stanwix, in November 1768.

125 Beta, *A Contribution to a Proper Understanding of the Oka Question; and a Help to its Equitable and Speedy Settlement*, pp. 4-5; Gabriel-Doxtator and Van den Hende, *At the Woods' Edge: An Anthology of the History of the People of Kanehsata:ke*, p. 57.

126 Reid, *Kahnawa:ke: Factionalism, Traditionalism, and Nationalism in a Mohawk Community*, pp. 13-14; Gabriel-Doxtator and Van den Hende, *At the Woods' Edge: An Anthology of the History of the People of Kanehsata:ke*, p. 55.

127 Judgment of Brigadier-General Ralph Burton, Governor of Montreal, 4 November 1763 as contained in Thompson, *Materials Relating to the History of the Land Dispute at Kanesatake*, p. 15.

128 Reid, *Kahnawa:ke: Factionalism, Traditionalism, and Nationalism in a Mohawk Community*, p. 16.

129 Miller, *Skyscrapers Hide the Heavens: A History of Indian-White Relations in Canada*, pp. 93-98; Watt, *Rebellion in the Mohawk Valley: The St. Leger Expedition of 1777*, Ch. 2-3.

130 Allen, *His Majesty's Indian Allies: British Indian Policy in the Defence of Canada, 1774-1815*, pp. 58-65.

131 Clarke, *The Bloody Mohawk*, pp. 347-350; Miller, *Skyscrapers Hide the Heavens: A History of Indian-White Relations in Canada*, pp. 93-99.

132 Paul Pasquaretta, *Gambling and Survival in Native North America* (Arizona: University of Arizona Press, 2003), p. 127; Clarke, *The Bloody Mohawk*, pp. 349-350.

133 Pasquaretta, *Gambling and Survival in Native North America*, pp. 127-128; Hall, *Warrior's Handbook*, p. 18.

134 Kahn-Tineta Horn, "Beyond Oka: Dimensions of Mohawk Sovereignty," Studies in Political Economy 35 (Summer 1991): pp. 34-35.

135 Hall, *Warrior's Handbook*, p. 18; Hall, *Rebuilding the Iroquois Confederacy*, pp. 6-7; Reid, *Kahnawa:ke: Factionalism, Traditionalism, and Nationalism in a Mohawk Community*, p. 17.

136 The 1794 *Jay Treaty*, <www.solon.org/misc/jay.html>. Specifically, Articles II and III recognized the right of free movement over the border and the nullification of import duties.

137 Johansen, *Life and Death in Mohawk Country*, p. 29; Hall, *Warrior's Handbook*, pp. 31-35; Goodleaf, *Entering the War Zone: A Mohawk Perspective on Resisting Invasion*, p. 10; Reid, *Kahnawa:ke: Factionalism, Traditionalism, and Nationalism in a Mohawk Community*, pp. 149-150; Pertusati, *In Defense of Mohawk Land: Ethnopolitical Conflict in Native North America*, p. 71.

138 House of Commons, *The Summer of 1990: Fifth Report of the Standing Committee on Aboriginal Affairs, Issue No. 59* (Government of Canada: Supply and Services Canada, April 1991), p. 7. Thompson, *Materials Relating to the History of the Land Dispute at Kanesatake*, p. 16.

139 J.R. Miller, "Great White Father Knows Best: Oka and the Land Claims Process," Native Studies Review 7, no. 1 (1991): p. 27.

140 Allen, *His Majesty's Indian Allies: British Indian Policy in the Defence of Canada, 1774-1815*, pp. 146-148.

141 Miller, *Skyscrapers Hide the Heavens: A History of Indian-White Relations in Canada*, pp. 110, 117; Allen, *His Majesty's Indian Allies: British Indian Policy in the Defence of Canada, 1774-1815*, p. 148. See: Guy St-Denis, *Tecumseh's Bones* (Montreal: McGill-Queen's University Press, 2005) for an excellent account of Tecumseh's death at the Battle of the Thames in 1813 and the subsequent search for his grave and bones.

142 Thompson, *Materials Relating to the History of the Land Dispute at Kanesatake*, pp. 18-19.

143 *Ibid*, p. 19.

144 Statute contained in Beta, *A Contribution to a Proper Understanding of the Oka Question; and a Help to its Equitable and Speedy Settlement*, pp. 83-92; Patricia Begin, Wendy Moss and Peter Niemczak, *The Land Claim Dispute at Oka* (Canada: Minister of Supply and Services Canada, 1992), pp. 1-2.

145 Thompson, *Materials Relating to the History of the Land Dispute at Kanesatake*, p. 24.

146 Miller, "Great White Father Knows Best: Oka and the Land Claims Process," p. 31; Gabriel-Doxtator and Van den Hende, *At the Woods' Edge: An Anthology of the History of the People of Kanehsata:ke*, p. 95.

147 As quoted in Thompson, *Materials Relating to the History of the Land Dispute at Kanesatake*, p. 24.

148 Gabriel-Doxtator and Van den Hende, *At the Woods' Edge: An Anthology of the History of the People of Kanehsata:ke*, p. 91.

149 Protestant Defence Alliance of Canada. *The Indians of the Lake of Two Mountains and the Seminary of St. Sulpice*, pp. 4-5; Miller, "Great White Father Knows Best: Oka and the Land Claims Process," p. 30.

150 Thompson, *Materials Relating to the History of the Land Dispute at Kanesatake*, p. 25.

151 Gabriel-Doxtator and Van den Hende, *At the Woods' Edge: An Anthology of the History of the People of Kanehsata:ke*, pp. 103-105.

152 *An Historical Notice on the Difficulties Arisen between the Seminary of St. Sulpice of Montreal and certain Indians, at Oka, Lake of Two Mountains: A Mere Case of Right of Property. "By No Means a Religious Question,"* p. 18.

153 Gabriel-Doxtator and Van den Hende, *At the Woods' Edge: An Anthology of the History of the People of Kanehsata:ke*, pp. 108-109.

154 Thompson, *Materials Relating to the History of the Land Dispute at Kanesatake*, p. 30; Gabriel-Doxtator and Van den Hende, *At the Woods' Edge: An Anthology of the History of the People of Kanehsata:ke*, Ch. 5.

155 Thompson, *Materials Relating to the History of the Land Dispute at Kanesatake*, p. 30.

156 Gabriel-Doxtator and Van den Hende, *At the Woods' Edge: An Anthology of the History of the People of Kanehsata:ke*, pp. 136-138.

157 Miller, "Great White Father Knows Best: Oka and the Land Claims Process," p. 32; Robert Vachon, "The Mohawk Nation and its Communities," INTERculture, Vol. XXIV, No. 4 (Fall 1991): p. 18.

158 Hayter Reed to Chief John Tewisha, 26 May 1894 as contained in Gabriel-Doxtator and Van den Hende, *At the Woods' Edge: An Anthology of the History of the People of Kanehsata:ke*, p. 168.

Chapter 5

159 Royal Commission on Aboriginal Peoples, *Treaty Making and the Spirit of Co-existence*, pp. 29-30.

160 John L. Tobias, "Protection, Civilization, Assimilation," contained in J.R. Miller ed, *Sweet Promises: A Reader on Indian-White Relations in Canada* (Toronto: University Press, 1991), pp. 127-144.

161 Miller, *Skyscrapers Hide the Heavens: A History of Indian-White Relations in Canada*, pp. 145-146; Gabriel-Doxtator and Van den Hende, *At the Woods' Edge: An Anthology of the History of the People of Kanehsata:ke*, pp. 129-130. It was at Confederation that the town of Oka got its name. At the urging of the steamboat company, Canada Post changed the name from Lake of Two Mountains to Oka. Mohawk tradition states that Oka was the last name of a French settler, Paul Oka, who after failing to trap enough meat for the winter ate his daughter. He is said to have died in 1882.

162 Frideres, *Native Peoples in Canada: Contemporary Conflicts*, pp. 8-10. Revisions to the Indian Act occurred in: 1880, 1884, 1885, 1894, 1895, 1911, 1920, 1922, 1927, 1933, 1951 and 1985.

163 Miller, *Skyscrapers Hide the Heavens: A History of Indian-White Relations in Canada*, pp. 254-255; Tobias, "Protection, Civilization, Assimilation," pp. 127-144. The U.S. Government also passed numerous similar pieces of legislation: 1830 *Indian Removal Act*, 1887 *Dawes Severalty Act* and the 1934 *Indian Reorganization Act.*

164 Frideres, *Native Peoples in Canada: Contemporary Conflicts*, p. 393.

165 House of Commons, *The Summer of 1990: Fifth Report of the Standing Committee on Aboriginal Affairs, Issue No. 59*, p. 3.

166 Indian and Northern Affairs Canada, *Mohawk Band Government* (DIAND: 1990), pp. 1-4; House of Commons, *The Summer of 1990: Fifth Report of the Standing Committee on Aboriginal Affairs, Issue No. 59*, p. 3.

167 Corinthe, Superior Court of Montreal, Record of Proceedings, 10 February 1909, as quoted in Thompson, *Materials Relating to the History of the Land Dispute at Kanesatake*, p. 34; Gabriel-Doxtator and Van den Hende, *At the Woods' Edge: An Anthology of the History of the People of Kanehsata:ke*, pp. 227-232.

168 Chief Joseph Gabriel to His Majesty, Edward VII, 28 May 1909, as quoted in Thompson, *Materials Relating to the History of the Land Dispute at Kanesatake*, p.35.

169 *Ibid*, p. 36.

170 House of Commons, *The Summer of 1990: Fifth Report of the Standing Committee on Aboriginal Affairs, Issue No. 59*, p. 8; Begin, Moss and Niemczak, *The Land Claim Dispute at Oka*, p. 2.

171 Commission des droits de la personne du Québec (prepared by Monique Rochon and Pierre Lepage), *Oka-Kanehsatake – Summer 1990: A Collective Shock: Report of the Commission des droits de la personne du Québec* (Quebec: 1991), p. 47; Thompson, *Materials Relating to the History of the Land Dispute at Kanesatake*, p. 38-39;

172 House of Commons, *The Summer of 1990: Fifth Report of the Standing Committee on Aboriginal Affairs, Issue No. 59*, p. 8.

173 Commission des droits de la personne du Québec, *Oka-Kanehsatake – Summer 1990: A Collective Shock: Report of the Commission des droits de la personne du Québec*, p. 48.

174 Thompson, *Materials Relating to the History of the Land Dispute at Kanesatake*, p. 40.

175 *Ibid*, p. 40; Gabriel-Doxtator and Van den Hende, *At the Woods' Edge: An Anthology of the History of the People of Kanehsata:ke*, p. 238.

176 Michel F. Girard, "The Oka Crisis from an Environmental History Perspective, 1870-1990," contained in *Readings in Canadian History Post-Confederation*, R. Douglas Francis and Donald B. Smith ed. (Toronto: Harcourt Brace & Co., 1994), pp. 581-582. The Oka forest is one of the only remaining white pine forests in Quebec. It is home to numerous rare bird species including the pine warbler, bald eagle and the golden eagle.

177 *Ibid*, pp. 584-589; House of Commons, *The Summer of 1990: Fifth Report of the Standing Committee on Aboriginal Affairs, Issue No. 59*, p. 16.

178 *Ibid*, pp. 590-591.

179 Johansen, *Life and Death in Mohawk Country*, p. xxii.

180 1969 White Paper as quoted in Miller, *Skyscrapers Hide the Heavens: A History of Indian-White Relations in Canada*, pp. 331-332.

Chapter 6

181 As quoted in Ward Churchill and Jim Vander Wall, *Agents of Repression: The FBI's Secret Wars Against the Black Panther Party and the American Indian Movement* (Boston: South End Press, 1990), p. 119.

182 Churchill and Vander Wall, *Agents of Repression: The FBI's Secret Wars Against the Black Panther Party and the American Indian Movement*, p. 119; Ward Churchill and Jim Vander Wall, *The Cointelpro Papers: Documents fro the FBI's Secret Wars Against Dissent in the United States* (Boston: South End Press, 1990). p. 233.

183 Churchill and Vander Wall, *Agents of Repression: The FBI's Secret Wars Against the Black Panther Party and the American Indian Movement*, pp. 119-120; Churchill and Vander Wall, *The Cointelpro Papers: Documents fro the FBI's Secret Wars Against Dissent in the United States*, pp. 233-234.

184 Krotz, *Indian Country: Inside Another Canada*, p. 75.

185 Tugwell and Thompson, *The Legacy of Oka*, p. 10.

186 Ted Means as quoted in Peter Matthiessen, *In the Spirit of Crazy Horse* (U.S.A.: Penguin Books, 1992), p. 75.

187 Churchill and Vander Wall, *The Cointelpro Papers: Documents fro the FBI's Secret Wars Against Dissent in the United States*, pp. 188, 276, 297; Churchill and Vander Wall, *Agents of Repression: The FBI's Secret Wars Against the Black Panther Party and the American Indian Movement*, pp. 290-299.

188 FBI document 5 June 1975 as quoted in Matthiessen, *In the Spirit of Crazy Horse*, p. 133.

189 Churchill and Vander Wall, *Agents of Repression: The FBI's Secret Wars Against the Black Panther Party and the American Indian Movement*, pp. 143-145.

190 Louis Hall, Toronto Star, 25 November 1990 as quoted in Johansen, *Life and Death in Mohawk Country*, p. 116.

191 Louis Hall speech, Tulsa Oklahoma 30 June 1984. Hall, *Rebuilding the Iroquois Confederacy*, p. 34.

192 Mike Mitchell as quoted in York and Pindera, *People of the Pines: The Warriors and The Legacy of Oka*, p. 182.

193 Cartoon as quoted in Thompson, *The Long Fall of the Mohawk Warriors*, p. 2.

194 Hall, *Warrior's Handbook*, p. 30.

195 Pertusati, *In Defense of Mohawk Land: Ethnopolitical Conflict in Native North America*, p. 58, 61-62.

196 *Ibid*, p. 58, 61-62.

197 Johansen, *Life and Death in Mohawk Country*, pp. 115-116.

198 Indian Time, 30 May 1990 as quoted in Johansen, *Life and Death in Mohawk Country*, p. 116.

199 Hall, *Rebuilding the Iroquois Confederacy*, p. 2.

200 Hall, *Ibid*, p. 47; Hall, *Warrior's Handbook*, p. 2; Johansen, *Life and Death in Mohawk Country*, p. 115.

201 As quoted in Ciaccia, *The Oka Crisis: A Mirror of the Soul*, p. 349.

202 Johansen, *Life and Death in Mohawk Country*, pp. 22-27; Canada. DND ATI, "Intelligence Report—Op AKWESASNE, 17 August 1990."

203 Pasquaretta, *Gambling and Survival in Native North America*, p. 131.

204 E.J. Dickson, *Communities, Contraband and Conflict: Considering Restorative Responses to Repairing the Harms Implicit in Smuggling in the Akwesasne Mohawk Nation* (Ottawa: Research and Evaluation Branch, Royal Canadian Mounted Police, 2002), p. 25; Tugwell and Thompson, *The Legacy of Oka*, p. 15; Confidential Source.

205 Krotz, *Indian Country: Inside Another Canada*, p. 84;

206 Gail H. Landsman, *Sovereignty and Symbol: Indian-White Conflict at Ganienkeh* (Albuquerque: university of New Mexico Press, 1988), pp. 26, 150.

207 *Ibid*, p. 29; Canada. DND ATI, "Letter: Grand Council of the Six Nations Confederacy to President Gerald Ford, 24 November 1974."

208 Landsman, *Sovereignty and Symbol: Indian-White Conflict at Ganienkeh*, p. 150; York and Pindera, *People of the Pines: The Warriors and The Legacy of Oka*, pp. 178-179.

209 Tugwell and Thompson, *The Legacy of Oka*, pp. 13-14.

210 Tugwell and Thompson, *The Legacy of Oka*, p. 15; Mohawk Council of Kahnawake, *Institutions of Mohawk Government in Kahnawake: An Overview*, p. 15. The Peacekeeper Force at Kahnawake was created in 1979. Prior to this however, Kahnawake had its own police force created in 1966.

211 Loran Thompson, "Fighting Back," contained in *Nation to Nation: Aboriginal Sovereignty and the Future of Canada*. Diane Engelstad and John Bird ed. (Canada: Anansi Press, 1992), pp. 173-178.

212 Tugwell and Thompson, *The Legacy of Oka*, p. 14; York and Pindera, *People of the Pines: The Warriors and The Legacy of Oka*, pp. 180-183.

213 Johansen, *Life and Death in Mohawk Country*, pp. 26, 51.

214 Tugwell and Thompson, *The Legacy of Oka*, p. 16; Krotz, *Indian Country: Inside Another Canada*, p. 85; Johansen, *Life and Death in Mohawk Country*, pp. 28-29.

215 Art Kakwirakeron Montour as quoted in Hornung, *One Nation Under the Gun: Inside the Mohawk Civil War*, pp. 30-31.

216 Tugwell and Thompson, *The Legacy of Oka*, pp. 15-16.

217 Pertusati, *In Defense of Mohawk Land: Ethnopolitical Conflict in Native North America*, p. 73.

218 Concept adopted from Tugwell and Thompson, *The Legacy of Oka*, p. 17.

219 *Ibid*, pp. 17-18.

220 Thompson, *The Long Fall of the Mohawk Warriors*, p. 3.

Chapter 7

221 Miller, *Skyscrapers Hide the Heavens: A History of Indian-White Relations in Canada*, pp. 343, 373.

222 Pierre Trudeau as quoted in Miller, "Great White Father Knows Best: Oka and the Land Claims Process," p. 38. This is the same Trudeau who in 1969 while speaking in Vancouver denied the existence of treaty rights because, "no society can be built on historical might-have beens."

223 House of Commons, *The Summer of 1990: Fifth Report of the Standing Committee on Aboriginal Affairs, Issue No. 59*, p. 8.

224 Department of Indian Affairs, *Land Claim Policy* (DIAND: July 1990), pp. 1-2.

225 House of Commons, *The Summer of 1990: Fifth Report of the Standing Committee on Aboriginal Affairs, Issue No. 59*, p. 9; Department of Indian Affairs, *An Overview of the Oka Issue*, p. 3.

226 House of Commons, *The Summer of 1990: Fifth Report of the Standing Committee on Aboriginal Affairs, Issue No. 59*, p. 9; Department of Indian Affairs, *An Overview of the Oka Issue*, p. 3.

227 Frideres, *Native Peoples in Canada: Contemporary Conflicts*, p. 369.

228 Begin, Moss and Niemczak, *The Land Claim Dispute at Oka*, p. 2; Department of Indian and Northern Affairs, *Land Claims Policy*, pp. 4-5. By March 1990, 578 Specific Claims had been submitted, with 205 being resolved.

229 House of Commons, *The Summer of 1990: Fifth Report of the Standing Committee on Aboriginal Affairs, Issue No. 59*, p. 10; Begin, Moss and Niemczak, *The Land Claim Dispute at Oka*, p. 2.

230 House of Commons, *The Summer of 1990: Fifth Report of the Standing Committee on Aboriginal Affairs, Issue No. 59*, pp. 9-10.

231 Begin, Moss and Niemczak, *The Land Claim Dispute at Oka*, p. 2.

232 Vachon, "The Mohawk Nation and its Communities," pp. 14, 18; DIAND, *How DIAND Programs are Administered at Akwesasne, Kahnawake and Kanesatake* (DIAND, 1990), pp. 1-2.

233 Commission des droits de la personne du Québec, *Oka-Kanehsatake – Summer 1990: A Collective Shock: Report of the Commission des droits de la personne du Québec*, p. 49.

234 Gabriel-Doxtator and Van den Hende, *At the Woods' Edge: An Anthology of the History of the People of Kanehsata:ke*, p. 245.

235 Letter 12 April 1988, Chief Gabriel to Bill McKnight as quoted in House of Commons, *The Summer of 1990: Fifth Report of the Standing Committee on Aboriginal Affairs, Issue No. 59*, p. 14.

236 *Ibid*, p. 15.

237 Commission des droits de la personne du Québec, *Oka-Kanehsatake – Summer 1990: A Collective Shock: Report of the Commission des droits de la personne du Québec*, p. 51.

238 Guy Gilbert, *Rapport D'Enquête du Coroner: Guy Gilbert sur les Causes et Circonstances du Décès de Monsieur Marcel Lemay, English Version* (Quebec, 1995), p. 77a.

239 House of Commons, *Minutes of the Proceedings and Evidence of the Standing Committee on Aboriginal Affairs, Issue No. 55* (Government of Canada: Supply and Services Canada, 19 March 1991), pp. 41-42

240 House of Commons, *Minutes of the Proceedings and Evidence of the Standing Committee on Aboriginal Affairs, Issue No. 55*, pp. 43-44.

241 Commission des droits de la personne du Québec, *Oka-Kanehsatake – Summer 1990: A Collective Shock: Report of the Commission des droits de la personne du Québec*, p. 55.

242 DIAND, *Mohawk Band Government*, p.1.

243 *Ibid*, p. 1.

244 *Ibid*, pp. 1-2.

245 Interview with Ellen Gabriel, Kahnawake, M.T., 1 September 2005. All sources give 11 March as the date of the first occupation of the Pines.

Chapter 8

246 Department of Indian and Northern Affairs, *Mohawk Band Government*, pp. 2-3.

247 *Ibid*, p. 3.

248 Harold Tarbell as quoted in Hornung, *One Nation Under the Gun: Inside the Mohawk Civil War*, p. 31.

249 Harold Tarbell interview with Jennifer Westaway, CBC: The House, 28 July 1990, "Are Mohawks Criminals?" (Ottawa: Bowdens, 1990), pp. 2-4.

250 Johansen, *Life and Death in Mohawk Country*, pp. 76-84; Canada. DND ATI, "Press Dispatches, 02 May 1990."

251 Lieutenant-Colonel Robin Gagnon, "Operation SALON-Briefing Given to the Infantry Conference, Ottawa, 18 November 1990."

252 Johansen, *Life and Death in Mohawk Country*, pp. 79-84; Hornung, *One Nation Under the Gun: Inside the Mohawk Civil War*, pp. 150-160.

253 Canada. DND ATI, "Letter: Mohawk Councils of Akwesasne to Major General L.P. Flynn, 25 April 1990."

254 Canada. DND ATI, "Letter: Mohawk Council of Akwesasne to Prime Minister Brian Mulroney and Minister of Indian Affairs Tom Siddon, 25 April 1990."

255 Canada. DND ATI, "Statement by Governor Mario Cuomo, 30 April 1990."

256 Harold Tarbell as quoted in Hornung, *One Nation Under the Gun: Inside the Mohawk Civil War*, p. 157.

257 Mike Mitchell as quoted in *Ibid*, p. 157.

258 Canada. DND ATI, "National Contingency Plan-Akwesasne, 30 April 1990."

259 Canada. DND ATI, "National Contingency Plan-Akwesasne, 30 April 1990."

260 *Ibid*.

261 Johansen, *Life and Death in Mohawk Country*, pp. 109-110.

262 Doug George as quoted in Hornung, *One Nation Under the Gun: Inside the Mohawk Civil War*, p. 163.

263 Canada. DND ATI, "Possible CF Involvement on the Akwesasne Indian Reserve, 25 April 1990."

264 *Ibid.*

265 Canada. DND ATI, "Possible CF Involvement on the Akwesasne Indian Reserve, 25 April 1990;" Canada. DND ATI, "Air Photo-Akwesasne, 30 April 1990."

266 Canada. DND ATI, "Possible CF Involvement on the Akwesasne Indian Reserve, 25 April 1990."

267 Canada. DND ATI, "Op Feather War Diary, 26-27 April 1990."

268 Canada. DND ATI, "Force Mobile Command Warning Order, 28 April 1990;" Canada. DND ATI, "Request for Security Intelligence Assessment-Akwesasne Indian Reserve, 30 April 1990;" Canada. DND ATI, "Support to Law Enforcement Agencies-Akwesasne Indian Reserve, 27 April 1990."

269 Canada. DND ATI, "Threat Assessment-St. Regis Akwesasne Indian Reserve, 27 April 1990;" Canada. DND ATI, "Intelligence Report—Threats St. Regis Indian Reserve, 28 April 1990."

270 Canada. DND ATI, "Threat Assessment-St. Regis Akwesasne Indian Reserve, 27 April 1990;" "Intelligence Report—Threats St. Regis Indian Reserve, 28 April 1990."

271 Canada. DND ATI, "Air Photo-Akwesasne, 30 April 1990."

272 Eric Siblin, "Mohawk Factions Fight Nine-hour Gun Battle," The Globe and Mail, 2 May 1990.

273 Canada. DND ATI, "Op Feather War Diary 01 May 1990."

274 Canada. DND ATI, "Op Feather War Diary 01-03 May 1990."

275 Canada. DND ATI, "CF Support to Police Activities at Akwesasne, 02 May 1990."

276 E.P. Craig, "In Light of Oka: A Need to Re-Examine *Aid to the Civil Power*," contained in Military Operations in Unique Environments: Domestic Operations Précis, (Canadian Land Force Command and Staff College, 1995), ANX I- p. 2.

Chapter 9

277 Craig, "In Light of Oka: A Need to Re-Examine *Aid to the Civil Power*," , ANX I- pp. 3-4.

278 Desmond Morton, "Bayonets in the Streets: The Canadian Experience of *Aid to the Civil Power* 1867-1990," Canadian Defence Quarterly 20(5), (April 1991): p. 30.

279 Craig, "In Light of Oka: A Need to Re-Examine *Aid to the Civil Power*," ANX I- p. 4.

280 Morton, "Bayonets in the Streets: The Canadian Experience of *Aid to the Civil Power* 1867-1990," p. 30.

281 Maloney, "Domestic Operations: The Canadian Approach," p. 137.

282 *Ibid*, pp. 137-138.

283 *Ibid*, p. 138.

284 Government of Canada, *National Defence Act* R.S. c. N-5 (Ottawa: 1987), pp. 112-116.

285 *Ibid*, pp. 112-116.

286 *Ibid*, pp. 112-116.

287 Queen's Regulations and Orders 23.09(2) as quoted in Craig, "In Light of Oka: A Need to Re-Examine *Aid to the Civil Power*," ANX I- p. 3.

288 Government of Canada, Department of National Defence, *Queen's Regulations and Orders, Vol. I Administration* (Ottawa: Queen's Printer, 1968), Section 5, 23:15, Note D.

289 Maloney, "Domestic Operations: The Canadian Approach," pp. 136-137.

290 Government of Canada, *War Measures Act* R.S.C. c. W-2 (Ottawa: 1985), Section 3(1).

291 Maloney, "Domestic Operations: The Canadian Approach," p. 137.

292 Canada. DND ATI, "Aide Memoire: Assistance to Civil Authorities," p. 3.

293 Maloney, "Domestic Operations: The Canadian Approach," p. 139.

294 Craig, "In Light of Oka: A Need to Re-Examine *Aid to the Civil Power*," ANX I- p. 5.

295 Maloney, "Domestic Operations: The Canadian Approach," p. 139.

296 Tommy Douglas as quoted in Morton, "Bayonets in the Streets: The Canadian Experience of *Aid to the Civil Power* 1867-1990," p. 36.

297 Craig, "In Light of Oka: A Need to Re-Examine *Aid to the Civil Power*," ANX I- p. 3.

298 *Ibid*, ANX I- pp. 7-8.

299 Canada. DND ATI, "Backgrounder: Canadian Forces in *Aid to the Civil Power*, July 1990;" Maloney, "Domestic Operations: The Canadian Approach," p. 140.

300 Government of Canada, *Emergencies Act*, R.S.1988 c. 29 (Ottawa: 1988), Section 3 (B).

301 Craig, "In Light of Oka: A Need to Re-Examine *Aid to the Civil Power*," ANX I- p. 11.

302 Government of Canada, *Emergencies Act*, Section 25(3).

303 Craig, "In Light of Oka: A Need to Re-Examine *Aid to the Civil Power*," ANX I- p. 11.

304 *Ibid*, p. 12.

305 Morton, "Bayonets in the Streets: The Canadian Experience of *Aid to the Civil Power* 1867-1990," p. 34.

306 Maloney, "Domestic Operations: The Canadian Approach," p. 137; Bland and Maloney, *Campaigns for International Security: Canada's Defence Policy at the Turn of the Century*, pp. 255-265.

Chapter 10

307 Lieutenant-Colonel Derald Prosser as quoted in Captain Tony Keene, "Guns Among the Mohawks," *Sentinel: Magazine of the Canadian Forces* Vol. 26, no. 4 (Ottawa: National Defence Information Services, 1990/4): p. 2.

308 Canada. DND ATI, "Operation Orders: Op FEATHER, 02 May 1990."

309 Lieutenant-Colonel Norris Pettis as quoted in Captain Tony Keene, "Guns Among the Mohawks," p. 3. Pettis was replaced by Major B. Bowes on 13 May 1990.

310 Canada. DND ATI, "Op Feather, Groupings and Tasks, 02 May 1990."

311 Canada. DND ATI, "Op Feather/Akwesasne, Tasked Equipment and Support;" Canada. DND ATI, "Op FEATHER, Personnel and Equipment List, 08 May 1990."

312 Canada DND ATI, "Situation Report, 02 May 1990."

313 Canada. DND ATI, "Intelligence Reports, 03-04 May 1990."

314 Canada. DND ATI, "Situation Report, Deployment of SIGINT Resources, 06 May 1990."

315 Canada. DND ATI, "Situation Report, Deployment of SIGINT Resources, 06 May 1990."

316 Canada. DND ATI, "Op FEATHER War Dairy, 06 May 1990."

317 Canada. DND ATI, "Op FEATHER War Dairy, 06 May 1990."

318 Canada. DND ATI, "Intelligence Summary, 04-06 May 1990."

319 Canada. DND ATI, "Situation Reports, 04-10 May 1990."

320 Canada. DND ATI, "Situation Reports, 04-10 May 1990."

321 Canada. DND ATI, "Joint Security Intelligence Report—Oka and Akwesasne Reserves, 10 May 1990."

322 *Ibid.*

323 Canada. DND ATI, "Situation Report, 25 May 1990."

324 Canada DND ATI, "Intelligence Support—Op AKWESASNE, 17 May 1990."

325 Canada. DND ATI, "Situation Reports, 10-23 May 1990; "Intelligence Summaries—Op AKWESASNE, 18-30 May 1990."

326 Canada. DND ATI, "Intelligence Summary—Op AKWESASNE, 18-22 May 1990."

327 Canada. DND ATI, "Intelligence Summaries—Op AKWESASNE, 18-30 May 1990."

328 Canada. DND ATI, "Intelligence Summary—Op AKWESASNE, 28-30 May 1990."

329 Canada DND ATI, "Situation Reports—Op AKWESASNE, 3-10 June 1990."

330 Canada. DND ATI, "Akwesasne—Gaming Report, 30 June 1990."

331 Canada. DND ATI, "Warning Order-Standby Force, 07 June 1990;" "Situation Report—Op AKWESASNE, 25 June 1990."

332 Canada. DND ATI, "Situation Report—Op AKWESASNE, 12 June 1990."

333 Canada. DND ATI, "Situation Reports—Op AKWESASNE, 16-19 June 1990."

334 Canada. DND ATI, "CTI Unit Intercept Activity Report, 17 June 1990."

335 Thompson, *The Long Fall of the Mohawk Warriors*, pp. 3-5.

336 Canada. DND ATI, "Op AKWESASNE Redeployment and Reduction of Readiness, 27 June 1990;" Canada. DND ATI, "Situation Report—Op AKWESASNE, 05 July 1990."

Chapter 11

337 Canada. DND ATI, "Situation Report—Op AKWESASNE, 14 June 1990."

338 Dan Gaspe as quoted in House of Commons, *The Summer of 1990: Fifth Report of the Standing Committee on Aboriginal Affairs, Issue No. 59*, p. 19.

339 Interview with Ellen Gabriel, Kahnawake M.T., 1 September 2005.

340 *Ibid.*

341 Hornung, *One Nation Under the Gun: Inside the Mohawk Civil War*, p. 182.

342 Canada. DND ATI, "Intelligence Reports—Op AKWESASNE, 26 April-4 May 1990."

343 Harold Tarbell interview with Jennifer Westaway, CBC: The House, 28 July 1990, "Are Mohawks Criminals?," pp. 4-6.

344 Oka Mayor Jean Ouellette as quoted in House of Commons, *Minutes of the Proceedings and Evidence of the Standing Committee on Aboriginal Affairs, Issue No. 55*, pp. 51-52.

345 Canada. DND ATI, "Intelligence Report—Op AKWESASNE, 2 May 1990;" York and Pindera, *People of the Pines: The Warriors and The Legacy of Oka*, pp. 66-67.

346 Canada. DND ATI, "Security Intelligence Report—Akwesasne and Oka, 8 May 1990."

347 Canada. DND ATI, "Air Photo Request, 4 May 1990."

348 York and Pindera, *People of the Pines: The Warriors and The Legacy of Oka*, pp. 65-74.

349 Canada. DND ATI, "Situation Reports—Op AKWESASNE, 25-30 June 1990."

350 Commission des droits de la personne du Québec, *Oka-Kanehsatake – Summer 1990: A Collective Shock: Report of the Commission des droits de la personne du Québec*, pp. 56-57; York and Pindera, *People of the Pines: The Warriors and The Legacy of Oka*, pp. 65-74.

351 Interview with Ellen Gabriel, Kahnawake M.T., 1 September 2005; York and Pindera, *People of the Pines: The Warriors and The Legacy of Oka*, pp. 65-74.

352 Interview with Ellen Gabriel, Kahnawake M.T., 1 September 2005.

353 Guy Gilbert, *Rapport D'Enquête du Coroner: Guy Gilbert sur les Causes et Circonstances du Décès de Monsieur Marcel Lemay, English Version* (Quebec, 1995), pp. 155-157.

354 House of Commons, *The Summer of 1990: Fifth Report of the Standing Committee on Aboriginal Affairs, Issue No. 59*, pp. 21-22.

355 Interview with Ellen Gabriel, Kahnawake, M.T., 01 September 2005.

356 Anthime Bergeron as quoted in York and Pindera, *People of the Pines: The Warriors and The Legacy of Oka*, p. 73; House of Commons, *Minutes of the Proceedings and Evidence of the Standing Committee on Aboriginal Affairs, Issue No. 55*, pp. 53-54.

357 House of Commons, *Minutes of the Proceedings and Evidence of the Standing Committee on Aboriginal Affairs, Issue No. 55*, pp. 53-54; York and Pindera, *People of the Pines: The Warriors and The Legacy of Oka*, pp. 73-74.

358 House of Commons, *The Summer of 1990: Fifth Report of the Standing Committee on Aboriginal Affairs, Issue No. 59*, pp. 23-24; House of Commons, *Minutes of the Proceedings and Evidence of the Standing Committee on Aboriginal Affairs, Issue No. 55*, p. 55.

359 Letter Municipality of Oka to Director General SQ, Robert Lavigne, 10 July 1990 as quoted in House of Commons, *The Summer of 1990: Fifth Report of the Standing Committee on Aboriginal Affairs, Issue No. 59*, p. 24.

360 Brigadier-General Armand Roy as quoted in House of Commons, *Minutes of the Proceedings and Evidence of the Standing Committee on Aboriginal Affairs, Issue No. 55*, pp. 88-89.

361 Gilbert, *Rapport D'Enquête du Coroner: Guy Gilbert sur les Causes et Circonstances du Décès de Monsieur Marcel Lemay, English Version*, pp. 39-40.

362 *Ibid*, pp. 40-41.

363 *Ibid*, pp. 41-42

364 *Ibid*, p. 312; Canada. DND ATI, "Oka Indian Reserve-Situation Report 1, 11 July 1990."

365 Canada. DND ATI, "Situation Report—Op AKWESASNE, 10-11 July 1990."

366 Gilbert, *Rapport D'Enquête du Coroner: Guy Gilbert sur les Causes et Circonstances du Décès de Monsieur Marcel Lemay, English Version*, p. 313; York and Pindera, *People of the Pines: The Warriors and The Legacy of Oka*, p. 80.

Chapter 12

367 Gilbert, *Rapport D'Enquête du Coroner: Guy Gilbert sur les Causes et Circonstances du Décès de Monsieur Marcel Lemay, English Version*, pp. 8-9, 42-46. It should be noted that the request for an investigation on the events of 11 July was forwarded by all levels of the SQ, the Municipalities of Oka (village and parish), and the Mohawk communities of Kanesatake and Kahnawake.

368 *Ibid*, pp. 42-46, 348.

369 *Ibid*, pp. 295, 307-310.

370 *Ibid*, pp. 65-66, 347-356. Of the 14,611 cartridges seized in the Treatment Centre on 26-27 September 6,506 were 5.56mm (.233 Rem.). Of these, 37 were equipped with a penetrator, all bearing NATO trademark numbers.

371 *Ibid*, p. 353.

372 *Ibid*, pp. 351-352.

373 *Ibid*, pp. 408.

374 Confidential Source.

375 Canada. DND ATI, "Oka Indian Reserve Intelligence, 11 July 1990;" MacLaine and Baxendale, *This Land is Our Land: The Mohawk Revolt at Oka*, pp. 21-23.

376 Gilbert, *Rapport D'Enquête du Coroner: Guy Gilbert sur les Causes et Circonstances du Décès de Monsieur Marcel Lemay, English Version*, p. 314.

377 Cookie McComber as quoted in Hornung, *One Nation Under the Gun: Inside the Mohawk Civil War*, p. 201.

378 Kenneth Deer as quoted in *Ibid*, p. 203.

379 Johansen, *Life and Death in Mohawk Country*, p. 140.

380 Gilbert, *Rapport D'Enquête du Coroner: Guy Gilbert sur les Causes et Circonstances du Décès de Monsieur Marcel Lemay, English Version*, p. 314.

381 Canada. DND ATI, "Intelligence Summary—Op AKWESASNE, 11-15 July 1990."

382 Canada. DND ATI, "Situation Reports—Op AKWESASNE, 11-13 July 1990;" Canada. DND ATI, "Operation Order: Operation CROSSBELT, 17, 19 July 1990."

383 Confidential Source.

384 Canada. DND ATI, "Intelligence Summary—Op AKWESASNE, 11-15 July 1990."

Chapter 13

385 Dan Smith, *The Seventh Fire: The Struggle for Aboriginal Government* (Toronto: Key Porter Books, 1993), pp. 88-89. Quebec-Native relations had not been as peaceful as in other Provinces.

386 The deadline was 23 June 1990.

387 John Howse, "A new native hero," Maclean's Magazine (16 July 1990): p. 13. Newfoundland Premier Clyde Wells vetoed Meech Lake the next day, and the Federal government tried to pin the defeat on him to take away Harper's "fame" or credibility.

388 Elijah Harper as quoted in Miller, *Skyscrapers Hide the Heavens*, p. 377. At the Charlottetown Accord in 1992, the Aboriginals did get some recognition and although it represented progress for self-determination, the Accord did not survive the October 1992 national referendum.

389 Phil Fontaine as quoted in Brian Bergman, "Drumbeats of Anger," Maclean's Magazine (2 July 1990): pp. 28-29.

390 Mercredi and Turpel, *In the Rapids: Navigating the Future of First Nations*, p. 174.

391 Marc Grenier, "Native Indians in the English-Canadian Press: the case of the Oka Crisis," *Media, Culture & Society* Vol. 16, Issue 2 (April 1994): pp. 315-318; Johansen, *Life and Death in Mohawk Country*, p. 136.

Chapter 14

392 Canada. DND ATI, "Op SALON Update, 12-17 July 1990;" Lieutenant-Colonel Robin Gagnon, "Briefing to the Infantry Conference at Ottawa, 18 November 1991 (Private Collection). The Company of Grizzlys came from 2R22eR.

393 Canada. DND ATI, "Situation Reports—Op SALON, 17-20 July 1990."

394 Canadian Red Cross Society, Quebec Division, *Report on the Intervention by the Canadian Red Cross Society at Kanesatake, Kahnawake, Oka and Chateauguay during the Indian Crisis in the Summer of 1990* (CRCS: Records Management, January 1991), pp. 1-2.

395 Letter 13 July 1990, Francine Chartrand to Chief George Martin.

396 See: Commission des droits de la personne du Québec (prepared by Monique Rochon and Pierre Lepage), *Oka-Kanehsatake – Summer 1990: A Collective Shock: Report of the Commission des droits de la personne du Québec* (Quebec: 1991).

397 *Ibid*, p. 35.

398 Canada. DND ATI, "Intelligence Summary—Op SALON, 21 August-02 September 1990."

399 Hornung, *One Nation Under the Gun*, p. 221; Johansen, *Life and Death in Mohawk Country*, pp. 144-145; MacLaine and Baxendale, *This Land is Our Land: The Mohawk Revolt at Oka*, pp. 79-80; Goodleaf, *Entering the War Zone: A Mohawk Perspective on Resisting Invasion*, pp. 73-75; Ciaccia, *The Oka Crisis: A Mirror of the Soul*, pp. 85-86.

400 York and Pindera, *People of the Pines: The Warriors and The Legacy of Oka*, pp. 80, 210, 240.

401 Ciaccia, *The Oka Crisis: A Mirror of the Soul*, p. 85; Canada. DND ATI, "Motion for Injunction, 26 September 1990." Audrey McLaughlin was contacted by this author in September by both email and letter. No reply was received. She filed a law suit against General de Chastelain, Lieutenant-General Foster and Brigadier-General Roy for limiting the access of journalists at Kanesatake during the TC holdout.

402 Kahnawake Hospital Director as quoted in Peeter Kopvillem, "Summer Faceoffs," Maclean's Magazine (6 August 1990), p. 25.

403 Ciaccia, *The Oka Crisis: A Mirror of the Soul*, p. 139.

404 Ciaccia, *The Oka Crisis: A Mirror of the Soul*, pp. 142-143; York and Pindera, *People of the Pines: The Warriors and The Legacy of Oka*, p. 240.

405 Canada. DND ATI, "Situation Reports—Op SALON, 14-20 July, 1990."

406 Canada. DND ATI, "Situation Reports—Op SALON, 14-20 July, 1990."

407 Canada. DND ATI, "NDHQ Situation Reports—Op SALON, 24-25 July 1990;" Canada. DND ATI, "NDHQ Command and Control Volume 3: A Case Study Operation SALON (The Oka Crisis), December 1993."

408 Canada. DND ATI, "NDHQ Situation Reports—Op SALON, 24-25 July 1990;" Canada. DND ATI, "Op SALON—Lessons Learned Vice Chief of the Defence Staff, 25 January 1991;" Canada. DND ATI, "NDHQ Command and Control Volume 3: A Case Study Operation SALON (The Oka Crisis), December 1993."

409 Canada. DND ATI, "NDHQ Situation Reports—Op SALON, 24-25 July 1990."

410 *Ibid*; House of Commons, *Minutes of the Proceedings and Evidence of the Standing Committee on Aboriginal Affairs, Issue No. 55*, pp. 75-76.

411 Canada. DND ATI, "NDHQ Command and Control Volume 3: A Case Study Operation SALON (The Oka Crisis), December 1993."

412 House of Commons, *Minutes of the Proceedings and Evidence of the Standing Committee on Aboriginal Affairs, Issue No. 55*, p. 84.

Chapter 15

413 Canada. DND ATI, "Letter Sam Elkas to General John de Chastelain, 6 August 1990."

414 Canada. DND ATI, "DND's Civil Emergency Response Capability, June 1990."

415 Canada. DND ATI, "Op SALON Summary Record of Discussions, 7-9 August 1990."

416 Canada. DND ATI, "*Aid to the Civil Power*—Armed Assistance to the Government of the Province of Quebec—Op SALON, 8-9 August 1990."

417 Canada. DND ATI, "CDS War Diary—Op SALON, 6-12 August."

418 Canada. DND ATI, "Summary Record of Discussion of a Special Briefing to the CDS by Commander Mobile Command, 1930 hrs, 10 August 1990.;" House of Commons, *Minutes of the Proceedings and Evidence of the Standing Committee on Aboriginal Affairs, Issue No. 55*, pp. 84-86. However, the CF under *Aid to the Civil Power* was required to stay as long as the Province of Quebec deemed necessary.

419 Canada. DND ATI, "*Aid to the Civil Power*—Armed Assistance to the Government of the Province of Quebec—Op SALON, 11 July 1990."

420 Interview Lieutenant-Colonel (Captain) R. Landry, via telephone Valcartier, QC, 22 September 2005.

421 Canada. DND ATI, "*Aid to the Civil Power*—Armed Assistance to the Government of the Province of Quebec—Op SALON, 11 July 1990."

422 Canada. DND ATI, "Situation Report—Op SALON—Request for Assistance to the Province of Quebec, 9 August 1990."

423 Canada. DND ATI, "First Bank of Questions and Answers for the Military Assistance Operation at Oka and Kahnawake, 9 August 1990."

424 Canada. DND ATI, "Letter General John de Chastelain to Premier Robert Bourassa, 11 August 1990."

425 Canada. DND ATI, "Situation Report—Op SALON, 12 August 1990."

426 York and Pindera, *People of the Pines: The Warriors and The Legacy of Oka*, pp. 291-293; MacLaine and Baxendale, *This Land is Our Land: The Mohawk Revolt at Oka*, pp. 47-48.

427 York and Pindera, *People of the Pines: The Warriors and The Legacy of Oka*, pp. 291-293.

428 Interview with Ellen Gabriel, Kahnawake M.T., 1 September 2005.

429 York and Pindera, *People of the Pines: The Warriors and The Legacy of Oka*, pp. 296-297; Canada. DND ATI, "Situation Reports—Op SALON, 12-14 August, 1990."

430 Interview with Colonel (Major) Alain Tremblay, Ottawa, ON, 15 September 2005.

431 Interview with Lieutenant-Colonel (Major) Colin Magee, via telephone, Leavenworth, Kansas, 25 October 2005.

432 Interview with Lieutenant-Colonel (Captain) R. Landry, via telephone Valcartier, QC, 22 September 2005.

433 "Briefing Op SALON 2R22eR, Major Alain Tremblay, 15 July 1991." (Private Collection); Interview with Lieutenant-Colonel (Major) Rusty Bassarab, Kingston, ON, 6 September 2005.

434 Interview with Colonel (Major) Alain Tremblay, Ottawa, ON, 15 September 2005.

435 Interview with Colonel (Major) Jacques Morneau, Toronto, ON, 19 September 2005.

436 Confidential Source.

437 Interview with Colonel (Major) Alain Tremblay, Ottawa, ON, 15 September 2005.

438 Confidential Source.

439 Lieutenant-General Kent Foster as quoted in Lieutenant-Colonel Bernd Horn, *Bastard Sons: An Examination of Canada's Airborne Experience, 1942-1995* (St. Catherines: Vanwell Publishing Ltd., 2001), p. 186.

440 DND, *Report of the Somalia Commission of Inquiry,* Vol. 2, Ch. 10 (Ottawa: Public Works and Government Services Canada, 1997).

441 Interview with Lieutenant-Colonel (Major) Colin Magee via telephone, Leavenworth, Kansas, 25 October 2005; Interview with Lieutenant-Colonel (Major) Rusty Bassarab, Kingston, ON, 6 September 2005.

442 "Briefing Op SALON, 01 November 1990." (Private Collection); Canada. DND ATI, "Intelligence Summary—Op SALON, 12-15 August 1990;" Confidential Source.

443 Lieutenant Roland Lavoie, "Behind the Scenes at Op SALON," Sentinel: Magazine of the Canadian Forces Vol. 27 no. 1 (1991): 8-9.

444 Confidential Source.

445 Confidential Source.

446 Interview with Major (Lieutenant) David Lambert, Kingston, ON, 8 September 2005. See: Frank Kitson, *Low Intensity Operations: Subversion Insurgency & Peacekeeping* (New Delhi: Natraj Publishers, 1992).

447 Kitson, *Low Intensity Operations: Subversion Insurgency & Peacekeeping*, p. 14.

448 Interview with Major (Lieutenant) David Lambert, Kingston, ON, 8 September 2005.

449 Canada. DND ATI, "Intelligence Reports, 15-26 August 1990."

450 York and Pindera, *People of the Pines: The Warriors and The Legacy of Oka*, p. 241; Canada. DND ATI, "Op AKWESASNE—War Diary, 17-23 July 1990."

451 Canada. DND ATI, "Op SALON Target Lists/Operational Maps/Photos, Op SALON—90 War Diary, 26 August 1990."

452 Canada. DND ATI, "Debrief-SIU Informant, 12 September 1990."

453 Interview with Colonel (Major) Alain Tremblay, Ottawa, ON, 15 September 2005.

454 "Briefing Op SALON 2R22eR, Major Alain Tremblay, 15 July 1991." (Private Collection); Canada. DND ATI, "Debrief-SIU Informant, 12 September 1990."

455 *Ibid*; Canada. DND ATI, "Intelligence Report—Op SALON, 31 August 1990;" Canada. DND ATI, "Debrief-SIU Informant, 12 September 1990."

456 Confidential Source.

457 Canada. DND ATI, "Intelligence Reports—Op AKWESASNE, 8-12 August 1990;" Confidential Source.

458 Canada. DND ATI, "Confidential Overview of Native Weapons Purchase;" Canada. DND ATI, "Director General Information: List of Weapons Purchased by Warriors." The disclaimer on the second source reads: "The information was obtained through reliable intelligence sources. We are not in a position to discuss these sources."

459 Canada. DND ATI, "Confidential Overview of Native Weapons Purchase;" Canada. DND ATI, "Director General Information: List of Weapons Purchased by Warriors."

460 Canada. DND ATI, "Confidential Overview of Native Weapons Purchase;" Canada. DND ATI, "Director General Information: List of Weapons Purchased by Warriors."

461 Confidential Source.

462 Canada. DND ATI, "Lieutenant-General Foster-Press Release, 9 August 1990."

463 General de Chastelain as quoted in House of Commons, *Minutes of the Proceedings and Evidence of the Standing Committee on Aboriginal Affairs, Issue No. 55*, p. 88.

464 General de Chastelain as quoted in *Ibid*, p. 97; Canada. DND ATI, "Lieutenant-General Foster Briefing 20 August 1990."

465 *Ibid*, p. 97.

466 Interview with Colonel (Major) Jacques Morneau, Toronto, ON, 19 September 2005.

467 Lieutenant-General Foster as quoted in *Ibid*, p. 97.

468 Colonel (Major) Alain Tremblay, "Séquence des événements—Op SALON." (Private Collection).

469 Lieutenant-Colonel Robin Gagnon, "Briefing to the Infantry Conference at Ottawa, 18 November 1991 (Private Collection).

470 Canada. DND ATI, "Op SALON—Situation Reports, 17-19 August 1990;" "Briefing Op SALON 2R22eR, Major Alain Tremblay, 15 July 1991." (Private Collection).

471 Lieutenant-Colonel (Major) Rusty Bassarab, "Mohawk Crisis: Presentation to United Services Institute." (Private Collection).

472 Canada. DND ATI, "Statement by the CDS, 17 August 1990."

473 Canada. DND ATI, "Situation Reports—Op SALON, 19-21 August 1990."

474 Canada. DND ATI, "CDS War Diary, 20-26 August 1990."

475 Interview with Lieutenant-Colonel (Major) Brad Boswell Kingston, ON, 08 September 2005.

476 Canada. DND ATI, "Situation Report—Op SALON, 21-22 August 1990."

477 House of Commons, *Minutes of the Proceedings and Evidence of the Standing Committee on Aboriginal Affairs, Issue No. 55*, p. 65. The trees cut were appraised by a firm hired by the municipality and were estimated at $6,000.

478 Canada. DND ATI, "Situation Reports—Op SALON, 19-22 August 1990."

479 "Briefing Op SALON 2R22eR, Major Alain Tremblay, 15 July 1991." (Private Collection); Canada. DND ATI, "Situation Report—Army Advances at Rang Sainte-Germaine, 23 August 1990."

480 "Briefing Op SALON 2R22eR, Major Alain Tremblay, 15 July 1991." (Private Collection)

481 Canada. DND ATI, "CDS War Diary—Chronology of Events, 9 October 1991."

482 Canada. DND ATI, "Statement by the Chief of the Defence Staff, 27 August 1990."

483 Canada. DND ATI, "Situation Report—Op SALON, 27 August 1990."

484 Canada. DND ATI, "Stabilized Binocular Project, 25 August 1990."

485 Canada. DND ATI, "Situation Report—Op SALON, 27 August 1990."

486 Canada. DND ATI, "Op SALON—Chronology of Events, 9 October 1990."

487 Canada. DND ATI, "Press Conference—Lieutenant-General K. Foster, Brigadier General A. Roy, 28 August 1990."

488 *Ibid.*

489 Canada. DND ATI, "Op SALON—Press Release, 28 August 1990."

490 York and Pindera, *People of the Pines: The Warriors and The Legacy of Oka*, pp. 244-246.

491 Cookie McComber as quoted in *Ibid*, p. 245.

492 Canada. DND ATI, "Intelligence Reports—Op SALON 30-31 August 1990."

493 Canada. DND ATI, "Record of Discussion of a Special Briefing on Operation SALON—Intelligence Briefing, 28 August 1990."

494 Interview with Major (Lieutenant) David Lambert, Kingston ON, 08 September 2005.

495 CBC Newsworld, *This Country: Special Report, Brian Mulroney Press Conference* (Ottawa: Media Tapes and Transcripts Ltd., 28 August 1990).

496 *Ibid.*

Chapter 16

497 *Ibid*; Confidential Source.

498 Canada. DND ATI, "Op AKWESASNE—War Diary 17-23 July 1990."

499 Canada. DND ATI, "Situation Reports—Op AKWESASNE, 27 July-10 August 1990;" York and Pindera, *People of the Pines: The Warriors and The Legacy of Oka*, p. 283.

500 Canada. DND ATI, "CAT Meeting, 19 August 1990."

501 Canada. DND ATI, "NDHQ National Situation Report, 26 July 1990;" York and Pindera, *People of the Pines: The Warriors and The Legacy of Oka*, pp. 281-283.

502 Canada. DND ATI, "Intelligence Report—Op AKWESASNE, 30 August 1990."

503 York and Pindera, *People of the Pines: The Warriors and The Legacy of Oka*, p. 274.

504 Canada. DND ATI, "Op SALON—War Diary 23 July 1990;" Canada. DND ATI, "SIU Intelligence Report, 28 July 1990;" Canada. DND ATI, "Summary Record of Discussion of a Special Briefing Op SALON/Op FRICTION, 27 August 1990."

505 Canada. DND ATI, "Summary Record of Discussion of a Special Briefing Op SALON/Op FRICTION, 27 August 1990."

506 Tugwell and Thompson, *The Legacy of Oka*, p. 28; Grenier, "Native Indians in the English-Canadian Press: the case of the Oka Crisis," p. 329.

507 Canada. DND ATI, "Situation Reports—Op SALON, 23 September 1990."

508 United Nations ATI, "Economic and Social Council: Discrimination Against Indigenous Peoples—Notes and Letters of the Chairman, 31 August 1990;" Per Bauhn, Christer Lindberg and Svante Lundberg, *Multiculturalism and Nationhood in Canada: The Cases of the First Nations and Quebec* (Sweden: Lund University Press, 1995), p. 31; York and Pindera, *People of the Pines: The Warriors and The Legacy of Oka*, pp. 161-163. After the First World War, the Iroquois sent a delegate to the Paris Peace Conference believing it was their right as they were a distinct nation that sent soldiers to fight and die in conjunction with Canada and her Allies. During the early 1920s an Iroquois Chief, Deskeheh, travelled around Europe campaigning for recognition of Iroquois sovereignty, including the League of Nations. In 1945, upon the formation of the United Nations, the Iroquois immediately put forth a submission of their right to be sovereign.

509 Anthony Wilson-Smith and Nancy Wood, "Starting Over," *Maclean's Magazine* (8 October 1990): p. 30. The 1986 census revealed that 37.2% of First Nations Peoples did not have a Grade 9 education compared to 17.1% of all Canadians.

510 Canada. DND ATI, "Situation Reports—Op SALON, 20-22 August 1990."

511 Canada. DND ATI, "NDHQ Command and Control Volume 3: A Case Study Operation SALON (The Oka Crisis), December 1993."

512 Ciaccia, *The Oka Crisis: A Mirror of the Soul*, pp. 113-115.

513 Canada. DND ATI, "Situation Reports—Op SALON, 23-24 September 1990;" Tugwell and Thompson, *The Legacy of Oka*, p. 29.

514 Johansen, *Life and Death in Mohawk Country*, p. 147.

515 McDonald, "Following the Oka Example," p. 34.

516 Red Cross Correspondence with Grand Chief George Martin, Six Nation Traditional Hereditary Chiefs, 13 July 1990; with Mohawk Nation Kahnawake Branch, 14 July 1990; with Kahn-Tineta Horn, 12 December 1990; Ciaccia, *The Oka Crisis: A Mirror of the Soul*, pp. 138-139, 148-157; Commission des droits de la personne du Québec, *Oka-Kanehsatake – Summer 1990: A Collective Shock: Report of the Commission des droits de la personne du Québec*; Canadian Red Cross Society, Quebec Division, *Report on the Intervention by the Canadian Red Cross Society at Kanesatake, Kahnawake, Oka and Chateauguay during the Indian Crisis in the Summer of 1990*.

517 Ciaccia, *The Oka Crisis: A Mirror of the Soul*, p. 139.

518 Ed Broadbent as quoted in Taylor, "Rough Justice," p. 19. Ed Broadbent was contacted for an interview request that was declined.

519 Interview with John Allen, Office of Archbishop Desmond Tutu via email Johannesburg, S.A., 11 July 2005; Canada. DND ATI, "Situation Report—Op AKWESASNE, 05 July 1990."

520 United Nations ATI, "Mohawk Nation Six Nations Confederacy—An Urgent Message to the United Nations, 2 September 1990;" United Nations ATI, "Economic and Social Council: Discrimination Against Indigenous Peoples—Notes and Letters of the Chairman, 31 August 1990."

521 United Nations ATI, "Mohawk Nation Six Nations Confederacy—An Urgent Message to the United Nations, 2 September 1990;" United Nations ATI, "Economic and Social Council: Discrimination Against Indigenous Peoples—Notes and Letters of the *Chairman, 31 August 1990;" Frideres, Native Peoples in Canada:* Contemporary Conflict, pp. 374-376;

Hornung, *One Nation Under the Gun*, p. 243; Ciaccia, *The Oka Crisis: A Mirror of the Soul*, pp. 155-56.

522 Ciaccia, *The Oka Crisis: A Mirror of the Soul*, p. 156.

523 European Parliament ATI, "The European Parliament—Resolution on Indigenous Peoples, 13 September 1990;" European Parliament ATI, "European Parliament: Report for Delegation for Relations with Canada, 2 May 1991."

524 Decima Research, *Report on Public Opinion Surrounding the Events at Oka, Quebec* (Ottawa: Decima Research, October 1990), pp. 6, 20-26.

525 Tom Siddon as quoted in Ciaccia, *The Oka Crisis: A Mirror of the Soul*, p. 127.

526 Harry Swain as quoted in York and Pindera, *People of the Pines: The Warriors and The Legacy of Oka*, p. 219; Hornung, *One Nation Under the Gun*, p. 222.

527 As quoted in Ciaccia, *The Oka Crisis: A Mirror of the Soul*, p. 133.

528 Tugwell and Thompson, *The Legacy of Oka*, pp. 10, 34-35; Johansen, *Life and Death in Mohawk Country*, pp. 156-157; Hornung, *One Nation Under the Gun*, p. 280; Thompson, *The Long Fall of the Mohawk Warriors*, pp. 1-5. AIM leader Vernon Bellecourt had visited Libya as a guest of Khaddafi on a number of occasions and had facilitated visits for many AIM and Warrior Society members between 1986-1988. In June of 1991, a delegation of three Warriors went to Libya to collect a $250,000 "Human Rights Award for the Red Race of America."

529 Canada. DND ATI, "Communications—Op SALON, 28 August 1990."

530 Interview with Lieutenant-Colonel (Major) Rusty Bassarab, Kingston, ON, 06 September 2005.

531 Canada. DND ATI, "Provision of Services to the Media at Oka by the Canadian Army."

532 Interview with Colonel (Major) Alain Tremblay, Ottawa, ON, 15 September 2005.

533 Canada. DND ATI, "NDHQ Command and Control Volume 3: A Case Study Operation SALON (The Oka Crisis), December 1993."

Chapter 17

534 Confidential Source.

535 Lieutenant-General Kent Foster as quoted in House of Commons, *Minutes of the Proceedings and Evidence of the Standing Committee on Aboriginal Affairs, Issue No. 55*, p.99.

536 Canada. DND ATI, "Op SALON—War Diary, 28-29 August 1990;" Tugwell and Thompson, *The Legacy of Oka*, p. 31; Captain Tony Keene, "Drug-Net," Sentinel Vol. 28 no. 2 (1992): 7-9.

537 York and Pindera, *People of the Pines: The Warriors and The Legacy of Oka*, pp. 332-334; Interview with Ellen Gabriel, Kahnawake, M.T., 01 September 2005.

538 Confidential Source.

539 Interview with Lieutenant-Colonel (Captain) R. Landry, Valcartier, QC via telephone, 22 September 2005.

540 Canada. DND ATI, "New Release—Light Aircraft Activity—Kahnawake, 3 September 1990."

541 Lieutenant-Colonel Robin Gagnon, "Briefing to the Infantry Conference at Ottawa, 18 November 1991 (Private Collection).

542 Lieutenant-Colonel (Major) Rusty Bassarab, "Mohawk Crisis: Presentation to United Services Institute." (Private Collection); Canada. DND ATI, "Op SALON Update, 29 August 1990."

543 Canada. DND ATI, "News Release—Lieutenant-General Kent Foster, 29 August 1990."

544 Canada. DND ATI, "NDHQ Command and Control Volume 3: A Case Study Operation SALON (The Oka Crisis), December 1993."

545 Canada. DND ATI, "Intelligence Reports—Op SALON, 30-31 August 1990;" Canada. DND ATI, "Situation Report—Op SALON, 31 August 1990;" Dickson, *Communities, Contraband and Conflict: Considering Restorative Responses to Repairing the Harms Implicit in Smuggling in the Akwesasne Mohawk Nation*, p. 28.

546 Canada. DND ATI, "Situation Report—Op SALON, 30 August 1990."

547 Canada. DND ATI, "NDHQ Command and Control Volume 3: A Case Study Operation SALON (The Oka Crisis), December 1993."

548 Interview with Lieutenant-Colonel (Lieutenant) John Fife via telephone Gagetown N.B., 05 October 2005.

549 Canada. DND ATI, "Situation Reports—Op SALON, 30 August-01 September 1990;" "Briefing Op SALON 2R22eR, Major Alain Tremblay, 15 July 1991." (Private Collection); Interview with Colonel (Major) Alain Tremblay, Ottawa, ON, 15 September 2005.

550 York and Pindera, *People of the Pines: The Warriors and The Legacy of Oka*, pp. 350-352; Interview with Colonel (Major) Alain Tremblay, Ottawa, ON, 15 September 2005.

551 Interview with Colonel (Major) Alain Tremblay, Ottawa, ON, 15 September 2005.

552 Canada. DND ATI, "SIU—Situation Report, 1-2 September 1990;" Canada. DND ATI, "Op SALON—Situation Report, 02 September 1990."

553 Canada. DND ATI, "SIU Situation Report, 03 September 1990."

554 "Briefing Op SALON 2R22eR, Major Alain Tremblay, 15 July 1991." (Private Collection); Interview with Colonel (Major) Alain Tremblay, Ottawa, ON, 15 September 2005.

555 Lieutenant-Colonel (Major) Rusty Bassarab, "Mohawk Crisis: Presentation to United Services Institute." (Private Collection); Interview with Lieutenant-Colonel (Major) Rusty Bassarab, Kingston, ON, 6 September 2005.

556 Canada. DND ATI, "SIU—Situation Reports, 1-2 September 1990."

557 Canada. DND ATI, "NDHQ Command and Control Volume 3: A Case Study Operation SALON (The Oka Crisis), December 1993."

558 Canada. DND ATI, "Situation Reports—Op SALON, 04 September 1990;" York and Pindera, *People of the Pines: The Warriors and The Legacy of Oka*, pp. 361-362.

559 Confidential Source.

560 Lieutenant-Colonel (Major) Rusty Bassarab, "Mohawk Crisis: Presentation to United Services Institute." (Private Collection); Interview with Lieutenant-Colonel (Major) Rusty Bassarab, Kingston, ON, 6 September 2005.

561 Canada. DND ATI, "Situation Reports—Op SALON, 04 September 1990;" Lieutenant-Colonel (Major) Rusty Bassarab, "Mohawk Crisis: Presentation to United Services Institute." (Private Collection).

562 Canada. DND ATI, "Situation Reports—Op SALON, 04-05 September 1990."

563 Canada. DND ATI, "News Release: Army and SQ Conduct Joint Operations, 3 September 1990."

564 Interview with Lieutenant-Colonel (Major) Bradley Boswell, Kingston, ON, 08 September 2005.

565 Canada. DND ATI, "Situation Reports—Op AKWESASNE, 04 September 1990."

566 Interview with Lieutenant-Colonel (Major) Bradley Boswell, Kingston, ON, 08 September 2005.

567 Canada. DND ATI, "SIU Situation Repors, 03 September 1990."

568 Interview with Ellen Gabriel Kahnawake M.T., 01 September 2005.

Chapter 18

569 Interview with Colonel (Major) Alain Tremblay, Ottawa, ON, 15 September 2005; Canada. DND ATI, "Situation Reports—Op SALON, 14 September 1990."

570 Canada. DND ATI, "NDHQ Command and Control Volume 3: A Case Study Operation SALON (The Oka Crisis), December 1993."

571 *Ibid.*

572 Canada. DND ATI, "Situation Reports—Op SALON, 04 September 1990."

573 Minister of Justice and Attorney General of Canada, The Warriors and Criminal Law (Ottawa: Communications and Public Affairs, Department of Justice, 9 September 1990).

574 Interview with Colonel (Major) Alain Tremblay, Ottawa, ON, 15 September 2005.

575 Confidential Source; Canada. DND ATI, "Intelligence Reports—Op SALON, 03-06 September 1990."

576 Interview with Lieutenant-Colonel (Major) Rusty Bassarab, Kingston, ON, 6 September 2005; Canada. DND ATI, "Situation Report—Op SALON, 10 September 1990."

577 Canada. DND ATI, "Crisis Action Team-Records of Decisions, 07 September 1990;" Canada. DND ATI, "NDHQ Command and Control Volume 3: A Case Study Operation SALON (The Oka Crisis), December 1993."

578 Canada. DND ATI, "NDHQ Command and Control Volume 3: A Case Study Operation SALON (The Oka Crisis), December 1993."

579 *Ibid.* Canada. DND ATI, "Situation Report—Op SALON, 08 September 1990;" Canada. DND ATI, "New Release-CF Questions and Answers-Fight at Oka, 08 September 1990."

580 Canada. DND ATI, "Situation Report—Op SALON, 08 September 1990;" York and Pindera, *People of the Pines: The Warriors and The Legacy of Oka*, pp. 369-372.

581 Canada. DND ATI, "Situation Report—Op SALON, 08 September 1990;" York and Pindera, *People of the Pines: The Warriors and The Legacy of Oka*, pp. 369-372.

582 Interview with Colonel (Major) Alain Tremblay, Ottawa, ON, 15 September 2005.

583 Interview with Waneek Horn-Miller, Montreal, Quebec, 26, 30 January 2006; Interview with Ellen Gabriel, Kahnawake, M.T., 1 September 2005; York and Pindera, *People of the Pines: The Warriors and The Legacy of Oka*, pp. 369-372.

584 Canada. DND ATI, "New Release—CF Questions and Answers-Fight at Oka, 08 September 1990."

585 Canada. DND ATI, "Situation Report—Op SALON, 10 September 1990."

586 Canada. DND ATI, "Situation Report—Op SALON, 10 September 1990;" Canada. DND ATI, "Op SALON-Intelligence Report, 13 September 1990."

587 Canada. DND ATI, "Situation Reports—Op SALON, 08-10 September 1990;" Canada. DND ATI, "G Coy (2 RCR)-War Diary, OP Reports 12-13 September 1990;" Canada. DND ATI, "H Coy (2 RCR) —War Diary, OP Reports, 09 September 1990;" Canada. DND ATI, "Army Cuts Telephone Lines to Detoxification Centre, 13 September 1990."

588 Canada. DND ATI, "Op SALON—Native Indian Activity-Intelligence Report, 14 September 1990."

589 Canada. DND ATI, "Situation Reports—Op SALON, 13-14 September 1990."

590 Canada. DND ATI, "Situation Report—Op SALON, 16 September 1990."

Chapter 19

591 Interview with Lieutenant-Colonel (Major) Bradley Boswell, Kingston, ON, 08 September 2005.

592 Interview with Lieutenant-Colonel (Major) Rusty Bassarab, Kingston, ON, 06 September 2005.

593 Interview with Lieutenant-Colonel (Major) Bradley Boswell, Kingston, ON, 08 September 2005.

594 Note: The names used for houses simply refer to ownership and registration. This does not infer that charges or legal actions are tied to these specific people.

595 Canada. DND ATI, "NDHQ Command and Control Volume 3: A Case Study Operation SALON (The Oka Crisis), December 1993;" Lieutenant-Colonel Rusty Bassarab, "Mohawk Crisis: Presentation to United Services Institute." (Private Collection); Confidential Source.

596 Canada. DND ATI, "Intelligence Report—Op SALON, 15 September 1990;" Lieutenant-Colonel Rusty Bassarab, "Mohawk Crisis: Presentation to United Services Institute." (Private Collection).

597 Canada. DND ATI, "Intelligence Report—Op SALON, 15 September 1990."

598 Canada. DND ATI, "Situation Reports—Op SALON, 16-17 September 1990."

599 Interview with Lieutenant-Colonel (Major) Rusty Bassarab, Kingston, ON, 6 September 2005.

600 Lieutenant-Colonel Rusty Bassarab, "Mohawk Crisis: Presentation to United Services Institute." (Private Collection).

601 *Ibid*; Interview with Lieutenant-Colonel (Major) Rusty Bassarab, Kingston, ON, 6 September 2005; Canada. DND ATI, "Press Release-Raid on Tekakwitha Island, 21 September 1990."

602 Canada. DND ATI, "Op SALON—Incident Report, 19 September 1990;" Canada. DND ATI, "NDHQ Command and Control Volume 3: A Case Study Operation SALON (The Oka Crisis), December 1993;" Lieutenant-Colonel Rusty Bassarab, "Mohawk Crisis: Presentation to United Services Institute." (Private Collection); Interview with Lieutenant-Colonel (Major) Bradley Boswell, Kingston, ON, 08 September 2005; Interview with Lieutenant-Colonel (Lieutenant) John Fife via telephone Gagetown, N.B., 05 October 2005. The persons driving the truck were actually the two males Major Boswell had helped under the wire at the rail road track when being chased by the crowd that torched their car.

603 Canada. DND ATI, "Op SALON—Incident Report, 19 September 1990."

604 Confidential Source; Interview with Lieutenant-Colonel (Major) Bradley Boswell, Kingston, ON, 08 September 2005.

605 Interview with Lieutenant-Colonel (Captain) Pat McAdam via telephone Gagetown, N.B., 29 September 2005.

606 Interview with Lieutenant-Colonel (Lieutenant) John Fife via telephone Gagetown, N.B., 05 October 2005.

607 Canada. DND ATI, "Op SALON—Incident Report, 19 September 1990."

608 *Ibid*; Confidential Source.

609 Canada. DND ATI, "Situation Report—Op SALON, 19 September 1990;" Lieutenant-Colonel Rusty Bassarab, "Mohawk Crisis: Presentation to United Services Institute." (Private Collection); York and Pindera, *People of the Pines: The Warriors and The Legacy of Oka*, pp. 382-384.

610 Canada. DND ATI, "SIU Report, 19 September 1990;" Interview with Lieutenant-Colonel (Major) Rusty Bassarab, Kingston, ON, 6 September 2005.

611 Interview with Lieutenant-Colonel (Major) Rusty Bassarab, Kingston, ON, 06 September 2005.

612 Interview with Lieutenant-Colonel (Captain) Pat McAdam via telephone Gagetown, N.B., 29 September 2005; Interview with Lieutenant-Colonel (Lieutenant) John Fife via telephone Gagetown, N.B., 05 October 2005.

613 Interview with Lieutenant-Colonel (Captain) Pat McAdam via telephone Gagetown, N.B., 29 September 2005; Interview with Lieutenant-Colonel (Lieutenant) John Fife via telephone Gagetown, N.B., 05 October 2005.

614 Canada. DND ATI, "Situation Report—Op SALON, 23 September 1990;" Interview with Lieutenant-Colonel (Major) Rusty Bassarab, Kingston, ON, 6 September 2005.

615 Canada. DND ATI, "SIU/Informant Source Meeting Debrief, 21 September 1990."

616 Canada. DND ATI, "NDHQ Command and Control Volume 3: A Case Study Operation SALON (The Oka Crisis), December 1993."

617 Canada. DND ATI, "SIU/Informant Source Meeting Debrief, 21 September 1990."

618 Interview with Lieutenant-Colonel (Captain) Pat McAdam via telephone Gagetown, N.B., 29 September 2005.

619 Interview with Colonel (Major) Alain Tremblay, Ottawa, ON, 15 September 2005.

620 Confidential Source.

621 House of Commons, *Minutes of the Proceedings and Evidence of the Standing Committee on Aboriginal Affairs, Issue No. 55*, pp. 117-118; York and Pindera, *People of the Pines: The Warriors and The Legacy of Oka*, pp. 344-346.

622 Canada. DND ATI, "Op AKWESASNE—Summary of Feeding Situation in St. Regis, 19 May 1990;" Canada. DND ATI, "Op AKWESASNE—Costs, 31 May 1990."

623 Confidential Source.

624 Canada. DND ATI, "Situation Report—Op SALON, 15 September 1990."

625 Kitson, *Low Intensity Operations: Subversion, Insurgency & Peacekeeping*, p. 200.

626 Interview with Lieutenant-Colonel (Major) Rusty Bassarab, Kingston, ON, 6 September 2005; Canada. DND ATI, "Situation Report—Op SALON, 12 September 1990."

627 Interview with Lieutenant-Colonel (Major) Rusty Bassarab, Kingston, ON, 6 September 2005.

628 Canada. DND ATI, "Situation Report—Op SALON, 12 September 1990;" Canada. DND ATI, "Situation Report—Op SALON, 19 September 1990."

629 Interview with Lieutenant-Colonel (Major) Bradley Boswell, Kingston, ON, 08 September 2005.

630 Canada. DND ATI, "Special Meeting-Commander's Remarks, 18 September 1990."

631 Canada. DND ATI, "An Agreement to Ensure the Safety and Protection of Persons who Voluntarily Agree to Lay Down their Arms and to Place Themselves Under Military Control and Custody."

632 Canada. DND ATI, "Operational Instruction #7, FMC Op SALON, 10 September 1990."

Chapter 20

633 Canada. DND ATI, "Lieutenant-General Foster-Army Details New Measures to be Taken to Resolve Crisis, 20 September 1990."

634 Canada. DND ATI, "Special Meeting-Commander's Remarks, 18 September 1990." Capital letter used as per the original document.

635 Canada. DND ATI, "Situation Report—Op SALON, 19 September 1990." The name derives from a 1973 hostage incident in Stockholm, Sweden. At the end of six days of captivity in a bank, several kidnap victims actually resisted rescue attempts, and afterwards refused to testify against their captors.

636 Canada. DND ATI, "Briefing Note for the Deputy Minister and the Chief of the Defence Staff: Legal Action Concerning the Deactivation of Cellular Telephones at Oka, 13 September 1990;" Canada. DND ATI, "Military Stops Passage of Tapes and Film of Journalists, 16 September 1990;" Interview with Geoffrey York, via email Beijing, China, 11 July 2005.

637 Canada. DND ATI, "Situation Reports—Op SALON, 18-23 September 1990."

638 Canada. DND ATI, "Intelligence Summary— Op SALON, 19 September 1990." The number Lasagna gave on the radio was traced to Akwesasne.

639 Canada. DND ATI, "Situation Report—Op SALON, 26 September 1990."

640 Canada. DND ATI, "Media Summary—Op SALON, 26 September 1990."

641 Canada. DND ATI, "Situation Reports—Op SALON, 23-25 September 1990."

642 Interview with Waneek Horn-Miller, Montreal, Quebec, 26, 30 January 2006.

643 Interview with Colonel (Major) Alain Tremblay, Ottawa, ON, 15 September 2005.

644 Canada. DND ATI, "Situation Report—Op SALON, 27 September 1990;" Interview with Waneek Horn-Miller, Montreal, Quebec, 26, 30 January 2006; Interview with Colonel (Major) Alain Tremblay, Ottawa, ON, 15 September 2005.

645 Interview with Colonel (Major) Alain Tremblay, Ottawa, ON, 15 September 2005.

646 Canada. DND ATI, "Operation SALON—Chronology of Events, 9 October 1990;" MacLaine and Baxendale, *This Land is Our Land: The Mohawk Revolt at Oka*, p. 93.

647 Confidential Source.

648 Interview with Waneek Horn-Miller, Montreal, Quebec, 26, 30 January 2006; Canadian Human Rights Commission, *Investigation Report—Waneek Horn Miller*, 27 March 1991.

649 Canada. DND ATI, "Situation Report—Op SALON, 27 September 1990;" Interview with Captain (Lieutenant) Howard Chafe, Ottawa ON, 14 September 2005; Canada. DND ATI, "Service Custody Area Regulations."

650 Canada. DND ATI, "Secret: Mohawk Alert System for Kahnawake in the Event of Military Searches/Movements, 28 September 1990;" Canada. DND ATI, "Situation

Report—Op SALON, 27 September 1990;" Lieutenant-Colonel (Major) Rusty Bassarab, "Mohawk Crisis: Presentation to United Services Institute." (Private Collection).

651 Canada. DND ATI, "Situation Report—Op SALON, 27 September 1990;" Lieutenant-Colonel (Major) Rusty Bassarab, "Mohawk Crisis: Presentation to United Services Institute." (Private Collection); Interview with Lieutenant-Colonel (Major) Bradley Boswell, Kingston, ON, 08 September 2005.

652 Canada. DND ATI, "Situation Report—Op SALON, 27 September 1990;" Lieutenant-Colonel (Major) Rusty Bassarab, "Mohawk Crisis: Presentation to United Services Institute." (Private Collection); Interview with Lieutenant-Colonel (Major) Bradley Boswell, Kingston, ON, 08 September 2005.

653 Canada. DND ATI, "Secret Ops, 27 September 1990."

654 Canada. DND ATI, "Situation Report—Op AKWESASNE, 27 September 1990."

655 Canada. DND ATI, "Situation Report—Op SALON, 01 October 1990."

656 House of Commons, *Minutes of the Proceedings and Evidence of the Standing Committee on Aboriginal Affairs, Issue No. 55*, p. 117.

657 Interview with Colonel (Major) Alain Tremblay, Ottawa, ON, 15 September 2005.

658 Confidential Sources; Interview with Waneek Horn-Miller, Montreal, Quebec, 26, 30 January 2006.

659 Canada. DND ATI, "NDHQ Command and Control Volume 3: A Case Study Operation SALON (The Oka Crisis), December 1993."

660 *Ibid*; House of Commons, *Minutes of the Proceedings and Evidence of the Standing Committee on Aboriginal Affairs, Issue No. 55*, p. 94; COS TF, "Briefing Op SALON, 01 November 1990" (Private Collection).

661 Canada. DND ATI, "Situation Reports—Op SALON, 07-26 October 1990."

662 Canada. DND ATI, "NDHQ Command and Control Volume 3: A Case Study Operation SALON (The Oka Crisis), December 1993."

663 Canada. DND ATI, "Op AKWESASNE—Redeployment 13-21 November 1990, 27 November 1990;" Canada. DND ATI, "DEM—Op SALON/Op AKWESASNE Update, 9 December 1990."

Conclusion

664 Canada. DND ATI, "Final Cost Report—Operation AKWESASNE, 7 March 1991."

665 Canada. DND ATI, "Operation SALON Sustainment Costs—Final Version, 25 November 1990."

666 Canada. DND ATI, "Oka Crisis—Financial Assistance to Quebec, 03 October 1994."

667 Office of the Auditor General of Canada, Review of the Request by the Province of Quebec for Financial Assistance Related to the Emergency in July 1990 Affecting Oka, Kahnawake and Chateauguay (Ottawa: Office of the Auditor General of Canada, August 1995), pp. 8-32.

668 Canada. DND ATI, "Operation SALON Sustainment Costs—Final Version, 25 November 1990."

669 Canada. DND ATI, "Op FEATHER—Tasks Summary, 17 May 1990."

670 Canadian Red Cross Society, Quebec Division, *Report on the Intervention by the Canadian Red Cross Society at Kanesatake, Kahnawake, Oka and Chateauguay during the Indian Crisis in the Summer of 1990*, p. 13.

671 Todd Fitzgerald and Michael A. Hennessy, "An Expedient Reorganization: The NDHQ J-Staff System in the Gulf War," Canadian Military Journal (Spring 2003): 25.

672 Canada. DND ATI, "NDHQ Command and Control Volume 3: A Case Study Operation SALON (The Oka Crisis), December 1993."

673 Canada. DND ATI, "Briefing Note for J3 Plans, Op SALON—CF *Aid to the Civil Power*, August 1992."

674 Canada. DND ATI, "Comments Armed Assistance to the Civil Authorities, Major-General Armand Roy, 8 February 1994."

675 Canada. DND ATI, "Op SALON After Action report, Lieutenant-General K. Foster, 31 January 1991."

676 Canada. DND ATI, "Op SALON—Lessons Learned, 29 January 1991."

677 *Strengthening Relationships Between the Canadian Forces and Aboriginal People* (Recruitment Guide 1999), as quoted in Victoria Edwards, *Don't Mention It! The Oka Crisis and the Recruitment of Aboriginal Peoples* (Ottawa: Department of National Defence, 2002), p. 5. As of 2002, there were 130 Status Natives and 1170 non-Status Natives in the CF. The total of 1,300 was two and one half times below the number it should have been (3,700) in relation to the overall First Nations population in Canada.

678 Interview with Major (Lieutenant) David Lambert, Kingston, ON, 08 September 2005.

679 Canada. DND ATI, Office of the Prime Minister, "Notes for an Address to the House of Commons by Prime Minister Brian Mulroney on the House Resolution with Respect to Oka, 25 September 1990."

680 Letter to author from The Chancellery of Honours Rideau Hall, 8 November 2005.

681 Canada. DND ATI, "Op SALON After Action report, Lieutenant-General K. Foster, 31 January 1991."

682 Canada. DND ATI, "Media Advisory, 24 August 1990."

683 Canada. DND ATI, "The Total Force Experiment—Op UNIQUE."

684 Government of Canada. Prepared by Mary C. Hurley, Law and Government Division, *Bill S-24: The Kanesatake Interim Land Base Governance Act* (Ottawa: Law and Government Division, 8 June 2001).

685 *Ibid.*

686 Dan David, "Anarchy at Kanesatake: drug trade, child porn, death threats. Why the band council and government aren't stopping rising community violence," THIS Magazine Vol. 29 no. 5 (January 1996): 11-15.

687 Guy Gilbert, *Rapport D'Enquête du Coroner: Guy Gilbert sur les Causes et Circonstances du Décès de Monsieur Marcel Lemay, English Version*, p. 419.

688 Dickson, *Communities, Contraband and Conflict: Considering Restorative Responses to Repairing the Harms Implicit in Smuggling in the Akwesasne Mohawk Nation*, p. 25; Thompson, *The Long Fall of the Mohawk Warriors*, pp. 1-4.

689 David Pugliese, *Canada's Secret Commandos: The Unauthorized Story of Joint Task Force Two* (Ottawa: Esprit de Corps Books, 2002), pp. 33-36.

690 Thompson, *The Long Fall of the Mohawk Warriors*, pp. 4-5.

691 Pugliese, *Canada's Secret Commandos: The Unauthorized Story of Joint Task Force Two*, pp. 33-36.

692 Interview with Ellen Gabriel, Kahnawake, M.T., 01 September 2005.

693 Interview with Waneek Horn-Miller, Montreal QC, 26, 30 January 2006; Joan Walters, "An Angry Generation: Aboriginal young people full of pride—and fury," Hamilton Spectator, 22 April 2006. Half of Canada's Aboriginal population is under 25 years of age.

694 CBC News, "Cigarette Smuggling on the Rise, Mounties say," 05 May 2006.

695 E.J. Dickson-Gilmore and Chris Whitehead, *Aboriginal Organized Crime in Canada: Developing a Typology for Understanding and Strategizing Responses* (Ottawa: Research and Evaluation Branch, Royal Canadian Mounted Police, 2005), p. 16; Dickson, *Communities, Contraband and Conflict: Considering Restorative Responses to Repairing the Harms Implicit in Smuggling in the Akwesasne Mohawk Nation*, p. 19.

696 Confidential Source.

697 Brigadier-General Armand Roy as quoted in Major Gerald Baril, "Mission Accomplished," Sentinel: Magazine of the Canadian Forces Vol. 26 no. 6 (1990): 8.

698 Interview with Ellen Gabriel, Kahnawake, M.T., 01 September 2005.

Epilogue

699 Canada. DND ATI, "Op SALON—War Diary, 23 July 1990;" Canada. DND ATI, "Liaison Between DND and DIAND, The Next Oka, 6 September 1990."

700 Canada. DND ATI, "Situation Reports—Op SALON, 02-16 September 1990."

701 Confidential Source.

702 Thompson, *The Long Fall of the Mohawk Warriors*, pp. 4-5.

703 John Thompson, *Ipperwash... Again* (Toronto: The Mackenzie Institute, 2003), p. 2.

704 See: P. Whitney Lackenbauer, "Combined Operation: The Appropriation of Stoney Point Reserve and the Creation of Camp Ipperwash," Journal of Military Strategic Studies, Vol. 2, No. 1 (Fall 1999): pp. 1-38.

705 Ontario Executive Council, Order in Council, *Establishment of Inquiry—Ipperwash* (Toronto: Executive Council, 12 November 2003).

706 Thompson, *Ipperwash... Again*, p. 2. For a detailed account see: Peter Edwards, *One Dead Indian: The Premier, the Police and the Ipperwash Crisis* (Toronto: McClelland and Stewart, 2003). OPP Acting Sergeant Ken Deane was convicted of criminal negligence causing death and sentenced to two years less a day to be served in the community not in custody.

707 Thompson, *The Long Fall of the Mohawk Warriors*, p. 5.

708 Bland and Maloney, *Campaigns for International Security: Canada's Defence Policy at the Turn of the Century*, p. 259; Pugliese, *Canada's Secret Commandos: The Unauthorized Story of Joint Task Force Two*, pp. 53-55; Confidential Source.

709 Interviews conducted with those behind the barricade, Caledonia, ON, 23 March 2006.

710 Ontario Reports, 82 O.R. (3d), *Henco Industries Ltd. v. Haudenosaunee Six Nations Confederacy Council et al. Superior Court of Justice,* Marshall, J.* (Toronto: Law Society of Upper Canada, 2007), pp. 347-350.

711 *Ibid.*

712 CBC News Indepth: Caledonia Land Claim, Historical Timeline, 21 April 2006.

713 Department of Indian and Northern Affairs Canada, *Backgrounder on the Claims of the Six Nations of the Grand River Band of Indians*, April 2006; Interviews conducted with those behind the barricade, Caledonia, ON, 23 March 2006.

714 Graham Darling, *Land Claims and the Six Nations in Caledonia* (Calgary: Centre for Constitutional Studies, University of Calgary, September 2006), p. 1.

715 Interviews conducted with those behind the barricade, Caledonia, ON, 23 March 2006.

716 Ontario Reports, 82 O.R. (3d), *Henco Industries Ltd. v. Haudenosaunee Six Nations Confederacy Council et al. Superior Court of Justice,* Marshall, J.*, p. 351.

717 Interviews conducted with those behind the barricade, Caledonia, ON, 23 March 2006; CBC News, "Native protestors face deadline to leave subdivision," Wednesday 22 11:00hrs March 2006.

718 Don Henning as quoted in Paul Legall, "Six Nations protestors say land 'stolen.' Developer says it's the federal government's problem," The Hamilton Spectator. March 2006.

719 Interviews conducted with those behind the barricade, Caledonia, ON, 23 March 2006.

720 Department of Indian and Northern Affairs Canada, *Press Release*, 24 March 2006.

721 "Standoff—Native protestor prepared to die over rights to land," The Hamilton Spectator. 30 March 2006; Paul Legall, "Natives vow to stand their ground: Mood tense as sheriff visits," The Hamilton Spectator, 31 March 2006. Laughing, 40, a high steel worker assisted in the 9/11 rescue and recovery operation in New York City.

722 Carmela Fragomeni, "Native Standoff is a Provincial Matter: Ottawa," The Hamilton Spectator, 07 April 2006.

723 Signe Katz, "Caledonia Protest," CBC: The National, 05 April 2006.

724 CBC News Indepth: Caledonia Land Claim, Timeline of Recent Events, 13 June 2006.

725 Canadian Press, "Que. Mohawks raise banner in support of Ont. Native dispute;" "Natives block rail line in eastern Ontario." 21 April 2006.

726 CBC News Indepth: Caledonia Land Claim, Timeline of Recent Events, 13 June 2006.

727 *Ibid.*

728 Marissa Nelson, "Harper rapped on Caledonia issue," The Hamilton Spectator, 26 May 2006.

729 David Peterson as quoted in Joan Walters, "Peterson fears another Oka," The Hamilton Spectator, 23 May 2006.

730 Marissa Nelson, "Clan mothers seek UN's help: Doreen Silversmith says 'genocidal practices' of Canada must stop," The Hamilton Spectator, 3 May 2006.

731 CBC News Indepth: Caledonia Land Claim, Timeline of Recent Events, 20 June 2006.

732 *Ibid.*

733 *Ibid.*

734 The Ottawa Citizen, "Ontario: Police seek arrest warrants after violence at native blockade," 11 June 2006.

735 Ontario Reports, 82 O.R. (3d), *Henco Industries Ltd. v. Haudenosaunee Six Nations Confederacy Council et al. Superior Court of Justice,* Marshall, J.*, 351-355. As of 20 June only one of the seven was arrested. Audra Ann Taillefer of Victoria, B.C., was arrested in conjunction with the swarming of the elderly couple's vehicle.

736 Canadian Press, "Government to buy disputed Caledonia land," 16 June 2006, 23 June 2006.

737 CBC News, "Six Nations protestors to excavate site," 20 June 2006.

738 Ontario Reports, 82 O.R. (3d), *Henco Industries Ltd. v. Haudenosaunee Six Nations Confederacy Council et al. Superior Court of Justice,* Marshall, J.*, 351-355.

739 *Ibid*, p. 361.

740 *Ibid*, pp. 343-344.

741 Ontario Secretariat for Aboriginal Affairs, *Press Release—Structure of Negotiations*, February 2007.

742 Ontario Secretariat for Aboriginal Affairs, *Press Release—Frequent Questions and Answers*, February 2007.

743 MPP Toby Barrett as quoted in CBC News, "Dozens of Police contain Caledonia Rally," 15 October 2006.

744 Julian Fantino as quoted in CBC News, "OPP's Job to 'preserve the peace' in Caledonia: Top Cop," 30 October 2006.

745 As quoted in CBC News, "Feds Scrap planned Caledonia Meeting," 31 October 2006.

746 Michael Coyle, *Senate Committee Submission on Specific Land Claims*, Ottawa: 3 October 2006.

747 Ontario Secretariat for Aboriginal Affairs, *Press Release—Frequent Questions and Answers*, February 2007.

748 CBC News, "Archaeological finds on disputed Ont. Land strengthen claims, Natives say," 17 January 2007.

749 Ontario Secretariat for Aboriginal Affairs, *Press Release—Six Nations (Caledonia) Negotiations Costs to Date*, February 2007.

750 All as quoted in CBC News, "Mohawks dispute development in Deseronto," 7 November 2006.

751 CBC News, "Deseronto hopeful after land claim meeting with government," 10 November 2006.

752 Samantha Craggs, "Heated confrontation with Mohawks at development," The Belleville Intelligencer, 15 November 2006; Montreal Gazette, "Aboriginals in land dispute end barricade of eastern Ontario highway, 15 November 2006.

753 Shawn Brant as quoted in Craggs, "Heated confrontation with Mohawks at development," 15 November 2006.

754 CBC News, "Mohawks take control of disputed property near Deseronto," 17 November 2006.

755 Ministry of Indian and Northern Affairs Canada, *Press Release—Minister Appoints Chief Federal Negotiator on Claim Talks with the Mohawks of the Bay of Quinte*, 9 January 2007.

756 CBC News, "Deseronto quarry blocked by Mohawk protest," 10 January 2007.

757 Jeremy Ashley, "Mohawk Protestors Charged," Belleville Intelligencer, 12 January 2007.

758 Department of Indian and Northern Affairs Canada, *Specific Claims Branch, Director General—Overview; Comprehensive Claims Branch, Agreements, Plans and Claims Index*, February, 2007.

Glossary

1 CMBG	1 Canadian Mechanized Brigade Group
1 RCR	1st Battalion, The Royal Canadian Regiment
1 Int Coy	1 Intelligence Company, 1st Canadian Division
2 CER	2nd Combat Engineer Regiment
2 EW Sqn	2 Electronic Warfare Squadron
2 R22eR	2nd Battalion, Royal 22e Régiment
2 RCHA	2 Royal Canadian Horse Artillery
2 RCR	2nd Battalion, The Royal Canadian Regiment
3 R22eR	3rd Battalion, Royal 22e Régiment
5 CMBG	5 Canadian Mechanized Brigade Group
ADATS	anti-aircraft missile defence system
ATI	*Access to Information Act*
AIM	American Indian Movement
AIRCOM	Air Command
APC	armoured personnel carrier
AR	automatic rifle
ATV	all-terrain vehicle
AVGP	armoured vehicle, general purpose
BNA Act	*British North America Act*
CAR	Canadian Airborne Regiment
CBC	Canadian Broadcasting Corporation
CDS	Chief of the Defence Staff
CF	Canadian Forces
CFB	Canadian Forces Base
CO	commanding officer
CP	command post
CS gas	2-chlorobenzalmalononitrile, tear gas
CSIS	Canadian Security Intelligence Service
DIAND	Department of Indian Affairs and Northern Development
DND	Department of National Defence
EW	Electronic Warfare

FBI	Federal Bureau of Investigation (United States)
FIA	*Freedom of Information Act* (United States)
FLN	Front de Libération nationale (Algeria)
FLQ	Front de la Libération du Québec
FMC	Force Mobile Command
GPMG	general purpose machine gun
HMCS	Her Majesty's Canadian Ship
HMG	heavy machine gun
hp	horsepower
hrs	hours
HQ	Headquarters
HUMINT	Human Intelligence
IAT	Indians of All Tribes
ICAC	Intelligence Collection and Analysis Centre
ICOM	intercepted communications
IRA	Irish Republican Army
IS	internal security
ISAF	International Security Assistance Force
JIC	joint intelligence cell
JOC	Joint Operations Centre
JTF 2	Joint Task Force 2, Canada's Special Forces
LAW	Light Anti-Tank Weapon
LEA	outside law enforcement agencies
MBT	main battle tank
MND	Minister of National Defence
NCM	Non-Commissioned Member
NDA	National Defence Act
NDHQ	National Defence Headquarters
NTM	notice to move
OP	observation post
OPP	Ontario Provincial Police

PA	Public Affairs
PLO	Palestine Liberation Organization
psyops	psychological operations
QR&O	Queen's Regulations and Orders
RCD	Royal Canadian Dragoons
RCMP	Royal Canadian Mounted Police
RCO	Regroupement des Citoyens d'Oka
ROEs	rules of engagement
RPG	rocket-propelled grenade
RPK	Russian-designed light machine gun
RRF	rapid reaction force
RSM	regimental sergeant-major
RTU	Returned to Unit
RV	recreational vehicle
SIGINT	Signal Intelligence
SIU	Special Investigations Unit
SQ	Sûreté du Québec (Quebec Provincial Police)
SSF	Special Service Force
TC	Rehabilitation Treatment Centre
TOW	tube-launched, optically tracked, wired-guided missile
UN	United Nations
U.S.	United States
VCDS	Vice Chief of Defence Staff
VHF	very high frequency
WHO	World Health Organization
WWII	World War Two

Index

A

B

C

D

E

F

G

H

I

J

K

N

O

P

Q

R

S

T

U

V

W

Y

Z